DATE DUE

MY 28 '98			
MY 19 '99			
JE 1 '00			
AP 18 '05			

DEMCO 38-296

UN PEACEKEEPING, AMERICAN POLITICS,

and the

UNCIVIL WARS OF THE 1990S

Edited by
William J. Durch

A Henry L. Stimson Center Book

St. Martin's Press
New York

UN PEACEKEEPING, AMERICAN POLITICS, AND THE UNCIVIL WARS OF THE 1990s
Copyright © 1996 by William J. Durch. All rights reserved. Printed in the United States of
America. No part of this book may be used or reproduced in any manner whatsoever without
 ̣uotations embodied in critical articles or
Press, 175 Fifth Avenue, New York, N.Y.

Library of Congress Cataloging-in-Publication Data

UN peacekeeping, American politics and the uncivil wars of the 1990s /
edited William J. Durch.
    p. cm.
"A Henry L. Stimson Center book."
Includes bibliographical references and index.
ISBN 0-312-12930-0 (cl.) ISBN 0-312-16075-5 (pb.)
   1. United Nations—Armed Forces—History. 2. International
police—History. 3. United States—Foreign relations—1989-
I. Durch, William J.
IN PROCESS
341.5'8—dc20   96-34880
                                       CIP

Design by Acme Art, Inc.

First edition: December, 1996
10 9 8 7 6 5 4 3 2 1

TABLE OF CONTENTS

ACRONYMS

AAs—Assembly Areas
AOR—Area of Responsibility
APCs—armored personnel carriers
ARENA—Alianza Republicana Nacionalista (El Salvador)
ASEAN—Association of Southeast Asian Nations
BBC—British Broadcasting Corporation
BSA—Bosnian Serb army
CAO—chief administrative officer
CCF—Cease-Fire Commission (Mozambique)
CCPM—Joint Political Military Commission (Angola)
CDR—Coalition for the Defense of the Republic (Rwanda)
CENTCOM—US Central Command
CEO—chief electoral officer
CINCSOUTH—commander in chief, Allied forces Southern Europe
CIS—Commonwealth of Independent States
CIVPOL—civilian police
CMO—chief military observer
CMOC—Civil-Military Operations Cell
CMVF—Joint Verification and Monitoring Commission (Angola)
COMINFO—Commission on Information (Mozambique)
COMPOL—Commission on Police Affairs (Mozambique)
COPAZ—National Commission for the Consolidation of the Peace
    (El Salvador)
CORE—Reintegration Commission (Mozambique)
CPAF—Cambodian People's Armed Forces
CPP—Cambodian People's Party
CSCE—Conference on Security and Cooperation in Europe
DART—Disaster Assistance Response Team
DCA—director of civil affairs
DCEO—deputy chief electoral officer
DCMO—deputy chief military observer
DHA—UN Department of Humanitarian Affairs
DoD—US Department of Defense
DPA—UN Department of Political Affairs
DPKO—UN Department of Peacekeeping Operations
DSRSG—deputy special representative of the secretary-general
EC—European Community
ECMM—European Community Monitoring Mission (former Yugoslavia)
FAA—integrated Angolan armed forces
FAES—armed forces of El Salvador
FAO—Food and Agriculture Organization
FAR—Armed Forces of Rwanda to mid-1994
FENESTRAS—National Trade Union Federation of Salvadoran Workers
FLEC—Front for the Liberation of the Enclave of Cabinda
FMLN—Faribundo Marti National Liberation Front (El Salvador)

FNLA—National Front for the Liberation of Angola
FRY—Federal Republic of Yugoslavia
FUNCINPEC—United National Front for an Independent, Neutral, Peaceful, and Cooperative Cambodia
FYROM—Former Yugoslav Republic of Macedonia
GNP—gross national product
GPA—General Peace Agreement (Mozambique)
HCHR—UN high commissioner for human rights
HDZ—Croatian Democratic Party
HRS—Humanitarian Relief Sectors
HVO—Croatian Defense Council
I MEF—1st Marine Expeditionary Force
ICFY—International Conference on Former Yugoslavia
ICRC—International Committee of the Red Cross
IFOR—NATO Implementation Force in Bosnia
IMF—International Monetary Fund
ISE—Intelligence Support Element (US Forces, Somalia)
JCS—US Joint Chiefs of Staff
JNA—Yugoslav National Army
KMS—Collective Peacekeeping Forces (in Tajikistan)
KPNLF—Khmer People's National Liberation Front
KR—Khmer Rouge (Party of Democratic Kampuchea)
MPLA—Popular Movement for the Liberation of Angola
MRND—Movement for Reconciliation and Development (Rwanda)
NAC—Northern Atlantic Council
NATO—North Atlantic Treaty Organization
NEC—National Election Commission
NGO—non-governmental organization
NIS—newly independent states
NMOG—OAU Neutral Military Observer Group (Rwanda)
NSC—National Security Council
NSDD—National Security Decision Document
OAS—Organization of American States
OAU—Organization of African Unity
OIC—Organization of the Islamic Conference
OMB—Office of Management and Budget
ONUCA—UN Observer Group in Central America
ONUMOZ—UN Operation in Mozambique
ONUSAL—UN Observer Mission in El Salvador
OSCE—Organization for Security and Cooperation in Europe
OSD—Office of the Secretary of Defense
OSOCC—On-Site Operations Coordinating Center (Rwanda)
PDD—Presidential Decision Directive
PDK—Party of Democratic Kampuchea (Khmer Rouge)
PRD—Presidential Review Directive
PRK—People's Republic of Kampuchea
PRM—Mozambique Police
QRF—Quick Reaction Force
RENAMO—Mozambique National Resistance
ROE—rules of engagement
RPF—Rwanda Patriotic Front
RPG—rocket-propelled grenade
RRF—Rapid Reaction Force
RSK—Republic of Serbian Krajina
RTLM—Radio/Television Libre des Mille Collines (Rwanda)

SNA—Somali National Alliance
SNC—Supreme National Council (Cambodia)
SNM—Somali National Movement
SOC—State of Cambodia
SPM—Somali Patriotic Movement
SRSG—special representative of the secretary-general
SSDF—Somali Salvation Democratic Front
SWAPO—South West Africa People's Organization
TDF—territorial defense unit
TNC—Transitional National Council
TOW—Tube-launched, Optically-tracked, Wire-guided (antitank missile)
UN—United Nations
UNAMIC—United Nations Advance Mission in Cambodia
UNAMIR—UN Assistance Mission for Rwanda
UNAVEM—UN Angola Verification Mission
UNCRO—UN Confidence Restoration Operation (Croatia)
UNDP—UN Development Program
UNESCO—UN Educational, Scientific, and Cultural Organization
UNHCR—UN High Commissioner for Refugees
UNICEF—UN Children's Fund
UNITA—Union for the Total Independence of Angola
UNITAF—Unified Task Force (Somalia)
UNMO—UN military observer
UNOHAC—UN Office for Humanitarian Assistance (Mozambique)
UNOMUR—UN Observer Mission Uganda-Rwanda
UNOSOM—UN Operation in Somalia
UNPAs—UN Protected Areas (Croatia)
UNPROFOR—UN Protection Force
UNPROFOR-BH—UN Protection Force in Bosnia-Herzegovina
UNREO—UN Rwanda Emergency Office
UNTAC—UN Transitional Authority in Cambodia
UNTAG—UN Transition Assistance Group (Namibia)
USAID—US Agency for International Development
USC—United Somali Congress
USLO—US Liaison Office (Somalia)
USUN—US Mission to the United Nations (New York)
WEU—Western European Union
WFP—World Food Program
WHO—World Health Organization
YA—Yugoslav Army
ZANU—Zimbabwe African National Union

LIST OF FIGURES

LIST OF TABLES

PREFACE

Over the past five years, with generous support from the Ford Foundation, the Henry L. Stimson Center has undertaken a series of projects on United Nations peacekeeping. Our initial project mapped the UN's decision-making process and derived political and operational lessons from the first 43 years of peacekeeping missions (1948-1991), leading to publication of *Keeping the Peace: The United Nations in the Emerging World Order* (Stimson Center, 1992) and *The Evolution of UN Peacekeeping: Case Studies and Comparative Analysis* (St. Martin's Press, 1993). The second project examined needs for better-trained peacekeeping troops and civilian staff; its final report, *Training for Peacekeeping: The United Nations' Role* (Stimson Center, 1994), recommended a pilot training project coordinated by UN Headquarters. The UN accepted the recommendation and started the pilot project in early 1995.

The third Stimson peacekeeping project, which led to this volume of case studies, addressed peacekeeping and US foreign policy, particularly the ways in which US policy, action, and inaction have affected the setup and implementation of peacekeeping and related operations since the end of the Cold War. US influence on these operations has been substantial, as it was during the Cold War, but US support has been attenuated. Increasingly of late, US foreign policy programs and objectives, particularly those involving multilateral institutions like the United Nations, have been skewed by domestic politics, with troubling results. This book is not about US foreign policy or domestic politics per se, but these two factors may be the most important determinants of the future course of conflict containment and resolution efforts by institutions like the UN. (Both are addressed at some length in chapter one.)

This volume is a companion to *The Evolution of UN Peacekeeping* that takes up the operational narrative where the earlier volume leaves off. It makes use of the same basic case structure to facilitate comparisons across cases and, like the earlier volume, it is designed for advanced undergraduate or graduate courses in contemporary conflict, conflict management, conflict resolution, or international organizations. It assumes, for example, that readers know the basic makeup and functions of the UN General Assembly, Security Council, and Secretariat.

In the course of conducting this study, I had the opportunity to speak with a number of scholars and practitioners to whom I would like to offer my thanks for their time and their insights. They include Kofi Annan, Margaret Anstee, Aldo Ajello, Maurice Baril, Joseph Bebel, Denis Beissel, Wolfgang Bierman, Hans Binnendijk, Samuel Butler, Timothy Byrne, Timothy Carney, Jay Carter, Christopher Coleman,

Staffan de Mistura, Alvaro de Soto, Albert Djemba, Michael Doyle, Manfred Eisele, Jonathan Howe, Angela Kane, Bert Koenders, Robert Loftis, Eric Lubin, Andrew Mainer, Douglas Manson, Ian McCloud, Ken Menkhaus, James Meyer, Robert Oakley, Giandomenico Picco, Hassan Reza Syed, Anne C. Richard, Greg Saunders, Michael Sheehan, David Stockwell, Shashi Tharoor, Waldemar Thiim, Richard Thornburgh, Gregory Vucsich, John Washburn, Melissa Wells, Warren Zimmermann, and Anthony Zinni.

I would like to specially thank those who took time out from busy schedules to read parts of this book in draft, including Stephen Blank, Mike Dziedzic, Robert Gravelle, Dennis Jett, Jane Sharp, Stephen Stedman, Jonathan Stromseth, and Susan Woodward. Of course, responsibility for any remaining errors or omissions rests solely with the authors and the editor.

Special thanks are also due to Shepard Forman, Geoffrey Wiseman, and Mahnaz Ispahani of the Ford Foundation for their sustained sponsorship of the Stimson Center's peacekeeping studies; to the Center's chairman, Barry Blechman, and president, Michael Krepon, for their ongoing intellectual, organizational, and moral support; to Pamela Reed, Michele Siders, Brian Curran, and Jolie Wood for their assistance with the research; and to Laurie Boulden, Sony Devabhaktuni, Stacy Gunther, Khurshid Khoja, Susan Kincade, Melinda Lamont-Havers, Kate Walsh, and Susan Welsh for their help with the hundreds of procedural details that make a project work.

Lastly, in this brave new world where the workplace is all too portable, relationships are often all too fleeting, and the pace of change can exhaust even its hardiest disciples, I feel lucky to have had the enduring support of one special person. Jane, who says the long missions are not the successful ones?

W.J.D.
Arlington, Virginia
July 1996

ONE

KEEPING THE PEACE: POLITICS AND LESSONS OF THE 1990S

WILLIAM J. DURCH

I n 1995, the world marked the fiftieth anniversary of the birth of an organization intended by its founders to provide global collective security. The Cold War confined the United Nations (UN) to the margins of global security, yet, over the decades, it helped to keep the margins from unraveling. UN peace observers attended the birth of Israel in 1948, for example, and armed peacekeepers still referee the Golan Heights, positioned between Syrian and Israeli armed forces. Elsewhere, UN peacekeepers helped to keep East and West from direct military confrontation, serving Western interests in political-military stability.

As the Cold War came to an end in the late 1980s, a number of conflicts that it had helped to sustain came to an end as well. United Nations observers or peacekeepers witnessed several of these endings on behalf of the international community. Other conflicts—locally grown but sometimes Cold War fortified—continued to take lives both directly and indirectly. That is, fighting destroyed the infrastructure needed to make economies go, drove farmers from their land, and decimated livestock. Where drought compounded the effects of such conflicts, as in eastern and southern Africa, the stage was set for large-scale loss of civilian life.

At the same time, the revolution in electronics allowed the news media to drop into remote, troubled areas and to broadcast live images using portable, satellite-linked equipment. Television crews extracted graphic images of mass suffering and over-stretched relief workers and broadcast them around the world. The images tended to give rise, first, to increased support for those agencies, private or international, who were attempting to deal with the crisis and, second, to public pressure on governments, at least among the industrial democracies, to do something as well.

But while military interventions into the affairs of states can promote humanitarian ends, that result is usually incidental to more realpolitik motivations. India challenged the Pakistani army in 1971 only after its months-long rampage in then-East Pakistan had introduced a flood of refugees into India's West Bengal state. The result of Indian intervention was the partition of Pakistan, which permitted refugees to be repatriated but also removed a "back door" threat to Indian security. Similarly, Vietnam invaded Cambodia in 1978, driving the bloodthirsty Khmer Rouge from power but securing de facto control of the government as well. American forces swept down on the Caribbean Island of Grenada in 1983, nominally to rescue endangered American students but equally to overthrow a nasty, radical regime that was too close to Cuba, politically, for Washington's taste.

At the end of the Cold War, the United Nations seemed to offer a way to do the humanitarian intervening without the realpolitik. After the stunning success of the UN-blessed, US-led coalition in the Second Gulf War, it seemed for a time that the age of collective security had finally arrived. US leaders began to see the UN as a vehicle through which America's security burdens might be shared, much as the burden of Cold War security in Europe had been shared with NATO (the North Atlantic Treaty Organization). The analogy was inexact, and would prove to be unfortunate, as it led important elements of the US government to assume that the UN was much more like NATO—a functioning military alliance with compatible forces, operational doctrine, and elaborate structures of command and control—than it actually was.

By the time the differences were truly appreciated, the UN had been given military jobs that were largely beyond its ken. Sent into places like Bosnia and Somalia, asked to carry burdens that its members were reluctant to shoulder themselves, and given contradictory jobs to do once it arrived, the organization stumbled and occasionally fell. These well-publicized failures distracted attention from the UN's successful peacekeeping ventures and its work in other fields. By the time the United Nations celebrated its fiftieth anniversary in October 1995, there was some risk that the experience of failure would prevent the organization from undertaking any new peace operations in the future, however promising.

WHAT THIS BOOK IS ABOUT

This book is, in part, an effort to clarify the record. It looks in some detail at a number of operations undertaken since 1991, picking up the thread where a companion volume, *The Evolution of UN Peacekeeping*, leaves off.[1] Where the former volume focused on the internal structure of the UN and how it sets up and pays for operations, this book focuses on America's role in UN operations and the lessons to be learned from the more "muscular" efforts undertaken since 1991 in the heady aftermath of the Second Gulf War. This introductory chapter establishes basic definitions of terms; addresses the impact of American politics and decision making on UN operations;

pulls together themes of American engagement from each of the cases; and summarizes political and operational lessons learned. Chapter 2 examines the process that developed the first US policy for peacekeeping, Presidential Decision Directive 25 (PDD-25). It is followed by chapters on UN operations in El Salvador, Angola, Mozambique, Rwanda, Somalia, Cambodia, and the former Yugoslavia. (The operation in Haiti occurred too late to receive full case treatment.) The closing chapter looks at Russian peacekeeping efforts as instances where US influence on the course of events is marginal, partly by circumstance and partly by choice.

DEFINITIONS OF TERMS[2]

Although a wide variety of mission objectives, participating organizations, and configurations of military units and civilian personnel can be found among peace operations undertaken to date, these operations can be reduced to four basic types: traditional peacekeeping, multidimensional peace operations, humanitarian intervention, and peace enforcement. The Stimson Center developed these categories to facilitate a succinct description of activities that have spawned a wide variety of terminology.[3]

Traditional Peacekeeping Missions

During the Cold War, the UN developed the format for traditional peacekeeping, which served US and Soviet desires to avoid direct clashes of arms in regions of tension. With the exception of the Congo operation (1960-64) and a small political transition mission in West New Guinea (1962-63), all UN missions between 1945 and 1988 were of this type and involved military components only. A traditional peacekeeping force is positioned between former belligerents and monitors a cease-fire, creating the political space for negotiation of the underlying dispute. Diplomatic efforts to resolve the dispute proceeded separately.

These missions are conducted with the full consent of the parties involved in the conflict and only after a cease-fire has been achieved: for example, after the Suez Crisis (1956), the October War (1973), and the Iran-Iraq War (1988). Use of force by the peacekeepers is authorized only for self-defense or defense of the mission, and then largely to deter small-scale threats, not to prevent a general resumption of fighting. Facing the latter threat, peacekeepers generally have been withdrawn (Sinai 1967), or have stood aside after token resistance (Lebanon 1982); although in one instance, at the airport in Nicosia, Cyprus, in 1974, UN units put up stiff resistance to invading Turkish forces.

Multidimensional Peace Operations

Multidimensional peace operations emerged near the end of the Cold War, as a number of conflicts with East-West dimensions came to a close and the permanent members of the UN Security Council were able to agree on more ambitious missions to help belligerents make the transition to a sustainable peace. These operations often have a mandate not only to facilitate the reduction of tensions between former foes (as in traditional peacekeeping), but also to help implement a peace accord that addresses the causes of the underlying conflict. In most cases, and unlike traditional peacekeeping, multidimensional operations have an implementation schedule and a timeline. When the tasks on the schedule have been completed, the operation folds its tents and departs. An operational deadline gives the UN and other external actors more leverage over the local parties than would an open-ended mandate, and the UN deployed that leverage in its operations in Cambodia and Mozambique, offering the local factions one, time-limited chance to implement their peace accords with outside help. However, the local parties must believe that the worst consequences of compliance (losing a UN-supervised election, for example) are preferable to taking up arms once again. Otherwise, peace may fall apart, as it did in Angola in 1992.[4]

Because multidimensional peace operations primarily involve the settlement of internal conflicts, they operate in a much more complex domestic political environment than does traditional peacekeeping. Moreover, although they usually operate with the full consent of the local parties, their military component may be authorized to use limited force against local elements that actively hinder implementation of the peace accord. Thus, multidimensional peace operations can entail greater risk of casualties than traditional peacekeeping, and greater pressure to use force to keep a peace accord on track.

Multidimensional UN operations have civilian components that may outnumber the military, and a civilian chief of mission who usually carries the title, "Special Representative of the Secretary-General." The civilian components may include administrators, election supervisors and/or poll watchers, an information section to educate the public about electoral processes and help develop grass-roots democratic institutions, a refugees and displaced persons resettlement unit, a component to monitor and report human rights abuses, and civilian police observers. The military help to maintain a secure environment in which the civilian components can work, a role that may involve a number of tasks not found in traditional peacekeeping, such as guarding polling stations, transporting refugees to resettlement areas, and assisting with the demobilization and disarmament of local forces.

Humanitarian Intervention

Whereas traditional and multidimensional operations help to secure an emerging peace, humanitarian interventions have been undertaken to relieve suffering in the midst of an ongoing conflict or situation of anarchy. They are considered a temporary measure to help non-combatants survive the stresses of war and to relieve acute suffering, but as the UN discovered in the former Yugoslavia, once deployed they can be difficult to terminate unless the conflict is brought to an end or, as in Somalia, the circumstances on the ground literally drive them out of the country. Humanitarian interventions may parallel diplomatic initiatives to reach a negotiated settlement of the conflict, as in Bosnia, or that task may be assigned to the leadership of UN forces on the ground, as in Somalia.

At first glance, humanitarian intervention appears to violate local sovereignty. Indeed, by finding that a situation constitutes a "threat to international peace and security," the Security Council overrules the UN Charter's otherwise blanket prohibition on interventions "in matters which are essentially within the domestic jurisdiction" of a state. Such declared threats to peace and security have included the risk of a conflict spreading to other states or an exodus of refugees that threatens political and economic stability in a region. But humanitarian interventions may also be viewed as an effort to protect the source of a state's sovereignty, namely, its populace, from the ravages of civil war or a renegade government. Examples of such operations would include the US- and UN-led operations in Somalia (1992-95), the UN operation in Bosnia-Herzegovina (1992-), and the US-led Operation Provide Comfort in northern Iraq (1991-).

Humanitarian interventions are a rather new type of peace operation and are operationally quite difficult. Intervenors may be violently opposed by one or more of the fighting factions as the intervention force tries to support and perhaps to protect the civilian, non-combatant population of a country, using the minimum amount of force authorized and necessary to achieve their objectives. The intervention force may take limited offensive measures to counter local parties that threaten the mission, but at the risk of the whole operation sliding into peace enforcement (see next section).

In practice, limiting humanitarian interventions to the safeguarding of civilian food and medical supplies has proven difficult, as demonstrated in both Somalia and Bosnia. One mission requirement leads to another. Once supplies have been escorted to regional distribution centers, they may need safeguarding from local looters. If further distribution to needy populations is not supervised and protected by the intervention force, supplies may be siphoned off by local power brokers. Thugs and militias may have to be reasoned with forcefully but, conversely, the whole operation may have to look the other way at times to avoid being dragged wholesale into whatever local disputes caused the humanitarian crisis in the first place. Such assiduous efforts to draw a line between protecting food and protecting its recipients may eventually come to be seen as morally (and politically) untenable, leading to a broadening of the intervenors' mandate anyway.

Part of the inherent complexity of humanitarian intervention stems from the presence of multiple national, international, or nongovernmental relief groups whose activities on the scene may predate the UN's intervention and whose protection may have been the proximate cause of that intervention. These organizations, even those nominally part of the UN system, have their own policy priorities, field objectives, and sources of funding.[5] The peace force must interact with these groups to coordinate activities and share information. Moreover, they may need direct assistance with transportation and communications, in addition to intelligence briefings and medical support. But while they may need the military for security of supply depots and relief convoys, aid providers are often reluctant to cooperate, out of concern that such cooperation will damage their image of neutrality and thus their effectiveness, and make them even more prominent targets of local factions. They may also have preexisting security arrangements with local "protectors" who may prove reluctant to give up their (extorted) incomes.

Peace Enforcement Operations

Peace enforcement may use coercive means to suppress conflict and create a de facto cease-fire and facilitate negotiations among local belligerents, or to protect non-combatant populations facing a general collapse of governance (as in the case of the US-led intervention in Somalia in late 1992). A peace enforcement operation may also be authorized to use coercive means to maintain a cease-fire or implement a peace accord in particularly dangerous circumstances (as in the case of the NATO-led Implementation Force (IFOR) for Bosnia-Herzegovina in late 1995). A humanitarian intervention operation can evolve into peace enforcement if the intervenors possess the political will to escalate their involvement and decide that the only way to protect civilians is to suppress or stop the conflict through use of coercive force.

Unlike a good police force that responds to trouble when called, the international community's responses to dire emergencies have been sporadic, reflecting its basically anarchic nature and its members' disparate definitions of national interests. Enforcement operations are thus the exception, so far, even in response to something as egregious as genocide. The UN Security Council weighed sending a peace enforcement operation into Rwanda, for example, to stop the interethnic massacres taking place there in spring 1994, but the notion received little support and the idea was shelved, at least insofar as UN action was concerned.

The rules of engagement for a peace enforcement operation, which define the circumstances under which deadly force may be used, will seek to minimize casualties, among both the peace enforcers and the local population. In consequence, peace enforcement may place much greater reliance than a traditional combat force on nonlethal weaponry. An enforcement operation may also attempt to maintain the appearance of impartiality, using minimum necessary force evenhandedly (against any party violating a cease-fire, for example).

Implementing such a mandate generally requires clear superiority over combined local forces. In practice, although such superiority may suppress fighting by formally organized combat forces, accompanying diplomatic action must work to resolve underlying disputes, lest fighting reemerge at lower levels in the form of guerrilla or terrorist activities. Ultimately, successful conclusion of any kind of peace operation must entail some form of political settlement.

The 1994-95 multilateral intervention in Haiti may be considered a peace enforcement operation. Its aim was to restore democracy and, by doing so, to stop the human rights violations of the de facto military regime. It was designed to suppress and, eventually, to eliminate that regime. It differed from traditional combat in that US forces did not plan to destroy the Haitian military unless it offered resistance as the legitimate government was restored. Once the threat of coercive force was effective in obtaining a negotiated settlement, the Haiti operation shifted from peace enforcement to multidimensional peacekeeping with residual responsibility for maintenance of civil order.

The UN deployment on the border between Serbia and the Former Yugoslav Republic of Macedonia can be considered a latent form of enforcement that I prefer to label a "deterrent deployment."[6] Although some consider these preventive deployments to be a variation on traditional peacekeeping, they may have consent from one party only—the potential victim—and symbolize the international community's will to take action against aggression. Thus they serve both as a deterrent and as a tripwire force. To the extent, however, that border tensions arise from mutual mistrust, such a deployment may serve the same function as traditional peacekeeping, that is, as a military confidence-building, but without the usual intervening war. Such a pre-conflict confidence-building mission should be deployed on, or at least be able to monitor equally, both sides of an international border.

Comparing the Categories

The four types of peace operations are compared and contrasted graphically in figure 1.1, according to the level of local consent to the operation's presence and the complexity of its mission objectives. Traditional peacekeeping involves full local consent and single mission objectives. Multidimensional operations also involve nominally full consent, but their mandates tend to be much more complex than a traditional operation, and they may encounter reduced levels of acceptance as some local factions maneuver for advantage.

Peace enforcement operations may have the consent of one party in a conflict, or one or more factions in a civil war, but they may also be directed against all combatants equally; that is, they may operate without local belligerent consent. The complexity of peace enforcement operations can, in principle, vary a great deal, from relatively straightforward operations to resist or suppress minor cross-border aggression to all-azimuth conflict suppression followed by the rebuilding of shattered governance. The arrow from peace enforcement to multidimensional peace operations indicates such a postconflict transition, as in Haiti.

Humanitarian intervention may vary considerably over time both in operationally complexity and in the level of consent accorded them by the local parties. The arrows within the humanitarian intervention box in figure 1.1 indicate the progression of international intervention in Somalia (points 1, 2, 3, and 4), and in Bosnia-Herzegovina (points A, B, C, D, and E). The Somali operation was first envisaged as primarily an exercise in suasion (point 1 on the graph) with the few peacekeepers of the first UN Operation in Somalia (UNOSOM I) sent to provide largely symbolic military escorts for food convoys, a strategy that proved ineffectual. The subsequent US-led Unified Task Force (UNITAF, or Operation Restore Hope [point 2]), launched

Fig. 1.1

COMPLEXITY VERSUS CONSENT IN PEACE OPERATIONS

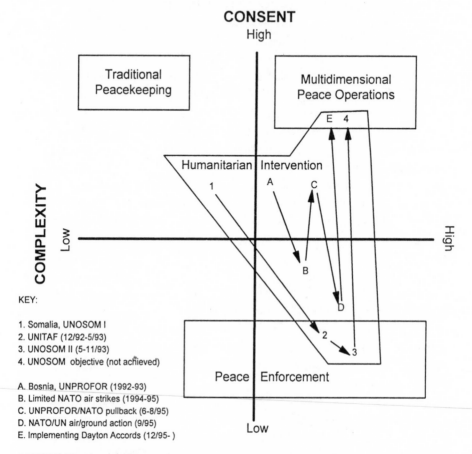

CONSENT
High

Traditional
Peacekeeping

Multidimensional
Peace Operations

E   4

Humanitarian | Intervention

1   A   C

COMPLEXITY
Low   High

B

D

2

3

Peace | Enforcement

Low

KEY:

1. Somalia, UNOSOM I
2. UNITAF (12/92-5/93)
3. UNOSOM II (5-11/93)
4. UNOSOM objective (not achieved)

A. Bosnia, UNPROFOR (1992-93)
B. Limited NATO air strikes (1994-95)
C. UNPROFOR/NATO pullback (6-8/95)
D. NATO/UN air/ground action (9/95)
E. Implementing Dayton Accords (12/95-)

SOURCE: The Henry L. Stimson Center, with thanks to Michael E. Brown
for suggesting the dimensions..

in December 1992, had an enforcement mandate insofar as the delivery of relief supplies was concerned. Its successor, UNOSOM II, had the additional burden of reestablishing government (point 3), which brought it into conflict with one major local faction. It failed to reach its ultimate objective of elections in a consensual environment (point 4).

The UN operation in Bosnia, although conducted with partial authority to use force, used it primarily within the self-defensive rules of engagement of traditional peacekeeping (point A). Its mission was complicated, and local consent was eroded, by limited NATO use of air power to coerce compliance with certain NATO and UN Security Council ultimata (point B). The willingness of NATO to use force abated in late 1994, leaving the UN to attempt to regain local consent in a more turbulent political-military environment (point C). Heavier applications of force in August-September 1995 (point D), in conjunction with other shifts in the balance of power

Fig. 1.2
PEACE OPERATIONS AND STAGES OF CONFLICT

Level of Conflict

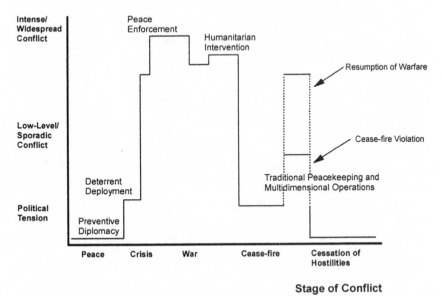

SOURCE: The Henry L. Stimson Center.

on the ground, pushed the local parties toward a US-brokered political settlement and set NATO to planning an IFOR to implement the settlement. Although designed to be deployed with local consent, the IFOR faced a very complex political and military situation on the ground (point E), and reserved the right to use force to support its mission objectives, suggesting the possibility of further short-term plunges into enforcement.

Figure 1.2 makes a different comparison, locating the various types of peace operations according to the phase and intensity of conflict that they typically face when first deployed. The vertical axis represents the nominal intensity of conflict, from political tension through high-intensity warfare. The horizontal axis portrays the nominal phases of a conflict, from startup through cessation of hostilities, although an actual timeline could show repeated cycles of fighting and cease-fires, as suggested by the dotted lines in the graph.

Preventive diplomacy makes an effort to defuse political tensions before they erupt into warfare. If it appears that rising tensions might be tempered by the presence of international forces, then the UN or other suitable regional organizations might resort to a deterrent deployment. The outbreak of war might occasion a peace enforcement operation to suppress conflict; after war has taken a toll on the population, a humanitarian intervention may be mounted to mitigate that toll. In both instances, the international force may be intervening in the midst of ongoing combat, which makes their task much more difficult, troops harder to recruit, and unified command and control harder to achieve and maintain than is the case for consent-based operations deployed before conflict has begun, or when it has ended.

Traditional peacekeeping and multidimensional operations deploy after peace has been achieved but, as noted earlier, the area may still face more or less serious outbreaks of fighting. Where that probability is thought especially high, or where any substantial outbreak of violence might shatter a fragile peace accord, the international operation may be configured for peace enforcement in an effort to deter such outbreaks, as was the IFOR in Bosnia.

AMERICA'S ROLE

During the Cold War, American support of UN operations—political, financial, and military—was vital to their success. The US influenced other states' attitudes toward new missions, it paid the largest single share of UN peacekeeping expenses, and its military logistics capabilities were often essential to move UN forces into position to support cease-fires or force separations. When Washington supported an operation, other UN member states generally supported it as well, and sometimes did so even when Washington's ideas were not particularly sound and the local parties to the conflict were not keen to have the UN around, as in the case of Lebanon.[7] But peacekeeping has been just one element influencing US-UN relations over time.

The Politics of US–UN Relations

Through the 1960s, the United Nations served largely Western interests. Peacekeeping stabilized conflict zones, and press coverage of Security Council meetings provided a direct line to world public opinion. During the Cuban Missile Crisis, for example, US Ambassador Adlai Stevenson displayed aerial reconnaissance photos of Soviet missile installations with television cameras running, and demanded an explanation from his Soviet counterpart.

By the 1970s, the organization had increasingly come to be seen as a tool by which the new voting majority of poor, "Third World" or "non-aligned" states, with the voting support of the socialist bloc, could press an agenda designed to redistribute wealth from North to South. UN bureaucracy grew as the General Assembly's majority established programs and agencies that the West was obliged to pay for, but over which the West maintained little political control and from which it saw little apparent return on investment. Ranging far from its original support of Israel, in 1975 the General Assembly voted to equate Zionism with racism.[8] By the time the Reagan administration took office in 1981, the UN Educational, Scientific, and Cultural Organization (UNESCO) had become a vehicle for Third World states' efforts to censor Western press coverage of their countries. The US, in turn, charged UNESCO's entrenched leadership with mismanagement and overspending. In 1984, the US withdrew from the organization.[9]

In following years, Congress took measures to halt what it viewed as uncontrolled growth in UN expenditures—virtually all attributable to UN economic and social programs. (Peacekeeping remained a relatively low-key, low-cost exercise, except for the mission in southern Lebanon.) Congress voted to withhold a significant fraction of US contributions to the organization unless the General Assembly agreed to pass all future budget resolutions by consensus, rather than simple majority vote. Consensus voting gives every state, including the US, a de facto veto over UN spending and greatly dilutes the influence of the developing states over money matters.

These heavy-handed tactics paid off, in the sense that funding for the UN Secretariat has, since the mid-1980s, only kept even with inflation, and all budgets have passed by consensus.[10] The director general of UNESCO was replaced in 1987, and from 1989 onward some steps were taken to reduce the number of upper-level managers in the Secretariat.

Reform in the 1990s

The prevailing image of the UN on Capitol Hill, however, remains one of inefficiency and overstaffing, and not undeservedly. Management remains the UN's weak suit. Its top leaders tend to be diplomats, its personnel system is chaotic, and even the secretary-general cannot guarantee that administrative reforms will stick. Shortly after taking office in February 1992, Secretary-General Boutros-Ghali reorganized elements of the Secretariat, but too many constituents among the UN's member states objected to his efforts to consolidate the large economic and social departments into a single unit, and it was broken up within a year into three separate departments.[11]

There is some appreciation on the Hill that certain elements of the Secretariat are more efficient than others and have been grossly *under*staffed for what they are expected to do. One example would be the UN's peacekeeping staff. In 1990, just a handful of civilians and military officers on loan from member states tracked the handful of peacekeeping operations then underway. As the number of operations tripled over the next three years and the number of troops supported rose from 10,000 to 80,000, the UN's Department of Peacekeeping Operations (DPKO) developed a staff of several hundred that were capable of supporting these forces in at least rudimentary fashion. Undersecretary-General Kofi Annan, who became head of DPKO in early 1993, also took steps to make the department more responsive to field requirements, setting up a 24-hour Situation Center and more effective planning and support capabilities. These remain well short of what the Pentagon would devote to similar-sized field operations, but they are a step in the right direction for the UN.[12]

Reform of other parts of the organization is far less advanced than in DPKO. The basic system for hiring, promoting, transferring, and firing personnel, for example, has been a shambles for years, with the result that a core of dedicated and competent international civil servants must work around a larger number of time-servers. This happens to some extent in any large bureaucracy but is particularly acute in the main Secretariat, where the 2,500 or so professional slots are distributed by national quota.[13] The US government has been emphasizing for some years the need to make this workforce more efficient, that is, to increase its per capita productivity, and its withholdings of funds have been intended in part to encourage such reforms. More recently, the United States began to pay equivalent attention to the Secretariat's effectiveness—its ability to accomplish the tasks assigned to it by the Security Council—as the UN moved from the margins of international security to an increasingly front-and-center position.

The Politics of Peacekeeping in the 1990s

As the Cold War wound down in the late 1980s, relatively small and reasonably successful UN operations in Afghanistan, Central America, and Angola, and between Iran and Iraq suggested that the UN might have a useful security role to play in the post–Cold War world. Then, after a successful UN mission overseeing Namibia's transition from South African rule in 1989, UN peacekeeping came to be seen as a kind of magic bullet for dealing with regional conflict. Demands for UN operations began to multiply and from spring 1991 to fall 1993 the Security Council (on which the United States sits as a permanent member, with a veto) agreed to send UN operations into ever more complex and dangerous environments, including unfinished civil wars.

It was during this period that the United States, with that peculiar mix of generosity, power, and multiple personalities that characterizes American foreign policy, jumped into peace enforcement with gusto, just as the domestic consensus around US foreign policy and America's role in the world was coming unglued. US political leaders recoiled when this activity produced military casualties, and the various facets of America's personality fell to fighting among themselves about the utility of peacekeeping, about Washington's fair share of UN costs, about "foreign command" of American forces, and about US participation in a future UN or NATO force to implement a peace accord in Bosnia.

A change of the party in power in the White House in early 1993 hobbled high-level US foreign policy decision-making at a crucial juncture while the new administration slowly staffed up. The Clinton administration's early enthusiasm for "assertive multilateralism" (as articulated by its UN ambassador, Madeleine Albright) and Mr. Clinton's well-publicized preference for domestic over foreign affairs allowed conservative members of Congress to caricature the new administration's approach as an abdication of responsibility for US foreign policy to Boutros Boutros-Ghali.[14]

The Republicans' victories in November 1994 gave them control of both houses of Congress for the first time in forty years and gave US-UN relations an even harder political edge. Many of the incoming freshmen members of the House brought with them a suspicion of the United Nations that runs deep within the right wing of the US body politic, where in some quarters the United Nations has replaced the

Soviet Union and communism as the principal identifiable external threat to the United States.

Far from dominating the foreign policies or behavior of its member states, however, the United Nations is both subservient to and dependent upon them. The need to balance its members' many policy interests contributes to the inefficiency that Washington decries, and limits the UN's effectiveness in advancing the interests of any one member. But by using its veto, the United States can stop any security-related UN action contrary to US interests before it even starts, and by withholding financial contributions it can cripple ongoing UN actions, although at some external political cost. The organization has no power to tax, or even to borrow. When its members fail to contribute their dues, the UN's coffers rapidly run dry, and the only sanction for nonpayment written into the Charter is loss of vote in the General Assembly. The image, painted by some ultra-conservatives, of a threatening UN would be funny if the organization's reality weren't so sad.

The Issue of Money

Looming over the political disputes about the United States and the UN was the continuing spectre (and all-purpose excuse) of the federal budget deficit. Indeed, the rising cost of peacekeeping was a growing source of friction between Congress and the White House even before party politics intervened. That cost increased sixfold between 1990 and 1993 at a time when Congress and the Executive were struggling to reduce the deficit and regular defense budgets were falling. Defense spending was, of course, falling from the historic heights of the mid-1980s, and the target of that heavy spending (the Soviet Union) had ceased to exist. But "defense" still resonates with generations of voters who have grown up inured to a large, external security threat, while "peacekeeping" gets pigeonholed closer to "foreign aid," and not without reason. The US financial contribution to UN operations is contained, not in the defense budget, but in the foreign affairs budget submitted by the Department of State. Although the cost of defense in the mid-1990s still exceeded the US financial contribution to UN peacekeeping by about 200:1, it has been the UN and peacekeeping that have taken the latest hits in the new American climate of fiscal stringency.[15] Neither the UN nor peacekeeping has a built-in domestic constituency of known, vote-casting beneficiaries back in the home district, few legislators tend to UN affairs, and not until well into the Clinton administration did the executive branch make more than a perfunctory effort to raise their level of understanding. Indeed, Congress grew increasingly irritated at the manner in which the bills for peacekeeping were presented for payment.

Although State Department budget planners made an effort to anticipate upcoming UN operations, the number and cost of those operations escalated much more rapidly than anticipated. In the spring of 1993, for example, the UN billed its members for large new UN operations in Bosnia and Somalia, which together entailed an American funding obligation of roughly $625 million that was not included in the State Department budget request submitted to the Congress only two months before, obliging the State Department to return to the Hill with "supplemental" budget requests.

Normally, federal agencies laboriously craft their requests for funds for up to two years before the requests are placed before the Congress, and Congress equally laboriously works them over, with hearings and markups, logrolling and pork-barreling. The peacekeeping supplementals, on the other hand, were presented to Congress not only outside the regular budget cycle but as international obligations to be met rather than requests to be bargained over—which further rubbed legislators the wrong way. Nor were the appropriate congressional leaders always given advance warning that costly new UN missions might be on the horizon.

This problem spanned administrations but came to a head under President Clinton. The new administration, which inherited both the Bosnia crisis and the intervention in Somalia from its Republican predecessor, did not get its foreign affairs and peacekeeping policy shops organized soon enough to shepherd the funding for either operation through Congress quickly. It did ultimately succeed in squeezing the extra money out of Congress in 1993, but disaster in Somalia that autumn made it very difficult to get full funding for UN operations thereafter, even from a Democrat-controlled Congress. The Republican majority in control from January 1995 proved unwilling to provide full funding either for peacekeeping or for the US share of the regular UN budget.

UN member states' shares of the regular UN budget are based roughly on their share of global gross national product (GNP), with a multitude of adjustments for per capita wealth, international indebtedness, and the like. In 1946, when it possessed one of the few intact economies in the world, the United States paid a 40 percent share of UN costs. In 1948, the General Assembly accepted in principle a ceiling of 33 percent on budget shares; in 1952, the Congress prohibited US contributions in excess of 33 percent. In 1972, the United States persuaded the Assembly to reduce its share of the regular budget from 31.6 to 25 percent.[16] That share, still somewhat less than the US share of global GNP, remains in effect in 1996.

In late 1973, as the UN got ready to deploy the first new peacekeeping mission in ten years to be paid for by its general membership, the General Assembly, mindful of the funding crises caused by the organization's previous peacekeeping operations, stipulated that developing countries would be assessed a reduced share of the costs (only 10 or 20 percent of their regular share), the shortfall to be made up by a surcharge on the five permanent members of the Security Council (or "Perm Five": the United States, Russia, France, Great Britain, and China). Since the Perm Five have a special responsibility for international security under the UN Charter, and any one of them can veto new UN operations, an extra increment of costs seemed fair enough at the time. Other economically developed UN member states pay the same share for peacekeeping as they do for the regular budget, while developing states pay at the discounted rate.[17]

As the US share of UN peacekeeping expenses passed $1 billion in 1993, members of Congress began to look for ways to reduce the bill, arguing that the US was being made to pay more than its fair share. The Foreign Relations Act for Fiscal Years 1994 and 1995, passed in April 1994 while Congress remained under Democratic control, stipulated that the United States unilaterally limit its payments for UN peacekeeping to 25 percent of total costs beginning in fiscal year 1996.[18] Meanwhile, at the end of US fiscal year 1995 the United States owed the UN $525 million in back dues for the regular budget and $740 million for its share of peacekeeping—arrears equal to about half of the regular UN budget for 1995 and one-third of the peacekeeping budget. In the great budget battles between Congress and the Clinton administration during the winter of 1995-96, Congress cut the administration's fiscal 1996 peacekeeping request by 30 percent, to $359 million. The fiscal 1997 request included $142 million to pay some of the United States' back dues, contingent on serious structural reform at the UN. By mid-1996, congressional action suggested that this "grand bargain" was not going to protect the budget from major (20-30 percent) cuts once again.[19]

Shortfalls in US payments to the UN have become, in turn, a source of friction between the United States and the rest of the UN's membership, especially those wealthier countries whose share of the regular budget is, in proportion to their respective gross national product, equivalent to that of the United States. The speeches delivered by heads of state at the UN's fiftieth anniversary celebration in the fall of 1995 were replete with references to fiscal deadbeats who nonetheless expected to wield great influence in the organization. Yet on Capitol Hill, the withholding of funds was expected to generate just such influence.

The Politics of American Participation

Although voting for a UN peacekeeping operation entails obligations to pay for a share of its operating costs, it does not entail a commitment of troops. The politics of the Cold War generally weighed against permanent members of the Security Council sending troops into UN peace operations.[20] Although post–Cold War politics pose fewer intrinsic obstacles to such deployments, and the United States has deployed a reinforced company of infantry with the UN operation on the Serbian-Macedonian border since mid-1993, direct participation of American combat forces in most UN operations remains problematic, for a number of reasons.

First, because American foreign policy objectives in the new era are much less focused, US domestic politics have tended to dictate the choice, extent, and duration of US support for and participation in UN operations. As the largest military power in the world, the United States faces, ironically, a uniquely limiting set of political risks when it joins a UN operation. Other states expect to win a few and lose a few; that is the price of being a low or middle-ranking member of the international pecking order. Successes here and failures there adjust their relative power and prestige at the margins. The United States, however, is "King of the Hill." Its military engagements are both grander and more publicized than most, so both its successes and its failures are splashier than most.

Moreover, the failures are more keenly felt. Being military King of the Hill contributes to a psychology of primacy that runs through American culture. Americans do not like to turn the other cheek when challenged, which peacekeeping sometimes requires and which other countries' troops accomplish, when necessary, without national disgrace. But Americans find such behavior excruciatingly difficult and take it personally when their troops are treated with disrespect. Being by and large a sentimental people, Americans also take it badly when, trying to do good as they see it, they stumble into political battles that they do not fully understand and the subjects of US assistance start to bite the hands that feed them.

Third, the lack of a sharp focus in post–Cold War US foreign policy means that American leaders have not been able to articulate clearly to the public at large just why it is that American troops are still being sent overseas—to Germany and Japan, let alone Iraq or Bosnia. During the Cold War, there was ready shorthand language available to explain operations whose specific rationales were always much more complex (and maybe even dubious). Today, the buzzwords like "containment" that previously evoked shared images and policy consensus no longer work. Leaders must sell operations on their specific merits and they have been hard put to do so. The Bush administration searched for months for a gripping rationale to support Operation Desert Storm before settling on Iraq's threat to Persian Gulf oil reserves and its looming nuclear weapon capability. When the Clinton administration came into office, it had a much tougher time rationalizing, in simple terms, the continuing US troop presence in Somalia.

When the public has not been effectively convinced that such missions are necessary, it may press for withdrawal if things get nasty; certainly, elected officials anticipate such pressure and attempt to get out in front of it. The result can be a kind of unseemly stampede for the exits, as happened in Somalia when US forces took casualties (see chapter eight). Or public officials may promise to withdraw forces by a certain date, regardless of whether the task at hand has been finished. Thus, in early December 1992 some Bush administration spokesmen promised that US forces would leave Somalia by Inauguration Day, after just six weeks on the ground. In fall 1995, Clinton administration spokesmen, and the president himself, stressed that US troops would be out of Bosnia in "about" 12 months.

Officials worry that American troops in UN operations may become targets for disgruntled local parties, but US behavior contributes to that risk. To the extent that the United States has tended to take sides where its troops have deployed nominally as peacekeepers (as in Lebanon in 1983 and Somalia in 1993), it has invited local retribution. And when US officials imply that the reasons they have given for America's military presence do not justify US casualties, foreign faction leaders pick up on it; that is, a reputation for pulling out when casualties occur invites concerted efforts to create such casualties.

America's risk-averse tendencies take their toll. Americans are accustomed to the deference accorded a global leader and the United States still has the largest national economy and the strongest military power projection capability. But during the Cold War its position of leadership was hard-earned; since the end of the Cold War it cannot be assumed. Direct US participation in first negotiating and then implementing the peace accord for Bosnia demonstrated the Clinton administration's belated recognition of that fact.

MEASURING SUCCESS

Generic measures of success for peace operations are difficult to formulate because each operation's mandate (that is, its operational objective) is different. Paul Diehl of the University of Illinois suggests, however, two basic criteria for evaluating traditional peacekeeping operations that can be applied in partial evaluation of more complex missions as well: how well an operation deterred or prevented violent conflict in its area of deployment; and how much it facilitated "resolution of the disagreements underlying the conflict."[21] These are useful and seemingly straightforward criteria, yet surprisingly difficult to apply in practice, even to traditional operations, because what host and troop contributing states, and members of the Security Council, want from peacekeeping operations varies from state to state and from mission to mission.

For example, to take a (relatively) simple case, some consider the UN operation on Cyprus, separating Greek and Turkish communities there, to be a success because it has prevented substantial armed conflict for more than twenty years (first criterion); others consider it a failure for essentially the same reason: it has so successfully prevented violence that the local parties have no pressing incentives to settle their grievances (second criterion). Countries that did not want to deal with Greek-Turkish enmity during the Cold War valued the UN operation on Cyprus for keeping a sticky intra-NATO dispute on the back burner. The Greek Cypriot government, on the other hand, sees a continuing division of the island that allows the self-proclaimed Turkish Cypriot regime in the north to become a de facto government under Turkish army protection.

On the other hand, the UN force on the Golan Heights between Syria and Israel is considered a success. Both parties want it to continue to occupy a neutral buffer zone in the contested area. No one chafes at its twenty-year history, possibly because no one expected its presence to do more than freeze the status quo after the disengagement agreements that followed the October 1973 Middle East War.

Peacekeeping forces are likely to remain on the Heights if there is ever a peace treaty between Israel and Syria, much as peacekeepers have continued to occupy and monitor a buffer zone between Egypt and Israel as stipulated in their 1979 peace treaty. In such instances, peacekeepers will generally meet both of Diehl's criteria for success: conflict is unlikely because the underlying causes have been removed. The source of this success lies primarily with the political process that produced the peace accord, yet the peacekeepers function as a confidence building measure, a little extra guarantee of pacific intent, a visible symbol of the outside world's continuing investment in peace, and potentially a vehicle through which the outside world might be drawn into the fight against whichever side breaks that peace.

If the cases contained in this volume were measured against these criteria, most would come up short. The UN operations in El Salvador and Mozambique would score highest on both counts: limiting conflict and resolving it. In El Salvador, as Fen Hampson writes in chapter three of this volume, the UN was both an active mediator and an active promoter of human rights and reconciliation. In Mozambique, the UN did not mediate the peace accords but was essential to their implementation. As Pamela Reed concludes in chapter seven, the operation kept the peace process on track, facilitated military demobilization, jawboned both parties into moving ahead with national elections, oversaw those elections, and verified their fairness. In Angola, on the other hand, as Yvonne Lodico notes in chapter four, an understaffed operation failed completely in its mission to implement a political settlement there and the country fell back into war. UN mediators continued to press for a cessation of hostilities and after two more years the effort produced a second settlement, Lusaka, Zambia in November 1994. But where El Salvador remained essentially free of cease-fire violations after its peace accord was signed and Mozambique suffered only a handful, cease-fire violations in Angola were still running at 110 per month in July 1995, eight months after the Lusaka Protocol entered into force.

In Cambodia, the UN racked up a partial win on both conflict limitation and conflict resolution. In chapter five, James Schear assesses this large UN multidimensional operation, deployed on the strength of a peace accord signed by all local factions to run multiparty national elections. The net result was not wholly peace but a more muted civil war with much-reduced international support for the remaining rebel faction (the Communist Khmer Rouge) and universal international recognition of the government in Phnom Penh for the first time in 25 years.

With its relatively force-prone operations in the former Soviet republics of Moldova, Georgia, and Tajikistan, the Russian Federation may have reduced armed conflict but resolution of the underlying grievances remains a rather distant hope. Kevin O'Prey's account in chapter ten shows how Russia's deployments demonstrate both the good and bad side of regionally-based peacekeeping, which is sometimes advanced as an alternative to UN operations: regional powers are nearby and their interests in stability on or near their own borders may be sufficient to energize efforts to bring conflicts there to a halt. But those same interests mean that the regional power does not enter the fray as a neutral and whatever it does or proposes may be viewed with suspicion by one or more parties involved in the fight, unless it is acting with the blessing of a wider international community. Russia did seek UN Security Council support for its operations, as well as financial assistance, and succeeded in getting UN observers for Georgia and Tajikistan. The request for funds fell on deaf ears (and empty pockets), however.

The Security Council is rightly reluctant to give member states a blank check to conduct military operations, even (perhaps especially) in their own backyards. It did write a blank check for Operation Desert Storm, the US-led coalition that expelled Iraqi troops from Kuwait in 1991, but that coalition effort would have been internationally legitimate even without Council action. Kuwait had the right under the UN

Charter to ask for assistance to defend its own territory, and other UN members had the right to provide it.[22]

In instances of internal upheaval where one or more local parties request outside help, or third parties deem it necessary, the legal situation is far less clear.[23] Where such plans to intervene involve a permanent member of the Security Council, the situation can be further clouded by political logrolling. Russia, for example, received support for its operations in Georgia in part by threatening to oppose the Council's blessing of American intervention in Haiti. Because Russia and the United States are permanent members of the Security Council, such expressions of support for essentially unilateral military action may come to be viewed as product endorsements for major sponsors rather than contributions to regional peace and security, unless the Council sets conditions on its support. For example, it might establish political and operational norms to be followed in the operation, require that UN observers accompany the intervention to monitor how well such norms are followed, and withdraw its support if these norms are violated.

The four operations that would receive the lowest scores on Diehl's two criteria for successful peacekeeping are the ones in Croatia, Bosnia, Somalia, and Rwanda. Although peacekeepers in Croatia helped maintain an uneasy cease-fire for three and a half years between Croats and Serbs in that country, there were sporadic outbreaks of fighting, and they were ultimately swept aside when Croatian army forces rolled into three out of four "UN protected areas" in May and August 1995.

In Bosnia, note James Schear and William Durch in chapter six, UN forces struggled to cope with a mandate to protect the delivery of humanitarian relief as war raged first between Bosnian Serbs and Bosnian Muslims, and later between Bosnian Muslims and Bosnian Croats. The UN Protection Force (UNPROFOR) helped to keep open the Sarajevo airport, and thus frustrated the Serb siege of the city, but Sarajevo's population continued to suffer casualties. When the UN Security Council created six urban "safe areas" around Bosnian-government-controlled cities and gave UNPROFOR a mandate to deter attacks on those safe areas, the Council plunged the force into a partisan role that it was not prepared to take on, and one that conflicted with its "neutral" role as relief provider to all parties. (Moreover, only 20 percent of the troops dubbed necessary by field commanders to execute this mandate were ever authorized by the Council.) A final mandate to supervise "weapon exclusion zones" around two of the safe areas, zones that primarily affected Bosnian Serb forces, managed at one and the same time to antagonize the Serbs and, because of their relatively porous enforcement, to antagonize the Bosnian government as well.

Still, the operation in Bosnia did get a chance to do some actual peacekeeping, after the United States brokered a deal between two factions in the conflict—Croats and Muslims—that ended hostilities between them and created, at least on paper, a federation of the two confessional communities. UNPROFOR separated forces, restored utilities and communications, and otherwise promoted the emergence of a semblance of normal life in central Bosnia.

However, not until the Croatian army had routed most Serb forces (and population) from its territory, Bosnian Serb forces had routed Muslim populations from two of the safe area enclaves, combined Croat-Muslim forces were threatening key Serb strongholds within Bosnia, and NATO had pummelled Bosnian Serb military targets in a two-week air campaign, was the way opened for a serious cessation of hostilities and peace talks under US leadership. Implementation of the peace accords reached at Dayton, Ohio, on 21 November 1995 after marathon negotiations, and signed at Paris, France, on 14 December, was assigned to NATO rather than United Nations forces.

Intervention in Somalia came almost a year after the last remnants of national government in that country had dissolved, after millions were at risk of starvation (war and drought having disrupted the growing of crops in those limited areas of Somalia with sufficient ground water to support crops), and after some 300,000, mostly children, had already starved. The United States asked for and received Security Council support for a military expedition to bring relief to the neediest; relief that had been piling up in port warehouses because to move it was to lose it to well-armed street gangs.

The US-led Unified Task Force for Somalia (UNITAF) that arrived in Somalia in late 1992 provided the security necessary to deliver relief, and that was its only specified mandate. Fearing that an immediate relapse into anarchy would follow a precipitate withdrawal, but fearing equally an indefinite troop commitment, the United States urged a follow-on mission upon a reluctant United Nations. Where UNITAF had been able to reduce armed conflict in southern and central Somalia by dint of its relatively overwhelming presence, the UN operation was militarily weaker and more vulnerable to challenge. Conflict levels rose as the UN, with assistance from American forces, found itself turning into yet another faction in Somalia's civil war, struggling for mastery of the capital, Mogadishu. American forces left the country in March 1994, having suffered painful losses the previous October, and the entire UN force pulled out under US protection in March 1995. Civil war continued in Somalia, although, since most international relief organizations and their cash wages were gone and the factions needed export earnings, fighters were less prone to disrupt agriculture and animal husbandry this time around. So while drought remains a problem, famine of 1992 proportions has not, as yet, returned. Somalia remained without a national government (unrecognized claims of pretenders notwithstanding) well into 1996. The northern half of the country has long since proclaimed its independence (also unrecognized internationally). Since no country seems poised to seize its territory, this state of anarchy might well persist for some time to come.

Finally, and sadly, there is Rwanda, the case that all of the post–Cold War, post–genocide-in-Cambodia rhetoric about new world orders, human rights, and the human community was supposed to prevent, and if not prevent then suppress. The "human community" did neither in Rwanda, proving itself both less than a community and less than humane, except after the fact, when conditions were safer.

Rwanda and its twin, Burundi, are bi-ethnic societies in which most residents are members of the Hutu tribal group and relatively small minorities belong to the

Tutsi. Long histories of minority political and military dominance, from precolonial through colonial times, have honed ethnic animosities and fostered periodic episodes of bloodshed over the last four decades. In the case of Rwanda, as detailed by Matthew Vaccaro in chapter nine of this volume, a three-year civil war waged by exile Tutsi forces against the Hutu-dominated government had apparently reached a negotiated end in August 1993. The agreement incorporated a UN peacekeeping force to oversee implementation. But extremist elements in the Hutu-dominated government, in its political party, and in the paramilitary militias associated with it were determined to implement a final solution to Rwanda's minority problem before the agreement took practical effect. Staging the assassination of Rwanda's president as a pretext, they set upon moderate Hutus and all Tutsis, in a savage hand-to-hand campaign that is estimated to have killed more than a half million people in April-May 1994.

Belgium withdrew its peacekeeping contingent after ten of its peacekeepers were brutally murdered by the extremists, depriving the UN operation of its best combat unit and most of its mobility, and demonstrating, as graphically as possible, that United Nations peace operations remain voluntary associations of national units, not field armies. No army in the world would tolerate—indeed, be able to survive—the wholesale withdrawal of fighting units on their own volition.

The Canadian general in command of UN forces pleaded for reinforcements, but none were forthcoming. The United States objected to expanding the operation, on economic grounds. The civil war reignited when Tutsi-dominated forces of the Rwandan Patriotic Front (RPF) poured back into the country from base areas in Uganda and swept south. France, erstwhile ally of the Rwandan government, deployed foreign legionnaires to cordon off the southwestern quarter of the country, stopping the killing but also stopping the advance of the RPF, whose rapid battlefield successes generated a tidal wave of Hutu refugees (civilian, military, and militia) who expected to be done to by the RPF as they had done to their Tutsi neighbors, and thus fled en masse, primarily into Zaire. As the cameras of international television focused on *their* plight in impromptu cross-border camps, the United States dispatched military engineers to run water lines and stem an outbreak of cholera. But the realization gradually dawned on the international relief community that it was sustaining, among the refugees, the very people responsible for genocide in Rwanda. That group reorganized and to some extent rearmed itself in exile and planned to reclaim power, hoping to undermine the largely agrarian economy of a now RPF-governed Rwanda by preventing the return of non-combatant refugees. By late fall 1995, the government of Zaire was pressing for the repatriation of all refugees, and an international conference chaired by former US president Jimmy Carter was working out a regional plan to do so. But the problem of the exile army remained, and there were periodic clashes between it and the RPF. The RPF-dominated government in Rwanda terminated the UN operation in early 1996, even as the United Nations and other outside groups worked to prevent Burundi from sliding into civil war—without notable success.

If one were to summarize the record of United Nations peace operations from 1991 through 1995 using Diehl's two criteria, one would be forced to conclude that the record is decidedly mixed. But because it is mixed, there are positive as well as negative lessons to be drawn.

LESSONS LEARNED

The late Joseph Campbell wrote about the power of myth, stories that illuminate human experience through analogy and metaphor.[24] Until 1990 or thereabouts, the myth most identifiable with peacekeeping was that of Sisyphus, the mortal condemned forever to push a boulder almost to the top of a hill, only to have it roll back down. Most peacekeeping operations have been similarly open-ended affairs: the observer missions in Kashmir and the Middle East have been in place since 1948, the mission in Cyprus since 1964, the mission on the Golan Heights since 1974, and the one in southern Lebanon since 1978. The UN's first operation in the Sinai Peninsula, separating Egyptian and Israeli forces, lasted from 1956 to 1967, and its second operation there lasted from 1973 to 1979. (This last mission was succeeded, in 1982, by the independent Multinational Force and Observers, which is still there and to which the United States contributes a battalion of troops.).

There are, however, exceptions to every myth. Even prior to 1990, some UN operations were of much shorter duration. The large and costly Congo operation wound down after four years, the observer mission in Yemen after two years, and the transfer-of-governance mission in western New Guinea after seven months.[25]

Since 1993, the prevailing myth has gone from Sisyphus to Icarus, the aeronaut who flew so high that the sun melted the wax in his wings and he plunged to his death. In going into places like Somalia, Angola, Bosnia, and Rwanda, the United Nations has overextended itself and risked complete meltdown. But like the myth of Sisyphus, the analogy in this instance is inexact. Icarus' failure involved a serious case of hubris. The UN did not fly too high on its own; rather, it was flown up to a certain altitude and dropped. The members of the Security Council opted to use a particular system of quasi-military operations in situations to which it was maladapted. They did so under press of events and to reduce political pressures to take, or to continue, unilateral military action.

But in other instances the UN adapted reasonably well to its new tasks, especially if the emphasis is placed on overall political outcomes and not the details of operations. The UN has done reasonably well, for example, where multidimensional operations have been invited in to implement peace accords, the local parties have reached the conclusion that political jousting is really preferable to war, and the UN has had an active rather than passive/observational role in their implementation. As one of the case authors puts it, peace agreements are "not self-catalyzing." Even if the local parties are sincerely interested in implementing peace, *they may not know how to do it*. (How much practice could they have had?) In any case, the local parties do not trust each other. Where wars are settled by victors' justice, the outcomes may be much starker and more unpleasant but they are relatively simple compared to the outcomes

and requirements of a negotiated stalemate. The UN gets involved, almost by definition, in the negotiated stalemates.[26]

Multidimensional Operations

The political situations into which multidimensional operations deploy are much more
dynamic than those faced by traditional operations. Whereas traditional peacekeepers
maintain political-military stasis, multidimensional missions encourage, oversee, and
sometimes directly manage political change. Because they concern the resolution of
internal or mixed internal-external conflicts, multidimensional operations involve far
more variables than traditional peacekeeping, as well as political-military situations
that are, in their details, unique. Yet such missions share certain basic characteristics
and objectives: they are generally time-limited; their mandates grow out of local
political settlements rather than cease-fires; and the requirements for a successful
mission build on the requirements for traditional peacekeeping (maintaining local
consent and heavy-duty outside political support; executing the mandate impartially;
and using force only in self-defense and then sparingly).

Lessons to be drawn from multidimensional operations are, as might be
expected, more complex (and tentative) than those drawn from traditional peacekeeping. Successful missions require the integration of civilian and military people, tasks,
and objectives; extensive coordination with other aid providers; and measures to
diminish the risk (and cost to the mission) of local factions defecting from the peace
accords. Such defections may prompt calls for the use of force to bring all parties back
into compliance. In Cambodia, the UN command resisted such calls, knowing that
the forces available to it were neither equipped, trained, nor intended by their
governments to engage in jungle warfare against the Khmer Rouge (the "Party of
Democratic Kampuchea," or PDK—the group responsible for genocide in Cambodia
in the 1970s) on the PDK's home turf. Political pressure from the Perm Five helped
to keep the PDK in check while the UN operation edged around it in order to hold
successful elections in May 1993.

Several multidimensional missions (those in Angola, Mozambique, Cambodia,
and El Salvador) involved peace accords that called for the disarmament and demobilization of local military forces. In the best of circumstances, the UN cannot reliably
disarm local parties. Most groups will hedge their bets with caches of hard-to-find
arms, even if they are sincere about peace, out of concern (as in the game of "prisoner's
dilemma") that another party will defect from the settlement, with deadly consequences for themselves. But while the cost of another's defection is higher if one has
relinquished all means of self-defense, retention of the means of war can make effective
defection possible. The UN's best hope therefore in a transition from war to peace is
to alter local attitudes and expectations about the need or the value of a return to
warfare. The UN can help to break the prisoner's dilemma by providing reliable,
transparent communications between the local parties; by providing reliable,

independent news to the local population; by imposing political penalties for defection (up to and including withdrawal of the transition force); and by providing or facilitating side-payments of various sorts to encourage cooperation (in Mozambique, these took the form of cash payments to rebel faction leaders, government officials, and their respective parties).

Most of the peace accords that the UN has helped to implement have involved national elections, sometimes to elect delegates to a constitutional convention, sometimes to elect presidents and legislatures. Whatever their objective, they may be the first elections ever held in the country under conditions that are fair and free of wholesale vote-rigging or intimidation. The populace will be skeptical about the value of their votes unless convinced otherwise. In Namibia and Cambodia, in particular, the UN operations engaged in substantial public relations campaigns to "sell" the concept of free and fair elections and went to great lengths to convince would-be voters that their choices would be secret and that all ballots would count once. In Cambodia, United Nations radio proved particularly effective in countering factional propaganda and making objective information about the peace process available to the average Cambodian.

In developing societies with low rates of literacy, radio may be the medium that can reach the most people. It may be a crucial tool of education and counter-propaganda both in multidimensional operations and in humanitarian interventions, where closed systems of communication may have been accustomed to pumping out the doctored news that totalitarians find so useful as a means of controlling their populations, or the hate-mongering that rabid nationalists use to promote attacks against out-groups. In both types of operations, objective accounts of local events have political ramifications that may be resented by at least one local party most of the time and thus may risk reprisals by the offended group even as they provide a service to the general populace.

In several cases, the UN was slow to incorporate the results of its own success in this area, failing to build broadcast facilities into initial plans for subsequent operations in other unstable places. It was not until the secretary-general's revised edition of *Agenda for Peace* in early 1995 that the UN formally endorsed the need for a broadcast capability in "future" operations. Still, the watchdog committee of funders that screens UN spending requests has been reluctant to support funds for radio stations.[27]

The heavier the international presence in the electoral process, the greater the likelihood of *credible* results. The peace accords governing the UN's role in Angola in 1991-92, for example, only allowed for a small operation to monitor the peace process without authority to manage it. The UN mission had no direct influence on the mechanics of the 1992 elections and had only enough observers to visit just a small fraction of polling stations during the vote. Although the UN endorsed the very close election results, when the loser claimed fraud there was no independent data to disprove his charge. In Cambodia, on the other hand, the United Nations ran the electoral process and even had the authority to manage government ministries that could influence the elections. Despite widespread threats to candidates of the opposition parties by the ruling faction, and attempted intimidation of voters by the PDK,

Cambodians went to the polls in droves and, when announced by the UN, the results were accepted as legitimate.

Power-sharing arrangements may help to diminish the risk of defection by giving both (all) sides a stake in the new political system established by the elections (and, to be frank, its spoils). Power-sharing arrangements were a pronounced feature of the transition to all-race democracy in South Africa (where the UN played a small but visible civil observer role before and during national elections). In Angola, the 1994 Lusaka Accords prominently featured power-sharing arrangements, as did the postelection deal struck in Cambodia, where two co-prime ministers were appointed from competing parties. As these countries gain experience with democratic governance and its institutions, the concept of a "loyal opposition" may appear less of an oxymoron, and parties may be willing to risk an outright loss at the polls in confidence that such a loss will not shut them out of power permanently.

In societies where civil order may still be only tentative, violent (and well-armed) crime is likely to be a major problem for the populace and the international force, but police powers and capabilities have been a rarity in UN operations. Infantry units are not trained for police work and generally detest it. UN civil police (CIVPOL) rarely receive more than a few days of postdeployment training in their mission tasks. Those tasks have mostly involved monitoring local police behavior, looking out for and reporting human rights abuses, or training new police forces, not patrolling and crime-fighting. Yet civil order and crime control may be a paramount concern in that uncertain period between the end of a war and the establishment of a new government. Indeed, if there is a role for a standing United Nations force of some sort, it is in this very area of deployable interim police forces, which no country keeps in surplus peacetime reserve as they do military forces.[28] Local police are always "deployed" in their home countries and few are trained to do the missions that UN multidimensional operations involve, much less perform general police work in foreign countries. Language alone is a significant impediment to effectiveness. While some preliminary spadework has been done in this area of UN police training and availability by, among others, the United States Mission to the UN and the Lester B. Pearson Peacekeeping Training Center in Canada, there is much work left to be done to improve UN CIVPOL capacity.

Finally, the international community must somehow come to grips with the fact that large, multinational missions that pay their staff and contractors world-class wages and buy what they can on local markets may, for the period of their deployment, be responsible for a substantial fraction of a prostrate host country's gross national product. Salaries paid to locally-hired employees, of which there may be several thousand, are often several times higher than prevailing local wages, and mission requirements for staff housing and office space may send rental prices into orbit.[29] When operations depart, on the other hand, the economic boost (or shock) they have given to the local economy leaves with them, making it all the more important that the political-military objectives and timetable of the UN's operation dovetail with others' plans for reconstruction and development assistance and do not derail efforts to put the local economy back on its feet.

Humanitarian Intervention

The complexities and hazards of humanitarian intervention were noted earlier and they in turn suggest a number of sobering lessons to be taken into account before the Security Council votes to commit UN forces to future such operations. The lessons have to do with the value of military power, the difficulty of maintaining neutrality, and the dilemmas created by partial solutions to conflict.

Although much is made of UN's moral authority as both a source of effectiveness and shield for its people in traditional peacekeeping and in multidimensional missions, operations that move into situations where conflict continues need greater capacity to use force in response to challenge and in some circumstances may need the capacity to maintain at least a temporary peace to facilitate the work that they are assigned to do, for example, escorting relief. When UNITAF landed in Somalia, it was strong enough to intimidate the one faction that resented its intrusion and was welcomed by the other factions because of that capability. It used force judiciously and proportionately, and stayed in close political touch with the faction(s) it engaged, projecting restrained strength with respect, which was more or less reciprocated. The subsequent UN operation in Somalia was not strong enough to maintain that respect on the part of General Mohammed Farah Aideed and his faction, and did not, in turn, harbor much respect for them, nor did it maintain the political bridges built by UNITAF. At the same time, it was not strong enough militarily to justify that policy. It could not protect itself, let alone the civilian population.

Much the same was true of UNPROFOR in Bosnia. Tasked to protect relief efforts, and then to deter attacks on "safe areas," it never possessed the wherewithal to do the job. Moreover, mutual respect eroded very quickly as fighting continued, cease-fires collapsed, and local political-military agendas were thwarted. It was much easier for the UN to assert its impartiality than it was to make local factions believe the assertion, because humanitarian intervention favors whatever faction is nearest to defeat when the intervention occurs and whatever faction can make greater use of time to summon other resources to its cause. Moreover, the UN's attempts to remain neutral were subject to manipulation by all local belligerents, as might be expected, because neutral intent does not translate into neutral impact on war outcomes. *Every* action taken by outsiders in a civil war situation affects the local balance of power. Outsiders' professed altruism may even make local parties suspicious or contemptuous of the intervention, rather than supportive or respectful, and the most aggrieved local parties may be more contemptuous than the local predators. The aggrieved parties want rescue, not solace.

Finally, interventions in active war zones may encounter painful dilemmas. Partial cease-fires without weapon impoundment may bring respite to one area but increase fighting in others. (The Yugoslav army withdrew weapons from Croatia into Bosnia in early 1992, for example, positioning them for the next round of fighting.) Components of an operation that deal with displaced persons may rescue individuals who are under physical threat, but in so doing can both increase the numbers of displaced citizens and abet the ethnic cleansing objectives of their tormentors.

Although the UN Secretariat may try to fashion the mandates for its operations so as to reflect a disinterested internationalism and a generic commitment to peace, any mandate to operate in an active war zone is bound to be charged politically. Since the United Nations is not equipped politically or temperamentally to accept the risks of partisanship in any given conflict, the Security Council should be wary of putting peacekeepers in harm's way.

Peace Enforcement

The above statement also holds for peace enforcement, that is, conflict suppression missions. UN operations are voluntary aggregations of disparate military forces whose governments' motives for participating range from a desire to do good to a desire to earn cash, but do not include a desire to lose troops in combat. It may be that, at some point in the future, nation states will see fit to set up the sort of collective security system envisaged by Article 43 of the UN Charter, including on-call air, land, and sea forces. It is possible that they will be willing to commit those forces in cases of internal conflict as well as international aggression. Until that time, however, it is not advisable to think or plan in terms of forceful multinational operations functioning under direct UN command and control.

This is not to say that the Security Council should never authorize actions to defeat aggression or suppress internal conflict. Its role as a legitimizing force for the actions of coalitions of member states may be crucial to establishing the international acceptability of such actions and to encouraging states to grant coalition forces the right to overfly, refuel in, or stage from their territory. But the political and military leadership of such operations needs to be provided by a member state with the political clout to rally support and the military capacity to provide the fighting and logistical core of the operation. This is the model followed in the Second Gulf War, applied to UNITAF, and used to restore democracy in Haiti. It is the model followed for the Implementation Force deployed in support of the December 1995 accords to end the war in Bosnia, and the model that the Russian Federation would like to see applied to its operations with and among the newly independent states on its borders. It has worked fairly well when the United States has been the coalition leader, partly because the country is reluctant to make long-term commitments of forces in Third World countries and its deployments are thus self-limiting. The Russian Federation may not be so shy in its own contiguous border areas and the UN has treated its requests with circumspection.

Because the UN is the improper locus of the command and control of fighting forces, it follows that building a full command staff capable of managing combat operations would not be a good use of funds. However, because of the difficulty of assembling experienced operational staffs on short notice for any large UN operation, the Canadian government proposed the establishment of a 30-50 person command staff within the UN Secretariat that would be able to deploy on short notice to jump-start new UN field operations.[30] Of course, a staff able to deploy on a few days' notice would be more useful if the troops and civilian staff it was designed to direct also were to show up where they were needed within days or, at worst, weeks of the need. As demands for United Nations forces rose sharply in the early 1990s, it was not uncommon for promised forces to arrive six months after the initial call for troops. This was true for the operations in Cambodia, Croatia, Bosnia, Mozambique, and Somalia. Although the UN has since created a list of "standby" forces that member states have said would be available, actual availability varies with the danger level of the operation. When the invitations went out for troops to send into Rwanda, there was a lot of staring at the floor and shuffling of feet, but no hands in the air. When Paris finally sent a battalion under unilateral command, France's history of support for the former Rwandan government raised questions as to its motives and its neutrality.

Some concerns about the objectives and behavior of coalition leaders might be alleviated by making Security Council blessings of coalition operations contingent, as suggested earlier, upon the presence of a force of UN military observers large enough, and with sufficient freedom of movement, to monitor coalition actions with respect to any conditions the Council may have placed on its endorsement of the operation. In the absence of such conditioned and actively monitored endorsement, Council members may wake up one day to find they have endorsed the demolition of the world's next Chechnya.

WHAT NEXT?

In the first years of the 1990s, the Security Council explored, reached, and exceeded the United Nations' capacity to undertake UN-run military and military-related field operations. The risk in the second half of the decade, on the rebound from the Somalias and Bosnias, is that the institution may be underutilized for the sorts of tasks that it has learned to do well and for which it may well be irreplaceable. As American politics moves through an inward-looking, privatizing phase, the UN and many other institutional objects of US foreign policy may suffer serious financial reverses that could hit the reformed and the hidebound elements of these institutions with equal force. The UN's peacekeeping department could be hit even harder than unreformed departments because a large part of its growth in a period of otherwise flat regular budgets was financed by a percentage of each peacekeeping mission budget. As the size and number of missions shrinks (from a peak of 78,500 military personnel deployed in 1993 to not more than 25,000 in 1996), DPKO's ranks will likely thin out as well, potentially dropping beneath the minimum needed to effectively plan, recruit, and support complex field operations. A standing force or a rapid-response capacity might be nice to have, but this basic support capability is crucial to maintain.

UN military forces have increasingly functioned as support and security elements for civilian agencies and civilian objectives, from elections to refugee repatriation. Although some of the UN's future tasks will doubtless require soldier-peacekeepers, many of them will entail the application of civilian, not military expertise. Yet the departments and agencies of the UN that deal with these areas are not well structured to work together or to interact smoothly with their non-UN counterparts in national governments and the nongovernmental relief and development community. Agencies like UNHCR (the UN High Commissioner for Refugees) and UNICEF (the United Nations Childrens' Fund) are relatively effective but largely autonomous actors, and the office of the UN Commissioner for Human Rights remains, as yet, in an embryonic state.

The United Nations' fiftieth anniversary came and went in October 1995 in a flurry of pomp and penury. Whether the UN becomes a more effective tool of international conflict prevention, containment, and resolution in the future or lapses back into earlier, more passive roles will depend on how the US government resolves its foreign policy personality crisis, and on what persona emerges as the dominant one in the years ahead. While American support is not sufficient to make the institution more effective, it is certainly necessary.

NOTES

1. William J. Durch, ed., *The Evolution of UN Peacekeeping: Case Studies and Comparative Analysis* (New York: St. Martin's Press, 1993).

2. This section builds on material in Pamela L. Reed, J. Matthew Vaccaro, and William J. Durch, *Handbook on UN Peace Operations* (Washington, D.C.: The Henry L. Stimson Center, April 1995), 1-6.

3. Some of these frameworks look at broader categories of action than we do in this volume, for example, diplomatic activities undertaken to head off a crisis. See, for example, United States Army, *Peace Operations,* Field Manual 100-23 (Washington, D.C.: Headquarters, Department of the Army, December 1994). The army uses the categories "Support to Diplomacy" (subsuming categories of preventive diplomacy, peacemaking, and postconflict peace building), "Peacekeeping," and "Peace Enforcement." NATO is developing its own categories (conflict prevention, peacemaking, peacekeeping, peace enforcement, peace building, and humanitarian operations). See Supreme Headquarters Allied Powers Europe, *ACE Doctrine for Peace Support Operations,* ACE (Allied Command Europe) Directive No. 80-62, Draft Revision (Mons, Belgium, 22 September 1995). The UN refers to preventive diplomacy and peacemaking, peacekeeping (under which is subsumed protection for humanitarian operations), postconflict peace building with "multifunctional" operations, disarmament, sanctions, and enforcement actions. See Secretary-General Boutros Boutros-Ghali, *An Agenda for Peace,* 2nd ed. (New York: UN Department of Public Information, February 1995), 5-29. Colonel Charles Dobbie developed a conceptual framework that has been adopted as British army doctrine; it distinguishes peacekeeping, "wider" peacekeeping, and peace enforcement. Wider peacekeeping incorporates tasks including conflict prevention, protected humanitarian relief operations, military

assistance to civilian authority, demobilization of local belligerents, and "guarantee and denial of movement," for example, implementing economic sanctions on Serbia (1992-95) or escorting oil tankers through a Persian Gulf war zone (1987-88). See his "A Concept for Post–Cold War Peacekeeping," *Survival* 36, no. 3 (autumn 1994): 121-25. Many of these efforts build on earlier conceptual work done by John Mackinlay and others at Brown University's Watson Institute for International Studies. Their notion of "second generation" operations covered a wide range of military tasks short of war. See John Mackinlay and Jarat Chopra, *A Draft Concept of Second Generation Multinational Operations 1993* (Providence, R.I.: The Thomas J. Watson Institute for International Studies, Brown University, 1993).

4. For further discussion, see Stephen John Stedman, "The New Interventionists," *Foreign Affairs* 72, no. 1 (winter 1992-93): 1-16.

5. UN relief agencies include the High Commissioner for Refugees (UNHCR), the Children's Fund (UNICEF), and the World Food Program. The mix is also likely to include national relief and development entities like the US Agency for International Development (USAID), private global relief groups (CARE, Save the Children, and dozens of others), and local grass-roots relief organizations.

6. The UN secretary-general's *An Agenda for Peace* refers to "preventive deployments," emphasizing their role as preconflict reassurance and confidence building measures. But unless conflict is preventable just by the mere presence of such a force, the fundamental utility of such a force is as a tripwire designed not just to warn of imminent aggression but to trigger an international response, the expectation of which would alter a would-be aggressor's calculation of costs and benefits. See Boutros Boutros-Ghali, *An Agenda for Peace, 1995,* 2nd ed., 49-51.

7. The United States pushed for the rapid deployment of UN peacekeepers into southern Lebanon following Israel's invasion of the country in March 1978 in reprisal for Palestinian terrorist attacks in northern Israel. The peacekeepers were supposed to monitor Israeli withdrawal and the reestablishment of Lebanese government authority in the border area. Unfortunately, Lebanon was in the midst of civil war at the time, and would remain so for another decade. The model applied in this instance, that of the Sinai and Golan Heights peacekeeping forces, worked in those instances because the antagonists were two organized states with disciplined armies and both sides wanted the UN to come in. In the case of Lebanon, Israel did not want it, and Lebanon was a seething mass of communal militias and guerrilla forces. The UN Interim Force in Lebanon (UNIFIL) remains in place in 1996, doing largely humanitarian work. See Mona Ghali, "United Nations Interim Force in Lebanon: 1978-Present," in William J. Durch, ed., *Evolution of UN Peacekeeping* (New York: St. Martin's Press, 1993), 181-205.

8. This resolution finally was rescinded by the Assembly on 16 December 1991.

9. William Branigin, "Nations Object to Spending," *Washington Post,* 22 September 1992, A15.

10. The budgets of many of the UN's operating agencies, like UNICEF or UNHCR, come from largely voluntary contributions from UN member states. Their budgets have

grown enormously in response to the surge in crises and refugee populations in the Third World in recent years. These agencies are also, by and large, considered to be effective at what they do. Unfortunately, in the decentralized system of the United Nations, there is no way to take operational or managerial lessons learned from one agency and apply them authoritatively to any other agency. Agencies have made efforts to coordinate their field actions, however. For example, the High Commissioner for Refugees and the Children's Fund signed a memorandum of understanding in March 1996 "designed to promote coordinated responses" to planning and executing field operations. "UNHCR and UNICEF Sign Agreement on Strengthening Coordination," Press Release No. 871 (Geneva: UNHCR Information Section, 14 March 1996).

11. Close observers suggest, however, that the original consolidation, by bringing a host of sometimes overlapping programs under common direction, laid the groundwork for creation of three better-rationalized departments for policy development, statistics, and program execution. See Bhaskar Menon, "UN Begins with Turmoil of Reform Within and Worsening Crises Around the World," *International Documents Review* [IDR] 4, nos. 1-2 (1-31 January 1993): 2; and Menon, "Dadzie Report Defines Second Phase of Reform in UN Economic and Social Sectors," *IDR* 4, no. 4 (15 February 1993): 3-4.

12. Many of the additional staff slots are paid for by a portion of the UN's peacekeeping mission budget called the "peacekeeping support account," rather than the regular budget. For a more thorough treatment of the UN's bureaucratic woes, see William J. Durch, "Structural Issues and the Future of UN Peace Operations," in Donald C. Daniel and Bradd Hayes, eds., *Beyond Traditional Peacekeeping* (London: Macmillan, Ltd., 1995).

13. Ibid.

14. US Congress, Senate Foreign Relations Committee, *FY94 Foreign Relations Authorization Act: Budget Requests, Hearings before the Subcommittee on Terrorism, Narcotics, and International Communications,* statement of Amb. Madeleine Albright, 9 June 1993, 103rd Cong., 1st sess., S.Hrg.103-330. For the Congressional Republican reaction, see, for example, reports of House floor debates in Associated Press, "House votes against UN peacekeeping fund," *Washington Times,* 14 September 1993, 4; and for reporting on Senate debates, see Donna Cassata, "Congress—Somalia," Associated Press newswire, 4 October 1993, 9:05 pm EDT, Internet.

15. In addition to paying its share of direct costs for UN peacekeeping operations, the United States supports the UN indirectly. In fiscal year 1994, in addition to its directly assessed $878 million share of UN peacekeeping costs, the United States spent roughly $1.7 billion in voluntary support of UN Security Council resolutions, helping to enforce sanctions against Iraq and Serbia, the arms embargo on all of the republics of the former Yugoslavia, and the "no fly zone" over Bosnia, in conjunction with other NATO countries. The US also enforced UN sanctions on Haiti and launched "Operation Restore Democracy" to bring elected civilian government back to Haiti. See Reed, et al., *Handbook,* A7. The cost of voluntary operations is cited in US Congress,

House, *To Revitalize the National Security of the United States,* 104th Cong., 1st sess., February 1995, H.R. 7, 5.

16. David W. Wainhouse, *United Nations Peacekeeping at the Crossroads* (Baltimore and London: Johns Hopkins University Press, 1973), 545-47.

17. When an operation is approved by the Security Council, the United States does incur an automatic financial obligation to support that operation. The United States was assessed 30.4 percent of the cost of each operation through 1992. The breakup of the USSR reduced Russia's overall share of the UN budget and the decline of the Russian economy further lowered its ability to pay, leading to higher surcharges on the other permanent members just as peacekeeping costs shot up. From 1993 through 1995, the United States was assessed 31.7 percent of peacekeeping costs but refused to remit more than its former share of 30.4 percent. See United States General Accounting Office, *United Nations: How Assessed Contributions for Peacekeeping Operations Are Calculated,* GAO/NSIAD-94-206, August 1994, 2.

18. US Congress, House Committee on Foreign Affairs, "Conferees Agree on State Department, Peacekeeping Bill," News Release, 20 April 1994, and House Committee on Foreign Affairs, *The Foreign Relations Authorization Act for Fiscal Years 1994 and 1995,* sec. 404, 103rd cong., 2nd sess., 1994, H. Doc. 103-482. The Clinton Administration agreed with this particular congressional move. See US Department of State, Bureau of International Organization Affairs, *The Clinton Administration's Policy on Reforming Multilateral Peace Operations,* Publication 10161 (Washington, D.C.: May 1994).

19. "The United Nations Financial Crunch: the US Role in Creating the Crisis," (Washington, D.C.: Council for a Livable World Education Fund, Project on Peacekeeping and the United Nations, October 1995); "Final Results: 1996 US Funding for United Nations Peacekeeping" (Washington, D.C.: Council for a Livable World Education Fund, Program on Peacekeeping and the United Nations, May 1996), mimeograph; and "Status of 1997 US Funding for United Nations Peacekeeping," (Washington, D.C.: Council for a Livable World Education Fund, Program on Peacekeeping and the United Nations, July 1996), mimeograph

20. Exceptions have included Cyprus, where British peacekeepers have served since 1963. French infantry served with the UN in Lebanon in the first half of the 1980s. US officers have served as military observers in UN operations since the late 1940s but prior to 1993 only one US military unit had ever been subordinated to UN operational command. The unit was a small Air Force transport detail used to resupply a UN operation in West New Guinea that was overseeing the transition of that territory from Dutch to Indonesian rule in the early 1960s.

21. Paul F. Diehl, *International Peacekeeping* (Baltimore and London: Johns Hopkins University Press, 1993), 34, 37. For a critical review of Diehl's criteria, see Robert C. Johannsen, "U.N. Peacekeeping: How Should We Measure Success?" *Mershon International Studies Review* 38 (1994): 307-10.

22. Article 51 of the United Nations Charter provides that, "Nothing in the present Charter shall impair the inherent right of individual or collective self-defense if an

armed attack occurs against a Member of the United Nations, until the Security Council has taken measures necessary to maintain international peace and security."

23. There are a number of excellent recent collections on norms of military intervention. They include Laura W. Reed and Carl Kaysen, eds., *Emerging Norms of Justified Intervention* (Cambridge, MA: Committee on International Security Studies, American Academy of Arts and Sciences, 1993), especially chapters by Ernst Haas, Virginia Gamba, and Lori Fisler Damrosch, and commentary by Anne-Marie Slaughter Burley; Lori Damrosch and David J. Scheffer, *Law and Force in the New International Order* (Boulder, CO: Westview Press, 1991), especially chapters by Thomas Franck, Tom Farer, and Lori Damrosch; Anthony Clark Arend and Robert J. Beck, *International Law and the Use of Force* (London: Routledge, 1993), 80-137; and Lori Fisler Damrosch, ed., *Enforcing Restraint: Collective Intervention in Internal Conflicts* (New York: Council on Foreign Relations Press, 1993).

24. Joseph Campbell, *Myths to Live By* (New York: Bantam Books, 1973).

25. These cases are detailed in Durch, *Evolution of UN Peacekeeping*, chapters 12, 17 and 19.

26. The military stalemate established in Rwanda in 1993 had fallen apart by spring 1994. The UN redeployed in summer 1994, however, as though the situation remained a stalemate, and the international community focused on relief instead of rapidly rebuilding the government's capacity to govern. (See Vaccaro, "The Politics of Genocide," in this volume.) On problems with negotiating and implementing settlements of civil wars, see I. William Zartman, ed., *Illusive Peace: Negotiating an End to Civil Wars* (Washington, D.C.: The Brookings Institution, 1995); Paul Pillar, *Negotiating Peace: War Termination as a Bargaining Process* (Princeton, NJ: Princeton University Press, 1983); and Stephen John Stedman, *Peacemaking in Civil War: International Mediation in Zimbabwe, 1974-1980* (Boulder, CO: Lynne Rienner Publishers, 1990).

27. The entity in question is the Advisory Committee for Administrative and Budgetary Questions (ACABQ), which filters Secretariat requests for funds before they reach the financial committee of the General Assembly. Its 16 members include representatives from the finance ministries of the United States and most of the UN's other major funders; as such, it pays more attention to the bottom line than to the impact of its decisions on mission execution. It meets in closed session. Most of its recommendations are accepted by the Assembly, especially since budget resolutions must be passed by consensus at US insistence. Interview by the author, UN Secretariat, 23 February 1994; see also William Branigin, "17-Year Reign of Chairman of Watchdog Panel Questioned," *Washington Post,* 23 September 1992, A33.

28. One State Department official familiar with US operations in Haiti observed that had there been a deployable international police force available to move into Haiti on short notice, the United States would have been able to send home most of its troops "in two weeks." Author's interview, 27 October 1995.

29. For further details and discussion, see William J. Durch, "The Components of Peace Operations and Their Impact on Economic Development and Welfare" (background paper for the Organization for Economic Cooperation and Development Workshop

on Peacekeeping Operations and Development, Paris, November 1993, mimeo-graph). Copy available from the author on request.

30. The Government of Canada, *Towards a Rapid Reaction Capability for the United Nations* (Ottawa: Department of Foreign Affairs and International Trade and Department of Defence, September 1995), 50-51.

KNOWING WHEN TO SAY NO: THE DEVELOPMENT OF US POLICY FOR PEACEKEEPING[1]

IVO H. DAALDER

The early 1990s witnessed a wave of optimism about the effectiveness of a revived United Nations in what was then called the "New World Order." For decades, the UN Security Council had been shackled by Cold-War politics and the frequent use of the veto power. But with the end of the Cold War and the success of the UN-authorized action against Iraq in 1991, the United Nations suddenly seemed reborn. The five permanent members now cooperated in (or at least did not block) efforts to address an ever wider array of threats to international peace and security. As a result, the number of peacekeeping operations exploded, and their scope and objectives expanded. As the one remaining superpower, the United States was intimately involved in promoting the expansion of UN peace operations and proved increasingly willing to participate in these operations, contributing US forces to protect Kurdish refugees in northern Iraq and to provide famine relief in Somalia.

The rapid expansion in the number and scope of UN operations, led first the Bush administration and then its successor to review the US role in multilateral peace operations. Starting late in its tenure, the Bush administration was only able to sketch the bare outlines of a full-fledged US policy toward peace operations. In contrast, the Clinton administration placed a high priority on its review immediately upon entering office in early 1993 and aimed to produce a comprehensive statement on US policy toward peace operations.

Contrary to its expectations, however, the policy review—known as Presidential Review Directive (PRD) 13—became highly controversial for a variety of domestic and international political reasons. As UN operations in Bosnia, Cambodia, and Somalia teetered on the brink of failure throughout the spring and summer of 1993, there was growing skepticism about the United Nations and its ability to meet the expanding demand for ever more complex peace operations. As a result, congressional opposition to US involvement in UN operations mounted steadily. By early fall, the policy review had become the prime target of this opposition, with critics of the administration charging that the review reflected a misguided attempt to subvert US foreign policy to whims of an ineffective United Nations. Consequently, the administration was forced to state explicitly what had been implicit in the review: that peace operations were a limited, though important, element of US national security strategy, but not a substitute for or an alternative to such a strategy. Equally significant, those parts of the bureaucracy opposed to the early direction of the policy review seized on the growing criticism to buttress their arguments in favor of limited US engagement in UN operations.

In the end, therefore, President Clinton in May 1994 approved a policy, codified in Presidential Decision Directive (PDD) 25, that extended, but did not radically alter, the conclusions reached late in the Bush administration. Rather than expanding and strengthening what had initially been portrayed as an essential element of US security policy in the post–Cold War era, the objective of the new policy was to promote a "more selective and effective" approach to multilateral peace operations. In public explanations of the new policy, administration officials stressed that the circumstances under which the United States would participate in such operations would be guided by strict conditions designed to reduce the risks to American forces.

This chapter examines how domestic and international political realities helped shape deliberations on peacekeeping policy and limited the scope of the policy reviews. It starts with a discussion of the Bush administration's review of US peacekeeping policy, an effort that highlighted some of the major hurdles that the Clinton administration would face, notably in overcoming longstanding resistance by the US military to participate actively in UN operations. Next, the chapter details the evolution of the Clinton administration's efforts to develop a comprehensive policy and how it ultimately was forced to adapt to bureaucratic, domestic, and international political constraints. The PDD that emerged from these efforts in May 1994 was the first comprehensive statement ever on US policy toward multilateral peace operations, but one nevertheless significantly different from what many had expected when the effort began in early 1993.

THE BUSH ADMINISTRATION
DISCOVERS THE UNITED NATIONS

Although largely an American creation, the United Nations played little if any role in US foreign policy for most of its existence. The end of the Cold War and US success during the Gulf war changed all that. Thenceforth, the United Nations was to be a central player in President Bush's New World Order, especially as it related to peacekeeping. During an unprecedented summit meeting of the UN Security Council's heads of state in January 1992, the United States suggested that the Council ask the new UN secretary-general, Boutros Boutros-Ghali, to examine ways to strengthen UN peacekeeping capabilities.[2] The resulting report, *An Agenda for Peace,* set out an ambitious agenda dealing with preventive diplomacy, peacemaking, peacekeeping, and peace building activities. It even urged member states to negotiate special agreements with the United Nations to make military forces available to the Security Council on a permanent basis, as called for under Article 43 of the UN Charter.[3]

The expanding number and scope of UN peace operations inevitably raised a question about whether the United States should participate in these operations and, if so, how. During the Cold War, US participation in UN operations had necessarily been limited to logistical support, transportation (especially airlift), and a few observers sent to selected missions, but Cold War constraints no longer existed. By the summer of 1992, the Bush administration concluded that this limited role was no longer tenable and that, if the United Nations was to succeed, the United States would have to weigh in more heavily. In early August, therefore, a small working group was established under the direction of the National Security Council (NSC) to review the nature and extent of US participation in peacekeeping operations. The immediate goal of this review was to develop ideas in time for the president's speech to the United Nations General Assembly scheduled for late September.

Given this short time span, the NSC decided to focus its attention initially on ways to strengthen the UN's capacity to conduct peace operations and on ways in which the United States could contribute to this end. The results of this rapid review were announced by President Bush in his UN speech on 21 September 1992. Referring to peacekeeping, the president urged that "as much as the United Nations has done, it can do much more." He set out five areas that required improvement: better peacekeeping equipment and training at the national level; enhanced interoperability, planning, and training of multinational peacekeeping forces; an improved system for providing logistic support; an enhanced capability for planning, crisis management, and intelligence capabilities; and adequate and equitable financing of UN operations.[4]

In addition, Bush stated, "the United States is ready to do its part to strengthen world peace by strengthening international peacekeeping." Specific actions by the United States would include: a new emphasis on peacekeeping operations within the Department of Defense (DoD); providing lift, logistics, communications, and intelligence capabilities in support of UN operations; teaching peacekeeping doctrine in the curricula of all US military schools; providing US military expertise to the UN; making available US military bases and facilities for joint training; and reviewing how to fund peacekeeping operations to ensure "adequate" US financial support.[5]

The initial review had not addressed the politically more sensitive issue of US military participation in peacekeeping operations, confining itself instead to developing ways to enhance and support the United Nations. Immediately following the president's speech, however, a formal review of US peacekeeping policy was launched to examine this issue in depth.[6] The most important questions addressed in this review were, first, whether the United States should commit to participate in UN operations on a regular basis and, second, what form such participation would take.

Although it was generally agreed that the United States could no longer sustain the Cold War posture of nonparticipation, there was no agreement within the Bush administration on whether the United States should participate in the full range of UN operations. Some officials argued that both UN and US credibility demanded full participation. Supporters included members of the NSC staff and officials at State and the United Nations. Some middle-ranking military officers on the army staff and seconded to other agencies also supported full US participation, believing that peace operations represented a permanent fixture of the post–Cold War security environment and an important new mission for the army. Others within the administration, however, were adamantly opposed to full US participation. Opposition centered in the Joint Chiefs of Staff (JCS), especially around General Colin Powell, the JCS chairman, and in the Office of the Secretary of Defense (OSD), where Defense Secretary Dick Cheney sided with the senior military. Their view was that the United States should only contribute its "unique" capabilities, like airlift, command, control, and communication, and intelligence capabilities. Ground forces and equipment, they argued, could be provided by other countries. As a result of this opposition, a statement originally included in a draft decision memorandum, that "the US military will participate in the full range of peace operations," was deleted from the final policy directive. Instead, the president's January 1993 *National Security Strategy of the United States,* which presumably drew on the directive, merely stated that the United States would take "an active role in the full spectrum of UN peacekeeping and humanitarian relief *planning and support.*"[7]

Another major issue confronting the interagency review related to the kind of capabilities the United States should declare to be available in principle to the United Nations for future peace operations. Officials in the National Security Council proposed the novel concept of creating a "skeletal" peacekeeping force, a concept that went beyond previous UN practices but would fall well short of the UN secretary-general's call for negotiating agreements on standing forces. Under the concept, at least one of the brigade-sized units stationed at US military bases for peacekeeping training purposes would be ready on a rotating basis to deploy for an operation if called upon by the UN Security Council. This unit would, therefore, provide the United Nations with a small, rapid reaction force for immediate deployment in crisis situations. The NSC proposal was not well received in other parts of the administration. The JCS flatly opposed committing US units on this basis (even if the commitment was only periodic, rotating among brigades from other countries as well). Many in the administration also feared "a slippery slope": feared that, with forces directly at its disposal, the UN Security Council would be more inclined to approve their deployment than if forces had to be marshalled for a new mission. As a result, the concept of a skeletal reaction force was dropped from consideration. Instead, it was decided that the United States would "advise the United Nations that a full range of military capabilities could be placed at UN disposal in appropriate circumstances," but without specifying what types of capabilities these might include.[8]

The Bush administration also debated how the United States would participate in UN operations once the decision to do so had been made, particularly whether US combat personnel should ever serve under the operational control of a UN commander.[9] The JCS was "flatly opposed" to this concept and no decision about UN operational control of US-contributed forces was made during the review.

The interagency review process resulted in the first policy document devoted to US support of UN peacekeeping. The two-and-a-half page directive—National Security Decision Directive (NSDD) 74—that President Bush approved shortly before he left office, represented a first step in committing the United States to support UN operations. Nearly all of the document was devoted to issues relating to how the UN capability for peacekeeping should be strengthened. It endorsed the creation of an enhanced peacekeeping planning staff and operations center, a 24-hour communications center, improved training and analytical capabilities for the UN Secretariat, and improved training for peacekeeping personnel. As to US participation, the final decision directive remained vague, only endorsing the participation of US forces if the use of their "unique" military capabilities was necessary for the success of the mission. It specifically opposed creating a small rapid reaction force and rejected concluding an Article 43 agreement with the UN to provide forces on a standby basis, believing that this raised "significant military, organizational, and political questions."[10]

In the end, NSDD-74 served its main purpose: to devise a policy committing the United States to support UN peacekeeping. It was the first such policy since the Truman Administration. Though many working on the policy would have preferred to have gone further, there was insufficient time, given that the process did not get fully underway until September 1992. Opposition in the Pentagon also proved too strong to overcome. Finally, with President Bush's defeat in November 1992, the process ground to a virtual halt, leaving it to the next administration to develop a more comprehensive policy.

ENTER THE CLINTON ADMINISTRATION

The Clinton administration began its review of US peacekeeping policy soon after taking office. (An early draft of the review directive was completed three days after Clinton was sworn in.) Many members of the new administration viewed both peacekeeping and the United Nations in a positive light. During the campaign, then-candidate Clinton had supported a more interventionist policy to end human rights abuses in China, help restore democracy in Haiti, and reverse the horrendous campaign of "ethnic cleansing" in Bosnia. He had also frequently expressed support for the United Nations, and in April 1992, he had urged exploration of the idea to create a "Rapid Deployment Force that could be used for purposes beyond traditional peacekeeping, such as standing guard at the borders of countries threatened by aggression, preventing mass violence against civilian populations, providing humanitarian relief, and combatting terrorism."[11] High-level officials entering the new administration were similarly predisposed. Many shared a sense that the end of the Cold War offered the United States a new opportunity to stress the importance of human rights and the spread of democracy, themes most had actively promoted when they had served in the Carter administration. They also believed that the measured use of force could help alleviate human suffering in places like Bosnia, Somalia, northern Iraq, and Haiti. In short, the foreign policy team shared with Anthony Lake, Clinton's national security advisor, a preference for "pragmatic neo-Wilsonianism," where the primary objective would be the defense of human rights, enlargement of democracy, and support for market-based economies.[12]

The new administration's support for multilateralism, peacekeeping, and the United Nations also had a practical, political basis. The president, after all, had been elected on a domestic agenda and he was deeply committed to focusing his energy and attention on domestic renewal. The mere fact of dwindling resources, combined with a predisposition to support a more interventionist policy, suggested the need for multilateral cooperation. A commitment to support and participate in multilateral peace operations, therefore, was essential to allow for greater burden sharing in efforts to create a sense of international order in an increasingly fragmented post–Cold War world.

Assertive Multilateralism

The strategy to achieve these ends was one that combined the continuing need for American engagement and leadership with the imperative for multilateralism. Dubbed "assertive multilateralism" by Madeleine Albright, the new US ambassador to the United Nations, the strategy suggested that,

> Though sometimes we will act alone, our foreign policy will necessarily point toward multilateral engagement. But unless the United States also exercises leadership within collective bodies like the United Nations, there is a risk that multilateralism will not serve our national interest well—in fact, it may undermine our interests. These two realities—multilateral engagement and US leadership within collective bodies—require an "assertive multilateralism" that advances US foreign policy goals.[13]

A central element in the strategy of assertive multilateralism had to be a commitment by the United States to strengthen UN peace operations, which would be possible only if the United States was actively committed to participate in such operations. In the early months of the new administration, senior officials repeatedly returned to this theme. At his confirmation hearings in January 1993, Secretary of Defense Les Aspin testified that "being present at the creation of a post–Cold War era . . . means creating new international organizations. And high on the list is this question of how do you create international peacekeeping organizations and peacemaking organizations."[14] In April, Secretary of State Warren Christopher noted that the administration was placing a "new emphasis on promoting multinational peacekeeping and peacemaking."[15] In June, Ambassador Albright maintained that "the time has come to commit the political, intellectual, and financial capital that UN peacekeeping and our security deserve."[16] And a few weeks later she told Congress that "Peacekeeping has become instrumental in meeting three fundamental imperatives of our national interest: economic, political, and humanitarian."[17]

Moreover, in a visible sign that the new civilian leadership in the Pentagon meant to throw its full support behind these pronouncements, it created a new position for an assistant secretary of defense for peacekeeping and democracy within the proposed reorganization of the Office of the Secretary of Defense. Frank Wisner, the undersecretary of defense for policy, was dispatched to Congress to indicate that peacekeeping "will no longer be an ancillary portion of the thinking of the Department of Defense; it will lie right at the *core* of our activities in the Office of the Secretary and the Uniformed Armed Forces." As to the specific issue of US participation, Wisner noted that

> the United States is truly unique in the skills that we can bring to bear in peacekeeping. And that is inherent in the nature of our forces, the mobility that we have, the capacity to deploy, command and control, [and] in intelligence assets. We are, to all serious peacekeeping undertakings in this world, the *central element*. There is no getting away from it.[18]

The Reluctant Military

Despite the different emphasis and tone that accompanied the change in administrations, there remained one crucial constituency that was less enamored with the prospect of greater US involvement in multilateral peace operations, and that was the American military. The main concern was eloquently addressed by General Powell in September 1993 when he provided a brief tutorial on the nature of the armed forces:

> Notwithstanding all of the changes that have taken place in the world, notwithstanding the new emphasis on peacekeeping, peace enforcement, peace engagement, preventive diplomacy, we have a value system and a culture system within the armed forces of the United States. We have this mission: to fight and win the nation's wars. . . .
>
> Because we are able to fight and win the nation's wars, because we are warriors, we are also uniquely able to do some of these other new missions that are coming along—peacekeeping, humanitarian relief, disaster relief—you name

it, we can do it. . . . But we never want to do it in such a way that we lose sight
of the focus of why you have armed forces—to fight and win the nation's wars.[19]

The warrior culture of US armed forces reflected not only the military's perceived
lessons of the Vietnam War but also its very limited experience with peacekeeping.
Except for a small number of Army units that had provided troops for the multinational
force in the Sinai and the disastrous experience by a limited number of Marines in
Beirut, the US military knew little about the nature and context of UN peacekeeping.
It therefore tended to distrust the enterprise or, at the very least, see it as an endeavor
to which US combat forces could contribute little. Although this attitude began to
change as UN peace operations became more numerous and as senior officers became
more exposed to the realities of peacekeeping in such places as northern Iraq, the
former Yugoslavia, and Somalia, the level of distrust remained high in many military
quarters, especially those around General Powell. Finally, while many demonstrated
an increasing willingness to learn more about the United Nations and help the
organization to improve its capacity to conduct effective operations, this willingness
never really translated into an interest to seek broader US participation in these
operations.

In conducting its review of US policy toward multilateral peace operations, the
Clinton administration was bound to take the views of the military into account.
Indeed, this administration was likely to be highly sensitive to the views of senior
military officers. President Clinton was the first postwar president not to have served
in uniform and the issue of his lack of service during the Vietnam War had been
repeatedly raised during the presidential campaign. Moreover, from the outset of his
presidency, Clinton had been on a collision course with the military over the question
of homosexuals serving in the nation's armed forces, something the president favored
but many in the military vehemently opposed. The last thing the administration
needed was to clash with the military on another issue of major importance.

Presidential Review Directive Thirteen

It was against this background that the Clinton administration conducted its review
of multilateral peace operations. Presidential Review Directive–13, signed in early
February 1993, provided an all-encompassing mandate to review the entire spectrum
of peace operations, from traditional peacekeeping to large-scale peace enforcement
operations falling just short of war. The review asked four basic questions:[20] When to
engage in peace operations? Who should conduct peace operations—the UN, regional
organizations, or ad hoc coalitions? How can UN peacekeeping be fixed? How can the
US system to support peace operations be improved?

The PRD also identified three fundamental problems that had to be addressed:
the inability of the United Nations to engage in expanded missions; the reluctance of
the United Nations to act in nonpermissive environments; and the increasing demands
being placed on the United Nations to engage in new operations.

To examine these issues, the PRD sought to devise "a plan for the long-term strengthening of UN peacekeeping and US capacity to participate."[21] Its mandate was all-encompassing, including a review of the overall role of peacekeeping, the role of regional organizations, the administrative and operational capabilities of the United Nations, financing, command and control mechanisms, the structure of the US governmental organization supporting these activities, and the executive-legislative relationship. The interagency review, which was chaired by the National Security Council, involved participants from the State Department, the Pentagon, the JCS, the US mission to the United Nations (USUN), the National Intelligence Council (NIC), and the Office of Management and Budget (OMB).

The PRD review was to be on a fast track. The goal was to complete the review and draft a Presidential Decision Directive outlining US policy on multilateral peace operations by April 1993. Many of the working-level people involved in the review had earlier participated in the development of NSDD-74. Indeed, Richard Clarke, the NSC's senior director for global issues and multilateral affairs, was the primary NSC person in charge of both the Bush and the Clinton administrations' reviews. The issues were therefore familiar, while some of the earlier constraints—notably the imminence of elections and lack of cooperation from OSD—were absent. As a result, the review proceeded smoothly, and many of the interagency differences had been resolved by April. In May, a full-fledged draft of the executive summary and decision paper was circulated by Richard Clarke to his assistant-secretary-level counterparts in other agencies. With one important exception, the draft was largely approved by these officials.

The Rapid Reaction Force

The exception concerned the issue of a UN rapid reaction force. During the transition between the Bush and Clinton administrations, a Clinton study group had tentatively endorsed the establishment of a standing UN army. However, when the group reviewed its conclusions with General Powell, he said: "As long as I am Chairman of the Joint Chiefs of Staff, I will not agree to commit American men and women to an unknown war, in an unknown land, for an unknown cause, under an unknown commander, for an unknown duration." According to a Pentagon official, "that was the end of the idea."[22] Except for some officials in USUN, no one seriously sought to reopen this question during the review except to endorse the idea that the issue might be studied in the future. Accordingly, while the draft acknowledged a need for the kind of capability proposed by the UN secretary-general, it rejected a large standing force "at this time."[23]

Having rejected a UN standing army or earmarking specific US military units for deployment on short notice upon the call of the UN Security Council, the interagency review then considered the alternative idea of creating a small rapid reaction force. Arguing that Clinton's campaign statements in favor of the force gave the idea new salience, NSC officials in charge of the review revived in a somewhat different form the concept of rapidly deployable units rejected by the previous administration. Thus, the draft decision paper specifically endorsed the establishment of a brigade-sized "on-call ready unit," which, while stationed in its home country, could be deployed within 72 hours of the UN Security Council having voted to reinforce existing operations or initiate a new one. The unit, which would be modeled after a brigade of the US 82nd Airborne division, would be made available on a rotating basis by different nations for six months at a time, although the country contributing the unit would always retain the final say over its deployment.

The concept of a small rapid reaction force had political appeal. It responded to one of the glaring weaknesses facing UN peace operations: the inability to respond rapidly in a crisis. And it was consistent with the idea the president himself had raised during the campaign. But critics of the force raised many practical problems: What kind of brigade should be made available? What sort of equipment should it possess? Who would guide its training? And who would bear responsibility for logistic support? Moreover, it was evident that formal endorsement of a rapid reaction force would face major opposition from the US military. The military had always hesitated about placing US troops under UN control and would certainly oppose doing so as a matter of stated policy. In view of this inevitable opposition, even some of those who supported the force warned that in pushing for its creation the administration risked a major battle with the JCS that might sour the entire effort to strengthen and expand multilateral peace operations.

Discussion of the proposed rapid reaction force exposed a major rift in the administration. Clearly in support of the idea were NSC officials in charge of the review and officials at USUN. The former believed that the force fulfilled the president's campaign commitment, while the latter argued that this capability was necessary to strengthen the UN's peacekeeping capabilities. Opposition crystallized in the Pentagon, especially in the JCS, where Powell's views on the concept were well known. The State Department was also unenthusiastic, believing that creation of the force would challenge its control over US peacekeeping policy. In what one Defense Department official described as the "night of the long knives," the issue was ultimately resolved when Frank Wisner wrote Samuel (Sandy) Berger, the deputy national security advisor, that, if the idea of establishing a rapid reaction force remained in the draft, his department would not support any part of the PRD. As a result of this intervention, the endorsement of a small rapid reaction force was deleted from the draft before the interagency working group chaired by Clarke met to consider the proposed policy.

Toward a Presidential Decision Directive

Following the approval of the PRD-13 decision paper in May, the interagency working group moved forward with drafting a final presidential decision directive on multilateral peace operations. By July 1993, the essential framework of the document was in place, with 95 percent of the text agreed upon. What remained in contention was the issue of who would be responsible for financing the increasing cost of present and future peacekeeping operations. Apart from this difference between State and Defense, a final draft of the presidential decision directive was approved on 19 July 1993, by the NSC's Deputies Committee, chaired by Sandy Berger and composed of the chief policy advisors (usually undersecretaries) of the relevant departments and agencies. What follows is an overview of its main contents.

The Role of Multilateral Peace Operations

The one-page introduction of the PDD draft was a forceful endorsement of multilateral peace operations. It suggested that peacekeeping often offered the best way for the international community to prevent, contain, and solve conflicts. The draft also expressed support for the "rapid expansion" of UN operations, noted the greatly expanded US role in peacekeeping, and committed the United States to support these operations "politically, militarily, and financially."[24] And while the draft PDD stated that the United States would maintain the capability to act unilaterally or in coalitions when US or allied interests were threatened, it maintained that "wherever appropriate" the United States would employ multilateral peacekeeping as a "key element" of its national security strategy. As one State Department official noted: "The difference with this Administration is that it envisions the United States, in principle, taking part in any peacekeeping operations in any capacity."[25] In this, the draft PDD represented a major departure from NSDD-74, which had merely endorsed the contribution of "unique" military capabilities.

When to Intervene

A key element of the draft PDD was the inclusion of two sets of specific guidelines (initially called criteria) to inform decisions relating to when the United States should (1) vote in favor of future UN peace operations and (2) participate in such operations.[26] These guidelines, elaborated in the PRD decision paper approved earlier, stipulated that before the United States would endorse establishing new UN operations it should be clear that there is a threat to international order, which could include threats arising from a "sudden and unexpected interruption of established democracy or gross violations of human rights";[27] a consensus within the international community to deal with the problem on a multilateral basis; clear objectives, including an understanding of where the mission fits on the continuum between peacemaking and peace enforcement; and available means, including forces, financing, and a mandate, to accomplish the mission.

A separate set of guidelines dealt with the issue of US participation in multilateral peace operations. According to the PDD draft, the United States might contribute troops if specific or general US interests would be advanced by US participation; forces are available without an unacceptable impact on military readiness; participation is necessary for the success of the mission or to persuade others to participate; the command and control relationship is acceptable; an end point to the US role can be identified; and there is domestic, including Congressional, support for participation.

Who's in Charge

The PDD draft also addressed the question of who would command and control American forces in multilateral peace operations. This section of the paper, which was drafted by the Pentagon with little input from other agencies, stated that while the president would always retain command authority over US forces, the United States could, on a case-by-case basis, allow American forces to be placed under the operational control of a UN or foreign commander. This conclusion had been presaged by a decision during the Bush administration in early 1993 to place US support troops in Somalia under the control of the UN force commander once the United Nations took over political and military command of the mission. Having set this precedent, the JCS conceded that future circumstances might warrant similar arrangements, hence the PDD's conclusion that American forces could serve under foreign or UN control so long as the decision was made on a case-by-case basis. The latter caveat was included to ensure that the commander was acceptable to the United States, implying that he or she had to come from a country with a first-rate military or from a NATO ally.

The PDD draft rejected participation in open-ended commitments and ordered US unit commanders to maintain separate channels of communication to US military authorities. It noted that American unit commanders operating as part of UN operations would be instructed not to comply with orders that they believed were outside the mandate of the mission, illegal under US or international law, or "militarily imprudent and unsound."[28] While the Pentagon insisted on this language, some officials acknowledged that particularly this last provision represented a "double-edged sword." Ambassador Albright acknowledged to an audience of US Army officers that this reservation of national decision-making powers would make for "serious command and control problems" in a UN force.[29]

A UN Data Base, Not a UN Army

The draft also addressed the issue of creating a standing UN force or earmarking military units and capabilities to be available to the UN Security Council on short notice. It stated that the United States would not support negotiating an Article 43 agreement "at this time," but it did call for subsequent revisiting of this issue as well as the rapid reaction force proposal rejected earlier. It also proposed the development of a UN data base of available forces modeled along the lines of the NATO Defense Planning Questionnaire (DPQ). In the DPQ, NATO countries list annually the forces and capabilities available in each of four categories: those already under NATO command, those that could be under NATO command within 72 hours, those that could be under NATO command within a set number of days, and those unlikely to be available for NATO command. NATO's military staff then uses these data to ascertain what forces would be available to NATO within what time frame in a crisis and does its force planning accordingly.

The draft PDD suggested that the NATO DPQ would be a useful model for planning UN peacekeeping operations. If members were to deliver detailed lists of the forces or capabilities that they could make available to the UN, then UN headquarters in New York could, like its NATO counterpart in Belgium, put together composite units for planning purposes. Even though notification would not imply commitment and any UN request for specific capabilities would necessarily have to be reviewed on a case-by-case basis, the advance information would allow the United Nations to conduct planning for future operations. The idea, as Ambassador Albright later noted, was to develop a "data base of who has what so that the Secretary-General doesn't have to go around with a tin cup."[30]

Professionalizing the United Nations

A major aim of the administration's review was to boost the prestige, staff, and resources of UN units dealing with peacekeeping and, more generally, to enhance the United Nations' capability to meet the growing demand for peace operations. In June, Ambassador Albright had suggested that serious shortcomings existed within the United Nations: "If I had to choose a single word to evoke the problems of UN peace-keeping, it would be 'improvisation.' . . . A kind of programmed amateurism shows up across the board."[31] Accordingly, the PDD draft, drawing on much of the previous work done as part of the NSDD-74 process, proposed that the staff at the UN's military headquarters be more than doubled (to 100 people), with 20 officials seconded (assigned temporarily) from the State and Defense Departments. It also proposed to reorganize the UN Department of Peacekeeping Operations by creating an information/research division (to analyze intelligence provided by the United States and other sources); an operations division with encrypted command, control, and communications facilities that would be staffed around the clock; a planning division to review future peacekeeping requirements; and a logistics division, which would command a standing airlift capability using commercial or leased Russian military transport aircraft. The draft also called for the establishment of a rapidly deployable headquarters team to support the startup of new operations.

Footing the Bill

When the draft PDD was presented to the NSC's Deputies Committee for approval, one final issue remained unresolved. This, not surprisingly, was the issue of financing, which was of growing concern both because the US share of UN peacekeeping assessments continued to increase and the overall cost of peacekeeping had steadily risen, reaching $3 billion in 1993.[32] The draft settled the question of how the Defense Department should be reimbursed for expenditures made in support of UN operations.

The United States would be fully reimbursed at the standard UN rate for US personnel. State could take a credit against its UN assessment if dedicated and appropriated peacekeeping funding were available to Defense to reimburse the armed services. If not, the reimbursement from the UN would first be used to cover DoD's cost. The Pentagon would also be directly and fully reimbursed by the UN for the provision of goods and services, although the president could waive this requirement in exceptional circumstances.[33]

The draft failed, however, to resolve differences between the State and Defense Departments over who would control peacekeeping funds and take lead responsibility for managing multilateral operations in the future. It was agreed that no DoD funds would be transferred to State for peacekeeping purposes or used to pay State's UN assessment.[34] But who would pay the mounting UN peacekeeping assessment was left unresolved. Though State saw the Pentagon's budget as a ready source of funds, it was fearful that a shift in financial responsibility would end up in a transfer of policy control. As one senior State Department official warned, "Peacekeeping funding and policy are inextricably intertwined."[35] The sentiment was correct, for Defense was unlikely to shift control over its own budget to another agency.

Notwithstanding the failure to resolve differences over financing and lead responsibility, the PDD draft represented a major, albeit evolutionary, change in US policy toward multilateral peace operations. Most important was the general tone of the document, which supported an enhanced use of multilateral operations, boosted the United Nations as a major actor on the world stage, and fully committed the United States to support such operations in all their political, military, and financial dimensions. This changing perspective was welcome news to the United Nations, where Kofi Annan, the undersecretary-general in charge of peacekeeping, gratefully acknowledged that there was "a definite change of mood and [a] willingness from the United States to be partners. . . . As UN operations become ever more complex and cumbersome to manage, US participation becomes ever more important."[36]

THE LIMITS OF PEACEKEEPING

Soon after the draft decision directive had been approved by the NSC's deputies, however, the dangers inherent in the new and expanding forms of peace operations became painfully apparent on the streets of Mogadishu, Somalia's war-ridden capital. As the summer of 1993 progressed, conflict mounted between US forces and the Somali faction of the dominant warlord in Mogadishu, Mohammed Farah Aideed, and American casualties mounted. Public unease and congressional criticism of American policy grew throughout the summer, and the administration scrambled to define the mission of the US forces and the UN Operation in Somalia (UNOSOM II) in a way that would help extricate American troops quickly yet not undermine the credibility of the United Nations in addressing new types of conflict.

Inevitably, the events in Somalia had a profound effect on American views of the utility of armed force in addressing the many intractable conflicts underway after the Cold War's end. Their impact was compounded by the continuing tragedy in Bosnia, where the UN appeared to be mired in its mandate to deliver humanitarian relief and the United States, constrained by its refusal to put troops on the ground, repeatedly failed to convince its NATO allies that Serb aggression deserved decisive punishment. Thus, while the development of the administration's new policy proceeded on the assumption that UN peacekeeping was a central element in the evolving world order, the difficulties confronting the UN's blue helmets in Somalia, Bosnia, and elsewhere were putting that assumption to a severe test.

The Somali Operation Goes Off Track

President Bush had sent 31,000 American troops to Somalia in December 1992 to create a "secure environment" that would enable feeding millions of Somalis, some 3,000 of whom were starving every day. Within weeks, this operation facilitated the food deliveries that averted the immediate threat of large-scale starvation, and in February 1993 the United States began to withdraw most of its forces. Control of the operation was handed to the United Nations in May. UNOSOM II's mandate was to disarm all Somali factions and aid the process of political reconciliation, both of which would be necessary to avoid a recurrence of the deplorable conditions that had prevailed in Somalia only a few months earlier.[37]

Within weeks of UNOSOM taking control, however, the nation-building mission went badly off track. On 5 June 1993, Aideed's faction decided to challenge the UN's authority in Mogadishu by ambushing a Pakistani patrol, killing 24. The next day, the Security Council called on UN forces to arrest and punish those responsible for the attack. Over the next four months, the UN operation in Mogadishu was essentially characterized by combat rather than reconciliation. A small task force of US Army Rangers was sent to Mogadishu in an attempt to find and capture Aideed. Inevitably, American forces themselves became targets in the war and on 8 August, four US soldiers were killed when their vehicle was blown up by a remote-detonated mine.

Congressional Criticism Mounts

As the conflict in the streets of Mogadishu escalated and American casualties mounted, congressional opposition to the mission began to grow. Writing in the *New York Times,* Senator Robert Byrd warned that the "death of four American soldiers in Mogadishu this month and the overt hostility of Somalis toward UN troops shows that the operation is quickly crumbling." The senator noted the lack of congressional and public consensus in favor of US participation in missions aimed at "forcing political reconciliation. . . . Without a consensus, the likely result of such an operation could be a cut-and-run failure similar to the Beirut disaster of 1982 to 1984. Lacking congressional and popular support, US combat forces in Somalia should be removed as soon as possible."[38] Weeks later, Senator Byrd sought to force the administration's hand by introducing a resolution proposing to cut off all funding for American forces in Somalia. Although support for a binding resolution was thin, Senator Byrd's criticism of administration policy was shared by many of his colleagues. On 10 September 1993, the Senate voted 90 to 7 for in a nonbinding resolution urging President Clinton to consult with Congress, report by 15 October on the administration's goals and objectives in Somalia, and receive congressional authorization by 15 November to continue the US deployment in Somalia. Three weeks later, the House adopted an identical resolution by a vote of 406 to 26.[39]

The Fatal Flaws of Multilateralism

While the congressional criticism was directed specifically at US policy in Somalia, it was part of an emerging, more general critique of the Clinton administration's emphasis on multilateralism. Led by former, mostly Republican, foreign policy officials, this wider critique faulted the administration for supposedly ignoring American national interests in its conduct of foreign policy. Representative of these views were two major broadsides by Jeane Kirkpatrick, President Reagan's ambassador to the United Nations, and former Secretary of State Henry Kissinger.

Kirkpatrick argued that Clinton had made American foreign policy subservient to the United Nations, contending that for "the Clinton team, implementing the decisions of the UN Security Council and the secretary general in Somalia, Bosnia, Cambodia, or wherever is our foreign policy." This, according to Kirkpatrick, is "a vision of foreign policy from which national self-interest is purged." She concluded that the "reason the Clinton administration's foreign policy seems indecisive is that multilateral decision-making is characteristically complicated and inconclusive. The reason Clinton policy seems ineffective is that UN operations—in Bosnia or Somalia or wherever—are characteristically ineffective."[40]

Kissinger focused his critique more specifically on the administration's policy toward multilateral peace operations, emphasizing in particular the drawbacks of Clinton's enthusiasm for US participation in UN peacekeeping operations:

> If these statements imply that international consensus is the prerequisite for the employment of American power, the result may be ineffective dithering, as has happened over Bosnia. If they mean that international machinery can commit US forces, the risk is American involvement in issues of no fundamental national interest, as is happening in Somalia.[41]

Referring specifically to the reported contents of the peacekeeping policy draft, which had been leaked to the *Washington Post* in early August, Kissinger noted that the administration had failed to relate the use of American force to a concept of the national interest: "the implication that the absence of any definable national interest is a viable criterion for risking American lives could erode the willingness of the American people to support any use of military power for any purpose."[42]

THE ADMINISTRATION RESPONDS

By mid-September 1993, then, the Clinton administration's foreign policy was under broad attack. The Somalia mission had gone badly off track, and the situation in Bosnia was getting worse by the day despite a large UN presence. In neither case did the administration have a convincing answer on how the situation could be rapidly improved. Critics also attacked the administration's commitment to multilateralism, arguing that this both undermined much-needed American leadership and subordinated US national interests to the concerns of multilateral bodies like the United Nations. These two strands of criticism coalesced in opposition to the administration's evolving peacekeeping policy. As details of the evolving policy appeared in the press, concern mounted regarding the administration's support for an expanded role for UN peacekeeping. Congressional and public opposition also focused on more parochial concerns, notably the administration's stated willingness to send American forces on new missions and under the control of UN commanders.[43]

In response to these concerns, the interagency redrafted key aspects of the policy originally approved by the NSC's Deputies Committee in July. This effort was directed less at changing substance than at clarifying implicit assumptions of the policy in order to address some of the critics' concerns. Thus, the new draft toned down the introduction, which had earlier been highly supportive of peacekeeping. For example, it noted that UN peace operations could not substitute for the necessity of fighting and winning wars, and that preparation for conducting these operations must not diminish the US ability to act unilaterally or in concert with others when American national interests demanded such action. Nevertheless, the draft still fully supported UN peace operations as a cost-effective tool for advancing US interests and, accordingly, suggested that US and UN capabilities for conducting peace operations be strengthened. And, like the earlier draft, it proposed that the United States expand its support for the United Nations "politically, militarily, and financially."

The new draft also sought to sharpen the guidelines on future peace operations and US participation. In particular, the document opted for a "three-tiered approach" in which stricter guidelines were introduced as decision-making moved from whether or not to back a UN operation, to the involvement of US troops, to the commitment of US forces to combat.[44] Regarding the first tier, the new draft added two guidelines (see table 2.1):[45] first, in the case of an operation conducted under Chapter VI of the UN Charter, a cease-fire should be in place and the parties to the conflict should consent to the UN presence; and, second, an end point to UN participation should have been identified. In addition, the draft underscored that peace operations should be linked to concrete political solutions, and not reflect open-ended commitments. In this regard, it noted that before the Security Council voted to establish a new UN peace operation, the operation should have a timetable tied to specific objectives, specified troop levels, provisions for mission termination, and a firm budget estimate.

Although the new draft made few changes to the guidelines governing a US decision to participate in peace operations, it repeatedly stressed that the greater the

Table 2.1

THE DRAFTING OF KEY ELEMENTS OF PDD-25

Key Element	July 1993 Draft	Sept. 1993 Draft	Final Policy
Guidelines for supporting UN operations	1. Threat to international order	1. Threat to international peace/security	1. (No change)
	2. Clear objectives, and agreement on whether mission is peacekeeping or enforcement	2. (No change)	2. (No change)
	3. Appropriate mandate, forces, financing available	3. (No change)	3. (No change)
	4. International consensus support	4. (No change)	4. International consensus and advances US interests
		5. If Ch. VI, cease-fire is in place and parties agree to UN presence	5. If Ch. VI, cease-fire in place; if Ch. VII, threat to peace and security is significant
		6. Identifiable end point to UN participation	6. Realistic criteria for ending operation
			7. Consequences of inaction unacceptable
Guidelines for US participation in UN operations	1. Advances US interests	1. (No change)	1. (No change)
	2. Necessary for mission success, or other states' participation	2. (No change)	2. If necessary for success of mission
	3. Identifiable end point	3. (No change)	3. Clear objectives and identifiable end point
	4. Acceptable command and control relationship	4. (No change)	4. (No change)
	5. Domestic/congressional support exists	5. Domestic/congressional support exists or can be marshalled	5. (No change)
	6. No unacceptable impact on military readiness	6. (deleted)	6. Unique/general risks to US troops are acceptable
		7. Funds/personnel available, acceptable risks	

Key Element	July 1993 Draft	Sept. 1993 Draft	Final Policy
Guidelines for US participation in combat	(None)	1. Sufficient forces to achieve clearly defined objectives	1. (No change)
		2. Decisive use of force	2. (No change)
		3. Adjust force size to achieve objectives	3. (No change)
		4. Commitment is last resort	4. (deleted)
		5. Domestic support exists or can be marshalled	5. (deleted)
Guidelines on UN command	1. Forces under US command, but can be under UN control	1. (No change)	1. (No change)
	2. Ignore orders that are outside mandate, illegal, or "militarily imprudent or unsound"	2. Appeal orders that are outside mandate or illegal, first to UN command then to US authorities	2. (No change)
		3. High-risk operations not under UN control	3. (No change)
Position on "Article 43 Agreements"	1. Reject "at this time"; study issue in future	1. (No change)	1. (No change)
	2. Notify UN of specific types of capabilities that can be made available on case-by-case basis	2. (No change)	2. (No change)

SOURCES: Barton Gellman, "Wider UN Police Role Supported," *Washington Post*, 5 August 1993, A1; Gellman, "US Reconsiders Putting GIs Under UN," *Washington Post*, 22 September 1993, A1; Madeleine K. Albright, "Remarks to the National War College" (Fort McNair: National Defense University, 23 September 1993), 7; Paul Lewis, "US Plans Policy on Peacekeeping," *New York Times*, 18 November 1993, A7; and Department of State, Bureau of International Organization Affairs, *The Clinton Administration's Policy on Reforming Multilateral Peace Operations*, publication 10161 (Washington, D.C., May 1994).

US role in any operation, the less likely it would be that the United States would allow a UN commander to exercise operational control over US forces. Instead, in these circumstances the United States would prefer to lead an international coalition acting under UN Security Council authority. Accordingly, the new draft added an entirely new tier of demanding guidelines for deciding whether US forces should engage in combat as part of peace enforcement operations (those authorized under Chapter VII of the UN Charter). These new guidelines had long been championed by the Pentagon but were specifically excluded in earlier drafts.[46] Following the events in Somalia, however, the Pentagon's longstanding preference was now explicitly included. This new set of guidelines suggested that the US might contribute troops to an enforcement operation when the operation is in the US national interest; there is a clear intention to achieve objectives decisively; political and military objectives are clearly defined and sufficient forces to achieve those objectives have been committed; the relationship between the size, composition, and disposition of forces and the objectives is reassessed and adjusted when necessary; the commitment of US forces to combat is a last resort; and there is domestic support for US involvement or this can be marshalled.

Aside from the guidelines, other changes in the new draft addressed the command and control relationship of US forces serving under the operational control of a UN commander. The statement that US personnel serving in UN missions could refuse to obey orders if they judged these to be "militarily imprudent and unsound" was deleted.[47] Finally, a high-level interagency task force had also resolved the question of how to finance the mounting cost of UN peacekeeping. Dubbed "shared responsibility," the proposed solution of the financing issue was that the State Department would take financial and leadership responsibility for all UN peacekeeping operations conducted under Chapter VI of the UN Charter, while Defense would be financially responsible and have authority over all operations, like Somalia and Bosnia, conducted under Chapter VII as well as any UN operations in which US combat units were present.[48]

The new draft was presented to the administration's top national security officials on 17 September 1993, when the NSC's Principals Committee met to discuss the new peacekeeping policy.[49] Meeting under the twin shadows of the mounting disaster in Somalia and growing political unease about UN and multilateral peace operations generally, the principals were not inclined to approve a draft policy directive on peacekeeping at this time. Despite the considerable changes in the new draft, moreover, some offices were said to be particularly concerned with the imprecise language of the guidelines for involvement in various UN operations.[50] There was also considerable unease about placing US forces routinely under UN operational control. Congressional criticism of the Somalia mission—which wrongly blamed the United Nations for US casualties even though US forces involved in the hunt for Aideed were under US, not UN, control—made such a commitment untenable. As a result, the Principals Committee meeting ended without the expected endorsement of the new policy, and the administration sought instead to deal with the growing criticism of its foreign policy.

A Public Retreat

In late September 1993, the administration turned to publicly defending its foreign policy. In a series of speeches, ending with the president's address to the United Nations on 27 September, top administration officials moved steadily away from their previous emphasis on multilateralism and support for peacekeeping. In the first speech, Secretary Christopher addressed the role of multilateralism in the administration's policies, linking its potential utility directly to American national interests: "Multilateralism is a means, not an end. It is one of the many foreign policy tools at our disposal. And it is warranted only when it serves the central purpose of American foreign policy: to protect American interests."[51] The next day, Anthony Lake sounded a similar theme: "Only one overriding fact can determine whether the US should act multilaterally or unilaterally, and that is America's interests. We should act multilaterally where doing so advances our interests—and we should act unilaterally when *that* will serve our purpose."[52]

The task of explaining the administration's evolving attitude toward UN peacekeeping was left to Ambassador Albright. Noting that the "UN emerged from 40 years of Cold War rivalry overweight and out of shape," Albright suggested the need for fundamental change: "reformed budget procedures, more dependable sources of military and civilian personnel, better training, better intelligence, better command and control, better equipment, and more money." Above all, UN decision-making procedures needed to be overhauled, and she spelled out tough questions (now included in the PDD draft) that had to be considered before new missions were approved. In short, she declared, no one "should be sent in harm's way without a clear mission, competent commanders, sensible rules of engagement, and the means required to get the job done."[53]

A similarly tough theme was sounded by the president in his speech to the UN General Assembly. Clinton told the gathering in New York that "the United Nations simply cannot become engaged in every one of the world's conflicts. If the American people are to say yes to UN peacekeeping, the United Nations must know how to say no." He suggested the need to ask some

> harder questions . . . Does the proposed mission have clear objectives? Can an end point be identified for those who will be asked to participate? How much will the mission cost? From now on, the United Nations should address these and other hard questions for every proposed mission before we vote and before the missions begins.[54]

Immediately following his speech, the president demonstrated what this new attitude would mean for decisions relating to future peacekeeping missions in which the United States participated. Referring to Bosnia, where the United States had pledged to contribute upwards of 25,000 troops to enforce a peace agreement, Clinton laid down a series of stiff conditions:

I would want a clear understanding of what the command and control was, and I would want the NATO commander in charge of the operation. I would want a clear timetable for the first review and ultimately for a right to terminate American involvement . . . . I would want a clear political strategy along with the military strategy . . . . And I would want a clear expression of support from the Congress. Now there are 20 other operational things I would want, but those are the big policy issues.[55]

The administration's public retreat came none too soon. On 3 October 1993 yet another US attempt to capture Aideed ended in a nine-hour gunfight, resulting in 18 Americans killed, 78 wounded, and 1 soldier taken hostage—a one-day US combat casualty total that exceeded any since the Vietnam War. With pictures of dead American soldiers being dragged triumphantly through Mogadishu streets appearing on every American TV screen, the congressional and public reaction was instantaneous and severe.[56] There were cries for the immediate withdrawal of all American forces, sometimes coupled with calls for swift and sure retaliation. Leading the pack, Senator Byrd resurrected his resolution calling for the withdrawal of US troops, saying that "Americans by the dozens are paying with their lives and limbs for a misplaced policy on the altar of some fuzzy multilateralism."[57]

On 7 October, President Clinton promised that all American forces would be withdrawn from Somalia within six months, but would be beefed up in the meantime "under American command . . . to protect our troops and our bases."[58] This retreat quieted the congressional uproar and found support from the American public. But the experience proved sobering for all concerned, including the president. In mid-October, Clinton questioned future American participation in operations that were not under US operational control:

My experiences in Somalia would make me more cautious about having any Americans in a peacekeeping role where there was any ambiguity at all about what the range of decisions were which could be made by a command other than an American command with direct accountability to the United States here.[59]

In so doing, the president followed Congress in placing the blame for the Somali debacle squarely on the United Nations. Lost in the commotion was the fact that the 3 October raid was instigated by US forces operating under US control and without the prior knowledge of UN commanders on the scene.[60] In blaming the UN, the administration may have somewhat limited political damage to itself, but it further soured congressional attitudes toward the United Nations.[61]

Back to the Drawing Board

In the aftermath of the political uproar following the disaster in Mogadishu, the working group preparing the new peacekeeping policy was ordered to take a fresh look at the document to see whether it needed to be revamped. At the same time, Ambassador Albright was sent to the Hill to reassure an increasingly jittery Congress that the administration was aware of its concerns. On 20 October, she told the Senate Foreign Relations Committee that it was "both necessary and appropriate, in the wake of the tragic death of American servicemen in Somalia, that we who make policy [on peacekeeping] take stock. Clearly, the bipartisan consensus that so recently guided our approach to UN peace-keeping has broken down."[62]

But even within the administration there were growing differences over the direction of US policy. On 26 October Defense Secretary Aspin telephoned Lake to urge a complete revision of the PDD draft. He suggested that senior policymakers "go back to the drawing board with it, send it to the deputies' committee" for redrafting.[63] Aspin's request resulted from his growing unease at involving US forces in nation-building exercises and the kind of police actions that had failed so miserably in Somalia. The secretary argued that American forces were ill-suited for these types of roles and that their participation would dull their fighting edge. In this, Aspin reflected the widespread sentiment among senior military officers who, following Somalia, were increasingly wary of getting involved in these types of missions, especially if it required that American troops be placed under foreign control.[64]

One immediate indication that the administration took these concerns seriously was a series of public statements by senior officials detailing new limits on the type and degree of American participation in future peace operations. Referring to possible participation in small-scale peacekeeping operations, Ambassador Albright told Congress that "the US contribution to such operations will most often be in areas such as logistics, intelligence, public affairs, and communications, rather than combat." She also stressed the limits of UN involvement in larger operations: "When large-scale or high-risk operations are contemplated and American involvement is necessary, we will be unlikely to accept UN leadership. Rather, we will ordinarily rely on our own resources or those of a regional alliance—such as NATO—or an appropriate coalition—such as that assembled during Operation Desert Storm."[65] Reflecting similar caution, the Pentagon proposed adding two new guidelines for deciding whether US forces should participate in multilateral peace operations, one suggesting that participation should be a last resort and another proposing that the stakes and interests be weighed against the risks to American forces.[66]

In short, by late 1993 the Clinton administration appeared to be circling back to where the Bush administration had ended up following its own policy review—the United States would participate in UN peacekeeping operations only to the extent that it could contribute "unique" capabilities, while large-scale operations would be subject to US control.

PRESIDENTIAL DECISION DIRECTIVE-25

The working group drafting the presidential directive on multilateral peace operations completed its careful scrubbing of the original document in mid-November 1993.[67] The administration next began an intense round of consultations to gain Congressional support. These made apparent that, in the aftermath of the Somali debacle, opposition to the United Nations in general and peace operations in particular remained strong on Capitol Hill. One important reflection of this new mood was the introduction in January 1994 of new legislation by Senator Robert Dole that barred placing US forces under UN or foreign operational control and proposed other restrictions on US participation in and support of UN peacekeeping operations.[68] The administration responded to this proposal by delaying the public release of the new policy and adding a new section to the directive on executive-congressional relations.

It was not until 3 May 1994 that the president signed Presidential Decision Directive–25, which contained the administration's new policy on multilateral peace operations.[69] Though many of the essential elements remained unchanged from previous versions, the new policy directive had adopted a fundamentally different tone, one that reflected the Pentagon's earlier skepticism much more than the rhetoric of incoming Clinton administration officials. Gone was the bold rhetoric of earlier versions supporting the "rapid expansion" of UN peacekeeping and committing the United States to support such operations "politically, militarily, and financially." Instead of emphasizing the centrality of multilateral peacekeeping in US security policy, the completely rewritten introduction of the PDD began by describing the limited role peacekeeping played in US national security and defense policy. The draft emphasized that the primary role of American military forces was to protect US national interests by deterring and, if necessary, fighting and winning wars. Peace operations could be useful in dealing with some, but certainly not all, of the new types of conflicts and human miseries that had become so prevalent in the post–Cold War world. But the goal of US policy was neither to expand the number of UN operations nor to enhance US involvement in such operations; rather, the United States would aim to ensure that peacekeeping would be "more selective and more effective" in the future.[70]

The policy also specifically excluded US support for a standing UN army or earmarking US military units for participation in UN operations, though it retained a commitment to study the issue in the future. At the same time, the policy affirmed that "participation of US military personnel in UN operations can, in particular circumstances, serve US interests," and it did not limit that participation to unique capabilities only. In addition, the policy stated that US military participation could "be necessary to persuade others to participate in operations that serve US interests." It could also provide "one way to exercise US influence over an important UN mission, without unilaterally bearing the burden."[71]

In most other respects, the new policy diverged little from the one that had evolved during the review process (See table 2.1). The guidelines for deciding which operations to support and when to participate were essentially the same as those agreed to in September 1993, with two small changes. At the suggestion of the Pentagon, "risks to American forces" was added as a factor to be considered in decisions relating to US participation in future operations. Moreover, following consultations with Congress, the "consequences of inaction" were to be considered in making decisions regarding future UN operations. The section on command and control was expanded considerably, but without changing the essential consensus reached a year earlier. The policy made an explicit distinction between command, which always rests with the president as commander in chief, and operational control, which could be exercised within a specified time frame and for a specified mission by foreign commanders, as, indeed, had been the case in the first and second World Wars, Korea, and Desert Storm. Proposals to strengthen UN management and administration of peacekeeping operations remained identical to ones endorsed in the first draft PDD. Indeed, some of these, notably the proposal to establish a 24-hour command center, had already been carried out. The policy also endorsed the concept of "shared responsibility" between the Departments of State and Defense as agreed upon the previous September. The Defense Department would have management and financial responsibility for all peace enforcement operations and any peace operation in which US combat troops participated (this was a change; previously this condition applied to combat "units" rather than "troops"). The State Department would be responsible for traditional peacekeeping operations in which no US combat troops participated. Finally, the policy addressed executive-legislative relations, committing the administration regularly to consult and "inform" Congress on new Security Council votes and future command and control arrangements involving US military units.

THE NEW REALISM

The Clinton administration's policy on multilateral peace operations was launched without much fanfare, with little press coverage, and almost no comment from Capitol Hill. Testifying before the House Foreign Affairs Committee two weeks later, Ambassador Albright suggested that "the purpose of the PDD is not to expand UN peacekeeping, but rather to help fix it."[72] In this, she expressed the administration's new realism. Multilateral peace operations were not to be at the core of the Clinton administration's policy toward the use of force as some had expected when the administration took office in early 1993. Instead, as Anthony Lake explained when first announcing the completion of the administration's review, "Let us be clear: peacekeeping is not at the center of our foreign or defense policy. Our armed forces' primary mission is not to conduct peace operations but to win wars."[73]

The move from "assertive multilateralism" to wary endorsement of UN peacekeeping was rooted in two factors that the Clinton administration could not overcome. The first related to the president's electoral mandate, which ensured that the administration would put domestic political concerns ahead of foreign policy considerations, especially in instances where US national interests were not directly at stake. Ironically, the impetus for the administration's endorsement of multilateralism and its efforts to strengthen the UN's capacity to conduct peace operations was partly attributable to this political imperative. Multilateral peace operations, it was thought, offered a way for the United States to remain engaged internationally without having to bear alone all the burdens of international leadership. But as domestic and congressional criticism of multilateralism and the United Nations mounted in the wake of the Somali debacle, the administration chose to join its critics rather than defend its policy, believing that in so doing it could better protect its domestic political agenda.

This decision was heavily influenced by the second reason for the change in policy: military opposition to an expansive US role in multilateral peace operations. As problems in Somalia, Bosnia, and elsewhere increased over time, the military's skepticism began to hold greater sway in internal administration debates. This was reflected in tougher decision-making guidelines, the addition of a third set of guidelines dealing with US participation in combat operations, and growing suspicion of placing US forces under UN operational control in all but traditional peacekeeping missions. In the end, the final guidelines on US participation in multilateral operations showed a remarkable resemblance to the Weinberger doctrine on the use of force enunciated in 1984—not surprising, since General Powell had a hand in drafting both sets of guidelines.[74]

The Clinton administration's peacekeeping policy therefore represented an evolutionary change from the policy developed by its predecessor. There were three significant changes in the new policy. First, the United States is now prepared to make available the full spectrum of its military capabilities to multilateral peace operations, not just its "unique" capabilities. Second, US contributions, even of combat forces, can be subject to the operational control of UN commanders. Third, the new formula for shared responsibility between the State and Defense Departments may increase available financing for UN operations.

However, these changes may be more significant on paper than in reality. In practice, the Clinton policy does not appear to have abandoned previous constraints on US participation. Thus, while it endorsed the idea of a UN force data base for planning purposes, the Defense Department has thus far refused to provide UN headquarters with data on specific forces or capabilities beyond suggesting the ten kinds of generic capabilities—like air and sealift, communications, and logistic support—it believes the United Nations can use most. In contrast, the United Kingdom and other countries have provided the UN with detailed lists of forces and capabilities that they expect to have available in most or some circumstances. The lists contain exact data on the number of personnel and kinds of equipment that could be deployed. Second, the administration frequently reiterates that large-scale and high-risk operations (presumably including those involving combat) will generally remain under US (or NATO) control, while US participation in traditional, low-risk missions will likely involve contributions of unique capabilities only. Finally, in regard to increased financing, although the new policy settles the bureaucratic debate on responsibility, Congress rejected the concept of shared responsibility by refusing to appropriate any DoD funds for peacekeeping.

Aside from the many useful suggestions on ways to strengthen the UN's capacity to conduct peace operations (the bulk of which were included in the Bush policy as well), the one remaining legacy of the year-long Clinton policy review is the set of guidelines for future US decisions on multilateral operations. Their significance, however, turns out to be less than it appears. Once the administration decided not to strengthen the United Nations by favoring the establishment of a standing force or earmarking US units for UN participation, decisions on future UN operations and US participation therein would necessarily be made on a case-by-case basis. This being so, the guidelines may provide a useful, common sense checklist, but not much more. Indeed, as the cases of Rwanda and Haiti indicate, decisions on whether or not to support new operations and send American troops need not even conform to the guidelines as written.

In the end, those who had hoped that the Clinton administration would opt for a fundamentally different attitude toward the multilateral use of force were sorely disappointed. But then they were bound to be. The administration's new realism is a reflection of both domestic political circumstances and the continuing absence of a clearly defined strategy in which the use of force in situations where less than vital national interests are at stake can garner significant and enduring political support. Despite several years of effort by two administrations, the need to devise such a strategy still remains.

NOTES

1. Research for this paper was funded in part by the Pew Faculty Fellowship in International Affairs, and completed while the author was Director of Research at the Center for International and Security Studies, University of Maryland. A different version has appeared as Ivo Daalder, *The Clinton Administration and Multilateral Peace Operations,* Pew Case Studies in International Affairs, No. 462 (Washington, D.C.: Institute for the Study of Diplomacy, Georgetown University, 1995). The author is grateful to the many individuals who consented to be interviewed for this chapter as well as for their comments on earlier versions. Responsibility for all interpretations of fact, omissions, and commissions are the author's alone.

2. "Security Council Summit Declaration: 'New Risks for Stability and Security,'" *New York Times,* 1 February 1992, 4.

3. Secretary-General Boutros Boutros-Ghali, *An Agenda for Peace: Preventive Diplomacy, Peacemaking, and Peacekeeping,* 2nd ed. (New York: UN Department of Public Information, February 1995), 13.

4. White House, "Address by President George Bush to the United Nations General Assembly," 21 September 1992, *Weekly Compilation of Presidential Documents* 28, no. 39 (1992): 1697.

5. Ibid.

6. This account of the interagency review is based on interviews with officials involved in the review. Aside from the president's United Nations General Assembly speech, the most detailed public statement of the Bush administration's peacekeeping policy is George H. Bush, *The President's Report on "An Agenda for Peace,"* a report to Congress

by the president pursuant to section 1341 of the National Defense Authorization Act for FY1993 (Washington, D.C.: White House, Executive Office of the President, 19 January 1993).

7. George H. Bush, *National Security Strategy of the United States* (Washington, D.C.: White House, Executive Office of the President, January 1993), 7. (Emphasis added.)

8. *The President's Report on "An Agenda for Peace,"* 3.

9. The president, as commander in chief, always retains command over US armed forces, wherever they are deployed. The issue is whether US forces can or should be placed under the operational control of non-US commanders for specific missions at any particular time. In its final, publicly released policy on peacekeeping, the Clinton administration went to great lengths to underscore this distinction. However, the public and congressional debate has continued to use the term "command" as meaning "operational control" when referring to participation of US forces in UN-controlled operations.

10. *The President's Report on "An Agenda for Peace,"* 6.

11. "Remarks Prepared for Delivery by Governor Bill Clinton," (New York: Foreign Policy Association, 1 April 1992), 9. (Mimeograph.) In August, Clinton unconditionally endorsed the creation of a "voluntary UN Rapid Reaction Force" as a way to share the burdens of maintaining international order. See "Remarks by Governor Bill Clinton" (Los Angeles: World Affairs Council, 13 August 1992), 6. (Mimeograph.)

12. Thomas L. Friedman, "Clinton's Foreign Policy: Top Adviser Speaks Up," *New York Times,* 31 October 1993, 8.

13. US Congress, House Committee on Foreign Affairs, *US Participation in United Nations Peacekeeping Activities, Hearings before the Subcommittee on International Security, International Organizations, and Human Rights,* 103rd cong., 2nd sess., statement by Amb. Madeleine K. Albright, 24 June 1994, 3-21.

14. US Congress, Senate Committee on Armed Services, *Consideration of Hon. Les Aspin to be Secretary of Defense,* 103rd cong., 1st sess., 20 January 1993, Exec. Rpt. 103-1.

15. US Congress, Senate Committee on Foreign Relations, *Foreign Policy Overview, Budget Requests for FY94, Hearing to review . . . the Administration's FY94 authorization request for foreign aid programs,* 103rd cong., 1st sess., statement by Secretary of State Warren H. Christopher, 20 April 1993, 2-39.

16. Madeleine K. Albright, "A Strong United Nations Serves US Security Interests," address before the Council on Foreign Relations, New York, 11 June 1993, *Dispatch* (formerly the Department of State *Bulletin*) 4, no. 26 (28 June 1993): 463.

17. US Congress, House Committee on Foreign Affairs, *US Participation in United Nations Peacekeeping,* statement by Amb. Albright.

18. US Congress, Senate Committee on Armed Services, *International Peacekeeping and Peace Enforcement, Hearings before the Subcommittee on Coalition Defense and Reinforcing Forces,* 103d Cong., 1st Sess., 14 July 1993, S.Hrg.103-353, 12-13. (Emphases added.)

19. US Congress, House Committee on Foreign Affairs, *U.S. Participation in United Nations Peacekeeping Activities,* statement by Colonel Harry G. Summers, Jr., 31-59.

20. This discussion of the interagency review is based on extensive interviews with officials in the Clinton administration, including many who directly participated in the review. Wherever possible, information gained through interviews was corroborated by public sources, including prepared statements by Frank Wisner and Karl F. Inderfurth, in US Congress, Senate Committee on Armed Services, *International Peacekeeping and Peace Enforcement*; Jeffrey Smith and Julia Preston, "U.S. Plans Wider Role in U.N. Peace Keeping," *Washington Post*, 18 June 1993, A1; Barton Gellman, "Wider UN Police Role Supported," *Washington Post*, 5 August 1993, A1; Steven A. Holmes, "Clinton May Let U.S. Troops Serve Under UN Chiefs," *New York Times*, 18 August 1993, A1; and Barton Gellman, "US Reconsiders Putting GIs Under UN," *Washington Post*, 22 September 1993, A1.

21. Douglas J. Bennet, "Statement at Confirmation Hearing before the Senate Foreign Relations Committee," *Dispatch* 4, no. 20 (17 May 1993): 361.

22. Cited in Jeremy D. Rosner, "Peacekeeping," *The New Tug of War: Congress, the Executive Branch, and National Security* (Washington, D.C.: Carnegie Endowment for International Peace, 1995), chapter 3, 69, n.14.

23. "The United States does not plan to earmark forces or to assign troops to the UN Security Council permanently under Article 43 of the UN Charter. Given the immediate challenges facing UN peacekeeping, these options are impractical *at this time*." US Congress, Senate Committee on Armed Services, *International Peacekeeping and Peace Enforcement*, statement by Frank Wisner, 69. (Emphasis added.) See also prepared statement by Inderfurth, ibid., 21.

24. Cited in Gellman, "Wider U.N. Police Role Supported," A1.

25. Cited in Holmes, "Clinton May Let US Troops Serve Under UN Chiefs."

26. The guidelines were to be used as factors to be considered in making these decisions, not as a strict checklist of criteria. While this was explicitly stated in both the draft PDD and the final policy directive, by February 1995 the administration reverted to calling them "rigorous criteria" in decisions relating to the participation of US forces in UN operations. See President William J. Clinton, *A National Security Strategy of Engagement and Enlargement* (Washington, D.C.: White House, 1995), 17.

27. Gellman, "Wider UN Police Role Supported," A22.

28. Gellman, "US Reconsiders Putting GIs Under UN," A32.

29. Gellman, "Wider UN Police Role Supported," A22. Most nations serving in UN operations maintain separate channels of communication to their capitals. However, the problems inherent in this arrangement were apparent in Somalia, where Italian units repeatedly ignored UN instructions on the orders of Rome.

30. Holmes, "Clinton May Let US Troops Serve Under UN Chiefs."

31. Albright, "A Strong United Nations Serves US Security Interests," 463.

32. The US share of UN peacekeeping assessments had risen from 30.4 to 31.7 percent in 1993 in response to Russia's inability to pay the share previously paid by the Soviet Union.

33. See US Congress, Senate Committee on Armed Services, *International Peacekeeping and Peace Enforcement*, report by Frank Wisner, 16-17.

34. Ibid.

35. Assistant Secretary of State for Politico-Military Affairs Robert Gallucci to Undersecretary of State for Political Affairs Peter Tarnoff, memorandum, 1 May 1993, Rosner, "Peacekeeping," 12, n34. Rosner's account, which is based in part on his own participation in the process as the NSC's senior director for congressional affairs, is the best perspective available on the issue of peacekeeping financing.

36. Smith and Preston, "US Plans Wider Role in UN Peace Keeping," A33.

37. For further details on this operation, see chapter 8 in this volume.

38. Robert C. Byrd, "The Perils of Peacekeeping," *New York Times,* 19 August 1993, A23. Even before the American casualties, Byrd had told his colleagues on the Senate floor that "this Senate did not vote to send American forces to Somalia to go from house to house to disarm participants in the internecine battles between Somalian warlords. . . . Some kind of understanding as to the rules of this game needs to be reached in the very near future before this Nation becomes embroiled in a quagmire somewhere on the globe which has zero support here at home." *Congressional Record,* 103rd cong., 1st sess., 15 July 1993, S8794.

39. Helen Dewar and Barton Gellman, "Senate Asks Clinton to Get Approval for Continued Troop Deployment," *Washington Post,* 10 September 1993, A31; and Clifford Krauss, "House Vote Urges Clinton to Limit American Role in Somali Conflict," *New York Times,* 29 September 1993, A1.

40. Jeane Kirkpatrick, "Where is Our Foreign Policy?" *Washington Post,* 30 August 1993, A19.

41. Henry A. Kissinger, "Recipe for Chaos," *Washington Post,* 8 September 1993, A19.

42. Ibid.

43. Although public support for US participation in UN operations remained high throughout 1993, support for placing US troops under UN control was much less enthusiastic. Thus, an ABC News survey conducted on 12 October 1993 found that while 58 percent of the public supported US participation in UN peacekeeping operations, 57 percent believed that US troops should not be placed under UN command. A month earlier, *Times Mirror* reported that 69 percent of the public agreed that "American forces always remain under an American officer," while only 25 percent favored contributing US military units to a permanent force under UN command. See ABC News survey, 13 October 1993, Internet; Steven Kull and Clay Ramsey, *U.S. Public Attitudes on UN Peacekeeping: Part I, Funding* (College Park, MD: Program on International Policy Attitudes, University of Maryland, March 1994), 7; and Times Mirror Center for the People and the Press, *America's Place in the World: An Investigation of the Attitudes of American Opinion Leaders and the American Public about International Affairs* (Washington, D.C.: Times Mirror Center for the People and the Press, November 1993).

44. Gellman, "US Reconsiders Putting GIs Under UN," A32.

45. See also Madeleine K. Albright, "Remarks to the National War College," Washington, D.C., press release USUN 139-(93) (New York: United States Mission to the United Nations, 23 September 1993), 7.

46. US Congress, Senate Committee on Armed Services, *International Peacekeeping and Peace Enforcement,* report by Frank Wisener, 39-40.

47. Gellman, "US Reconsiders Putting GIs Under UN," A32.

48. Elaine Sciolino, "US Narrows Terms for Its Peacekeepers," *New York Times,* 23 September 1993, A8; and Rosner, "Peacekeeping," 15.

49. The Principals Committee is chaired by the national security advisor, and includes the secretaries of state and defense, the chairman of the Joint Chiefs of Staff, the director of central intelligence, and the US ambassador to the United Nations.

50. Sciolino, "US Narrows Terms for its Peacekeepers"; and Gellman, "US Reconsiders Putting GIs Under UN."

51. Warren Christopher, "Building Peace in the Middle East," address at Columbia University, New York, 20 September 1993, *Dispatch* 4, no. 39 (27 September 1993): 657.

52. Anthony Lake, "From Containment to Enlargement," address to Johns Hopkins University (Washington, D.C.: White House, 21 September 1993), 13. (Mimeograph; emphasis in original.)

53. Albright, "Remarks to the National War College," 6-7.

54. White House, "Remarks of President Clinton to the 48th Session of the United Nations General Assembly in New York City," 27 September 1993, *Weekly Compilation of Presidential Documents* 29, no. 39 (1993): 1901.

55. White House, "The President's News Conference with Prime Minister Morihiro Hosokawa of Japan in New York City," 27 September 1993, *Weekly Compilation of Presidential Documents* 29, no. 39 (1993): 1908.

56. Even before the disastrous raid, public support for the Somalia mission had fallen drastically. In September, only a minority (43 percent) approved of the presence of US troops in Somalia, down from 84 percent in March. A majority (53 percent) said US troops should leave, and an even greater majority (57 percent) argued that military action against the warlords should be halted. After the raid, pressure to withdraw American forces increased. In the days following the disaster, polls indicated that between 37 and 50 percent of the public favored an immediate withdrawal. This sentiment waned somewhat as time passed; by mid-October only 28 percent favored an immediate withdrawal. But an additional 43 percent approved the decision to withdraw US troops within six months, and approval of US involvement in Somalia plummeted to 34 percent. Data are from Andrew Kohut and Robert Toth, "Arms and the People," *Foreign Affairs* 73, no. 6 (November-December 1994): 52; and Steven Kull and Clay Ramsey, *U.S. Public Attitudes on Involvement in Somalia* (College Park, MD: Program on International Policy Attitudes, University of Maryland, October 1993), 3-4.

57. Helen Dewar and Kevin Merida, "From Congress, More Questions," *Washington Post,* 5 October 1993, A25.

58. White House, "Address to the Nation on Somalia," 7 October 1993, *Weekly Compilation of Presidential Documents* 29, no. 39 (1993): 2022.

59. White House, "The President's News Conference," 14 October 1993, *Weekly Compilation of Presidential Documents* 29, no. 39 (1993): 2068.

60. See Patrick J. Sloyan, "How the Warlord Outwitted Clinton's Spooks," *Washington Post,* 3 April 1994, C3.

61. The Republican party's "Contract With America" that forms the legislative basis of the 104th Congress includes a proposal, since passed by the House, to prohibit the United States from participating in UN operations that would place American troops under foreign command, unless the president determines that participation is "vital to US national security interests" and Congress approves of the deployment. See House Republican Caucus, "National Security Restoration Act," *Legislative Digest* (27 September 1994): 1-2. Senator Robert Dole followed suit on the first day of the 104th Congress, when he introduced the "Peace Powers Act of 1995," Senate bill S.5, which contained similar provisions.

62. US Congress, Senate Committee on Foreign Relations, *US Participation in Somalia Peacekeeping,* 103rd cong., 1st sess., statement made by Amb. Madeleine K. Albright, 20 October 1993, S.Hrg.103-318.

63. Daniel Williams and Ann Devroy, "US Limits Peace-Keeping Role," *Washington Post,* 25 November 1993, A1.

64. Helen Dewar, "Senators Approve Troop Compromise: Clinton Authority is Left Unrestricted," *Washington Post,* 21 October 1993, A1.

65. US Congress, Senate Foreign Relations Committee, *US Participation in Somalia Peacekeeping,* statement by Amb. Albright.

66. Secretary of Defense Les Aspin, *Annual Report to the President and the Congress* (Washington, D.C.: Government Printing Office, 1994), 65 ff.

67. Paul Lewis, "US Plans Policy on Peacekeeping," *New York Times,* 18 November 1993, A7.

68. See *Congressional Record,* 103rd cong., 2nd sess., 26 January 1994, S180-83. See also Bob Dole, "Peacekeepers and Politics," *New York Times,* 24 January 1994, A15.

69. White House, "President Clinton Signs New Peacekeeping Policy," 5 May 1994, *Weekly Compilation of Presidential Documents* 30, no. 13 (1994): 998. An unclassified summary of key elements of the new policy was released at that time. See US Department of State, Bureau of International Organization Affairs, *The Clinton Administration's Policy on Reforming Multilateral Peace Operations,* Publication 10161 (Washington, D.C.: May 1994). By all accounts, the public version differs little from the classified PDD, except that certain passages dealing with US policy toward Russian peacekeeping have been omitted.

70. Department of State, *Reforming Multilateral Peace Operations,* 1-3.

71. Ibid., 2-3.

72. US Congress, House Committee on Foreign Affairs, *Tensions in US-United Nations Relations, Hearing before the Subcommittee on International Security, International Organizations, and Human Rights,* 103rd cong. 2nd sess., statement by Amb. Madeleine K. Albright, 17 May 1994, 5-62.

73. Anthony Lake, "The Limits of Peacekeeping," *New York Times*, 6 February 1994, sec. IV, 17.

74. On this point, see Harry Summers, "Assertive Multilateralism . . . and Haiti Basics," *Washington Times*, 5 August 1994, A18. Of Weinberger's six criteria, only one—that force be a last resort—was not included in the PDD, although it had been included in the September draft.

THREE

THE PURSUIT OF HUMAN RIGHTS: THE UNITED NATIONS IN EL SALVADOR

FEN OSLER HAMPSON[1]

The United Nations Observer Mission in El Salvador (ONUSAL) was the first UN peacekeeping mission to have a special focus on human rights in its mandate, and soon evolved into one that included responsibility for verifying all aspects of the cease-fire and separation of forces under the El Salvador Peace Agreement; responsibility for the monitoring of public order during the transitional period while a new National Civil Police was established; and, at the request of the Salvadoran government, responsibility for observing national elections held in March and April 1994. Among recent UN peacekeeping operations, it is regarded as one of the more successful.

ORIGINS

The UN-brokered settlement ended a protracted and brutal civil war during which neither the Salvadoran army (the Armed Forces of El Salvador, or FAES) nor the guerrilla resistance movement (Frente Farabundo Marti para la Liberacion Nacional, or FMLN) had managed to accomplish much in the way of political goals. During the war, the Salvadoran government had expanded the FAES to about 70,000 military and paramilitary personnel, an otherwise impossible feat except for the heavy assistance provided by the United States. No amount of military and economic assistance, however, could buttress the senior command's poorly conceived and unevenly implemented strategy of "sporadic infantry attacks supported by aerial bombings across extensive 'free fire' zones" for which "any military success . . . was gained at high cost to the civilian population." With less impressive resources, including outside support from Cuba, Nicaragua, and the Soviet Union, the FMLN sustained for ten years a well-organized campaign of "dispersed ambush attacks, urban terrorism and economic sabotage."[2]

Perhaps even more than the resources of the guerrilla movement, the difficult terrain of El Salvador helps account for how long the war lasted. El Salvador is a tiny country, slightly smaller than Massachusetts in area and population (5.3 million people living in about 8,100 square miles; see figure 3.1). Its five largest cities are each only a few miles from remote and inaccessible mountainous terrain, which provided convenient cover and the possibility of virtually undetectable bases to which retreat was quick and reliable. Maneuvering through the uplands of northern El Salvador, which stretch down to the coastal lowlands, makes a slow and difficult journey especially for heavy equipment and armed forces; enormous portions of the country were impossible therefore for the military to monitor, except by air.

Within this environment, then, the military, right-wing "death squads" (accused of collusion with the government and the conservative Alianza Republicana Nacionalista, or ARENA), and FMLN terrorist cells engaged in ceaseless retaliatory attacks on key figures associated with their opponents. In a campaign intended to embarrass, delegitimize, and expose the vulnerability of the government, the FMLN assassinated the attorney general, the minister of the presidency, a variety of local election officials, and other highly visible public officials. The death squads, on the other hand, sought to terrorize the civilian population, especially the peasantry, in order to frighten them away from supporting the FMLN. It is likely, however, that the death squads' campaign of assassinations, mass killings, disappearances, and torture of political activists, trade unionists, church leaders, local village leaders, and other suspected guerrilla "sympathizers" alienated at least as many government supporters as it frightened supporters of the FMLN.

The results for most Salvadorans were disastrous, as they watched city after city, town after town, village after village, transformed into bleak battlefields. At least 75,000 civilians and combatants were killed. As the fighting dragged on, the war and the military consumed about half of the annual government budget. Per capita income and other measures of economic development rolled back to levels not seen since the 1960s. The war destroyed crops, communication and transport infrastructures, and other essential components of the agrarian and export economies, which were also damaged by a severe earthquake in 1986 and a drought shortly thereafter, and beset by persistent corruption and incompetence within the government. Most foreign businesses left the country, and the combined rate of adult unemployment and underemployment rose above 50 percent. Many observers believe that without US assistance the economy would have collapsed. Not surprisingly, enormous numbers of people fled their homes as refugees, searching for jobs and in fear for their lives.

Fig. 3.1
MAP OF EL SALVADOR

Base 504510 8-80 (545437)

SOURCE: US Government

According to one estimate, about half (550,000, or over 10 percent of the population) relocated internally, while the rest abandoned the country altogether, escaping to the US or to neighboring countries in Central America.[3]

Numerous efforts, formal and informal, to negotiate peace between the government and the FMLN foundered on defining the future role, control, and structure of the military and the integration of the FMLN into national political life.[4] On the first issue, the FMLN demanded a reorganization of the military, including both a purge of the conservative elements that dominated the senior command and integration of FMLN leaders and troops into the armed forces. Pressure from the United States to undertake reform along these lines never achieved much success, largely because Jose Napoleon Duarte (president of El Salvador and commander in chief of the armed forces) could never assure control over the military and thus guarantee compliance with the terms of a peace agreement, even if one could be struck. On the second issue, the FMLN did not accept the legitimacy of the six elections held in El Salvador between 1982 and 1989, even though they were supervised by international teams of observers and praised as "reasonably free and fair contests."[5] As late as November 1989, just six months before the UN secretary-general chaired meetings in Geneva between the government and the FMLN that would ultimately lead to UN-brokered peace accords, the two parties fought bitterly on the streets of the capital, San Salvador, where the FMLN temporarily occupied more than half of the city's administrative divisions.[6]

This chapter traces the origins of the peace process and the UN's involvement in mediating the peace accords, then discusses political support for the operation by local parties and outside powers. Subsequent sections trace the mandate, funding, planning, and implementation of ONUSAL, finishing with an assessment of the operation and its broader implications for peacekeeping.

Origins of UN Involvement

By the late 1980s, it was evident that the people and government of El Salvador had grown weary of a civil war that was destroying the social, political, and economic fabric of the country. As Stanford's Terry Karl argues, this war between the US-backed Salvadoran government and the communist-backed guerrilla forces of the FMLN had reached a "hurting stalemate" by the mid 1980s.

> The stalemate consisted of a set of mutually reinforcing vetoes. The Reagan administration was committed to the defeat of a communist revolution on its watch, which ruled out a military victory for the FMLN. Congress, however, refused to condone either an open alliance with the violent ultra-right or intervention by US troops, which ruled out both the full restoration of the old Salvadoran regime and the FMLN's total defeat. Finally, the FMLN demonstrated that it was too strong to be defeated by the Salvadoran military alone or excluded from the consolidation of a new order. In sum El Salvador faced gridlock in a set of international and domestic circumstances that prevented either an authoritarian or a revolutionary outcome.[7]

Military gridlock was not in itself a sufficient condition to propel the parties to the negotiation table. Other events were required to turn the tide, such as the March 1989 presidential elections in El Salvador. These saw the election of Alfredo Cristiani to the presidency and the replacement of the moderate Christian Democratic Party (Partido Democrata Cristiano, or CD) by the more conservative ARENA party which enjoyed the strong backing of the armed forces. Ironically, Cristiani's relationship with the armed forces, as we see below, enabled him to make concessions that the CD had found difficult.

During the election campaign, the FMLN had indicated that they would lay down arms if the elections were postponed and they were allowed to participate. Their offer was rebuffed and their efforts to disrupt the electoral campaign were thwarted by El Salvador's armed forces, which continued to receive aid from the United States. However, in November, the FMLN launched a major new offensive, which demonstrated that it was still a major force to be reckoned with. The FMLN's attacks pushed into the heart of the nation's capital, San Salvador, and demonstrated to the government that a military "solution" to the conflict was not possible.

In September and again in October 1989, there were inconclusive discussions in Mexico and Costa Rica between the government of El Salvador and the FMLN on the matter of formal negotiations. The parties did agree at the meeting in Mexico that a credible third party was needed to help move the process forward and that this third party should be the United Nations.[8] A third meeting scheduled for November in Venezuela was canceled as a result of an FMLN attack on the offices of the National Trade Union Federation of Salvadoran Workers (FENESTRAS) and the subsequent all-out FMLN offensive. At the December 1989 Central American summit in San Isidro, Costa Rica, the participants called for the FMLN to begin talks with Cristiani's government to end the conflict. At the same time, UN Secretary-General Javier Perez de Cuellar, Canada, and the so-called "Group of Three"—Mexico, Venezuela, and Colombia—called upon the FMLN to immediately cease military hostilities in order to get negotiations underway.

By 1990, in the wake of the brutal murder of six Jesuit priests by army henchmen, the United States was threatening to cut off military assistance to the government and armed forces. The FMLN's own support in the general population was also declining because of growing public weariness with the civil war. On 31 January 1990, President Cristiani met with Mr. Perez de Cuellar in New York and formally asked him to use his good offices to persuade the FMLN to agree to peace talks under the terms of the agreement on "Procedures for the Establishment of a Firm and Lasting Peace in Central America," which had been signed by the Central American presidents at the 1987 Esquipulas II summit meeting.[9] Secretary-General Perez de Cuellar agreed to do so. Shortly thereafter, US Secretary of State James Baker and Soviet Foreign Minister Eduard Shevardnadze issued a joint statement at their February meeting in Moscow expressing their firm support for a peaceful settlement to the conflict in El Salvador and their firm backing of UN efforts to secure a permanent cease-fire and a resumption of negotiations between the government and the FMLN. The groundwork for the formal onset of peace talks was thus laid.

On 13 March 1990, the FMLN declared a partial suspension of its attacks on government officials and employees with no ties to the army or paramilitary groups and of its sabotage operations against public transport vehicles, commercial establishments, and telephone lines, as a goodwill gesture to the UN secretary-general. This action was followed a week later by an announcement from El Salvador's minister of information that the government was prepared to resume talks with guerrilla forces immediately, without preconditions. At the end of March, President Carlos Andres Perez of Venezuela met separately with senior government officials, leaders of the FMLN, and leaders of Convergencia Democratica (Democratic Convergence) at Caracas to review the possibilities of setting the dialogue in motion.

Negotiations

A formal agreement to begin talks was signed on 4 April 1990, in Geneva, under the auspices of the secretary-general, by a government delegation headed by Minister of the Presidency Oscar Santamaria; three ambassadors accredited to European countries; and an FMLN delegation comprising Commanders Shafik Handal, Ana Guadalupe Martinez, and Roberto Canas. The meeting was an important breakthrough insofar as (1) the parties agreed that the conflict was "political" and not ideological; (2) they reached a basic understanding on the need to promote the democratization of the country; and (3) they agreed that negotiations would have to be concluded within a reasonable period of time.[10]

The first round of full-fledged talks was held in Caracas in May and set the agenda and a tentative timetable for negotiations. It was decided that the first phase of the talks would deal with issues such as human rights, the Salvadoran armed forces, the judiciary, the electoral system, constitutional reform, socioeconomic reforms, a cease-fire, and the UN's role in verification. The second phase would focus on a cease-fire. Once a cease-fire was in effect, it was agreed that negotiations on the implementation of the political agreements would follow. The phased integration of these two aspects of the peace process, in the words of one observer, "cut the Gordian knot" and allowed the negotiations to move forward.[11]

The second round of negotiations held in Oaxtepec, Mexico in June dealt with the armed forces and human rights. The government proposed to restructure the army, while the FMLN proposed that the army be purged and its troop strength reduced, and that it be placed entirely under civilian control. The FMLN also insisted that paramilitary groups, civil defense forces, and the so-called "death squads" be disbanded, that a single police force be established under civilian control, and that penalties be imposed against military personnel implicated in human rights violations. The government responded positively to some of these demands. At the Oaxtepec session, the issue of human rights was also broached in terms of a possible mechanism, a "Commission on the Truth," to determine the real story of the war and address problems of military impunity.[12]

A human rights agreement was subsequently reached in San Jose, Costa Rica, in July. Both sides agreed to a draft UN proposal calling for each to pledge respect for human and civic rights and to allow the establishment of a UN human rights monitoring mission once a cease-fire went into effect. The mission would monitor the situation for one year and would have the authority to investigate specific cases of alleged human rights violations, to make recommendations, and to report to the secretary-general. The powers of the mission would be broad and would include the right to visit any place or establishment freely and without prior notice, to receive communications from any Salvadoran individual, group, or entity, and to conduct direct investigations.[13]

In mid-August, a fourth round of negotiations took place at San Jose that dealt with the armed forces. Interfactional differences within the FMLN prompted its negotiators to present a new 18-point proposal calling for the disbanding of the armed forces of El Salvador, which would take place simultaneously with the dissolution of FMLN forces.

On 19 September 1990, an electoral agreement was signed in El Salvador by all political parties, including the three left-wing parties. This agreement had been worked out by an interparty commission appointed for this purpose that Cristiani had set up in April. Electoral rules governing March 1991 legislative and municipal elections were revised and the number of seats in the legislative assembly was increased from 60 to 84.

Negotiations resumed on 31 October. Unresolved issues included the composition and procedures of the ad hoc commission that was to identify and discharge armed forces officers accused of human rights violations, and whether the security forces should be completely disbanded. When talks appeared on the verge of floundering, the so-called Four Friends of the secretary-general (Mexico, Colombia, Venezuela, Spain) offered encouragement to the parties in El Salvador and the UN representative to reach an agreement as soon as possible.

Both sides then asked that human rights verification begin without waiting for an agreement on a cease-fire. In December 1990, the secretary-general informed the UN Security Council that he intended to propose the establishment of a United Nations Observer Mission in El Salvador (ONUSAL) that would verify any peace agreement that was negotiated by the parties.[14] In March 1991, a preliminary mission consisting of human rights experts and technical advisers was sent to El Salvador to help determine the extent of human rights monitoring activities feasible before the cessation of armed conflict. The preliminary mission reported that there was a widespread desire in all sectors of opinion in El Salvador that the UN begin monitoring activities immediately, without waiting for a cease-fire. On 2 May, both the government of El Salvador and the FMLN reiterated their request that the mission be established before a cease-fire. The secretary-general endorsed the mission's conclusions and transmitted them to the Security Council.[15] The decision to deploy a human rights observer mission before a cease-fire went into effect was unprecedented in the history of UN peacekeeping. But it was a bold move that was to play a major role in curbing violence and instilling confidence in the peace process.

A partial agreement was signed in Mexico City on 27 April 1991. It was partial because it did not deal with all aspects of the Caracas agenda. It did provide, however, for certain constitutional reforms on which the parties had reached agreement; these needed to be submitted to the Legislative Assembly before its term expired on 30 April.[16] The reforms subordinated the armed forces to civilian authority; removed from the armed forces their autonomous role to defend the constitutional legal order; established a National Civil Police and a State Intelligence Agency that would be independent from the armed forces; reorganized the Supreme Court of Justice and established new procedures for the election of Supreme Court justices; created a Supreme Electoral Tribunal to replace the Central Electoral Tribunal; and established a Commission on the Truth entrusted with the task of investigating incidents of violence that had occurred since 1980.[17]

On 17 September 1991, a new round of negotiations began in New York City. The secretary-general proposed the creation of a Peace Commission to oversee the peace process, particularly during the implementation phase. On 25 September, the parties signed accords in New York that set conditions and guarantees to ensure the full implementation of previous agreements. First, agreement was reached on a Comision Nacional para la Consolidacion de la Paz (COPAZ), which would be responsible for overseeing the implementation of all the political agreements reached by the parties. COPAZ would include two representatives of the government (one of them from the armed forces), two representatives of the FMLN, and one representative of each of the parties or coalitions represented in the Legislative Assembly. The archbishop of San Salvador and a delegate of ONUSAL would serve as observers to the Commission. COPAZ's powers were to be quite broad and included "the power to issue conclusions and recommendations of any kind relating to the implementation of the peace agreements and to make them public"; the power "to prepare the preliminary legislative drafts necessary for the development of agreements which have been reached, both on the subject of the armed forces and . . . other items"; and access to and the power of inspection of "any activity or site connected with the implementa-tion of the peace agreements."[18]

In addition, the parties agreed to a process of "purification" of the armed forces, that is, the removal of those officers and personnel who had committed human rights abuses; a reduction in the size of the armed forces and a redefined role limited to defending the sovereignty of the state and the integrity of its territory; and professional training that placed emphasis on the "pre-eminence of human dignity and democratic values, respect for human rights, and the subordination of such forces to the consti-tutional authorities."[19] The parties also agreed to a compressed agenda for negotiations "and to secure, at one go, political agreements to: (a) coordinate an end to the armed conflict and to every act that violates the rights of the civilian population . . . [and] (b) establish the guarantees and conditions needed to reintegrate members of the FMLN into the civilian, institutional, and political life of the country in absolute legality."[20] The subjects for negotiation would include doctrine, training, and purification of the armed forces (all public security forces were to be replaced by the single National Civil Police); disbanding of the military-controlled National Guard, the Treasury Police, and the DNI; judicial and electoral reforms; ratification of the constitutional reforms agreed to in Mexico on 27 April 1991; economic and social questions; and conditions for the cessation of armed confrontation.[21]

During these talks, Washington held behind-the-scenes meetings with the FMLN and indicated that it was prepared to provide training for a new civilian police force to assist with national reconstruction. The FMLN informed Washington that its own combatants had to be included in the new civilian police force.

On 4 December 1991, as negotiations dragged on and Perez de Cuellar's tenure as secretary-general was about to end, he again proposed that talks be moved to New York; on 16 December they were. Much to everyone's surprise, the FMLN suddenly introduced new demands on land reform into the negotiations. The government responded that it wanted an agreement on a cease-fire before addressing broader social and political issues.

The FMLN agreed to cease-fire talks under the chairmanship of UN undersec-retary-general Marrack Goulding on 24 December. This encouraging move motivated

Cristiani to travel to New York for negotiations, although he did not meet directly with the FMLN. During the course of the negotiations, the UN played a key role in offering compromise formulas on key issues. One UN formula provided that the number of ex-FMLN in the new National Civil Police not exceed the number of former National Police officers drawn into the new organization; it was accepted by both sides. The UN also offered an agreed proposal that would make land available to former combatants and to former landholders in conflict zones (who had been forced to flee the fighting). Cristiani informed the secretary-general that he intended to reduce the size of Salvador's armed forces by 50 percent within two years and to immediately dismantle the army's notorious Immediate Reaction Battalions as the FMLN began to demobilize. The final agreement, including a cease-fire, was initialed at midnight 31 December 1991, and a formal signing was set for 16 January 1992.

The cease-fire agreement provided that the process of ending armed confrontation would begin on 1 February 1992 (D-day) and would be completed by 31 October 1992.[22] Any alleged violation of the cease-fire would be investigated by ONUSAL. Separation of forces would be carried out in two stages: the first ending 6 February 1992, and the second on 2 March 1992, with the Armed Forces of El Salvador (FAES) redeploying progressively to the positions they would normally maintain in peacetime and the FMLN concentrating its forces in "designated locations" within the areas of conflict. During the two weeks of informal cease-fire between 16 and 31 January, the chief military observer of ONUSAL, in consultation with the two sides, would define the locations for redeployment of FMLN forces, help plan the movement of the forces of both sides to their designated locations, and supervise these redeployments. After signing the agreement, both sides would convey to ONUSAL detailed information about the strength and armament of their forces.

As part of the overall peace agreement, two of Salvador's existing security bodies would be disbanded early in the process and the third—the National Police—would be phased out over a longer period of time as the National Civil Police took shape. The UN would play a role that entailed more than mere verification—it would now become directly involved in maintaining the public order, in particular by monitoring the operations and conduct of the existing National Police Force until the new National Civil Police was deployed throughout the country.

Chapultepec Peace Accords, Mexico City, 16 January 1992

The final peace accords, which were signed in Mexico City on 16 January 1992, represented the culmination of the negotiations on all substantive items of the Caracas Agenda and the New York Accord of 25 September 1991. The agreements contained five separate chapters dealing with (1) the armed forces; (2) the National Civil Police; (3) the judicial system; (4) the electoral system; (5) economic and social questions; (6) political participation by the FMLN; and (7) cessation of the armed conflict. It also contained numerous annexes and articles and came to some 95 pages in total. The key provisions in the accord, building on the various agreements, were as follows:

- redefining the mission of the armed services to defend the sovereignty of the country and its territory;
- bringing the armed forces under strict civilian control;
- establishing a new basis for training the members of the armed forces;
- purifying the armed forces "with a view to the supreme objective of national reconciliation;"
- reducing and reorganizing the armed forces;
- creating a new National Civilian Police force and a State Intelligence Agency;
- establishing a new National Public Security Academy;
- reform of the judicial system to include the establishment of a new Judicial Training School and an Office of National Counsel for the Defense of Human Rights;
- establishment of new economic and social instruments covering land reform, loans to the agricultural sector, measures required to alleviate the social cost of structural adjustment programs, and a forum for economic and social consultation and for the National Reconstruction Plan;
- transfer of agrarian lands with preference being given to former combatants of both parties and landholders in conflict zones;
- adoption of measures to guarantee former FMLN combatants full exercise of their civil and political rights and their reintegration into society;
- cessation of armed conflict in four elements involving a cease-fire, separation of forces, end of the military structure of the FMLN, and UN verification of these activities.

POLITICAL SUPPORT

In one sense the peace process in El Salvador was a direct beneficiary of the end of the Cold War between the United States and the Soviet Union and their desire to end proxy wars in regions like Central America. From 1981 to 1989, US policy toward El Salvador followed one track, namely military. During Ronald Reagan's presidency, the United States had provided massive aid to the Salvadoran government in order to defeat what it saw as a communist-led insurgency. The election of George Bush to the presidency, however, witnessed an important shift in US policy to a less obsessive focus on Central America. The United States began to reduce its aid to the Salvadoran military, and it is widely recognized that Bush threatened to cut off military aid altogether unless the government began to cooperate with efforts to find a negotiated settlement to the conflict. However, although the United States was strongly support-ive of UN efforts it was not directly involved in the negotiations and did not offer mediated solutions. The negotiations were, in that sense, "autonomous," although the

United States did help to nurture Salvadoran president Cristiani's stature as a moderate conservative who could retain the support of the nation's strong right-wing forces while winning the trust of rebel leaders. US diplomats also exerted useful pressure on Cristiani during the final round of negotiations in New York by pressuring him to make the necessary concessions that would clinch the deal.[23] Moreover, the United States, through its bilateral aid programs, continues to be a crucial player in the implementation of those aspects of the peace accords dealing with military, social, and economic reform.[24]

The FMLN received varying levels of military support not only from the Soviet Union but also from Nicaragua (when it was ruled by the Sandinistas) and Cuba. However, as the Cold War began to wind down and Nicaragua experienced its own change in regime with the ousting of the Sandinistas from power in national elections, the FMLN's external list of sponsors began to shrink. At the same time, the FMLN had developed a rather formidable guerrilla fighting machine capable of continuing its campaign of armed struggle against the government on its own. This autonomous capacity also meant that even if the Soviets were interested in bringing about a negotiated settlement to the conflict, their influence over the FMLN was quite limited. Nor were political relations between the Soviets and FMLN especially close. For example, when Soviet foreign minister Eduard Shevardnadze visited Managua in 1989 and indicated his desire to meet with the FMLN, FMLN leaders refused and sent a clear signal to the Soviets that they were not prepared to let Moscow negotiate on their behalf. According to a senior FMLN member, "the Soviets were not a factor in the negotiations."[25] When the FMLN launched its November 1989 offensive, the Soviets protested in vain.

The United States was the more important superpower player in the peace process but also had only limited leverage. The civil war in El Salvador was only marginally a proxy affair; it had its roots in a domestic insurgency unprovoked from the outside. Thus changes in US and Soviet policies toward the conflict were not enough to bring peace; internal conditions had to change as well before a settlement could be reached.

The regional security environment was also supportive of the peace process in El Salvador. Democratic governance took hold in country after country in Latin America in the 1980s, providing a base for regional support of real democratization in Salvador. As a result of the Contadora-initiated peace process that led to the Esquipulas II peace accords, the civil war in Nicaragua had been brought to a peaceful end, and El Salvador's neighbors were keen to see an end to its civil war as well. Once negotiations were underway, the leaders of the countries of the region continued to express their strong support for a negotiated settlement. In the same manner, officials from Colombia, Mexico, Spain, and Venezuela worked with both sides in support of and at the behest of the UN secretary-general to prevent a breakdown of talks. During the implementation of the Chapultepec Accords, El Salvador's neighbors did not try to disrupt or otherwise undermine the settlement. For example, when secret FMLN arms caches were found in Managua, authorities from the Nicaraguan government and specifically the Sandinista army worked closely with the UN investigating team that itemized and destroyed the weapons.

MANDATE

ONUSAL was formally established on 20 May 1991 by Security Council Resolution 693 (1991) for an initial period of 12 months. ONUSAL would monitor, as an integrated operation, all agreements concluded between the government and the FMLN. Its initial mandate was to verify compliance with the July 1990 San Jose agreement on human rights.

On 14 January 1992, two days before the formal signing of the El Salvador Peace Agreement, the United Nations Security Council enlarged ONUSAL's mandate to include verification and monitoring of the Agreement. ONUSAL would thus verify all aspects of the cease-fire and separation of forces, in addition to verifying the implementation of the 1990 Human Rights Agreement. ONUSAL would also be responsible for monitoring the maintenance of public order while the new National Civilian Police was set up.

With the cease-fire and demobilization firmly in place, the UN's job might have ended there. But it did not. On 8 January 1993, the government of El Salvador formally requested United Nations observation of the elections for the presidency, the Legislative Assembly, mayors, and municipal councils to be held in March 1994.[26] This request for further assistance was formally accepted by the Security Council on 27 May 1993.

FUNDING

ONUSAL was funded by UN assessment of member states under the normal procedures for peacekeeping (see chapter one of this volume for details). The total cost of ONUSAL for the first 12-month period, including initial procurement of vehicles and communications equipment, was first estimated to be approximately $32 million.[27] However, the initial 12-month budget adopted for the mission was $23 million.[28]

The General Assembly had estimated that the cost of the UN Observer Mission in El Salvador, from its inception on 1 July 1991 to its termination in April 1995, would be nearly $124 million, and member states were assessed that amount. Total payments received over the life of the mission came to just over $114.5 million. The actual cost of the operation, however, as of December 1995, was about $99.7 million—sufficiently below estimate to generate a modest surplus.[29]

More than two-thirds of the expenditure supported the civilian and military personnel employed by the mission to observe the election, to staff the regional offices, and to police the country until the National Civil Police was assembled and trained. Of the remaining budget, ground and air transportation entailed the most expense, about as much as the combined costs of mine-clearing, office equipment, data processing, communications, building rental and construction, UN flags and decals, insurance, medicine and healthcare, fuel, water purification, maps and numerous other items required to support such an operation.[30]

ONUSAL's budget did not finance activities such as the reintegration of former combatants into society or activities necessary to promote democratic institutions beyond electoral monitoring and assistance. Furthermore, as noted by UN Secretariat officials Alvaro de Soto and Graciana del Castillo, there was a "lack of transparency and coordination within the UN system as the International Monetary Fund (IMF) and the World Bank did not keep the UN abreast of the economic program they sponsored, and the UN neglected to inform the Bretton Woods institutions of the peace accords."[31] As a consequence, El Salvador's economic stabilization program worked at cross purposes with the peace program. El Salvador also found itself ineligible for concessional financing under IMF's structural adjustment program because its per capita income was higher than the ceiling allowable for concessional financing.

PLANNING AND IMPLEMENTATION

Initial planning for ONUSAL estimated that approximately 70 professional staff (such as coordinators, monitors, educators, and legal and political affairs officers), 28 police personnel, and 15 military liaison officers would be required. For the second phase, additional personnel would be deployed (approximately 20 professional and 38 police personnel). Given the tasks for which ONUSAL was responsible, it was also recognized that it would be important to equip the mission with a reliable communications system and transport to give its monitors mobility. ONUSAL was launched at the end of July 1991, headed by Chief of Mission Iqbal Riza, special representative of the secretary-general. (Riza served until March 1993, after which he was succeeded by Augusto Ramirez-Campo.) Philippe Texter was appointed director of the Human Rights Verification Mission. ONUSAL's military personnel functioned under the command of Chief Military Observer (CMO) Brigadier General Victor Suanzes Pardo (Spain), who had previously been the chief of the United Nations Observer Group for Central America (ONUCA).

By 15 September, a total of 101 international civil servants from 27 countries had joined the mission, including 42 human rights observers and advisers, legal advisers, educators, and political affairs officers; 15 military advisers; 16 police advisers; and 23 support and communications staff. Regional offices were set up in San Salvador (central region), San Vicente (paracentral region), San Miguel (eastern region) and Santa Ana (western region), with suboffices in Chalatenango and Usulutan (see figure 3.1). The mission embarked immediately on an extensive program of visits both to official institutions and to nongovernmental organizations working in the field of human rights, as well as to marginal populations, communities of returnees and other vulnerable sectors of Salvadoran society, and eventually to populations living in conflict zones.[32] During the first phase of its operations ONUSAL also made contacts in the field with the FMLN.

In its first report on the human rights situation in El Salvador, in September 1991, the director of ONUSAL's Human Rights Division noted several difficulties experienced by the mission. First, the absence of a cease-fire was complicating the mission's verification task in parts of the country. Second, the San Jose agreement was only a partial one, with no other agreements having been reached on issues that affected the human rights situation—the parties had originally intended human rights monitoring to take place only after a cease-fire and in the context of institutional reform of the judiciary and the armed forces designed to ensure respect for human rights. Moreover, extremist groups were launching efforts to intimidate mission members. Shortly after the mission was set up, groups such as the self-styled Salvadoran Anti-Communist Front and the Crusade for Peace and Work—offshoots of groups that had been active in the 1980s and had surfaced during the April 1991 negotiations on Constitutional reform—began to arouse hostility toward ONUSAL and to question its constitutionality. In addition, the mission was suffering from the problem of raised expectations. "Vast numbers of Salvadorans right across the political spectrum, believe the mission will be able to prevent, or at least punish, human rights violations in spite of the fact that its powers are limited to verification; the mission had neither the power to prevent violations nor the power to punish violators."[33] Nonetheless, the mission lent an element of stability to the peace talks by opening up an important channel of communication between the combatants and in areas of the country that hitherto had been wracked by violence and war.

On 1 October 1991, ONUSAL entered its second phase of operations, in which it began to investigate cases and situations involving human rights violations and to follow up these cases with relevant governmental bodies. ONUSAL also maintained an ongoing dialogue with the FMLN concerning its violations of the San Jose agreement. During this phase, ONUSAL significantly expanded its contacts with the parties by holding regular working meetings with an interagency group in the Salvadoran government coordinated by the executive secretary of the governmental Human Rights Commission. The group consisted of representatives of the Supreme Court of Justice, the Armed Forces General Staff, the Office of the Attorney General, and the Ministry of Foreign Affairs. In addition, ONUSAL expanded its contacts with local and regional political, judicial, and military authorities, making frequent visits to the mayors' offices, departmental governments, military and police units, law courts, and other public entities. It also held periodic meetings at Mexico City or Managua with the FMLN Political and Diplomatic Commission and maintained ongoing contact with FMLN leaders inside the country.

The mission also began its educational activities and an information campaign designed to publicize its function as widely as possible. The team of ONUSAL educators worked in consultation with human rights organizations to design a program to engender respect for human rights that was directed mainly at the armed forces, FMLN, and social organizations. In its first fours months, the mission received over 1,000 complaints of alleged human rights violations and was able to confirm that a number of summary executions by unidentified individuals or paramilitary groups had taken place. It noted that no special investigation had been made by security forces or the judiciary, and this was heightening the feeling of insecurity in El Salvador. The mission recommended that the government of El Salvador, the Office of the Attorney General of the Republic and the judiciary establish the necessary mechanisms to ensure that cases of attacks on the life of persons be systematically investigated, in order to find and punish the perpetrators. ONUSAL also recommended that vigorous action be taken to put an end to the practice of intimidation and threats by clandestine groups and that regulations be adopted prohibiting their broadcasting (on radio or television) of threatening messages.[34]

Although the political situation remained tense, there were some encouraging developments in November. COPAZ, having just been set up, was still in an "informal phase in which delegates from all the political parties represented in the Legislative Assembly came together to discuss and establish guidelines for the preliminary drafting of secondary legislation enabling the political agreements adopted at the negotiating table to be incorporated into El Salvador's legal system."[35] However, some parties had strong reservations about the direction and rate of negotiations, and apprehension about the political, legal, and social insecurity that might arise as a result of the end of the conflict: in the spring of 1991, while the Legislative Assembly was ratifying the constitutional reforms emanating from the negotiations, the fighting had intensified. However, tensions eased when the FMLN announced a unilateral cessation of offensive operations in the middle of November 1991.

Once the Chapultepec Accords had been signed, the United Nations moved swiftly to deploy ONUSAL's military contingent and to implement its military and public security monitoring and verification activities.[36] During the informal cease-fire (16-31 January 1992), the Military Division received its first personnel, who came both from ONUCA and directly from a number of contributing countries.[37] Military observers were deployed at all the verification points on 31 January and, one day later, as agreed, began their verification activities, operating from 4 regional military offices and 15 verification centers. Under UN supervision, the first stage of the separation of forces proceeded without incident. As of 25 February, the Military Division had 368 of 373 authorized observers deployed. The Military Division was responsible for monitoring the troops of the Salvadoran armed forces and the FMLN at the locations designated by the peace agreements, verifying the inventories of weapons and personnel furnished by the two parties, authorizing and accompanying the movements of both forces, and receiving and investigating complaints of violations.

At the beginning of February, the Police Division was established under the command of Colonel Pierre Gastelu (France), within the framework of the agreement on the establishment of the National Civil Police. Its job was to facilitate the military-to-civilian transition in public security, which was scheduled for completion in mid-1994. The division had deployed 147 of 631 authorized police observers by 25 February, with 120 more observers slated to arrive in the first week of March.

Security-Related Elements

Difficulties soon arose with regard to the definition of the 15 locations designated for the concentration of FMLN combatants and troops of the FAES. Where it was impossible to reach an agreed definition, both sides accepted the delimitation determined by the UN's CMO. In the case of the armed forces, the majority of troops were concentrated at the designated locations. However, forces remained at about 16 additional locations because the government claimed that they were necessary to protect installations of national importance, and at 20 others, on the grounds of a lack of space. ONUSAL pressed the armed forces to withdraw from these locations, which they gradually did. By 25 May, they remained at only one disputed location.

Difficulties also arose over the two public security bodies—the Treasury Police and the National Guard—which, under the peace agreement, were supposed to be abolished by 1 March 1992, with their members incorporated into the army. The government's failure to carry out the disbanding of these two bodies on that date contributed to the failure to complete the cantonment of the two sides' troops as agreed. For several weeks after their incorporation into the army, the former members of these two bodies remained in their original barracks, even though these were not included in the 62 locations designated for the armed forces. The FMLN denounced this as a violation of the peace agreement and refused to complete redeployment of its own forces until the problem was resolved. Although the majority of personnel from the former Treasury Police and National Guard were relocated, some 3,500 continued to remain in their barracks in San Salvador in violation of the agreement.

The FMLN had concentrated its forces at the 50 locations designated for the first stage, but the second stage of concentration scheduled for 2 March was not completed owing to a lack of infrastructure at the agreed locations and the government's noted failure to comply with the agreement. Further deadlines were established only to be broken.

On the positive side, the signing of the peace agreement and the cessation of military hostilities had a major, beneficial impact on the activities of ONUSAL's Human Rights Division.[38] Difficulties linked to armed conflict generally disappeared and freedom of movement was restored. The number of complaints about human rights abuses also declined. However, summary executions and violent deaths were still occurring in certain regions of the country and no action was being taken either to end them or to root out the perpetrators. There were recurring threats against nongovernmental organizations, trade unions, churches, and political leaders. ONUSAL made a number of specific recommendations to government authorities concerning these incidents and the state's duty and responsibility to prevent and investigate them, but these recommendations were not heeded in the manner prescribed in the San Jose agreement. However disturbing, these violations were not serious enough to throw the peace process off track.

As 1992 came to a close, implementation of the peace accords advanced steadily. The cease-fire held without incident and the FMLN engaged in political activities in anticipation of its full legalization as a political party, suggesting to the UN that the government and FMLN both intended to consolidate peace and make it "irreversible."[39] However, there were still major compliance problems. The most serious threat was the failure of both parties to comply with the 31 October date for ending the conflict. Related to this problem was the government's failure to comply with the schedule of the Ad Hoc Commission on the Purification of the Armed Forces as called for by the Chapultepec Accords. The government also had reservations about the inventory of weapons submitted by the FMLN—fearing that the FMLN was secretly retaining caches of arms—and about the FMLN's compliance with the demobilization schedule.

These delays and the reactions of each party to them were clearly leading the peace process into a cul-de-sac as each party held the other responsible for the delays while insisting on its own interpretation of key clauses in the accords. In order to break the impasse, the secretary-general sent Marrack Goulding and Alvaro de Soto, the secretary-general's senior political adviser, to San Salvador on 30 October to mediate a solution. De Soto had extensive discussions that were conducted separately with the government and the FMLN. The result was an adjustment in the Chapultepec timetable and an exchange of letters stipulating that compliance with specific undertakings by one side would be contingent upon compliance with specific undertakings by the other side. Under the new schedule, the dismantling of the military structure of the FMLN would begin on 31 October and be completed by 15 December 1992.[40]

There were also delays in the constitution of a new State Intelligence Agency and in forming the National Public Security Academy that would train the National Civil Police. The latter began its activities four months behind schedule on 1 September 1992. It had funding problems despite financial support from the governments of Norway, Spain, and the United States. Two groups totaling 622 students joined the academy on 1 September. Although Chapultepec required that applicants from the National Police be evaluated by the director-general of the National Civil Police before they took admission examinations, this requirement was not met and evaluations continued to remain behind schedule.

Contrary to the peace accords, the government had been transferring personnel from the Treasury Police and National Guard into the National Police. Following ONUSAL's intervention, the government halted the transfers. However, units from the demobilized Immediate Reaction Infantry Battalions, including officers, were also integrated into the National Police in spite of ONUSAL's position that such transfers were contrary to the spirit of the agreements. The government defended the practice on the grounds that it needed the personnel to deal with an increase in crime in rural areas where the former National Guard and Treasury Police had functioned.[41]

On 15 December 1992, in accordance with the adjusted UN timetable for implementing the peace accords, the armed conflict between the government of El Salvador and the FMLN formally came to an end. This event was preceded by legalization of the FMLN as a political party and, although it did not mark the end of the implementation of the Chapultepec Accords, was an important moment. The ceremony was attended by UN Secretary-General Boutros Boutros-Ghali, Shafik Handal of the FMLN, Vice-President Dan Quayle of the United States, Narcis Serra, the Vice-President of Spain (on behalf of the "Four Friends of the Secretary-General"), President Cristiani, and President Serrano of Guatemala.[42]

Land Transfer

The land tenure problem was also a major source of disagreement and conflict. It is crucial to keep in mind that the peace agreements did not sanction an overall land redistribution program (of the sort that many postrevolutionary regimes implement after a civil war). Rather, the peace accords specified a land transfer program as "the main venue . . . through which ex-combatants and supporters of the FMLN would be reintegrated into the productive life of the economy."[43] Land tenure questions were especially sensitive issues, given the importance of agriculture to the economy and the fact that arable land was in short supply and unevenly distributed. Ownership of land also made available other potential benefits, like housing credits and assistance for agricultural production. Additionally, because the peace accords themselves only reflected broad principles, the actual details of land transfer had to be worked out during the course of implementation with ONUSAL's help.

The peace accords stipulated that, pending agreement on various issues, the current land-tenure situation would be respected in former conflict zones and current landholding occupants would not be evicted. They also assigned COPAZ the task of verifying implementation of these provisions through a special commission. The special commission, which had the same composition as COPAZ, took up the problem of land tenure one week later than called for in the implementation timetable. One of the difficulties it faced derived from the peace agreement's failure to define the conflict zones. February and March 1992 saw tensions rise in the countryside after various peasant groups seized properties, only to be evicted by security forces. These actions were also of concern to FMLN combatants who were waiting to move into designated concentration areas. COPAZ's appeal to peasants and landowners to allow the dispute settlement provisions of the peace agreements (those involving evictions and property rights) to go into effect were only partially heeded. As conditions failed to improve, the secretary-general sent Undersecretary-General Goulding to El Salvador to meet with the parties, including Cristiani and the general command of the FMLN. On 13 March 1992, it was agreed that land seizures and evictions would be suspended in order to facilitate the processing of cases submitted to the special commission of COPAZ. In his report, the secretary-general noted that "ONUSAL is operating in an atmosphere of deep distrust, which may be an inevitable consequence of a long and bitter conflict. Its insistence on maintaining its impartiality is sometimes misperceived by each side as being partiality toward the other."[44] Threats against ONUSAL personnel again became a problem.

The accords required that arrangements for transferring land to former comba-tants of both sides, and for legalizing wartime occupations of land, be completed by

31 July 1992. Before then, COPAZ had to verify the inventory of affected lands presented by the FMLN; define the conditions of transfer (that is, determine potential beneficiaries, their entitlements, and terms of payment); and make the actual transfer of land titles. There were delays in meeting each one of these goals. The FMLN's inventory was incomplete and had to be revised several times before a complete inventory was submitted to COPAZ in June. Discussions in COPAZ about the inventory caused further delays, and the conditions for land transfer were only presented to the government at the end of August. The government itself was not happy about the transfer conditions and dragged its feet. ONUSAL became involved in the issue because of these delays and the fact that land transfers were supposed to have begun on 1 May 1992. The secretary-general commissioned a group of experts from the IMF, the World Bank, and the Food and Agriculture Organization of the United Nations (FAO) to visit El Salvador and work with ONUSAL on the land transfer issue. On 13 October 1992, the secretary-general submitted a proposal of his own to both sides, which both accepted.[45]

Truth Commission

The question of implementing the recommendations of the Commission on the Truth was also a source of major controversy. The commission was established in accordance with the Mexico Agreements of 27 April 1991 and entrusted with the task of investigating serious acts of violence that had occurred since 1980 and whose impact on society was deemed to require an urgent public knowledge of the truth.[46]

The commission was set up on 15 May 1992 and was to transmit to the parties and to the secretary-general, within six months of starting its work, a final report with conclusions and recommendations. The report, entitled *From Madness to Hope* and numbering over 200 pages, with annexes of several hundred pages, was delivered to the secretary-general and President Cristiani on 22 September 1992. It was originally scheduled for public release in January 1993, but, as a result of an agreement between the FMLN and the government, release was postponed until 15 March 1993. The commission received 22,000 complaints of serious acts of violence that had occurred between January 1980 and July 1991, of which 60 percent referred to illegal executions, 25 percent to "forced disappearances," and more than 20 percent to complaints of torture. It was able to confirm 7,312 specific cases of human rights abuses, including 6,566 deaths and disappearances, and to gather indirect evidence in support of 13,562 other victims of abuses, including 11,130 deaths and disappearances. The statistical results of the report suggested that the rightist military, paramilitary, security forces, and death squads were responsible for 97 percent of human rights violations and the FMLN the remaining 3 percent.

Cristiani had implored the commission not to release the names of the perpetrators of human rights abuses. He argued that if names were made public he would not be able to guarantee the personal safety of those who had testified before the Truth Commission. FMLN leader Joaquin Villalobos also reportedly requested that the names of the violators be suppressed. These pleadings went unheeded. Following examples set by similar commissions in Argentina and Brazil, the Truth Commission went public with the names on the grounds that the purpose of the exercise was to enable the country to come to grips with its past as a vital first step in national reconciliation.[47]

The commission recommended a wide range of administrative, legislative, and constitutional changes. The Legislative Assembly was asked to adopt new laws and to approve constitutional amendments. Cristiani indicated that he was willing to comply with those recommendations falling within his competence, but other government officials accused the commission of exceeding its mandate and usurping judicial functions. The FMLN leader, Shafik Handal, indicated that although he harbored a number of reservations about the commission's report, the FMLN accepted them in their entirety.

Although there was no violence directly attributable to the release of the report, five days after its release El Salvador's Legislative Assembly, controlled by Cristiani's ARENA party, passed legislation granting total amnesty to all those guilty of extrajudicial crimes during the war, thereby rejecting one of the principal recommendations of the report. The head of the Salvadoran military, Defense Minister General Rene Emilio Ponce, who resigned just before the report's release, also went on national television to repudiate the report's findings. Mauricio Gutierrez Castro, the chief justice of the Supreme Court of El Salvador, whose immediate resignation was called for by the report, also condemned its findings.[48]

Progress in implementing the recommendations of the Truth Commission Report was slow. The recommendation to dismiss from their posts and discharge from the armed forces officers who were named in the report, and who were personally implicated in the perpetration or cover-up of cases, was delayed for several months. The recommendation to dismiss civilian officials who covered up serious acts of violence or failed to investigate such acts also was not carried out immediately. The recommendation that current members of the Supreme Court of Justice resign their posts to enable constitutional reform concerning the election of judges to the court was simply ignored. Implementation of other recommendations was delayed or not carried out at all.[49]

Election-Related Activities

A technical mission visited El Salvador from 18 to 28 April 1993 to define the terms of reference, the concept of operations, and the financial implications of expanding ONUSAL's mandate to include electoral monitoring as requested by the government the previous January. The mission identified a number of serious problems with the existing electoral roll and impediments to the timely issue of electoral documents. Key among these were: (1) the large number of names belonging to expatriates and dead persons and insufficient controls at the national level to avoid double registration of voters; (2) differences between the names on the electoral rolls and those on electoral cards, and persons with valid electoral cards whose names did not appear on electoral rolls; and (3) large numbers of citizens whose names were not on the electoral roster, as many as one-third of potential eligible voters.

With these problems in the background, the Electoral Division of ONUSAL was established in September 1993 under the following terms of reference: (1) to observe that measures and decisions made by all electoral authorities were impartial and consistent with the holding of free and fair elections; (2) to observe that appropriate steps were taken to ensure that eligible voters were included in the electoral rolls; (3) to observe that effective mechanisms were in place to prevent multiple voting, given that a complete screening of the electoral rolls prior to the election was not feasible; (4) to observe that freedom of expression, organization, movement, and assembly were respected without restrictions; (5) to observe that potential voters had sufficient knowledge about how to participate in the election; (6) to examine, analyze, and assess criticisms made, objections raised, and attempts undertaken to delegitimize the electoral process and, if required, to convey such information to the Supreme Electoral Tribunal; (7) to inform the tribunal of complaints received regarding irregularities in electoral advertising or possible interferences with the electoral process, and to request information on corrective measures taken by the tribunal; and (8) to place observers at all polling sites on election day to verify that the right to vote was fully respected.[50]

The Electoral Division decided to conduct its operations in five stages: (1) a preparatory stage devoted to organization at the central and regional level; (2) verification of citizens' registration and following political activities; (3) observation of the electoral campaign; (4) observation of elections, counting of votes, and announcement of results; and (5) observation of a possible second round of elections for the presidency should the first round not yield a definitive result.[51]

The Electoral Division functioned for more than six months with a staff of 36 professionals working out of six regional offices. It was able to perform its duties, despite its small staff, by working closely with other elements of ONUSAL. In addition to observing the Supreme Electoral Tribunal, the political parties, other public organizations, and the media, ONUSAL provided technical and logistical support to aid the registration of voters throughout the entire country.

The Electoral Division initially focused on observing voter registration, which was to close on 20 November 1993, and on monitoring the election campaign. It also assisted in drawing up electoral rolls, in keeping with the appeal made by the Security Council on 5 November 1993.[52] The division held regular joint meetings with the Supreme Electoral Tribunal, the Board of Vigilance, which was made up of representatives of all political parties, and the party campaign managers in order to solve any problems that arose during the course of the campaign. The division asked the parties to provide a schedule of their campaign activities. It also set up a system to receive and process allegations of violations of the Electoral Code. These allegations were transmitted to the Supreme Electoral Tribunal, which had to report on follow-up action taken. The division also prepared a plan for the deployment of international observers who, working with mission staff, would bring the total number up to 900 to monitor events on election day.[53]

Six parties and one coalition registered to run in the presidential election: Armando Calderon Sol for ARENA; Fidel Chavez Mena for the Partido Democrata Cristiano (PDC); Ruben Zamora for the coalition composed of the FMLN, the Movimiento Nacional Revolucionario (MNR), and the Convergencia Democratica (CD, itself a composite of three smaller parties); Edgardo Rodriguez for the Movimiento de Solidaridad Nacional (MSN); Jorge Martinez for the Movimiento de Unidad (MU); Rina de Rey Prendes for the Movimiento Autentico Cristiano (MAC); and Roberto Escobar Garcia for the Partido de Conciliacion Nacional (PCN). The Pueblo Libre (PL) party failed to put forward any candidates.[54]

There were a number of reforms legislated during the campaign period that were intended to facilitate the electoral participation both of political parties and of Salvadoran citizens. The deadline for the closure of voter registration was extended to 19 January 1994 to facilitate the issuance of voter registration cards. The deadline for registering candidates running for the office of deputy in the Legislative Assembly and for the municipal councils was extended from 19 January to 31 January 1994, and publishing the results of surveys or projections of possible voting outcomes was prohibited from 15 days prior to the election until the final results were made public.

As a result of pressure from ONUSAL, a major reform of the Salvadoran electoral code succeeded in resolving a dispute between the Supreme Electoral Tribunal and the parties comprising the MNR/CD/FMLN coalition regarding the composition of the departmental and municipal elections boards. The dispute arose from the tribunal's decision to reduce the number of representatives of the coalition parties from three to one. ONUSAL asked that the problem be resolved by means of a broad interpretation of the law that would allow all parties running in the four elections to participate, and a legislative reform of 19 January did so.

Major improvements had been made in the voter registration process before the closure of voter registration on 19 January and the drawing up of provisional electoral rolls. The tribunal made its own procedures more flexible, and ONUSAL provided strategic and logistical support for registration. ONUSAL teams made at least 9 observation visits to each of the country's 262 towns, or more than 2,350 visits in total, and made 3,700 mobile team visits to other sites around the country. By 19 January 1994, voter registration cards had been issued to 2,653,871 people, or 80 percent of the estimated voting age population. Of these, 2,171,805 replaced voter registration cards issued in previous years and 482,066 were temporary cards that could be converted into permanent cards once they were claimed at distribution centers. However, the Electoral Division estimated that El Salvador had just 2.3 million potential voters. The discrepancy was due to deceased voters who remained on the rolls; about 300,000 unclaimed temporary registration cards; and Salvadorans residing outside the country who still possessed registration cards.[55]

Locating birth certificates in order to validate some 154,000 requests for registration posed another set of problems. El Salvador does not have a civil registry, and there is great latitude in the use of surnames. This problem was compounded by rural-urban migration and displacements caused by armed conflict, which made it difficult to verify place of birth. ONUSAL, the United Nations Development Program (UNDP), and the United States Agency for International Development (USAID), made efforts to recover more than 360,000 birth certificates from municipal offices, particularly in former conflict areas. As a result of their efforts, nearly 60,000 applications were validated. Some 80,000 remained unvalidated when the voter registration period closed.

The Political and Security Climate as Elections Neared

By late 1993, there were "disturbing signs of the reappearance of some ugly features of El Salvador's past" including politically motivated murders and assaults by death squads.[56] On 23 November 1993, the secretary-general reported that although the government was taking necessary steps to comply with the provisions of the peace accords relating to purging the armed forces of human rights offenders, several other key aspects of the accords "were suffering from serious delays."[57] The program for land redistribution was falling behind the targets agreed upon in October 1992. Delays were also affecting the programs to reintegrate former combatants and war disabled. There were startup problems with the National Public Security Academy and delays in the deployment of the National Civil Police. There was still no government plan for phasing out the National Police and establishing functional divisions of the National Civil Police, such as the Criminal Investigation Commission, or the Special Antinarcotics Unit. The roundup of weapons previously issued for exclusive use by the armed forces also remained far from complete.

Civilianization of the police was a crucial element of the whole peace settlement and necessary to create a proper climate for the elections. It was essential that the armed forces be structured to limit their role to external defense and that they be placed under full control of civilian authorities. In furtherance of these objectives, the government undertook to adopt laws on the possession of weapons and the regulation of private security services; to submit a plan for phasing out the National Police; to ensure the civilian character of the National Civil Police and its autonomy from the armed forces of El Salvador; to deploy the new force; to appoint former FMLN combatants to executive senior posts at the National Public Security Academy; and to accelerate both the transfer of land and the reintegration programs. The government and FMLN also agreed to cooperate in eradicating illegal armed groups and pledged to refrain from mutual accusations when serious incidents occurred. ONUSAL devised a timetable for implementation of these commitments and joint government-ONUSAL working groups were created or reinforced to monitor implementation.[58]

Increasing crime and security problems, however, led the government to decide unilaterally to deploy the armed forces in several areas of the country in a deterrent capacity. Under the peace accords the armed forces were to be used for public security functions only in exceptional circumstances, which were to be reported to the

Legislative Assembly. ONUSAL pressed the government to issue such a report as required by the Salvadoran Constitution, but the government failed to comply with this request.

The growing number of murders and assaults raised fears about the possible resurgence of illegally armed groups, including the death squads. In October, ONUSAL's Division of Human Rights raised this issue with the government and stressed the need to establish an independent authority to investigate these incidents. The killing of two senior FMLN leaders (Francisco Velis, a member of the FMLN National Council and candidate in the forthcoming elections, and Eleno Castro, another member of the National Council) along with the discovery of the bodies of several FMLN supporters, a member of ARENA, and two former municipal officials, further underscored the problem and led ONUSAL to call for the creation of an Interinstitutional Commission to investigate these crimes. At a meeting between President Cristiani and the FMLN leadership, with ONUSAL present, it was decided to invite foreign experts to cooperate in the investigation of the murder of the two FMLN leaders.

In February 1994, new problems surfaced that some observers feared would jeopardize the peace process and the upcoming elections in March. There was a great deal of concern that the former head of the Anti-Narcotics Unit and Army Captain Oscar Pena Duran, who was appointed Deputy Director of the National Civil Police (PNC), were violating the letter and spirit of the peace accords by monitoring activities of former FMLN colleagues in the PNC and by appointing old cronies to key posts in the organization. In January 1994, the government also suspended the demobilization of the National Police on the grounds that it needed extra forces to address the growing crime wave in the countryside. The government informed ONUSAL that it would complete the demobilization by the end of 1994, thus violating the July 1994 deadline it had earlier agreed to. The PNC also stopped accepting technical assistance and logistical support from ONUSAL and began to limit its overall contact thus preventing it from carrying out its human rights verification activities. According to one report, "Human rights violations attributed to PNC units . . . increased . . . with a sharp upturn in October [1993] after the discontinuation of the PNC's close collaboration with ONUSAL's Police Division in the field."[59]

The Electoral Campaign

Despite such problems, the presidential electoral campaign began on 20 November, the campaign for the election to the legislative assembly on 20 January, and the campaign for the municipal elections on 20 February. All proceeded without major incident, although uneven compliance with electoral norms prompted remedial efforts by ONUSAL and the tribunal. The political parties signed pacts of honor about the conduct of the campaign in all of the 14 departments of El Salvador. On 10 March, at ONUSAL headquarters, all presidential candidates signed a declaration in which they declared their rejection of violence and their commitment to respect the results of the elections and to comply with the peace accords. The parties held joint meetings at regular intervals under ONUSAL auspices to discuss the campaign. The Electoral Division also held joint meetings on a regular basis with the Supreme Electoral Tribunal, the Board of Vigilance (made up of representatives from all the political parties), and the party campaign managers to solve problems that arose during the electoral process. The Division met with some 70 delegations from governments, nongovernmental organizations, universities, and media seeking information about the electoral process. Finally, ONUSAL helped to mobilize some 2,000 international observers in addition to its own 900 observers of the elections.[60]

On 20 March 1994, national elections were held for the presidency, for the 84 seats of the Legislative Assembly subject to proportional representation, and for mayor in some 262 municipal districts. Table 3.1 describes the results of each of these elections. ARENA won a plurality in the first round, and a runoff election for the presidency was called for 24 April. The presidential candidates in the runoff were Armando Calderon Sol and Ruben Zamora, for ARENA and the Coalition, respectively.

Voter records indicated low turnout in the election with only 53 percent of those registered voting. Although this number was substantially higher than in previous elections, it fell well below expectations. Part of the problem was attributable to the cumbersome nature of the Salvadoran system of voting. First, the complex system of registration meant that citizens had to invest a considerable amount of time to obtain a voter card. Second, the limited number of polling stations meant that voters had to travel long distances, especially in rural areas, to cast their ballots. These problems generally were not remedied in time for the elections.[61] Although UN chief of mission Ramirez-Campo stated that only 25,000 people were unable to vote, other international observers charged that up to 300,000 citizens were not allowed to vote because their names did not appear on the voting lists. International election observers reported serious electoral anomalies but not sufficiently serious to have changed the outcome of the presidential election. In his report on the conduct of the elections, the secretary-general stated that ONUSAL observers performed their task without interference. There was no evidence of ballot-rigging, nor were there any serious incidents of violence on election day that could have affected the outcome. Problems that did arise involved organization of the voting, preparation of the electoral roll, shortages of public transport on election day, and citizens who were unable to vote because others had already used their names. This confusion in the election process created considerable tension and led to bitter feuding among the parties over the election results.[62]

To overcome some of the serious problems detected in the first round of elections, ONUSAL's Electoral Division made a number of recommendations to the Supreme Electoral Tribunal on 24 March concerning the number of polling centers, transport for voters, guidance and training of electoral officials on the polling station teams, and electoral publicity. Thirty-five additional polling centers were established and, with the assistance of USAID and UNDP, arrangements were made to provide free transportation to polling places in rural areas and in the San Salvador metropolitan

Table 3.1

ELECTION RESULTS FOR THE PRESIDENCY, LEGISLATIVE ASSEMBLY, AND MAYORAL DISTRICTS OF EL SALVADOR, 20 MARCH 1994

Party	Presidency[a]	National Assembly[b]	Mayoral Districts[c]
ARENA	49.03	39	206
Coalition	24.90	n/a	n/a
PDC	17.87	18	29
PCN	5.39	4	10
PMU	2.41	1	n/a
MSN	1.06	n/a	n/a
MAC	0.83	n/a	1
FMLN	n/a	21	16
CD	n/a	1	n/a

[a] Percentage of popular vote for party's candidate
[b] Number of seats contested (total= 84)
[c] Number of seats contested (total=262)
n/a Not applicable [party did not field candidate or did not win seat]

SOURCE: UN Security Council, *Report of the Secretary-General on the United Nations Observer Mission in El Salvador*, S/1994/536, 4 May 1994.

area. Some 15,000 names were added to the electoral roll and voters were given more information about how to find their proper polling stations.

On runoff election day, ONUSAL posted some 900 observers around the country to cover all polling centers from the time the stations opened until they closed and the first vote tally was completed. ONUSAL also observed the official vote-counting process in the Supreme Electoral Tribunal, concluding that the runoff was largely free of serious incidents affecting law and order or involving ballot-rigging, and that there was "a distinct improvement in the organization of the election, including the layout of the polling centers, the stationing of personnel to direct voters to the proper polling places, the finding of names on the electoral roll,"[63] transportation of voters to polls, and early broadcasts of the election results. There were some minor irregularities. For example, some polling stations closed before they were supposed to, some party members campaigned at polling centers in violation of the electoral code, and, as in the first round, "a considerable number of citizens were unable to exercise their right to vote even though they had voter cards."[64] But these were not considered serious enough incidents to call into question the final result. In the end, only slightly more than 50 percent of eligible voters cast their ballots, and conservative candidate Armando Calderon Sol won the presidential runoff election with 68.3 percent of the vote. His leftist opponent Ruben Zamora received 31.7 percent.

ASSESSMENT AND CONCLUSIONS

Although a military stalemate, brought about by a combination of internal and external pressures, helped to propel El Salvador's conflicting parties to the negotiating table, the fact that the parties had fundamentally conflicting political objectives meant that a political settlement was not preordained. The government's main goal was to end the war whereas the FMLN's goal was to change El Salvadoran society, initially by demobilizing the armed forces. There was no straight or easy quid pro quo, and it would take an outside mediator to help them reach a negotiated agreement. In this regard, although the conflict in El Salvador was, in one sense, "ripe for resolution," ripeness was not a sufficient condition in laying the foundations for a durable settlement. Given the high levels of mistrust and suspicion that characterized relations between the Salvadoran government and the FMLN, the potential for violence was high even after a cease-fire had been negotiated. The foundations of the peace settlement therefore had to be laid with the assistance of third parties who could not only help to define the terms of a negotiated settlement but see to it that once the settlement was negotiated, the parties adhered to its terms and lived up to their commitments.

The UN was chosen to be the mediator because it was able to "neutralize" outside parties and build on the new US and Soviet interests in defusing regional conflicts. The secretary-general discussed the situation with interested but neutral states and dealt separately with governments that had taken sides in Salvador's civil war. He tried to obtain a commitment very early on from the United States, the Soviet Union, and Cuba that they would support the negotiations and avoid taking positions that would jeopardize them. He also tried to invest the negotiations with such prestige that it would be seen as bad form to undermine them.[65] Among the warring parties in El Salvador, however, many thought it was impossible for the UN to be an effective interlocutor. The FMLN wanted the UN to be just a mediator, and, initially, the government did not want a mediator at all. However, once the UN secretary-general became involved, the UN came to be viewed as a more effective and desirable mediator than, for example, the Organization of American States because the UN's participation gave both superpowers an indirect seat at the table and made it more likely that they would support the initiative.[66] As a mediator, the UN helped energize the negotiations by being a source of proposals, by reframing the meaning of concessions, and by creating a sense of urgency, imposing deadlines, and offering side-payments, assurances, and the threat of sanctions if progress was not forthcoming. In undertaking these tasks the UN enjoyed the support of the "Four Friends" of the secretary-general (Mexico, Colombia, Venezuela, Spain), who lent their encouragement when negotiations appeared to be floundering.

Once a settlement was reached, the UN's role in the peace process became even more important. The UN-monitored cease-fire was crucial to consolidating the peace process. Participants have called the cease-fire "the most successful part of the whole peace process." There was not one violation, and ONUSAL's verification of the cease-fire and the subsequent demobilization of forces by both sides contributed to this result. However, the linking of the cease-fire with other political factors created its own problems and demobilization was slow because of linkage. Nonetheless, the "cease-fire brought about a level of maturity; parties saw that without armed conflict they could advance in different areas. The cease-fire thus helped to contain the conflict."[67]

Although the cease-fire was a crucial confidence-building measure, ONUSAL played a key role in addressing other problems as well. Its interventions ensured that these problems did not become serious enough to derail the peace process. For example, as noted above, the peace accords allowed a small number of former FMLN and National Police members to be admitted to the new civilian police but purposely excluded members of the armed forces. Yet several hundred former members of the army and the Treasury Police were transferred to the National Police in early 1992, raising concerns that these individuals might find their way into the new National Civil Police. ONUSAL tried, unsuccessfully, to secure personnel records to identify these individuals. More serious was the discovery that 11 superior-level candidates for the civil police, who were represented by the government as former National Police force members, had actually come from the army, Treasury Police, and National Guard, in direct violation of the peace accords. Following extensive discussions, the officers were permitted to remain in the training program because they were relatively young and had spent no more than three years in military service. ONUSAL secured a pledge from the government not to enroll any more former military personnel in the training academy and civilian police force.[68]

What factors helped to account for the widely observed success of the ONUSAL mission? Undoubtedly the groundwork laid by a serious process of negotiation greatly reduced the problems of implementation. That the negotiations directly and specifically addressed issues of human rights and political and military reform reduced the likelihood that these contentious issues would later threaten much-needed collaboration between the former disputants. Along these same lines, the ongoing availability of UN mediation services during the implementation phase preempted the emergence of unforeseen grievances and helped to resolve uncertainties about the accords, further affirming the perceived stability and appropriateness of the peace process.

Related to this point, the early deployment of human rights workers created a local climate of confidence in the UN, in the accords, and about the seriousness of the signatories. The ONUSAL human rights bureaucracy aimed the international spotlight directly at the Salvadoran government, putting it on the defensive as it tried to explain the appalling evidence of state-sponsored brutality. The government was compelled, one might even say shamed, by the intense international scrutiny to compensate for past atrocities by complying with the terms of the peace agreement and proving its commitment to a reinvigorated democracy. However, there was an obvious tension between the degree to which the UN could push for human rights reform and its need to keep the government and military "on side" and committed to the peace process.

For the FMLN, demobilization proved to be thorough, stable, and permanent, an accomplishment that effectively ended the guerrilla war and created a fresh climate for cooperation. A successful ONUSAL mission was inconceivable without disarming the FMLN, but demobilization had its double edge, removing as it did the FMLN's single most important source of leverage against the government. Demobilization secured cooperation from the government, but drastically reduced the ability of the FMLN and other domestic groups to force the government to treat them seriously, reform its practices, and stick to the agreement. ONUSAL had to address this inequity in power between the two parties throughout its mission.

Finally, the relatively small size of the UN force in El Salvador actually worked to the advantage of the peace process. Unlike the UN operation in Cambodia, for instance, with its far larger and more cumbersome bureaucracy, ONUSAL did not experience major delays in deploying its workers, setting up its offices, acquiring the necessary equipment, or generally going about its business. As the peace process gathered momentum, ONUSAL was in position to exploit the initial euphoria and the sense of urgent good will just as the parties were striving to cultivate the fruit of their negotiations. ONUSAL's logistical efficiency enhanced the perception that the peace accords could work.

Although the UN was instrumental in ensuring that the peace process stayed on track, some critics have charged that ONUSAL did not make sufficient use of its "moral authority" and "status as an objective interpreter of the accords." Scholars David Holiday and William Stanley argue that ONUSAL failed to criticize the government for its performance on human rights "in a timely fashion," and failed to distinguish adequately between state violations of human rights and "common crime" violations.[69] Moreover, because the personnel in ONUSAL responsible for implementing the accords were not those who negotiated them, disputed interpretations of the accords could not be easily or quickly resolved; the mediators were sometimes "forced to wait instead for clarification from U.N. headquarters."[70]

These are fair criticisms and there are certainly aspects of ONUSAL's involvement in the implementation of the peace accords that could have been carried out better than they were. On the other hand, these criticisms should not be allowed to detract from the more basic point that without ONUSAL's active and constructive involvement in the implementation of the peace accords, the process would have surely come unstuck. There were simply too many outstanding issues and points of contention between the parties that had to be negotiated—or, in some instances, renegotiated. There were also outright violations of the accords by both sides that engendered mutual feelings of hostility and mistrust. These could have easily escalated and gotten out of hand had the UN not been there to deal with them and secure the parties' continuing commitment to the peace process. Finally, there were clearly many aspects and functional activities related to the peace process that the parties were incapable, or unwilling, to perform entirely themselves. These included the management of the elections, rehabilitation and integration of former combatants into society, and military and police reform, where the UN found itself having to respond to appeals from the parties to do more. ONUSAL's mandate was therefore constantly having to be redefined and expanded so that it could take on the additional responsibilities being requested by the parties. Whether this kind of dependency relationship is ultimately healthy for a society in the long run remains to be seen, but without it, in the short run, the peace process could not have been sustained.

After the substantial withdrawal of the UN in the early months of 1994, there were a number of developments that suggested flagging commitment by both sides to the peace process. The government's "sluggish" attempt to dismantle the National Police suggested to Alvaro de Soto and Graciana del Castillo a "lingering reluctance to see it disappear." The revelation that the FMLN had hidden large stockpiles of arms from ONUSAL monitors fueled a longstanding "root fear that the undertakings of the government coupled with international verification were insufficient to ensure compliance" with the accords. Both the FMLN and the government contributed to "serious delays" in the implementation of the land transfer program and other strategies for reintegrating former combatants into the economy—a failure that resulted mainly from the "lack of political will among lower level government officials."[71]

The *Washington Post* reported in March 1995 that "former combatants from both sides of the war"—with automatic weapons and rocket-propelled grenades—were overwhelming the National Civil Police in their efforts to assure public order in postsettlement El Salvador.[72] While the spectre of political murders and disappearances had not yet been revived, this new criminal violence randomly terrorized all of El Salvador's major cities.

These challenges to the peace process had little to do with deficiencies in the peace accords or flaws in the ONUSAL operation itself but do raise questions about the timing of a UN mission's withdrawal from the field. In fact, the most significant lesson that de Soto draws from the ONUSAL experiment is that "deciding how and when to end such an operation . . . may well be as difficult and as important as deciding [when] to begin the operation." Judging the appropriate moment for exit after the implementation of a settlement should not be based on "whether things seem quiet or elections have taken place, but whether peace-related reforms have advanced enough to make the process durable, indeed irreversible."[73] ONUSAL is at an end. To judge whether peace in El Salvador has indeed been made irreversible, we still may have to wait a number of years.

NOTES

1. Research assistance for this chapter was provided by John T. Crist.

2. Dr. David Browning, "El Salvador—History," *South America, Central America and the Caribbean* (London: Europa Publications, 1995), 310.

3. Ibid., 310.

4. Ibid., 310.

5. Ibid., 310.

6. David Munro and Alan J. Day, "El Salvador." *A World Record of Major Conflict Areas* (Chicago: St. James Press, 1990), 254.

7. Terry Lynn Karl, "El Salvador's Negotiated Revolution," *Foreign Affairs* 71, no. 2 (spring 1992): 149.

8. Observation by a senior official of the government of El Salvador at an academic workshop, "Resolving Civil Conflicts: The Lessons of El Salvador," hosted by the Center for Latin American Studies and the Center for International Security and Arms Control, Stanford University, 5-7 May 1993 (hereafter referred to as "Stanford Workshop"). Participants at the high-level workshop, organized by Professor Terry Karl, Stanford University, included senior officials from the government of El Salvador, the FMLN, and the UN who were directly involved in the negotiations that led to the peace accords.

9. The Esquipulas II agreements (or Guatemala Procedure) were signed by the presidents of the five Central American nations on 7 August 1987. They agreed to launch a process of democratization in their countries, to promote a national dialogue, to decree general amnesty, to bring about a genuine cease-fire, and to promote the holding of free, pluralistic, and fair elections. They also requested all governments concerned to terminate support for irregular forces or insurrectional movements and reiterated their commitment to prevent the use of their own territory for destabilization of other countries in the region. To help achieve these objectives, the presidents also set up an International Verification and Follow-up Commission (CIVS) composed of the foreign ministers of the Contadora Group (Columbia, Mexico, Panama, and Venezuela), and the Support Group (Argentina, Brazil, Peru, and Uruguay), the Central American countries, and the secretaries-general of the UN and the Organization of the American States. Steps toward implementation of the Esquipulas II accords were taken by the five Central American presidents on 14 February 1989, when they signed the Costa del Sol Declaration requesting that their foreign ministers, assisted by the UN, arrange technical meetings to establish verification mechanisms. On 27 July 1989, in Resolution 637, the UN Security Council welcomed the Esquipulas II and other agreements made by the five presidents and indicated its full support for the mediation efforts of the UN secretary-general in the region.

10. Comment by senior Salvadoran government official, Stanford Workshop.

11. Comment by Salvadoran government official, Stanford Workshop.

12. UN General Assembly, *Report of the Economic and Social Council: Situation of human rights in El Salvador: Note by the Secretary-General*, A/45/630, 22 October 1990, 3-5.

13. United Nations Department of Public Information (hereafter, DPI), *The Agreement on Human Rights*, ONUSAL Fact Sheet No. 5, DPI/1149E (New York, July 1991).

14. UN Security Council, *Central America—Efforts Toward Peace*, S/22031, 21 December 1990.

15. UN Security Council, *Central America—Efforts Toward Peace, Report of the Secretary-General*, S/22494, 16 April 1991.

16. Constitutional amendments under the Salvadoran Constitution required ratification by two successive Legislative Assemblies. Had the 30 April deadline been missed, the reforms would have had to be ratified by the new assembly and then by its successor, stretching out the ratification process by two years, to 1993.

17. UN DPI, *ONUSAL: Mexico Agreements*, DPI/1149D-40697 (New York, July 1991).

18. UN General Assembly, *Letter dated 26 September 1991 from the Permanent Representative of El Salvador to the United Nations Addressed to the Secretary-General*, A/46/502, 26 September 1991, 3.

19. Ibid., 5.

20. UN General Assembly, *Letter dated 4 October 1991 from the Permanent Representative of El Salvador to the United Nations addressed to the Secretary-General*, A/46/502 Add.1, 7 October 1991, 2-5.

21. Ibid.

22. UN Security Council, *Central America: Efforts Towards Peace: Report by the Secretary General*, S/23402, New York, 10 January 1992, 2-3.

23. "Peace for El Salvador," *Christian Science Monitor*, 6 January 1992.

24. Observation by senior FMLN member, Stanford Workshop.

25. Observation by senior FMLN member, Stanford Workshop.

26. UN Security Council Res. 832, 27 May 1993.

27. UN DPI, *ONUSAL, El Salvador*, Fact Sheet No. 7, DPI/11449G-40697, July 1991, 4.

28. UN General Assembly, *Financing of the United Nations Observer Mission in El Salvador, Report of the Advisory Committee on Administrative and Budgetary Question*, A/45/1021, 12 June 1991.

29. UN General Assembly, *Financing of the United Nations Observer Mission in El Salvador—Report of the Secretary General*, A/50/735/Add.1, 29 February 1996.

30. The proportional contribution of these budget items is estimated from the actual expenditures reported for the period 1 December 1993 to 31 May 1994 and not from the total expenditures since the beginning of the mission. Please see UN General Assembly, *Financing of the United Nations Observer Mission in El Salvador—Report of the Secretary-General*, A/49/518, Annex I, 14 October 1994, 3-9.

31. Alvaro de Soto and Graciana del Castillo, "Obstacles to Peacebuilding," *Foreign Policy*, no. 94 (spring 1994): 74.

32. UN General Assembly, *The Situation in Central America: Threats to International Peace and Security and Peace Initiatives: Note by the Secretary-General*, A/45/1055, 16 September 1991.

33. Ibid., 11.
34. UN General Assembly, *Second Report of the United Nations Observer Mission in El Salvador, Annex, Report of the Director of the Human Rights Division,* A/46/658, 15 November 1991, 38.
35. Ibid., 2.
36. A useful account of some of the early problems of implementation of the peace accords is to be found in George Vickers and Jack Spence, *Endgame: A Progress Report on Implementation of the Salvadoran Peace Accords* (Cambridge, Mass.: Hemisphere Initiatives, 3 December 1992).
37. UN Security Council, *United Nations Observer Mission in El Salvador: Report of the Secretary-General,* S/23642, New York, 25 February 1992.
38. UN General Assembly, *The Situation in Central America: Threats to International Peace and Security and Peace Initiatives: Annex: Report of the Director of the Human Rights Division,* A/46/935, 5 June 1992.
39. UN Security Council, *Report of the Secretary-General on the United Nations Observer Mission in El Salvador,* S/24833, 23 November 1992, 16.
40. Ibid., 3.
41. Ibid., 10.
42. UN Security Council, *Report of the Secretary-General on the United Nations Observer Mission in El Salvador* (ONUSAL), S/25006, 23 December 1992.
43. Alvaro de Soto and Graciana del Castillo, "El Salvador: Still Not A Success Story," June 1994, 11-12. Mimeograph.
44. UN Security Council, *Report of the Secretary-General on the United Nations Observer Mission in El Salvador,* S/23999, 26 May 1992, 15.
45. The proposal provided that the total number of beneficiaries should not exceed 47,500 (15,000 former combatants from the armed forces; 7,500 FMLN former combatants; and approximately 25,000 landholders in the former zones of conflict). The proposal established a three-phased program of land transfer because of financing difficulties and the complexity of the transactions involved. Operational aspects of the land transfer activity were to be worked out by a supervisory committee. Since a large portion of the land to be transferred was under private ownership, international and regional organizations and bilateral donors would have to supplement the limited financing available for the purchase of land. On 31 October, the land transfer officially started with the signing by the government and FMLN, in the presence of ONUSAL, of an agreement to transfer state properties to FMLN former combatants and current landholders on these properties. See Security Council, S/24833, 12-13.
46. UN Security Council, *Letter Dated 8 October 1991 from the Permanent Representative of El Salvador to the United Nations Addressed to the Secretary-General, Annex, Mexico Agreements.* S/23130, 9 October 1991, 5 and 16-18. See also the secretary-general's remarks, "Presentation of the report of the Commission on the Truth" (New York: United Nations, 15 March 1993, mimeograph).
47. Lauren Weiner, "El Salvador Confronts the Truth Commission Report," *Freedom Review* 24, no. 6 (November-December 1993): 36.

48. Ibid., 37.

49. UN Security Council, *Further Report of the Secretary-General on the United Nations Observer Mission in El Salvador*, S/26581, Annex 1, 14 October 1993, 6-7.

50. UN Security Council, *Report of the Secretary-General on the United Nations Observer Mission in El Salvador*, S/1994/304, 16 March 1994, 1-2.

51. UN Security Council, *Report of the Secretary-General on the United Nations Observer Mission in El Salvador*, S/25812, 21 May 1993, 21-22.

52. UN Security Council, *Note by the President of the Security Council*, S/26695, 5 November 1993.

53. UN Security Council, *Report of the Secretary-General on the United Nations Observer Mission in El Salvador*, S/26606, 20 October 1993 and S/1994/179, 16 February 1994.

54. On the election process, see Jack Spence and George Vickers, *Toward a Level Playing Field? A Report on the Post-War Salvadoran Electoral Process* (Washington D.C.: Hemisphere Initiatives, January 1994).

55. UN Security Council, S/1994/179, 5.

56. UN Security Council, *Further Report of the Secretary-General on the United Nations Observer Mission in El Salvador*, S/26790, 23 November 1993, 19.

57. Ibid., 2.

58. Ibid.

59. Washington Office on Latin America (WOLA), *El Salvador Peace Plan Update #3: Recent Setbacks in the Police Transition* (Washington, D.C.: 4 February 1994), 6.

60. UN Security Council, *Report of the Secretary-General on the United Nations Observer Mission in El Salvador*, S/1994/536, 4 May 1994, 4.

61. See Security Council, *Report of the Secretary-General on the United Nations Observer Mission in El Salvador*, S/1994/375, 31 March 1994.

62. Ibid., 2-4.

63. Ibid.

64. UN Security Council, *Report of the Secretary-General on the United Nations Observer Mission in El Salvador*, S/1994/536, 3-4.

65. Comment by senior UN official, Stanford Workshop.

66. Senior Salvadoran government official, Stanford Workshop.

67. Senior Salvadoran government official, Stanford Workshop.

68. William Stanley, *Risking Failure: The Problems and Promise of the New Civilian Police Force in El Salvador*, (Washington, D.C.: Hemisphere Initiatives and Washington Office on Latin America, September 1993), 7-8.

69. David Holiday and William Stanley, "Building the Peace: Preliminary Lessons from El Salvador," *Journal of International Affairs* 46, no. 2 (winter 1993): 430.

70. Ibid., 437.

71. De Soto and del Castillo, "El Salvador," 9-17.

72. Douglas Farah, "Salvadorans Complain Postwar Crime Defeating Rebuilt Police Force," *The Washington Post*, 15 March 1995, A24.

73. De Soto and del Castillo, "El Salvador," 20.

A PEACE THAT FELL APART: THE UNITED NATIONS AND THE WAR IN ANGOLA

Y V O N N E   C.   L O D I C O [1]

I n May 1991, the Security Council unanimously endorsed the establishment of the second United Nations Angolan Verification Mission (UNAVEM II), an extension of the mission that had monitored the exodus of Cuban forces from Angola. After 32 years of war, Angola presented the United Nations with one of its most daunting challenges, and UNAVEM II was created to monitor and verify the implementation of essential elements of the first Acordos de Paz Para Angola (Peace Accords for Angola). However, the mission was given inadequate financial and human resources and insufficient international support to monitor and verify a very tenuous transition to peace and democracy. In light of the extensive role of foreign influences in fueling Angola's wars, it was incumbent upon the international community to give the entire peace process the support that it deserved. Regrettably, when the peace process was threatened and when UNAVEM's declaration for free and fair elections was rejected, its limited international support undercut UNAVEM's ability to maintain peace between the local parties. Tragically, a civil war resumed that turned into one of the worst humanitarian disasters in the world.

The political developments that led to the authorization of a verification mission in Angola, the unfortunate collapse of the peace accords, and the failures of UNAVEM II offer insight for more comprehensive mandates and more thoroughly managed peacekeeping missions. The lessons of UNAVEM II clearly demonstrate that for the third United Nations mission in Angola, the international community needed to ensure that it had the capacity to ensure finally that peace would endure in Angola. Most of all, however, the Angolan government and its principal opponent, the National Union for the Total Independence of Angola (Uniao Nacional para a Independencia Total de Angola, UNITA) had to decide finally that peace was better than war.

ORIGINS

Since 1961, Angola has been a fixture on the agendas of the Security Council and the General Assembly, in the context of the organization's focus on the struggle for self-determination in Africa. The General Assembly called for an end to colonial subjugation, and the Security Council demanded that Portugal recognize Angola's right to self-determination and desist in its repressive measures there. These resolutions were reinforced by Secretary-General Dag Hammarskjold's vision for an active United Nations role in the transformation of the African continent.[2]

For the following 13 years, the Security Council continued to endorse similar resolutions, including those calling for an arms embargo, which were directed at the colonial power, Portugal, and other parties supporting its policies. The United Nations, however, took no further action as the situation was considered "internal" and consequently not under United Nations jurisdiction.[3] It would be hard to find a time, however, in Angola's history in which there were not several external influences feeding its internal strife.

The War for Independence

Three principal "internal" forces waged the war against Portuguese colonial rule. The first party organized was the Popular Movement for the Liberation of Angola (Movimento Popular de Libertacao de Angola, MPLA) led by Dr. Augustino Neto. The second group formed was the National Liberation Front for the Liberation of Angola (Frente Nacional de Libertacao de Angola, FNLA) led by Holden Roberto. The third party to be formed, and the smallest and least financially equipped when it was formed, was UNITA, led by the now notorious Dr. Jonas Malheiro Savimbi.

In addition, an independence movement for Cabinda known as the Front for the Liberation of the Enclave of Cabinda (Frente para a Libertacao do Enclave de Cabinda, FLEC) also based its operations in Zaire (see figure 4.1).[4] With most of Angola's oil coming from Cabinda, FLEC remained a threatening movement regardless of who was in power in Luanda.

The three principal insurgent parties formed alliances with outside forces both within and beyond the African continent. MPLA received some support from the Congo and significant assistance from Tanzania and Zambia, which permitted the transportation of Chinese and Russian weapons over their borders. FNLA, originally based in Zaire, received funds from the Organization of African Unity (OAU), training

Fig. 4.1
MAP OF ANGOLA

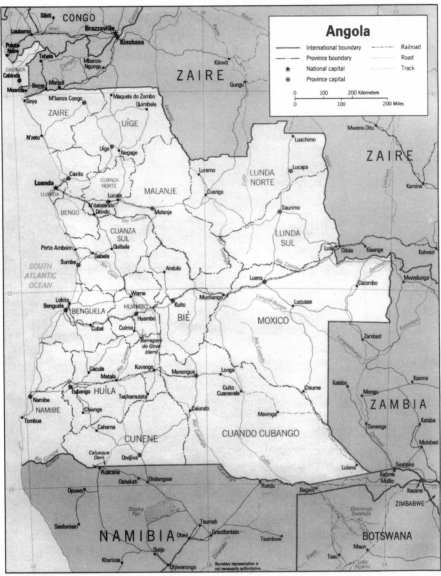

SOURCE: US Government

and arms from Algeria, and some financial assistance from the United States.[5] UNITA, which came into the arena in 1966, initially received training in China.

By 1964, MPLA's struggle for independence became increasingly aligned with the Marxist-Leninist cause, supported by military aid from the Soviet Union and Cuba.[6] In 1964, the Soviet Union demonstrated its exclusive support for the MPLA with its first large consignment of armaments.[7] Later, in 1965, Cuba began to train MPLA forces in Brazzaville.[8] This affinity with the Soviet Union and Cuba alarmed the government of South Africa, which perceived this union as a threatening communist expansion in the region. Thus, with a war already launched against insurgents in South West Africa (now Namibia) and its support for white rule in Rhodesia (now Zimbabwe), South Africa expanded its military campaign into Angola to expunge communism in the region.[9]

After 14 years of fighting a colonial war that fueled a military coup in Portugal, the Portuguese decided to relinquish their rule in an agreement known as the Alvor Accord. This agreement, devised in January 1975 and signed by MPLA, FNLA, and UNITA in June 1975, called for the establishment of a transitional coalition government composed of all three parties followed by general elections in October and full independence on 11 November 1975.[10] The Portuguese, however, provided no institutional support for a transitional government, no system for disarmament of insurgent forces, and no policy framework for keeping the parties together.[11] Therefore, when the Portuguese pulled out in November, they relinquished their power not to a government but to the people of Angola.[12] Without elections, the MPLA, with popular support in Luanda, filled executive government posts, and heavy fighting broke out between the three parties in an internal power struggle that would become ever more bitter and gruesome.[13]

The Civil War

As Angola finished its war for independence, it descended into another war, its factions supported by parties who were not indigenous and did not care about the country's real needs. The Angolans desperately needed assistance. With the country devastated from nearly 14 years of war, there was no functioning governmental or social infrastructure and very few people trained to take over the tasks the Portuguese abandoned. During colonialism, blacks were permitted to hold only those menial jobs that no Portuguese would take.[14] Therefore, upon its independence from Portugal, Angola was without any markets or expertise to maintain even minimal economic order, let alone growth.[15] Yet, Angola's potential was great, with oil reserves, abundant mineral deposits, and plentiful fisheries.

International Influences

To help Angola get on its feet during this fragile transition period, the former Soviet Union and Cuba, respectively, gave MPLA massive amounts of arms and deployed thousands of troops.[16] Despite its dreadful experience in Vietnam, and despite the fact that Angola represented only a "modest direct strategic interest," the United States remained concerned about communist expansion and its own credibility. Therefore, the United States intervened indirectly, supporting the FNLA and then UNITA, and working through South Africa and Zaire.[17] South Africa was increasingly apprehensive about the MPLA alliance with the South West African People's Organization (SWAPO) in Namibia, and it intervened forcefully in Angola, in support of UNITA. At the same time, while the US government sought to stem communism and to support the FNLA and UNITA, American oil companies continued to drill for oil in Cabinda and pay the MPLA, which helped to support the MPLA's war against the other two guerrilla forces and the South African army.

In October 1975, South Africa launched its first large scale intervention in support of UNITA. In November 1975, both the Soviet Union and Cuba stepped-up their support for the MPLA with the arrival of heavy Soviet weapons and a large contingent of Cuban soldiers. From that time on, more Cubans arrived and assisted the MPLA in its battles against South Africa and UNITA. As South Africa enhanced its intervention both directly and indirectly via UNITA, Cuba increased the deployment of its soldiers so that by the late 1980s, Cuba had 50,000 troops in Angola.[18] Due to the Clark Amendment, formalized in 1976, the United States was legally prohibited from giving direct assistance to any side in the Angolan conflict. In 1985, in the context of the Reagan administration's efforts to support counterrevolutionary movements (for example, in Afghanistan and Nicaragua) the Clark Amendment was repealed. In 1986, the United States began to make sizable military contributions to UNITA once again.

The turning point for outside intervention in Angola's civil war, however, was the battle of Cuito Cuanavale in 1988, which has been described as the biggest military campaign ever fought in southern Africa.[19] This battle, which badly bruised South African forces, was part of the Angolan government's overall strategy to weaken UNITA's hold in the southern region and to repel South African military intervention.

Following the debacle at Cuito Cuanavale, South Africa returned to the US-brokered negotiations that were aimed at implementing United Nations Security Council Resolution 435 (1978), which called for the independence of South African-ruled Namibia.[20] To coax South Africa into accepting this resolution as well as to quell its own concerns about Cuban forces in Angola, the United States proposed to link South Africa's departure from Namibia with Cuban withdrawal from Angola. Because the General Assembly had opposed the linkage of Namibia's independence to "extraneous issues," the United States pursued these mediation efforts outside the United Nations framework.[21] In New York in December 1988, Angola, Cuba, and South Africa finally reached an agreement for ending hostilities in southern Angola and for withdrawing South African forces from that country.[22] This agreement was an historic achievement: it enabled the implementation of Resolution 435; terminated South African military intervention in Angola; and facilitated the withdrawal of Cuba's 50,000 troops from Angola.[23] In the wake of this agreement, the United Nations deployed a peacekeeping force, named the United Nations Transition Assistance Group (UNTAG), to supervise Namibia's first democratic elections and its transition to independent statehood.[24] The agreement also led the way to United Nations involvement in Angola.

United Nations Engagement

From the beginning of the civil war, the United Nations denounced foreign intervention in Angola.[25] Although Angola's internal strife possessed an international dimension and threatened regional security, the United Nations could not authorize collective security action while the United States and the former Soviet Union were bitter enemies. Indeed, places like Angola had become the preferred battle grounds of the Cold War.

By the late 1980s, with the Cold War beginning to thaw, the environment for settling peace issues in Africa improved. The Cubans, after twenty years of involvement in Angola, were willing to leave as long as they did so with dignity, which was possible after the battle of Cuito Cuanavale. With the December 1988 agreement calling for the implementation of Resolution 435 in Namibia and the withdrawal of the Cubans, the UN was prepared to help secure peace in Angola.[26]

In late December 1988, after 28 years of deploring the situation in that country, the Security Council endorsed Resolution 626, which called for establishment of the United Nations Angolan Verification Mission (UNAVEM I) to validate the withdrawal of the Cuban troops over a 31-month period beginning 3 January 1989. This mission comprised 70 military observers from Argentina, Brazil, the Congo, Czechoslovakia, India, Jordan, and Norway, and was led by Chief Military Observer Brigadier General Pericles Ferreira Gomes, from Brazil.[27] As it was the first neutral international political presence in Angola, UNAVEM I was considered an important breakthrough.

By 25 May 1991, all Cuban troops had withdrawn from the country. The secretary-general attributed this mission's success to the full cooperation of all the parties involved.[28]

Despite the progressive withdrawal of Cuban and South African forces, the civil war continued as both the MPLA and UNITA persisted in seeking a military victory (a victory which continued to elude them). In April 1990, the Portuguese, with the United States and Russia as observers, began to mediate secret talks between the MPLA and UNITA at the Bicesse hotel school outside Lisbon. In May 1991, after more than a year of negotiations, the MPLA and UNITA finally relented and signed the Bicesse Peace Accords.

Conditions did not bode well for the agreed transitional arrangements, however. There were doubts that the prerequisites for fair and just elections would be in place for the September 1992 vote called for in the accords.[29] Also, as the Cold War ended, Angola was no longer a strategic trophy and therefore lost some of its international benefactors.[30] Unless Angola received the appropriate international support, in light of the country's miserable condition there were very real dangers that nationwide elections would not be enough to secure the achievement of peace and security. Unless they were widely accepted as legitimate, the elections could represent a serious threat to security. In this very fragile situation, the United Nations deployed its next Angolan verification mission.

The Peace Accords

On 17 May 1991, the minister of external affairs of Angola formally communicated to the United Nations secretary-general that the government of the People's Republic of Angola had signed, on 1 May 1991, a set of documents called the *Acordos de Paz para Angola* that established the principles for the implementation of peace in the country. The accords consisted of four documents: the cease-fire agreement, the principles for the establishment of peace, concepts for resolving the issues still pending between the government of Angola and UNITA, and the Protocol of Estoril.[31]

To demonstrate United Nations support for the peace accords, the Security Council adopted Resolution 696 on 30 May 1991, entrusting a new mandate to the United Nations Angolan Verification Mission (which thereafter became UNAVEM II).[32] The purpose of UNAVEM II was to help give effect to the peace accords, specifically by verifying the arrangements set out in the cease-fire agreement and by monitoring the neutrality of the Angolan police force as set out in the Protocol of Estoril.

The arrangements for the cease-fire agreement called for a total and definitive cessation of hostilities between the government and UNITA; the end of supplies of all lethal weapons by any government; and elimination of the two standing armies through a process of separation into assembly areas from which the soldiers would either join the new national army (Forcas Armadas de Angola, FAA), or be demobilized and reintegrated into society. By the time of the elections, only the national army would exist.[33]

To oversee the implementation of the cease-fire agreement, two political bodies were established. The primary political body was the Joint Political Military Commission (Comissao Conjunto Politico-Militar, CCPM) which was responsible for overall supervision of the cease-fire. It was composed of representatives from the government and UNITA, and observer-representatives from Portugal, Russia, and the United States. In addition, the United Nations was invited to monitor the CCPM. None of the international observers had any voting power.

To monitor the demobilization of the armies, the accords called for the establishment of a Joint Verification and Monitoring Commission (Comissao Mista de Verificacao, CMVF). The CMVF was to have monitoring sites in all regions and subregions of the country, and was responsible for the monitoring of the demobilization of the armies, including preventing, verifying, and investigating possible violations of the demobilization efforts. It reported to the CCPM and had the same observer group representatives as the CCPM.[34] The role of UNAVEM II was to verify that the CMVF monitoring groups carried out their responsibilities.

The Protocol of Estoril included agreements on political and military matters relating to elections, the CCPM, international security, political rights of UNITA, administrative structures, and the formation of the FAA.[35] The protocol called for the election of a president and national assembly through direct and secret suffrage in a majority vote, with a second round of voting if no presidential candidate won a majority of the votes cast in the first round. It stipulated that all adult Angolan citizens would be given the right to vote, to participate in the campaigning, and to stand for election without any discrimination or intimidation. In addition, it called for an international organization to provide technical advice on certain electoral matters. It did not, however, specifically designate the United Nations for technical advice or as an observer body for the elections.[36]

On the issue of internal security, the protocol called for the creation of a neutral police force under the supervision of a joint police monitoring force composed of both government and UNITA police monitoring and verification teams. In addition, it called for the monitoring and verification teams to include an expert in police affairs who would be designated by and subordinate to the United Nations command structure.[37]

MANDATE

The arrangements set forth in the peace accords entered into force on 31 May 1991, and it appeared that the Angolan people would finally get a chance at peace.[38] This hope was reinforced with the deployment of personnel under UNAVEM II starting on 1 June 1991.

The mandate for UNAVEM II called for a greater United Nations presence with the deployment of 350 military observers. In addition, rather than just verifying the withdrawal of readily distinguishable foreign troops under conditions of full cooperation, the new observer group had to verify activities of two Angolan standing armies who intensely distrusted each other. Although UNAVEM II, like UNAVEM I, had a passive mandate, its verification tasks were more difficult. The verification activities called not only for observing the cantonment of armies in certain areas but also for verifying the resignation of each army's weapons. UNAVEM II, however, was not given the responsibility to search for hidden weapons or to penalize the parties for their noncompliance.

In December 1991, the Angolan minister of external affairs submitted to the secretary-general a request for United Nations technical assistance for the electoral activities. In response to this request, the secretary-general recommended enlargement of the UNAVEM II mandate to include observation of the upcoming national elections. The secretary-general gave the following reasons for his recommendation: the situation already had a clear international dimension; the conduct of internationally supervised elections was a central element in the implementation of the peace accords; the fairness and impartiality of the elections in Angola required the monitoring of the entire electoral process, including voter registration; and there was broad public support for the United Nations to assume such a role.[39]

On 24 March 1992, the Security Council unanimously endorsed the secretary-general's recommendation and adopted Resolution 747, which enlarged UNAVEM II's mandate to include an Electoral Division to observe and verify the electoral process and the verification of free and fair multiparty elections.[40] The expanded mission's tasks included verifying the impartiality of the electoral authorities; freedom of organization, movement, assembly, and expression for political parties; and fair access of all political parties to State radio and television. In addition, the electoral observers would monitor all activities related to the registration process, the organization of the polls, and for the elections, the actual polling and counting of the ballot.[41]

FUNDING

UNAVEM II's projected initial budget was $122 million.[42] When the mission's mandate expanded, its budget was increased by $18.8 million. This revised budget, however, was still too low and reflected the lack of political attention and concern that UNAVEM received in comparison to other missions. When UNAVEM II was launched, it competed for resources and attention with the missions already established in El Salvador, Western Sahara, and Kuwait in the spring of 1991 and the very large missions established in Cambodia and Croatia in early 1992.[43]

The resources actually made available to UNAVEM II were even less than what was budgeted. From its inception in May 1991 until 31 October 1992, the operation received $105.2 million, while its operating costs for the same period were $106.5 million.[44] Underfunding continued. Through 15 September 1993, UNAVEM II's operating costs were $140.5 million and it had amassed an operating deficit of $27.3 million.[45] To help cover this deficit, a loan of $19 million from the Peacekeeping Reserve Fund and a loan of $18 million from UNTAG's special account were directed toward UNAVEM's operations.[46]

From 16 September 1993 to 30 September 1994, UNAVEM's total expenditures were $24.8 million. During this period, the mission ran an operating deficit of $1.26 million.[47]

When the civil war resumed in late October 1992, UNAVEM, facing extremely dangerous conditions, reduced its staff and its field sites. In the course of this withdrawal, many materials were stolen or abandoned, creating losses of $6.7 million. These losses included $1.9 million in vehicles and trailers, $0.4 million in communications equipment, $3.5 million in shelters, $0.6 million in generators, and $0.3 million in miscellaneous equipment.[48] Within six months of the resumption of the civil war, the size of UNAVEM's staff was reduced to 75 military observers, 30 police observers, and a small international civilian staff.[49] Any equipment that was salvaged was sent to the newly forming United Nations operation in Mozambique.

PLANNING AND IMPLEMENTATION

The secretary-general's March 1992 report, which called for enlargement of the UNAVEM mandate, noted delays in the implementation of the peace accords. As of 30 October 1991, less than 60 percent of the two armies' troops had been confined in assembly areas, three months after demobilization was supposed to have been complete.[50] Neither the government nor UNITA had established any police monitoring teams. These delays and continuing deterioration of internal security did not bode well for the maintenance of certain aspects of the accords.

The Problem of Decimated Infrastructure

Such delays notwithstanding, UNAVEM faced daunting challenges given the devastated conditions of the country (which, at 1.2 million square kilometers, is roughly the size of the eastern United States, or the countries of France, Spain, and Italy combined). When UNAVEM II personnel first arrived, there was almost no functioning infrastructure: about 70 percent of all roads were unusable because of mines; telephone and other communications were limited; and food and fuel supplies were scarce or nonexistent.[51] These awful conditions affected the mission's ability to execute its mandate and caused delays in implementing key provisions of the peace accords. For example, the formation of the assembly areas posed great logistical problems. There were inadequate means of transporting soldiers to the areas. In addition, many of the assembly areas were located away from population centers (for good reason: these were not highly disciplined armies), and therefore away from food markets. Also, in a country overwhelmed by economic and social problems, most of the soldiers had no job or training other than fighting, and therefore had little incentive for effective demobilization.

The lack of infrastructure impeded the extension of governmental administration, and the lack of order affected the free circulation of people and goods throughout Angola.[52] It also frustrated the voter registration process because areas remained inaccessible for delivery of registration materials, and there were no reliable communications networks to transmit registration data.

In addition to the inadequate infrastructure, there were very serious humanitarian problems, including widespread unemployment, drought, and population displacement.[53] Jobless demobilized soldiers often remained in their uniforms because they had no other clothing and no means to buy some. Humanitarian problems sometimes called for urgent United Nations attention and therefore diverted the UN from its role to observe and verify the electoral process.[54]

Security Problems

Along with harsh living conditions, all United Nations personnel had to cope with a lack of basic personal security and the tremendously high rate of crime in Angola.[55] With the end of the war, plenty of weapons had seeped out into the general population, and it was not safe to be in isolated areas or to drive at night, and not wise to walk on the streets, day or night.

Suspicion and mutual distrust between the MPLA and UNITA also continued after the war. Although the peace accords called for mechanisms to reduce suspicion, such as the establishment of a neutral police force, most of the mechanisms were never used. Instead, each side charged the other with noncompliance and secret build-ups of forces. The government alleged that UNITA maintained hidden arms reserves, and UNITA charged that the government's mobilization of riot police was a ruse to maintain a parallel army.[56] In fact, both parties' allegations proved correct after the elections. On the weekend of 31 October 1992, the government's "riot police" launched a military offensive in Luanda. UNITA's ready, standing army, which had already begun to occupy territory by force in central Angola, was equipped for revenge and for confronting government-held cities and villages throughout the rest of the country.

As the two sides charged each other with cheating, senior UNAVEM officials attempted to reduce the two parties' hostility, which often put UNAVEM personnel at risk. Often, after UNAVEM offered its good services, one of the parties would accuse the UN of siding with the other side and threaten to retaliate.

From the time the observers (military, police, and civilians) were first deployed, until the elections, UNAVEM personnel were subject to intimidation and, in some regions, were fired upon while in their camps. Every night gunfire could be heard, even in Luanda. In Malange, the conditions became so tense that it was no longer safe for the staff to stay in their prefabricated weatherhaven housing units. Once, one of the observers was forced to dance over machine-gun fire. In the contested Dundo/Saurimo area, the diamond region, both UNITA and the MPLA tried to intimidate UNAVEM personnel. During the political campaign period, UNAVEM personnel were forbidden to have cameras. Once, MPLA soldiers caught a UNAVEM observer, grabbed her camera and destroyed the film. During the month of August 1992, the MPLA increased its accusations that UNAVEM personnel were siding with UNITA; at night, stones were thrown at UNAVEM personnel while they were in their vehicles. Despite these incidents, everyone continued to hope that once the elections took place the situation would change and be peaceful.

Following the elections, the staff was steadily reduced in size. Many soldiers and police had already served their respective tours, and the majority of the civilian component, which was dedicated mostly to electoral activities, no longer served a purpose. In addition, many civilians were evacuated because the resumption of the war increasingly imperiled their safety.

Although the original objectives of the mission were destroyed when the elections failed, UNAVEM maintained a small presence in Angola to facilitate a mediating role for the UN. Nearly one year later, on 30 September 1993, UNAVEM's international staff totaled just 95 persons. This staff included 16 professional civilians, including the special representative of the secretary-general (SRSG); 54 military observers, 11 of whom were part of the medical unit; and 16 police observers.[57] Most of the staff was located in Luanda, but there were four other military team sites in Benguela, Lubango, Namibe, and Sumbe (See figure 4.1). In November 1994, however, in anticipation of the renewal of peace in Angola, the Security Council endorsed the restoration of UNAVEM's strength to its March 1992 level.[58] This was done to further demonstrate the United Nations commitment to Angola and to encourage the two parties to continue their peace efforts.

Composition, Command and Control

UNAVEM II had three goals: military demobilization, police neutrality, and a fair elections process. The UNAVEM staff was organized along these lines. At the head of the entire mission was the SRSG, a civilian, who outranked all other UN officials, including the chief military observer (CMO). Margaret Joan Anstee, a career international civil servant, was appointed the SRSG in March 1992.[59] The CMO, Major General Edward Ushie Unimna, was from Nigeria.

UNAVEM II initially comprised a total of 548 personnel, all of whom had been deployed by 30 September 1991.[60] They included 350 unarmed military observers who were deployed at 50 assembly areas as well as 12 other critical points to verify CMVF activities and to investigate and resolve alleged violations of the cease-fire.[61] Table 4.1 lists the countries that contributed military observers to UNAVEM II.

The military and the police were controlled by the CMO. In Luanda, in addition to the CMO, there was a deputy chief military observer (DCMO), initially from Egypt, later from Zimbabwe; a chief of staff; and a military staff in charge of logistics and the gathering of situation reports transmitted from the UNAVEM field sites. The police had their own operations rooms, and they reported to a chief inspector who in turn reported to the CMO. In each region, there was a regional commander, who was a colonel, and three to four military observers, with an average rank of major.

For observing the joint monitoring teams of the Angolan police, nine UN member states contributed 89 police officers who were deployed in 18 provincial centers (Table 4.1 shows contributions of police observers as well).[62]

At UNAVEM headquarters in Luanda, the Electoral Division comprised a small staff headed by a chief electoral officer (CEO); a deputy chief electoral officer (DCEO); a liaison officer; a statistician to tabulate registration and electoral figures; and, three administrative support personnel. This component was responsible for all electoral activities of the mission, including the actual monitoring of the polls during the election days. Through the CEO, the division reported to the SRSG.

As part of its efforts, the Electoral Division followed all National Electoral Council programs and policies in Luanda, as well as the activities of other contributors of international electoral monitors such as the National Democratic Institute and International Republican Institute, from the United States, and International Foundation for Electoral Systems (IFES). Although UNAVEM officials met with representatives of these organizations and attended some of their respective programs, UNAVEM remained independent of these groups in order to ensure its neutral position. In addition to international electoral groups, the Electoral Division consulted with the British company, Thomas De La Rue and Co., Ltd., which the Angolan government hired to develop the election kits, including the printing of the ballot sheets.

In addition, the Electoral Division was responsible for overseeing UNAVEM electoral activities in the field. Each week the electoral observers submitted reports describing the progress of activities in their respective areas, based on their participation in local political meetings, monitoring of polling stations during registration and then during the election days, and observance of any political rallies and incidents. These activities were undertaken at both the regional and provincial levels. The electoral division in Luanda synthesized this information and produced weekly reports that included projections of the political climate. These reports were submitted to the

Table 4.1

NATIONAL COMPOSITION OF UNAVEM II

Military Observers	Police Observers	Military Observers	Police Observers
Algeria		Malaysia	X
Argentina	X	Morocco	X
Brazil	X	Netherlands	X
Canada		New Zealand	
Congo		Nigeria	X
Czechoslovakia		Norway	
Egypt		Senegal	
Guinea Bissau		Singapore	
Hungary		Spain	
India		Sweden	X
Ireland	X	Yugoslavia	
Jordan		Zimbabwe	X

SOURCE: Security Council, *Report of the Secretary-General on the United Nations Angola Verification Mission II (UNAVEM II) for the period 31 May 1991–25 October 1991,* S/23191, 31 October 1991.

SRSG and then eventually to the substantive office in the Department of Peacekeeping Operations in New York. The CEO, DCEO, and liaison officer traveled in the field to check on the observers and hear their problems.

In the field, the electoral observers were deployed in the six regional centers and the 18 provincial centers, collocated with the military and police observers. Each center had an electoral coordinator to whom the other electoral observers reported. About once a month the regional coordinators came to Luanda for UNAVEM meetings and principal National Electoral Commission (NEC) meetings. The provincial coordinators were permitted to come to Luanda less frequently, in principle, generally when there was a national NEC meeting or meeting of all coordinators at headquarters. Observers who were not coordinators were only permitted to travel back to headquarters after written authorization. They could then visit Luanda on a very short term basis, either to make phone calls to their families or to receive medical attention, since there were few doctors in the provinces. Most of the time, observers received treatment for malaria, which was prevalent throughout the country. For many observers, the field situation was particularly stressful; except for a few centers such as Benguela, Lobito, and Lubango, conditions were very tough.

The military and police managed their respective commands in a similar fashion: observers could not leave their duty site without authorization, and most of the time it was for sick leave or calling their respective home countries.

Although Resolution 747 called for an additional 36 police monitors, the original function of the police was never realized and their role was ephemeral. The Angolans often misconstrued the role of the UNAVEM police as enforcers of law and order.

Because the mission continued without the Angolan parties ever establishing the neutral monitoring teams called for by the accords, the UNAVEM police themselves were not sure of their expected role. First, these officers were only trained as police in their home countries and not specially trained as human rights observers. Then, the mandate they were given never materialized, so their roles evolved as circumstances required, which many of them resented. Depending on their locations, they either worked with the military, to whom they were subordinate, or the electoral observers, who often regarded the police as their personal bodyguards and drivers. Nevertheless, the police assisted in staffing the radio centers and reported on any incidents they observed.

Logistics

For about the first nine months of the mission, the military and police lived like the Angolans and spent most of their time trying to meet the basics of survival. Due to extreme shortages of food and water, some of the observers had to spend most of their time getting water and trading for food. In some sites, water had to be carried as far as two kilometers to the UNAVEM camp or even shipped by air. Prior to the arrival of the prefabricated weatherhavens, living conditions in the field ranged from tents to war-ravaged buildings and grass huts, which gave little protection against poisonous snakes, rats, and insects.

By the time the electoral component started to work, which was nearly a year after UNAVEM II began, logistics had improved throughout the operation. Buildings had been repaired, and weatherhaven shelters were constructed with facilities for running water and electricity. At the main headquarters in Luanda, known as Villa Espa, a container base camp was erected. These containers, which were the same as those used for shipping cargo, were linked together and transformed into living quarters with air conditioning and beds. Critical shortages of vehicles and communications equipment remained, however.

All staple supplies had to be imported from Europe, Namibia, or South Africa. Flights to Namibia were made to obtain United States dollars because there was no real banking system in Angola. It was not possible, for example, to cash travelers checks or to use credit cards. The finance unit, therefore, instituted a policy of paying the staff a monthly stipend in dollars, after which they were able to trade on one of the streets, known as "Wall Street," for the local currency (kwanza) and then buy food and other basic items.

Moreover, Angola's telecommunications development had been interrupted in 1961 for a war that lasted about 32 years. It was nearly impossible to make a telephone call in Luanda and utterly impossible to contact other parts of the country. For international communications, UNAVEM installed satellite hookups in both its main headquarters at Villa Espa and in the SRSG's office in downtown Luanda. Although there were radio links to the field sites, these centers did not have satellite communications outside of Angola. During the actual election days, however, portable satellite telephones were installed to facilitate regional reporting for the quick count.

At UNAVEM headquarters, there were two radio operations rooms. One was dedicated to receiving all military situation reports. Another was dedicated solely to receiving situation reports from the entire northern region, which included Luanda. In addition, there was a room where staff members could sign up for making their long distance telephone calls, which could not exceed ten minutes.

In the city proper, the SRSG had established an office for receiving official visitors and conducting meetings with other United Nations representatives and international organizations. This office also had international satellite communications links. In comparison to the main headquarters at Espa, which was about a half hour from the center of the city, this office was close to other government offices and near other United Nations agencies in Luanda. The NEC and other international electoral groups, including the European Community technical assistance group, also had their offices in the same building. In view of the poor communications facilities, even in Luanda, this office offered a venue for the international community to exchange views.

For transportation and delivery of supplies to the provinces, UNAVEM had its own air support, which included helicopters and several fixed-wing aircraft. For local transportation, UNAVEM used Toyota and Nissan vehicles. When the war broke out, many of them were blown up by the UN to prevent local people from stealing and riding around in UNAVEM vehicles.

As the mission progressed and the security situation deteriorated, UNAVEM confronted more logistical problems. For example, in the province of Uige, there were three UNAVEM helicopter crashes in three consecutive weeks, which left UNAVEM with fewer helicopters for the election days. There were several reasons for the crashes, including unskilled subcontractor pilots, who lacked the requisite flying time, and poor maintenance. UNAVEM civilians were injured and a local Angolan staff member was killed.

Despite the obstacles, logistics for the actual elections operated relatively smoothly. For the election period, UNAVEM and United Nations Development Program (UNDP) organized the largest air support operation that the United Nations had ever mounted at that time, consisting of 45 helicopters and 15 fixed-wing aircraft. This equipment was used to deploy electoral teams, supplies, and equipment to the more inaccessible polling stations as well as to provide a communications network and fuel supply.[63] Unlike other aircraft at the airport (for example, US Air Force C-130s), the United Nations aircraft were painted white with "UN" clearly marked in black.

Verifying Demobilization

The peace accords stipulated that the disbandment of the two armies and the formation of the new unified armed forces should be achieved by the time of the elections. The first part of this process was the confinement of forces in assembly areas from which troops would be demobilized. By the end of June 1992, however, only 49 percent of the troops had been assembled.[64] In July 1992, therefore, this approach was abandoned for a speedier process that involved troops being selected either for demobilization or for the new Angolan armed forces without passing through assembly areas.

Demobilization, however, also ran behind schedule and in fact continued after the elections. By 2 September, with the elections only three weeks away, only 41 percent, or a total of 61,994, government and UNITA troops had been demobilized.[65] On the government side, 45 percent, or 54,737 troops, had demobilized while on the UNITA side, only 24 percent, or 7,270 troops, had done so.[66] UNITA justified its lack of demobilization on grounds that the government was really reassigning troops to other police or paramilitary forces rather than demobilizing them. Although the United States assured UNITA that its fears were overblown, UNITA's assertion about the formation of a secret paramilitary force was proven accurate, as noted earlier, on the weekend of 31 October in Luanda.[67]

The formation of the new Angolan armed forces also ran woefully behind schedule. By 2 September, only 19 percent of the new armed forces had been formed. Given the tardiness of both demobilization and the formation of the new armed forces, it became clear that unless drastic measures were taken, Angola faced the dangerous prospect of three standing armies on its soil at election time.[68]

To help speed up the demobilization of forces, the United States deployed several C-130s to Luanda. For nearly two months, one month prior to elections and one month after, the US Air Force moved thousands of mostly government soldiers from assembly areas to their home regions.[69]

Electoral Implementation

As the electoral process moved forward, most of UNAVEM's activities became oriented toward making the elections work. After a year of implementation, it became apparent that the original goals of the peace accords would not be attained. Therefore, the operations of the military and police components of the UNAVEM were altered to dovetail with the operations's election-related objectives.

For example, the military observers, though still monitoring CMVF activities, turned their attention to reporting on incidents, such as those that occurred during demobilization, that indicated levels of acceptance of the electoral process. A policy was also initiated to integrate the electoral observers' reports with military and police information to determine how smoothly the elections might proceed.

The progression of UNAVEM's mandate corresponded and reacted to the development of national electoral activities. Once the NEC was established in May

1992, to organize and supervise the elections, UNAVEM's role became more oriented toward ensuring (or wishing for) its success. The electoral process consisted of four phases: the registration of voters from 20 May to 31 July 1992 (subsequently extended to 10 August); the electoral campaign from 9 August to 28 September; the voting on 29 and 30 September; and, finally, the counting of the votes.[70] The United Nations, through the UNDP, provided some technical assistance in developing civic education programs. Although UNAVEM sought to have an electoral code of conduct instituted, and even developed one for the NEC, the code was never implemented.

The UNAVEM Electoral staff was aware that if there were any problems in the electoral process, particularly if certain regions were not adequately represented and registered for the voting, one of the parties could later cry foul. Therefore, in August, the SRSG made several appeals for the registration period to extend beyond 10 August 1992, to cover areas where there was a late extension of the central administration, where there was inadequate delivery of registration materials, and where there were returning refugees. The NEC, however, decided against the extension. UNAVEM was particularly concerned about the situation in Cabinda. The FLEC independence movement had successfully kept the province largely out of the peace and electoral process. Government troops stationed there had to be kept on combat duty because of the ongoing conflict. Only about one-fifth of Cabinda's eligible voters registered.[71]

Poor funding provided for scant electoral coverage. Until the election itself, UNAVEM had just 89 people in its Electoral Division. For the actual polling days of the first democratic elections ever held in Angola, UNAVEM had resources for 400 observers—300 international civil servants from the Secretariat and various United Nations agencies, and 100 personnel serving in other United Nations agencies in Angola and neighboring countries. In addition, military and police observers were assigned to electoral observation teams. By comparison, for the 1989 elections in Namibia, the United Nations had dedicated 6,000 people to electoral observation, even though Namibia's population was 12 percent of Angola's.

Despite logistical constraints and the two parties' lack of compliance with the peace accords, the NEC reported that 4.86 million eligible voters, or about 92 percent of an estimated voting population of 5.3 million, registered to vote. Although the SRSG had raised concerns about not every eligible voter having an opportunity to register, particularly in the provinces of Moxico, Cuando Cubango, and Vigo, the NEC decided by majority that 92 percent registration gave evidence that the process had in large part succeeded against great odds.

THE ELECTIONS AND THEIR AFTERMATH

On 29 and 30 September 1992, the Angolan people patiently stood in long lines to vote for a change to a lasting peace. Many were barefoot. The women as usual had their babies tied to their backs. UNAVEM's election days observers were put in two-person teams to visit about 4,000 polling stations, spending an average of 20 minutes at each, enough time to observe four voters complete the process. The observers monitored the organization of the polling stations and the general conduct of the voting. At each polling station they attended, the observers completed a standard form that UNAVEM's Electoral Division had prepared.

Angolan electoral law required that the counting of the votes take place at each polling station. With a limited number of observers, UNAVEM was not able to dedicate observers to the entire counting process at all polling stations. Therefore, UNAVEM carried out its own quick count of the presidential election at a selected sample of 166 polling stations where observers remained throughout the count. The results of the quick count turned out very close to final election results, that is, within 0.3 percent of the final result for President dos Santos and within 2 percent of that for Dr. Savimbi. (Although the UNAVEM quick count was supposed to have been a guarded secret, the results seemed to have leaked out and everyone apparently was aware of the results well before the official announcement.)

In view of the vast size of Angola and its near nonexistent infrastructure, the counting of votes and the investigation of complaints and alleged fraud was an extensive undertaking. Although the electoral law allowed eight days for the counting, the count was extended until 17 October. During this period, both the MPLA and UNITA announced over their radio stations that each had won the elections, which caused tensions between the two parties to rise even further.

According to the official election results, President Jose Eduardo dos Santos, the MPLA candidate, won 49.6 percent of the vote, and Jonas Savimbi of UNITA won 40.1 percent of the vote. Because neither won a majority, there would be a second round of elections.[72] The United Nations SRSG announced in Luanda on 17 October 1992 that the elections, "despite some irregularities, were generally free and fair" and requested that the international community respect and support the results.[73] UNITA, however, denounced the results and claimed massive and systematic fraud. It withdrew from the new national army and began to mobilize its forces, launching a nationwide operation to forcefully occupy municipalities and remove government administrative structures.

Return to Civil War

Violent incidents in the country rose steadily and became more serious. For example, there was an ammunition dump explosion four kilometers from UNAVEM's Espa headquarters. When the ammo dump exploded, the ground shook, missiles fired in all directions, the sky was filled with light, and there were loud booming sounds lasting for several hours. This incident, which occurred two weeks after the elections, provided an ominous sign of things to come. In its wake came the bombing of a hotel in Luanda used by UNITA. This incident coincided with a visit from members of the Security Council, who strongly urged UNITA not to abandon the peace process.

Then, on 31 October 1992, in reaction to the escalation of tensions, the MPLA launched an offensive now dubbed the "Halloween Massacre" because of the scores of victims slaughtered in Luanda that weekend. The victims were suspected or real UNITA supporters, including Salupeto Pena, the nephew of Jonas Savimbi and the leader of UNITA's delegation to the Joint Political and Military Commission. UNITA retaliated and carried out deliberate and arbitrary killings against MPLA supporters. Thus, the civil war resumed, engulfing Angola and shredding all aspects of human decency that had been nurtured during the 16 months of peace.

The lack of communications and transportation links to UNAVEM observers in the outstations put the lives of observers at risk because they were not always aware of hostilities beyond their immediate areas. When the civil war erupted on 31 October, one regional electoral coordinator was in a helicopter on his way to Luanda for a meeting. He had not been informed of the cancellation of the meeting or the outbreak of war; his helicopter was shot down by UNITA forces, and he was held captive in Huambo for 24 hours.

When the war broke out, all travel was forbidden. Therefore, the observers in most of the outstations were caught without adequate food supplies. Others, who were left in different parts of Luanda, were surrounded by fighting and the massacre of civilians by MPLA soldiers, riot police, and vigilantes.

Despite nonstop efforts by the United Nations, including sponsorship of cease-fire negotiations, civil war raged worse than ever before, killing as many as one thousand people a day, one of the highest fatality rates of any conflict in the world.[74] Widespread fighting produced anarchy in much of the country and led to severe and widespread hunger. Some viewed the humanitarian situation in Angola at this juncture to be worse than the tragedies in Somalia and Bosnia-Herzegovina.[75] The depths of atrocities visited upon the civilian populace prompted the United Nations World Conference on Human Rights in Vienna on 24 June 1993 to call for an end to the total disregard in Angola of international humanitarian law.[76]

Renewed Search for Peace

Following the outbreak of the war, the SRSG sought to mediate the crisis between the two parties. Meetings were first held in Namibe, Angola, in 1992, followed by talks in Addis Ababa in January 1993, and then in Abidjan in March and April 1993. The negotiations failed, however, and were considered by the SRSG as "very dispiriting experiences." During these negotiations, however, both the MPLA and UNITA agreed that when they did reach another cease-fire, the United Nations must have a very strong mandate and a much bigger role.[77]

In response to some Angolans' comment that the United Nations had somehow betrayed them, Margaret Anstee stressed UNAVEM's limited mandate, "which was not of its choosing" but was "handed down" by the negotiators of the Bicesse Accords. Those accords, she observed, permitted compromises that were not the best in terms of practical implementation.[78]

Diplomatic Initiatives

As the civil war raged on, the United Nations maintained its pressure for reconciliation. The Security Council endorsed numerous resolutions calling for an end to the conflict, including Resolution 864 in September 1993, which called for a Chapter VII action prohibiting any sale or delivery of weapons or lethal materials, as well as petroleum products, to UNITA if UNITA broke any cease-fire agreement.[79] Despite this embargo, some countries continued to sell lethal weapons to Angola, an act particularly egregious in view of the human misery in that country.[80]

Upon her request, the United Nations replaced Margaret Anstee as SRSG in July 1993 with Alioune Blondin Beye, a former foreign minister from Mali, who headed up negotiations that resumed in Lusaka, Zambia. The new chief military observer presiding over the mission as of September 1993 was Major General Chris Abutut Garuba, from Nigeria like his predecessor.

In May 1993, the United States government recognized the Angolan government and the election results of September 1992, in the hope that this would encourage a peace settlement. Also, in October 1993, US president Clinton appointed a special envoy, Paul J. Hare, to join the United Nations negotiations in Lusaka.

The Lusaka Protocol

After about a year and a half of very tenuous negotiations that continued through promises of cease-fire and resumptions of intensive combat, the government of Angola and UNITA finally agreed to reconcile and to establish a just and enduring peace. The document embodying their renewed commitment to peace, the Lusaka Protocol, was signed in Lusaka, Zambia, on 20 November 1994.[81] The Lusaka Protocol called on the parties to conclude the implementation of the 1991 peace accords, and called for monitoring of the cease-fire, the withdrawal, quartering, and demobilization of all UNITA military forces, the disarming of all civilians, the completion of the formation of the Angolan armed forces, the formation of a neutral police force, and the completion of the electoral process of 1992, that is, the holding of the second round of presidential elections.[82] Among the principles for reimplementing the cease-fire was the repatriation of all mercenaries.[83]

In contrast to the Bicesse Accords, which were orchestrated by Angola's former colonial rulers and Cold War interventionists, the Lusaka negotiations embraced the efforts of Africans to solve an African crisis. They were spearheaded by SRSG Blondin Beye, who sought the cooperation of African leaders to improve the political atmosphere in Angola and to facilitate the implementation of a new peace agreement.[84]

Also unlike the Bicesse Accords, the Lusaka Protocol stressed the role of the United Nations as not only an observer to the process but as an integral partner in ensuring the renewal of peace.[85] In fact, to oversee the implementation of the Lusaka Protocol, the United Nations was to do more than observe: it was to chair the new political supervisory body called the Joint Commission that replaced the CCPM.[86]

ASSESSMENT OF UNAVEM II

Unlike the United Nations' more recent Chapter VII intervention activities, UNAVEM satisfied the requirements of a traditional peacekeeping mission. It was deployed after the request and with the consent of the Angolan parties. In fact, in the case of UNAVEM, concern for Angolan state sovereignty was paramount. This meant that UNAVEM was not involved in the direct supervision or implementation of the peace accords, which remained the responsibility of the Angolan people.[87] The role of UNAVEM was to encourage the parties to fulfill their obligations under the peace accords by verifying that the two Angolan parties were shouldering those responsibilities.[88] By providing reliable accounts of the strengths and disposition of opposing forces, the verification and monitoring process was to have enhanced military transparency and helped build confidence between erstwhile adversaries.

Despite the absence of an enforcement capability, UNAVEM's mandate to verify compliance in a sense gave it an enforcement mechanism that was not used. When noncompliance was detected, as it was throughout the process, UNAVEM should have not only publicly denounced the lack of compliance and the parties' activities, but also declared that it would not sanction the continuation of the process. By not having a standard for verifying compliance or a set of procedures for correcting defects that the mission observed, UNAVEM simply became a rubber stamp for a process that collapsed into civil war.[89]

Although the peace accords included a provision by which enforcement would not infringe upon the sovereignty and territorial integrity of Angola, their full entry into force also required strict observance by the government and UNITA of the other provisions and of the decisions made by the verifying and monitoring bodies.[90] Therefore, as long as the United Nations did not encroach upon the sovereignty of the Angolan state, the United Nations through its verification role could have ensured compliance with the Peace Accords.

From the mission's inception, noncompliance with the peace accords was detected and reported by UNAVEM staff and even the political parties in Angola. In June 1992, with the elections only four months away, the political parties protested to the SRSG that the elections had a scant chance of being free and fair, mainly because of mutual distrust, slow extension of the central administration, proliferation of weapons, decline in law and order, and the lack of resources for effective multiparty elections.[91]

Although UNAVEM II noted noncompliance, its mission did not get the international media attention or support that might have helped bring more pressure on the parties to comply. With more international condemnation and action, it might also have been possible to halt the increase in tension that occurred after the elections. But the need for greater international attention would not have been so acute if the parties had in good faith really wanted peace and a democratic society.

Although UNAVEM's mandate recognized that the verification of democratically held elections was the ultimate requirement for instituting peace in Angola, it did not include the verification of integral aspects of democracy, like respect for human rights.[92] Although a one-week human rights seminar for Angolan officials was held, funded by the Raoul Wallenberg Institute in Sweden, this was hardly enough for the entire country. As more states make the transition to democracy, it is becoming increasingly clear that peace, democracy, and human rights are interdependent, with the success of one dependent on the existence and integrity of the others. Basic norms of tolerance and respect for human rights are essential for a stable democratic society.

One of the underlying notions of the Bicesse Accords was the establishment of a neutral police force, which was considered an essential element in creating an environment conducive to protecting human rights. UNAVEM's police contingent, created to monitor the organization and operation of the Angolan new police force, never performed that task.[93] Even if it had been more active, the UNAVEM police lacked training in human rights.

UNAVEM III

On 8 February 1995, the Security Council unanimously endorsed Resolution 976 calling for UNAVEM III, an enlarged United Nations mission in Angola.[94] This third United Nations mission was given a far more comprehensive mandate than its predecessor, reflecting in part lessons learned from the shortcomings of UNAVEM II. Unfortunately, the resumed civil war caused more destruction, and therefore, UN-AVEM III faced deployment under even more deplorable and tragic conditions than its predecessor.

The new operation deployed into a country in which the basic infrastructure was almost totally devastated and 35 percent of the population, approximately 3.5 million persons, had been displaced from their homes. Intensifying the humanitarian situation, land mines could be found throughout the country: Angola is now reported to be the most mine-polluted country in the world.[95]

The main components of UNAVEM III are political, military, police, and humanitarian. Their tasks include monitoring and verifying the implementation of the cease-fire; the assembly and demobilization, collection, storage, and custody of weapons; the formation of the new army; the creation of a neutral police force; the extension of central administration; assurance of the free circulation of people and goods; assurance of security for UNITA leaders; and supervision and verification of the second round of elections. The mission's original mandate, endorsed by the Security Council in February 1995, included a component for supervision and verification of elections. Development of this component has been deferred, however, in light of the government's decision to hold off elections until 2000, or later.

To ensure that these functions are carried out, this time around the United Nations can do more than monitor and verify; it is to be involved in and oversee each stage of the new peace process. For example, during the demobilization stage, the United Nations is to receive, guard, and transport all weapons, which are to remain under United Nations custody.

To carry out its enlarged role, UNAVEM III has an enhanced management structure and increased resources. The organizational structure includes an SRSG, who exercises complete authority over all personnel and units and is the chief negotiator between the Angolan parties and the observer states, a deputy SRSG to assist in the management of the mission, a director for political affairs who heads up the political component, a human rights office, and a legal staff. A small secretariat attached to the SRSG's office assists the SRSG in his or her duties as chair of the Joint Commission.

Heading the enlarged military component is the force commander, Major General Philip Sibanda of Zimbabwe. The police component is led by a chief police observer with the rank of chief superintendent, and the administrative component by a director of administration. Also under the UNAVEM III umbrella is a Unit for Coordination of Humanitarian Assistance, which was established by the UN's Department of Humanitarian Affairs in 1993, during the war.

Generally, the political component monitors and prepares analyses for the SRSG regarding difficulties that arise in implementing the renewed agreement for peace. Specifically, it monitors the conditions for national reconciliation, which are considered vital for a sustainable transition to peace.

The military component is far more robust than under UNAVEM II, incorporating six infantry battalions as well as military observers. These contingents patrol the perimeters of the troop quartering areas, supervise the quartering of troops and their demobilization, and facilitate the free circulation of people and goods. Specialized engineer squadrons are deployed to assist in mine clearance and to advise on the creation of a demining school. Finally, the military component is responsible for verifying the handing in and storage of weapons by UNITA.

Under UNAVEM III, the police component will again set out to help establish a neutral police force. This time, however, they have better-specified tasks. Their duties include monitoring the quartering of the government's rapid reaction police in eight locations throughout the country; verifying the collection of Angolan police arms now in the hands of the civilian population; verifying the integration of 5,500 UNITA personnel into the national police; receiving reports on violations of the Lusaka Protocol; and, visiting police facilities.

The Unit for Coordination of Humanitarian Assistance coordinates all humanitarian relief among Angolan, international, national, and non-governmental relief organizations, as well as the demobilization and reintegration of soldiers and demining. Since one of the obstacles to demobilization in 1992 was the lack of alternative employment for troops, the Humanitarian Assistance Unit includes an Office for the Demobilization of Former Combatants and Their Reintegration into Civilian Life. Since mines and explosives can disrupt the implementation of humanitarian assistance operations, the Humanitarian Unit also oversees a Central Mine Actions Office that coordinates activities with UNAVEM to ensure the safe deployment of United Nations personnel and resettlement of displaced persons.

To carry out its various functions, the UNAVEM III staff includes 6,770 military contingent personnel, 350 military observers, 260 civilian police monitors, 350 international civilian staff, 343 locally recruited staff, and 68 United Nations Volunteers.[96] This level of staff stands in remarkable contrast to the level allowed UNAVEM II.[97]

UNAVEM III was given a budget of $383.1 million for its first 12 months.[98] The government of Angola contributes to the support of the operation with about $500 million worth of in-kind services and facilities. This contribution includes provision of a residential compound for UNAVEM, an aircraft parking facility, harbor space for vessels, warehouses and office space in ports, fuel at rates below the international price and exemption from custom duties.[99]

The third UNAVEM mission, facing infrastructure in even worse shape than before, needed an efficient logistic network. The plans for UNAVEM III, therefore, called for the establishment of a main logistics base south of Luanda in the port city of Lobito, to avoid logistic bottlenecks. This main base is supplemented by one or two hub bases in the countryside. Although UNAVEM III maintains satellite communications between Luanda and New York and to its six regional headquarters in Angola, it does not have access to the intelligence gathering devices, such as aerial or satellite surveillance photos, that it should have.[100]

For the renewed peace effort to work, both parties *must* be ready to fully cooperate and be willing to build a peaceful society. In hindsight, it is now obvious that in the 1992 elections the parties did not trust each other; most likely neither was willing to accept a transfer of power to the other. In addition to this lack of trust, there was a misunderstanding about the role of UNAVEM II. Therefore, under UNAVEM III, to ensure that all Angolans receive the same information, the United Nations does a weekly television broadcast with updates on the peace process and explanations of UNAVEM's role. UNAVEM sought to install a radio station to disseminate information about the peace process throughout the country (since few Angolans have televisions), but this was not allowed by the government.

As UNAVEM II demonstrated, without a far-reaching program for protecting human rights, reconciliation and development cannot take place.[101] Therefore, to help facilitate conditions conducive to respect for human rights, UNAVEM III includes a human rights component attached to the SRSG's office at headquarters in Luanda and to various posts throughout the country. The component's observers help assess the country's progress in establishing an atmosphere of tolerance.[102]

Unlike the UNAVEM II mandate, UNAVEM III's mandate contains several enforcement mechanisms. The armed military contingent is authorized to use force in self-defense and against forcible attempts to impede implementation of the UN's mandate. In addition, the secretary-general has warned that if political will is found lacking or if the parties are uncooperative, he will invite the Security Council to reconsider its commitments in Angola.[103]

CONCLUSION

Peacekeeping missions, although not specifically stipulated in the United Nations Charter, symbolize the ideals embodied in the Charter and actualize its principles. As peacekeeping missions increasingly become a regular component of the promotion and maintenance of international security, it is particularly important that these missions fulfill their mandates and have the requisite resources and trained personnel to do so. Without a comprehensive and objective assessment of the political situations into which the UN sends its people, and without the necessary resources, the chances for a successful mission are slim. When the mission fails, the situation may become even worse than when the United Nations entered the country.

Already, however, the lessons of Angola have been absorbed at the United Nations and applied to the development of comprehensive mandates for the successful mission in Mozambique and the third mission in Angola. For the people of Angola, however, the collapse of the Bicesse Accords and the failures of UNAVEM II made it painfully clear that, without adequate international attention and support, efforts to end civil wars may bring only despair. Hopefully, by applying the lessons learned from UNAVEM II, its successor will help, finally, to ensure peace in this African country. As of mid-1996, peace seemed finally to be taking hold, as the government and UNITA showed increasing willingness to cooperate toward building a peaceful society in Angola once and for all.[104]

NOTES

1. The author served on the second and third UN Angola Verification Missions, as well as on the UN Operation in Mozambique. This chapter was prepared in the author's personal capacity and does not necessarily reflect the views of the United Nations.

2. United Nations General Assembly (UNGA) Resolution 1603, UN General Assembly Official Record, 15th sess., 992 mtg., 20 April 1961; see also UNGA A/4390/Add.1, 1961; for United Nations Security Council Resolution 163, S/4835, 9 June 1961, see Dusan J. Djonovich, *United Nations Resolutions, Series II: Resolutions and Declarations of the Security Council, Vol. IV, 1960-63* (Dobbs Ferry, NY: Oceana Publications, 1989), 45.

3. The UN Charter, Article 2(4), states: "All Members shall refrain in their international relations from the threat of use of force against the territorial integrity of political independence of any state." Compare with Article 2(7): "Nothing contained in the present Charter shall authorize the United Nations to intervene in matters which are essentially within the domestic jurisdiction of any state . . . ; but this principle shall not prejudice the application of enforcement measures under Chapter VII."

4. Thomas Collelo, ed., *Angola: A Country Study* (Washington, D.C.: Library of Congress, 1989), 34. In view of Cabinda's oil reserves, FLEC's international support has always been viewed as economically self-serving, rather than politically motivated.

5. Ibid., 28; Daniel Spikes, *Angola and the Politics of Intervention* (Jefferson, NC: McFarland & Co., 1993), 105-07.

6. Ws Van Der Waals, *Portugal's War in Angola, 1961-1974* (Johannesburg, S. Africa: Ashanti Publishing, 1993), 104-05; Spikes, *Angola and the Politics of Intervention,* 56. National liberation notwithstanding, the overriding objective of Moscow's renewed interest in the MPLA was to use the organization to support its operations against Portugal.

7. Van Der Waals, *Portugal's War in Angola,* 105.

8. Collelo, *Angola: A Country Study,* 31.

9. Ibid., 151. Revolutionary action in Angola was a threat to South West Africa because it allowed Angola to become a staging area and infiltration route for guerrilla forces fighting South African rule.

10. Collelo, *Angola: A Country Study,* 38.

11. Kenneth Maxwell, "The Legacy of Decolonization," in Richard J. Bloomfield, ed., *Regional Conflict and US Policy: Angola and Mozambique* (Algonac, MI: Reference Publications, Inc., 1988), 29.

12. Ibid., 25. At the end of colonial rule, the Angolan whites took with them almost everything that made the system of government and economy work, throwing an already confused situation into chaos.

13. Inge Tvedten, "US Policy Towards Angola Since 1975," *Journal of Modern African Studies* 30, no. 1 (1992): 31-35.

14. Fred Bridgland, *Jonas Savimbi: A Key to Africa* (Edinburgh, UK: Mainstream Publishing Co., 1986), 24.

15. Collelo, *Angola: A Country Study,* 113-15.

16. By November 1975, there were 4,000 Cuban troops in Angola. A February 1976 joint Soviet-Cuban airlift and sealift transported weapons to Angola. By March, weapons delivered included MIG-21 fighter aircraft, T-34 and T-54 tanks, armored personnel carriers, antitank and portable antiaircraft missiles, AK-47 automatic rifles, and 122 millimeter rocket launchers. (Ibid., 32-33.)

17. Ibid., 39. See also, Peter J. Schraeder, *United States Foreign Policy Toward Africa: Incrementalism, Crisis and Change* (Cambridge and London: Cambridge University Press, 1994); Michael Wolfers and Jane Bergerol, *Angola in the Frontline* (London: Zed Press, 1983), 9. On the American response in support of the MPLA's opponents, Holden Roberto and Jonas Savimbi, see John Stockwell, *In Search of Enemies* (New York: W.W. Norton, 1978).

18. Collelo, *Angola: A Country Study,* 45.

19. David Birmingham, *Frontline Nationalism in Angola and Mozambique* (Trenton, NJ: Africa World Press, 1992), 106.

20. Tvedten, "US Policy Toward Angola Since 1975," 41.

21. United Nations, *The Blue Helmets: A Review of United Nations Peacekeeping,* 2nd ed. (New York: United Nations Department of Public Information, 1990), 335. See also, Chester A. Crocker, "Peacemaking in Southern Africa, The Namibia-Angola Settlement of 1988," in David D. Newsom, ed., *The Diplomatic Record 1989-1990* (Boulder, CO: Westview Press, 1991), 14-18. This section describes the negotiations.

22. Chester A. Crocker, *High Noon in Southern Africa: Making Peace in a Rough Neighborhood* (New York: W.W. Norton, 1993), 37. In 1978, five members of the Security Council—Britain, Canada, France, Germany, and the United States—converted themselves into the so-called "Contact Group" to negotiate with South Africa to develop a peace plan leading to independence for Namibia. The result of these negotiations was UN Resolution 435.

23. Gerald Bender, "Washington's Quest for Enemies in Angola," in Bloomfield, ed., *Regional Conflict and US Policy: Angola and Mozambique* (Algonac, MI : Reference Publications, Inc., 1988), 194.

24. See Virginia Page Fortna, "United Nations Transition Assistance Group in Namibia," in William J. Durch, ed., *The Evolution of UN Peacekeeping: Case Studies and Comparative Analysis* (New York: St. Martin's Press, 1992), 353-75.

25. Security Council Res. 387, 31 March 1976; and Res. 428, 6 May 1978.

26. United Nations, *The Blue Helmets,* 349-50.

27. Security Council Res. 626, 20 December 1988; for details on UNAVEM I, see Virginia Page Fortna, "United Nations Angola Verification Mission I," in William J. Durch, ed., *The Evolution of UN Peacekeeping: Case Studies and Comparative Analysis* (New York: St. Martin's Press, 1992), 376-87.

28. United Nations, *The Blue Helmets,* 340.

29. Anthony J. Pazzanita, "The Conflict Resolution Process in Angola" *Journal of Modern African Studies* 29, no. 1 (March 1991): 83. These prerequisite conditions included a census, registration, electoral code, and infrastructure.

30. Christopher Coker, "'Experiencing' Southern Africa in the Twenty-first Century," *International Affairs* 67, no. 2 (April 1991): 281-82.

31. United Nations Security Council, *Peace Accords for Angola,* S/22609, 17 May 1991.

32. Security Council Res. 696, 30 May 1991.

33. Security Council, S/22609, Attachments I-IV.

34. Ibid., Annex 1.

35. Ibid., Attachment IV. The new Angolan army would be a combination of troops from both the government army (the People's Armed forces for the Liberation of Angola, FAPLA) and the UNITA army, (the Armed Forces for the Liberation of Angola, FALA).

36. Security Council, S/22609, Attachment IV, section 1.

37. Ibid., section III.

38. Ibid.

39. UN Information Note IHA/424, 20 December 1991. On 5 December 1991, the permanent representative of Angola to the United Nations delivered letters to the secretary-general formally requesting United Nations observers to follow the electoral process.

40. Security Council Res. 747, 24 March 1992; Security Council, *Further Report of the Secretary-General on the United Nations Angola Verification Mission: (UNAVEM II),* S/23671, 24 March 1992.

41. United Nations Press Release, SC/5387, 24 March 1992.

42. The secretary-general estimated the total cost of UNAVEM II at about $122 million for the period 1 June 1991 to 31 October 1992. (United Nations Document PS/DPI/5 Rev.1, November 1991.)

43. See Security Council, *Further Report of the Secretary-General on the United Nations Angola Verification Mission (UNAVEM II)*, S/24556, 9 September 1992, which refers to the secretary-general's statement on the budget increase; and United Nations Press Release, SC/5387.

44. UN General Assembly, *Financing of the United Nations Angola Verification Mission: Report of the Secretary-General*, A/47/744, 2 December 1992, 9.

45. UN General Assembly, *Financing of the United Nations Angola Verification Mission: Report of the Secretary-General*, A/48/836, 4 January 1994, 7-8.

46. Ibid. The Transition Assistance Group, which finished in 1990, cost less than was anticipated and so had surplus funds.

47. UN General Assembly, *Financing of the United Nations Angola Verification Mission: Report of the Secretary-General*, A/49/433, 27 September 1994, 7.

48. Security Council, *Further Report of the Secretary-General on the United Nations Angola Verification Mission II (UNAVEM II)*, S/25840, 25 May 1993, 11.

49. Ibid.

50. Security Council, *Further Report of the Secretary-General on the United Nations Angola Verification Mission (UNAVEM II)*, S/24145, 24 June 1992, 67.

51. Security Council, S/23671, 9.

52. United Nations Press Release, SC/5435, 7 July 1992.

53. Security Council, S/24145, 10. The United Nations High Commissioner for Refugees (UNHCR) estimated that its refugee operation would need to serve 270,000 refugees returning from Zaire and Zambia. This operation only began on 11 August 1992 due to severe lack of funds. (Ibid., 8.)

54. Ibid., 3.

55. See United Nations Press Release, UNAVEM II Special Representative, 27 May 1992 (commenting on the deterioration of security); Security Council, S/24145, 4 (stating that there was great concern for the political and security situation); United Nations Press Release, SC/5435; and Security Council, *Further Report of the Secretary-General on the United Nations Angola Verification Mission (UNAVEM II)*, S/24556, 9 September 1992, 3 (stating that the security situation throughout the country had deteriorated significantly). There were reports of intimidation and provocations directed against both government and UNITA supporters. Violent incidents, accompanied by killings, erupted in Malange, as well as in Huambo, Saurimo, and the provinces of Benguela and Bie.

56. Amnesty International, *Angola: An Appeal for Prompt Action to Protect Human Rights* (New York: Amnesty International Publications, May 1992), 4.

57. UN General Assembly, A/48/836, 13-14.

58. Security Council Res. 952, 27 October 1994.

59. In reference to the mission's scarce resources and limited staff allotment, Anstee often remarked that Resolution 747 was truly symbolic of her tasks because she was given the responsibilities of flying a Boeing 747-sized aircraft but only had fuel for a car.

60. Security Council, *Report of the Secretary-General on the United Nations Angola Verification Mission II (UNAVEM II)*, S/23191, 31 October 1991, 5.

61. United Nations Document, PS/DPI/5/Rev.1, November 1991.

62. Ibid. The UNAVEM II police teams were expected to visit police facilities, to examine activities of the police, and to investigate possible violations of political rights.

63. Security Council, *Further Report of the Secretary-General on the United Nations Angola Verification Mission (UNAVEM II)*, S/24858, 25 November 1992.

64. Ibid., 6.

65. Security Council, *Report of the Secretary-General on the United Nations Angola Verification Mission II (UNAVEM II)*, S/24245, 7 July 1992, 10.

66. Security Council, S/24556, 4.

67. United States government official, interview by author. UNITA contended that the government unilaterally and clandestinely transferred about 30,000 of its troops into the "anti-riot" police. (Security Council, S/24556.)

68. Security Council, S/24556, 7.

69. Ibid., 22. The northern area, particularly around M'banza Congo, which had become very volatile after the detonation of an ammunition site, was completely demobilized.

70. Security Council, S/24145, 10.

71. Ibid.

72. Kenneth B. Noble, "Tally in Angola Leads to Runoff," *New York Times*, 18 October 1992, A7.

73. United Nations Press Release, SC/1966, 19 October 1992.

74. Security Council, *Further Report of the Secretary-General on the United Nations Angola Verification Mission (UNAVEM II)*, S/26434, 13 September 1993, 5.

75. See United Nations Press Release, SC/5567, 12 March 1993 (noting that a humanitarian tragedy of grave proportion is developing in Angola); Paul Taylor, "Angola's Dual Reign of Terror: Government, Rebels both Committing Atrocities on Civilians," *Washington Post*, 23 March 1993, A1.

76. Amnesty International, *Angola: Assault on the Right to Life* (New York: Amnesty International Publications, August 1993), 13.

77. Press Briefing By Special Representative for Angola, Abidjan, Ivory Coast, 27 May 1993 (mimeograph).

78. Ibid., 4.

79. Security Council Res. 864, 15 September 1993.

80. John Darnton, "Civil War of Nearly Two Decades Exhausts Resource-Rich Angola," *New York Times*, 9 May 1994, A1, A6. Both sides spent huge sums on arms. UNITA bought black market weapons paid for by diamonds mined in the Lunda Norte, mining thought to bring in about $1 million a week. In addition, the Angolan government hired scores of South African mercenaries to help fight the offensives against UNITA.

81. Security Council, *Lusaka Protocol,* S/1994/1441, Annex, 22 December 1994.

82. Ibid., Annex 1.

83. Ibid., Annex 3.

84. See Security Council, *Report of the Secretary-General on the United Nations Angola Verification Mission (UNAVEM II),* S/1995/97, 1 February 1995, 2. The secretary-general took note of the SRSG's intensive negotiations not just with the president of Angola and the president of UNITA, but also with Presidents Mobutu Sese Seko of Zaire, Robert Mugabe of Zimbabwe, Frederick Chiluba of Zambia, and Sam Nujoma of Namibia.

85. Security Council, S/1994/1441, 3. The parties who signed, and thus are bound by the Lusaka Protocol are not only Jose Eduardo dos Santos and Jonas Malheiro Savimbi, but also Alioune Blondin Beye, on behalf of the secretary-general. Also, in Annex 8, both the government of Angola and UNITA reaffirmed their wish that the United Nations "play an enlarged and reinforced role." (Ibid., 47.)

86. Security Council, S/1994/1441, 47. The observers to the Joint Commission will be representatives from the United States, Portugal, and the Russian Federation.

87. Security Council, S/24145, 10.

88. United Nations Press Release, SC/5435.

89. Thomas M. Franck, "The Emerging Right To Democratic Governance," *American Journal of International Law* 86, no. 1 (January 1992): 46, 72. Verifying the electoral process requires more than merely recording the process, and should not stop short of correcting the defects.

90. Security Council, S/22609, Attachment I.

91. Security Council, S/24145, 9.

92. UN General Assembly, *An Agenda for Peace,* A/47/277, 17 June 1992, 22. The secretary-general affirmed that democracy requires respect for human rights and fundamental freedoms. See also, William J. Durch, "United Nations Forces and Regional Conflicts," in Patrick M. Cronin, ed., *From Globalism to Regionalism: New Prospects on US Foreign and Defense Policies* (Washington, D.C.: National Defense University Press, 1993), 181, 194.

93. Although the peace accords called for the government to invite UNITA to participate in the national police, only 39 percent of the 183 UNITA personnel offered for training were included in the first joint training effort. (Security Council, S/24556.)

94. Security Council Res. 976, 8 February 1995.

95. Ibid., 12. Angola is reported to have 10 million unexploded land mines scattered about its territory.

96. Security Council, *Further Report of the Secretary-General on the United Nations Angola Verification Mission (UNAVEM II),* S/1995/97/Add.1, 6 February 1995.

97. In comparison to UNAVEM II, other missions which have been considered successful, such as those in Cambodia and Mozambique, were well staffed and well financed. For example, the United Nations Transitional Authority in Cambodia (UNTAC) cost about $2.5 billion, deploying about 22,000 personnel. Also, for Angola's "poor cousin," Mozambique, the United Nations spent $600,000 and deployed about 6,000

people. See Inge Tvedten, "The Angolan Debacle," *Journal of Democracy* 4, no. 2 (April 1993): 114. In addition, the World Bank is pumping $1 billion a year into Mozambique.

98. Security Council, S/1995/97/Add.1.

99. Security Council, S/1995/97, 14.

100. On the informational requirements of peacekeeping, see William J. Durch and Barry M. Blechman, *Keeping the Peace: The United Nations in the Emerging World Order,* Report No. 2 (Washington, D.C.: The Henry L. Stimson Center, March 1992), 78-86.

101. Amnesty International, "Appeal to Protect Human Rights," Newsletter, September 1992.

102. Ibid., 5.

103. Security Council, S/1995/97, 6, 16.

104. In August 1996, the UN reported that 59,000 of 62,000 UNITA fighters had been disarmed, and the government agreed to spend some $65 million to finally demobilize the soldiers of both sides. *Reuters* newswire cited in *New York Times,* 16 August, 1996, A15.

FIVE

RIDING THE TIGER: THE UNITED NATIONS AND CAMBODIA'S STRUGGLE FOR PEACE

JAMES A. SCHEAR[1]

The United Nations Transitional Authority in Cambodia (UNTAC) was established to implement the 1991 Paris Accords, which were designed to end Cambodia's long-running conflict and to restore legitimate government with international assistance. UNTAC was a major departure in UN peacekeeping. While the concept of transitional political assistance was itself not new, nothing on the scale and complexity of UNTAC had ever been attempted before. The operation began on 15 March 1992 and ended in September 1993 amidst widespread praise and applause for a job well done.

Yet, during most of its existence, UNTAC was not the object of much praise. Despite the powers entrusted to it, the operation was far less assertive than many Cambodians (and some outside observers) thought it would be. Many of UNTAC's weaknesses were quickly apparent, while its strengths went largely unappreciated until the very end of its tour. More fundamentally, the Paris Accords began to unravel almost as soon as the operation deployed, embroiling UNTAC in a series of controversies with one local party or another. So intense was the torrent of complaints at times that UNTAC could fairly claim to have united the warring Khmer factions in opposition to itself.

Why, then, is UNTAC's experience trumpeted by so many as a success?[2] Specifically, what did the operation do, or not do, that enabled it to circumvent the obstacles created by the fraying of the Paris Accords in sufficient measure to yield more operational successes than failures? To answer these questions, this chapter explores the diplomatic build-up to UNTAC's deployment, its expansive mandate, its concept of operations, and the major challenges it encountered in carrying out its assigned tasks. It concludes with an assessment of UNTAC's overall impact and its implications, both positive and negative, for future efforts at peace implementation.

ORIGINS

Few countries during the twentieth century have endured more trauma than Cambodia. In the 1960s, the country's fragile neutrality was compromised by Vietnamese communist guerrillas, whose presence triggered the secret American bombing campaign of 1969. A parade of horrors followed: the overthrow of Cambodia's head of state, Prince Norodom Sihanouk, and the US-led intervention against Vietnamese sanctuaries (1970); a bloody struggle for power between a weak pro-Western government and the Maoist Khmer Rouge (1970-75); the Khmer Rouge's victory and rein of terror (1975-78); Vietnam's invasion of Cambodia (1979); and a seemingly interminable civil war that pitted a Vietnamese-installed regime in Phnom Penh against a coalition that included the ousted Khmer Rouge and two smaller non-communist opposition groups (1979-91). Overall, well over a million Cambodians, or roughly one-seventh of the population, may have perished during these years, while hundreds of thousands more fled the country to neighboring Thailand and beyond.[3]

The Vietnamese invasion of December 1978, presaged by rising tensions with the Pol Pot regime and Khmer Rouge border incursions into Vietnam, had triggered major shock waves throughout Asia.[4] The Vietnamese army did not stop at the eastern bank of the Mekong River but overran most of the country, pushing the Khmer Rouge into remote mountainous areas of Cambodia's frontier with Thailand. With Soviet backing, the Vietnamese installed a quisling government in Phnom Penh. The People's Republic of Kampuchea (PRK), consisting mainly of Khmer Rouge defectors, was led by Heng Samrin and, after 1985, by Prime Minister Hun Sen.

Meanwhile, the Khmer Rouge, defeated in battle, benefited politically from the international outrage triggered by Vietnam's invasion. They maintained the support of the Chinese and close links with the Thais, who felt particularly threatened by the Vietnamese. Although their full record of atrocities was finally coming to light, they also retained their seat at the United Nations, as very few countries outside the Soviet bloc were willing to recognize the PRK. In 1982, the Khmer Rouge, also known as the Party of Democratic Kampuchea (PDK), entered into an alliance with two, smaller opposition groups, creating the exile Coalition Government of Democratic Kampuchea, under the leadership of the former head of state, Prince Sihanouk. The coalition, which assumed Cambodia's UN seat, included the Front Uni National pour une Cambodge Indépendent, Neutre, Pacifique et Coopératif (FUNCINPEC), a royalist party led by Sihanouk and, subsequently, by his son Prince Ranariddh. It also included the Khmer People's National Liberation Front (KPNLF), a republican non-communist group led by Son Sann, a former prime minister. These two groups brought with them

Fig. 5.1
MAP OF CAMBODIA

Base 801646 (B00998) 2-91

SOURCE: US Government

the backing, in varying degrees, of major Western countries, including the United States, as well as the Association of Southeast Asian Nations (ASEAN).[5]

In the polarized atmosphere of the 1980s, international peacemaking efforts were stalemated. At the urging of the ASEAN states, the UN General Assembly convened the International Conference on Kampuchea in July 1981 but the event produced no real momentum, being seen as anti-Vietnamese and boycotted by Soviet-bloc states. Meanwhile, the armed struggle inside Cambodia settled down after

1985 into a pattern of sporadic, often desultory clashes during the dry season. The PRK remained ostracized internationally; the country it ruled was isolated, destitute, and starved of development funding.

By 1987, however, two developments began to break the diplomatic logjam. First, Indonesia undertook to promote contacts among the various Khmer factions, drawing in ASEAN and the Indochina states. Prince Sihanouk and Hun Sen began to meet on a regular basis. Second, Sino-Soviet rapprochement, and improving East-West relations more generally, increased both the flexibility of the patrons and the pressure on the parties to reach a settlement.

As part of a campaign to shed its communist trappings and open up toward the West, the PRK changed its name in 1989 to the State of Cambodia (SOC). Domestically, however, it continued to rule harshly, tolerating little dissent. The SOC's hand was weakened by Vietnam's declaration in April 1989 that, in light of shrinking Soviet support, it would be withdrawing its armies from Cambodia.[6] In the wake of Hanoi's announcement (and its actual withdrawal of troops by September 1989), Hun Sen sought improved relations with the Thais and other regional neighbors.[7] These turns of events prompted the other factions to press forward with negotiations, concerned that the Vietnamese withdrawal would result in greater international acceptance of the Hun Sen regime and reduced prospects for themselves.

At the initiative of France, the Paris Conference on Cambodia was held in August 1989, involving Indonesia (as cochair), the five permanent members of the Security Council (or "Perm Five"), and a range of other interested parties.[8] The central issues for negotiation were how to end the fighting among Cambodia's warring factions, in the wake of Vietnam's expected departure, and how to establish an internationally recognized government in Phnom Penh. The conference failed to achieve a breakthrough but did begin to map out some of the basic elements of a comprehensive settlement: a cease-fire; the verified withdrawal and nonreturn of any foreign forces; the cessation of outside military assistance; the creation of a transitional administration; the holding of internationally supervised elections leading to the formation of a new government; the voluntary repatriation of refugees and displaced persons; guarantees of Cambodia's neutrality, sovereignty, and territorial integrity; and international support for Cambodia's rehabilitation and reconstruction.[9] All of these elements, with further refinements, became part of the final settlement.[10]

The thorniest question in subsequent talks involved power-sharing during the political transition to a new Cambodian government. The idea of an "interim authority" including the four factions under Prince Sihanouk's leadership was generally agreed but its composition, powers, and relationship to the existing SOC administration were disputed. The three opposition factions were adamant that the SOC should cede its authority to a coalition government; just as adamantly, the SOC insisted that such a body be essentially advisory in nature.[11]

With the conference thus stymied, all eyes turned to the United Nations. The idea of drawing the organization into the Cambodian transition process, oddly enough, came from the halls of the US Congress, specifically from Representative Stephen

Solarz, a longtime Asia specialist and key member of the House Foreign Affairs Committee. Solarz persuaded Gareth Evans, Australia's foreign minister, as to the merits of the idea, and Evans campaigned energetically for the concept starting in late 1989.[12] During the summer of 1990, the approach gained momentum and the Perm Five began to step up pressure for a settlement. In early September, the Cambodian factions took a major step forward, agreeing to the formation of a quadripartite body—the Supreme National Council (SNC)—that would embody Cambodian sovereignty and represent the country during the transition. The SNC, it was agreed, would have twelve members, six from the SOC and two apiece from the other three factions, with Sihanouk as chairman and its thirteenth member. The SNC, in turn, would delegate to the United Nations "all powers necessary" to ensure the proper implementation of the settlement.[13]

It was a portentous moment for the United Nations. Within a short space of time, the organization had moved from being one player among many in the diplomatic process to being the key implementing agent in a complex peace settlement. The arrangement was clearly a gamble: delegating contentious jobs to the United Nations helped pave the way for agreement, but how the organization would wield the authority entrusted to it, and how durable the parties' consent to the arrangement would be, remained unclear. Few people had any illusions about the Paris Accords. They were fragile instruments, a product of intense pressure applied upon the parties by external powers operating in a climate of cooperation that did not yet exist inside Cambodia.[14]

POLITICAL SUPPORT

For all of the Khmer factions, the Paris Accords involved difficult tradeoffs, a balancing of the uncertainties involved in a transition process against the risks and costs of torpedoing an internationally supported peacemaking enterprise. For all of the local parties' external patrons, however, bringing this outdated relic of a Cold War conflict to an end was a shared paramount goal.

Local Parties

Arguably, the two non-communist groups, FUNCINPEC and KPNLF, stood to gain the most from the settlement itself. All of the basic elements of the deal—ending the civil war, opening up the country economically, leveling the playing field politically, and implementing widespread disarmament—would tend to cut very heavily in their favor and against the two larger, more heavily armed, authoritarian factions. Conversely, failure to implement the deal would tend to favor the SOC, as Cambodia's de facto authority, which could buy international acceptance over time with outwardly reformist policies. Finally, FUNCINPEC enjoyed strong support among Cambodia's diaspora communities in Europe and North America and was extremely eager to cash in on the popularity of its royalist pedigree inside the country.

For FUNCINPEC and KPNLF, the major potential downsides to the settlement were the sheer uncertainties of trying to reestablish a political presence in SOC-controlled areas of the country. They would be heavily reliant upon the international presence to provide a margin of safety as the country girded itself for multiparty elections.

The SOC, led by Hun Sen, was also heavily vested in the negotiating process but for different reasons. First and foremost, as noted earlier, its external support was drying up. Faced with the reality of Vietnam's pullout, the SOC attempted to make a virtue of necessity by using the Paris negotiations to chip away at its international isolation. But it was putting a good deal at risk in agreeing to the peace settlement. Fearful of its poor image in the countryside (and conversely, Sihanouk's popularity) the SOC had staunchly opposed the idea of multiparty elections. There were, in addition, disagreements between putative moderates and hardliners within the SOC hierarchy that were being worsened by the negotiation process.[15] And finally, the idea of accepting a role for the Khmer Rouge in the political process was a loathsome proposition for the SOC.

Khmer Rouge calculations about the Paris settlement were cloaked in mystery. Their leadership for the most part had not changed since their bloody rule during 1975-78.[16] External support for the Khmer Rouge, though of decreasing importance to their survival (given their commercial trade in timber and gems), was also drying up. The Chinese and the Thais were encouraging them to cooperate. Inclusion of the faction as a recognized player in the negotiating process had been a sine qua non for the Chinese and for Prince Sihanouk, but it gave the Khmer Rouge an the aura of legitimacy that galled many critics.[17] Whether the Khmer Rouge actually placed any stock in such legitimacy is unknown.

On the debit side, the basic terms of trade contained in the Paris Accords—that is, political "demobilization" of SOC in return for the nationwide cantonment and disarmament of all armed elements—was an inherently risky deal for the Khmer Rouge. As an insurgent force, they would, if they complied, be giving up their only real trump card in return for the uncertain prospect of UN supervision of SOC's security apparatus. Nor were they gaining any blanket amnesty for their record of previous atrocities.[18] Finally, the Khmer Rouge leadership must surely have been aware of the claims of Western governments involved in the negotiations that the Paris Accords would tend to marginalize the Khmer Rouge over time by shifting the struggle from the battlefield to the ballot box and by opening up the country for development assistance.

Given these considerations, it is hard to see what the Paris Accords really offered to the Khmer Rouge. Arguably, in fact, the agreement confronted them with a serious dilemma: whether to participate in the settlement at the risk of losing control over their soldiers and cadre, or reject the peace process and run the serious risk of seeing the emergence of an internationally recognized government in Phnom Penh anyhow. Possibly the most the Khmer Rouge could hope for was either that the Hun Sen regime itself would unravel as the accords were being implemented, or that political chaos in postelections Cambodia would give the Khmer Rouge new opportunities to exploit.

Outside Parties

From the outside world's vantage point, the Cambodian settlement was seen almost universally as a means to break down the Cold War-era barriers between communist Indochina and the rest of Southeast Asia. No outside party had any interest in seeing the conflict continue. The diplomatic challenge was to steer the process in a fashion that would not disadvantage current or erstwhile clients of major powers inside the country.

Vietnam was eager to pursue better relations with the non-communist world, to shore up its ailing economy and mitigate internal dislocations associated with the drying up of Soviet aid. The stalemated civil war in Cambodia and Vietnam's military presence there stood in the way of these priorities. Once Hanoi took the decisive step of withdrawing its occupation forces from Cambodia in 1989, and once its relations with the United States and other countries began to improve, the Paris Accords became a vital hedge against any backsliding.

China's overarching goal was to end Vietnamese hegemony over Indochina and to restore Prince Sihanouk, a longtime friend and ally. Vietnam's military withdrawal was an important step toward that goal, and the Paris Accords would make that disengagement irreversible. Once it was clear that Beijing's clients, the Khmer Rouge, would be accepted as participants in the negotiating process, China agreed to stop supplying its Khmer comrades with weapons.[19]

The ASEAN states saw the Paris Accords in much the same light and were eager to remove Cambodia as an impediment to better relations with Indochina. But Thailand's official support for the accords was also clouded by its military's longstanding coziness with anti-Phnom Penh insurgencies along its remote common border with Cambodia. At the same time, other regional powers such as Japan and Australia were looking to establish better relations with the Hun Sen regime. They saw the accords as a way to remove the Vietnamese taint from Cambodia while holding back the Khmer Rouge.

Within the United States, the Paris Accords were controversial, in large part because the Khmer Rouge were included. But the Bush administration saw the accords as a way to shift the emphasis in American policy from support of the opposition Cambodian coalition (of which the Khmer Rouge were, uncomfortably, members) to support for a political transition that, if done properly, could work to the benefit of those parties most committed to democratic reform. The Paris Accords could end Cambodia's isolation. Hun Sen's lobbying for the peace settlement in Washington during the spring of 1992 did much to negate direct opposition to the accords. At the same time, the United States took steps to confine its role in implementation mainly to logistical and financial support (via its UN-assessed share of 31 percent, as well as voluntary contributions to Cambodia's rehabilitation program). Given Americans' memories of previous military ground involvement in Indochina, the Bush administration did not want to see an American ground presence in Cambodia.[20]

Among the other permanent members of the Security Council (France, Great Britain, and Russia), support for the Paris Accords was equally strong, although only France, by dint of its colonial heritage, took an active role in both the negotiations and the implementation phase.

MANDATE

The Security Council expressed support for the Paris Accords in Resolution 718 (1991), and it authorized the establishment of UNTAC in Resolution 745 (1992) for a period not to exceed 18 months.[21] Shortly before the actual signing of the accords, on 23 October 1991, the Council authorized the establishment of the United Nations Advance Mission in Cambodia (UNAMIC), initially to monitor the cease-fire and then to initiate mine-clearance training and the repair of roads and bridges to prepare the way for UNTAC's arrival.[22]

Under the accords, the signatories agreed to confer upon UNTAC "all powers necessary to ensure implementation" of the comprehensive settlement.[23] This expansive delegation of authority was coupled with a decision process for resolving any disputes over implementation that might arise between UNTAC and the local parties; but that process was heavily weighted in UNTAC's favor.[24] As for specifically mandated tasks, the accords spelled them out in an annex to the agreement.

Military Elements

UNTAC was tasked to "supervise, monitor, and verify" the cease-fire, the withdrawal and nonreturn of foreign forces, the cessation of outside military assistance to the Cambodian factions, the regroupment, cantonment, and disarmament of regular forces of the four factions, the demobilization of at least 70 percent of these armies, and the disarmament of militia forces. It was also given the job of locating and confiscating caches of weapons and military supplies; assisting with clearing mines and undertaking mine awareness programs; and assisting, as necessary, the International Committee of the Red Cross (ICRC) in the release of all prisoners of war and civilian internees.

Civilian Elements

In this area, UNTAC's assignments were to supervise or control existing civil administrations of the four Cambodian factions; to organize and conduct nationwide multiparty elections for a new constituent assembly; to coordinate the repatriation of refugees and displaced persons; to develop and implement a human rights education program and to perform general human rights oversight; to investigate specific human rights complaints and, where appropriate, to take corrective action; and to coordinate the initial phases of an international program for Cambodia's rehabilitation and reconstruction.

Adjustments

Once UNTAC was up and running, the Council approved several adjustments in UNTAC's operations without substantially altering or enlarging its basic mandate.[25] The initial change involved a Council decision to apply economic pressure, or "soft sanctions," on the Khmer Rouge, essentially to penalize them for boycotting the peace process. In July 1992, the Council asked the secretary-general to ensure that international rehabilitation assistance would benefit only those parties cooperating with UNTAC.[26] As the boycott continued, the Council took further steps. In November 1992, it called upon parties to the accords to prevent the supply of petroleum products to Khmer Rouge areas; voiced support for an SNC-sponsored moratorium, promulgated by Sihanouk, on the export of round logs, asking UNTAC to take "appropriate steps to secure the implementation" of the SNC's action; and called for effective measures by UNTAC "to prevent the recurrence or escalation of fighting in Cambodia, as well as incidents of banditry and arms smuggling." Finally, in the same resolution, the Council approved the redeployment of UNTAC's military component in support of electoral preparations and accepted the secretary-general's proposal that UNTAC's peacekeeping battalions be kept at full strength throughout the operation, since UN troop reductions during the latter stages of the mission had originally been predicated on the cantonment, disarmament, and demobilization of 70 percent of local forces, which was not completed as planned.[27]

A subsequent moratorium on the extraction and export of minerals and gemstones was endorsed by the Council in March 1993. At the same time, the Council endorsed UNTAC's steps to address the petroleum import and timber export issues (mainly through additional checkpoints and patrolling).[28]

In spite of these adjustments, and the broad scope of UNTAC's functions, it is worth stressing that never *at any time* did the Council confer upon UNTAC compulsory authority provided for in Chapter VII of the UN Charter. This was somewhat at odds with the tenor of the Paris Accords, under which the Cambodian parties had entrusted UNTAC with powers to do such things as fire or reassign obstructive bureaucrats, seize arms caches, or take corrective action in the face of human rights abuse. But no enforcement provisions had been built into the Paris Accords and it is doubtful that the parties would have agreed to the inclusion of such provisions. Nor was there any real support in the Security Council for mounting or sustaining UNTAC on anything but a consensual basis. The UN's leadership was keenly aware of the low tolerance for casualties among UNTAC's troop contributors.[29] For these and other reasons, even relatively small enlargements of UNTAC's mandated tasks in areas such as the implementation of economic sanctions were limited to the jobs of monitoring and reporting noncompliant behavior, not of thwarting such activity.

PLANNING AND IMPLEMENTATION

The implementation plan developed by the secretary-general and presented to the Security Council on 19 February 1992 echoed the ambitiousness of the Paris

Accords.[30] (For summaries of the military and civilian aspects of the plan, see tables 5.1 and 5.2.) Actual implementation of some elements, especially on the military side, deviated considerably from the initial plans.

Design for the Security Elements

The security mission was to take precedence at the outset. Absorbing UNAMIC into its ranks by mid-March, UNTAC would continue to mark and clear land mines from high priority areas, in advance of the initial repatriation of refugees. UNTAC would also continue to provide good offices to the parties in the maintenance of the cease-fire, while preparing the ground for a more ambitious second phase of the operation, when it would assume responsibility for verifying the cease-fire. By June, at the outset of this second phase, the arduous job of regrouping, cantoning, and disarming factional armies would begin, with an estimated timeline of four months to completion. UNTAC's military component, consisting of 12 infantry battalions, 5 engineering battalions, and support units for signals, air, logistics, and medical services, would be deployed in a thin nationwide pattern, concentrating units in areas where the four factions were expected to regroup and canton their soldiers.

UNTAC's mix of infantry and engineering battalions drew heavily from Asia and the Pacific. Infantry battalions from Malaysia, Bangladesh, Pakistan, and Indonesia were earmarked for Cambodia's central and northwestern provinces; Uruguayan and Indian units would deploy into the remote northeast; a Dutch battalion was slated to deploy into western Battambang province, a Khmer Rouge stronghold; and Cambodia's populous and fertile southeastern regions, including greater Phnom Penh, would receive infantry battalions from France, Bulgaria, Tunisia, Ghana, and Indonesia. Engineering units would be provided by Thailand, France, Japan, Poland, and (interestingly) the People's Republic of China.

Cantonment of Local Forces

Based on its own field surveys and data provided by the various parties, the UN estimated that UNTAC would have to supervise the encampment, or cantonment, of some 200,000 regular troops dispersed at over 650 locations, while at the same time taking custody of over 300,000 weapons of all types along with some 80 million rounds of ammunition. UNTAC would also be receiving weapons from approximately 250,000 militia troops, who were to disarm (though not canton) under the agreement. During the period of cantonment and up to three months after it, a phased 70 percent demobilization of soldiers would be implemented, with a corresponding percentage of weapons removed from cantonments to centralized storage areas.[31]

As cantonment proceeded, UNTAC's military component would undertake a range of monitoring and control activities. The cessation of outside military assistance and the withdrawal of foreign forces would be monitored primarily by UN military observers (UNMOs) from border checkpoints and air- and waterborne patrols. Engineering units would be disposing of unexploded ordnance and arms caches, repairing roads and bridges, and installing water purification, all essentially in support of international field operations.

Rules of Engagement (ROE)

UNTAC's rules governing the use of force were drawn from standard UN peacekeeping practices. Broadly, UNTAC military personnel were authorized to use force in self-defense or in resisting forceful attempts to prevent UNTAC from accomplishing its mission. The rules distinguished between unarmed and armed force, with the latter category covering military as well as "nonmilitary" weapons (for example, batons, tear gas, rifle butts). Armed force was authorized for a wide range of cases falling within self-defense (for example, defense of self, of other UN personnel in mortal danger, of UN posts, positions, or vehicles). Within the larger "defense of the mission" category, armed force could be used to resist attempts to compel UNTAC personnel to withdraw from positions they had been ordered to occupy as well as attempts to prevent UN personnel from carrying out other orders.

UNTAC's ROE also identified "crimes against humanity" as a special category of activity warranting the use of all available means, including armed force. It defined such crimes as executions, or attacks on refugee columns, cantonment areas, or other soldiers—including prisoners of war (POWs) under UNTAC's care—who had laid down their weapons.

The use of force by UNTAC was to be minimal and proportionate to threats; applied in a controlled and discriminate fashion; and automatic fire was to be used only as a last resort. If possible, negotiation or persuasion was to precede any use of force; warning procedures, including verbal warnings or shots, were to be attempted first unless there was an immediate threat to UNTAC personnel or UNTAC casualties had been sustained; and fire was to cease once its aim had been achieved.

The ROE also established general guidelines for delegating authority to use various types of weapons, while acknowledging the need for commanders on the spot to retain flexibility in responding to various circumstances. Under these guidelines, the authority to order the use of heavy support weapons (for example, heavy machine guns and 120mm mortars) lay with the force commander or his designate. Sector commanders could authorize use of lighter weapons and mortars, and company commanders or warrant officers could authorize the use of personal weapons. The ROE nonetheless exhorted subordinate commands to inform higher-level headquarters before resorting to the use of armed force.[32]

Design for the Civilian Elements

With momentum building on the peacekeeping side, civil affairs activities would unfold on several fronts. (These are summarized in table 5.2.) UNTAC's repatriation component, staffed by officers of the United Nations High Commissioner for Refugees (UNHCR), would begin bringing back roughly 370,000 refugees from the Thai border

Table 5.1

THE PARIS ACCORDS:
MAJOR MILITARY PROVISIONS AND UNTAC TASKS

Phase One (23 October 1991-12 June 1992)[a]	
PARTIES AGREED TO	UNTAC TASKS
• Observe a cease-fire; disengage forces; and refrain from all hostilities and actions to extend control over territory.	• Provide good offices to assist in the observance of the cease-fire and related measures.
• Provide to the UN data on: — total strength, organization, number, and location of force deployments; — comprehensive lists of arms, ammunition, and equipment; — mine fields, including types of mines and booby traps; and — strength, organization, and location of police forces, including arms and equipment.	• Finalize plans for regroupment and cantonment of local forces, and for the storage of their arms and equipment, not later than four weeks prior to Phase Two. • Open regroupment sites one week prior to Phase Two. • Ensure the marking of known minefields. • Assist in the clearing of mines from repatriation centers and resettlement areas. • Establish Mixed Military Working Group (MMWG) to resolve problems arising in implementation.
• Provide data to UNTAC on foreign forces, their equipment and withdrawal plans (pending or already implemented), no later than two weeks prior to Phase Two.	• Investigate reports of foreign forces and deploy personnel with such forces until they withdraw. • Establish checkpoints at border crossings, withdrawal routes, and airfields to verify the withdrawal and nonreturn of foreign forces.
• Refrain from obtaining or seeking outside military assistance. • Laos, Thailand, and Vietnam to prevent their territories from being used for military resupply of the Cambodian parties.	

camps in March 1992 at a rate of up to 10,000 per week, providing resettlement assistance such as shelter, household kits, and food rations for an average period of one year. Paralleling this effort, a human rights component would launch training programs in human rights education and set up a nationwide network for reporting and investigations of human right violations; it would also review existing domestic law and propose initiatives for adoption by the SNC in order to provide a legal framework for human rights protection as the country prepared itself for transition to a multiparty system.

Meanwhile, UNTAC's civil administration component would begin deployment of its staff into bureaucracies in Phnom Penh and the 21 provinces, to exercise "direct control" over existing administrative bodies and agencies in the fields of foreign affairs, national defense, public security, finance, and public information, and to "supervise or control" a broader range of public sector activities. As part of this effort, on the public security side, UNTAC's civilian police component would be deploying roughly 3,600 unarmed officers nationwide to ensure the impartial administration of law and order by local police and to serve as monitors for human rights reporting.

Table 5.1

CONTINUED

Phase Two (13 June 1992-End of Operation)[a]	
PARTIES AGREED TO	**UNTAC TASKS**
• Continue to observe the cease-fire and related obligations on the withdrawal and nonreturn of foreign forces and the cessation of outside military assistance.	• "Supervise, monitor, and verify" the cease-fire and related measures.
• Regroup their forces within two weeks after start of Phase Two; proceed to cantonment sites. • In addition: -- hand over arms, ammunition, and equipment to UNTAC upon entry into sites; -- undertake a phase and balanced demobilization of at least 70 percent of soldiers by the end of voter registration (date to be determined by UN's special representative); -- demobilize remaining forces before or shortly after election, and incorporate them into a new national army; -- militia-held weapons to be turned in at designated sites.	• Escort soldiers from regroupment to cantonment sites, completing process within four weeks. • In addition: -- take custody of arms, ammunition, and equipment for on-site storage, checking arms, etc., against lists provided by parties; -- reduce numbers of arms, etc., in parallel with 70 percent demobilization, moving weapons to central storage depot(s); -- ensure orderly transfer of arms, etc., to the new government.
• Laos, Thailand, and Vietnam to: -- confirm in writing, no later than four weeks after start of Phase Two, that no forces or equipment of Cambodian parties are present on their territories; and -- receive UNTAC liaison officers to investigate reports of military resupply.	• Establish checkpoints, water-borne patrols and mobile teams to monitor non-resupply obligations; • Investigate and destroy caches of weapons and military supplies.
	• Undertake investigations of alleged violations, accompanied by personnel provided by parties

[a] Precise dates for the completion of Phase One and beginning of Phase Two were announced by the Force Commander of UNTAC on 9 May 1992.

SOURCES: *Agreements on a Comprehensive Political Settlement of the Cambodia Conflict,* (New York: UN Department of Public Information, 1992); Security Council, S/23613, 19 February 1992.

Contrary to popular mythology, UNTAC's civil administrative supervision and control mechanisms were never designed as a way to "run" Cambodia. UNTAC administrators were to have unrestricted access to administrative operations and information and authority to investigate noncompliance with the Paris Accords, to issue binding directives, and to require the removal or reassignment of personnel.[33] But their fundamental objective was narrowly crafted: to "ensure a neutral political environment conducive to free and fair general elections,"[34] by thwarting any overt political bias traceable to bureaucratic behavior—actions such as the issuing of passports to some but not others, selling off public assets to the benefit of certain constituencies, fomenting strife in opposition political parties, intimidating or harassing voters, authorizing public works projects in some villages but not others, or using public finance to underwrite political activities.[35]

Table 5.2

UNTAC'S CIVIL MANDATE

TASKS	PERFORMED BY[a]
HUMAN RIGHTS	
• Develop and implement human rights education program.	• Human Rights Component: 88 staff members at headquarters and in the province.
• Exercise human rights oversight of existing public administration (including penal institutions).	• Civil Police Component (CIVPOL): 3,600 CIVPOL to supervise local law enforcement and assist in HR investigations.
• Investigate reports of human rights abuse and, where appropriate, take corrective action.	
ELECTIONS	
• Organize and conduct elections for a constituent assembly.	• Electoral Component: 4,200 staff members at the headquarters, provincial, and district levels (580 international staff and 3,600+ local staff), plus up to 55,000 temporary local staff for registration and polling duties and 1,000 international polling station observers.
• Subordinate tasks include: drafting electoral law; civic education; recruitment and training of local field staff; registration of parties and voters; supervision of the polling and the vote count.	
CIVIL ADMINISTRATION	
• Control administrative agencies, bodies or offices in five fields (Defense, Foreign Affairs, Finance, Public Security, and Information), in order to ensure a "neutral political environment" conducive to free and fair elections.	• Civil Administration component: 540 staff members at headquarters and in the provinces.
	• CIVPOL (for public security supervision and contol).
• Supervise or control other agencies that could directly influence the outcome of elections.	• Office of the Economic Adviser (for financial supervision and control).
• Investigate allegations of administrative actions inconsistent with the Paris Accords and, when necessary, take appropriate corrective steps.	• Information/Education Division (for information-related supervision and control).
• Supervise civil police work, to ensure the impartial administration of law and order.	

To be sure, even this limited scope of authority was unprecedented. To wield it effectively, UNTAC would need the acquiescence of the parties. Indeed, the Paris Accords, as an expression of the parties' consent to the operation, presumed the active cooperation of all the factions with UNTAC's administration, and thus UNTAC would count upon that cooperation in rooting out bureaucratic malfeasance. Again, there was no provision in the accords for enforcing judgments against uncooperative parties, and very likely there would have been no accords at all had such a formulation been proposed.

The most significant and labor-intensive civilian activity was the organization of the election itself. UNTAC's electoral component would start from scratch, drafting an electoral law and presenting it for consultation by the SNC. It would also begin deployment of over 450 UN volunteers throughout Cambodia's 179 districts to conduct civic education and train locally recruited staff.[36] In April, it would initiate the provisional registration of political parties and party agents as a prelude to the commencement of voter registration, which was scheduled to take place in October, after the completion of the cantonment process. Voter registration was expected to

Table 5.2
CONTINUED

TASKS	PERFORMED BY
REPATRIATION	
• Facilitate the voluntary return of refugees and displaced persons to destinations of their own choosing within Cambodia, over a nine month period. • Provide food assistance for a 12-month period, and resettlement/reintegration packages of various kinds.	• UNHCR, operating as UNTAC's Repatriation Component.
REHABILITATION	
• Coordinate international rehabilitation assistance to Cambodia, focusing on food security, health, housing, training, education, transportation, and the restoration of the country's existing infrastructure and public utilities.	• Rehabilitation Component: 16 staff members. • Office of the Economics Adviser: 25 staff members.[b]
INFORMATION/EDUCATION	
• Organize and conduct information programs to acquaint Cambodians with the Paris Accords and with UNTAC, its purposes, activities, and goals.	• Information/Education Division: 160 staff members.

[a] Staffing figures are approximations and include both professional and general service staff categories (for international as well as local staff).

[b] UNTAC's Economic Adviser absorbed the rehabilitation mission during the operation. Staffing breakdown for rehabilitation versus other work is not available.

SOURCES: Security Council, *Report of the Secretary-General on Cambodia*, S/23613, 19 February 1992; General Assembly, A/47/133/Add.1, 27 July 1993, Annex V.

take three months. Once that hurdle was passed, UNTAC would begin to lay the groundwork for the polling phase, planning the location of polling stations, procuring ballot papers and other materials, and hiring and training over 50,000 local polling staff. By May 1993, after a six-week electoral campaign and cooling off period, UNTAC would be ready to conduct nationwide elections, with the assistance of an additional 1,000 international polling observers.

On the economic and developmental fronts, UNTAC's rehabilitation component would coordinate the early phases of internationally funded programs to restore basic infrastructure (for example, transport, telecommunications, and roads). In June, acting upon a consolidated appeal by the secretary-general, an international donors conference in Tokyo raised US $880 million for near-term rehabilitation and long-term needs.[37]

Beyond sketching out UNTAC's seven major components, the secretary-general's Implementation Plan also spelled out the need for a large-scale information/education program designed to familiarize Cambodians with the Paris Accords, to explain UNTAC's goals and activities, and to aid civic education efforts in human rights, the elections process, refugee repatriation, and mine awareness. The locus for these activities was UNTAC's Information and Education Division, which also picked up responsibility for supervising Cambodia's information activities and for evaluating

Fig. 5.2

UNITED NATIONS TRANSITIONAL AUTHORITY IN CAMBODIA (UNTAC) ORGANIZATIONAL CHART

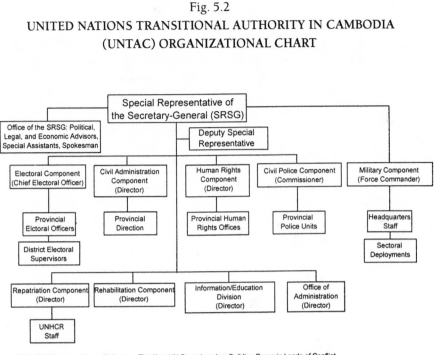

SOURCE: Based on Steven R. Ratner, *The New UN Peacekeeping: Building Peace in Lands of Conflict After the Cold War* (New York: St. Martin's Press, 1995), 165.

political, social, and public opinion trends in the countryside.[38] (Figure 5.2 portrays UNTAC's complex organizational structure.)

In disaggregated form, UNTAC's diverse array of activities often seemed haphazard and confusing to outside observers. But the underlying strategy for the operation was quite straightforward:

1. Obtain military stability through a verified cease-fire and associated measures (such as disarmament and demobilization) that would effectively end the war.
2. Neutralize the political influence of Cambodia's civil administrative structures while promoting human rights observance, civic education, the repatriation of refugees, and the rehabilitation of infrastructure, thereby laying the groundwork for a transition to democracy.
3. Organize and conduct national elections as a tool for deciding who would rule postwar Cambodia.

Reflecting the basic formula for compromise woven into the Paris Accords, the military and political aspects of the operation were tightly coupled—the Khmer Rouge (and the other opposition parties) would accept military demobilization if, and only if, the Hun Sen regime would accept the idea of political "demobilization" implicit in the civil administrative supervision and control arrangements that the accords established for the transition. In the abstract, this strategy looked sensible; whether it would prove feasible was very unclear.

UNTAC was given an 18-month timetable, from March 1992 to September 1993. Secretary-General Boutros-Ghali, as one of his first acts in office, appointed a senior secretariat official, Yasushi Akashi of Japan, to head UNTAC and serve as his special representative for Cambodia. The secretary-general also appointed Lieutenant General John Sanderson of Australia to serve as UNTAC's force commander. Under Akashi and Sanderson, UNTAC would fan out across Cambodia as a large, diverse organization of nearly 22,000 international staff members (including 16,000 peacekeeping troops) and an additional 60,000 Cambodian staff. Eventually, the operation would draw staff members from over 100 countries. Its costs would run to an estimated $1.9 billion. Perhaps most significantly, it would have no dress rehearsal.

Implementing the Plans

Though not fully appreciated early on, UNTAC was bound to be a tumultuous operation. It was, after all, a tool for transition assistance, not static peacekeeping. It was meant to shake Cambodia's warring factions out of their stalemated, decade-long civil war and end the country's crippling isolation; and it could only do these things by being a large, highly invasive enterprise. UNTAC touched virtually every part of Cambodia. It required the largest foreign military presence in the country since the Vietnamese invasion of 1978, and its concept of operations called for the largest movement of civilian population, albeit in a cooperative way, since the forced evacuation of Phnom Penh and other cites by the Khmer Rouge in the fateful days of April 1975.

Looking at UNTAC in retrospect, the operations unfolded as a kind of drama in four parts, loosely related to the formal operational phasing stipulated in the initial implementation plans but with some significant deviations on the military side. Chronologically, the parts overlap to a degree but each is distinctive in terms of the issues and challenges that the operation faced.

Part One: Starting Up (March–October 1992)

For the first eight months, most of UNTAC's energies were devoted to getting itself up and running. Nearly five months elapsed between the signing of the Paris Accords and initial UNTAC deployments, and the projected pace of full deployment was anything but reassuring. The delays generated tensions between UNTAC and UN headquarters in New York.[39] UNTAC's leadership understood the psychological and other advantages of timely deployment but lacked the resources to seize the initiative.

The Military Component. UNTAC's military component deployed in a somewhat fragmented fashion, though by July it was substantially in place, ahead of the rest of the operation. The woeful state of Cambodia's air- and seaport infrastructure made it

Table 5.3

UNTAC MILITARY COMPONENT, NATIONAL CONTRIBUTIONS

Country	Number[a]	INF.	UNMOS	ENG.	LOGS & COMMS	MINES	OTHER
Algeria	16		X				
Argentina	2		X				
Australia	685				X		X
Austria	17		X				X
Bangladesh	942	X	X			X	X
Belgium	5		X				
Brunei Darussalam	3		X				
Bulgaria	748	X	X				X
Cameroon	14		X				
Canada	218				X		X
Chile	52						X
China	444		X	X			X
France	1,350	X	X	X		X	X
Germany	137						X
Ghana	912	X	X				X
India	1,336	X	X			X	X
Indonesia	1,779	X	X				X
Ireland	11		X				

extremely difficult to phase in 16,000 troops from more than 30 countries (see table 5.3). Compounding this problem, UNTAC's 12 infantry battalions generally arrived prior to the engineering units that were to have repaired and demined roads and established camp facilities.[40] UNTAC's logistics units turned out to be undersized and reached the mission area only after the infantry elements had arrived. This sequence would have been manageable if all the infantry units had possessed the basic supplies and equipment necessary to be self-sufficient for sixty days, in line with standing UN requirements and UNTAC's Implementation Plan. Unfortunately, several under-equipped units generated immediate demands for everything from tents to food supplies.[41]

Several factors lay behind the slow startup. First and foremost, UNTAC found itself in competition with the UN operation in the former Yugoslavia. The Secretariat's understaffed peacekeeping and field operations units were overwhelmed by the near-simultaneous requirements to assemble large, multicomponent UN operations

Table 5.3

CONTINUED

Country	Number[a]	INF.	UNMOS	ENG	LOGS & COMMS.	MINES	OTHER
Japan	605		X	X			
Malaysia	1,090	X	X				X
Namibia	43		X				X
Netherlands	809	X			X	X	X
New Zealand	67				X	X	X
Pakistan	1,106	X	X		X	X	X
Phillipines	127						X
Poland	666		X	X	X		X
Russian Federation	52		X				X
Senegal	2		X				
Singapore	35		X				X
Thailand	716			X			X
Tunisia	883	X	X				X
United Kingdom	130		X			X	X
United States	49		X			X	
Uruguay	940	X	X				X
Total	15,991						

[a] At peak strength, June 1993

KEY: INF= infantry; UNMOS= military observers; ENG= engineers; LOGS & COMMS= logistics and communications; OTHER= headquarters staff, military police, medical units, and air units.

SOURCES: United Nations, *The United Nations and Cambodia, 1991-95* (New York: United Nations, 1995), 13; Office of the Spokesman, UNTAC HQ, Phnom Penh, Cambodia, 5 March and 5 April, 1993.

for Cambodia and Croatia. The January 1992 changeover in secretaries-general also proved to be a distraction. The outgoing incumbent, Mr. Perez de Cuellar, declined to appoint UNTAC's leadership echelon, leaving that job to his successor. This delayed other management appointments. Moreover, the organization's time-consuming procedures for generating troop contributions and its complex web of procurement regulations (designed more for cost control than promptness) greatly compounded the problem.[42]

Yet, it was also apparent that the Secretariat had not made good use of the slow negotiation of the Paris Accords to prepare the ground adequately for UNTAC. According to the congressional General Accounting Office, the Secretariat had only begun *informal* contacts with member states regarding possible troop contributions in late 1991, after the accords themselves had already been signed. UN survey missions had been dispatched to

Cambodia as early as 1989 in support of advance planning but, except in the electoral area, the assessments produced by these efforts were generally fragmentary, inaccurate, and of limited value.[43] There were also problems of coordination between those parts of the Secretariat engaged in the diplomatic effort and those responsible for implementation. General Sanderson was particularly critical: "No substantial planning had taken place in anticipation [of UNTAC] and, other than on the initiative of some contributing countries, no contingents had been earmarked for the operation."[44] Scrambling for time, the Secretariat sought to plug the gap by dispatching UNAMIC. Essentially a liaison mission, it did little to prevent a growing sense of drift in Phnom Penh.[45]

From the military angle, the most serious question raised by UNTAC's slow deployment concerned the process of regrouping, cantoning, and disarming Cambodia's factional armies. Pressures were mounting to begin this part of the operation as soon as possible: the cease-fire was growing more fragile by the day and civil unrest was increasing. Yet to start this effort too soon would throw an under-manned UN force into confusion. With the Khmer Rouge already stonewalling certain aspects of the implementation plan by this time, there was strong sentiment in UNTAC to adopt an incremental approach to cantonment, taking whatever units were ready to cooperate, in the hope that the Khmer Rouge would jump aboard the train as it began to leave the station.[46] If, however, cantonment officially commenced and soldiers did not appear for demobilization, UNTAC would look quite ineffectual.[47]

Ultimately, however, Force Commander Sanderson opted for the incremental approach. With support from Akashi and UN headquarters, and with assurances from the four factions, he announced on 9 May that Phase Two of the operation would begin on 13 June.[48] As it became clear that the Khmer Rouge were not going to participate in cantonment, Sanderson adjusted the ground rules: cantonment would be partial and strictly voluntary, to be implemented only in areas where cantoning units felt reasonably secure and where cantonment would not upset the military balance. Also, cantoning units could choose to keep their weapons and leave or reinforce their encampments if they came under attack.[49]

In retrospect, the Khmer Rouge decision to boycott Phase Two, discussed further below, saved UNTAC from the operational nightmare that might have ensued if full cantonment had actually begun on time, in June 1992. One-third of UNTAC's peacekeeping units had yet to deploy in early June, so it would have been impossible for UNTAC to open all the regroupment and cantonment sites on time.[50]

The overall impact of the UN's molasses-like military deployments a full nine months after the signing of the Paris Accords was damaging to the operation. An opportunity to establish early momentum was lost. Perversely, the slower than expected startup also meant that UNTAC ran well under budget during 1992.

Civilian Components. Among UNTAC's several civilian components, there was wide variation in the speed and effectiveness of the startup. UNHCR, already established in country, was well postured to operate effectively as UNTAC's repatriation arm, providing refugees with transport as well as various forms of assistance to facilitate reintegration, including grants of land. Small returns were begun in March, with rates increasing throughout the period. The most serious challenges facing the repatriation program were a serious shortage of available arable land in the northwestern provinces of Cambodia, where most of the returnees wanted to settle, and the slow pace of demining efforts in agricultural areas. To get around these bottlenecks, UNHCR in May broadened the range of assistance options to include cash payments in lieu of land, building materials, or other assistance. This adjustment proved popular and by September about one-third of the repatriation (roughly 130,000 persons) had been completed.[51]

The electoral component suffered annoying delays in staff recruitment and equipment procurement but it still managed to be fully operational by the summer of 1992. It benefited greatly from a highly effective advance survey unit that had mapped out Cambodia, demographically and cartographically, down to the communal level, enabling UNTAC to anticipate staffing and logistics needs for its civic education, voter registration, and polling efforts.[52] UNTAC's electoral managers, drawn heavily from the electoral commissions of several British Commonwealth countries, had extensive field experience. The electoral component was also able to tap into a pool of talented personnel provided by the United Nations Volunteer program in Geneva; although these "UNVs" came largely from economic development backgrounds, they were accustomed to the spare existence of village life in underdeveloped areas and proved very adept at performing civic education and other electoral tasks at the communal level.[53]

Other UNTAC civilian components fared less well. Its civil administration component, in particular, suffered from painfully slow recruitment of key staff and a dearth of useful advance information about the problems it would encounter in attempting to supervise or control Cambodia's public sector. Unlike the electoral component, which did not require a major infusion of manpower to meet some of its initial goals (for example, drafting Cambodia's electoral law), UNTAC's corps of civil administrators needed to make an impact early in order to establish authority. This simply did not happen. Civil administrative oversight was a highly experimental endeavor, and the UN Secretariat lacked a ready reservoir of personnel from which to draw quickly and had apparently done little to anticipate its needs for specialized expertise in such areas as weapons procurement, public security, finance, and other areas.[54] UNTAC nonetheless initiated "direct control" in Phnom Penh on 1 July and UNTAC's 21 provincial civil administration offices were opened two weeks later. But full staffing was not achieved until October and numerous practical and conceptual problems began to surface almost immediately.

UNTAC's 3,600-strong civilian police component (CIVPOL) drawn from over 30 countries, was not fully staffed until the end of 1992, and even so, the quality of its personnel was extremely uneven. Many came from constabulary and paramilitary backgrounds and were not particularly adept at community-based policing techniques; some lacked basic policing and investigative skills; and a significant number could speak neither English nor French, the operation's two official languages, let alone Khmer. Moreover, a variety of problems soon arose regarding effective utilization of CIVPOL by UNTAC in the deteriorating security conditions plaguing parts of Cambodia during the latter phases of the operation.

By September 1992, six months after its initial deployments and nearly a year after the signing of the Paris Accords, UNTAC was more or less fully operational but encountering turbulence. Its slow-motion start contributed to nagging doubts and uncertainties about the whole political transition, feeding a situation in which the Khmer Rouge and the Hun Sen regime began to back away from their commitments under the accords. General Sanderson, for one, saw a steady erosion of confidence in the United Nations and growing assertiveness by reactionary elements in the country: "I could feel the ground moving away from under myself and those moderates of all the military factions who were committed to the process."[55]

Part Two: Struggling to Stay Afloat (October–December 1992)

During this period, UNTAC struggled to keep the parties on board an increasingly unstable peace process. The Khmer Rouge, having sent mixed signals during the preceding months, drifted into a posture of passive boycott (as opposed to active obstruction) of the transition. The SOC was backtracking on aspects of the Paris Accords most inconvenient to it, namely the civil administrative control provisions. Meanwhile, Cambodia was opening up to the diverse influences of the outside world, for good (trade and investment, political pluralism, tourism) and ill (crime, inflation, prostitution, AIDS). UNTAC was beginning to achieve key milestones in its own efforts. But it was becoming clearer that full implementation of the comprehensive peace settlement would be hard, if not impossible, to achieve.

It seems scarcely surprising, in retrospect, that the Khmer Rouge disowned a peace settlement that, if fully implemented, would have surely eliminated the advantages they enjoyed as a radical insurgent force. Initially, however, Khmer Rouge actions evinced a cautious "wait and see" attitude about the process. Although they pursued low-level military operations, mainly in Kompong Thom province in central Cambodia during early 1992, they certainly were not alone in doing so. UNTAC interposed a company-sized unit between the Khmer Rouge and government forces that calmed the situation down considerably.[56] Meanwhile, a number of Khmer Rouge field commanders welcomed contact with UNTAC, and UNTAC field personnel detected credible indications that some Khmer Rouge units were preparing for demobilization.[57] They also were forthcoming in their cooperation with UNHCR repatriation efforts, and somewhat gingerly allowed UN personnel to reconnoiter possible regroupment and cantonment areas within their zones.[58]

Cantonment Stillborn.   During May and June, however, the Khmer Rouge's field posture shifted considerably. After having given assurances to UNTAC regarding UN freedom of movement and the provision of data on their force dispositions, in line with Phase Two obligations, the Khmer Rouge increased interference with UNTAC's freedom of movement, blocking the deployment of the Dutch battalion into Battambang province. On 30 May, in a highly publicized incident, Khmer Rouge checkpoint guards prevented an UNTAC motorcade carrying Akashi and Sanderson from traveling out of Pailin to the Thai border.[59] Then, on 9 June, just four days prior to the beginning of Phase Two, Khmer Rouge representatives formally notified UNTAC that they would not give the UN access to their areas.[60]

In explaining their decision, the Khmer Rouge professed readiness to enter into Phase Two arrangements but complained that the Paris Accords were not being implemented fairly and that they would withhold cooperation until their concerns were met. Their representatives claimed that "a great number" of Vietnamese forces remained in Cambodia, many disguised as civilians, in violation of the foreign forces withdrawal and nonreturn provisions of the accords. They produced a list of allegations for UNTAC but refused to accompany UNTAC personnel dispatched to investigate the charges.

The Khmer Rouge also argued that the Supreme National Council was not wielding its full range of powers and, as a result, was failing to ensure a neutral political environment for the forthcoming elections, as envisaged by the accords.[61] Instead, they said, there was a continuing, if disguised, Vietnamese presence within "the political and administrative structures of the regime installed in Phnom Penh."[62] To correct this problem, the Khmer Rouge proposed that the SNC should establish consultative committees *within* each existing administrative structure, including police forces, in order to "depoliticize" these bodies, while UNTAC would carry out its mandated civil administrative responsibilities. Rather creatively, they proposed a four week timetable linking a phased process of troop cantonment with the progressive "depoliticization" of ministries in Phnom Penh.[63]

With respect to foreign forces, the Khmer Rouge allegations had no real foundation.[64] Nonetheless, UNTAC took steps to augment its monitoring efforts, expanding its checkpoints and patrolling activity along the Laotian- and Vietnamese-Cambodian borders and establishing a number of mobile "strategic investigation teams" (SITs) to check out alleged sightings of foreign forces and cease-fire violations; these efforts produced no evidence of any military units or soldiers operating in-country under the control of Vietnamese authorities. Unfortunately, the Paris Accords had not defined exactly what was meant by "foreign forces" and thus could not preclude the Khmer Rouge from contorting the term to cover virtually anyone of Vietnamese descent, including settlers and civilians whom KR representatives often characterized as instruments of Vietnam's strategy to colonize Cambodia.[65]

UNTAC rejected any suggestion that migrants or civilian foreign residents should be in any way subject to the military withdrawal provisions of the Paris Accords. Nonetheless, to avoid whipping up the anti-Vietnamese sentiment shared, in greater or lesser degrees, by all the Cambodian opposition factions, UNTAC gained agreement within the SNC on a definition of "foreign forces" that, while narrower than the Khmer Rouges' absurdly broad construction, was still broader than a common sense reading of the Paris texts.[66] The consequence of this action was that several Vietnamese residents who had served with the Vietnamese armed forces in Cambodia, but subsequently married Cambodians and either demobilized or joined the Hun Sen regime's armed forces, were deemed to be in technical violation of the accords and subject to repatriation. But UNTAC continued to reject the suggestion that these paltry results in any way validated Khmer Rouge claims of a foreign military presence in-country.[67]

UNTAC maintained its voluntary cantonment efforts in the face of these challenges, mainly to mop up surplus weaponry (with which the countryside was awash) and to see if individual Khmer Rouge units could be lured into self-demobilization. The Khmer Rouge would have none of it. Sensing a trap, they began to rotate field commanders, bringing in officers with a more hostile attitude toward UNTAC. Eventually, some 55,000 soldiers from the three other factions came into the cantonments.[68] But only about 200 or so Khmer Rouge troops came in, and the process was effectively suspended by the end of the year.

Civil Administration: A Bridge Too Far.   As for the Khmer Rouges' criticisms regarding implementation of civil administrative control aspects of the Paris Accords, UNTAC found itself on the defensive. On the one hand, there was no basis to the claim that the SNC was not performing its functions as foreseen by the Paris Accords. The SNC was never meant to act as a de facto transitional government. It was intended, rather, as a symbolic authority that would convey practical power for supervising and controlling Cambodia's public administrations to UNTAC.[69] For this reason, the Khmer Rouges' proposal for establishing an SNC presence within existing administrative structures was resisted by UNTAC. (The SOC, of course, rejected the idea altogether.) On the other hand, it was also clear that UNTAC's supervisory mechanisms were not performing on par with the spirit or the letter of the peace settlement.

On paper, UNTAC's oversight apparatus was highly developed. It established a number of distinct units, or "services," to latch up with counterpart Cambodian administrations in the fields of defense, foreign affairs, finance, public security, and information; it also created an investigations service to handle complaints lodged by Cambodian citizens regarding bureaucratic excesses; and it set up a catchall "specialized control" service to extend oversight to a number of related public sectors—health, education, agriculture, and transport, among others—deemed to be sensitive enough to warrant scrutiny.[70] By the latter stages of the operation, UNTAC personnel could be found doing such things as probing into the country's penal code, investigating its defense procurement decisions, vetting editorials in state-run media, reviewing regulations on national heritage preservation, scrutinizing admissions policies at public educational institutions, monitoring passport and visa procedures, managing monetary and fiscal decisions, and delving into a host of other civil administrative activities.

UNTAC's modes of supervision and control were largely of its own making. It developed a three-part, experimental methodology under which UNTAC inspectors could exercise control authority: (1) a priori (where advanced warning enabled preemption of actions that could skew the neutral political environment); (2) a posteriori (where reviewing the "paper trail" on previous decision-making and bureaucratic operations could lead to changes in those decisions and actions); and (3) by appraisal (identifying and correcting problems in administrative operations). Armed with these procedures, UNTAC's civil administrators would be placed alongside high ranking Cambodian officials within specific civil administrations, attending meetings, issuing codes of conduct, and tapping into flows of information.[71]

Unfortunately, the degree of physical and cognitive access into bureaucratic operations generally fell short of expectations. During the stage at which UNTAC might have been able to aggressively insert its personnel into key Cambodian administrations (prior to the Khmer Rouge backtracking), UNTAC was not prepared to do so.[72] By the time the necessary UN assets were in place, the SOC was much less willing to open bureaucratic doors to UNTAC.

Nor was it clear where such doors would lead, for the whole concept of administrative oversight presumed the existence of coherent bureaucracies to supervise. Such was not the case. Some of the key ministries in Phnom Penh scarcely functioned at all.[73] Effective power most often resided with provincial governors, party chiefs, and army officers, individuals who shared partisan loyalties and (often) kinship with national leaders but were generally accustomed to running their own fiefdoms without much intrusion from Phnom Penh. Moreover, as University of Texas law professor Steven Ratner has pointed out, Cambodian decision-making was rarely done through "formal processes." Rather, "key individuals made decisions on their own and conveyed them to subordinates, usually without any [written] record."[74] Given the personalized character of authority, techniques such as monitoring a bureaucratic "paper trail" or attending a staff meeting would not necessarily help to supervise a decision process, let alone control it.

The socialist, one-party character of the Cambodian state compounded all of these problems significantly. From UNTAC's standpoint, the key to effective mission performance was keeping the country's bureaucracies out of politics. But as UNTAC found out, the SOC's governmental structure was comingled with its Cambodian People's Party (CPP) to an extent that defied most efforts at disentanglement.[75] There is some anecdotal evidence that certain parties to the Paris Accords agreed to the UN oversight measures confident that state-party relationships would tend to render the accords' provisions meaningless.[76]

UNTAC's most intensive oversight efforts were made in the field of finance, including taxation, monetary policies, and public expenditure. Exploiting its leverage as the disbursing authority for World Bank and International Monetary Fund assistance, UNTAC introduced a fair amount of transparency into Cambodia's financial institutions. The country's erratic currency issuance practices were brought under control.[77] State revenue flows were tracked on a spot-check basis. Expenditure controls were also applied: payment orders submitted by national or provincial offices to the Cambodian Treasury would require the countersignature of an UNTAC financial controller, who would examine the payment's propriety and political impact. Disputed payments (usually involving questions raised by UNTAC provincial staff with the local governor) could be processed but UNTAC reserved the right to hold up disbursements.[78] In addition, UNTAC managed to increase public revenues through new taxes (and to a degree, improved tax collection) on commercial and sales activity in Phnom Penh, then experiencing the boom-town effects of UNTAC's purchasing power, expanded tourism, and the sudden influx of overseas private investment. Somewhat less successfully (due to SOC stonewalling), UNTAC tried to establish a register for the sale of public assets, so that the fair market value of properties could be determined and the flow of funds generated by the transaction could be tracked back to the treasury.

Outside the financial area, UNTAC's difficulties were far greater. During the latter part of 1992, Cambodia witnessed an upsurge in politically inspired violence and intimidation, aimed largely at the newly resident opposition parties, in particular FUNCINPEC and the KPNLF's main successor, the Buddhist Liberal Democratic Party (BLDP). While the Khmer Rouge were mainly responsible for attacks on indigenous Vietnamese, elements loyal to the SOC were widely believed to be the instigators of violence against the non-communist parties.[79] In some of the more unstable provinces, most notably Battambang, Siem Reap, and Kompong Thom, UNTAC personnel saw an expanding pattern of harassment, arrest, or abduction of political activists, bombings of party offices, and execution-style murders. Voter intimidation was also widespread, the most familiar tactic being the "registration" and/or confiscation of voter identification cards by local authorities. As these cases began to pile up, the complicity of SOC police and CPAF personnel became clearly established, and yet UNTAC seemed unable to curb the violence through its civil administrative powers.[80]

In retrospect, it is fair to ask whether the operation could have seized effective control of the SOC's public security apparatus even without the burdens of slow deployment, personnel deficiencies, poor pre-mission analysis, and other constraints: the sheer predominance of the SOC at all levels of Cambodian society was not something that UNTAC was going to alter fundamentally in a mere 18 months. The faction's large assemblage of local party functionaries, hacks, and thugs was totally unaccustomed to political pluralism and had little inclination to adjust gracefully to the competitive pressures created by opposition parties. Moreover, there were simply too many ways to evade UNTAC's scrutiny; and without a functioning, independent judicial system to investigate, apprehend, and prosecute suspects (something that the Paris Accords left for a post-transition constitution), there was little expectation that criminal acts would carry any consequences.

Picking its fights carefully, UNTAC did expose the SOC's most flagrant abuses of administrative and police power. In early 1993, it created a so-called "Control Team" and dispatched it to various provinces on a series of surprise inspections to assess the SOC's behavior vis-à-vis the political opposition.[81] The data collected in these investigations confirmed suspicions of the SOC's involvement in efforts to foment violence against political opposition parties and to intimidate voters.[82] As discussed below, UNTAC also established a public prosecutor's office. A number of recalcitrant bureaucrats were removed or reassigned, and UNTAC sought to oust Ung Sami, Battambang's particularly notorious provincial governor.[83] None of these steps made a major impact on the problem of political violence, however, and each would trigger howls of protest back in Phnom Penh, where SOC leaders complained that they were not being treated in an evenhanded fashion.[84]

Given the SOC's bureaucratic heft relative to the other factions, it was no surprise that its behavior would be subject to the greatest scrutiny. Unhappily, the fragile state of the overall settlement weighed heavily against UNTAC in its efforts to cajole the SOC back into line.[85] Built upon the fundamental principle of consent, the Paris Accords could work only if the leaderships of the warring factions cooperated with UNTAC in enforcing compliance at lower levels within their own administrations. Once the Khmer Rouge backed off their obligations, the SOC leadership's incentive to play that internal enforcing role simply dried up; not unexpectedly, the Khmer Rouges' boycott seemed to strengthen the harder-line elements within the SOC and the CPP. To be sure, the SOC leadership was desperate to have an election as a way to achieve international respectability, but it was also well aware that the UN was not about to cancel the polling in order to penalize the SOC's misbehavior.

UNTAC's difficulties with the SOC only fed Khmer Rouge intransigence. The lack of effective civil administrative control, General Sanderson would later point out, lent "a measure of credence" to the Khmer Rouge charge that UNTAC was not properly implementing its mandate. This, he said, "probably preempted any prospect for bringing the Khmer Rouge into the process."[86]

By the end of 1992, it was becoming clear that peace would not come to Cambodia in the manner foreseen by the Paris Accords. The SOC and the Khmer Rouge were like two boats drifting apart, with a beleaguered sailor, UNTAC, caught astraddle and straining mightily to keep them together. The soft sanctions, noted earlier, combined with diplomatic overtures by Thailand, Japan, and others did not budge the Khmer Rouge back into compliance.[87]

UNTAC's Other Woes.   Meanwhile, socioeconomic dislocations were adding to the burdens of the transition. Cambodia's shaky economy was overheating; it was trying to privatize, staunch its hemorrhaging public sector deficit, and open up to the outside world all at once. Speculative capital and foreign migrant workers flooded into Phnom Penh, attracted by the lure of quick investment returns and a spiraling demand for services due to the influx of UNTAC personnel, tourists, and foreign entrepreneurs. Construction crews and traffic clogged the streets. The presence of Vietnamese workers triggered some unrest. Inflation shot up by about 250 percent during the first three quarters of 1992 before spiking and declining toward the end of the year.[88] Common crime jumped. Unpaid police and soldiers increasingly resorted to banditry and extortion on Cambodia's highways.

UNTAC was not well postured to compensate for these instabilities, or indeed to offset the disruptive side effects of its own deployment. Economically, it did stimulate new construction and local employment; it also helped to stabilize Cambodia's soaring public deficit and probably inhibited at least the more egregious forms of civil corruption. On the other hand, its presence tended to fuel social tensions in some respects. For every Cambodian hired by UNTAC, mainly for electoral preparations, many other eager job-seekers were turned away and resented losing a chance to earn several times the average Cambodian's annual income in short-term UN employ.[89] To boost its information dissemination efforts, UNTAC distributed thousands of transistor radios donated by a Japanese non-governmental organization. The radios rapidly became prized status symbols, and this goodwill gesture triggered a spate of riots and robberies as well as acts of violence against Cambodians who were fortunate enough to receive one.

Such episodes did little to boost UNTAC's media image. Stories of poor morale, incompetence within its civil police ranks, and instances of misconduct by some of its soldiers contributed grist for press depictions of UNTAC as a bunch of brawling soldiers and disorderly keystone cops. Such stories often overlooked the organization's many good works at the grass-roots level and greatly exaggerated the impact of specific problems.[90] Still, they did expose the organization's Achilles heel: the wide variation in the quality of its personnel, especially at mid-levels. Such variations perhaps were inevitable in a diverse, multicultural organization operating under extremely tight timetables and stressful conditions, but they nonetheless raised doubts that UNTAC would be able to cope with the climate of violence and instability that was marring the transition.

Part Three: Adapting to Circumstances (January - May 1993)

If UNTAC's work had been limited to missions like cantonment and civil administrative oversight that required the active cooperation of the Khmer parties, the operation likely would have collapsed by the end of the 1992. In fact, other aspects of UNTAC's activities that required only minimal cooperation or passive acquiescence by the parties were running much more smoothly.[91] Approaching the May 1993 elections, UNTAC sought to insulate these activities from the disruptive effects of SOC and Khmer Rouge misbehavior while shepherding the process to a decisive conclusion.

Preparing the Way to Elections.   Overshadowed by the hue and cry over Khmer Rouge and SOC backtracking, UNTAC's electoral and civic education activities were moving ahead expeditiously. By August 1992, nearly twenty Cambodian political parties had provisionally registered, a step that made it possible for voter registration to proceed (with party agents in place to monitor the process), and for UNTAC to authorize the opening up of party offices, eventually at hundreds of locations around the country. In the meantime, UNTAC's electoral component assembled and trained 834 registration teams, each consisting of 5 locally hired registration officers and a team leader. Voter registration commenced in Phnom Penh in early October and then fanned out in a "rolling" pattern from the populous southeastern provinces to the more remote areas in the north and west. By the end of January 1993, the operation had managed to register over 4.6 million Cambodians, or about 96 percent of the eligible population, including many voters in areas nominally controlled by the Khmer Rouge.[92]

Successful voter registration was no mean feat. Few Cambodians possessed civil documentation that could easily and reliably be used to establish ancestry, age, or domicile. Moreover, all of the Khmer factions, except the SOC, had complained that UNTAC's racially blind voter eligibility requirements would allow hundreds of thousands of Vietnamese settlers to vote, thereby skewing the elections. Akashi and his managers, while very conscious of Khmer antipathies toward the Vietnamese, opposed any measure that would exclude non-Khmers on a purely racial basis. Apartheid, they said, was no more acceptable in Cambodia than in South Africa.

Akashi had presented UNTAC's draft electoral law to the SNC in April 1992 and allowed the parties to subject it to seemingly endless debate. In a bow to Khmer preferences, he also accepted certain amendments, one of which tightened up on voter eligibility, albeit in a nonracial fashion.[93] Even though he could have promulgated the law at any time, and was urged to do so by some advisors, Akashi regarded a lengthy review as a necessary step in vesting the Cambodians in what was, after all, their own electoral process. The law was eventually adopted by the SNC in early August (with the Khmer Rouge in dissent), and Akashi could fairly claim to have been spared from the "dilemma of imposing democracy on a reluctant people."[94]

These moves paid off. With party agents in place to monitor the voter registration process, only about .03 percent of all registrants were challenged.[95] Thus no Cambodian party could disown the process on the basis of unfair or poorly applied eligibility criteria, and UNTAC had achieved a great rarity in Cambodian political history—an authentic voter roll. Meanwhile, the process of registration itself had inspired great public enthusiasm. One item in particular, UNTAC's flashy laminated photographic registration cards, proved to be extremely popular, so much so that when UNTAC flirted with the idea of temporarily repossessing the cards during polling as a further hedge against voter fraud, the measure was rejected on the grounds that voter turnout might shrink.

Refugee Repatriation and Human Rights Promotion.   UNTAC was pressing ahead on other fronts as well. By April 1993, it had largely completed its voluntary repatriation program, closing the remaining camps on the Thai-Cambodian border and resettling about 370,000 refugees. Although a high degree of secondary migration among returning populations (largely to reunite with family members) impeded efforts to fully monitor the situation of returnees, no signs of major disruption in the reintegration process came to light. Fortunately, the return proved to be far less physically dangerous than feared. Only a handful of casualties occurred as a result of land mines, for example, and UNTAC's mine awareness education programs seemed to be paying off.[96]

The operation also made progress in planting the seeds of civil society. UNTAC's human rights component, despite its small size, managed to secure the release of hundreds of political prisoners from SOC prisons. It conducted hundreds of training programs in human rights for lawyers, judges, journalists, teachers, police, and administrators. It established a process for receiving, verifying, and, where possible, remedying individual complaints of human rights violations. Filling a void created by the absence of international human rights NGOs, UNTAC actively promoted the growth of local human rights organizations, whose ranks eventually swelled to over 150,000 members, providing manpower for human rights monitoring efforts at the provincial level. Meanwhile, a lively, uncensored press began to flourish in Phnom Penh. Political parties established a highly visible presence in the city as well as in Cambodia's larger provincial towns.[97]

All these developments stirred a great deal of public excitement. They also marked such a rapid departure from Cambodia's past authoritarian traditions that violence was certain to flare, absent any externally imposed restraints. As noted earlier, UNTAC was not capable of imposing such restraints. Nor were UNTAC's peacekeeping units in any position to "secure" the countryside against a sputtering civil conflict that was supposed to have been brought to closure by cantonment, disarmament, and demobilization. What UNTAC tried to do, instead, was enhance protection for specific activities, mainly electoral preparations, while pressing ahead with initiatives to sidestep the main obstacles presented by the Khmer Rouge and the SOC's security apparatus.

The Military Component's Redeployment.   By January 1993, UNTAC had shifted into a new deployment pattern. Partially used or empty cantonment sites were closed down and peacekeeping units took up a configuration that mirrored UNTAC's other components. The stated aim of the redeployment—"to create a secure environment conducive to the preparations, and subsequent conduct of, an election in Cambodia"—was not a startlingly new mission but one that would henceforth be achieved through concurrent operations with civilians.[98] The secretary-general had foreshadowed this move to the Security Council in late November, when he sought and received support for maintaining UNTAC's full complement of infantry battalions until the elections.[99] The Council also identified 31 January 1993 as the effective deadline for Khmer Rouge participation in the transition process.[100]

Operationally, the redeployment involved a major clockwise rotation of troops. Within Cambodia's more unstable regions, for example, the Malaysian battalion moved westward into Battambang province, enabling its Dutch counterpart to consolidate positions to the north, in Banteay Meanchey, a strategically located province separating the two largest Khmer Rouge-controlled zones in the country. The Bangladeshi battalion, meanwhile, expanded eastward into Siem Reap, freeing up the Pakistani battalion to redeploy farther eastward, to accessible areas of Preah Vihear province. UNTAC carried out smaller-scale redeployments throughout Cambodia's southeastern areas, close to and around the KR's more disparate "leopard spot" operating areas.[101]

These adjustments allowed UNTAC to augment its presence within the roughly 25 percent of the country nominally contested by both the Khmer Rouge and SOC forces. UNTAC's military units increased the tempo of their reassurance and anti-banditry patrols, and provided greater assistance to CIVPOL and local police in operations to reduce the number of illegal weapons held by the civilian population. The provision of transportation, security, and logistics support for electoral preparations at the local level became a much higher priority. UNMOs were freed up to do more local liaison and information-gathering work in Cambodia's countryside. Twelve mobile reserve units were organized at the company-level to react quickly to problems.

Concomitantly, civil-military coordination became a much higher priority for UNTAC at the field level. Its sector boundaries were realigned to correspond with Cambodia's existing provincial frontiers, so that a given commander's area of responsibility would overlap with those of UNTAC's local civilian provincial directors. As Sanderson put it,

> Sector Commanders have the responsibility for understanding their patch. Putting their people out everywhere, operating with the Cambodian people . . . are all parts of this. They must know which places are dangerous to go, which are not. Part of that understanding involves cooperating with the Electoral Component to work out the best way to see this electoral process through, right down to this district level.[102]

Given the Khmer Rouges' growing hostility toward the transition process, taking steps to reduce electoral vulnerabilities seemed only prudent. Even so, there were sharp limits, recognized even at the time, to what UNTAC could do. Apart from the repatriation program, the original UN implementation plan had not envisaged extensive integration of civil and military efforts and trying to achieve it midway into the mission was a gamble. Yet UNTAC felt it was a risk worth taking: the Khmer Rouge were stretched thin militarily and not well postured to pose threats to ongoing electoral preparations on a large scale. They held only one provincial town, Pailin, and about 5 percent of the overall population.[103]

UNTAC also reckoned that the growing popularity of electoral preparations would tend to inhibit obstructionism. It would be difficult for any Khmer faction to attack voters or polling staff without also putting in jeopardy their claim to be guardians of the public will. The Khmer Rouge had not interfered with UNTAC's hitherto unprotected civilians performing civic education and voter registration tasks in and around their areas. Reports indicated that a number of KR soldiers even registered to vote.[104]

Still, UNTAC doubted that the Khmer Rouges' laid back attitude would last indefinitely, for the SOC was benefiting politically from the atmosphere of tension created by the KR's boycott of the transition process. Some in UNTAC felt that SOC police and soldiers were deliberately laying low in some areas, allowing the security situation to deteriorate, hoping to reap political benefits later.[105] Everyone's nightmare scenario was a sudden, desperate Khmer Rouge move to prevent an SOC victory at the ballot box. UNTAC's military redeployment—"hoping for the best while preparing for the worst," as Akashi put it—was intended to keep things from reaching that point. The Khmer Rouge were not pleased to see larger numbers of blue berets moving closer to their areas and played a "cat-and-mouse" game of detaining UNMOs and peacekeepers, threatening them if rescue attempts were made, and then releasing them unharmed.

Keenly aware of the larger issues at stake, Sanderson worked hard to imbue his subordinate commanders with the mission's new emphasis. Not all units, however, were comfortable in a supporting role. Some saw the job as little more than a glorified taxi and escort service. Worried about being stretched too thin, military sector commanders sometimes found themselves at odds with their civilian counterparts over how much manpower and equipment to allocate to the support of nonmilitary activities. Worse, a few units were loath to release security information to civilian staff members, drawing sharp criticism from UNTAC's other components which argued (correctly) that civilians were supposed to be the main beneficiaries of such information. In some cases, language and cultural barriers compounded civil-military problems.[106]

UNTAC's military had its own complaints about the civilians, most of whom lacked prior experience with highly unstable environments. Beyond land mine awareness, few had much training in safety and security procedures. Undisciplined use of mobile radios, which local factions would monitor, was a problem, and many civilians chafed at restrictions on their freedom of movement. Electoral personnel, in particular, wanted maximum flexibility as well as maximum protection, and it took awhile for some of them to recognize that these priorities could clash and that UNTAC's military could not be omnipresent.

In March, UNTAC developed more detailed plans for military operations before, during, and after the elections. Sector commanders began producing daily assessments of low, medium, and high risk districts and the appropriate security measures to be observed in each case. Guidelines were issued for security arrangements at campaign events and polling stations. Evacuation plans were reviewed. Meanwhile, military and electoral planners restudied plans for polling station distribution. Reluctantly, the electoral component agreed to cut the number by about 25 percent, to 1,600 sites.[107] UNTAC reckoned that a better (and more secure) distribution of the remaining sites could confine the highest risks to a small percentage of the population.[108] And the military agreed to take on more burdensome arrangements, transporting ballot boxes to and from the polling stations each day.

Despite these efforts, the atmosphere remained tense. During March and April, the Khmer Rouges' anti-UNTAC propaganda turned vitriolic. KR leaders vilified the upcoming elections as a "stinking farce" and made dark references to the possibility of bloodshed. They intensified their attacks on indigenous Vietnamese, triggering a wholesale flight of floating villages off the Tonle Sap (the Great Lake) and down the Mekong and Bassic rivers toward Vietnam.[109] They also began to selectively target UNTAC with hostile fire. In one particularly flagrant episode, KR cadre murdered several Bulgarian peacekeepers in Kompong Speu, a province close to Phnom Penh; in another episode, they ambushed an electoral convoy in Banteay Meanchey, killing a CIVPOL officer. In April, when a Japanese electoral worker and his Cambodian interpreter were murdered (probably not by Khmer Rouge, as it turned out) in

Kompong Thom province, the operation came to a virtual standstill. For a few anxious days it appeared that UNTAC's district electoral staff might leave the mission en masse.[110] Akashi and Sanderson quickly organized a civil-military conference to review the security situation, and in the end only a small number of electoral workers left the country.

Even at the time, however, it was never very clear that the Khmer Rouge were fully prepared to torpedo the Cambodian elections by force. Their strategy seemed geared more to frightening UNTAC personnel out of Cambodia than to waging war against the operation. Khmer Rouge guerrillas could have inflicted far more casualties upon UNTAC had they wished to do so. With few exceptions, they did not use lethal force against international civilian staff and justified their resort to violence as protecting Cambodians against UNTAC's more unsavory military elements.

In the end, then, UNTAC's military redeployment was an absolutely vital step in keeping the operation moving forward. Both operationally and psychologically, it provided valuable protective cover. For the Khmer Rouge, it reduced easy targets of opportunity and increased the costs of obstruction. Although it left UNTAC's military units more exposed in some remote areas, the shift also helped to keep a line of reasonable distance between Khmer Rouge-controlled zones and locations where UNTAC planned to concentrate its electoral assets.[111] At the same time, it demonstrated UNTAC's resolve to stay the course, contributing to heightened confidence among the Cambodian people that polling could be conducted safely in the major population areas. Without the military's direct involvement, the elections could not have been held under the tense conditions that prevailed at the time.

Containing the Impact of Political Violence. Meanwhile, politically inspired violence and abuses of administrative power continued to plague the run-up to the May elections. Increasingly, UNTAC found itself in daily squabbles with the SOC over such matters as police excesses, voter intimidation, the rights of opposition parties to fair media access, and the confiscation of campaign materials and media equipment by customs agents. While UNTAC managed occasionally to resolve problems, the objective of maintaining a "neutral political environment" seemed more elusive than ever.[112]

Unable to penetrate the SOC's security apparatus, UNTAC tried to curb political violence by indirect means. It launched surprise "Control Team" inspections in a number of provinces and moved into civil policing, deploying both static guards and mobile patrols to deter attacks on vulnerable party offices. After numerous appeals failed to prod the SOC and other factions into acting upon his staff's investigations of human rights violations, Akashi established an UNTAC Special Prosecutor's Office with powers to arrest and detain suspects and to prosecute cases before Cambodian trial and appellate courts.[113] Later, he issued a directive prohibiting the unauthorized possession of firearms and explosives (in effect to enforce the SOC's own gun licensing laws), and soon thereafter UNTAC and local police began jointly enforcing the directive with weapons confiscation checkpoints.[114] Again, the common aim in all these actions was the deterrence of violence.

These steps may have helped at the margins. Attacks on political party offices dropped off somewhat after UNTAC posted its guards. A decrease in violent crime was reported after UNTAC's weapons directive came into effect.[115] UNTAC's highly visible presence at campaign events most likely inhibited organized violence at these venues. Yet, the limited character of these measures was obvious. UNTAC's military component was not prepared to assume responsibility for protecting party candidates, recognizing (correctly) that VIP security would quickly overwhelm its limited manpower and field intelligence resources. Nor did UNTAC press its prosecutorial powers very far, fearing adverse reactions from the SOC.[116] UNTAC's unarmed CIVPOL were distinctly unenthusiastic about escorting UNTAC personnel or arresting suspected human rights violators.[117] They had come to Cambodia to monitor law and order, not to administer it.

Fortunately, UNTAC had other cards to play. On the electoral side, the operation devised systems and procedures that helped to insulate the process from the corrosive effects of political violence and intimidation. The key to this effort was, ironically, opacity. The ballots, for example, listed political parties rather than candidates, and this fact allowed UNTAC to delay the release of the lists of actual candidates in some cases until very late in the campaign. When the SOC's internal security officials demanded such information, UNTAC's electoral component refused.[118] Moreover, the balloting and counting procedures were designed to protect not only the electoral choices of individual voters but also localities below the provincial level. Prior to counting, returns from a number of districts would be mixed together, so that no one could learn how a given commune had voted (and thus could not threaten reprisals on that basis).[119] To thwart the most common form of political harassment—the confiscation of voter IDs—UNTAC adopted a so-called "tendered ballot" procedure, to enable registered voters without their IDs to cast ballots.[120] All these steps helped to ensure that at least within the polling booth the environment was conducive to free and fair elections.

UNTAC also participated actively in the electoral campaign. When the SOC's information ministry preempted the campaign's official start date by airing political messages for its party, the CPP, UNTAC implemented an "equal access, equal time" policy, giving all registered political parties broadcast time on Radio UNTAC.[121] Akashi banned public opinion polls to prevent their abuse for harassment or intimidation purposes. When the SOC's notorious transportation minister, Prince Norodom Chakrapong, denied his half brother, Ranariddh, the use of a private aircraft for campaigning, UNTAC gave FUNCINPEC leaders helicopter "lifts" to rallies in SOC areas. UNTAC also sponsored and provided security for multiparty debate forums and other events.

UNTAC's largely unforeseen involvement in the campaign was risky, raising as it did perceptions of partisanship. Even though UNTAC's leadership was careful to include all registered political parties in its offers of assistance and based its actions on provisions of the Paris Accords, the SOC complained bitterly of bias on numerous occasions.[122] Yet, UNTAC was aware that FUNCINPEC and other opposition parties were giving serious thought to withdrawing from the elections to protest the violence of pro-SOC elements; rumors were also rife that the Khmer Rouge were trying to bribe opposition leaders into bailing out. Consequently, UNTAC saw little choice but to actively assist the opposition.[123]

UNTAC's information/education effort also proved highly effective. Despite the priority given to public information in the secretary-general's implementation plan, delays in personnel recruitment and equipment procurement slowed the effort. Radio broadcast capability was a novelty for a UN operation. The secretary-general was initially skeptical about the idea but Akashi and other aides managed to change his mind. By November 1992, UNTAC was broadcasting its programs over an antiquated vacuum-tube transmitter located in Phnom Penh.[124] In the interim, the Voice of America provided critical support by beaming UNTAC programs into Cambodia from its large, Bangkok-based transmitter. With relay stations installed (finally) by late March 1993, Radio UNTAC reached all parts of Cambodia.[125] In the weeks preceding the elections, the station expanded its diverse menu of news, civic education, and variety programs to 15 hours a day. It gained a reputation as the most popular and credible radio station in the country, and it was widely listened to in Khmer Rouge areas.[126]

While radio broadcast helped to neutralize the abundant anti-UNTAC propaganda and misinformation aired on KR and SOC radio stations, other UNTAC products also captured attention. A dizzying array of Khmer-language posters, banners, brochures, videos, cassette tapes, T-shirts, comic books, and stickers were produced and disseminated to explain such things as the mechanics of voter registration and polling, ways of dealing with political intimidation, and how one's ballot would be kept secret.[127] UNTAC's electoral staff made extensive use of such materials at the village level and UNTAC's Khmer specialists kept tabs on how the overall program was shaping public perceptions of UNTAC's mission. Arguably, UNTAC's hardest audience were the non-Khmer speakers on its own senior staff, who professed skepticism about the effectiveness of the whole endeavor.[128] It was not until the elections that the full effects of the information campaign were seen.

By the time the campaign gathered steam in late April 1993, UNTAC's fortunes seemed to be improving. The violence that was widely expected to flare up at campaign events did not materialize. While campaign activities started off slowly in the more stable areas, they soon spread throughout most of the provinces. By the end of the six-week period, according to UNTAC's tally, nearly 1,600 meetings and rallies, involving nearly one million people, had been held around the country without any serious incident.[129] It appeared that the SOC's security forces were exercising some restraint, perhaps out of a belief that victory at the polls was assured. On the other hand, there were indications that Khmer Rouge were beefing up their units, possibly in anticipation of orders to disrupt the polls.

Part Four: Turning a Corner (May–September 1993)

The elections of 23-28 May were a culminating point for UNTAC. Amidst a tense atmosphere, international polling observers and foreign media descended on the country. UNTAC pared down the number of polling stations, finalized plans to secure ballot boxes at safe havens each evening after polling, distributed protective gear (for example, US-provided flak jackets and helmets) and medical equipment to its field staff, and deployed additional troops and helicopters brought in for the event. With Akashi's support, Sanderson authorized CPAF to take up defensive positions in support of the elections, and he consented to a request by the other factions to take back some of their weapons stockpiled in UN depots.[130] On 15 May, the secretary-general informed the Security Council of his decision to go ahead with the elections. While conditions "are not those anticipated in the Paris Agreements," he stated, UNTAC was prepared to conduct the "most impartial election in conditions that are not susceptible to its full control."[131] The Council supported his decision.[132]

The polling itself was a stunning spectacle. As early monsoon rains swept across the country, Cambodians thronged to the polls in a festive mood. Almost 90 percent of registered voters, approximately 4.2 million people, cast ballots, the bulk of them in the first 48 hours. The process was remarkably peaceful and the Khmer Rouge, for the most part, sat quietly on the sidelines. In some areas, Khmer Rouge soldiers could be seen watching crowds of voters assembling around polling stations. It was unclear whether the Khmer Rouge leadership actually ordered their units to disrupt the voting with force; some defectors would later claim that they had.[133] But the massive turnout meant that any concerted attacks would have been exceedingly bloody. In a sense, the Cambodian voters provided their own protective cover for the election. In the last few days of the election, possibly to boost their erstwhile FUNCINPEC allies, Khmer Rouge commanders began to truck their people to the polls.

The days following the polling witnessed a political earthquake and numerous aftershocks. On 29 May, Akashi certified that the polling had been free and fair. The same day, UNTAC's electoral staff began to count ballots under the watchful eyes of international observers and party agents. When early returns showed FUNCINPEC moving into the lead, nonplussed SOC officials raised a flurry of complaints about irregularities in the polling and counting procedures. Akashi agreed to investigate these charges, mainly as a face-saving gesture to the SOC, while asserting that the allegations fell short of anything approaching fraud and, even if true, would not affect the outcome.[134] But the SOC kept up the drumbeat of criticism, insisting that new elections should be held in seven provinces and Phnom Penh; Akashi refused. The SOC then appealed to Prince Sihanouk for action, hinting darkly of civil war. On 4 June, with ballots still being counted, Sihanouk announced the formation of a "national government of Cambodia," with himself in near-total control. A day later, he backed off, rather petulantly, under a barrage of criticism by FUNCINPEC, UN sources, and some foreign governments.

By 7 June, FUNCINPEC emerged victorious. The party took over 45 percent of the vote and won 58 of the 120 seats in the new Constituent Assembly. The SOC's party, the CPP, finished in second place with roughly 38 percent of the vote, giving it 51 seats; embarrassingly, however, its total of about 1.5 million votes was considerably less than its claimed party membership. BLDP came in a distant third with only about

4 percent, though the proportional representation formula gave it 10 seats in the assembly.[135] On 10 June, Akashi certified the results of the election and appealed to all sides to respect the outcome.

At this point, the SOC upped the ante considerably. A group of hardliners led by Sihanouk's son, Prince Chakrapong, staged a "secession" in Cambodia's eastern provinces, instigating riots against UNTAC and FUNCINPEC personnel and forcing several thousand civilians to flee. A few days later, the scheme collapsed when Sihanouk called for national unity but its underlying goal, to lever FUNCINPEC into accepting the principle of power-sharing, had been achieved.[136] The SOC accepted the electoral outcome. On 16 June, Sihanouk announced the formation of an Interim Joint Administration, with himself as head of state and Ranariddh and Hun Sen as co-prime ministers. Ministerial portfolios would be split equally between FUNCINPEC and the SOC.

With Sihanouk's announcement, the crisis atmosphere subsided. FUNCINPEC, in effect, had conceded its winning margin in the interests of stability. What all these developments implied for the final phases of the settlement process was not clear, however. An interim government had not been scripted by the Paris settlement, and it highlighted the lack of attention the accords paid to the critical period between the elections and the formation of a new government. UNTAC found itself in a curious position. The election had clearly given it an enormous boost. Cambodians who had scorned the operation previously were suddenly more compliant and respectful.[137] On the other hand, its refurbished reputation did not translate into much political clout. With the SNC in eclipse, UNTAC lost its main forum for political influence. UNTAC's postelectoral civil administrative authority, already ambiguous, eroded quickly. Those in the Constituent Assembly involved in drafting the new constitution kept UNTAC at arms length.

Greater Cambodian self-reliance was not an unwelcome development. With the end of their mission looming on the horizon, some in UNTAC argued that the operation should in fact be stepping back, allowing the Cambodians to take control of their own political affairs. But it was also clear that moving to the sidelines too quickly could result in renewed factional infighting eclipsing the democratic aspirations reflected in the election.

Thus, UNTAC sought a middle course, to remain in the fray but as a behind-the-scenes player. In the tumultuous days during the vote count, Akashi maneuvered quietly to open up lines of communication between Ranariddh, then in hiding, and SOC leaders Hun Sen and Chea Sim. Convinced that some form of power sharing was an absolute necessity, Akashi lobbied FUNCINPEC to offer the olive branch as a way to pacify the SOC's disoriented and defiant membership. At the military level, Sanderson brokered an agreement among the three factional chiefs of staff to form a new national army and to support whatever government emerged from the elections.[138] The Mixed Military Working Group, developed and utilized extensively by Sanderson, became the nucleus of a unified military command structure, and the group's 10 June agreement served to deflate the SOC's provocations in the eastern provinces. Somewhat later, the group became an implementing mechanism for "Operation Paymaster," an UNTAC-proposed initiative to pay the salaries of soldiers, police, and civil servants who agreed to pledge support to the new government.[139]

By the end of UNTAC's mandate, in late September, the prospects for Cambodia's transition looked brighter than at any time since the signing of the Paris Accords. A new constitution (incorporating some modifications urged by UNTAC and human rights groups) was adopted overwhelmingly by the constituent assembly. Prince Sihanouk, as head of state, promulgated the constitutional monarchy and was elected king by a newly established Royal Council of the Throne. At the same time, a new "Royal Government of Cambodia" was proclaimed. Prince Ranariddh was appointed "first" prime minister and Hun Sen "second" prime minister.[140] FUNCINPEC and the SOC split up the ministries once again, codifying their (uneasy) relationship as coalition partners. The Khmer Rouge, meanwhile, were in retreat, politically isolated, weakened by widespread defections, and facing, for the first time, unified Cambodian armed forces.

When Akashi and Sanderson bid a final farewell to Phnom Penh on 26 September 1993, the key questions for Cambodia were how durable its new governing coalition would be and what role the international community would play in assisting its post-transition recovery.

ASSESSMENT

UNTAC accomplished a great deal in its 18 month lifespan. In the face of prodigious difficulties, it organized an electoral process that inspired great public enthusiasm, produced an internationally recognized government and helped to end Cambodia's years of crippling isolation. The operation brought home hundreds of thousands of refugees; helped to open up Cambodian society in unprecedented ways; and assisted in the unification of factional armies. In steering a shaky transition process forward, UNTAC aided a major realignment of domestic political power in the country, one in which Cambodia's royalist non-communist opposition party moved into coalition with the Hun Sen faction, leaving the Khmer Rouge out in the cold. UNTAC also helped to remove Cambodia from the ranks of international conflict. By codifying Vietnam's disengagement, it played a part in promoting reconciliation between Indochina and the ASEAN states.

These numerous achievements appear all the more remarkable in light of the difficulties that UNTAC encountered in fulfilling its mandate. The Paris Accords were built upon a foundation of post–Cold War international harmony that, alas, was not much in evidence inside Cambodia. The tasks given to UNTAC were breathtakingly ambitious in scope, and the UN and its member states did not lay adequate groundwork for key aspects of the operation. Even with better preparation and swifter deployment, however, some of the tasks were simply not feasible while others took insufficient account of the political dynamics of implementation.

It was technically within UNTAC's grasp to help end the civil war inside Cambodia, if the Khmer Rouge had fully implemented the Paris Accords' provisions for a cease-fire as well as for the cantonment, disarmament, and demobilization of troops. But the Khmer Rouge leadership balked, and UNTAC lacked the authority and the means to force them into compliance. One cannot rule out the theoretical possibility that the Khmer Rouge might have complied if UNTAC had been able to rein in the SOC's security apparatus, as called for by the Paris Accords. At the very least, such control would have denied the Khmer Rouge an attractive pretext for boycotting the process. Still, it strains credulity to imagine that the KR leadership, given its history and character, was really prepared to honor the Paris Accords if that meant accepting multiparty elections to decide who would govern Cambodia.

The most plausible reading of the Khmer Rouge's behavior is that their strategy, if they had one at all, was simply opportunistic: to go along with the peace process in the hope that the SOC would unravel once UNTAC arrived; or to exploit any opportunities to chisel away at the accords with selective violations.[141] But UNTAC was not scripted for muscular, Haitian-style intervention. Hun Sen was not Raoul Cedras, Haiti's erstwhile military dictator. In fact, UNTAC's presence tended to bolster the SOC. The operation's purchasing power revived a local economy that had been decimated by the drying up of Soviet assistance. In addition, foreign aid from Asian and Western sources was beginning to flow into the country. UNTAC's engineering units were repairing roads and bridges destroyed by years of war, stimulating commercial activity in the countryside.[142] UNTAC's technical advisors disseminated valuable know-how to Cambodia's bureaucrats even as the UN operation sought to control them. All these developments must have left the Khmer Rouge uneasy about their prospects in the peace process.

UNTAC's poor performance in civil administrative oversight was a major disappointment, given the centrality of that mission in the Paris Accords. Better preparation by the UN Secretariat, in concert with leading member states, to pull together human resources for this mission could have made a critical difference, for there appeared to be a window of opportunity early on, when the SOC was ready to accept outside bureaucratic intrusions. Yet, it is doubtful that any amount of civil administrative control could have moderated the SOC's behavior at the provincial levels. There were simply too many police, soldiers, and party hacks whose livelihoods were threatened by political pluralism; UNTAC could not restrain them all.

In hindsight, the operation could have acted more aggressively to deter political violence with its Special Prosecutor's Office and associated measures. But it is hard to say how much further UNTAC could have pushed human rights enforcement without triggering a crisis with (and within) the SOC that could have imperiled the election. It is very clear that UNTAC's decision to proceed with the elections, despite Cambodia's instability, was the right choice.

In performing its diverse tasks, UNTAC faced numerous handicaps. Some of these problems stemmed from the forbidding character of Cambodia itself: its inaccessibility, poor infrastructure, mine fields and malaria-infested jungles, and the difficulty of finding Khmer linguists. But other problems emerged as the result of unforeseen crosscurrents in the transition itself. UNTAC's rehabilitation program, for example, which might have bred greater stability early on, crept along at a snail's pace when certain donors decided to hold off on disbursements prior to the election lest the SOC reap political benefits. The injection of political pluralism into the country, though welcome in many respects, opened the door to an upsurge in violence that UNTAC was ill prepared to handle. And UNTAC's postelectoral powers were grounded in the Paris Accords, creating uncertainties about how to manage the "transition" from the transition.

While these factors impeded UNTAC's efforts, others greatly aided the operation. Cambodia's high degree of ethnic homogeneity was certainly a plus. UNTAC was spared the complications of trying to forge peace among different ethnic groups; the Vietnamese issue, while sensitive, was essentially a sideshow during UNTAC's stay. The operation also benefited from the Khmer Rouges' own limitations. Their geographical remoteness and military deficiencies made it possible to hold elections without the antecedent steps of cantonment, disarmament, and demobilization. Had they occupied downtown Phnom Penh, as Mohammed Farah Aideed's clan did in Mogadishu, the Khmer Rouge might well have stymied UNTAC completely. Finally, Prince (now King) Norodom Sihanouk was of inestimable value to the transition process. Paternalistic, erratic, and manipulative, Cambodia's "papa tres venere" gave UNTAC fits on occasion. He vilified the operation when it served his purposes. Yet he was a unifying force in the country, eliciting the allegiance of all the factions (and their militaries). Sihanouk's return to Cambodia on the eve of the election provided a critical last-minute boost; and his efforts to forge a FUNCINPEC-SOC coalition served stability and prevented massive bloodshed.

None of this should imply that UNTAC was simply a bystander in its own success. On the contrary, UNTAC's leadership (in tandem with top officials in the UN Secretariat) proved adept at moving the operation forward. Their preference for utilizing "soft" sanctions in responding to Khmer Rouge noncooperation, derided by some outside observers, was very much in sync with the constellation of interests represented on the Security Council and in Southeast Asia. The pressures created by the sanctions were strong enough to prod Thailand and China into urging restraint upon their erstwhile allies, but were not so strong as to prompt these countries to withdraw from the peace process in deference to the Khmer Rouge. In this regard, UNTAC knew its limits. Akashi and Sanderson understood that political pressure applied by external patrons would do far more to influence the behavior of various Khmer factions than ill-advised excursions by UNTAC into the realm of peace enforcement. They were also savvy about utilizing the Paris Accords' statutory bodies, the SNC and the Mixed Military Working Group, to forge some habits of cooperation among the parties that would most likely participate in Cambodia's future government.[143]

CONCLUSIONS

With United Nations field operations currently in retreat, future historians may well look back at UNTAC as the organization's high point in multidimensional peacekeeping. Its large size and diverse functions were not a product of organizational hubris but a reflection of a negotiated peace settlement that sought to deal with a conflict comprehensively, in its military, social, and political dimensions. Future peace settlements of equal complexity that attempt to translate agreements crafted by diplomats into a durable measure of conflict resolution will generate operations on UNTAC's scale, or greater. One need only look at the NATO-led peace implementation operation in Bosnia circa 1996 for confirmation.

UNTAC showed how dramatically a field operation's fate hinges upon the durability of its international backing. For UNTAC, the durable consensus forged in the Paris negotiations was an enormous asset. The accords were marred by numerous glitches and ambiguities, some of which came to light only during implementation, but their basic principles (halting the fighting and organizing elections to support a process of political transition) were clear and accepted by all the major powers. At times, it was difficult for UNTAC to reconcile its role as a partisan for the settlement with its need to remain impartial vis-à-vis the parties. Yet the durability of its international backing assured that it could count on unified outside support when crises arose. No Cambodian party could disown the process and count on the unwavering support of a patron.

Operationally, one can glean several important lessons from UNTAC's track record. One lesson, surely, is that promptness counts. UNTAC's slow-motion deployment deprived it of precious momentum early on; it never fully recovered. Another lesson is the importance of rapport-building at the grass-roots level. UNTAC's reputation was sullied by instances of misconduct on the part of some of its soldiers and civilians. The Khmer Rouge tried to exploit that problem, casting themselves as the people's protectors against UNTAC's "bad" elements. Some of their attacks on UNTAC personnel were justified by the Khmer Rouge on such grounds. In other respects, however, UNTAC did an excellent job in establishing its good intentions with the people. Its electoral work, information/education programs, and the refugee repatriation inspired great enthusiasm.

Still another lesson, and an essential one, is the importance of civil-military coordination for multicomponent operations. Except at very senior levels, UNTAC was poorly prepared to mount joint operations but was able to improvise reasonably well when deteriorating security conditions required it to do so. Other operations may not be so fortunate.

A final lesson, clearly evident in UNTAC's case, is the absolute importance for multicomponent operations to be followed by coherent packages of post-transition assistance. UNTAC's hefty size and price tag guaranteed not only that it would be a short-lived phenomenon but that its departure would be politically deflationary for

Cambodia. "You don't go from 22,000 personnel to effectively zero," as one diplomat observed, "without some negative impact."[144] Still, a long-run international presence beyond a certain level is risky. It can stifle self-reliance and incur resentments against UN-style "neocolonialism."

Sensitive to these concerns, the UN opted to establish a small liaison office to coordinate residual tasks arising from the Paris Accords, for example, reconstruction, reintegration of returning refugees, mine clearance, and human rights promotion, in the wake of UNTAC's departure.[145] Some larger states augmented their diplomatic presence. Unhappily, international attention since UNTAC's departure has been sporadic, at best, and resistance by some ASEAN states to internationally sanctioned human rights monitoring has tended to shelter the Cambodian government from pressure on its human rights record.[146]

Without safeguards in place, the goods that complex peacekeeping operations can deliver are bound to be perishable. Even at the time, many worried about the impermanence of UNTAC's numerous accomplishments; and subsequent events have served only to heighten that concern. By mid-1996, Cambodia was still struggling to avoid slipping back into old patterns of repression and violence. On the other hand, the Khmer Rouge threat had dwindled, and the country was far more open and economically stable than it had been prior to the Paris settlement. Nevertheless, Cambodia's fragile ruling coalition was racked by internal crises; corruption was rampant; and political violence presented a continuing threat to human rights advocates and critics of the government.[147] No longer the source of regional conflict in Southeast Asia, Cambodia still had not found peace with itself.

ANNEX I: FINANCING UN OPERATIONS
IN CAMBODIA 1991–1993

UNAMIC and UNTAC were funded by all UN member states according to the standard UN peacekeeping scale of assessments. Within UNTAC, the functions covered by these assessments included military (peacekeeping) operations as well as a variety of civilian activities: elections, human rights, civil police, civil administration supervision, public information, and UNTAC administration. Two additional civilian activities—repatriation and rehabilitation—were funded through voluntary contributions and are not included in the cost figures. Originally estimated to cost $1.9 billion, the actual expenditures of UNAMIC and UNTAC were some $350 million less than that (as table 5.A indicates).

Table 5.A
UNAMIC and UNTAC Expenditures (US dollars)
(1 November 1992 through 30 September 1993)

Categories	Amount
Military Activities	
Peacekeeping Units*	376,759,500
Military Observers*	64,162,900
Mine Clearing Programs	7,787,500
Assistance for Disarmament and	3,482,900
Military Subtotal	**452,192,800**
Civilian Activities	
International and Local Staff	183,705,000
Civilian Police	204,764,600
Election-Related Supplies and Equipment	17,832,100
United Nations Volunteers	16,199,000
Public Information Programs	6,210,300
Civilian Subtotal	**428,711,000**
Support Activities	
General Operations**	369,395,800
General Administration***	273,396,400
Support Subtotal	**642,792,200**
Grand Total	**1,523,696,000**

* Inclusive of UN budgeted travel.
**Inclusive of air, sea, and land transport costs (including purchase and maintenance of vehicles), communications, and support for peacekeeping units. Exclusive of military unit rations.
***Inclusive of supplies and services, office rental, equipment not provided by troop contingents, and training programs. Exclusive of civilian and military subsistence allowance.

SOURCE: United Nations General Assembly, *Report of the Secretary-General on the Financing of the United Nations,* A/48/701, 8 December 1993, Annex II.

NOTES

1. The author wishes to acknowledge the Abe Fellowship Program and its sponsoring institutions—the Social Science Research Council, the American Council of Learned Societies, and the Japan Foundation Center for Global Partnership—for financial support that assisted in the preparation of this chapter. He is also grateful to Maren Zerriffi for research assistance. The opinions expressed in this chapter are the author's own and should not be attributed to any organization.

2. At the official level, pronouncements were uniformly positive. See, for example, United Nations Security Council, *Statement by the President of the Security Council concerning the successful completion of the mandate of UNTAC,* S/26531, 5 October 1993. Among scholars and journalists, assessments of UNTAC's efforts are more varied. Among the more favorable treatments are William Shawcross, *Cambodia's New Deal* (Washington, D.C.: Carnegie Endowment for International Peace, 1994); Janet E. Heininger, *Peacekeeping in Transition: The United Nations in Cambodia* (New York: The Twentieth Century Fund, 1994); Michael W. Doyle, *UN Peacekeeping in Cambodia: UNTAC's Civil Mandate* (London: Lynne Rienner, 1995); and Trevor Findlay, *Cambodia: The Legacy and Lessons of UNTAC,* SIPRI Research Report No. 9 (Oxford: Oxford University Press, 1995). More mixed reviews come from Steven R. Ratner, *The New UN Peacekeeping: Building Peace in Lands of Conflict After the Cold War* (New York: St. Martin's Press, 1995) and Jarat Chopra, *United Nations Authority in Cambodia,* Occasional Paper No.15 (Providence, RI: Thomas J. Watson Institute for International Studies, 1994). A sharply negative perspective is presented by Sheri Prasso, "Cambodia: A $3 Billion Boondoggle," *The Bulletin of the Atomic Scientists* (March/April 1995): 36-40.

3. Estimates of fatalities vary widely. According to Ruth Leger Sivard, war-related deaths in Cambodia from 1970 to 1989 may have amounted to slightly in excess of 1.2 million people. For specific breakdowns, see Sivard, et al., *World Military and Social Expenditures, 1993* (Washington, D.C.: World Priorities, 1993), 21.

4. Portions of this section are drawn from James Schear, "Beyond Traditional Peacekeeping: The Case of Cambodia," in Donald C. F. Daniel and Bradd C. Hayes, eds., *Beyond Traditional Peacekeeping* (New York: St. Martin's Press, 1995), 248-66.

5. ASEAN members at the time included Brunei, Indonesia, Malaysia, the Philippines, Singapore, and Thailand. For useful background, see Shawcross, *Cambodia's New Deal,* 8-9.

6. Shawcross, *Cambodia's New Deal,* 10.

7. Frederick Z. Brown, *Cambodia and the Dilemmas of U.S. Policy,* Critical Issues Series 1991 2/3 (New York: Council on Foreign Relations Press, 1991), 14-16.

8. These included the ASEAN and the other Indochina states (Vietnam and Laos), plus Australia, Canada, Japan, India, and Zimbabwe.

9. Senate of Australia, *Prospects for a Cambodian Peace Settlement,* statement by Senator Gareth Evans, Minister of Foreign Affairs and Trade, Australia, 6 December 1990.

10. For the text of the *Agreement on a Comprehensive Political Settlement of the Cambodia Conflict,* see Security Council, *Letter dated 30 October 1991 from the Permanent Representatives of France and Indonesia to the United Nations addressed to the Secretary-General,* S/23177, 30 October 1991, Annex.

11. Ratner, *The New UN Peacekeeping,* 144.

12. Evans, in February 1990, produced an exhaustive analysis of how a UN-supervised transition process might be created and implemented. This exploratory work on an international control mechanism later become the blueprint for UNTAC. See Australian Department of Foreign Affairs and Trade, *Informal Meeting on Cambodia: Issues for Negotiation in a Comprehensive Settlement,* Working Papers for the Jakarta meeting, 26-28 February 1990 (Canberra: 1990).

13. General Assembly, *Letter Dated 11 September 1990 from France and Indonesia, as Co-chairmen of the Paris Conference on Cambodia,* A/45/490, 17 September 1990.

14. This point is well developed by Ratner, *The New UN Peacekeeping,* and by Julio A. Jeldres, "The UN and the Cambodian Transition," *Journal of Democracy* 4, no. 4 (October 1993): 107.

15. Ibid., 15.

16. For a revealing perspective on dynamics within the Khmer Rouge leadership, see the letter from Akashi to Secretary-General Boutros-Ghali, 27 July 1992, in United Nations, *The United Nations and Cambodia, 1991-1995* (New York: UN Department of Public Information, 1995), 206-7.

17. For a representative sample, see Ben Kiernan, "The Failures of the Paris Agreement on Cambodia, 1991-93," in Dick Clark and William Nell, eds., *The Challenge of Indochina: An Examination of the U.S. Role,* Congressional Staff Conference, 30 April– 2 May, 1993 (Queenstown, MD: The Aspen Institute, 1993), 7.

18. One of the more contentious provisions in the Paris Accords was contained in Annex 5, Para. 2, which barred the retrospective application of criminal law under Cambodia's new constitution. In fact, this provision, which also benefited the Hun Sen faction (given that the SOC's leaders were, for the most part, former Khmer Rouge), did not give the Khmer Rouge protection against prosecution for violations of international humanitarian law.

19. Shawcross, *Cambodia's New Deal,* 11.

20. The administration, after some delay, did agree to the dispatch of 40 or so American officers to serve as UN military observers (UNMOs). One of their lesser-known jobs was to search for any indications of US missing-in-action from the Vietnam war.

21. Security Council Resolution 718, 31 October 1991, and Resolution 745, 28 February 1992.

22. United Nations, *The United Nations and Cambodia, 1991-1995,* 10-11. UNAMIC's enabling resolution was Security Council Resolution 717, 16 October 1991.

23. Security Council, S/23177, 11.

24. Under the Paris Accords, UNTAC was bound to comply with the SNC's "advice," provided there was a consensus among SNC members and provided the advice was

consistent with the objectives of the agreement. If the SNC could not reach a consensus, Prince Sihanouk could make the decision on what advice to offer, taking into account the views expressed in the SNC. If, however, Prince Sihanouk could not reach a decision, the authority to make decisions would pass to the UN's special representative. In all cases, the authority to determine whether advice was consistent with the accords would be held by the special representative. Ibid., 21-22.

25. These actions were taken with almost total unanimity among the permanent Council members. On one occasion, China abstained on a vote to impose a deadline for Khmer Rouge participation in the elections, but otherwise Beijing was part of the consensus and took steps to gradually distance itself from the Khmer Rouge. Yasushi Akashi, *UNTAC in Cambodia: Lessons For U.N. Peacekeeping,* The Charles Rostov Annual Lecture on Asian Affairs (Washington, D.C.: Johns Hopkins University, Paul H. Nitze School of Advanced International Studies, 14 October 1993).

26. Security Council Resolution 766, 21 July 1992.

27. Security Council Resolution 792, 30 November 1992. "Round logs" referred to unprocessed teak and other exotic timber exports, made through Thai military entrepreneurs, revenues from which were used to sustain Khmer Rouge operations. To greater or lesser degrees, however, all of the Cambodian factions engaged in such timber exports to generate revenues.

28. Security Council Resolution 810, 8 March 1993.

29. Author's interviews, UNTAC headquarters, Phnom Penh, 11 June 1992. UNTAC's deputy force commander, Brigadier General Jean-Michel Loridon of France, professed a willingness to risk several hundred casualties in a gambit to challenge the Khmer Rouge for control of their territories. Loridon's criticisms of UNTAC's unwillingness to confront the Khmer Rouge with force created some media waves but his prescriptions were not popular with other troop contributors, nor (apparently) with Paris, and he was soon replaced. Loridon's skeptics wondered how 16,000 UN troops could do what nearly 200,000 Vietnamese were unable to do, namely dislodge the Khmer Rouge from their sanctuaries.

30. Security Council, *Report of the Secretary-General on Cambodia,* S/23613, 19 February 1992.

31. Ibid., 9-12.

32. Author's interviews, UNTAC headquarters, Phnom Penh, 11 June 1992.

33. UNTAC Spokesman's Office, briefing memo on civil administration, Phnom Penh, 7 May 1993 (mimeograph).

34. Security Council, S/23177, 11.

35. In general, UNTAC had oversight authority with respect to any public administrative entity whose actions or omissions could influence the conduct of the forthcoming electoral campaign or the conduct or outcome of the elections themselves. In practice, this could have been any entity with assets—physical or financial—that could be used to support a favored political party and/or oppose others. Supervision and control could also be undertaken with the aim of preventing or correcting for bureaucratic actions impeding UNTAC's operations.

36. The UN Volunteer (UNV) Program, headquartered in Geneva, was established by the General Assembly in 1970 to support local and community-based development projects financed by the United Nations Development Program (UNDP) or other UN agencies. Much like the US Peace Corps personnel, UN volunteers live and work in local settings providing skills and technical training for humanitarian and developmental-related activities. The UNV program reports to the governing council of the UNDP and works through UNDP field offices around the world.

37. *United Nations Transitional Authority in Cambodia,* DPI/1352 (New York: UN Department of Public Information, March 1993), 12.

38. Heininger, *Peacekeeping in Transition,* 110.

39. At an early stage, Special Representative Akashi and his deputy, Behrooz Sadry, had to resort to rotating back and forth between North America and Cambodia so that one would always be at UN headquarters in New York to "backstop" the operation and break administrative logjams.

40. Chopra, *United Nations Authority in Cambodia,* 29.

41. The self-sufficiency requirement is spelled out in S/23613, 15. For enumeration of the deficiencies, see United States General Accounting Office (GAO), *UN Peacekeeping: Lessons Learned in Managing Recent Missions,* GAO/NSIAD-94-9 (Washington, D.C.: GAO, December 1993), 39.

42. GAO, *Lessons Learned,* 37, 41.

43. Ibid, 34, 41.

44. Lieutenant General John M. Sanderson, "UNTAC: Successes and Failures," a paper presented at an international conference on *The United Nations Transitional Authority in Cambodia: Debriefing and Lessons,* cosponsored by the Institute of Policy Studies of Singapore and the United Nations Institute for Training and Research (UNITAR), 2-4 August 1994, released in a compendium of conference papers (Geneva: UNITAR, December 1994), 80. (Cited with permission.)

45. Sanderson states that UNAMIC was ill prepared for its task, but created a "false sense of security" in the UN bureaucracy that the gap between the Paris Accords and its implementation could be managed. Ibid., 81.

46. With the rainy season approaching and a lull in military operations already apparent, UNTAC's military command felt that partial cantonment was worth the risk. Cantonment would make the military environment more transparent; cease-fire violations would decline; and operational effectiveness would be curtailed. It was also known that a number of local commanders and their soldiers, including several in the Khmer Rouge, favored cantonment. Author's interviews, UNTAC headquarters, Phnom Penh, 11 June 1992.

47. Author's interviews in Phnom Penh, 9 June 1992.

48. Security Council, *Special Report of the Secretary-General on UNTAC and Phase II of the Cease-fire,* S/24090, 12 June 1992, 1.

49. Author's interviews, UNTAC headquarters, Phnom Penh, 11 June 1992.

50. GAO reported complaints among Cambodian military commanders about lack of UN presence at cantonment sites, which raised concerns about protection. See GAO, *Lessons Learned,* 42.

51. United Nations, *The United Nations in Cambodia, 1991-1995*, 19.

52. Michael Maley, "Reflections on the Electoral Process in Cambodia," in Hugh Smith, ed., *Peacekeeping: Challenges for the Future* (Canberra: Australian Defence Force Academy, 1993), 89. See also UNTAC, *Report on UNTAC's Activities: The First Six Months, 15 March–15 September 1992* (Phnom Penh, October 1992, mimeograph), 12.

53. Reginald Austin, "Election-Monitoring: Preparation and Conduct," in Nassrine Azimi, ed., *The United Nations Transitional Authority in Cambodia: Debriefing and Lessons* (London: Kluwer Law International, 1995), 182.

54. Ratner points out a mismatch between talent and availability in the area of recruitment. Recruitment efforts within the system could generate personnel at the required grade levels but not always with the needed expertise. On the other hand, efforts to recruit outside the UN system produced applicants with relevant experience but lacking knowledge of the UN system. See Ratner, *The New UN Peacekeeping*, 167.

55. Lieutenant General John M. Sanderson, "UNTAC: The Military Component View," in Nassrine Azimi, ed., *The United Nations Transitional Authority in Cambodia* (London: Kluwer Law International, 1995), 129.

56. As UN military observers were progressively fielded, it became increasingly clear to UNTAC that the SOC's military element, the Cambodian People's Armed Forces (CPAF), was responsible for a large number of cease-fire violations that occurred during this initial phase. Once the Khmer Rouge did not comply with the final deadline set by the Security Council at the end of the January 1993, CPAF launched military operations in western Battambang, pushing toward Pailin, the only provincial town of any size held by the Khmer Rouge anywhere in the country.

57. These indicators were drawn from numerous contacts with local Khmer Rouge units, from debriefs of a number of so-called "self-demobilizers," and from a discernible movement of Khmer Rouge soldiers and their families from the mountainous sections of northern and northwestern Cambodia into more fertile sections in the southeast. (Author's interviews, UNTAC headquarters, Phnom Penh, 11 February 1993.) The most authoritative public analysis of this issue is found in Steve Heder, "The Resumption of Armed Struggle by the Party of Democratic Kampuchea: Evidence from . . . 'Self-Demobilizers,'" in Steve Heder and Judy Ledgerwood, eds., *Propaganda, Politics, and Violence in Cambodia* (London: M.E. Sharpe, 1996), 73-113.

58. Security Council, *First Progress Report of the Secretary-General on the United Nations Transitional Authority in Cambodia*, S/23870, 1 May 1992, 2.

59. Security Council, *Special Report of the Secretary-General on UNTAC and Phase II of the Cease-fire*, S/24090, 12 June 1992, 3. According to members of the UNTAC party, while blocking Akashi and Sanderson, Khmer Rouge sentries allowed a Thai vehicle to pass through the checkpoint.

60. Reported in the statement of Special Representative Yasushi Akashi to the Supreme National Council, 10 June 1992 (Phnom Penh: UNTAC, mimeograph).

61. Amplifications on these positions were given by the Khmer Rouge's president and Supreme National Council representative, Khieu Samphan, at SNC meetings in June

and August 1992. Statements of H.E. Mr. Khieu Samphan to the Supreme National Council, 10 June and 24 August 1992. (Phnom Penh: UNTAC, mimeographs).

62. Khieu Samphan, statement to the SNC, 10 June 1992.

63. See texts of Khmer Rouge proposals of 27 June and 12 July 1992, in United Nations, *The United Nations and Cambodia, 1991-1995,* 198-201.

64. As early as September 1992, UNTAC stated that "there is little serious doubt that the repeated written assurances by Viet Nam that its forces left Cambodia in 1989 are true." (UNTAC, *Report on UNTAC's Activities: The First Six Months,* 16.) At the same time, UNTAC was also well aware of a fact conveniently overlooked by the Khmer Rouge, namely that Thai army units were present in KR-controlled zones. Ibid., 17.

65. In a statement to the SNC, Khieu Samphan stated that the Paris Accords dealt with the withdrawal of foreign "forces," not merely "troops," because the framers of the accords had intended to address the political as well as the military aspects of the Vietnamese occupation. (Khieu Samphan, Statement to the SNC, 10 June 1992.) For revealing analysis on how this issue was blurred in the Paris Accords, see Steve Heder and Judy Ledgerwood, "Politics of Violence: An Introduction," in Heder and Ledgerwood, eds., *Propaganda, Politics, and Violence in Cambodia* (London: M.E. Sharpe, 1996), 11.

66. At the SNC's meeting of 20 October 1992, Akashi proposed that foreign forces be defined as "any foreign regular, paramilitary and auxiliary forces, advisers and military personnel who remained in Cambodia upon entry into force of the agreement or entered Cambodia thereafter." (UNTAC press release, Phnom Penh, 20 October 1992, mimeograph.) This definition opened the door to treating demobilized Vietnamese soldiers or CPAF advisers (including retirees and deserters) resident in Cambodia and no longer under Hanoi's command, as "foreign forces" within the meaning of the Paris Accords. Eventually, three or four such people were identified, although Vietnam declined to have them repatriated. See Security Council, *Fourth Progress Report of the Secretary-General on UNTAC, S/25719,* 3 May 1993, 11.

67. Ibid., 11-12.

68. With the soldiers came roughly 52,900 weapons, 19 aircraft, 26 tanks and 25 armored personnel carriers. Press conference by Force Commander John Sanderson, UNTAC headquarters, 13 November 1992.

69. Akashi, statement to the SNC, 10 June 1992.

70. For enumeration of the various offices and their functions, see Security Council, *Third Progress Report of the Secretary-General on UNTAC, S/25154,* 25 January 1993, 12-16.

71. See Security Council, *Second Progress Report of the Secretary-General on UNTAC, S/24578,* 21 September 1992, 6-7.

72. See Ratner, *The New UN Peacekeeping,* 149, for useful background on early concepts for UN involvement in civil administrative affairs. For delays in developing procedures, see Findlay, *Cambodia: The Legacy and Lessons of UNTAC,* 61.

73. See "Report and Recommendations," in Nassrine Azimi, ed., *The United Nations Transitional Authority in Cambodia: Debriefing and Lessons* (London, Kluwer Law International, 1995), 21. (No author.)

74. Ratner, *The New UN Peacekeeping*, 173.

75. UNTAC succeeded in getting the Cambodian People's Party (CPP) dropped from the SOC's regular budget but extra-budgetary flows of revenue into CPP coffers, as well as to certain other political parties, almost certainly continued without UN detection. In the provinces, UNTAC observed a common pattern of transfers of tangible assets (cars, buildings, and so forth) from the SOC to the CPP in the period preceding the electoral campaign. UNTAC's approach was to expose such practices while attempting to thwart the most blatant cases. Author's interviews, UNTAC headquarters, Phnom Penh, 2 February 1993.

76. According to Ratner, Soviet participants at the Paris negotiations later acknowledged that they had agreed to the provisions on civil administrative control because of the ease with which the SOC could resist it. See Ratner, *The New UN Peacekeeping*, 175.

77. See Roger C. Lawrence, "Economics/Rehabilitation," in Nassrine Azimi, ed., *The United Nations Transitional Authority in Cambodia: Debriefing and Lessons* (London: Kluwer Law International, 1995), 159-60. Cambodia is certainly not the only country to print money as a way of trying to bail itself out of a public sector deficit, but the process had some interesting twists in Phnom Penh. Typically, UNTAC would observe a transport aircraft flying in with a cargo of freshly minted Cambodian riel notes, presumably from a point of origin in the former Soviet Union. Soon thereafter, wage payments would be made, inflation would jump and the value of the riel would swing wildly. By late 1992, UNTAC brought money creation under control.

78. The effectiveness of such measures varied widely from province to province. Author's interviews, UNTAC headquarters and Takeo province, 9-10 February 1993.

79. The worst of the violence occurred between March and mid-May 1993. During this period, UNTAC confirmed 200 deaths, 338 injuries, and 114 abductions. The SOC was suspected of complicity in 15 deaths and 9 injuries, while the Khmer Rouge were thought to be responsible for 131 deaths, 250 injuries, and 53 abductions. Press statement by Director Dennis MacNamara, UNTAC Human Rights Component, UNTAC Headquarters, 23 May 1993.

80. Philip Shenon, "Cambodian Factions Use Terror Tactics in Crucial Election, *The New York Times*, 10 May 1993, A1.

81. For details, see the Security Council, *Fourth Progress Report of the Secretary-General on the United Nations Transitional Authority in Cambodia*, S/25719, 3 May 1993, 13-14.

82. For a public account, see Mary Kay Magistad, "Cambodian Rulers Cited in Anti-Voting Violence," *The Washington Post*, 10 June 1993, A29.

83. Unfortunately for UNTAC, it turned out that the offending governor in Battambang was a relative of Chea Sim, president of the CPP. SOC Prime Minister Hun Sen told Akashi that if he were intent upon sacking Ung Sami, he (Akashi) might as well sack Hun Sen first. See David Ashley, "The Nature and Causes of Human Rights Violations in Battambang Province," in Steve Heder and Judy Ledgerwood, *Propaganda, Politics, and Violence in Cambodia* (London: M.E. Sharpe, 1996), 172.

84. At one stage, after UNTAC had launched its surprise inspections program, an angry Hun Sen summoned Akashi and senior UNTAC officials to meet with a group of

provincial governors visiting Phnom Penh to protest UNTAC's "Pol Pot tactics." Whatever impact Hun Sen may have sought from the meeting, however, was blunted when almost all of the governors used their allotted time to extol the virtues of UNTAC's work in their provinces. Author's interviews, UNTAC headquarters, Phnom Penh, 20 April 1993.

85. UNTAC's provincial "civadmin" directors were also keenly aware that they needed the cooperation of local SOC officials to sustain the UN's diverse array of electoral, administrative, civil police, refugee, human rights and related offices in the provinces. Having to deal with local officials daily, UNTAC administrators at times found it difficult to strike the proper balance between a cordial working relationship and the assertive "in your face" attitude that the supervision and control mission required. This conflicted posture sometimes strained relations between UNTAC's provincial civadmin directors and the operation's other civilian field elements. Some UN field staff complained, rather sardonically, that UNTAC's provincial civadmin directors, having failed to control SOC governors adequately, were trying to control UNTAC instead, with no greater success. Author's interviews, Takeo and Kampot provinces, Cambodia, 22-23 August 1992.

86. Sanderson, "UNTAC: Successes and Failures," 82.

87. For discussion of diplomatic steps vis-à-vis the Khmer Rouge, see Security Council, *Second Special Report of the Secretary-General on UNTAC,* S/24286, 14 July 1992, and Security Council, *Report of the Secretary-General on the Implementation of Security Council Resolution 783 (1992),* S/24800, 15 November 1992.

88. Report by UNTAC's Economic Advisor, *Impact of UNTAC on Cambodia's Economy,* UNTAC headquarters, December 1992 (mimeograph).

89. The starkest example of this problem was the murder of a Japanese electoral worker, Atsuhito Nakata, and his Cambodian interpreter, most likely by a disappointed job-seeker in the Kampong Thom province on 8 April 1993. UNTAC personnel received threats from local police and CPAF personnel because members of the armed forces and police were ineligible for the elections jobs. "Civpol Completes Investigation on Kampong Thom Murders," *Free Choice: Electoral Component Newsletter,* no. 18 (30 April 1993): 27.

90. To no small degree, these issues were hyped by Prince Sihanouk himself, in an effort to maneuver the factions (and UNTAC) into acceptance of a presidential election, for himself, as an alternative to a faltering transition process. For example, in one of many highly publicized interviews, the Prince thundered, "I have had enough. UNTAC is a terrible cocktail of races who do not even understand each other, who cannot even agree with each other. There is jealously within UNTAC. There is anarchy. There are people in UNTAC who behave very badly. . . ." Nayan Chanda and Nate Thayer, "I Want to Retake Power," *Far Eastern Economic Review,* 4 February 1993, 21.

91. Michael W. Doyle and Nishkala Suntharalingam have introduced the important distinction between missions requiring active versus passive cooperation. See their article, "The UN in Cambodia: Lessons for Complex Peacekeeping," *International Peacekeeping* 1, no. 2 (summer 1994): 117-47.

92. Maley, "Reflections on the Electoral Process," 92-94.

93. The most significant amendment refined the term "Cambodian," used in the Paris Accords, in a manner that required a potential voter to show a firmer connection to the country. The Paris Accords had provided that persons must be 18 years old and either born in Cambodia or the child of a person born in Cambodia, in order to be eligible to vote. The electoral law, as amended, defined "Cambodian persons" as an individual born in Cambodia, with at least one parent born in Cambodia. Eligible voters could be a "Cambodian person" of sufficient age *or* a person born elsewhere with at least one parent who met the definition of a Cambodian person. (See Security Council, S/24578, 2.) In effect, a potential voter born in the country would have to show at least one generation tie to Cambodia, and a person born anywhere else would have to show a two generation connection, within the same blood line. UNTAC also accepted an amendment to allow overseas polling, provided that voters first came to Cambodia to register. At the same time, Akashi rejected demands to extend the franchise to the so-called "Khmer Krom" populations (ethnic Cambodians living in Vietnam), despite the awkward fact that one of the faction leaders, Son Sann (KFNLF), was such a person and not technically eligible to vote. Later on, the electoral law was amended to extend the franchise to any Cambodian person, "wherever born, who is a member of the Supreme National Council." UNTAC, *United Nations Electoral Legislation for Cambodia, Amendment Law (No. 2),* UNTAC headquarters, January 1993 (mimeograph).

94. Akashi, "UNTAC in Cambodia," 13.

95. Security Council, *Third Progress Report of the Secretary-General on UNTAC,* S/25124, 25 January 1993, 7.

96. For example, with over 300,000 refugees returned by February 1993, there had only been three mine casualties, and these were farmers who had ignored UN warnings about mines in areas where they wanted to settle. UNTAC attributed this low casualty rate to UN-sponsored mine awareness training undertaken in the camps. As for actually clearing mines, the story was less favorable. UNTAC trained some 2,300 Cambodians in mine clearance. It helped to establish the Cambodian Mine Action Center (CMAC), a nonprofit Cambodian institution to conduct programs in mine related activities. Overall, some four million square meters of land were cleared of about 37,000 mines and unexploded ordnance during UNTAC's stay. But this was only a dent in the problem and factions continued to lay mines sporadically. Press release, *U.N. Department of Public Information,* 31 October 1993.

97. Dennis McNamara, "UN Human Rights Activities in Cambodia: An Evaluation," in Alice H. Henkin, ed., *Honoring Human Rights and Keeping the Peace: Lessons from El Salvador, Cambodia and Haiti* (Queenstown, MD: The Aspen Institute, 1995), 75-76. See also Shawcross, *Cambodia's New Deal,* 15.

98. John M. Sanderson, "Preparation for Deployment and Conduct of Peacekeeping Operations: A Cambodia Snapshot," in Kevin Clements and Christine Wilson, eds., *UN Peacekeeping at the Crossroads* (Canberra: Australian National University, 1994), 109-10.

99. See Security Council, S/24800, 15 November 1992. The Council's approval of the recommendation is recorded in Resolution 792 (1992), 30 November 1992. Originally, UNTAC had been due to shrink from 12 to 6 infantry battalions after the cantonment and demobilization tasks had been completed. Security Council, S/23613, 19 February 1992, Annex 2.

100. It did so by authorizing UNTAC to proceed with preparations for elections to be held in the April/May time frame within areas of the country to which UNTAC had access by 31 January 1993. See Security Council, Resolution 792, Operative Para. 5.

101. UNTAC's Military Component issued Operation Order No. 2 on 9 December 1992, and the redeployment was largely completed before the year's end. A public discussion of its basic purposes is found in "Interview: Lt. Gen. John Sanderson," *Free Choice: Electoral Component Newsletter* no. 11 (15 January 1993): 12-14.

102. Ibid., 12.

103. Arguably, UNTAC's greatest electoral-related vulnerability was at its headquarters in Phnom Penh, the site of its computerized voter and party registration lists and its supply depots. For this reason, UNTAC's security measures at its electoral component offices were among the most extensive undertaken anywhere in the country.

104. See Reginald Austin's discussion, "Election-Monitoring: Preparation and Conduct," 183. While critics of UNTAC berated its unwillingness to march its peacekeeping forces into Khmer Rouge territory without permission, the fact is that UN civilians were doing just that without much fanfare.

105. Author's interviews, UNTAC headquarters, Phnom Penh, 20 April 1993.

106. Lack of fluency in English or French in some military units created serious problems. At critical moments, additional interpreters had to be brought in from overseas. Also, civilian workers in some areas complained that military units were too passive, unwilling even to defend UNTAC storage areas against attack.

107. Reginald Austin, "Election-Monitoring: Preparation and Conduct," 184.

108. Even in Siem Reap and Kompong Thom, two of Cambodia's most unstable provinces, UNTAC still felt it could service the majority of the people who lived close to the main road, Highway 6. "Interview: Chief Electoral Officer Reginald Austin," *Free Choice: Electoral Component Newsletter* no. 18 (30 April 1993): 13. Planners anticipated that in the worst case perhaps 6 or 7 percent of the population might be affected by the curtailment of polling stations. Author's interviews, UNTAC headquarters, Phnom Penh, 22 April 1993.

109. United Nations, *The United Nations and Cambodia,* 42. UNTAC was criticized by some foreign diplomats and private observers for not taking more energetic steps to protect fleeing Vietnamese. UNTAC leaders felt caught in a no-win situation: not to protect the Vietnamese would be criticized on moral and humanitarian grounds; to protect them, on the other hand, would give the Khmer Rouge a major propaganda coup and a tool for undermining the elections. Neither the Khmer factions nor Cambodia's new human rights groups saw fit to condemn anti-Vietnamese violence, and UNTAC was fearful of being portrayed as pro-Vietnamese. In the end, UNTAC dispatched armed marine UNMOs to patrol the rivers in order to deter extortion of the Vietnamese by

bandits and soldiers, and it quietly ordered UNTAC personnel to return hostile fire directed at the Vietnamese if the targets could be identified. (Author's interviews, UNTAC headquarters, Phnom Penh, 20 April 1993.)

110. Mary Kay Magistad, "U.N. Workers in Cambodia Give Ultimatum," *Washington Post,* 16 April 1993, 1. For a useful narrative of the problem, see Findlay, *Cambodia: The Legacy and Lessons of UNTAC,* 78-79.

111. Author's notes from remarks by Lieutenant General John Sanderson to UN volunteers, Phnom Penh, 20 April 1993.

112. UNTAC, for example, managed to free-up campaign materials and a television transmitter seized by the SOC's customs agents, after Akashi took the matter up with Hun Sen. "On the Campaign Trail: Election Countdown," *Free Choice: Electoral Component Newsletter* no. 18 (30 April 1993): 8. On the whole, however, the problems were so numerous that UNTAC had to pick and choose which ones to press.

113. Security Council, S/25124, 22. The directive establishing procedures for the prosecution of human rights violations is reprinted in McNamara, "UN Human Rights Activities in Cambodia," 80-83.

114. UNTAC Spokesman's Office, daily press briefing, UNTAC headquarters, Phnom Penh, 17 March 1993 (mimeograph).

115. Starting in April 1993, approximately 14 random checkpoints were set up daily, and an average of 15 weapons were confiscated per day, including AK-47s, rocket launchers, pistols, and assorted ammunition. These measures coincided with a decline in reported crime in Phnom Penh. Security Council, S/25719, 3 May 1993, 19. The assertion of a direct cause and effect relationship remained unproven, however.

116. Heininger, *Peacekeeping in Transition,* 99. Although a number of arrest warrants were issued (for both SOC and Khmer Rouge suspects), only three arrests were actually made. Moreover, UNTAC could not find a Cambodian judge who was willing to try the cases in accordance with accepted international standards, and it could not rely on SOC jails to reliably detain suspects. The latter issue was resolved when UNTAC established its own facility; the former issue was never resolved. Findlay, *Cambodia: The Lessons and Legacy of UNTAC,* 66-67.

117. McNamara, "UN Human Rights Activities in Cambodia," 67. McNamara, director of UNTAC's human rights component, argues that UNTAC's prosecutorial effort could have been more effective as a deterrent to political violence had it been used more extensively.

118. UNTAC's electoral component told surprised SOC officials that it would honor the request of any party to delay the release of lists of its candidates and registered party members. If the SOC wanted to avail itself of that protection, it was free to do so. Author's interviews, UNTAC headquarters, Phnom Penh, 21 April 1993. Reportedly, four parties requested such treatment. Security Council, S/25719, 7.

119. "Confiscation of Registration Cards Will Not Deter Secret Balloting," *Free Choice: Electoral Component Newsletter* no. 14 (26 February 1993): 7.

120. This procedure, in essence, involved placing a marked ballot in a special envelope containing data about the voter that could be verified by a subsequent check of registration records back at UNTAC headquarters. Safeguards were in place to protect the voter's identity. Ibid., 7. During the polling, roughly 244,000 valid tendered ballots were cast. United Nations, *The United Nations in Cambodia: A Vote for Peace* (New York: United Nations, 1994), 92.

121. "Interview: Timothy Carney," *Free Choice: Electoral Component Newsletter* no. 16 (26 March 1993): 14. Carney directed UNTAC's Information/Education Division.

122. Reginald Austin argues that using ad hoc campaign interventions rather than clearly spelled out civil administrative authority (for example, circumventing Prince Chakrapong with free airlifts to FUNCINPEC rather than firing him) in order to level the political playing field simply fueled the SOC's paranoia and exposed UNTAC to charges of bias. See Austin, "Election-Monitoring: Preparation and Conduct," 187.

123. Akashi, "UNTAC in Cambodia," 10.

124. According to Timothy Carney, the secretary-general initially thought that UN broadcasts over the factions' transmitters and from neighboring countries would suffice. Timothy Carney, "UNTAC's Information/Education Programme," in Nassrine Azimi, ed., *The United Nations Transitional Authority in Cambodia: Debriefing and Lessons* (London: Kluwer Law International, 1995), 173. UNTAC's difficulties in getting its programs aired by the SOC, and the mis- or disinformation about UNTAC aired by SOC and Khmer Rouge radio stations may have been factors in his change of mind. In the meantime, with delays in procurement consuming precious time, Carney spent thousands of dollars of his own money in Bangkok for the purchase of studio production equipment.

125. "Interview: Timothy Carney," *Free Choice,* 13.

126. Based on defector reports and other indications, Sanderson argues that Radio UNTAC was instrumental in bringing many rank and file Khmer Rouge members into the political mainstream and in convincing others not to interfere with the elections. See Sanderson, "UNTAC: Successes and Failures," 83.

127. "Interview: Timothy Carney," *Free Choice,* 14.

128. In the face of constant mutterings, UNTAC's information/education staff members mounted an eye-catching English-language poster with the slogan "your vote is secret" splashed across it, next to the entrance at UNTAC headquarters where senior staff arrived every day. The complaints soon subsided.

129. UNTAC's Spokesman, daily press briefing, UNTAC headquarters, Phnom Penh, 20 May 1993.

130. In April 1993, without much fanfare, Sanderson negotiated an agreement with the parties' military chiefs in UNTAC's Mixed Military Working Group on security arrangements for elections. He regarded the effort as a catalyst for the unification of the armed forces following the election. See Sanderson, "UNTAC: Successes and Failures," 90.

131. Security Council, *Report of the Secretary-General in pursuance of paragraph 6 of Security Council Resolution 810 (1993) on preparations for the election for the constituent assembly in Cambodia,* S/25784, 15 May 1993, 5.

132. Security Council Resolution 826 (1993), 20 May 1993.

133. The Khmer Rouge in fact seemed uncertain of their own stance. Some defectors reported that they had received orders to disrupt the elections; other stated that those orders had been canceled. Some Khmer Rouge units did mount a few sporadic attacks, in Kampot and Kompong Cham, without much effect. In a few areas they prevented people from going to the polls. UNTAC commanders were told that the KR leadership had passed down orders to vote for FUNCINPEC just prior to the election. See Shawcross, *Cambodia's New Deal*, 22. See also, Security Council, *Report of the Secretary-General on the conduct and results of the election in Cambodia*, S/25913, 10 June 1993, 1-2.

134. Security Council, S/25913, 10 June 1993, Annex II. Akashi's willingness to investigate the SOC's allegations triggered strenuous objections among his electoral aides, but he saw it as a useful maneuver to head off the SOC's complete rejection of the electoral result. Akashi, "UNTAC in Cambodia," 6.

135. United Nations, *The United Nations in Cambodia: A Vote for Peace*, 92.

136. Shawcross argues, persuasively, that the secessionist bid was little more than a ploy to blackmail FUNCINPEC into power-sharing. Chakrapong fled to Vietnam but later returned to Phnom Penh and went unpunished for his misdeeds. See *Cambodia's New Deal*, 27.

137. For example, during the electoral campaign, two of the SOC's more vociferous anti-UNTAC officials, Prince Chakrapong and Khim Bo, the governor of Sihanoukville, had each been fined $5000 by UNTAC for repeated violations of the electoral law. At about 4:30 P.M. on the second day of the polling, two members of Chakrapong's staff suddenly showed up at UNTAC's finance office to deliver a large bag and a suitcase containing 15 million riels, the local cash equivalent of the fine, in 500 riel denominations. Ten minutes earlier, Khim Bo had appeared in person at UNTAC's office in Sihanoukville, carrying his fine in bags containing 500, 200, and 100 riel notes. UNTAC's press spokesman reported that proper receipts were issued. UNTAC daily press briefing, Phnom Penh, 25 May 1993.

138. Cambodian Armed Forces, Chiefs of the General Staff, communique, 10 June 1993, issued by UNTAC's press spokesman, Phnom Penh (mimeograph). In an unusual vote of confidence, Sihanouk asked Gen. Sanderson to serve as the new supreme commander of Cambodia's armed forces. Sanderson declined, politely, and Sihanouk assumed the role. (Shawcross, *Cambodia's New Deal*, 28.)

139. See Security Council, *Letter Dated 14 July 1993 from the Secretary-General to the President of the Security Council*, S/26095, 16 July 1993, contained in United Nations, *The United Nations and Cambodia, 1991-1995*, 325.

140. For details, Security Council, *Further Report of the Secretary-General on the implementation of Security Council resolution 745 (1992)* [by which UNTAC was established], S/26529, 5 October 1993.

141. Supporting this contention was a February 1992 internal Khmer Rouge memorandum that came into UNTAC's possession and is regarded as authentic. It states, *inter alia:* "the contents of the Paris agreement are to our advantage . . . if the Agreements

are incorrectly implemented we are dead (disarmed), but if they are correctly implemented then we will win." The passage is cited in Doyle and Suntharalingam, "The UN in Cambodia," 146.

142. UNTAC's infrastructure repair may have had a significant impact on Khmer Rouge attitudes. According to some analysts, a longstanding trademark of the Khmer Rouge approach to insurgency was to destroy road access after taking over a piece of territory, to ensure that local communities would remain isolated from the outside world. Author's interviews, Phnom Penh, 9 February 1993.

143. Skeptical that the Cambodian factions could work together, the architects of the Paris Accords had not intended the Supreme National Council to be an activist body. It was created mainly as a device to invite the UN into Cambodia. But Akashi viewed the SNC as a useful consensus-building instrument among the non-Khmer Rouge factions. During UNTAC's lifespan, the SNC convened over thirty times and deliberated on items such as the electoral law, principles for a new constitution, natural resource preservation measures, and rehabilitation and reconstruction programs. The SNC also established its own secretariat that fostered pragmatic working relationships among the senior staff of the various factions and later became a talent pool for the new government. On the latter point, see Takahisa Kawakami, "Exercising the Transitional Authority," in Nassrine Azimi, ed., *The United Nations Transitional Authority in Cambodia: Debriefing and Lessons* (London: Kluwer Law International, 1995), 98.

144. Author's interview, Phnom Penh, 21 April 1993.

145. United Nations, *The United Nations and Cambodia, 1991-1995,* 51.

146. The Paris Accords *inter alia* provided for a post-UNTAC human rights monitoring presence in Cambodia, but a number of regional states took issue with this initiative when the UN Commission on Human Rights considered the establishment of an operational field presence. In the resulting compromise, a local office for the UN Center for Human Rights was authorized but its monitoring mandate considerably watered down. McNamara, "UN Human Rights Activities in Cambodia," 79.

147. See Barbara Crossette, "Outsiders Gone, Cambodia Unravels," *New York Times,* 3 December 1995, D4. Also, Keith B. Richburg, "Cambodia Shows Signs of Returning to Old Patterns of Violence, Repression," *Washington Post,* 9 December 1995, A1.

FAULTLINES:
UN OPERATIONS IN THE
FORMER YUGOSLAVIA

WILLIAM J. DURCH
AND JAMES A. SCHEAR[1]

Yugoslavia's violent breakup shattered the conceit that post–Cold War Europe was somehow immune to war. In early 1990, as a rising tide of competing nationalisms, socioeconomic decline, and the near-complete paralysis of federal institutions swept the old Yugoslavia toward the abyss, European states and regional organizations found themselves ill prepared to cope with the impending crisis. When the implosion finally occurred in 1991, the international community turned first to diplomacy, then to a major UN-led field operation intended to help contain the violence, reduce civilian hardships, and open up space for a negotiated settlement in which all the peoples of former Yugoslavia could live peacefully. The results of the first four years of UN efforts left a lot to be desired: although the violence, at certain stages, was contained and lives were saved, the conflicts in Croatia and Bosnia-Herzegovina defied resolution by measured UN action. Croatian military victories and sustained NATO bombing in Bosnia ultimately created a balance of suffering that paved the way to a US-brokered settlement whose long-term viability was a matter of debate.

By any measure, the former Yugoslavia represented a massive commitment for the United Nations. By mid-1995, two out of every three blue-helmeted peacekeepers that the United Nations fielded globally were located there, escorting relief convoys, monitoring cease-fires, patrolling buffer zones, repairing roads and bridges, and performing a multitude of other tasks, often at very high levels of risk. But the UN operations were pulled in competing directions by difficult and, at times, inconsistent mandates. Some tasks were performed well, even heroically, but in other areas the UN's performance was uneven at best, its mandates a substitute for stronger armed intervention that the United States and its allies were reluctant to undertake. In Croatia and Bosnia, UN field personnel were tempting targets for manipulation and abuse by all parties, as the UN found itself embroiled in seemingly intractable conflicts that it could not master and that gravely threatened its credibility.

This chapter examines the conduct and impact of the UN's field operations in the former Yugoslavia between 1992 and 1995. It begins with background on the sources of the conflict and the roles played by outside states and organizations at various stages. Then, it looks in depth at the planning and implementation of the UN-led efforts in Croatia and Bosnia, and how these distinctive operations have evolved over time in response to ongoing crises.[2] It concludes with a general assessment of mission effectiveness and observations on what the experience of former Yugoslavia may imply for the future of UN peace operations.

ORIGINS

The causes of conflict in the former Yugoslavia are complex and debated among scholars, practitioners, and participants alike. To some observers, the war is traceable to Serb aggression and efforts to carve a Greater Serbia out of the remains of the disintegrating Yugoslav state.[3] Others attribute the country's disintegration to the rise of ethnic-nationalist leaderships, not only in Serbia but in Croatia, Bosnia, and Slovenia and lay stress upon the role of Western influences—cultural, economic, financial, and political—in accelerating the pace of internal fragmentation.[4] What all observers recognize, however, is that the wars of Yugoslav succession involved competing claims for self-determination. They broke out as economic conditions declined, as the collective presidency established to "succeed" Tito proved unable to act decisively, and as other social and economic organizing principles began to supplant "Yugoslavism" and socialism.[5]

The Role of Ethnic Nationalism

Sociologist Anthony Smith describes a three-step process by which self-identified ethnic groups (those with a sense of "homeland," common history of struggle, a unifying religion, and a myth of "chosenness") can be mobilized by ethnic nationalism. The first step is "vernacular mobilization," the rediscovery and dissemination of the memories, symbols, and languages of the group—a task for the intelligentsia. The second is the "cultural politicization" of that rediscovered shared heritage: "what were formerly venerated traditions now become weapons in a cultural war," wielded by nationalist politicians. The third step is "ethnic purification," which "sanctifies" the culture and its symbols and aims to protect its adherents "through the relegation, segregation, expulsion, deportation and even extermination of aliens," a task for soldiers.[6]

This process roughly describes the march of events in Serbia and among Serb populations in the other republics of the former Yugoslavia through the 1980s and early 1990s, and to a lesser extent the reactions from those republics. The Albanian majority in the impoverished region of Kosovo began to agitate against Serb rule as early as 1981. The crisis there persisted through the 1980s and provided the spring-board for Slobodan Milosevic's 1987 campaign for the leadership of Serbia's Communist Party. He benefited from the growing nationalist leanings of the Serbian Academy of Arts and Sciences. Its 1986 Memorandum is considered the manifesto of Greater Serbian nationalism.[7] In 1989, his campaign for president of the Serb Republic included an elaborately staged six-hundredth anniversary visit, complete with imported crowds, to Kosovo Polje, the valley in present-day Kosovo where Turkish forces routed the Serbs in 1389.[8]

Although not every Serb obsesses about their defeat by the Turks in 1389 and not every Croat fears the recrudescence of extreme Chetnik nationalism, enough do to have made these things rallying points for ambitious politicians like Serbian Milosevic and Franjo Tudjman in Croatia. They proved especially potent for those segments of the rural population whose world was neither Europe nor Yugoslavia but a mountain, valley, or village.

Modern means of communications cannot fully bridge the differences that such people see between themselves and other groups. Indeed, communications media can easily be used to accentuate differences and exploit latent fears, especially when economic times are tough. Firm control of the media enabled politicians in Serbia and Croatia in particular to fan ethnic nationalism on behalf of their respective agendas, while muzzling dissent.

The nonmilitarized, intermixed urban populations of the larger towns in Bosnia (and to some extent Croatia) generally functioned according to a more tolerant, cosmopolitan notion of "civic" nationalism—the notion of belonging based on birth or permanent residence within a given national territory and adhering to its laws and customs[9]—and thought that was enough to insulate their world from the rising tide of militancy around them. They were wrong. Not only were the more segregated rural areas of Bosnia and Croatia susceptible to ethnic propaganda, they had access to most of the guns and help from the Yugoslav army.

The defense strategy that Yugoslavia developed to defend against Soviet and Warsaw Pact attack facilitated the country's breakup. Weapons cached around the country gave rural militias ready sources of armaments. Weapons cached in the mountains, valleys, and villages of Croatia and Bosnia gave the poorest, least educated, least cosmopolitan, most disenfranchised, rumor-susceptible, and envious segments of the population the means and, when central control slipped away, the opportunity to right old wrongs, guard against new ones, and maybe grab a share of urban wealth. Yugoslavia's defense strategy made conflict more difficult to control in another way, since "the post-1968 constitution formally outlawed a repetition [of the Yugoslav army's surrender of 1941,] . . . Local defense militias were therefore constitutionally directed to ignore cease-fires."[10]

The Role of History

Historically, the region that was Yugoslavia has offered little security to either persons or groups. As a crossroads between Europe and Asia, the Balkans have been a borderland of empire since the heyday of the Romans. The modern border between Croatia and Bosnia-Herzegovina—the Sava River, its western tributaries, and the northern reaches of the Dinaric Alps—was a key segment of the military frontier (or *krajina*) between the Austro-Hungarian and Ottoman Empires for nearly 200 years, a frontier maintained by the ancestors of contemporary "mountain Serbs." Empire brought religion in its wake (separation of church and state being a recent Western invention), so the Balkans are also riven by religious fault lines—not just Christian and Muslim, but Catholic and Orthodox.[11]

While geography has made the Balkans a crossroads, topography has confined its easy lines of communications to a handful of river valleys running east and south of Belgrade, and down from the mountains of Bosnia. The terrain outside these corridors made the region hard to subdue, historically. The Ottoman Turks spent the better part of two centuries trying to conquer it, although Bosnia was perhaps the easiest conquest.

The Ottomans spent another three centuries losing control of their northern empire, one section at a time. Serbia became independent in 1878, after a long struggle, under the Treaty of San Stefano, which ended the Russo-Turkish War. The Congress of Berlin in that same year gave Austria-Hungary control over Bosnia-Herzegovina and otherwise rearranged Balkan boundaries to most local parties' displeasure.[12] That displeasure erupted into two short, brutal wars that rearranged the political face of the Balkans once again in 1912-13.[13] They also set the stage for the well-known assassination of Austrian archduke Franz Ferdinand by a Serbian nationalist, Gavrilo Princip, in Sarajevo in June 1914, which set in motion the machinery that ground all of Europe into the mud of World War I. The postwar Versailles settlement glued Serbia, Macedonia, and Montenegro together with several fragments of the old Austro-Hungarian domain (Slovenia, Croatia, Bosnia, and Vojvodina) into a new, Serb-dominated Kingdom of Serbs, Croats, and Slovenes, renamed the Kingdom of Yugoslavia in 1929.[14] Under Nazi assault in 1941, the kingdom swiftly dissolved, to be replaced by the pro-Nazi "Ustashe" regime in Croatia and by a brace of guerrilla forces—the Serbian Chetniks and Tito's polyglot Communist Partisans—who fought the invaders, the Ustashe, and each other in a war that mimed all the horrors for which World War II is infamous, including concentration camps, particularly the death camps run by the Ustashe.[15]

Yugoslavia was stitched back together by Tito and the Communists in 1945. Under Tito's charismatic rule lived Serbs, Croats, Slovenes and Muslims, Hungarians, Montenegrins, Kosovars, and Macedonians. When Tito died in 1980, a collective presidency, with one representative drawn from each republic, replaced him—a solution indicative of the already tenuous state of national identity. As the economy slipped, so did political cohesion. Throughout the 1980s the average Yugoslav's income, which had grown steadily during Tito's lifetime, shrank in real terms.[16] The country's cohesiveness was further undermined when the principal external threat to the country, the Soviet Union, began to withdraw its forces from Eastern Europe in 1989, democratic forces were elected to power in neighboring Hungary (Spring 1990), and the Soviet-led Warsaw Pact crumbled. The Pact formally ceased all military functions in March 1991 and dissolved in July 1991. The Soviet Union experienced an abortive military coup in late August, and dissolved itself four months later.

The Wars of Yugoslav Secession

As the external threat to the country was disappearing, the internal pressures became too much for Yugoslavia's Communist Party, the country's major unifying force since the 1940s. At its 14th Congress in January 1990, the party fell apart. In April 1990, multiparty elections in Croatia gave Franjo Tudjman's Croat nationalist party a majority in the republican legislature and made Tudjman himself president of Croatia. Six months later, Serb nationalists in Croatia set up their own parliament and declared autonomy. By the end of the year, multiparty elections had been held in all of Yugoslavia's constituent republics, and non-communist parties had won parliamentary majorities in Slovenia, Macedonia, and Bosnia, while Slobodan Milosevic's Social Democratic (ex-Communist) Party took about two-thirds of the vote in Serbia and Montenegro.[17]

Slovenia was the first to move toward secession after a December 1990 referendum overwhelmingly supported independence. Slovenian leaders set a six-month deadline for negotiating a new, confederal political arrangement for Yugoslavia, a deadline to which Croatian leaders subscribed in February 1991. If a new confederation of semi-autonomous units could not be formed, they would both declare independence. Serbia's Milosevic, on the other hand, threatened to secede if Yugoslavia *did* adopt a confederal scheme.[18]

The Yugoslav National Army (JNA), which viewed itself as the only remaining pan-Yugoslav institution, formed its own political party at the end of 1990 and became a political player in its own right. With a legal basis in federal Yugoslav law, the JNA was determined to fight separatist tendencies in Yugoslavia and, failing that, reattach to Serbia proper the Serb communities within the breakaway republics. If Croats and Slovenes chose to defend themselves, then the breakup of Yugoslavia would ultimately be bloody.

Yugoslavia's collective presidency fell apart in the spring of 1991, and from that point on Yugoslavia's federal government began to crumble as well. In early May, in the first major clash of the looming war, Croatian police fought militiamen who had crossed over from Serbia to the largely Serb border village of Borovo Selo. On 25 June 1991, Slovenia and Croatia both declared independence; two days later, the JNA moved to crush the secessions.[19]

Ethnically, Slovenia is much more homogeneous than other former Yugoslav republics. Although the JNA made some effort to retake it, Slovenia's lack of a Serb population to protect meant that the JNA was not highly motivated, and concerted resistance at a few points by Slovenian infantry led it to pull back and leave Slovenia alone.[20]

Croatia's prewar population was 12 percent Serb, with the biggest concentrations in three areas: the old Krajina region, one central pocket (Western Slavonia), and near the eastern river border with Serbia. When the JNA pulled out of Slovenia, elements of its forces set about carving out defensible space for Croatia's Serb minority while the rest tried to extricate themselves from garrisons besieged by hostile local populations and Croat irregular forces. Two months into a siege that started in late August 1991, JNA artillery pounded the eastern city of Vukovar into rubble (wasting time and firepower in the course of a seemingly obsessive campaign to break the city's tenacious resistance). Fighting continued as cease-fire negotiators from the European Community (EC) and the United Nations tried to bring it to a halt (see below).[21]

When a UN-brokered cease-fire in Croatia was achieved on 23 November, it called for the JNA to withdraw forces from Croatia. Most of them moved into Bosnia-Herzegovina, setting the military stage for the next phase of the war.

Bosnia-Herzegovina's prewar population was 31 percent Serb, most heavily concentrated in two regions: the western third of the country and the eastern border areas abutting Serbia and Montenegro.[22] In October 1991, the Muslim-Croat majority in Bosnia's Republican assembly voted in favor of independence; Serb deputies walked out and formed their own assembly. On 16 December, when the European Community set the timetable for recognizing Croatia and Slovenia, it also gave other Yugoslav republics thirty days to apply for recognition. Bosnia applied on 24 December but also asked for UN peacekeepers to help prevent an outbreak of conflict. That request was refused.[23]

One month before an independence referendum required by the EC, Bosnian Serb leaders declared their community's autonomy from Bosnia, and Serb voters boycotted the vote. On 29 February, the rest of Bosnia's voters chose independence by a wide margin, and on 3 March President Alija Izetbegovic declared Bosnia's independence.[24] Immediate negotiations under EC auspices led to a concept of loose confederal rule that seemed on the brink of all-around acceptance when it was rejected, in late March, by the Bosnian government.[25] Two days later, on 27 March, the Bosnian Serbs adopted a constitution for their "Republika Srpska," which had, at least initially, merger with the other Serbian entities of the former Yugoslavia as its ultimate goal.

As these political events unfolded, fighting broke out in the northern Bosnian border town of Bosanski Brod, situated on the line of communication linking Serbia proper, Serb-majority northwestern Bosnia, and the upper Drina Valley.[26] On 6 April 1992, the EC recognized Bosnia-Herzegovina, and Serb shelling of Sarajevo and other Muslim-majority areas began in earnest. Earlier, Chetnik bands had crossed Bosnia's eastern, Drina River border to apply the terror tactics developed a year earlier in Croatia to non-Serb populations and towns in the lower Drina Valley.[27]

The UN Security Council demanded withdrawal of the JNA from what was, after 22 May 1992, a sovereign member of the United Nations. However, rather than physically withdraw most forces, the authorities in Belgrade instead gave up titular control of them, so that Serb forces in Bosnia, still relatively short on manpower, gained a near-monopoly on heavy weapons vis-à-vis the Bosnian government.[28] That weaponry was used to lay siege to Sarajevo, in particular, and to maintain control of supply routes into most of Bosnia's other major towns and cities.

In central Bosnia and western Herzegovina, Bosnian Muslims and Croats maintained an uneasy alliance. Based in Mostar, the Croatian Defense Council (HVO) was equipped by and owed allegiance to Tudjman's regime in Zagreb. Because its principal objective was political affiliation with Croatia, HVO was an unpredictable ally for the Sarajevo government and eventually turned on it. Muslim populations were driven from western Herzegovinian towns like Prozor and Gornji Vakuf beginning in October 1992, and from Mostar itself the following spring. Muslim forces returned the favor against Croat towns in central Bosnia.[29] At this point, UN forces had been present in both Croatia and Bosnia for more than a year.

Before turning to their stories, however, it is important to have some grasp of the positions of major external actors with regard to this conflict, as it was to the outside world that the local parties turned initially for ratification of their actions and for political and material support.

THE INTERNATIONAL RESPONSE

The peoples of Yugoslavia have long-established links to the outside world, both within and beyond the Balkan peninsula. Those very linkages, however, pose problems from the standpoint of international security. Whereas a unitary Yugoslavia could be accepted as a given of the post–World War II European political order, its various national groups maintained a complex, disparate web of foreign affinities. The Germans and Austrians were and are closely connected to Yugoslav Croats and Slovenes; the Greeks and, more distantly, the Russians have cultural and religious ties to Serb communities; and Turkey's interests have clearly focused on the fate of Albanian and Bosnian Muslims. As the centrifugal forces of hypernationalism began to tear Yugoslavia apart, these divergent international affinities became more apparent. Along with other factors, discussed below, they acted to generate strong countervailing diplomatic pressures among the major powers to try to keep a lid on the Yugoslav crisis at a time of historic transformation in East-West relations. As a result, pressures that might have been dissipated by concerted international action early on were allowed to build to explosive levels.

This section examines briefly the roles and objectives of the United States, Russia, France, the United Kingdom, and Germany, and it assesses the diplomatic efforts leading up to the UN's engagement in the crisis.

The United States

From the outset of the conflict in the former Yugoslavia, the United States tried to get Europe to assume and to retain primary responsibility for dealing with the looming conflict on its doorstep, but tried to do so without permanently damaging the US position of leadership within NATO. The European Union (EU) took up the gauntlet; indeed, the EU insisted that it should handle the crisis.[30]

The United States, largely preoccupied with the crisis and war in the Persian Gulf from August 1990 to mid-1991, paid scant attention to the burgeoning crisis in Yugoslavia and, when it did, viewed the building separatist movements there not in terms of local politics but as a bad precedent for the tottering Soviet Union.[31] In late March 1991, President Bush told Yugoslav prime minister Markovic that the United States would "neither encourage nor reward" Yugoslavia's breakup. In late May, the American ambassador in Belgrade, Warren Zimmerman, publicly opposed independence for Slovenia. In late June, less than a week before the independence deadline, Secretary of State Baker visited the region, arguing against forceful maintenance of the Yugoslav state, but suggesting no penalties if force were used. The day before the secession deadline, Deputy Secretary of State Eagleburger said that the United States would ignore the declarations of independence, which he called a "threat to the stability and well-being of the peoples of Yugoslavia."[32] Even after the Soviet Union broke apart in December 1991, the United States delayed recognizing Yugoslavia's breakaway republics, leaving that initiative in European hands.

Seen from the outside as a somewhat even match, the conflict that raged in Croatia in the second half of 1991 did not create anywhere near the pressure for outside intervention that the subsequent fighting in Bosnia did. In the latter case, the United States was pulled by two forces: a sense of public outrage fed by televised images of suffering, balanced by reluctance on the part of political leaders to risk an engagement that could be lengthy, bloody, and fatal to the career of whoever inaugurated it. Thus the United States cooperated with others to contain the violence and relieve human suffering, but only to the extent feasible without US combat troops on the ground. It supported multilateral peace proposals but only when they promised to reunify the country in some fashion and give back to displaced populations—mainly the Bosniacs[33]—much of what they had lost to ethnic cleansing. These policies proved difficult to implement, as the United States relied on economic sanctions against Serbia to get Belgrade to press the Bosnian Serbs to give up lands that they were under no direct military pressure to surrender.

US policy, while in one sense more "principled" than the policies of its European allies, nonetheless held out to the Bosnian government more hope of better days than Washington was willing or able to deliver, and critics of US policy averred that it merely prolonged the war. On the other hand, prolongation gave the Bosniacs the time to scramble for (covert) money and arms and to train troops, and the ability to bloody the Croat HVO, facilitating a US-brokered truce on that front in early 1994. But by mid-1995, with the siege of Sarajevo well into its third year and tighter than ever, it was not clear that prolongation would ultimately buy any more land, peace, or security than could have been had under the earliest proposals for partition made in 1992. By urging Bosniac rejection of the early plan in favor of a more advantageous (but undefined) outcome, the United States bought a share of responsibility for the subsequent outbreak of fighting.

The Russian Federation

The Soviet, later Russian, role in the crisis and war that engulfed the former Yugoslavia has been critical from the beginning, in a number of ways. Like the United States, Moscow has a veto on the Security Council. Russia has long, pre-communist ties with Orthodox Christian Serbia (its alliance with Serbia helped trigger World War I). Finally, Russia's volatile internal politics have shaped UN and Western responses to the Yugoslav conflict from the outset.[34]

Moscow has made the best of this conflict, seeking opportunities to play the role of a great power and ultimately joining other major powers in the 1994-95 "Contact Group" to present a united diplomatic front to the three main Bosnian parties. Like the United States, Yeltsin's government has taken unilateral steps when opportune. Such actions demonstrated independence to its diplomatic partners and, equally if not more importantly, to its domestic constituents and critics.[35] Showing greater sympathy for and dealing more closely with the Serbs helped to cover Yeltsin's domestic right flank, and the unprecedented participation of Russian troops in UNPROFOR gave Moscow the same kind of implicit veto over unwanted UN or NATO action in Bosnia possessed by France and the United Kingdom.

France and the United Kingdom

Paris and London had no more desire to become bogged down in a Balkan war than did Washington, but since the conflict was in their backyard they had more trouble avoiding troop commitments than did the United States. Their common stance, however, was to try to contain the conflict while relieving civilian hardships, promoting negotiations, and avoiding a partisan ground combat role. Both capitals could point to the costs and risks of their participation in UNPROFOR, and to their support for a negotiated peace, anytime domestic critics demanded greater action to end the conflict. They could (and did) emphasize risks to their peacekeepers anytime the question arose in NATO councils of sustained air action to punish Bosnian Serb transgressions or enforce a political deadline. This strategy, however, risked trapping French and British forces in Bosnia for as long as the war continued, since any mission to extract them under fire was likely to involve precisely the sort of combat engagement that both had sought to forestall.

France had additional, implicit reasons to participate fully in UNPROFOR. First, the UN operation offered France, which has not been party to NATO's military command structure for thirty years, an opportunity to participate fully in a field operation with its allies, and even exercise command over their forces (by seconding a French general to serve as UN force commander). Second, the Yugoslav crisis offered France an opportunity to take a leading role within NATO and the European Union on an issue where history has limited Germany's voice, as well as its options.

Germany

World War II and the complicity of the Wehrmacht in the deaths of several hundred thousand Yugoslav citizens kept Germany and Austria from playing an active role on the ground when the new Yugoslav crisis brewed up, but did not keep Germany from pressing fellow members of the European Community, in the latter half of 1991, for early recognition of Slovenia and Croatia. The outbreak of war had sent shockwaves through the German body politic, fanning the flames of deep resentment at what many Germans saw as hardline repression by old guard (mainly Serb) Communists in Belgrade of the democratic aspirations of the Croats and Slovenes. Not surprisingly, the fighting created an enormous groundswell of sympathy for Croat and Slovene self-determination claims. Although Foreign Minister Hans-Dietrich Genscher had previously opposed early recognition (due in part to pressure from Moscow), growing domestic pressure led him to switch course in the fall of 1991. On 27 November, Chancellor Helmut Kohl announced that the German government would recognize Slovene and Croat independence by the end of the year, a move that threatened to short-circuit the laboriously constructed EC common position that recognitions could only be seen as part of an overall settlement.[36]

From the German perspective, recognition was a tool that would deprive federal Yugoslav authorities any pretext for staying in Croatia and would thus transform an internal conflict into a "Kuwait situation" with a clearly defined (and stigmatized) aggressor, for example, the Serb-dominated JNA.[37] It would also tend to open doors to international involvement that had previously been closed while Croatia remained a component of Yugoslavia. Whether the move would actually help stop the fighting was less than clear, however, even at the time. The JNA withdrew, but into Bosnia-Herzegovina where the precedent of recognizing the independence of a state despite the objections of a significant minority community put the Bosnian Serbs further on edge.[38]

The Tangled Path of Multilateral Diplomacy

The warning signs of Yugoslavia's demise, so clear in retrospect, were overshadowed by the turmoil created by the sudden collapse of Cold War divisions in Europe. The increasing stridency of Serb nationalists in Belgrade, the suppression of Albanian dissent in Kosovo, the demise of the Yugoslav Communist Party in January 1990, the electoral victory of the nationalist Croatian Democratic Party (HDZ) several months later in Zagreb, and rising tensions in the Serb-majority communities of Croatia, seemed to fit into the larger pattern of communism's failing health and regime transformation elsewhere in Eastern Europe and the Soviet Union. These events did not convince many observers that Yugoslavia itself might collapse violently until the country stumbled into a constitutional crisis in early 1991, and the Slovene and Croat republics appeared ready to make good on their oft-stated threats to break away.[39]

During mid-1991, with the Persian Gulf war and its aftermath dominating international attention, it was the EC that took up the baton on the Yugoslav question. Italian foreign minister Gianni de Michelis actively promoted the idea of EC diplomatic engagement, using as a lure to the Yugoslav parties membership in the community and an aid package that was designed to keep the country together while promoting constitutional and economic reforms to help stem separatist pressures. Eager to deflect growing support in Austria, Germany, and Hungary for Croat and Slovene independence, and to strengthen Italy's European credentials, de Michelis's initiative resonated with mainstream Western sentiment on Yugoslavia at a time when the country's unity and territorial integrity ought to have been preserved and unilateral secessions strongly discouraged. In late May, during a high visibility visit to Belgrade, EC president Jacques Delors and Luxembourg prime minister Santer promised to seek $4.5 billion in aid from the EC membership, provided Yugoslavia remained united and heading down the path of reforms.[40]

The EC's interest reflected more than simply the lack of attentiveness of the major powers. With European states poised to take a leap toward economic and monetary union at the Maastricht summit in December 1991, Europeanists were eager to test their capacity to achieve greater self-reliance on political and security matters. Reflecting this mood, Luxembourg's foreign minister Jacques Poos at one point exclaimed: "If anyone can do anything here [in Yugoslavia], it is the EC. It is not the US or the USSR or anyone else."[41] Washington, as noted above, had little incentive to disabuse Europeans of this view; indeed, it dovetailed nicely with US preferences to keep Yugoslav troubles confined to Europe's backyard. In the end, however, the levers of economic assistance and other incentives were simply not enough. Some critics argue that insistence upon a unified Yugoslavia—the linchpin of the EU's involvement—simply fed Serbian intransigence and reinforced stalemate in the negotiations.[42] Others argue that Western actions tended on balance to send mixed messages to the parties, fueling the dispute and encouraging Croatia and Slovenia to go their separate ways.[43]

From Preventive Diplomacy to Conflict Management

Whichever thesis is more accurate, by mid-1991 it was clear that the EC's foray into conflict prevention was on the verge of failing. Croatia and Slovenia staunchly opposed anything more binding than loose confederal ties to Serbia, whose dominance of federal institutions and claim on the national wealth they bitterly resented. Belgrade, in turn, was dead set against any arrangement in which dispersed Serb communities outside of Serbia would suddenly become minorities within new sovereign states; such an outcome, Milosevic warned repeatedly, would prompt his government to redraw existing inter-republican borders.

Following Ljubljana's and Zagreb's declarations of independence on 25 June, the outbreak of hostilities between the JNA and Slovene territorial defense units produced a new flurry of international diplomacy. A troika of EC foreign ministers sought to arrange an immediate cease-fire and a standdown of forces. Meanwhile, the Conference on Security and Cooperation in Europe (CSCE) put some of its newly established institutions into action. At the initiative of Austria, the conference utilized an "emergency mechanism" in order to convene a meeting between senior CSCE officials and the key Yugoslav parties, in Belgrade, on 4 July. The CSCE's Conflict Prevention Center also levied a requirement upon Belgrade to explain the role of the federal army in suppressing the rebellion. CSCE action, however, required consensus among its members, including Yugoslavia and it soon faded into the background.[44]

EC mediation appeared more promising, at least initially. On 7 July, the troika managed to broker a package deal among Croatian, Slovenian, and federal Yugoslav authorities; its elements included a cease-fire, a three-month suspension of Croatian and Slovene activities aimed at independence, the deployment of observers to monitor compliance, and (rather vague) commitments to negotiations on Yugoslavia's future.[45] Diplomatic efforts were also set in motion to convene a peace conference of all parties, something the CSCE had tried to arrange until Belgrade's opposition put an end to it. The effect of the EC's July agreement, however, was to help Ljubljana in its bid for independence, and it became much harder for the EC to avoid the appearance of favoring Croat and Slovene self-determination.

By the time the EC's peace conference got underway in the Hague in early September under the chairmanship of former British foreign secretary Lord Peter Carrington, the Serbs had begun to chafe at the EC's role.[46] A progression of cease-fires brokered by Carrington during the fall did not hold. A settlement plan pieced together by the EC's Council of Ministers, and presented to the parties by Carrington and Council president Hans van den Broek, attracted widespread interest. But its central elements—a loose confederation of sovereign Yugoslav republics, a bar on border changes except by mutual agreement, and a restoration of autonomy for Kosovo and Vojvodina—required potentially large concessions from Belgrade with little compensation attached.[47] By early November, the plan had run aground. Meanwhile, the EC was caught up in its own internal disagreements over a proposal, advocated initially by the Netherlands, to deploy an interposition force under the auspices of the Western European Union (WEU) to separate the combatants in Croatia.[48]

The Europeans, in fact, had strong incentives to want to keep Yugoslavia from breaking up. Britain and France, among the larger powers, were extremely sensitive to the issue of nationalist dissent in their own backyards—whether Scottish, Irish, or Corsican—and wished to avoid any step that might encourage problems at home. Moreover, a disintegrating Yugoslavia might encourage the breakup of other multi-ethnic states in Eastern Europe. On the other hand, amidst a diplomatic stalemate and continued escalation of violence in Croatia, irresistible pressures began to build in Western Europe to impose punitive sanctions on the Belgrade authorities and to weigh the recognition of Croatia and Slovenia, if only as a way to maneuver the Serbs into a more cooperative stance before that bridge was crossed. For assistance on recognition questions, the EC turned to an international arbitration commission of jurists chaired by a French constitutional lawyer, Robert Badinter. Established by the EC's peace conference to deal with economic and other technical aspects of Yugoslav secession, Badinter's panel was given the politically explosive task of vetting requests for recognition from the various republics against a set of criteria: respect for individual and minority rights, a commitment not to alter existing borders by force, democratic government, and acceptance of the EC's peace process. Slovenia and Macedonia passed muster, but the commission raised questions about Croatia's commitment to human rights, and it asked the government of Bosnia and Herzegovina to hold a referendum to determine public support for independence.[49]

The deliberative pace of the Badinter process in the end proved too much for Germany, and its go-it-alone decision on recognition provoked no small amount of angst among its allies and EC partners. To preserve unity within the EC at a critical moment in its evolution was very important but to preserve it on Germany's terms would mean a humiliating retreat from the proposition that Yugoslavia's unity or dissolution should be a matter of negotiation among the parties. In the end, despite the strongly stated misgivings of Carrington and other international officials regarding Germany's stance, the EC's membership, preferring retreat to disunity, decided to go along. The EC recognized Croatia and Slovenia on 15 January 1992. Croatian and Slovene state-run television played the tune "Danke, Deutschland."[50]

Enter the United Nations

As the EC's internal disagreements began to sap its energies and undermine its mediating role, the United Nations moved into the forefront of diplomatic activity. The Security Council, meeting in ministerial session on 25 September 1991, took the first step, voting unanimously under Chapter VII of the UN Charter to impose a country-wide arms embargo on Yugoslavia and inviting UN secretary-general Perez de Cuellar to offer his assistance to the Yugoslav parties, the EC, and other countries' ongoing negotiating efforts.[51] Acting on the Council's initiative, Perez de Cuellar appointed former US secretary of state Cyrus Vance to be his personal envoy for the region.

Energizing a reluctant UN on the Yugoslav question made sense for frustrated Europeans. Germany's unilateralist gambit on recognition, in particular, had prodded France and Britain to look for a new venue like the Security Council where these two countries enjoyed special status. Russia and the United States, whose absence from Balkans diplomacy had tended to make European divisions more visible, could be brought into the mix as members of the Council. The UN also enjoyed good credentials in nonaligned Yugoslavia: the Serbs, in particular, were eager for UN mediation, sensing it could be more impartial (and less imperial) than a German-led EC. Finally, the United Nations had peacekeeping, humanitarian, and field operations resources to apply in implementing whatever agreements could be worked out on the ground. No European regional organization had such tools, and NATO's military assets were optimized for forceful intervention (a non-starter for the United States and most other allies), not consensual peacekeeping.

By late 1991, a broad framework of international policy on Yugoslavia could be seen falling into place. It was, in essence, a strategy of containment and indirect pressure, aimed at maneuvering the Yugoslav parties toward a settlement, and its core elements were threefold: an arms embargo to limit the scope of outside involvement; economic and political sanctions to punish aggressive behavior; and a field operation to alleviate civilian hardships, operating with the consent of the parties. At a later stage, no-fly zones, safe areas, and other nonconsensual techniques for conflict control would be added to the mix, as would a war crimes tribunal designed to exact justice for the victims of the fighting.

On the spectrum of options these elements, taken together, occupied a precarious midpoint between total disengagement and forceful intervention, which raised the spectre of a Balkan quagmire and even competing interventions. It was never considered an ideal policy or a solution to the conflict. Rather, it was the least unacceptable option among a range of unsavory choices.

CROATIA: THE ADVENT OF UNPROFOR

In early 1992, UN peacekeeping personnel began to deploy into Croatia's conflicted areas, tasked by the Security Council to be an "interim arrangement to create the conditions of peace and security required for the negotiation of an overall settlement of the Yugoslav crisis."[52] The UN Protection Force (UNPROFOR) marked an uncertain turning point in the crisis. For many outsiders the arrival of a foreign presence on the ground carried with it hope that the warring parties—the Croats, local Serbs, and an increasingly Serb-dominated JNA—could finally be induced to show military restraint after six months of bitter fighting. Whether greater diplomatic flexibility would flow from this development was unknown.

The context of UNPROFOR's deployment was anything but auspicious. Initially, a cease-fire/disengagement agreement that Cyrus Vance had negotiated in late November appeared to unravel, going the way of a string of previous EC-brokered truces. Continued blockage by the Croatians of JNA facilities was provoking, and being provoked by, ongoing attacks by JNA and Serb militia upon civilian areas. By the end of the year, however, Vance appeared to have made headway toward final agreement among the parties on arrangements to permit initial UN deployments, and the fighting died down perceptibly.[53]

It is, nonetheless, difficult to imagine that the cease-fire was premised on anything more than tactical calculations. Serbia and the JNA, in the face of internal problems, had begun to apply heavy pressure on the *krajina* Serbs to accept, if only begrudgingly, the UN's presence.[54] Croatia appeared eager to adopt an accommodating stance on the eve of its recognition by the EC. The lull in the fighting quickly produced international pressures on the UN to seize the initiative. Secretary-General Boutros-Ghali, acknowledging a risk of backsliding, urged the Security Council to act quickly. "The danger that a United Nations peace-keeping operation will fail for lack of cooperation from the parties," he observed, "is less grievous than the danger that a

Fig. 6.1
MAP OF CROATIA

SOURCE: US Government

delay in its dispatch will lead to a breakdown of the crease-fire and a new conflagration in Yugoslavia."[55] The Council agreed with this judgment.

The Pattern of Conflict

The impulse to do something was understandable. Despite the lengthy political prologue, no one had been prepared for the intensity of the communal strife that engulfed Croatia in the latter half of 1991. Mixed nationality towns such as Gospic and Karlovac, as well as large areas of the Dalmatian hinterland, suffered in the village-to-village combat between Croat and Serb fighters. JNA facilities throughout the republic saw violent confrontations between army units and local Croatian militia.[56] Croatian villagers in Krajina were driven out by Serb irregular units, which set up a base of operations in Knin, an old fortress town and the capital of the self-styled "Republic of Serbian Krajina," or RSK. Serbs, in turn, had reportedly fled or been forced out by the thousands from places such as Ogulan, Sisak, Daruvar, Gospic, and parts of Western Slavonia and the Dalmatian coast. To the east, Serb militants from villages near Osijek, Vukovar, and Serbia proper began to expel large numbers of non-Serbs from Eastern Slavonia and Baranja. The JNA laid siege to Vukovar, mercilessly shelling the town and killing or driving its Croatian majority population out of the area.

Civilian population dislocation was the most obvious consequence of the fighting and in no small measure its basic objective. Unlike the violence that would later engulf Bosnia-Herzegovina, where the lion's share of ethnic cleansing was performed by Bosnian Serbs, population dislocation in Croatia was a genuinely two-sided affair. A quarter of a million Serbs were displaced from their homes or fled Croatia entirely, more than the number of Croats forced out of Serb-held areas.[57] Estimates of the dead, overwhelmingly civilian, were placed at 6,000-10,000.[58] The economic consequences of the conflict went beyond just physical destruction of infrastructure. Oil pipelines connecting Adriatic ports to central Croatia via the Krajina were shut off and the krajina Serbs blocked road and rail links connecting Zagreb to other parts of Croatia, including the Dalmatian coast, thus curtailing tourism and trade. Zagreb, in turn, had cut Krajina's electricity and water supplies and its commercial access.

The irregular pattern of fighting in Croatia presented several daunting problems for any UN deployment. First, the localized character of the violence made it very difficult to disengage the opposing forces along clear and well-established lines, in traditional peacekeeping style. Even more significant were the number and diversity of armed elements to be dealt with. Serb factions included a mix of locally based militia (so-called territorial defense units, or TDF), certain JNA units, special police, as well as paramilitary groups and criminal-turned-nationalist groups from Serbia such as the Arkanovci.[59] Croat partisans were found in the Zengas (National Guard), the special police and local militia, and the still evolving Croatian army. The variety of armed elements made for fragile command and control and created a tendency for even the smallest local incidents to escalate quickly.[60]

Finally, the substantial population displacement created tensions *within* Croatian and Serbian communities, pitting the generally more angry, extremist, and armed displaced population that had been driven into a given area against the more moderate local communities. Tensions of this type introduced enormous difficulties in maintaining law and order and stemming the cycle of atrocities and revenge killing.[61]

To have any chance of consolidating a cease-fire under these difficult conditions, it was clear that UNPROFOR's concept of operations would have to go far beyond traditional peacekeeping. The secretary-general acknowledged this fact early on, expressing misgivings about the pressures upon UNPROFOR to assume "quasi-governmental" functions and the tendency of the evolving situation to draw the United Nations into the conflict ever more deeply—prescient concerns, as it turned out.[62]

Mandates for the Operation in Croatia

The general parameters for the operation were laid out in a concept paper that came to be known as the "Vance Plan."[63] For its first two years UNPROFOR deployments followed the Vance Plan. They were subsequently adjusted by a Serb-Croat agreement of March 1994 and in response to Zagreb's threat in January 1995 to withdraw the UN's welcome unless the force were reconfigured.

The primary feature of the Vance Plan was the extraction of JNA units from Croatian territory and the temporary establishment of several zones, known as United Nations Protected Areas (UNPAs), that encompassed the main areas of fighting in which local Serbs constituted the majority or a substantial minority of the population. As JNA elements withdrew, the new peacekeeping force, including not only UN-assigned infantry battalions but also military observers, civil police, and civil affairs officers, would deploy in a so-called "inkblot" pattern, concentrating at points of tension throughout the UNPAs.[64]

In essence, the Vance Plan foresaw UNPROFOR as a stabilizing agent for public security, pending a diplomatic solution to the conflict. Its main task was to ensure that all persons residing in the UNPAs were "protected" from the fear of armed attack and human rights abuse.

Superimposed upon the ethnic-nationalist character of the conflict, this novel protective function was to shield non-Serbs remaining in and returning to the UNPAs from intimation or violence; at the same time, the force would also seek to protect Serbs residing inside the UNPAs from threats posed by Croatian police and army elements operating outside. This concept of dual protection—stated nowhere explicitly but arguably the linchpin of the operation—was never intended to be a service that UNPROFOR could render on its own. The Vance Plan presumed large amounts of forbearance and cooperation on all sides in order to achieve a reasonable level of public security inside the areas of UN jurisdiction.

Disarming UN Protected Areas

The first step in implementing the plan was demilitarization. Units from 12 UN-assigned infantry battalions would supervise the withdrawal or disarming of combatants in the protected areas. JNA, Croatian army, or any other units not based in the UNPAs would be obliged to withdraw; all other units, both regular and irregular forces, would be disbanded and demobilized.[65] Weapons not being withdrawn from the UNPAs would be handed over to UNPROFOR for safe custody. Only side arms for local police would be allowed. UNPROFOR's military component would verify these arrangements by establishing checkpoints in and around the UNPAs, with authority to stop and search vehicles for proscribed materials. UN military units and military observers (UNMOs) would also patrol intensively, by land and air; they would have authority to conduct investigations of complaints of arms violations; and in the event of renewed tensions, they could be interposed between two sides to prevent hostilities, even without the consent of the parties.[66]

UNPROFOR's rules of engagement, that is, the ground rules governing the use of force, were derivative of standard UN peacekeeping rules. The one exception was additional latitude to conduct cordon and search operations. The rules devised for Croatia were also applied in Bosnia.[67] The use of armed force was permitted:

- to defend oneself, other UN personnel, or persons and areas under their protection against direct attack;
- to resist, by forceful means, attempts to prevent UNPROFOR from discharging its duties; and
- to resist deliberate military or paramilitary incursions into the UN Protected Areas (of UNPROFOR-C/UNCRO).

Under normal conditions:
- personnel authorized to carry arms could carry them loaded;
- upon encountering hostile intent [actions preparatory to aggressive action], UN personnel were to observe, not to withdraw, and to establish liaison with the forces concerned;
- in response to hostile action, UN forces were to warn verbally, fire warning shots, then fire for effect if hostile acts continued and lives were threatened, at the option of the local troop commander; and finally,
- firing for effect without initial verbal challenge was authorized at all times in self-defense when delay could lead to death or injury to UN personnel or to protected persons or property.

UN personnel did not have general authority to disarm individual local soldiers, the paramilitaries, or civilians.

Public Order

Once demilitarization was accomplished, the focus of the operation would shift to the restoration of public order under the authority of local *opstine* (county) councils. A corps of 530 unarmed UN civilian police (CIVPOL) would monitor the work of local police to ensure the impartial administration of law and order. In addition to this field work, a contingent of UN civil affairs officers would play a more intrusive role: to monitor the reconstitution of local administrations and their police elements, specifically to determine whether the composition of local police reflected the prewar ethnic balances in a given local area; and to work out modifications in the makeup of the local police if individual units did not conform to those percentages.[68] Again, all of these procedures were premised upon the active cooperation of the parties. Problems encountered in the field would be referred to senior levels, and the factions would be responsible for enforcing the compliance of their own subordinates.

Return of Displaced Persons

With these steps completed and a reasonable degree of security achieved, the plan foresaw the voluntary return of civilians displaced by the fighting. Here, the UN's role would be essentially humanitarian: to assist returning populations and to monitor human rights compliance. Issues of compensation for personal or property losses were not addressed. The whole thrust of these interim arrangements was to try to establish a modicum of social stability while not prejudging in any way the negotiations that would determine the future political status of these conflicted areas. That, in any case, was the hope.

The Vance Plan as Calculated Risk

In fact, the Vance Plan was seen as a risky gamble, featuring a mixture of elements whose inclusion reflected the necessity of obtaining the acquiescence of all parties rather than considerations of practicality. In particular, the notion of restoring a public security *status quo ante* by, among other steps, bringing back displaced inhabitants and somehow assuring that local police would be mixed ethnically seemed very unrealistic when the underlying causes of the dispute—Croatia's secession from the old Yugoslavia and self-determination claims by local Serbs—remained unresolved. So too was the notion that the UN could somehow be an agent for protection and "affirmative action" in the presence of an unresolved communal conflict. What lured the UN into experimenting with these novel functions was the idea that cooperation of the parties could, in principle, make any or all of them doable, no matter how far-reaching, and that once the UN deployed the fighting would at least die down.

It is clear, however, in retrospect that the parties were never fully on board with the plan. While they accepted the UN's disclaimer that the plan would not prejudge the outcome of negotiations on a comprehensive settlement, all sides sought to use the plan for precisely that purpose; that is, to advance irreconcilable political objectives.

For local Serb authorities, the Vance Plan was a potential gateway to independence. It provided for UN rather than Croatian control over the UNPAs during an open-ended interim period.[69] The presumption that prewar Yugoslav republican borders could be changed by peaceful means certainly did not preclude the possibility that Krajina-controlled regions might eventually become independent. As for the Belgrade Serbs, the Vance Plan was an artful way to disengage from the Krajina militarily while still offering political support. UNPROFOR was, in effect if not by design, a contrivance to provide cover for departing JNA forces.

The Croatian government, on the other hand, saw the plan as a prelude to the eventual (re)incorporation of the UNPAs. The plan's provisions for disarming Serb combatants (requiring in exchange only the redeployment of Croatian forces to locations outside of the UNPAs), coupled with the return of displaced populations into the UNPAs, clearly worked to Croatia's advantage.[70] The Zagreb authorities were correspondingly resistant to any action that might tend to freeze or codify the division of their newly independent country. Under such circumstances UNPROFOR was bound to become embroiled in the ongoing dispute between the parties, as both sought to use the UN force to advance their own agendas.

Changes in the Mandate

As a result of a cease-fire agreement reached at the end of March 1994 between Zagreb and the *krajina* Serbs, UNPROFOR acquired the task of patrolling a newly enlarged buffer zone along the line of confrontation separating the forces of the two sides. The agreement provided that Croatian and RSK forces would separate up to a distance of two kilometers, with UNPROFOR taking exclusive control of the zone between these lines. All indirect fire weapons would be redeployed out of range of the lines of separation to specified storage areas on each side (for mortars and AA-guns, not less than ten kilometers; for artillery and tanks, not less than twenty kilometers), and both sides would begin lifting mines affecting UNPROFOR deployments within the area of separation. The cease-fire and heavy weapons withdrawal/non-redeployment obligations would be monitored jointly by UNPROFOR and the European Community Monitoring Mission (ECMM), and several storage areas exempted from the withdrawal requirement would be subject to UNPROFOR supervision. A number of new crossing points would be opened. UNPROFOR would also supervise the work of a limited number of civil policemen from each side in villages located within the area of separation. To oversee implementation of the agreement and to resolve violations, joint commissions of the parties working under UNPROFOR's chairmanship would be established in all sectors and at the national level.[71]

A year later, in response to threats by President Tudjman to revoke UNPROFOR's welcome unless further changes were made in its deployments, the UN split its forces in the former Yugoslavia into three quasi-autonomous operations. The force in Croatia was renamed (somewhat optimistically) the UN Confidence Restoration Operation in Croatia (UNCRO).[72] The inconvenient task of somehow brokering the consent of both parties to the details of the new mandate was consigned to "implementation discussions" to be managed by UN diplomats.

Not surprisingly, Knin's attitude toward these changes was frosty, but it avoided outright rejection in favor of lengthy negotiations. Anticipating the problem, the Council crafted the most sensitive language in the revised mandate to ensure that UNCRO's border presence, while intrusive, would remain consensual. Thus, among other things, UNCRO's mandate would include: "*assisting in controlling, by monitoring and reporting,* the crossing of military personnel, equipment, supplies and weapons, over the international borders between the Republic of Croatia and the Republic of

Bosnia and Herzegovina, and the Republic of Croatia and the Federal Republic of Yugoslavia" (emphasis added).[73]

In the end, however, diplomatic fine-tuning of the UN's mandate could not head off a military resolution of Croatia's ethnic difficulties.

Implementation in Croatia

UNPROFOR's initial deployments were largely completed by July 1992.[74] For administrative purposes, the UN protected areas were divided into four sectors. Each had its own distinctive features. Sector East, bordering Serbia and spanning the agricultural area of Baranja and the oil producing areas of Eastern Slavonia, became operational on 15 May 1992 with the deployment of Belgian and Russian infantry battalions. Sector West (Western Slavonia), an ethnically mixed farming region with both Croat and Serb areas of control, came into being on 20 June, staffed by battalions from Argentina, Canada, and Nepal. The Krajina itself, a rugged, mountainous area bordering Bosnia and the largest of the designated UNPAs, was divided into Sectors North and South. After some delays, discussed below, these sectors were declared operational on 2 July and initially included battalions from France, Denmark, Poland, the Czech Republic, and Kenya.

Command and Control

The overall command of UNPROFOR was entrusted to its force commander, Lieutenant General Satish Nambiar (India), who served until March 1993. Reporting to the force commander in Croatia were four military sector commanders, each a brigadier general; a director of civil affairs (DCA) who served as political adviser to the force commander; and civil police and military observer elements.[75] UNPROFOR's headquarters was initially established in Sarajevo, partly in the hope that a UN presence might inhibit the outbreak of fighting in the Bosnian capital.[76] Subsequently, as the violence in Bosnia sharply escalated in May 1992, UNPROFOR headquarters was moved to Belgrade and then, finally, to Zagreb.

From the start, UNPROFOR's command structure did not promote unity of effort (see figure 6.2). In addition to serving as chief political adviser, the DCA directed the civil police monitors. The operation's chief administrative officer (CAO) controlled the purse strings and reported directly to New York, in a traditional UN arrangement. Finally, the chief military observer (CMO) commanded the mission's several hundred unarmed UNMOs. The DCA, CAO, and CMO had personnel in each of the military sectors who reported directly to them and were not organizationally responsive to the military sector commanders, that is, the force had four separate internal chains of command.[77]

Jurisdictional Disputes

In setting up the UNPAs, the Vance Plan had deliberately defined these areas in terms of *opstine* or parts of *opstine;* it had avoided delineation of UNPA boundaries on the

Fig. 6.2

UNPROFOR COMMAND STRUCTURE, EARLY MAY 1992

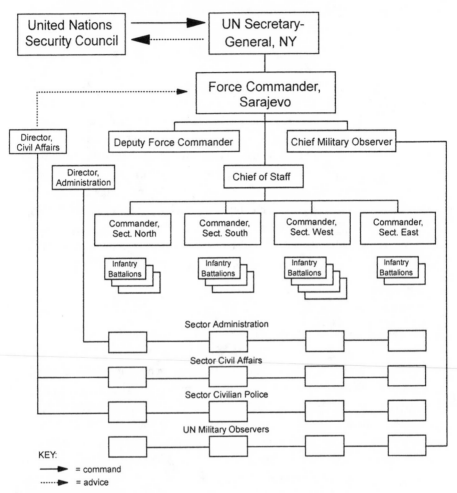

KEY:

→ = command

····▶ = advice

SOURCE: Based on Security Council,

Report of the Secretary-General Pursuant to Security Council Resolution 743 (1992), S/23777, 2 April 1992.

basis of existing confrontation lines for fear of eliciting Croatian rejection of the plan as a de facto partition of the country.[78] While the plan allowed some scope for small adjustments in UNPA borders, certain pockets of Serb population abutting Sectors North and South—dubbed "pink zones"—were to be left outside the UNPAs, and it was expected that the Croatians would reassert authority in these areas. Yet, as JNA units began to withdraw, Serb irregulars moved up to cover their departure and to block any advances by the Croatian police or army. A tense standoff ensued, punctuated by Croat attacks upon Serb positions in "pink zones," areas adjacent to Sector South in late June 1992.

For Belgrade, the solution to this problem was simply to incorporate the "pink zones" into the UNPAs. This idea was quickly rejected by the Croatians as an unacceptable contravention of the original deal. UNPA enlargement got a sympathetic hearing at senior levels at UN headquarters, on the grounds that the expansion would give UNPROFOR a mandate to control access to, and weapons flows within, what had been the "pink zones," and to demobilize local militia in the zones, something it could not otherwise do. Even so, the secretary-general agreed with the Zagreb government's contention that the boundary adjustments necessary to incorporate the zones would exceed any contemplated by the Vance Plan, and that the Croatians therefore were under no obligation to accept UNPA enlargement.[79]

To break the impasse, the secretary-general proposed a joint commission of parties to oversee the demilitarization of the "pink zones" under UN supervision and to enable the Croats gradually to reestablish their authority subject to certain safeguards to protect the local population. The Council accepted this proposal and expanded UNPROFOR's mandate on 30 June 1992.[80] This largely procedural fix helped to defuse tensions to an extent and cleared the way for UNPROFOR's final deployments in Sectors North and South, but subsequent efforts to implement the joint commission process yielded little result, and the "pink zone" problem was left to linger unresolved.

Disarming the UNPAs

Following the Vance Plan's proposed sequence, UNPROFOR concentrated initially on the weapons control/demilitarization aspects of the operation, and with some early success. JNA units were substantially withdrawn from Croatia by late July, and Croatian army units pulled back from the front lines. Tanks and artillery were withdrawn to a distance of thirty kilometers from existing confrontation lines. Serb forces appeared to be meeting their obligation to hand over heavy weapons (that is, tanks, artillery, mortars, antiaircraft guns) for UN-supervised storage. A "dual-lock" system was established whereby weapons in storage could not be removed without the joint concurrence of the local *opstine* council leader and the UN sector commander. During this period, cease-fire violations involving heavy weapons were largely eliminated. All these steps were characterized as early achievements.[81]

Nonetheless, with jurisdictional disputes creating tensions on the fringes of the UNPAs, problems began to impede the demilitarization process. Throughout the protected areas UNPROFOR observed a cascading of weapons, vehicles, and even personnel from departing JNA units to the local armed elements variously called the "border police" or the "multipurpose police brigades." The Belgrade authorities acknowledged this cascading phenomenon but argued that it simply reflected a return to normality—many local police, they asserted, had joined JNA ranks when the fighting broke out, and they were simply returning to their duties.[82] By November, the UN estimated that there were roughly 16,000 Serb militia in the UNPAs equipped with mortars, heavy machine guns, and other prohibited equipment, and that these units were clearly not performing police duties, as asserted by the Knin authorities.

By the end of the year, apart from Sector West, no appreciable demobilization of paramilitary forces had been achieved. UNPROFOR had experimented with small doses of coercive disarmament in Sector East in late July, launching several cordon and search operations to barricade and forcefully disarm local militia. After some tense standoffs, about 500 personal weapons were seized in these operations but the militia units continued to resist compulsory disarmament, and UNPROFOR, in the end, was not prepared to resolve the problem through the use of deadly force.[83] UN Undersecretary-General Marrack Goulding (then head of the Department of Peacekeeping Operations) traveled to Knin in September 1992 and reached agreement on a timetable for the final demobilization of militia but its deadlines passed without apparent result, and RSK officials increasingly took the line that Croatian army behavior was making it impossible for them to implement the Vance Plan's commitments.[84]

The Serbs had reason to be concerned about Croatian activities, although their obduracy in implementing the Vance Plan only fueled Croatian impatience and set the stage for subsequent military actions. In June, Croatian army units launched small-scale attacks near the town of Drnis and the Miljevci plateau, located in a "pink zone" on the edge of Sector South, causing Serb defenders to retreat several kilometers. The Croatians refused to pull their troops back unless the Serbs withdrew entirely into the UNPA. UNPROFOR managed to broker partial withdrawal and attempted to initiate talks in the joint commission on the repair of hydroelectric and road infrastructure. The only tangible result of these efforts was agreement that the UN should take control of the (dangerously damaged) Peruca dam complex, which UNPROFOR's Kenyan battalion accomplished on 14 September.[85]

UNPROFOR fared somewhat better further to the south, in the strategically sensitive Dubrovnik area. During the final stages of JNA withdrawal, the Belgrade government informed UNPROFOR commanders that it would not complete its withdrawal along the Dalmatian coast unless the Prevlaka peninsula, which controls the entrance to the Gulf of Kotor in Montenegro (site of the Yugoslav navy's principal Adriatic base), was demilitarized. A package of arrangements involving JNA withdrawal, a ban on military deployments on the peninsula, and the withdrawal of heavy weapons from both sides of the border area was hammered out by international mediators and accepted in mid-September. Once again, the Council authorized enlargement of the mandate to incorporate monitoring of the agreement.[86]

Ongoing Ethnic Cleansing and Border Control Issues

The continuing displacement of mainly non-Serb populations in the UNPAs posed another problem. With UNPROFOR's arrival, mass expulsions had begun to ebb but individual acts of intimidation and violence against non-Serb property-holders continued, especially in Sector East, often with the involvement or acquiescence of local police or militia. One factor fueling the problem was the large influx of Serb refugees from elsewhere in Croatia and Bosnia who were intent upon seizing property and exacting revenge for their own losses.

On top of this, the newly recognized Croatian government began to press hard for the establishment of international border controls to prevent Serbs from moving industrial infrastructure and natural resources out of the UNPAs and into Serbia, a point with which the Vance Plan offered little help.

Negotiated prior to Croatia's recognition, the Vance Plan had not addressed these nonmilitary, cross-border flows of people and property. Moreover, any provision acknowledging Croatia's frontiers as international borders, even after its recognition, would have unglued Serb support for the plan. To compound matters, the Vance Plan clearly forbade the Croatians from controlling customs and immigration along the 600 or so kilometers (and 66 crossing points) where UNPA boundaries and international frontiers coincided. The only logical choice was to enable UNPROFOR to do the job, even though the UN had no prior experience with international customs and immigration control. The Security Council authorized this expansion in UNPROFOR's mandate in August 1992. Not surprisingly, the Knin Serbs balked, citing a derogation of their own sovereignty.[87]

By the latter part of 1992, it had become clear that the Vance Plan would never be more than partially implemented. Indeed, seven months after UNPROFOR's deployment, the secretary-general bluntly concluded that "no system of law and order exists in the UNPAs."[88] Although major fighting had died down in most areas, widespread patterns of lawlessness, economic collapse, lack of social services, extremist politics, and violence against minorities effectively precluded the safe return of refugees. Successive efforts by UNPROFOR to defuse such problems as the "pink zones," immigration, and border controls quickly ran afoul of disputes between the two parties that no amount of mediation could bridge.

1993: Unhappy Hosts and House Guests

On 22 January 1993, Croatian forces launched a major offensive to reestablish links between isolated Croat-held areas along the Dalmatian coast. The attack, which drove into and around areas of UN control in Sector South, provoked a sharp rebuke from the Security Council and a demand for cessation and withdrawal.[89] It also triggered remobilization of Serb forces within the UNPAs, as RSK soldiers broke into UN-controlled arms depots to retrieve their heavy weapons, nullifying one of UNPROFOR's few successes, and redeployed forces along the confrontation line.[90] The Croats were subjected to daily shelling and rocket attacks that made it difficult to consolidate their gains, while the Serbs bitterly complained that the UN had failed to protect them from Croatian incursions.[91] Thereafter, they adopted a much more aggressive attitude toward UNPROFOR, which once again found itself searching for ways to reestablish stability as a gateway for negotiations.

Through most of 1993, Bosnia attracted international attention while the situation in Croatia reflected stalemate and drift. Sporadic fighting occurred around the fringes of the UNPAs and the security situation inside the areas grew more precarious. Serb militia fighters remained armed and defiant. Without any real local police activity to monitor, UNPROFOR found itself drawn into policing directly.

Among the scattered, mostly elderly, residual Croat populations, it established a protection program for the most vulnerable villages, to deter "hard" cleansing.[92] It also encouraged small-scale, voluntary repatriation efforts in Sector West, the most quiescent of the UNPAs, and it continued to support humanitarian relief efforts. In early September, a third Croat incursion, into the so-called Medak pocket, a "pink zone" abutting Sector North, triggered widespread Serb shelling against Croat-populated areas and sent UNPROFOR scrambling to broker yet another local cease-fire and to interpose itself between the local forces.[93]

On the diplomatic front, much time and energy during 1993 was devoted to debating the terms of the UN's continued presence. Seeing the expiration of UNPROFOR's initial mandate on the horizon in February, Tudjman left little doubt that Croatia would oppose a renewal unless the force were directed to take stronger measures against the *krajina* Serbs, including forcible disarmament and return of refugees.[94] There was no inclination at the UN or among troop contributing states to give UNPROFOR in Croatia an enforcement mandate, but it was also painfully apparent that this consent-based UN peacekeeping force, confronting increasingly hostile attitudes on both sides, was not creating openings for negotiations, as had been hoped.

In fact, the contrary was true: the Serbs were using UNPROFOR to try to freeze the territorial status quo and advance their demands for an independent mini-state; and the Croats were giving up on UNPROFOR as a way station to an "overall political settlement" of the Yugoslav conflict. That settlement, the Zagreb government asserted, had already been achieved with Croatia's recognition; the only issue to negotiate with local Serbs was how to reincorporate the UNPAs into the Croatian body politic. Frustrated by this stalemate but loath to withdraw the peacekeepers and risk a major flareup in the fighting, the Security Council approved three "interim" extensions for UNPROFOR in Croatia while the secretary-general sought to energize talks on Vance Plan implementation and on a larger settlement.[95]

By the fall, a few faint glimmers of hope appeared. The Zagreb government agreed to a longer-term renewal of UNPROFOR's mandate, in exchange for its restructuring into separate commands for Croatia, Bosnia-Herzegovina, and the new operation in the Former Yugoslav Republic of Macedonia (FYROM).[96] Under the aegis of the International Conference on Former Yugoslavia (ICFY), Croats and *krajina* Serbs agreed in principle to a new, three-step process for negotiation: first, discussion of a more durable cease-fire/cessation of hostilities regime; second, consideration of cooperation on economic and reconstruction questions; and third, negotiations on a political settlement.[97]

UNPROFOR units, meanwhile, were having better success in arranging UNPA-specific cease-fires and creating local joint commissions to monitor cease-fire compliance. A Christmas truce was agreed to and extended into the new year.

1994: Temporary Reprieve

After nearly two years of being mired in controversy, UNPROFOR's prospects for 1994 were gloomy. But, somewhat surprisingly, on 29 March, Zagreb and Knin signed a comprehensive cease-fire agreement that was heralded as a major step forward and did, in fact, significantly lessen military tensions throughout the UNPAs. Then, in December, a package of economic measures was agreed upon that produced the first concrete steps toward cooperation on infrastructure repair and other issues. Both agreements had a significant impact on UNPROFOR's operations during 1994 and 1995, although they were not enough, in the end, to deflect Croatia from a military solution to the standoff.

The March agreement was a significant boost to the *krajina* Serbs. By reinforcing the military status quo, the agreement relieved Croatian pressure on Serb positions within the UNPAs and deflected, at least temporarily, the question of Croatian control over the so-called "pink zones" left on the Serb side of the separation lines. UNPROFOR redeployed some of its peacekeepers and civil police monitors into the newly created areas of separation and the secretary-general requested an additional mechanized infantry battalion, four engineering companies, and a helicopter squadron to meet UNPROFOR's increased obligations under the agreement.[98]

The Croatian government's surprising willingness to give the *krajina* Serbs some breathing space militarily did not, however, signify a change of heart in Zagreb but a sense of growing confidence that time was on its side. The Croatians were getting stronger, militarily and economically, while the UNPAs were being dragged under by persistent economic deprivation, rampant unemployment, crime, and political unrest.[99]

Internationally, support for Croatia was growing as well, despite criticism of its military involvement in the Bosnian conflict next door. To address Zagreb's criticisms of UNPROFOR, the Security Council in 1993 had begun to give greater weight in its resolutions to the reintegration of Croatian territory than to the reconciliation of parties.[100] In particular, Resolution 820 (intended mainly to punish the *Bosnian* Serbs for rejecting the Vance-Owen Peace Plan, discussed below) barred the import, export, or transshipment of nonhumanitarian goods through the UNPAs without Croatian government authorization. This decision delighted Zagreb and was seen as a major political win, much to the consternation of the Serb leadership in Knin.[101]

The step-by-step diplomatic process as scripted by the ICFY also worked to the advantage of Croatia. Having achieved a cease-fire, the *krajina* Serbs would be reluctant to imperil that achievement by resisting joint initiatives on economic cooperation and infrastructure repair. Benignly conceived as confidence-building measures, these joint projects nonetheless cut two ways. While they could help alleviate the most immediate social and economic needs by unblocking fuel, power, water, and agricultural supplies, they also gave Zagreb a tool for promoting mutually beneficial commercial ties between individual Serb-held regions (notably Sectors East and West) and neighboring Croat areas, which could in time undermine Knin's authority. The *krajina* Serb leadership was sensitive to this "divide and conquer" potential and sought to reduce it by floating initiatives that would assure their control over implementation of joint projects.[102]

In the end, the March breakthrough did not impart any immediate momentum to the larger peace process, but the cease-fire itself took hold remarkably well in all sectors. Within a month or so, 1,400 square kilometers were opened up between the two sides, allowing UNPROFOR to establish a military presence with 150 observation posts, despite serious hazards from mines.[103] Meanwhile, UN civil police arranged to conduct joint patrols with Croat and Serb police in the numerous villages within the area of separation. A degree of normality returned to previously tense areas near the confrontation lines.[104]

However, certain sectors of the political community in Zagreb objected to the accord, which in their view consolidated a still unsatisfactory status quo. In July and August, amidst local media fanfare, displaced Croats began organizing around-the-clock blockades of UN checkpoints, disrupting UNPROFOR's logistics operations and scheduled troop rotations. The Croatian government's relaxed attitude toward this interference was aggravating to the UN, but Croatia did not otherwise block renewal of UNPROFOR's mandate, either in March 1994 or the following September.[105]

During the fall of 1994, the ICFY-sponsored negotiations seemed to gather steam. Croat/Serb working groups discussed measures of cooperation in various fields, leading to an Agreement on Economic Cooperation on 2 December. Both sides agreed to restore certain water supply systems and electrical transmission lines spanning war-torn areas. The Adriatic oil pipeline was to be opened in part and a joint company set up to sell and distribute oil products in the UNPAs. A segment of the Zagreb-Belgrade highway running though Sector West was to be opened to Croatian traffic, and transportation between Sectors East and West through Croatian areas was agreed upon. UNPROFOR assumed a leading role in implementation, supervising damage assessment, demining, restorative work, and providing security arrangements for vulnerable sites. The initial results were encouraging.[106]

Meanwhile, behind the scenes, the so-called "Z-4" mini-contact group (including the US and Russian ambassadors to Zagreb, along with ICFY representatives) was hard at work finalizing a proposed political settlement that would confer substantial autonomy, though not outright independence, on Krajina.

1995: Beginning of the End?

The sense of optimism generated by these year-end developments proved to be short-lived. On 12 January, as the UN completed a review of UNPROFOR's mandate, President Tudjman announced that Croatia would not accept a further renewal of the mandate after its expiration at the end of March.[107] While Croatia's unhappiness with the Vance Plan implementation was widely known, the announcement's tone of finality caught many by surprise. Knin reacted badly, refusing even to receive the Z-4 proposals in January and suspending implementation of the economic agreement in February until UNPROFOR's future was clarified. The number of cease-fire violations on both sides increased noticeably, as the stability of the previous few months seemed to be slipping away.

Zagreb's unsettling behavior appeared to be motivated by several factors: impatience with the deliberate pace of ICFY-sponsored negotiations; frustration at being taken for granted by major Western states; and, perhaps most of all, deep concern that Knin's increasingly active participation in the Bosnian conflict might in time lead to a political union between the Bosnian and *krajina* Serbs in a "Western Serbia." Although Tudjman would later claim that his January announcement had been mainly designed to change rather than terminate UNPROFOR's mandate, the force's nonpartisan character and largely Third World composition clearly were very unappealing to the Zagreb authorities. At the time of his January statement Tudjman's government in fact had already launched a flurry of initiatives to see whether NATO or some other European regional institutions might replace the UN operation. No one signed up.

In meetings with US Vice-President Albert Gore in Copenhagen in early March, Tudjman agreed to let the UN force stay, if it were renamed and redeployed.[108] "UNCRO" would be reduced from roughly 13 infantry battalions to 8. About 1,200 of its troops would redeploy along Croatia's frontiers, in line with Zagreb's longstanding demands that the UN do more to secure its borders.

In the end, however, fine-tuning of the UN's mandate in Croatia proved to be of little consequence. With war flaring once again in Bosnia and the likelihood that the Bosnian Serbs would be hard pressed to aid their cousins in Krajina, Croatia saw an opportunity to take action. Seizing upon an incident that had prompted the Serbs to close the Zagreb-Belgrade highway, on 1 May 1995 the Croatian army attacked Serb positions in Sector West, completely overrunning them in a few days, and triggering a major refugee flight into northern Bosnia.[109] Though described by Zagreb as a "limited police action," the assault had all the trappings of a preplanned military operation aimed at seizing and holding territory. And it was only the beginning.

Three months later, on 5 August, Croatian armed forces launched a full-scale assault on the Krajina region, presaged by an intense artillery bombardment of Knin from positions in both Croatia and Bosnia. Apart from scattered locations in Sector North, the blitz ("Operation Storm") met with surprisingly little resistance.[110] Croatian forces occupied the entire region within days, sparking a massive exodus of upwards of 200,000 Serb civilians and soldiers and leaving scores of towns and villages in Krajina virtually depopulated.

For the UN, the Croatian actions effectively closed an unhappy chapter in its Yugoslav-based operations. Peacekeepers could do little but watch as Croatian forces drove around and through their positions; a few soldiers were caught in the crossfire; and some were used, egregiously, as human shields. The UN's leadership sought and received (for the most part) Croatian assurances to allow an orderly departure of civilians and soldiers, as well as access for humanitarian organizations.[111] Local UN commanders brokered disengagement accords, allowing for the departure of besieged *krajina* Serb fighters on the condition that they leave their weapons behind. Much less successful were UN efforts to gain access for UNMOs and human rights monitors into affected areas, and reports of looting, destruction of property, and revenge killing continued to filter out of Krajina in the weeks following the attack.[112]

By mid-November 1995, UNCRO had been reduced to less than half of its former strength.[113] Although it maintained its position in strategically sensitive Sector

East, where a Croatian attack seemed likely in the absence of any peace settlement, its presence in other former Croatian war zones was much reduced. Having reintegrated much of its territory through force, Zagreb was more than happy to see large contingents of peacekeepers leaving the country. Only 6,000 Croatian Serbs remained in the Krajina region (former UN Sectors North and South), many of them elderly or disabled, and UN monitors that did gain access confirmed continuing "harassment, looting of property, burning of houses," and killing of civilians.[114]

Assessment of UNPROFOR-C/UNCRO

Much bitterness and controversy has surrounded the UN's experience in Croatia. UN peacekeepers sought to implement a risky, experimental arrangement that proved far too ambitious to be feasible. Casting UNPROFOR (rather uncomfortably) as a protector of people, the Vance Plan conditioned performance of that protection mission upon the unstinting cooperation of the parties. Such cooperation was not to be found, however. UNPROFOR could do little to thwart sporadic violence against remaining non-Serb minorities in the UNPAs, and the Serbs themselves continued to feel extremely vulnerable to the increasingly capable Croatian army.

The Vance Plan, moreover, gave UNPROFOR no license to implement agreed provisions by force, and in all likelihood the parties would not have accepted a de facto intervention force whose guns might at some point be turned on them. Even more problematic was the fact that the Vance Plan scripted procedures for a return to normality—demilitarization, the return of displaced people, restoration of law and order, and so on—even though the issue that had triggered the conflict in the first place, that is, who rules the Serb communities in Croatia, remained unresolved.

Once it was clear that implementing the Vance Plan was impractical, the UN operation turned its attention to other tasks. It can justifiably claim credit for having helped to maintain a shaky cease-fire, preventing a larger conflict that, as one US diplomat observed, would have "all the civility of the war in Bosnia with ten times the firepower."[115] In the broader scheme of things, cease-fires may seem trivial, except of course to those whose lives are spared by them.

The UN also managed to shield small numbers of minorities from violence in the higher risk areas (mainly Sector South), and it shouldered an enormous humanitarian burden, sustaining hundreds of thousands of refugees and displaced people during the bleak period following the 1991 war. Finally, although very hard to measure, the UN's scrutiny of human rights practices within Croatia may have helped to heighten sensitivities to this issue in a country whose historical record on human rights observance leaves much to be desired.

Yet, in the end, UNPROFOR/UNCRO and the diplomatic efforts that ran in conjunction with it could not find a pathway to a durable political settlement. The conditions in Croatia were not ripe for this. As time went on, the relative power positions of the two parties moved increasingly out of balance. The *krajina* Serbs were politically and economically destitute, cut off by their erstwhile benefactors in Belgrade and by the rest of the world as a consequence of UN-imposed sanctions. They were too weak and internally divided to negotiate with confidence, and thus they largely played for time and marginal advantages.

The Croats were well aware of the weakness of the Serb position, which left them with little incentive to negotiate. They had pocketed international recognition, maneuvering Knin into a corner diplomatically. They were not subject to economic sanctions or, apparently, hampered very much by a leaky arms embargo. Indeed, despite their vociferous protests that UN peacekeepers were supporting an unfair status quo in the country, it was the Croats who clearly gained the most from the UN's presence. For without the UN's arrival in 1992, the JNA might have remained engaged in Croatia, working increasingly to the advantage of the local Serbs. Once the UN deployed, the JNA departed, and the stability provided by UNPROFOR gave the Croats the necessary breathing space to gain strength, economically and militarily. In retrospect, absent a diplomatic capitulation by the *krajina* Serbs, it was only a matter of time before Zagreb would try to settle matters by force.

UNPROFOR IN BOSNIA-HERZEGOVINA

United Nations military forces sidled into Bosnia-Herzegovina, not to monitor a cease-fire (as in Croatia), nor to impose peace, but to keep the population alive while the war—and diplomatic efforts to end it—continued. UNPROFOR's multilayered mandate in Bosnia was the end product of Security Council efforts to reconcile the national objectives of the four permanent members (the United States, Great Britain, France, and Russia), who are active players on most international security issues.[116] Despite their patchwork nature, UNPROFOR's mandates broke new ground for UN forces (not all of it welcome to those *on* the ground). Bosnia in particular taxed command, control, communications, and tactical intelligence more than any previous UN field operation. Because a large part of its job was to escort humanitarian relief, unlike most UN operations some of its forces were always on the move. Because Bosnia was an active war zone where central political control of undisciplined, often drunk, local fighting units was sometimes tenuous at best, UN convoys and observation posts faced threats that changed unpredictably, sometimes in response to local conditions and sometimes to larger political events. Once inserted into the conflict, moreover, UNPROFOR became an element of it.

Peacemaking: The Tortuous Path

From the outset, Bosnia's communal conflicts have spawned, and defied, a seemingly endless parade of mediation efforts. Initially, the EC led the effort, but after the collapse of its Lisbon initiative in the spring of 1992 (mentioned above), the UN and the EC teamed up in August 1992 to establish the ICFY. There followed over the next three years a dizzying array of statements of principles, suggested constitutional arrange-

Fig. 6.3

MAP OF BOSNIA-HERZEGOVINA

SOURCE: US Government

ments, and territorial maps: two major ICFY initiatives, the United States-sponsored effort to establish a Muslim-Croat federation, the five-nation "contact group" plan in 1994, and finally, the United States-led mediation in late 1995. On the ground, meanwhile, UNPROFOR sought to put into place a cease-fire/cessation of hostilities regime, initially in mid-1994 and again in early 1995. Some of these efforts fared better than others; all bumped up against the same vexing problems of multiethnic governance that had pushed Bosnia into the abyss in the first place.

The first, and most significant problem, was the character of the Bosnian state itself. Would independence from Yugoslavia lead to a unitary Bosnia within its prewar administrative borders, to a federated state, to a rump Bosnia with parts of the country annexed by Serbia and Croatia, or to a loose confederation of mini-states? The second problem was how to draw boundaries. Who would control which areas, especially the major cities, like Sarajevo, which were ethnically mixed and could not be easily assigned to one group or another?

The 1992 rebellion had been fomented by Serb nationalists who played upon the deep anxieties of their kin regarding the emergence of a Muslim-led unitary state, effectively consigning Bosnia's Serbs to minority status. As rebel Serb leader Radovan Karadzic put it, "If the Muslims were not willing to remain in a multi-ethnic and multi-cultural Yugoslavia ruled by non-Muslims, why should we be willing to live in a Bosnia ruled by non-Serbs?"[117] The Muslim-led Bosnian government, on the other hand, favored independence from Yugoslavia but rejected any constitutional arrangement that would dilute Bosnian sovereignty or legitimize the Bosnian Serb Army's (BSA's) land-grab, for fear that the country's Muslims would sooner or later would be consigned to a twilight existence, sandwiched between a greater Serbia and a greater Croatia.

Bosnia's Croats were no more enthusiastic than the Muslims about remaining in Yugoslavia, but they shared the Serbs' anxiety about a unitary Bosnian state. Croatian nationalists in western Herzegovina, especially, leaned heavily toward integration into Croatia and, as an ominous step in that direction, established their own "Croat Republic of Herzeg-Bosna" based in Mostar.

Given staunch opposition, from one party or another, to the polar extremes of a strong unitary state or a Serbian-Croatian carve-up of Bosnia, nearly all diplomatic efforts have focused on constitutional principles embracing various degrees of decentralized authority. The first of these initiatives was the Vance-Owen Plan (named after the ICFY cochairs, UN envoy Cyrus Vance and the EC's chief mediator, Lord David Owen), which was formally presented to the parties on 4 January 1993. Sidestepping the failed strategy of promoting ethnic cantons, Vance and Owen proposed the creation, within a single state, of ten semi-autonomous provinces for Bosnia. One ethnic group or another would predominate in each province and "most governmental functions" would be carried out at the provincial level, although there would be a loosely organized central authority.[118]

Initially, the reactions of the parties to the Vance-Owen Plan appeared promising: all three signed up to the basic constitutional principles. There was, however, much haggling over a proposed map of provincial boundaries and other details, and the Serbs in the end refused to accept the plan.[119]

The failure of the Vance-Owen Plan, coupled with the outbreak of fighting between Bosnia's Croats and Muslims, prompted ICFY's negotiators to return to a looser construction of Bosnian governance. Owen, along with Vance's successor, former Norwegian foreign minister Thorvald Stoltenberg, put forward a new blueprint for a peace settlement after a round of talks with Presidents Tudjman and Milosevic during June 1993.

Under the Owen-Stoltenberg approach, Bosnia would be recast as a confederation, or "union," of three ethnically based constituent republics. There would be a number of common institutions—for example, a collective presidency and a parliament drawn from the three republic's assemblies—and no republic could withdraw from the union without the prior agreement of the others. At the same time, all governmental authorities would flow to the republics except those expressly given to the common institutions by the constitutional agreement or subsequently by the 120-member union parliament (requiring a majority vote of members from *each* of the three republics).[120] Again, the general outline of this deal seemed to elicit a positive reaction, but it unraveled toward the end of the year when the Bosnian government insisted on territorial adjustments opposed by both Croat and Serb sides.[121]

At this point, the peacemaking process shifted toward lesser goals. Germany, the United States, and other countries began to press hard on Sarajevo and Zagreb for an end to the Croat-Muslim fighting in central Bosnia, and in late February, UN commanders were able to broker a bilateral cease-fire/cessation of hostilities agreement between the two. This was quickly followed on 1 March in Washington by agreements on a Muslim-Croat federation of the two communities and, as an inducement to the Croats, a *con*federation between the new Bosnian federation and Croatia.[122] The partiality of the achievement was clear enough: little effort was made to leave the door open to a future Serb association; the transition from the two existing Muslim-led and Croat political entities to the federation was not fully clarified; nor were the precise character of the confederal links to Croatia specified in any detail. The fighting, nonetheless, died down in the central and southern parts of the country. With UNPROFOR's assistance, the quality of life improved as infrastructure was repaired and the EU assumed administration of Mostar. There was at long last some peace to keep.

With "piecemeal peace" breaking out in Bosnia, there was hope in mid-1994 for a larger deal. The major vehicle for that effort was now the so-called "Contact Group," a loose coordinating committee of ambassadors from the United States, Great Britain, France, Russia, and Germany, that eclipsed ICFY. In July 1994, after prior contact with the parties, the group devised a proposal that aggregated territory in a manner similar to the Owen-Stoltenberg Plan (51 percent for the Muslims and Croats; 49 percent for the Serbs), except that it placed Sarajevo under a transitional UN administration. The map was presented to the parties initially on a "take it or leave it" basis.[123]

Proposed constitutional arrangements also echoed the Owen-Stoltenberg Plan. The group weighed whether Bosnia's Serbs should be able to confederate with Serbia in exchange for their acceptance of a loose Bosnian Union, without a unilateral right to secede. This idea was not proposed as part of the original Contact Group package, however, for fear that the Muslims would oppose it. The Muslims did accept the map, albeit begrudgingly; the Serbs did not. The process ground to a screeching halt, and the members of the Contact Group fell to arguing among themselves over how to pressure the Bosnian Serbs into accepting the plan, at least as a basis for further negotiation.

With stalemate setting in, it was left to events on the ground to provide future diplomatic openings. A four-month cessation of hostilities, brokered by the UN's special representative, Yasushi Akashi, in the wake of former president Jimmy Carter's intercession with both sides in late December 1994, gave rise to hope in early 1995. (The Bosnian side, ever skeptical of cease-fires that would simply freeze the status quo, had consistently rejected such proposals.) But the arrangement produced no momentum at the bargaining table, and within three months the Bosnian government resumed military operations. The Serbs, in turn, tightened their stranglehold on Sarajevo and the besieged enclaves held by the government in eastern Bosnia.

Mandates

UNPROFOR's Bosnian mandate expanded and its force levels grew year by year. Although its work can be divided, analytically, into phases based on these added tasks, readers should understand that the old responsibilities continued even as each new task was added.

All of these tasks were carried out under peacekeeping rules of engagement (ROE), that is, impartiality and nonuse of force except in self-defense or defense of the mandate. Both of these elements of the ROE caused problems and misunderstandings from the outset. It was, however, the consensus of the UN's leadership (both political and military), as well as UNPROFOR's major troop contributors, that the force could not sustain a tougher ROE given its equipment, physical disposition, and increasingly variegated nationality.

Phase One: Aid to Sarajevo

On 5 June 1992, two months after Sarajevo came under attack from Bosnian Serb forces, UNPROFOR's director of civil affairs, Cedric Thornberry, negotiated an agreement with the Bosnian government and Bosnian Serb representatives to open the Sarajevo airport under UN control for "humanitarian purposes." A security corridor, run by UNPROFOR, would be established for aid convoys between the airport and the city. All antiaircraft weapons were to be withdrawn out of range of the airport, and all heavy weapons in range of the airport were to be concentrated and subject to monitoring by UNPROFOR.[124]

Three days later, the Security Council unanimously passed Resolution 758, implementing the airport agreement. At the end of June, Resolution 761 increased the UN presence in Sarajevo to one infantry battalion, and in mid-July Resolution 764 increased it further, to two battalions. Both votes were unanimous.

Phase Two: Escort of Humanitarian Relief

Only days after the Council voted to expand UNPROFOR's presence in Sarajevo, the London Conference on the Former Yugoslavia adopted its declaration on the concentration of all heavy weapons into monitored areas (along the lines of the airport agreement) and asked the UN to assume responsibility for monitoring them. On 17 July 1992, a statement by the president of the Security Council agreed, in principle, to that request. Unfortunately, Secretary-General Boutros-Ghali had not been sitting in on the Council session that produced the statement and reacted angrily when apprised of it. On 21 July, the Secretariat produced a report for the Council that detailed requirements to implement the London accord (some 10,000 military observers, which seemed a lot at the time). Three days later, the Council recanted in another presidential statement that described the London agreement as premature.[125]

One month later, in response to increasingly lurid press accounts of mass murder, kidnappings, torture, and concentration camps in Bosnia that ascribed responsibility primarily to Bosnian Serb forces, the Council passed Resolution 770 (13 August). The resolution referenced Chapter VII of the UN Charter in calling upon states to take "nationally, or through regional agencies or arrangements, all measures necessary" to facilitate the delivery of humanitarian assistance to Bosnia-Herzegovina.[126] In using language reminiscent of that used to previously invite member states to expel Iraqi forces from Kuwait, the Council gave its members, and organizations like NATO, a green light to act as they saw fit to get the aid through to beleaguered civilians.

NATO military planners estimated that 100,000 troops would be needed to ensure distribution of relief in Bosnia-Herzegovina. The US Joint Chiefs of Staff estimated that 60,000-120,000 troops would be needed to guarantee relief for Sarajevo and 400,000 would be required to quell fighting and occupy the country at large. Political leaders on both sides of the Atlantic quailed before these numbers and, despite such gestures as a US Senate resolution supporting forceful intervention to secure relief and open up detention camps, ultimately backed away from the use of coercive military force. An emergency meeting of NATO ambassadors on 14 August reviewed existing military options and asked for new ones; at the review of modified options on 24 August, the United States reportedly backed away from the use of force and supported British and French proposals to deploy NATO-contributed units under the UN flag.[127]

In apparent response to Resolution 770, the BSA turned down the heat, allowing a UN food convoy into Gorazde, in eastern Bosnia. At the London Conference in late August, Serb envoys agreed to lift sieges, close detention camps, cooperate with the relief operations, and turn over heavy weapons to the UN. Two weeks after passage of Resolution 770, NATO offered forces to the UN for escorting humanitarian relief convoys in Bosnia. The Secretariat recommended that these units be folded into UNPROFOR and operated under standard peacekeeping rules of engagement, that is, not as a fighting force. But it also reaffirmed that self-defense could be interpreted to include "situations in which armed persons attempt by force to prevent United Nations troops from carrying out their mandate."[128]

On 14 September, the Security Council, without reference to Chapter VII, endorsed this recommendation in Resolution 776, which gave UNPROFOR a mandate to protect humanitarian relief convoys in Bosnia-Herzegovina. The same resolution approved deployment of up to five infantry battalions and a transport battalion and establishment of a subcommand for Bosnia within UNPROFOR, under the command of a major general. The troop contributing countries initially agreed to absorb their own marginal costs of deploying these forces.[129]

Under Resolution 776, UNPROFOR was to provide protection to humanitarian assistance activities as requested by the UN High Commissioner for Refugees (UNHCR), which retained responsibility for assigning priorities to relief activities, scheduling convoys, and negotiating safe passage. UNPROFOR would also provide ground transportation for "difficult routes."

Resolution 776 maintained the fiction, invented thirty years earlier for another UN operation a continent away in the Congo, that impartial intervention was really nonintervention and should be viewed as such by the local parties. But in a war in which civilians and their domiciles were principal targets, aid to that population was aid to the enemy, no matter that it flowed in all directions at once. Relief supplies were political currency, subject to constant decisions by the Bosnian factions and their local unit commanders to constrict or expand the flow as political—not humanitarian—requirements dictated. Often, the greater the humanitarian need, the greater the political utility in constricting the flow of aid. UN indignation and, for a time, threats of air attack usually served to reopen the flow of aid, but usually in exchange for something valuable to the side controlling the flow, which was frequently (but not always) the Bosnian Serbs.

Shortly after giving UNPROFOR the relief escort job, the Security Council decided (in response to continuing, if desultory, attacks by Yugoslav and BSA aircraft on Croat and Bosniac targets) to ban military aircraft from Bosnian airspace (Resolution 781, 9 October 1992), except as authorized by UNPROFOR. In a companion resolution (786 of 10 November), the Council approved a system of implementation that relied on ground-based inspectors. All flights destined for Bosnia were to pass through the airports at Split or Zagreb, in Croatia, or through Belgrade, where they would be inspected before departure by ECMM observers (at Split), UN military observers (at Zagreb), or UN civilian police (at Belgrade). The ECMM and UNMOs divided responsibility for reinspecting aircraft arriving at and departing from 13 other airfields in Croatia, Bosnia, and Yugoslavia. NATO early warning aircraft would monitor Bosnian airspace and provide information on all flights to UNPROFOR headquarters.[130]

Within a week of this action on military overflights, in Resolution 787 (16 November 1992), the Council tightened the embargo on Serbia and Montenegro (the self-declared Federal Republic of Yugoslavia, or FRY), banning transshipment of goods through the country (thereby trying to close a large loophole in the original sanctions). Member states were directed to enforce sanctions, and naval vessels were given the right to stop, board, and search vessels bound for FRY ports. (China abstained on this vote, as it did on all resolutions imposing sanctions.) On 22 November, NATO/Western European Union ships, already on picket duty in the Adriatic, began enforcement of sanctions in operations called Maritime Guard and Sharp Fence. These were merged on 15 June 1993 into Operation Sharp Guard.[131]

In mid-December, NATO also offered to enforce the "no-fly zone" if the UN were to authorize such action.[132] After more than 400 violations of the zone had been noted in its first few months of existence, the Council voted, in Resolution 816 (31

March 1993), to authorize enforcement of the flight ban by member states or "regional arrangements," under Chapter VII of the Charter, subject to "close coordination" with UNPROFOR. Although zone violators could be engaged in flight, the resolution did not permit bombing of ground targets. Enforcement by NATO aircraft commenced on 12 April 1993.[133]

Phase Three: Protection of Safe Areas

At roughly the same time, in response to a deteriorating humanitarian situation spawned in part by renewed BSA offensives against the isolated areas of eastern Bosnia still held by the government, the Security Council, acting under Chapter VII of the Charter, passed Resolution 819 (16 April 1993), declaring the town of Srebrenica and its (unspecified) surrounding territory to be a UN-protected "safe area" free "from armed attack or any other hostile act."[134] The resolution, which passed unanimously, demanded withdrawal of Bosnian Serb paramilitary units from the area, but not government forces. Although it demanded Serb compliance, the resolution did not give UNPROFOR responsibility for *defending* Srebrenica.

Three weeks later, the Council unanimously declared Sarajevo, Bihac, Tuzla, Zepa, and Gorazde to be safe areas as well (Resolution 824, 6 May 1993). On 3 June, in Resolution 836, the Council extended UNPROFOR's mandate to "*deter*" attacks on all six safe areas, "*promote*" the withdrawal from them of all but government forces, "*monitor*" cease-fires, and "*occupy some key points on the ground*" (emphasis added). UNPROFOR was further authorized,

> *acting in self-defense,* to take the necessary measures, including the use of force, in reply to bombardments against the safe areas by any of the parties or to armed incursion into them or in the event of any deliberate obstruction in or around those areas to the freedom of movement of UNPROFOR or of protected human- itarian convoys. (Emphasis added.)

The resolution also allowed member states, in the now-standard formula ("acting nationally or through regional organizations or arrangements"), to take "all necessary measures, through the use of air power, in and around the safe areas . . . , to *support UNPROFOR in the performance of its mandate,* . . . subject to close coordination with the Secretary-General and UNPROFOR" (emphasis added).[135]

In practice, these resolutions were interpreted to mean that UNPROFOR would take action if its forces in or near the safe areas were subject to attack and could call for NATO close air support in those circumstances. They were not interpreted by UNPROFOR's leadership or its major troop contributors to give the operation general responsibility for defending the safe areas, nor were they interpreted to give NATO carte blanche to do so. Nonetheless, by singling out the Bosnian Serbs as the party in the wrong, and by demanding their withdrawal from the designated areas without quid pro quo from government forces, the Security Council gave UNPROFOR a mandate that was decidedly partisan in nature. But it neither provided the means to implement that mandate nor revoked earlier elements of the mandate, such as food distribution, that were still to be implemented impartially.[136] What had merely been a trip through the Twilight Zone for UN forces became an increasingly Orwellian exercise in which safe areas were not safe, protection was extended to food but not people, and the vicious customs of war in the Balkans were condemned without consequence to the perpetrators.

As it added the safe areas to UNPROFOR's task list, the Security Council also took steps to further tighten economic sanctions on Serbia and Montenegro as punishment for their continued support of Serbian forces in Croatia and Bosnia. And it extended the embargo to Serb-held areas in those countries. Resolution 820 (17 April 1993) authorized the freezing of all FRY financial assets abroad, closed the ports of Serbia and Montenegro to all shipping not explicitly exempted by the UN's Sanctions Committee (or under force majeure), and authorized the detention and impoundment of vessels, vehicles, and rolling stock found to be in violation of UN sanctions. Thus, after nearly a year, the trade embargo on the FRY acquired serious teeth; ships of what would shortly become Operation Sharp Guard could seize, not merely board and inspect, other ships and cargoes violating sanctions.

Phase Four: Weapons Exclusion Zones and the Muslim-Croat Federation

The detonation of a large mortar round in Sarajevo's busy Markale Market on 5 February 1994 killed 68 people and wounded 197 in the single bloodiest incident in Sarajevo in 22 months of war. Although Serb forces denied responsibility, Secretary-General Boutros-Ghali immediately asked his NATO counterpart, Manfred Woerner, for a NATO commitment to support UNPROFOR with air strikes (that is, ground attacks whose aim was something other than protection of UN troops and facilities). NATO agreed, and went a step further.

On 9 February 1994, NATO's governing body, the North Atlantic Council (NAC), issued an ultimatum that assigned to the Bosnian Serbs the "main responsibility" for loss of life in Sarajevo; condemned the continuing "siege" of the city; and called for

> the withdrawal, or regrouping and placing under UNPROFOR control, within ten days, of heavy weapons . . . of the Bosnian Serb forces located in an area within 20 kilometres of the centre of Sarajevo, and excluding an area within two kilometres of the centre of Pale [Bosnian Serb headquarters].[137]

NATO also called upon

> the Government of Bosnia-Herzegovina, within the same period, to place the heavy weapons in its possession within the Sarajevo exclusion zone described above under UNPROFOR control, and to refrain from attacks from within the current confrontation lines in the city.[138]

Any heavy weapons (specified as tanks, artillery pieces, mortars, multiple-rocket launchers, missiles, and antiaircraft weapons) found within the exclusion zone after midnight, Greenwich Mean Time, 21 February 1994, and not under UNPROFOR "control," would be subject to NATO air strikes, along with their support facilities.

In addition, the NAC gave the commander in chief of Allied Forces Southern Europe (CINCSOUTH), based in Naples, Italy, the authority to undertake air strikes against any artillery or mortar positions near Sarajevo, in or outside of the exclusion zone, "which are determined by UNPROFOR to be responsible for attacks against civilian targets" in Sarajevo—provided the UN agreed.[139]

Although the UN Security Council met to consider the situation in Bosnia at the request of Russia and Pakistan, and debated the issue for two days (14-15 February), no resolutions or statements were issued, which may seem strange given the momentous events underway and the Council's verbose track record on Yugoslavia. Indeed, the Council's main action throughout the rest of 1994 was to extend the reach of air power into Croatian territory to protect UN troops and support safe areas (Resolutions 908 and 958, 31 March and 19 November 1994).

This apparent lapse into relative passivity derived in large part from US, British, and French desires not to give presumed Serb-sympathizer Russia a voice (let alone a veto) on the use of NATO air power in the former Yugoslavia, preferring to terminate the UN chain of command on this issue at the secretary-general's office. Thus the Council watched events unfold, increasing UNPROFOR's authorized strength to monitor the weapon exclusion zones (and to help implement the Muslim-Croat Federation accord) without further altering the operation's mandates.[140] Once the command and control procedures for the use of air power had been agreed to in the spring of 1994, key decisions influencing the course of events were made by Secretariat officials in New York and in the field.

The 1994 Muslim-Croat cease-fire brokered by UN commanders in late February, and the federation accord brokered by the United States in March conferred upon UNPROFOR an additional set of tasks in central Bosnia that looked more like postconflict, multidimensional peacekeeping than did the rest of the operation. UNPROFOR monitored Muslim-Croat zones of separation and weapons control points, helped to rebuild local infrastructure, and staffed checkpoints on key routes within the federation area, although the Security Council had passed no resolutions specifically calling upon it to do so (in part because of concerns that the "anti-Serb" character of the federation would trigger Russian opposition).[141]

Implementation in Bosnia

The UN Protection Force in Bosnia-Herzegovina (UNPROFOR-BH), initially calved off the main force in Croatia, proved to be the most complex and frustrating operation ever undertaken by the United Nations, Somalia included. This section traces its planning and implementation, by phase, from June 1992 through June 1995.

Implementing the Sarajevo Airport Agreement

UNPROFOR's initial deployment into Bosnia was in direct response to the growing humanitarian crisis in Sarajevo that led to the 5 June 1992 Sarajevo Airport Agreement. That agreement was to be implemented in the beginning by UN military observers. Sector Sarajevo—initially headed by Canadian brigadier general Lewis Mackenzie, UNPROFOR's chief of staff—was created to operate the airport. Mackenzie arrived in Sarajevo on 10 June with 50 UNMOs (at roughly the same time that UNPROFOR achieved full deployment in Croatia). They were met with flowers. Two weeks later, they were reinforced by a Canadian mechanized battalion and a company of French marines. The Canadians' armored personnel carriers were stuffed with TOW antitank missiles—higher firepower than authorized by the UN but thought by Canada to be necessary for its troops' self-defense.[142] By this time, however, Sarajevans had tumbled to the fact that the UN had not come to save them or to defeat the BSA, but instead to feed and clothe them while the siege continued. Now booed by local residents as often as bouqueted, Mackenzie requested early transfer, reportedly after receiving death threats.[143]

Implementation of the Airport Agreement illustrated and foreshadowed some of the political and moral tradeoffs that the UN would face everywhere as it went about its humanitarian tasks in Bosnia. The Serbs granted UNPROFOR control of the Sarajevo Airport, for example, in exchange for a UN pledge to block non-UN access to the city through the airport (which lay between Bosniac-held Mount Igman, south of the city, and the city itself; Serb forces held the lowlands at either end of the airfield). UN illumination of the runways, intended as a deterrent to nocturnal crossings, incidentally facilitated Serb sniping at individuals who did try to cross. The government spent the better part of a year completing work on an under-airport pedestrian tunnel in response, thereby linking the city to trails over Mount Igman that connected with supply routes in central Bosnia.

Canada's battalion in Sarajevo was replaced in July by a unit from Egypt that was in turn reinforced later that month by a battalion from Ukraine (then independent for just six months and starved for the hard currency that would be paid for service in a UN mission).[144]

The airport was opened up to relief flights in late June following a brief, flak-jacketed visit by French president François Mitterand, although BSA heavy weapons had not been pulled out of range as stipulated in the airport agreement. The relief airlift, coordinated by UNHCR, kept the otherwise isolated city resupplied for nearly three years. (In April 1995, as the Bosnian government reinitiated military operations on the tail end of a four-month cease-fire, the Serbs forced the airport to close, citing abuse by the UN and the Bosnian government of agreed rules on passenger use of the cargo aircraft. It remained closed for nearly six months, precipitating a food crisis in the city and unconsented resupply efforts by UNPROFOR over Mount Igman, until the NATO bombing campaign of September 1995 forced the Serbs to back off once again.)

Escorting Relief Convoys

Once Resolution 776 expanded UNPROFOR's mandate to include relief escort, its command staff busied itself with operational planning. UNPROFOR headquarters, under the leadership of Major General Phillipe Morillon, the deputy force commander, studied the operational implications of relief convoy escort with UNHCR field representatives even before it received mandate for the mission, thereby smoothing the transition to phase two. When Major General Morillon was appointed UNPROFOR-BH commander, he gathered civilian and military representatives from troop contributing countries for a ten-day pre-deployment meeting in Zagreb on command and control and the mission. Moreover, initial operational orders were sent by UNPROFOR to national battalions before they left their home garrisons for the Balkans.

During this phase of its operations, UNPROFOR-BH grew from three to seven infantry battalions, and acquired three support battalions as its operations moved beyond Sarajevo to encompass (at least on paper) all parts of the country. BH Command headquarters, formed from part of a NATO Central Front command group, was set up in the Croat town of Kiseljak, near Sarajevo but outside the siege line and, for awhile, outside the fighting. (At this time, UNPROFOR's director of civil affairs Thornberry acquired a second hat as deputy chief of mission, making him deputy to Force Commander and Chief of Mission Nambiar, and more clearly the senior civilian in UNPROFOR.)

What had been largely a two-sided fight, with Croats and Muslims fending off Serb attacks, began to decay into a three-way struggle in September 1992, when leaders of the Bosnian Croats broke ranks with the Bosnian government and called for a three-way partition of the country. In exchange for a deal that demilitarized the Prevlaka Peninsula near Dubrovnik, in the far southeastern tip of Croatia, Croat forces pulled out of the joint Muslim-Croat defense of Bosanski Brod, a town in northern Bosnia on the Sava River, which allowed the Serbs to create a land corridor linking Serbia with Serb-held areas of Croatia and northern and western Bosnia. This "Posavina Corridor" was a major Serb territorial objective in the war.[145] Shortly after this event, radical nationalist Croat forces in western Herzegovina began to murder Muslims in Prozor and other towns, scouring out a Croat-only area consistent with what seemed at the time to be a budding Serb-Croat deal to carve up Bosnia between themselves.[146]

As the war thus became more complex, the first NATO-member units assigned to convoy protection attempted to deploy into Bosnia, but found that a UN flag did not automatically open the way. In November 1992, the French battalion group sent into Bihac was blocked by Serb forces from deploying further south to Serb-held Bosanski Petrovac, a junction of main roads south to the Dalmatian coast and east to central Bosnia. Deployments of a Canadian battalion and a Belgian-Dutch supply company slated for Banja Luka, in Serb-held northwestern Bosnia, were also blocked by the BSA. UN military observers did operate within Serb-held areas and a Russian battalion deployed, from the spring of 1994 onward, within Serb-held parts of

Sarajevo, but UNPROFOR deployed mainly on the Muslin/Croat side of the "line of confrontation."

As relief escort operations got underway, Bosnian Serb forces resumed the offensive against government-held enclaves in eastern Bosnia (especially Cerska, Zepa, and Srebrenica). Muslim commando units were, in turn, ambushing Serb vehicles and convoys.[147] For ten days (12-22 February), the Bosnian government refused aid for Sarajevo as long as no aid was getting through to the enclaves, in an effort to pressure the UN to try harder. Miffed, UNHCR shut down all aid deliveries and the secretary-general, equally miffed at UNHCR, ordered aid resumed. An UNHCR convoy reached Zepa on 21 February, and the Sarajevo government's aid boycott ended.[148]

To help ease the supply crisis in the eastern enclaves, the United States announced the start of an airdrop operation in late February. Its first target was Cerska, which fell to Serb forces on 5 March; nearby Konjevic Polje, also an airdrop target, fell nine days later. More civilians fled into neighboring Srebrenica and its environs, swelling a town of 7,000 to roughly 30,000 persons.[149] BH commander Morillon went to Srebrenica in mid-March and stayed there for two weeks in a personal gesture of solidarity with the besieged population. In the meantime, nonaligned members of the Security Council pressed it to act on Srebrenica's behalf. The net result was the safe areas concept and a further expansion of UNPROFOR's mandate.

As these events that attracted Western attention were taking place in eastern Bosnia, and as Vance and Owen pressed for both local and international acceptance of their cantonal peace plan, central Bosnia erupted into wholesale fighting between Muslims and Croats that shut down UNHCR's main convoy routes into Bosnia from the south. Using back mountain roads, convoys took double the normal time to reach warehouses in Zenica and Sarajevo, delivering only half of the supplies that UNHCR calculated were needed for the first six months of 1993.[150]

Implementing Safe Areas

At about the same time that UNPROFOR received its new safe areas mandate, it also received its first civilian chief of mission, former Norwegian foreign minister Thorvald Stoltenberg, then also UN envoy to ICFY, in Geneva. Appointed special representative of the secretary-general (SRSG), and thus UNPROFOR's first civilian chief of mission, Stoltenberg continued to be based in Geneva. UNPROFOR also changed force commanders. Lieutenant General Lars Erik Wahlgren of Sweden replaced Lieutenant General Nambiar in March 1993. Wahlgren remained in his post only until July, however, when he was replaced by General Jean Cot of France.

Lieutenant General Morillon was replaced as commander of UNPROFOR-BH at about the same time that Cot took command in Zagreb.[151] His successor, Lieutenant General Francis Briquemont of Belgium, grew increasingly frustrated at not having the troops required to implement even the "light" option for safe area protection. By the end of 1993, only 2,000 of the 7,600 troops authorized had actually been deployed. Briquemont asked to be relieved and was replaced in January 1994 after six months on the job.[152]

Fig. 6.4

UNPROFOR COMMAND STRUCTURE, MAY 1993, MILITARY ELEMENTS

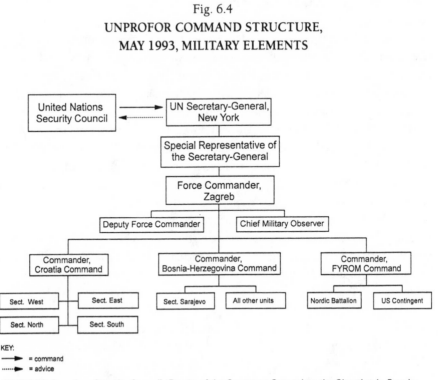

KEY:
——▶ = command
······▶ = advice

SOURCES: Based on Security Council, *Report of the Secretary-General on the Situation in Bosnia and Herzegovina,* S/24540, 10 September 1992; and Security Council, *Further Report of the Secretary-General Pursuant to Security Council Resolution 743 (1992),* S/25264, 10 February 1993.

During this phase, BH Command grew from 7 to 12 infantry battalions and to 8 support-battalion equivalents, including the large British logistics unit based at Split, Croatia, on the Dalmatian coast. To cope with the growing operation, the Security Council restructured UNPROFOR into three subordinate military commands (Croatia, Bosnia, and Macedonia) under General Cot's overall direction. Figure 6.4 reflects this change and the fact that UNPROFOR now had a nominal civilian boss not based in New York.

The safe area declarations produced mixed results. Fighting died down around Srebrenica, food aid reached the town, and the sick and wounded were evacuated, but the BSA refused to allow housing materials (which they deemed to be nonhumanitarian supplies) into the town and in withdrawing from the area blew up the local water treatment plant (as was done a year later at Gorazde). However, Gorazde's 65,000 people (half of them already displaced from elsewhere) were cut off from resupply for more than a month after the town was declared a safe area. At the same time, threats to UNHCR and other relief personnel increased throughout Bosnia, making it "virtually impossible to move without UNPROFOR military escort or in armored vehicles."[153] Muslim-Croat fighting blocked aid through central Bosnia such that by mid-year, UNHCR's Zenica warehouse held only 20 percent of the supplies reckoned necessary to meet the immediate needs of the beneficiary populations that it served.[154]

Sarajevo's airlift could bring in food and medicine, but not water, fuel, or power, which were blocked by Serb or Croat forces. To work around the worst bottlenecks, British engineers spent several months creating a new road (dubbed "Route Triangle") out of the mud tracks that crossed the mountains between Tomislavgrad and Prozor, bypassing Mostar, the Neretva River Valley, and its blown bridges, and linking Route Square coming from Split with Route Diamond going north to Zenica.[155]

The BSA also pressed in on Sarajevo during the summer of 1993, fighting closer to the city from the south and capturing the flanks of Mount Igman on 4 August, which cut the last land route into Sarajevo, a dirt track over the mountain. UN mediators brokered an agreement for Serb withdrawal from Igman by 14 August. NATO threatened air strikes against Serb forces if they failed to withdraw by the agreed deadline and set up command and control procedures with UNPROFOR to govern the use of NATO air power. Shortly after the 9 August NATO ultimatum, however, French forces with UNPROFOR were deployed on Igman, intermingling with Serb units (and effectively forestalling air strikes).[156]

The Muslim-Croat fighting produced some of the same horrors originally attributed to Serbian paramilitaries. Both the Bosnian government and the Croat HVO militia held prisoners under marginal conditions and both engaged in ethnic cleansing in central Bosnia, but the Croats tended to take the initiative and to use more horrific tactics, more consistently, than Bosniac forces. A number of villages were totally razed, their inhabitants driven out or slaughtered, and the entire Muslim population of Mostar was driven into the eastern half of the city and shelled for several months, without relief.

Although the HVO received substantial material and manpower assistance from Croatia proper and was widely viewed as being under the Zagreb defense ministry's direct control, the small Croat population of central Bosnia was no match for the Bosniacs' numbers. While simultaneously holding the line against the (equally man-power-strapped) BSA, government forces pushed back the HVO on some fronts and surrounded it, eastern-enclave-style, on others.

How the government managed to do this while under attack on two fronts (three counting the defection of a large group of Muslims in Bihac) is a matter of much conjecture. As much as a year earlier, in July 1992, members of the Organization of the Islamic Conference (OIC, the "commonwealth" of Islamic states) had voted to underwrite arms acquisitions by the Bosniacs. Croatia was more than willing to peddle arms to the Bosniacs if the price was right (and the share of the shipment—often one-third to a half—was large enough). Serb forces sold arms to perpetuate Muslim-Croat fighting, and over time the government managed to revive the production of small arms, rocket launchers, and heavy mortars in former JNA factories that had been abandoned quickly in the spring of 1992.[157]

By September, Bosniac forces had advanced on Croat communities in central Bosnia, effectively isolating them, and were pressing south toward Mostar.

Government advances were sufficient by early 1994 to cause Croatia to draft "Bosnia-born male citizens of Croatia" into the HVO. Serbia did the same for male Serb refugees in Serbia, and the Yugoslav Army (YA) was openly moving troops and supplies into Bosnia, across the Drina River. Toward the south, some 5,000 Croatian army regulars were operating in Bosnia in support of the HVO as far north as Gornji Vakuf.[158]

The continued fighting meant that, for all of 1993, the UN managed to meet only 57 percent of identified humanitarian needs in Bosnia. But the tide of battle on the Muslim-Croat front created a new opportunity for diplomacy that the United States seized with uncharacteristic skill. In between grand designs for peace in Bosnia, the United States brokered a deal by which the country's Muslim and Croat factions would federate and present a single military and diplomatic front to the Serbs. As those talks continued, the two factions agreed on 23 February 1994 to a general cease-fire, brokered by UNPROFOR, and Muslim-Croat fighting in Bosnia effectively ended.[159]

While Muslims and Croats were making peace, Serb forces stepped up the shelling of Sarajevo, starting 21 December as peace talks resumed in Geneva. On Christmas Day nearly 700 shells were fired at the city. Shelling resumed after a few days' lull, apparently in response to a Bosnian army infantry assault into Serb-held parts of Sarajevo. In the first half of January 1994, shells killed Sarajevans at the rate of about six a day.[160]

NATO, gathering in early January for a summit meeting of the North Atlantic Council, threatened air strikes in Bosnia for the second time in six months, unless the siege of Sarajevo were lifted. (The first time had been during the Igman crisis the previous August.) Over the next few weeks, NATO and UN officials brushed up procedures for the summoning of NATO close air support by UN commanders, setting the stage for the next phase of UNPROFOR.[161]

Weapon Exclusion Zones and the Muslim-Croat Federation

Moving toward the fourth phase of its involvement in the former Yugoslavia, the United Nations replaced its entire top level of management in the field. In early January, Yasushi Akashi, who had led the UN's large peace operation in Cambodia, took up his duties as UNPROFOR's first resident special representative, replacing Thorvald Stoltenberg. Relieving BH commander Briquemont in late January was Lieutenant General Sir Michael Rose, a British officer with special forces background and combat experience in the 1982 Falklands-Malvinas War. Deputy Chief of Mission and Director of Civil Affairs Cedric Thornberry also departed after 22 months with UNPROFOR, replaced on 3 February by Sergio Vieira de Mello, UNHCR's former chief operating officer in Cambodia and thus a familiar of Akashi's. Finally, Force Commander Cot was replaced on 16 March by fellow countryman General Bertrand de Lapresle.[162]

UNPROFOR-BH was still expanding (table 6.1 shows the progression). It peaked at about 22,500 troops (plus roughly 300 military observers, 250 international civilian staff, and 500 local hires). From early spring 1994 onward, most of the new

Table 6.1
TROOP CONTRIBUTIONS TO UNPROFOR - BOSNIA-HERZEGOVINA

Troop Contributors	Feb-93	Mar-94	Apr-94	Sep-94	Mar-95	Nov-95
Bangladesh	0	0	0	0	1238	334
Belgium	129	278	425	416	100	95
Canada	829	783	780	785	820	189
Denmark	214	302	292	289	280	280
Egypt	416	429	429	429	418	413
France	2,509	4,206	4,518	4,904	3781	3,938
Indonesia	0	0	0	0	0	469
Jordan	0	0	120	94	100	102
Malaysia	0	1,487	1,487	1,555	1545	971
Netherlands	615	1,216	1,766	1,647	1482	633
New Zealand	0	0	0	266	249	250
Norway	36	292	292	665	636	729
Pakistan	0	0	0	2,995	2983	2,622
Portugal	0	7	7	0	0	0
Russian Federation	0	0	453	498	472	498
Spain	758	1,153	1,327	1,396	1372	1,237
Sweden	0	822	800	1,019	1030	1,000
Turkey ·	0	0	0	1,460	1469	1,450
Ukraine	398	582	579	584	460	566
United Kingdom	2,626	2,642	3,407	3,255	3155	1,637
BH HQ Company	193	234	241	275	380	171
Rapid Reaction Force (UK, France, Netherlands)	0	0	0	0	0	6,046
Subtotal BH Cmd	**8,723**	**14,433**	**16,923**	**22,532**	**21,970**	**23,630**

SOURCES: Security Council, *Further Report of the Secretary-General Pursuant to Security Council Resolution 743 (1992)*, S/25264, 10 February 1993, annex 1; Security Council, *Report of the Secretary-General Pursuant to Resolution 871 (1993)*, S/1994/300, 16 March 1994, annex 1; United Nations Protection Force, *Fact-Sheet* (Zagreb: UNPROFOR Press and Public Information Office, 13 April 1994), 7-10; United Nations Protection Force, *Fact Sheet* (Zagreb: UNPROFOR Press and Public Information Office, 20 September 1994), 8-11.

troops were provided by Islamic countries (Bangladesh, Indonesia, Jordan, Malaysia, Pakistan, and Turkey; Egypt had deployed a battalion in Sarajevo since mid-1992).

The growing numbers necessitated further delegation of command responsibility within UNPROFOR. Separate commands were established for northeastern and southwestern Bosnia. Sector Northeast was headquartered near the city of Tuzla. Sector Southwest was headquartered in the town of Gornji Vakuf, about 60 kilometers

Fig. 6.5

UNPROFOR–BOSNIA-HERZEGOVINA COMMAND STRUCTURE, APRIL 1994, MILITARY ELEMENTS

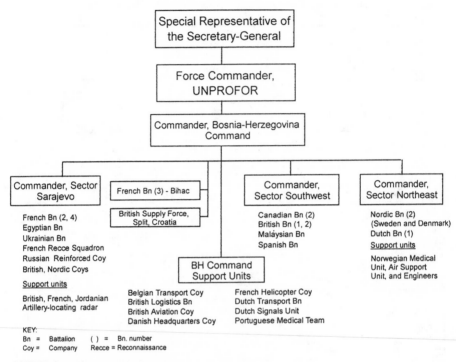

KEY:
Bn = Battalion   ( ) = Bn. number
Coy = Company   Recce = Reconnaissance

SOURCE: Based on United Nations Protection Force, *Facts Sheet*

(Zagreb: UNPROFOR Press and Public Information Office, 13 April 1994).

west of Sarajevo. Figure 6.5 depicts these new command arrangements and the military units associated with each.

Rose proved to be the most visible of BH commanders, using the media as one of the tools in his kit bag for countering what he soon came to see as the relentless propaganda of all parties in the conflict. Because he tended to assume that nobody believed the Serbs and their reflexive political hyperpole, he devoted most of his public energy to debunking what he considered the inflated claims of the Bosnian government, especially regarding civilian casualties. This earned him no friends in government circles or among the Bosniacs' political supporters in the United States.

Rose's stormy encounters with the Sarajevo government reflected deep-set tensions in the Bosniac-UNPROFOR relationship. The government, for example, was extremely suspicious of negotiated cease-fires, fearing these would only codify an unacceptable division of the country, whereas UNPROFOR supported such measures to engage the Serbs diplomatically and make humanitarian operations easier. Government forces repeatedly violated the Mount Igman demilitarized zone and fired mortars from inside the city at Serb areas, actions seemingly designed more to trigger Serb retaliation (and NATO intervention) than to break the siege of the city.

While such provocations angered UN commanders, there was little they could do to deal with them, given the need to maintain operational impartiality. They knew that the local parties viewed impartiality either as weakness or as hostility-by-omission, but they also knew that taking sides would undermine the UN's basic mission of providing humanitarian relief, and would place UN troops in great danger. Such increased risk would likely result in contingents being called home by their governments and possibly in the withdrawal of the entire force under hostile circumstances.

The tasks of phase four made it even more difficult for UNPROFOR to maintain an impartial image among Bosnian Serbs, in particular. Although the Security Council passed few additional resolutions affecting UNPROFOR's mandate, NATO's ultimata singled out the BSA as the target for most of the threats to use air power, and UNPROFOR was the trigger for that power. Thus the relationship between NATO and UNPROFOR, in Serb eyes, was not so much "bad cop, good cop," as "bad cop, stoolie," and the stoolie had friends and they were vulnerable.

This attempt to graft tasks that required the application of coercive force onto a mission conducted under peacekeeping rules of engagement did not work very well. Yet it fit with evolving British doctrine for peace operations, dubbed "wider peacekeeping," that called for just enough force to do the job, but not too much.[163] Too much force was what Americans tended to do (they "crossed the Mogadishu line"); just enough force was whatever worked without making one look like an American.

The Security Council may have been a spectator in the establishment of the exclusion zones around Sarajevo and Gorazde, but UNPROFOR was not. Substantial portions of the 9 February 1994 NATO ultimatum to the Serbs and the Sarajevo government were crafted within BH Command in negotiation with the local parties and transmitted to Brussels, so that BH Command knew exactly what to expect in terms of operational requirements from the North Atlantic Council.

Almost as soon as NATO issued its February ultimatum, Serb forces around Sarajevo agreed both to withdraw heavy weapons and to permit the UN to establish buffer zones between BSA and government lines. As NATO's 21 February deadline approached, however, few weapons had been removed or placed under UN control. On 17 February, Russian mediator Vitaly Churkin, in close coordination with Akashi, obtained Serb compliance in exchange for a reassuring deployment of 800 Russian peacekeeping troops in Sarajevo. Although a number of (mostly inoperable) BSA weapons remained in the exclusion zone and not under UN supervision when the deadline passed, several hundred weapons were removed and both Akashi and Rose felt that compliance was sufficient to forego requests for air strikes. In their view, substantial compliance with the spirit of the ultimatum was more important than total compliance with the letter. The object of the exercise was to end the shelling of Sarajevo, not to find and eliminate every Serb gun, given the scarce resources that UNPROFOR had available for that task. This attitude caused frustration in NATO military headquarters and may have encouraged incremental violations of the exclusion zones and safe areas later on.[164] Indeed, the exclusion zones, like the safe areas, gave the BSA another (and the government yet another) way to probe for UNPROFOR weaknesses.

One of the problems with the air strike option was the sheer familiarity of NATO air power. The Serbs recognized the damage that NATO could do to them but after a year of operating under constantly buzzing Western jets they largely discounted it, gambling that the same countries who were unwilling to confront them on the ground would be loathe to risk the lives of their peacekeepers if push came to shove. Eager to find ways of recouping their position after the Sarajevo episode, the BSA tried to press forward elsewhere. One week after the original Sarajevo ultimatum expired without NATO air power being called into play, six Serb jets bombed and strafed the town of Novi Travnik. American F-16 fighters on patrol over central Bosnia immediately engaged and shot down four of them in NATO's first-ever air action.[165]

One month after this incident, on 30 March 1994, using some of the guns withdrawn from Sarajevo, BSA forces launched a major offensive against Gorazde in eastern Bosnia. The choice of Gorazde, one of the six UN safe areas and the largest government enclave in Drina Valley, seemed calculated to test the UN's resolve and to derail the incipient Muslim-Croat cooperation by provoking another massive flight of Muslim refugees into central Bosnia, upsetting its fragile ethnic balance.[166] On the twelvth day of its offensive, the BSA surprised UNPROFOR's military analysts by seizing high ground on the east bank of the Drina overlooking the town, encroaching upon what the UN considered the safe area. Secretary-General Boutros-Ghali warned the Serbs to pull back. The following day, 10 April, US jets under NATO command were called in, nominally to provide close air support for threatened UN observers, and ended up striking a Serb command post when they had trouble locating the tanks that were their primary targets. Two more US aircraft attacked Serb armor in the area the following day.[167]

In reaction, the BSA closed access to Sarajevo, began to take UN military hostages, and refused to talk with either Akashi or Rose. Russian envoy Vitaly Churkin flew in at the UN's behest to talk with the Bosnian Serbs, while Akashi flew to Belgrade to urge Serbian president Milosevic to intercede with Pale.

On 18 April, the UN secretary-general asked NATO to give CINCSOUTH authority to conduct air strikes, similar to those approved for Sarajevo, in and around Gorazde and the other four safe areas. On 22 April, NATO agreed and issued new ultimata to the BSA: cease attacks on Gorazde, pull all forces at least three kilometers from city center, and allow the UN free access to the city by one A.M. local time, 24 April—or face air strikes on heavy weapon and other military targets within 20 kilometers of the city.[168] In a separate statement, NATO established a 20-kilometer heavy weapon exclusion around Gorazde and called on the BSA to withdraw such weapons from that zone by one A.M. local time, 27 April. NATO also warned that if heavy weapons were moved within 20 kilometers of any of the safe areas, or used to attack them, the threatened areas would themselves be declared military exclusion zones and any heavy weapons or support facilities (including fuel and ammo dumps) used in attacks by the Bosnian Serbs on any of the safe areas would be subject to NATO air strikes.[169]

These ultimata established the framework for what might have been a robust air campaign against the BSA, but the campaign did not materialize at that time. The Serbs haltingly complied, and UNPROFOR held back air strike authorization (NATO air strikes were subject to approval by UNPROFOR, and UNPROFOR's basic mandates and vulnerability to retaliation remained unchanged). Like the UN Security Council, the NAC could talk tough but member states whose troops were in the field were no more likely to sacrifice them after Gorazde than before. Indeed, the command arrangements of UNPROFOR, starting in January 1994, gave Britain and France de facto additional insurance against undesired NATO use of force because their nationals commanded UN forces in Bosnia and the mission as a whole. Fusible links in the UN's chain of command, one or the other commander could veto UN field units' calls for air support or NATO staff suggestions for air strikes.[170]

As the crisis in Gorazde gradually eased and central Bosnia returned, if not to normal, than at least to a semblance of peace, two different initiatives—one diplomatic and one military—shook up the emerging stalemate. In early June 1994, France, Britain, Germany, the United States, and the Russian Federation came together as the "Contact Group" to release a commonly agreed territorial settlement for Bosnia. The group gave all Bosnian parties until 19 July to accept its proposal for a 51-49 percent Federation-Serb allocation of territory under a loose confederal central government, or face unspecified consequences. The Bosnian Serbs rejected the plan, saying that it failed to give them contiguous territory and to allow confederation with Serbia and Montenegro as Bosnian Croats were allowed to do with Croatia.[171]

Serbian president Milosevic soon broke with the Bosnian Serbs, and the Security Council embargoed political contact and trade, other than humanitarian items, with Bosnian Serb-held areas of Bosnia-Herzegovina. Observers reported reduced resupply of Serb-held areas of Bosnia from Serbia.[172] But many Bosnia-watchers believed that the Bosnian government counted on Bosnian Serb rejection of the Contact Group plan, hoping that it would finally induce the outside world to give the BSA a good pounding.

In the battlefield initiative, the newly confident Bosnian army's Fifth Corps, based in Bihac, launched an August offensive against the dissident Muslim forces of Fikret Abdic.[173] Pushing them across the border into Serb-held Croatia, the Fifth Corps wheeled, in late October 1994, to mount an offensive against BSA positions on the confrontation line south and east of Bihac, pushing the Serbs off the plateau overlooking the city and taking nearly 100 square kilometers of territory. The BSA reinforced, counterattacked, and, aided by Croatian Serb units, undertook the kind of infantry assaults they had rarely used against organized opponents in this war. The counter-attack pushed the Fifth Corps back toward the city, precipitating in the process a new air strike crisis for the UN and NATO.[174]

When Serbian aircraft based at Udbina airfield in Serb-held Croatia attacked Bihac in mid-November (their targets including, but not limited to, Bosnian Fifth Corps headquarters), the UN requested air strikes and on 21 November NATO bombed Udbina, cratering the runway but taking care *not* to strike any of the aircraft or facilities on the airfield. Two days later, twenty NATO aircraft struck two Serb air defense sites in response to missiles fired at NATO aircraft. Serb forces took 450 UN personnel hostage to ward off further attacks. No more air strikes occurred and the hostages were released unharmed.[175]

The Bihac air raids actually seemed to hurt NATO and UNPROFOR's ability to maintain the safe areas and exclusion zones more than they hurt the Serbs. For a few days after the raids, Washington pushed its NATO allies for a wide-ranging air campaign against the Serbs. The allies resisted, pointing to their stake on the ground in Bosnia and the lack of a similar US stake and bridling at US willingness to put others' troops in jeopardy with such a campaign. Rather than risk a major political clash with the allies, the Clinton administration relented.[176] Without the willingness of Washington, Paris, and London to back the UN with force (via NATO), a large chunk of what UNPROFOR was supposed to be doing became virtually moot.

In late December, the warring parties agreed to a UN plan for a four-month cease-fire/cessation of hostilities, brokered with last-minute help from former president Jimmy Carter. It was, however, no more than a temporary respite, and the government side in particular used this period to train, equip, and position its forces. Adding tension was Croatia's seemingly serious threat (noted in the previous section) to expel UNPROFOR when its mandate expired at the end of March 1995.[177] As that crisis passed, and as the cease-fire period drew to an end, the Bosniacs launched a series of small offensives, seeking to sever Bosnian Serb lines of communication.[178] The Serbs replied predictably, ratcheting up the pressure on Sarajevo. They also upped the ante, removing some heavy weapons from UN-guarded collection points within the weapon exclusion zone and closing down the airport as well as road access into the city.[179]

A Summer of Discontent

The rising tempo of military action left UNPROFOR with little room to maneuver. UN Bosnia commander, Lieutenant General Rupert Smith (who replaced Rose when the latter's one-year tour ended in January) expected the BSA to sharply increase pressure against the safe areas, as a way to check the Bosnian army's further advances. On the other hand, the renewed pressure on Sarajevo was prompting the Bosnian government to hit Serb supply lines in and around the city. On 8 May, Smith requested air strikes to stave off a further deterioration of the situation, but Force Commander Janvier and SRSG Akashi turned down the request, citing its possible incendiary effect on fighting in Croatia, which was then poised on the brink of war following Serb losses in Sector West.

However, on 24 May, in the face of continued Serb violations of the exclusion zone, the UN issued an ultimatum demanding Serb compliance and government restraint. When the Serbs balked, UNPROFOR authorized NATO air strikes. Over two days, NATO aircraft destroyed ammunition dumps near the Serbs' Pale headquarters east of Sarajevo. The Serbs responded by shelling Tuzla and killing 71 people at an outdoor cafe; by rounding up several hundred UNPROFOR hostages as guarantees against further NATO air action; and by emptying the Sarajevo weapons collection points. By the end of May, the weapon exclusion zone around Sarajevo had ceased to exist and the Bosnian Serbs had declared all UN Security Council resolutions null and void. Shelling of Sarajevo resumed, as aid, water, and power continued to be blocked.[180]

After much back and forth within NATO and the loss of an American F-16 by BSA surface-to-air missiles, France, Britain, and the Netherlands offered to form a "Rapid Reaction Force" (RRF) to buttress UNPROFOR on the ground. By early July, the first elements of the force included a battalion consisting of British and Dutch mechanized units already with UNPROFOR, and a brigade of French foreign legionnaires, to be equipped with antitank helicopters and heavy artillery. The total size of the force was to be 10,000-12,000 troops.[181] Backed up by initial RRF deployments, UNPROFOR, for the first time, began delivering aid over the perilous Mount Igman road into Sarajevo. The convoys ran under the cover of darkness. White-painted UN vehicles were covered with mud, and the old requirement to obtain the BSA's consent vanished.

In mid-summer, the Bosnian Serbs continued their campaign to force the war to a conclusion. The BSA attacked the government enclave of Srebrenica in early July, overrunning it 12 July despite resistance by a platoon of Dutch UN troops attached to the Dutch battalion in Srebrenica. Most of the population was bundled out of town, but thousands of male inhabitants were unaccounted for. A few thousand, mostly soldiers, walked to Tuzla. Hundreds, and possibly thousands, appear to have been executed en masse by the BSA; US high-altitude reconnaissance photographs shown to a closed session of the Security Council on 10 August showed fields full of people, later empty, and other empty fields, later freshly dug-up, suggesting mass burials.[182] The photos dispelled any thoughts that the BSA had mellowed in three years or that earlier atrocities were attributable only to paramilitary gangs from Serbia proper. They also assured that the Bosnian Serbs would be unable to garner outside sympathy from any quarter in the weeks that lay ahead.

The Serbs next advanced on the nearby enclave of Zepa. Gorazde, with 65,000 people (as many as Srebrenica and Zepa combined), was considered at serious risk as well. Newly elected President Jacques Chirac of France volunteered to reinforce Gorazde with French troops from the Rapid Reaction Force if the United States would chip in with transport helicopters. The United States declined, but at a meeting of NATO countries and UNPROFOR troop contributors in London on 21 July, the United States won support for extensive use of NATO air power to protect the remaining safe areas. Events subsequently conspired to make this new option viable.

First, Zepa fell to the Serbs on 25 July. At about the same time, Croatian army forces began a northward drive into Serb-held areas of Bosnia adjacent to the Krajina. As related earlier, the Croatian army then attacked and routed the *krajina* Serbs in four days, and the Serb army and population alike fled into Bosnia and onward to Serbia. Not only was Serb pressure on the Bihac enclave eliminated, but the myth of the invincible Serb warrior was destroyed, and Slobodan Milosevic and the Yugoslav Army made no move to assist the *krajina* Serbs. These psychological, territorial, and population shifts opened up both the possibility of a grand diplomatic settlement induced by the selective use of force.[183] Gorazde, the last isolated government enclave and better defended by the government than the other eastern enclaves, was evacuated by UNPROFOR at the end of August except for a handful of UNMOs. Thereafter, no UN troops aside from the Russian contingent in Sarajevo remained behind Serb lines as potential hostages to NATO-UN action.

America Shifts Its Weight

The Clinton administration had been looking for a new policy in the Balkans since before the fall of Srebrenica and was increasingly willing to take stronger action, since further inaction could have led to American ground troops being knee-deep in a Balkan rescue operation sometime during the 1996 presidential primary season. national security adviser Anthony Lake convened weekly cabinet-level meetings in July and August, attended by UN ambassador Albright, defense secretary Perry, Secretary of State Christopher, and Joint Chiefs chairman Shalikashvili. On 7 August, President Clinton approved their recommendations for a new US diplomatic initiative for the Balkans, and Lake flew to brief the Europeans.[184] By 17 August, US Assistant secretary of state Richard Holbrooke was in Belgrade briefing Milosevic on the initiative. Among the items on the table were a wider Posavina Corridor to link the eastern and western Bosnian Serb holdings, and the option of confederating Bosnian Serb areas with Serbia. The Bosnian Muslims would get additional territory around Sarajevo and reconstruction assistance from the West if they signed onto the plan's territorial arrangements. Sanctions on Serbia would be lifted if it recognized Croatian and Bosnian independence. If the Bosnian Serbs failed to accept the plan, they would be subject to NATO air strikes, the arms embargo on the Bosnian government would be lifted, and no objections would be raised to Muslim countries contributing troops to Bosnia's defense.[185]

The diplomatic initiative was gathering steam in late August: in four days of talks Slobodan Milosevic had wrested from Bosnian Serb leader Karadzic the right to represent Bosnian Serb interests in talks with the United States. At this point, the BSA or some element in it gave NATO the excuse it was looking for to implement its new air strike policy. On 28 August, a mortar shell exploded near the Sarajevo marketplace where 68 had died in a Serb shelling in February 1994; this one killed 37 and wounded 80. After waiting a day for UN "crater analysis" to finger the Serbs as the perpetrators, NATO unleashed a two-week, 3,400-sortie air campaign against Bosnian Serb targets.[186]

NATO warplanes targeted Bosnian Serb air defenses, communications, command and control, and ammunition depots. That is, NATO did its best to destroy the Bosnian Serbs' capacity to ward off further NATO strikes and their ability to mount a coordinated and sustained military campaign. Air action was complemented by the recently arrived artillery of the UN Rapid Reaction Force on Mount Igman, whose guns fired hundreds of shells at Serb targets around Sarajevo.[187] At the same time, Bosnian Croat militias, Croatian army units, and Bosnian army units attacked Serb positions in western and northern Bosnia, seizing additional territory. (Figure 6.6 shows the positions of the lines of confrontation as of mid-September.) On 15 September the BSA relented, began to remove most of its heavy weapons from around Sarajevo, and agreed to allow access into the city by air and road.

By the fall of 1995, UNPROFOR and NATO were increasingly difficult to separate in terms of policy and actions taken against the Bosnian Serbs. What NATO was doing from the air, elements of UNPROFOR were doing on the ground. The objective of both was to force a negotiated settlement, and for once there appeared to be a viable, realistic diplomatic alternative on the table, backed by the sort of sustained American leadership that had been lacking in efforts to settle this conflict.

Thus, even as NATO air strikes in Bosnia continued, Holbrooke pressed forward with negotiations in Geneva. Relying heavily upon the intercessions of Milosevic with the Pale Serbs—something the Americans had been loath to do before—Holbrooke pushed the parties to accept the principles of (1) a sovereign Bosnian state within its current borders (to preclude annexations by Croatia or Serbia); (2) the existence of two substantially autonomous entities within Bosnia (the federation and a "Republika Srpska"); (3) a parallel right of each entity to create (undefined) associations or special relationships with neighboring countries; and (4) a 51-49 percent split of territory, consistent with the Contact Group formula. On 8 September, the Bosnian, Serbian, and Croatian foreign ministers signed onto these political principles.[188]

The substance of Holbrooke's approach was applauded by European governments, for it was very much in sync with the mainstream European view that a Serbian entity within Bosnia, having rights of association with Serbia proper, should be explicitly acknowledged. The NATO air campaign against the BSA placed the Clinton administration in a strong position to deliver the Bosnian government's acceptance of a Serbian entity with such associative rights.

Follow-up talks in New York produced agreements in principle on new all-Bosnian governmental institutions and early elections. On 5 October, Holbrooke brokered a Bosnia-wide cease-fire that took effect 12 October; the opening of supply routes to relief convoys (including routes into Gorazde); the restoration of public utilities to Sarajevo and the reopening of the city's airport; and commitments to attend so-called "Proximity Peace Talks" in the United States, to be followed by a peace conference in Europe.[189]

On 1 November, the proximity talks convened in Dayton, Ohio, within the spare but high-tech confines of the Wright-Patterson Air Force Base. This time, the delegations were headed by the three presidents (Izetbegovic, Milosevic, and Tudjman). Opened by Secretary Christopher and once again brokered by Holbrooke, the Dayton talks turned into a three-week marathon that, in its later stages, seemed on the verge of breakdown, even on the night before the final accord was reached. In a surprise move, Milosevic conceded Sarajevo to the Muslim-Croat federation. The

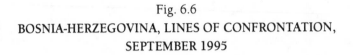

Fig. 6.6
BOSNIA-HERZEGOVINA, LINES OF CONFRONTATION,
SEPTEMBER 1995

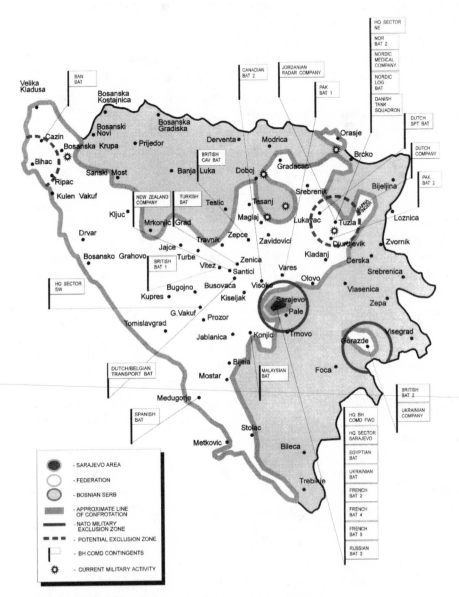

SOURCE: UN High Commissioner for Refugees,

Information Notes on Former Yugoslavia no. 9/95 (September 1995).

Bosnian delegation (often internally split) raised last-minute objections about the width of a corridor linking two Serb-held sections of the country and about the status of a town (Brcko) within that corridor. Brcko was set aside for arbitration at a later date, and the General Framework Agreement for peace in Bosnia, along with 11 annexes, were initialled on 21 November 1995.[190]

The Framework (or Dayton) Agreement fleshed out the Geneva deal, including the "inter-entity" boundaries delineating federation and Republika Srpska territory. (Negotiators had access to American mapping and display technology that allowed them to see, in simulated but life-like detail, where any proposed boundary line would fall.[191] Figure 6.7 shows the resulting boundaries.) In addition, all sides agreed to a new constitution for Bosnia with federal institutions, free and democratic elections, full cooperation with the War Crimes Tribunal in the Hague, unrestricted access for human rights monitors, the right of refugees and displaced persons to return to their homes or receive just compensation, an arms control mechanism for setting limits on heavy weapons, and, finally, the deployment of a NATO-led Peace Implementation Force (IFOR), whose task it would be to monitor the cease-fire and separate the warring factions. The UN, however, would remain engaged in the peace effort, supervising and training local police and organizing the repatriation of refugees and displaced persons.

The UN Security Council gave its formal blessing to the IFOR on 15 December, one day after the Dayton Agreement was formally signed in Paris.[192] Most sanctions on Serbia were lifted conditional upon its (and the Bosnian Serbs') compliance with the Dayton Agreement. On 20 December, IFOR took over operations in Bosnia from UNPROFOR. Upon that transfer of authority, the Security Council terminated UNPROFOR's mandate and nullified a number of resolutions (including the safe areas' regime) that had been promulgated prior to the peace agreement.

Several elements that had been part of UNPROFOR transferred to NATO command at that point. General Janvier became deputy to IFOR commander Admiral Leighton Smith, who as NATO CINCSOUTH had been in command of NATO air forces operating over Bosnia. French and British peacekeepers traded blue helmets for NATO camouflage, and the majority of UNPROFOR's remaining NATO and non-NATO contingents also transferred to NATO command. The rest headed home.

Assessment of UNPROFOR-BH

UNPROFOR faced impossible odds in Bosnia. It was an improvised, last-resort operation, burdened by mandates that were at times inconsistent and well in excess of its resource base. It also was buffeted by sharp disagreements among its main sponsors on when and how to use force beyond self-defense. Ultimately, however, UNPROFOR could not surmount the rising resentment of the local Bosnian factions. While the Bosnian government condemned the operation for failures to protect safe areas, the Serbs increasingly chafed at aspects of UNPROFOR's work that appeared to abet Bosniac-Croat cooperation at the Serbs' expense. UNPROFOR, neither loved nor

Fig. 6.7

"INTER-ENTITY" BOUNDARIES ESTABLISHED BY THE DAYTON AGREEMENT, 21 NOVEMBER 1995

SOURCE: The White House, National Security Council Staff, December 1995.

feared by any of the parties, found itself handicapped in promoting dialogue and lacking the clout necessary to compel hostile parties to negotiate.

In terms of mandated activities, UNPROFOR's track record was mixed. On the humanitarian side, a comparison of UNHCR's calculations of relief needed versus relief delivered suggests that UNPROFOR did a reasonably good job, although shipments continued to be delayed for political reasons and delivery remained impossible in areas of heavy fighting, even with UNPROFOR escort. The airlift into Sarajevo was the longest-running effort of its kind in history. From July 1992 until April 1995, when Bosnian Serb threats shut it down, the airlift brought roughly 175,000 tons of food and other relief items into the city. Road convoys over the same period brought in another 90,000 tons. At the same time, UN efforts to halt Serb artillery and sniping attacks on the city produced mixed results.[193]

UNPROFOR never had the resources to implement the safe areas concept, which relied heavily on the "moral force" of Security Council edicts to protect their populations, particularly in the eastern enclaves. The UN's presence probably delayed the collapse of Srebrenica and Zepa for more than two years, but there was really no political will in the outside world to prevent their collapse when the Serbs decided to move. Moreover, the fixed-wing NATO air power available for use at Srebrenica in 1995 was of little use once the BSA changed tactics and moved infantry through the forest into the enclave. Without willingness on the part of major powers to airlift substantial numbers of troops into the enclaves and their commitment to keep them supplied by air, if necessary, the concept of "safe area" was always a misnomer.

Bihac and Tuzla survived, as did Gorazde, because they had substantially larger populations and stronger government garrisons, not because UN protection was that much better. Sarajevo hosted six UN battalions by the spring of 1995, but apart from the French, their effectiveness was open to question. That situation finally changed in late August, as British and French troops of the UN Reaction Force joined NATO aircraft in shelling Serb positions. Although the mortar shells that exploded in Sarajevo in February 1994 and August 1995 probably killed, between them, fewer people than ethnic cleansing killed on an average day near the start of the war, the visibility of the victims and their familiarity to Western eyes prompted a collective response that the razing of villages and killing of peasants (of whatever faith) failed to evoke. NATO ministers also put the alliance's reputation on the line in late July 1995; if NATO had not made good on its threat to respond forcefully to new Serb attacks on safe areas, NATO's credibility as a security organization might have been damaged beyond repair.

In taking action against the BSA, UNPROFOR and NATO also sought to restore the Sarajevo heavy weapon exclusion zone. Both exclusion zones (Sarajevo and Gorazde), mainly the products of NATO ultimata, proved difficult to maintain in Bosnia's fluid political and military situation. As government forces grew stronger and challenged the BSA more openly, the Serbs' willingness to accept the constraints imposed by the UN and NATO diminished correspondingly, whereas the political will of the outside parties to act remained the same or decreased. It did not increase substantially until Milosevic signaled, with his acquiescence to Croatia's retaking of the Krajina, that the war was unlikely to widen dramatically if NATO lit into his Bosnian cousins. Once UN forces were no longer as susceptible to Serb hostage-taking, moreover, British and French objections to substantial NATO air strikes melted away.

The fall 1995 air and artillery campaign was aimed initially at restoration of the Sarajevo exclusion zone and reopening of the airport. Bosnian Serb military leader General Ratko Mladic gambled that Western publics or their leaders would tire of the air campaign, that NATO would begin to divide against itself, and, perhaps, that

Russian counter-pressure would bring the campaign to a halt.[194] That he finally succumbed was a major victory for the UN and NATO.[195]

The Security Council's strategy of indirection in Bosnia from 1992 through the first half of 1995 was a faithful reflection of the policies—and the political disagreements—of the United States, Britain, France, and Russia. Smaller members of the Council were generally more favorable to stronger, earlier international action in Bosnia but were in no position to take such action themselves, or to pay for it. The UN's initial strategy of impartiality allowed it to bring several hundred thousand tons of relief supplies into Bosnia, sustaining over 2.2 million civilians as well as their respective fighters. Overall, the intervention probably stretched out the Bosnian conflict and changed its outcome from a quick Serb win and bilateral division of Bosnia (actively abetted by many Bosnian Croats for nearly a year) to a war of attrition in which Muslims and Croats had a growing capacity to balance Serb military power, and even exceed it (thanks in part to a leaky arms embargo and American willingness, in particular, to look the other way).

It is noteworthy that UNPROFOR managed some actual peacekeeping in Bosnia, overseeing removal of troops and weapons from a four-kilometer buffer zone along the Muslim-Croat line of confrontation. On the whole, it performed this role very effectively. Aid routes through central Bosnia were reopened to traffic, and by late 1994, locally produced food was meeting most local needs in the areas. UN engineering units helped to restore power and water to villages throughout the federation, and UN checkpoints replaced checkpoints manned by fighters from either side. All these efforts represented a substantial military boost to the Muslims, giving them strategic depth and interior lines of communication, and the Serbs viewed them as such. However, not until after the Bosnian Serb offensives of April - May 1995 did Croat and Muslim military leaders begin seriously to coordinate their actions, and although a Bosnian Croat, Stepan Klujic, was named federation president, few of the institutions of joint governance had been established 18 months after the initial framework agreement was signed.[196]

In the end, the shifting military balance, the continuing atrocities committed by Bosnian Serb forces, and their avowed intent to ignore Security Council edicts, combined with Serb territorial losses to Croat-Muslim forces, prompted UNPROFOR's major troop contributors to reconsider their strategy and lay the military groundwork for a more robust approach. By late August 1995, UNPROFOR had become "militarily engaged," to use the UN's words, with NATO against the BSA and was no longer by any definition an impartial operation.[197] Humanitarian intervention had metamorphosed into peace enforcement, though only part of UNPROFOR—the Rapid Reaction Force—was actively engaged. Fortunately, events in and around Bosnia conspired to keep this engagement brief; had the fighting continued much longer than a month, the political stresses of continued military action would have taken an increasing toll on both the UN and NATO, and Mladic's gamble might have paid off, not necessarily in Bosnian Serb victory but in continuing, low-level conflict with a prospect of spreading.

OVERALL CONCLUSIONS

The UN experience in the former Yugoslavia offers a number of larger lessons for peace operations, almost all of them sobering. First, the cascading deployments of UN forces in the former Yugoslavia show both the danger and the utility of deploying such forces to support partial cease-fires in larger conflicts. In Croatia, the UN came between breakaway Serbs and nationalist Croats, each with unfinished political agendas. Although UNPROFOR's mandate there entailed a certain amount of weapons impoundment, most of the Yugoslav army's troops and equipment were withdrawn, not impounded. The UN presence thus helped to "push the conflict around," even as UN troops acted, in effect, as guardians of a new territorial status quo that the Zagreb government rejected as a long-term solution. However, the relative stability that the UN force maintained bought Croatia the time to build an army out of the ragtag bands with which it had started life as a state. Peacekeeping in Croatia was thus a prelude to further war and civilian suffering.[198]

In Bosnia, where UNPROFOR helped to implement the federation arrangement, Muslim and Croat forces were freed for other fighting fronts at the Serbs' expense. Once again, UN presence tended to channel the conflict in certain directions, but in this case the cause of political settlement was probably helped rather than hurt.

Second, peace operations trying to remain neutral in a war zone are subject to manipulation by all local belligerents. Humanitarian intervention delivers relief goods that all sides want and value, and these are obvious targets of manipulation. But deliveries of "lethal goods" by the intervenors are equally subject to manipulation: Bosnian government forces attempted to induce UN/NATO punitive reactions against the BSA, at times by drawing the UN into the line of fire, while the Serbs took hostages on several occasions to intimidate the UN into not pulling that trigger.

Third, *every* action taken by outsiders in a civil war situation affects the local balance of power. Humanitarian intervention in particular favors whatever faction is nearest to defeat when the intervention occurs and whatever faction can make greater use of time to summon other resources to its cause. It may be just one faction that benefits in this way, or it may be different ones at different times, but such an impact is unavoidable and sure to anger those factions who lose political-military leverage as a result.

Impartiality in humanitarian interventions is thus much easier to assert than it is to maintain in the minds of the local belligerents. Outsiders' professed altruism may even make local parties suspicious or contemptuous of the intervention, rather than supportive or respectful, and the most aggrieved local parties may be more contemptuous than the local predators. Food and medicine sustain life but aggrieved parties want to end their predicament, not just sustain it—hence the mutual bitterness expressed by the Bosnian government and several former UN commanders in Bosnia. One side wanted rescue, the other gratitude.

Fourth, mandates that rely upon the consent of all parties cannot easily be reconciled with those that require a peace operation to become a partisan of one side or another. This was the central dilemma of the safe-area mission. Although it is conceivable that adequately equipped and trained UN forces could have maintained "safe areas" for segments of local populations caught up in conflict, UNPROFOR was never so endowed and in any event could not have performed that mission in a neutral fashion. UNPROFOR was always acutely conscious that on acting to protect specific safe areas in Bosnia, it would trigger BSA retaliation that would imperil its humanitarian relief efforts *throughout* Bosnia. Conceivably, the UN force could have been augmented with better passive self-protection (armored vehicles with mine-protection built in, for example), better local intelligence, and greater firepower, in order to fend off major attacks in safe areas. If, however, the international community had been willing to go that far in deploying multilateral forces to a conflict zone, it might have been better advised to take stock of the conflict and throw its support to the less-objectionable side in the conflict in an effort to end or stalemate it quickly.

The United Nations' experience in the former Yugoslavia demonstrates clearly that UN field operations are derivatives of, and can be placeholders for, the foreign policies of the organization's major member states. A weak and divided international response to a conflict will always breed a cautious, risk-averse field operation. Although the UN Secretariat may try to fashion such operations to reflect a disinterested internationalism and a generic commitment to peace, any mandate to operate in an active war zone is bound to be charged politically. If the United Nations is not equipped politically or temperamentally to accept the risks of partisanship in a given conflict, the Security Council should be wary of putting peacekeepers in harm's way.

ANNEX I: FUNDING THE UN PROTECTION FORCE

UNPROFOR was funded by all UN Member States according to the standard UN peacekeeping scale of assessment. The following table reflects actual United Nations expenditures through 30 November 1995 and cost estimates through 31 December 1995. It does not reflect the cost of independent NATO air and sea operations in support of the no-fly zone over Bosnia, the cost to NATO of answering close air support requests from UNPROFOR, or the costs of conducting air strikes. Finally, it does not include the cost of maintaining sanctions against Serbia or enforcing the Security Council arms embargo against all of the republics of the former Yugoslavia.

Table 6.A
COSTS OF UNPROFOR THROUGH 31 DECEMBER 1995
(US$ MILLIONS)

Time Periods	Final Expenditures							UN Estimates	Totals
	12 Jan 92–31 Mar 93	1 Apr 93–30 Jun 93	1 Jul 93–31 Mar 94	1 Apr 94–30 Sep 94	1 Oct 94–31 Mar 95	1 Apr 95–30 Jun 95	1 Jul 95–30 Nov 95	1–31, Dec 95	12 Jan 92–31 Dec 95
Expenditures Based on UN Assessments[a]	541.01	261.05	805.34	767.99	842.89	367.06	746.67	113.87	4,445.85
Value of Voluntary Contributions In-kind	8.4	0.43	0.15	8.28	5.00	----	50.17	n/a	72.44
FYROM[b] (Macedonia)	2.1	2.1	6.3	4.2	4.2	n/a	n/a	n/a	n/a
Croatia	503.71	148.23	458.04	314.52	323.96	n/a	n/a	n/a	n/a
Bosnia-Herzegovina	43.6	111.15	386.47	535.02	658.72	n/a	n/a	n/a	n/a

NOTES: [a] Expenditures for UN operations in Macedonia, Croatia, and Bosnia-Herzegovina combined. The value of in-kind contributions for 1 July–30 November 1995 includes $31.9 million from the United States to support the UNPROFOR rapid reaction capability. In addition to in-kind contributions, the UN received about $9.3 million in voluntary cash contributions toward its operations in the Former Yugoslavia.
[b] Not separately reported; estimated from January 1993 at about US$700,000 per month.

SOURCES: Security Council, *Further Report of the Secretary-General Pursuant to Security Council Resolution 721 (1991)*, S/23592/Add.1, 19 February 1992; Security Council, *Further Report of the Secretary-General Pursuant to Security Council Resolutions 757 (1992), 758 (1992) and 761 (1992)*, S/24263/Add.1, 10 July 1992; UN General Assembly, *Financing of the United Nations Protection Force*, A/49/540, 19 October 1994; and UN General Assembly, *Financing of the United Nations Protection Force, Report of the Secretary-General, Addendum*, A/50/696/Add.4, 13 March 1996, annex xiv.

NOTES

1. James A. Schear wishes to acknowledge the Abe Fellowship Program and its sponsoring institutions—the Social Science Research Council, the American Council of Learned Societies, and the Japan Foundation Center for Global Partnership—for financial support that assisted in the preparation of this chapter. He is also grateful to Maren Zerriffi for research assistance. The opinions expressed in this chapter are the authors' own and should not be attributed to any organization.

2. This chapter does not treat the preventive, deterrent deployment by about 1,000 UN troops in the Former Yugoslav Republic of Macedonia (FYROM), which seceded from rump Yugoslavia in 1992. (The awkward name was derived from Greek objections to the use of the term "Macedonia," which is also the name of a Greek province; the dispute took three years to work through, with a Greek embargo on the new state in the meantime wrecking its economy and contributing to 30 percent unemployment.) To help prevent the spread of regional conflict into the FYROM—which in turn risked the involvement of several neighboring states—the Security Council took the novel step of pre-deploying peacekeepers (Security Council Resolution 795, 11 December 1992). A Canadian infantry company in Croatia deployed temporarily in January 1993, replaced shortly thereafter by a composite Nordic battalion. A reinforced US infantry company—the first American infantry unit to serve under UN command in a peacekeeping operation—joined the operation in July 1993. Not seriously challenged, the operation was considered a success. (Two years into the operation, casualties totaled 18, none from hostile action, and included just one fatality.) Had "UNPROFOR-M" been challenged—a risk in preventive operations that has not been fully thought through—the UN and the United States would have then had to decide whether to substantially reinforce or withdraw the mission. In March 1995, as part of a general restructuring of UN operations in former Yugoslavia, the Macedonian deployments were redesignated UNPREDEP (UN Preventive Deployment Force). See Security Council, *Report of the Secretary-General Pursuant to Security Council Resolution 795*, S/26009, 13 July 1993; and Security Council, *Report of the Secretary-General Pursuant to Security Council Resolution 947*, S/1995/222, 22 March 1995.

3. See, Branka Magas, *The Destruction of Yugoslavia: Tracking the Breakup, 1980-92* (London: Verso, 1993).

4. Susan Woodward, *Balkan Tragedy: Chaos and Dissolution After the Cold War* (Washington, D.C.: The Brookings Institution, 1995), 145, 148-162.

5. The political and economic decay of Yugoslavia and the violence that it spawned has been traced in a number of recent books whose detail cannot be replicated here but whose analyses are drawn upon in the following sections. See, in addition to Magas, *Destruction . . .*, and Woodward, *Balkan Tragedy,* Lenard J. Cohen, *Broken Bonds: The Disintegration of Yugoslavia* (Boulder, Colo.: Westview Press, 1993); Robert J. Donia and John V. A. Fine, Jr., *Bosnia and Herzegovina: A Tradition Betrayed* (New York: Columbia University Press, 1994); Brian Hall, *The Impossible Country: A Journey through the Last Days of Yugoslavia* (Boston: David R. Godine, Publisher, 1994); Misha

Glenny, *The Fall of Yugoslavia: The Third Balkan War*, revised and updated ed. (New York: Penguin Books, 1993); Mark Pinson, ed., *The Muslims of Bosnia-Herzegovina: Their Historic Development from the Middle Ages to the Dissolution of Yugoslavia* (Cambridge, Mass.: Harvard University Press, 1994); Robert D. Kaplan, *Balkan Ghosts: A Journey through History* (New York: Vintage Books, 1993); and Roy Gutman, *A Witness to Genocide* (New York: Macmillan Publishing Co., 1993).

6.   Anthony D. Smith, "The Ethnic Sources of Nationalism," *Survival* 35, no. 1 (spring 1993): 56-58. Smith stresses that the final step, purification, is not "an expression of an ethnic inferiority complex or an exaggerated ethnic defensiveness," but "is common to all ethnic nationalisms." It varies only in severity, according to local circumstances.

7.   Magas, *The Destruction of Yugoslavia*, 66, 122, 199.

8.   Despite victories in most of their modern wars from 1878 onward, what seems to rally the Serbs (and, for that matter, their Croat neighbors and, since 1992, many Muslims as well) is not pride in accomplishment but recollection of wrongs, events that underline the need for group solidarity, strength, and revenge. Thus originated the four Cyrillic C's ("Only Unity can Save the Serbs"), that are the de facto heraldry of Serbian forces in the present wars. The red-and-white checkerboard heraldry of Croatia, the "Sahovnica," serves the same purpose for Croats. Although it has ancient significance, it was also the hated symbol of the Ustashe regime, and only reinforces Serb fears.

9.   Jack Snyder, "Nationalism and the Crisis of the Post-Soviet State," *Survival* 35, no. 1 (spring 1993): 7.

10. See Cohen, *Broken Bonds*, 266-70; and Hall, *The Impossible Country*, 64.

11. Given the common ethno-linguistic heritage of the majority of Yugoslavia's population, group identities there derived largely from religion and the shared, partly mythic, history of the confessional group, either Catholic Christian (Slovenians, Croats, and ethnic Hungarians), Orthodox Christian (Serbs), or Muslim (Bosnian Muslims, Sanjak Muslims, Albanians). See Hall, *The Impossible Country*, 7; Donia and Fine, *Bosnia and Herzegovina*, 81-83; and Ivo Banac, "Bosnian Muslims: From Religious Community to Socialist Nationhood and Post-Communist Statehood, 1918-1992," in Mark Pinson, ed., *The Muslims of Bosnia-Herzegovina* . . . (Cambridge, Mass.: Harvard University Press, 1994), 131-34, 141, 145.

12. William T. Johnsen, *Deciphering the Balkan Enigma: Using History to Inform Policy* (Carlisle, Pa.: US Army War College, Strategic Studies Institute, 25 March 1993), 11-14.

13. Just how brutal is related in George F. Kennan, introduction, *The Other Balkan Wars: A 1913 Carnegie Endowment Inquiry in Retrospect*, by the Carnegie Endowment for International Peace (Washington, D.C.: The Carnegie Endowment for International Peace, 1993).

14. Cohen, *Broken Bonds*, 13.

15. Hall, *The Impossible Country*, 23-24; Banac, "Bosnian Muslims," 141-44; and Donia and Fine, *Bosnia and Herzegovina*, 139-46.

16. Cohen, *Broken Bonds*, 31, 35. Real income in Yugoslavia averaged 6 percent annual growth through 1972 but less than 3 percent annual growth in the later 1970s, and turned negative in the 1980s. By 1974, the population of Slovenia, the richest republic, was eight times wealthier, on average, than the population of Kosovo, the poorest.

17. See Magas, *The Destruction of Yugoslavia*, 331-33; and Cohen, *Broken Bonds*, chapters 4 and 5.

18. See Samantha Power, comp., *Breakdown in the Balkans: A Chronicle of Events, January 1989 to May 1993* (Washington, D.C.: The Carnegie Endowment for International Peace, 1993), 5, 9-10; and Magas, *The Destruction of Yugoslavia*, 263.

19. Power, *Breakdown in the Balkans*, 16.

20. Anton Bebler, "Yugoslavia's Agony," *International Defense Review* no. 9 (1992): 814-15. In its halfhearted efforts to keep Slovenia from seceding, the JNA used less than 10 percent of the troops at its disposal in or near Slovenia and sent armored units without infantry protection or adequate logistics, leaving them prey to road-blocks and flanking attacks.

21. JNA mechanized forces used Croatia's main road network to seize major towns while Serb irregulars fought "a partisan war for the hills and forests between." Irregulars were local Serb villagers (who operated within a day's march of their homes) plus fighters from the Krajinas and from self-styled Chetnik units "recruited from southern Serbia" and intermixed with JNA special forces. Chetnik units were used to terrorize and drive out non-Serb populations from territory that the JNA hoped to seize. Tammy Arbuckle, "Yugoslavia: Strategy and Tactics of Ethnic Warfare," *International Defense Review* no. 1 (1992): 19-21.

22. Cohen, *Broken Bonds*, 141, has a good map of Serb population distribution by *opstina* (commune). Of Bosnia's remaining population, 44 percent was Muslim and 19 percent Croat.

23. Such an operation in Bosnia would have been difficult to implement if accepted. The later preventive operation in Macedonia deployed along that country's border with Serbia (about one-quarter of its total length); it did not deploy internally, to police the boundaries of Macedonia's ethnic communities. Bosnia would have required an internal presence as well as a substantial military presence all along the country's rugged border with Serbia and Montenegro.

24. Power, *Breakdown in the Balkans*, 35-37.

25. Donia and Fine, *Bosnia and Herzegovina*, 235-36.

26. Control of this "Posavina Corridor" and expulsion of non-Serb populations from the Drina River border between Serbia and Bosnia were the two key territorial elements in the establishment of a greater Serbia.

27. Chuck Sudetic, "Shelling by Serbs in Bosnia Intensifies," *New York Times* (hereafter *NYT*), 7 April 1992, A3; and "Serb-Backed Guerrillas Take Second Bosnia Town," *NYT*, 10 April 1992, A14.

28. Glenny, *The Fall of Yugoslavia*, 200. Belgrade's continued military involvement with Bosnian Serb forces belied its public distancing, however. On 9 May 1992, the

commander of the JNA's Knin Corps, a Bosnian Serb named Ratko Mladic, was appointed "temporary" head of the JNA in Bosnia. Ibid., 201. He soon became commander of the Bosnian Serb army but evidently remained in frequent contact with Yugoslav army headquarters in Belgrade. Such communications are reported to be an important source of evidence implicating General Mladic in war crimes. See Elaine Sciolino, "US Says it is Withholding Data from War Crimes Panel," *NYT*, 8 November 1995, A10.

29. See Paul Lewis, "Two Leaders Propose Dividing Bosnia into Three Area," *NYT*, 17 June 1993, A3; Chuck Sudetic, "Serbs and Croats Mount Joint Attack on Muslim Town," *NYT*, 28 June 1993, A3; Chuck Sudetic, "Once Again, Bosnian Peace Talks Appear to Crumble," *NYT*, 21 September 1993, A3; David Ottaway, "Bosnian Muslims' Gains May Have High Cost," *Washington Post* (hereafter *WP*), 12 September 1993, A37; and John Lancaster and Daniel Williams, "US Begins to Shape Terms for Security Role in Bosnia," *WP*, 26 September 1993, A42.

30. Roy Gutman, *A Witness to Genocide* (New York: Macmillan Publishing Company, 1993), xxv.

31. Many factors contributed to the largely peaceful way in which the USSR finally did break up but a crucial one has to have been the attitudes of top leaders: Mikhail Gorbachev, as president of the Soviet Union, Boris Yeltsin, as president of Russia, and the leaders of the newly independent states themselves. Many ethnic Russians living in what had been republics of the Soviet Union, such as Kazakhstan, suddenly found themselves in foreign countries when the USSR broke up, but there was at the time no Russian leader in power willing to use raw force to save it, either in its basic form or as a kind of greater Russia.

32. Power, *Breakdown in the Balkans,* 12, 14-16.

33. "Bosniacs," as it is used here, refers to the mainly Muslim communities represented by the internationally-recognized government in Sarajevo.

34. When the USSR broke up in December 1991, the United States was freed to recognize Slovenia, Croatia, and Bosnia-Herzegovina with less concern for the impact of its actions on Moscow. In April 1993, the Security Council delayed implementation of further sanctions on Serbia and Montenegro (under Resolution 820) until the day after a referendum in Russia on Boris Yeltsin's rule. In October 1993, Russia delayed the renewal of UNPROFOR's mandate while Yeltsin engaged a rebellious parliament with tank fire.

35. Steven Erlanger, "Yeltsin Adamant on Role in Bosnia," *NYT*, 16 February 1994, A7; and John Kifner, "Serbs Withdraw in a Russian Plan to Avert Bombing," *NYT*, 18 February 1994, A1.

36. Woodward, *Balkan Tragedy,* 183.

37. For helpful background on the German perspective, James Schear is most grateful to Christoph Bertram, former resident associate at the Carnegie Endowment.

38. Glenny, *The Destruction of Yugoslavia,* 188-93.

39. The crisis reached a climax on 15 May 1991, when Serbia blocked a scheduled rotation of Yugoslavia's collective federal presidency to Stipe Mesic, the Croatian

representative. Previously, in December 1990, Slovenes had voted overwhelmingly in a referendum to secede should efforts to agree on a new, looser Yugoslav confederation fail. In February, the Slovene and Croat republics had issued a joint statement saying they would secede by July "if Yugoslavia did not become a community of sovereign republics." See Power, *Breakdown in the Balkans,* 8, 10. One of the few European officials sounding the alarm over Yugoslavia was Austrian foreign minister Alois Mock, who toured capitals in 1990 in an effort to generate action, without much success. For details see Woodward, *Balkan Tragedy,* 148. Austria's sympathies with Croat and Slovene grievances, however, may have cast its appeals in a partisan light. Reportedly, intelligence analysis performed within the US government during this time frame also raised deep concerns. See David Binder, "Evolution in Europe: Yugoslavia Seen as Breaking up Soon," *NYT,* 28 November 1990, 7.

40. James B. Steinberg, "International Involvement in the Yugoslavia Conflict," in Lori Fisler Damrosch, ed., *Enforcing Restraint: Collective Intervention in Internal Conflicts* (New York: Council on Foreign Relations, 1993), 34. It is not clear, however, that the aid package would have passed muster with all EC members. Great Britain opposed the initiative at the time. See Woodward, *Balkan Tragedy,* 459.

41. Power, *Breakdown in the Balkans,* 14.

42. James Gow, "Deconstructing Yugoslavia," *Survival* (July - August 1991): 310.

43. See Woodward, *Balkan Tragedy,* 161-62. As one piece of evidence, among others, Woodward (*Balkan Tragedy,* 158) points to the European parliament's resolution of 13 March 1991, which declared that Yugoslav republics "must have a right freely to determine their own future in a peaceful and democratic manner and on the basis of recognized international and *internal* borders." (Emphasis added.)

44. See Steinberg, "International Involvement," 35; and John Zametica, *The Yugoslav Conflict,* Adelphi Paper 270 (London: IISS, 1992), 58-59. As a result of this episode, the CSCE changed its voting rule from consensus to a qualified majority (that is, consensus minus one), but by that time the EC had eclipsed the CSCE on this issue.

45. "Brioni Declaration," *Yugoslav Survey* 32, no. 2 (1991): 45-48.

46. A series of EU actions during the summer of 1991, according to Woodward, had the effect of convincing the Serbs that the EU had abandoned its commitment to Yugoslavia. See Woodward, *Balkan Tragedy,* 178.

47. The compensating element in the plan, reportedly, was a provision that minorities be permitted to hold dual citizenship in another republic. For details on the proposal, see Michael Brenner, "The United State Perspective," in Mario Zucconi, ed., *Western Responses to the Conflict in Yugoslavia* (New York: St. Martin's Press, forthcoming, 1997), passim.

48. According to Woodward, Luxembourg, the Netherlands, and Germany initially supported the idea, and the French appeared open to the proposal, seeing it as a step toward greater European self-reliance and a vehicle to further the concept of a German-French Eurocorps. Britain, on the other hand, professed skepticism (rather presciently) that such a force would simply become embroiled in the fighting. The United States, also, was

strongly opposed, raising questions about US relations to NATO. See Woodward, *Balkan Tragedy,* 174-80.

49. Steinberg, "International Involvement," 37.

50. Power, *Breakdown in the Balkans,* 33. Other countries who followed the EC's lead were Austria, Finland, Norway, Sweden, Switzerland, and Turkey. Britain and France indicated that they would refuse to send ambassadors to Zagreb until human rights issues were resolved, and the United States refused to extend recognition. To smooth the way, Croatia agreed to make some changes to its constitution at Germany's request, changes widely viewed as cosmetic. Steinberg, "International Involvement," 38.

51. Security Council Resolution 713, 25 September 1991. China and nonaligned Council members voted in favor after the government of Yugoslavia indicated that it would not object. Steinberg, "International Involvement," 39. Arming of nationalist groups had been an issue. Hungary reportedly sold over 36,000 AK-47s to Croatia, creating a parliamentary scandal in Budapest when the shipment was revealed. Woodward, *Balkan Tragedy,* 149.

52. Security Council Resolution 743, 21 February 1992.

53. Chuck Sudetic, "Cease-Fire Stills Gunfire in Croatia," *NYT,* 4 January 1992, A3.

54. *Krajina* Serb leader Milan Babic openly criticized Serbia's desires to see the JNA withdraw as well as the disarmament aspects of the UN's plan. See Chuck Sudetic, "Yugoslavia Truce Is Largely Holding," *NYT,* 5 January 1996, 3. According to Woodward, the JNA was facing substantial pressure to withdraw from Croatia. See *Balkan Tragedy,* 191.

55. Security Council, *Further Report of the Secretary-General Pursuant to Security Council Resolution 721 (1991),* S/23592, 15 February 1992, 7.

56. Glenny, *The Fall of Yugoslavia,* 101.

57. Figures from the United Nations High Commissioner for Refugees (UNHCR) are contained in Security Council, *Report of the Secretary-General Pursuant to Security Council Resolution 815 (1993),* S/25777, 15 May 1993, 4. See also "Nations on the Move," *The Economist,* 19 August 1995, 42. These numbers exclude the population exodus that accompanied the Croatian reconquest of the Krajina in August 1995.

58. Stockholm International Peace Research Institute, *SIPRI Yearbook 1993: Armaments, Disarmament, and International Security* (New York: Oxford University Press, 1993), Table 3A.1, 121.

59. Reportedly, there was some sharp variation in JNA behavior. Local JNA units in Krajina actively fought with Serb irregulars while in Western Slavonia and other places they acted more as non-combatants and peacemakers. Glenny, *The Fall of Yugoslavia,* 101.

60. For this reason, among others, the cease-fire plan reportedly included an obligation by the parties not to return fire even if attacked without first raising a protest through a liaison network set up to link sector commanders on both sides. See Chuck Sudetic, "Yugoslav Factions Agree to U.N. Plan to Halt Civil War," *NYT,* 3 January 1992, 1.

61. One consequence of this phenomenon was the rising frequency of Serb-on-Serb crime in the UN Protected Areas during 1994, with indigenous Serb communities and political moderates being most at risk. (James A. Schear's visit to Sector East, interviews, 24 June 1994.)

62. Security Council, *Report of the Secretary-General Pursuant to Security Council Resolution 762 (1992)*, S/24353, 27 July 1992, 9.

63. Security Council, *Report of the Secretary-General Pursuant to Security Council Resolution 721 (1991)*, S/23280, 11 December 1991, annex III.

64. Chuck Sudetic, "U.N. Envoy Wins Yugoslav Peace Move," *NYT*, 30 December 1991, A3.

65. Security Council, S/23280, 18-19.

66. UN forces had no authority to seize proscribed weapons or materials, however. Confirmed violations would be taken up with the offending party and would, if necessary, be reported the Security Council. Ibid., 17.

67. These were revised as of July 1993. See Bruce D. Berkowitz, "Rules of Engagement for UN Peacekeeping Forces in Bosnia," *Orbis* 38, no. 4 (fall 1994): 635-46. Berkowitz's article appends, "Force Commander's Policy Directive Number 13, Rules of Engagement Part 1: Ground Forces." For a reaction to Berkowitz's commentary, see Major General John A. MacInnis, "The Rules of Engagement for UN Peacekeeping Forces in Former Yugoslavia: A Response," *Orbis* 39, no. 1 (winter 1995): 97-100. Interviews by William Durch established that the same ROE were used in UN-PROFOR-BH at least through December 1994.

68. Security Council, S/23592, 4-5.

69. The secretary-general, for instance, pointed out that the application of Croatian laws in such areas as trade, banking and currency, traffic, and police within the UNPAs would be inconsistent with the spirit of the plan. See Security Council, S/23592, 2. As for Serb motivations, Woodward points out that Milosevic saw the plan as a way to buy time for the *krajina* Serbs and to save face in Serbia. *Balkan Tragedy*, 189-90.

70. While there was great agitation among displaced Croats to return to their homes in the UNPAs, there was much less desire on the part of displaced Serbs to return to their homes in other parts of Croatia.

71. The March agreement is appended to Security Council, *Letter Dated 30 March 1994 from the Secretary-General Addressed to the President of the Security Council*, S/1994/367, 30 March 1994.

72. Security Council Resolution 981, 31 March 1995.

73. Ibid., para. 3. The secretary-general's implementation plan correctly interpreted this weasel-worded injunction as monitoring cross-border traffic and notifying parties of violations of UN resolutions, but not physically controlling the border. See Security Council, *Report of the Secretary-General Submitted Pursuant To Paragraph 4 of Security Council Resolution 981 (1995)*, S/1995/320, 18 April 1995, 7.

74. Data on initial deployments are drawn from Security Council, S/24353, 27 July 1992, 1.

75. The Vance Plan had foreseen the appointment of a civilian chief of mission, but the secretary-general later decided against this in order to maintain a clear distinction

between the diplomatic and peacemaking roles of the EC and the peacekeeping roles of the United Nations. See Security Council, S/23592, 4.

76. General Nambiar reportedly opposed the idea of locating the headquarters in Sarajevo but was overruled by superiors in New York. For details see Brigadier General John Wilson, "Lessons from UN Operations in Yugoslavia," in Hugh Smith, ed., *Peacekeeping: Challenges for the Future* (Canberra: Australian Defence Studies Centre, 1993), 113.

77. For further discussion of UNPROFOR's early command, control, and logistics problems, see Mats Berdal, "United Nations Peacekeeping in the Former Yugoslavia," in *Beyond Traditional Peacekeeping,* edited by Donald C. F. Daniel and Bradd C. Hayes (London: Macmillan Press Ltd., 1995), 236-39.

78. Interviews by James A. Schear, UNPROFOR Headquarters, Zagreb, Croatia, 17 April 1994.

79. Security Council, *Further Report of the Secretary-General Pursuant to Security Council Resolution 752 (1992),* S/24188, 26 June 1992, 1.

80. Security Council Resolution 762 (1992), 30 June 1992.

81. See Security Council, S/24353, 1-2.

82. Security Council, *Further Report of the Secretary-General Pursuant to Security Council Resolution 749 (1992),* S/23844, 24 April 1992, 4. UNPROFOR noted that such practices made it difficult to reestablish local administration and law enforcement. In September, the UN reported that civil police in the UNPAs were impotent in the face of the continued presence of irregular units and that in some instances local police chiefs had been replaced with extremists. See, Security Council, *Further Report of the Secretary-General Pursuant to Security Council Resolution 743 (1992) and 762 (1992),* S/24600, 28 September 1992, 5.

83. These operations involved UNPROFOR's Belgian battalion, in Baranja, and the Russian battalion near Lipovac. The experience tended to harden Serb attitudes towards the UN in Sector East. For details see Security Council, S/24600, 3. Canadian units also carried out cordon and search operations in Sector West.

84. Ibid., 4.

85. Security Council, S/24600, 9. UN forces were pushed off the dam, however, in fighting that erupted in January 1993. John Darton, "Serb-Croat Battle for Dam Grows, Ousting U.N. Force," *NYT,* 27 January 1993, A3.

86. Security Council Resolution 779, 6 October 1992. (See below, however, the associated impact on fighting in northern Bosnia.)

87. Security Council Resolution 769, 7 August 1992. The secretary-general's recommendation on this matter is found in Security Council, S/24353, 9. On Serb reactions, see Security Council, *Further Report of the Secretary-General Pursuant to Security Council Resolution 743 (1992),* S/24848, 24 November 1992, 7.

88. Security Council, S/24600, 6. Cedric Thornberry, UNPROFOR's director of Civil Affairs, was especially blunt: "The trend is toward anarchy in sectors East and South, with gangs of terrorists roaming the area, with police who don't police, with prosecutors who don't prosecute and with courts that are afraid to sit." Blaine Harden, "Grim Winter Seen in War Zones," *WP,* 6 November 1992, A20.

89. Security Council Resolution 802, 25 January 1993, operative para. 1.

90. Wilson, "Lessons from Operations in Yugoslavia," 113. In retrospect, the so-called "dual-lock" system implemented by UNPROFOR may have played an unhelpful role in this episode. Among certain UNPROFOR military commanders, there was a view that the Croats may have developed an exaggerated notion of the system's durability and felt that they could exploit the one-sided restriction on the Serbs by launching conventional attacks; the success of Serb raids upon the depots, however, quickly disabused them of that misperception. The Serbs, on the other hand, felt that the dual-lock arrangement denied them the means of self-defense at a critical moment. Both sides complained bitterly about the UN's role, and subsequent arrangements on storage of heavy weapons in Croatia conspicuously avoided any such dual-lock systems. (Interviews by James A. Schear, UNPROFOR Headquarters, Zagreb, 13 April 1994.) There were also reports that the dual-lock system was misapplied in Sector East, see Jonathan C. Randal, "Russian Unit Dismays U.N. Brass in Croatia," WP, 21 February 1993, A30.

91. David B. Ottaway, "Croat Attack Last Month Said to Fail," WP, 21 February 1993, A25.

92. In nine villages in Sector South, for example, it established a 24-hour military presence. See Rob Williamson, "UN Protection for Civilian Victims of War," UN-PROFOR News, no. 2, November 1993, 10.

93. In this action, the Croats seized three Serb villages that were then turned over to UNPROFOR control. The reported massacre of several dozen Serb villagers in the operation, however, tended to heighten threats against Croats in Sector South and created additional protection demands upon UNPROFOR. Marc McEvoy, "Villagers Decide Their Own Future," UNPROFOR News, no. 2, November 1993, 5.

94. John Darnton, "Croatia's Chief Vows 'Liberation' of More Land in Serbian Enclave," NYT, 1 February 1993, A3.

95. Security Council Resolution 807, 19 February 1993; Resolution 815, 30 March 1993; and Resolution 847, 30 June 1993.

96. Security Council, Further Report of the Secretary-General Pursuant to Security Council Resolution 743 (1991), S/26470, 20 September 1993, 5. One dimension of Croatian frustration was the UN's increasing preoccupation with Bosnia, and this adjustment was seen as a way to help correct that.

97. Security Council, Report of the Secretary-General to the Security Council Pursuant to Security Council Resolution 871 (1993), S/26828, 1 December 1993, 2.

98. Ibid., 2.

99. It is possible that Croatia was trying to influence the political balance of power in Knin. The RSK's hardline "president," Milan Martic, was at the time locked in a struggle with his own parliament, and some in the UN were fearful that he might seek to manufacture a military crisis with Zagreb as a way to consolidate his power base. If Zagreb shared this view, it may have seen a "charm" offensive as a way to check any capricious action on Martic's part. Croatia also was making good use of a lull in the fighting to consolidate and improve its military posture. For a report on

its arms-acquisition efforts, see John Pomfret, "Croatia Slips Closer to Renewed War," *WP,* 14 November 1993, A21.

100. Security Council Resolution 815, for example, supported the efforts of ICFY to "help define the future status of those territories comprising the United Nations Protected Areas (UNPAs), *which are integral parts of the territory of the Republic of Croatia*" (emphasis added). See Security Council Resolution 815, 30 March 1993, para. 5.

101. See Security Council Resolution 820, 17 April 1993, para. 12.

102. Thus, for example, Knin proposed in April 1994 that the "RSK" and UNPROFOR enter into a bilateral agreement governing all forms of reconstruction and economic-related projects in the UNPAs. UNPROFOR resisted this invitation to become independent agent for the Krajina's redevelopment. (Interviews by James A. Schear, Knin, 13 April 1994.)

103. Some UNPROFOR commanders regarded this new phase of operations as more dangerous for the UN than previous phases, given the greatly increased exposure of personnel to land-mine hazards. Many units lacked adequate equipment to perform demining in and around their own sites, and the two parties' records of mine laying left much to be desired. In Sector South, for example, over 500 mine fields were declared by both sides, but some 150 of these had been laid by JNA/TDF forces during 1991 and were not well marked. (Interviews by James A. Schear, Knin, 13 April 1994.)

104. For background, see Mark Baskin, "Building Peace With Patience," *UNPAs Monitor,* no. 1, 9 September 1994, 1. Newsletter published by UNPROFOR headquarters, Zagreb.

105. Security Council Resolution 947, 30 September 1994.

106. International Conference on the Former Yugoslavia, "Agreement on Economic Co-operation," 2 December 1994, issued by UNPROFOR headquarters, Zagreb. Mimeograph. For details on UNPROFOR operations in support of the highway reopening, see Susan Manuel, "Pact Set to Inject New Life into 'Alley of Ghosts,'" *UNPROFOR News,* no. 14, December 1994, 4.

107. "Statement by the Secretary-General," UNPROFOR Press Release, Zagreb, 12 January 1995. Mimeograph.

108. Barbara Crossette, "Croatian Leader Agrees to Continuation of UN Force," *NYT,* 13 March 1995, A9.

109. John Pomfret, "Croatian Army Launches Blitz against Serbs," *WP,* 2 May 1995, A1.

110. It appeared, in fact, that Serb forces in Krajina were ordered to evacuate. Roger Cohen, "Serbs of 'Greater Serbia' Find Suffering and Decay," *NYT,* 17 September 1995, A1. It was widely reported that a Serbian major general, Milan Mrksic, who was sent by Belgrade to assume command of *krajina* forces in May 1995, overruled the objections of local Knin authorities and ordered a speedy withdrawal of troops, including their heavy weapons, during the first hours of the Croatian attack.

111. On 6 August 1995 an agreement was reached between UN Special Representative Yasushi Akashi and the Croatian government to allow for access by UNCRO and humanitarian organizations to civilian populations, "to the extent allowed by objec-

tive security considerations." Croatia undertook additional obligations not to fire into areas vacated by combatants, or forcibly remove refugees or UN personnel from UN premises. UN Peace Force press release, Zagreb, 6 August 1995.

112. Chris Hedges, "Arson and Death Plague Serbian Region of Croatia," *NYT,* 1 October 1995, A6.

113. In Sector East, 693 Belgian and 912 Russian troops remained on duty along with 48 UNMOs and 16 CIVPOL; in former Sector North, a rump Polish battalion of 462, a Danish company of 116, a dozen troops from Jordan and Ukraine, 31 UNMOs and 61 CIVPOL remained; in former Sector South, a 523-strong Czech battalion and a handful of Canadian, Jordanian, and Kenyan soldiers were complemented by 34 UNMOs and 71 CIVPOL; in former Sector West, a Nepalese company of 165 remained, along with a dozen UNMOs and 99 CIVPOL. Security Council, S/1995/987, annex I.

114. Security Council, *Report of the Secretary-General Pursuant to Security Council Resolutions 981 (1995), 982 (1995), and 983 (1995), S/1995/987,* 23 November 1995, para. 7.

115. Samantha Power, "Guns and Pigs," *The New Republic,* 22 May 1995, 14. The quotation is attributed to US Ambassador Peter Galbraith. The relative ease of the Croatian conquest of Krajina in August 1995 does not invalidate Galbraith's point, because the Serbs chose to withdraw rather than fight. A future showdown over Eastern Slavonia might turn out differently.

116. China votes in favor of Council resolutions or abstains, only rarely threatening a veto. The non-permanent majority of the Council tended to favor greater international action on Bosnia, in particular. While the non-permanent members constitute a blocking vote on the Council, they cannot force it into action on a substantive matter over a permanent member's veto. They do, however, have the ability to transfer an issue to the General Assembly, on a veto-proof procedural vote, if the Security Council is deadlocked by veto. (The precedent is the "Uniting for Peace" Resolution, A/1775, adopted 3 November 1950 when the Council was deadlocked over Korea [5 UN General Assembly Official Records, Supp. 20, at 10].) In the case of Bosnia, however, the Council did not seize up; indeed, it spewed resolutions.

117. Stephen Kinzer, "Serbs Get Subtle Reminder on Day Full of Symbolism," *NYT,* 29 June 1995, A12.

118. Nevertheless, to emphasize Bosnia's sovereignty, the constitutional principles clearly forbade any province from entering into agreements with foreign states and international organizations. See Security Council, *Report of the Secretary-General on the Activities of the International conference on the Former Yugoslavia: Peace Talks on Bosnia and Herzegovina, S/25479,* 26 March 1993, 21, annex II.

119. Karadzic, under much pressure, finally signed the Vance-Owen plan boundary map and other documents on 2 May 1993 in Athens, but linked its final acceptance to ratification by the Bosnian Serb "Assembly," which did not happen. The Bosnian Serbs also made it very clear that they did not favor the constitutional arrangements under the Vance-Owen approach, even though they had signed them, and wanted

to continue their "Republika Srpska" as one of three independent Bosnian states. Ibid., 4.

120. See Security Council, *Letter Dated 6 August 1993 from the Secretary-General Addressed to the President of the Security Council*, S/26260, 6 August 1993, 13, appendix I.

121. United Nations Department of Public Information (DPI), *The United Nations and the Situation in the Former Yugoslavia*, 15 March 1994, 33. The overall territory division would have given the Muslims 33.5 percent, the Croats 17.5 percent, and the Serbs 49 percent.

122. The texts are appended to Security Council, *Letter Dated 3 March 1994 from the Permanent Representatives of Bosnia and Herzegovina and Croatia to the United Nations Addressed to the Secretary-General*, S/1994/255, 4 March 1994.

123. The map is found in Security Council, *Letter Dated 21 September 1994 from the Permanent Representatives of France, Germany, Russian Federation, United States of America, and the United Kingdom of Great Britain and Northern Ireland to the United Nations Addressed to the Secretary-General*, S/1994/1081, 21 September 1994. The "take it or leave it" approach, in fact, was never fully agreed upon within the Contact Group. Reportedly, the Americans favored it; the Russians opposed it; and the Europeans were dubious about it.

124. This element of airport accord was not implemented until February 1994, under NATO ultimatum.

125. Seth Faison, "UN Chief Rejects Plan to Collect Bosnian Arms," *NYT*, 23 July 1992, A3; UN Security Council, *Report of the Secretary-General on the Situation in Bosnia-Herzegovina*, S/24333, 21 July 1992; and "Statement by the President [of the Security Council], 24 July 1992," *The United Nations and the Situation in the Former Yugoslavia* (New York: UN Department of Information, May 1993), 53-54. This episode demonstrated the extent to which the Council can act in serious crisis situations without adequate substantive staff input. Its statement endorsed a plan that the UN could not implement, especially in the short time span envisaged by the London accord, in part because the organization at that time was also supporting two other very large operations, in neighboring Croatia and in Cambodia, with entirely inadequate headquarters staff.

126. Security Council Resolution 770, 13 August 1992, operative para. 2.

127. Michael R. Gordon, "60,000 Needed for Bosnia, a US General Estimates," *NYT*, 12 August 1992, A8; Gordon, "NATO Seeks Options to Troop Plan in Bosnia," *NYT*, 14 August 1992, A6; Theresa Hitchens, "West Skirts Military Action on Yugoslav Strife," *Defense News*, 17-23 August 1992, 4; and Trevor Rowe, "Allies Drop Plan for Military Role in Bosnia," *WP*, 25 August 1992, 1.

128. Security Council, *Report of the Secretary-General of the Situation in Bosnia and Herzegovina*, S/24540, 10 September 1992. A broad interpretation of the ROE could have allowed UN convoys to push their way through roadblocks and other obstacles without waiting to be fired upon first. In practice, this happened rarely, as convoy commanders knew that what got them through one roadblock could get them (or some third party hostage) killed at the next one.

129. The arrangement came unstuck six months later when the troop contributors refused to shoulder as well all of the support costs that the UN associated with the operation of these forces (for 20 international professional staff and 60 other civilian staff for administrative support, political support, public information, and liaison). Security Council, *Report of the Secretary-General on the Situation in Bosnia-Herzegovina*, S/24540, 10 September 1992, para. 17.

130. Security Council, *Report of the Secretary-General Pursuant to Security Council Resolution 781*, S/24767, 5 November 1992.

131. NATO/Western European Union, *Fact Sheet: Operation Sharp Guard* (Naples, Italy: NATO AFSOUTH Public Information Office, 5 January 1995).

132. Paul Lewis, "NATO to Help U.N. on Yugoslav Plans," *NYT*, 16 December 1992, A3; and Elaine Sciolino, "NATO Offers Support," *NYT*, 18 December 1992, A14. Bosnian Serb leader Radovan Karadzic threatened retaliation against UNPROFOR if the no-fly zone were enforced.

133. Mr. Karadzic kept his promise to retaliate by shelling the Muslim-held towns of Bihac and Srebrenica, as well as Sarajevo. (See further discussion of Srebrenica in the section on implementation.)

134. Security Council Resolution 819, 16 April 1993, operative para. 1.

135. Security Council Resolution 836, 3 June 1993, operative para. 10.

136. After lengthy debate, the Council rejected the secretary-general's request for 34,000 additional UN troops to deter attacks on the six safe areas. The request is detailed in Security Council, *Report of the Secretary-General Pursuant to Security Council Resolution 836 (1993)*, S/25939, 14 June 1993. Resolution 844, 18 June 1993, instead authorized 7,600 troops.

137. NATO Press Release (94)15 (Brussels: NATO Press Service, 9 February 1994).

138. Ibid.

139. Ibid.

140. Security Council Resolution 908, 31 March 1994, authorized a 3,500-troop increase in UNPROFOR; Resolution 914, 27 April 1994, authorized another 6,500.

141. Security Council, *Report of the Secretary-General to the Security Council Pursuant to Security Council Resolution 900 (1994)*, S/1994/291, 11 March 1994. The Council's resolutions "welcoming" these activities were deemed to provide sufficient mandate.

142. The 170 French marines arrived in Sarajevo 1 July. The Canadian battalion, with 80 armored personnel carriers and 220 other vehicles, arrived 2 July after multiple delays crossing Serb-held northern Bosnia from Croatia. John F. Burns, "First Airlifted Food Supplies Reach a Needy Sarajevo," *NYT*, 2 July 1992, A10; and author's interview, US Army War College, Carlisle Barracks, Pa., 25 February 1994.

143. Blain Harden, "Beset Sarajevo Doubts Will of Blue Helmets," *WP*, 19 June 1992, A30; and *The Independent (UK)*, 17 July 1992, 1. Mackenzie's plague-on-both-your-houses view of the conflict was colored in part by an incident early in his tenure with UNPROFOR in which a convoy of JNA troops evacuating Sarajevo under UN protection was attacked by Bosnian government forces. The incident escalated the shelling of Sarajevo and convinced Mackenzie that there were no innocents in this

war. Glenny, *The Fall of Yugoslavia,* 176-177; and then-Major General Mackenzie, interview by Terry Gross, "Fresh Aire," National Public Radio, 15 June 1995.

144. Ukrainian troops operating counter-battery radars were immediately targeted by Serb gunners. John F. Burns, "A Debut for the Ukrainian Peacekeepers in Bosnia," *NYT,* 31 July 1992, A3. The unit was also dogged by reports of black marketeering in fuel and other UN-supplied commodities. See, for example, David Rieff, *Slaughterhouse: Bosnia and the Failure of the West* (New York: Simon and Schuster, 1995), 149; and Giles Elgood, "UN in Sarajevo Probes Corruption Allegations," *Reuters* newswire, 26 August 1993, 12:14 GMT.

145. Power, *Breakdown in the Balkans,* 60, 62-63.

146. Glenny, *The Fall of Yugoslavia,* 192-94.

147. John F. Burns, "Bosnia 1992: The Paradox of Swords to Plowshares," *NYT,* 31 December 1992, A1.

148. High Commissioner Sadako Ogata's decision to halt convoys was made without consulting other senior UN officials outside UNHCR, for example, Lieutenant General Morillon, force commander of UNPROFOR-BH, the Security Council, or mediators at the International Conference on the Former Yugoslavia. John F. Burns, "Most Relief Operations in Bosnia Are Halted by UN Aid Agency," *NYT,* 18 February 1993, A1; Paul Lewis, "Condemnation at the UN," *NYT,* 18 February 1993, A8; and Paul Lewis, "UN Chief, Overruling High Aide, Orders Bosnian Relief to Resume," *NYT,* 20 February 1993, A1.

149. Peter Maas, "Enclave in Bosnia Falls to Serb Force," *NYT,* 7 March 1992, A1; Chuck Sudetic, "Serbs Overrun Muslim Enclave in Bosnia's East," *NYT,* 15 March 1992, A3; and UNHCR, *Information Notes on Former Yugoslavia,* no. 5/93, 25 April 1993, 2.

150. UNHCR, *Information Notes on Former Yugoslavia,* no. 6/93, 25 May 1993, 3; and no. 7/93, 30 June 1993, 16.

151. At that point, Morillon had been with UNPROFOR for 16 months, from its inception, and deserved a break but his independent style may also have contributed to his relief.

152. Chuck Sudetic, "Killings in Bosnian Monastery Widen Croat-Muslim Divide," *NYT,* 31 December 1993, A1; and "Commander in Bosnia Quits," *NYT,* 5 January 1994, A3. Briquemont was able to send two companies into Srebrenica and one company into Zepa, but no units to Gorazde, Tuzla, or Bihac.

153. In one instance, a 500-truck UNPROFOR-escorted convoy moving toward Tuzla from Vitez was ambushed the night of 10-11 June 1993 by Bosnian Croat militia (HVO) forces. Eight drivers were reported killed, and thirty kidnapped. The British military escorts lost two armored personnel carriers along with their weapons. The following day the escorts returned fire after warning shots, killing two HVO soldiers—UNPROFOR's "first blood" in Bosnia. James Rupert, "British UN Troops Kill 2 Croat Gunmen," *WP,* 12 June 1993, A15. Overall, despite its risk-averse reputation, UNPROFOR very likely inflicted more casualties acting in self-defense than were inflicted upon it by the warring factions.

154. UNHCR, *Information Notes on the former Yugoslavia,* no. 7/93, 30 June 1993, 2-3.

155. *NYT*, 17 July 1993, 5; UNHCR, *Information Notes on the former Yugoslavia*, no. 8/93, 1 August 1993, 16; and *UNPROFOR News*, November 1993, 7.

156. John F. Burns, "Bosnia Serbs Drive to Take Sarajevo," *NYT*, 22 July 1993, A1; and John F. Burns, "In Orchards of Sarajevo, a Key Battle," *NYT*, 3 August 1993, A9. BSA forces used helicopters with impunity, violating the no-fly zone, to shuttle troops and supplies into the offensive south of Sarajevo. (Indeed, all sides used helicopters, day and night, to ferry troops and supplies, and NATO had difficulty distinguishing one side's choppers from the other's, so none were attacked.)

157. Power, *Breakdown in the Balkans*, 82, 112, 116, 121; Stephen Kinzer, "Croatia Reportedly Buying MiGs, Defying UN," *NYT*, 23 September 1993, A9; Chuck Sudetic, "Bosnia is Using Islamic Money for Serb Arms," *NYT*, 17 January 1994, A3; Chuck Sudetic, "Serb Gunners Hit Gorazde Hospital and Refugee Sites," *NYT*, 21 April 1994, A8; John Pomfret, "US Says Serbs Plan to Fake Arms 'Airdrop'," *WP*, 10 February 1994, A23; John Pomfret, "Iran Ships Material For Arms to Bosnians," *WP*, 13 May 1994, 1; John Pomfret, "Bosnian President Demands Statement of Intent," *WP*, 25 May 1994, A30; Daniel Williams and Thomas W. Lippman, "US Is Allowing Iran to Arm Bosnia Muslims," *WP*, 14 April 1995, A1; Paul Beaver, "Iran uses Russian planes to supply Bosnian Muslim, Croat troops," *Washington Times*, 2 August 1994, 3; and "Arms to Bosnia: Serbs Still Win," *Economist*, 12 August 1994, 41. In early 1996, the *Washington Post* reported that Saudi Arabia channeled $300 million to the Bosnian government to purchase arms, primarily through Croatia, and that Washington acquiesced in this effort. See Michael Dobbs, "Saudis Funded Weapons for Bosnia, Official Says," *WP*, 3 February 1996, A1. In spring 1994, as NATO threatened air strikes against the Bosnia Serbs, the US government opted not to dissuade Croatian president Tudjman from funnelling arms to the Bosnian government. See Tim Weiner and Raymond Borne, "Gun-Running in the Balkans," *NYT*, 29 May 1996, A1.

158. John Kifner, "Yugoslav Army Reported Fighting in Bosnia to help Serbian Forces," *NYT*, 27 January 1994, A1; Chuck Sudetic, "Asserting Croatia Invaded, Bosnia Appeals to UN," *NYT*, 29 January 1994, 3; John Kifner, "Foe's Troops Pouring In, Bosnia Says," *NYT*, 31 January 1994, A9; Jonathan S. Landay, "Force Remains Tool of Choice on Run-Up to Bosnia Talks," *Christian Science Monitor*, 11 January 1994, 7; Jonathan S. Landay, "Yugoslav Army Troops Active Inside Bosnia," *Christian Science Monitor*, 28 January 1994, A1.

159. William Schmidt, "Croats and Muslims Reach Truce to End the Other Bosnia Conflict," *NYT*, 24 February 1994, A1; and Elaine Sciolino, "US and Russians Broker New Pacts for a Bosnia Peace," *NYT*, 2 March 1994, A1. The federation accord did not, however, produce automatic political or military cooperation between Croats and Muslims. More than a year passed before the two sides were reported to have mapped out a "joint battle plan" against the Serbs. Michael Dobbs, "Bosnian Serbs Test West's Will as Settlement Options Dissolve," *WP*, 12 June 1995, A14.

160. "Heavy Shelling Kills 15 People in Sarajevo," *WP*, 4 January 1994, A8; Chuck Sudetic, "UN Accuses Bosnia Army of Setting Off New Attacks," *NYT*, 8 January 1994, 6; Chuck Sudetic, "In Death, Sarajevo Woman Becomes a Symbol," *NYT*, 13 January

1994, A1; and Chuck Sudetic, "Bosnian Army Seen in Big Gain and Setback," *NYT,* 14 January 1994, A11.

161. *NYT,* 13 January 1994, A1; and William Claiborne and Daniel Williams, "UN Chief Prods NATO on Bosnia Airstrikes," *WP,* 7 February 1994, A1. Close air support procedures—including procedures for identifying targets, and command and control arrangements giving the initiative to the UN secretary-general—had been worked out during the Mount Igman crisis and approved by the NAC on 9 August 1993. NATO Press Release (93)52 (Brussels: NATO Press Service, 9 August 1993), 2. Secretary-General Boutros-Ghali and Force Commander Cot differed over whether authority to call in close air support should be pre-delegated to Cot. When Boutros-Ghali denied the request, Cot reportedly tried to bypass him and communicate with the Security Council directly. Boutros-Ghali then asked France to recall Cot, who announced his departure from UNPROFOR on 20 January.

162. "Personnel Corner," *UNPROFOR Magazine* no. 1, May 1994, 44-45.

163. Charles Dobbie, "A Concept for Post–Cold War Peacekeeping," *Survival* 36, no.3 (autumn 1994): 121-148.

164. Fred Cuny, a humanitarian expert, charged in a widely circulated broadside that haphazard UN implementation of the Sarajevo exclusion zone taught the Serbs that violation of these zones would not entail a substantial military penalty. See "An Analysis of Serb Violations of the Sarajevo Exclusion Zone," *Intertect,* 28 May 1994. Mimeograph.

165. Michael Gordon, "NATO Crafts Down 4 Serb Warplanes Attacking Bosnia," *NYT,* 1 March 1994, A1. Interestingly, the Bosnian Serb reaction to this incident was nil; apparently air-to-air exchanges were considered tit for tat.

166. It was also the case that Bosnian government forces based in Gorazde had been launching attacks on Serb villages outside the safe area.

167. Chuck Sudetic, "NATO Jets Bomb Serb Forces Assaulting Bosnian Haven," *NYT,* 11 April 1994, A1; Chuck Sudetic, "US Planes Bomb Serbian Positions for a Second Day," *NYT,* 12 April 1994, A10; and Jonathan Randal, "US Jets Strike Serb Forces Near Bosnian Town," *WP,* 11 April 1994, A1. On 16 April, a British Harrier jump jet on a close air support mission was brought down near Gorazde by a Serb surface-to-air missile; the pilot was rescued.

168. NATO Press Release (94)31 (Brussels: NATO Press Service, 22 April 1994).

169. NATO Press Release (94)32 (Brussels: NATO Press Service, 22 April 1994).

170. A proposal by NATO Allied Forces South (AFSOUTH) commander Admiral Leighton Smith to threaten Serb artillery positions around Tuzla, for example, was rejected by UN force commander de Lapresle. Roger Cohen, "UN Rebuffs NATO Plan on Bosnia," *NYT,* 24 May 1994, A11.

171. David B. Ottaway, "Bosnian Serbs' Reply to Peace Plan is Secret," *WP,* 20 July 1994, A26; and David B. Ottaway, "Bosnia Serb Reply to Peace Plan Seeks More Talks on Maps, Six Issues," *WP,* 22 July 1994, A20.

172. In September 1994, Milosevic agreed to a small (150-member), largely civilian force to monitor Serbia's borders with Bosnia. Paul Lewis, "Serbian President Is Said to Accept Trade Monitoring," *NYT,* 9 September 1994, A1.

173. John Pomfret, "Thousands Flee as Bosnian Government Troops Rout Rebel Muslim Force," *WP*, 22 August 1994, A12.

174. Roger Cohen, "Defeated Serbs in Northwest Bosnia Retreat into Croatia," *NYT*, 31 October 1994, A1; Kurt Schork, "All Bosnian Factions Pitch into Fighting," *Reuters* newswire, 1 November 1994, 6:17 P.M.; Chuck Sudetic, "Serbs Recover Land Lost to Bosnian Army," *NYT*, 12 November 1994, A7; Chuck Sudetic, "Bosnia Army Retreating in North as Serbs Press Attacks, UN Says," *NYT*, 15 November 1994, A1; Richard D. Lyons, "UN Considers Authorizing NATO to Retaliate for Serbian Attacks," *NYT*, 19 November 1994, A6; Chuck Sudetic, "Serbian Jets Bomb a Muslim Enclave, Flouting UN Ban," *NYT*, 20 November 1994, A1; Roger Cohen, "NATO, Expanding Bosnia Role, Strikes a Serbian Base in Croatia," *NYT*, 22 November 1994, A1; Roger Cohen, "Fighting Rages as NATO Debates How to Protect Bosnian Enclave," *NYT*, 24 November 1994, A1; and UNPROFOR Division of Information, "Daily Public Information Summary No. 322," Zagreb, 23 November 1994.

175. Between the Gorazde crisis and the attack on Udbina, NATO aircraft were called in twice to strike Bosnian Serb targets near Sarajevo, once on 5 August in connection with violations of the weapons exclusion zone and once on 22 September in response to Serb attacks on French troops. Tom Post, "Mission Accomplished—Barely," *Newsweek*, 15 August 1994, 55; Kurt Schork, "Bosnian Serbs Pull Guns at Sarajevo," *Washington Times*, 22 September 1994, 13; and Roger Cohen, "NATO Jets Strike Serbs Near Sarajevo," *NYT*, 23 September 1994, A8.

176. Daniel Williams and Ruth Marcus, "US Favors Making Concessions to Serbs," *WP*, 29 November 1994, A1.

177. The agreement worked out with Croatia divided the UN effort in the former Yugoslavia into three nominally separate operations with new civilian chiefs of mission (UNCRO, the UN Confidence Restoration Force in Croatia; UNPREDEP, the UN Preventive Deployment in the Former Yugoslav Republic of Macedonia; and UNPROFOR, in Bosnia-Herzegovina). All three civilians continued to report to a single UN SRSG in Zagreb, however, and all three military force commanders reported to a single theater commander, also in Zagreb. William Drozdiak, "Croatia Will Allow UN Forces to Stay," *WP*, 13 March 1995, A1.

178. Roger Cohen, "Bosnian Army, On the Attack, Breaking Truce," *NYT*, 21 March 1995, A1; and "Bosnian Offensive Draws UN Warnings," *NYT*, 28 March 1995, A3.

179. Roger Cohen, "Bosnian Serbs Shell a Town and Steal Arms," *NYT*, 22 March 1995, A8. The weapon removals, starting in March, were technically violations of the NATO exclusion zone liable to reprisal by NATO, at UN request. But since the BSA actions were taken in response to government ground offensives, air strikes would have further confirmed, in Serb eyes, UNPROFOR's partiality to the Bosniac cause.

180. UNHCR, *Information Notes on Former Yugoslavia*, no. 7/95, July 1995, i, iv; Joel Brand, "NATO Strikes Threatened in Sarajevo," *WP*, 25 May 1995, A33; Kurt Schork, "Serbs Shell Sarajevo after NATO Air Raid," *Reuters* newswire, 25 May 1995, 2:04 P.M. EDT; "Serbs Threaten Remaining UN Arms Depots," *Reuters* newswire, 27 May 1995, 1:09 P.M. EDT; and Rick Atkinson, "Strategy to Make War, not Peace," *WP*, 1 June 1995, A1.

181. Sean Maguire, "French Clash with Serbs on Sarajevo Convoy Road," *Reuters* news-wire, 14 July 1995, 4:20 P.M. EDT; Chris Hedges, "UN Combat Force Sent to Sarajevo to Counter Serbs," *NYT*, 24 July 1995, A1; and Hedges, "British Set Up Guns above Sarajevo, but Serbs Go On Pounding City," *NYT*, 25 July 1995, A6.

182. Barbara Crossette, "US Seeks to Prove Mass Killings," *NYT*, 11 August 1995, A3; and Security Council, *Report of the Secretary-General Pursuant to Security Council Resolution 1019 (1995) on Violations of International Humanitarian Law in the Areas of Srebrenica, Zepa, Banja Luka, and Sanski Most*, S/1995/988, 27 November 1995, paras. 4-37.

183. Within a week of the Serbs' flight from the Krajina, there began mass expulsions of Croats and Serbs remaining in Serb-held areas of Bosnia, especially Banja Luka. Mike O'Connor, "Split Divides President and Premier in Bosnia," *NYT*, 16 August 1995, A8.

184. Steven Engelberg, "How Events Drew US into Balkans," *NYT*, 19 August 1995, A1.

185. Ibid.; and Roger Cohen, "In Balkans: Power Shift," *NYT*, 18 August 1995, A1.

186. "Operation Deliberate Force" involved roughly 850 air strike sorties and 2,350 support sorties (tankers, surveillance, reconnaissance, electronic support measures, and combat air cover). *Reuters* newswire, 14 September 1995, 11:57 A.M. EDT.

187. Rick Atkinson and Daniel Williams, "NATO Jets Hit Serbs Again; Bad Weather Curtails Raids," *WP*, 1 September 1995, A26.

188. Chris Hedges, "Three Enemies Agree to Serbian State as Part of Bosnia," *NYT*, 9 September 1995, A1.

189. Alison Mitchell, "Bosnian Enemies Set a Cease-Fire, Plan Peace Talks," *NYT*, 6 October 1995, A1; and Security Council, S/1995/987, paras 15-17.

190. Elaine Sciolino, "Accord Reached to End the War in Bosnia; Clinton Pledges U.S. Troops to Keep Peace," *NYT*, 22 November 1995, A1.

191. Eric Schmidt, "High-Tech Maps Guided Bosnia Talks," *NYT*, 24 November 1995, A14.

192. Security Council Resolution 1031, 15 December 1995.

193. UNPROFOR's overall contribution to relief delivery is difficult to gauge from aggregate statistics, as UNHCR does not report relative success rates for escorted and unescorted convoys through equally hostile areas. UNPROFOR rarely pushed its way through closed checkpoints, but its escort forces probably reduced the rate of enroute hijacking, and its armored vehicles were rolling refuges for the drivers of aid trucks who came under fire. Without that recourse, many drivers might have refused to undertake deliveries. Moreover, the majority of aid reaching Sarajevo came in by air, and that access was made possible by UNPROFOR's control of the airport. Some 60 percent of relief delivered by road was non-food (fuel, medicines, housing materials, clothing, personal sundries), and delivery rates improved over time. In 1993, while Muslims and Croats were fighting in Central Bosnia, UNHCR managed to meet just 56 percent of its food delivery targets. In 1994, after the federation agreement and cease-fire, the delivery rate rose to 82 percent, and to 94 percent in the first four months of 1995. In May and June, deliveries fell sharply due to resumed hostilities and closure of the Sarajevo airport by the Bosnian Serb army. For detailed statistics,

see UNHCR, *Information Notes on former Yugoslavia*, 1/94, January 1994; 1/95, January 1995; and 7/95, July 1995.

194. The first twinges of discomfort in NATO circles came after an attack by US Navy cruise missiles against communications and air defense targets around the Serb stronghold of Banja Luka in northwestern Bosnia. They became more pronounced when the United States sought to deploy F-117 stealth fighter-bombers to Italian bases. Both weapons were closely associated with the devastating 1991 strategic air campaign against Iraq. Eric Schmitt, "Wider NATO Raids on Serbs Expose Rifts in Alliance," *NYT*, 12 September 1995, A1.

195. The United States, however, allowed the BSA to keep smaller heavy weapons around Sarajevo, in part as a face-saving device for the BSA and in part as an acknowledgment of the BSA's argument that it needed to deter government attacks on Serb sections of greater Sarajevo.

196. See Security Council, S/1995/222.

197. Security Council, S/1995/987, para. 11.

198. On 12 November 1995, while participating in the Bosnian peace talks at Dayton, Ohio, Presidents Milosevic and Tudjman signed an agreement to return the last Serb-held part of Croatia, known in UN parlance as Sector East, to Croatian government control in a transition of up to two years to be overseen by the UN. Sector East was to be demilitarized, with security provided by approximately 5,000 UN troops. Displaced persons were accorded the right to return to their properties. The UN would also help to establish and train a temporary police force. See Security Council, *Letter dated 15 November 1995 from the Permanent Representative of Croatia to the United Nations addressed to the Secretary-General*, S/1995/951, 15 November 1995 (text of the agreement); *Report of the Secretary-General Pursuant to Security Council Resolution 1025 (1995)*, S/1995/1028 (reissued), 13 December 1995 (Secretariat's concept of operations for the new force); and Security Council Resolution 1037, 15 January 1996 (authorization of the force).

The Sector East accord represented, to all intents and purposes, a slow-motion surrender by local Serb militias to forestall further armed action by Croatia. Slobodan Milosevic opted to hand control of the territory back to Zagreb rather than risk a conflict that could derail a settlement in Bosnia and prevent the lifting of international sanctions on Serbia.

The United States declined to contribute troops to the new UN operation, known as UNTAES (short for UN Transitional Administration for Eastern Slavonia, Baranja, and Western Sirmium). However, a former American general, Jacques Klein, was appointed to head it. By year's end, he and the UN were attempting to recruit forces to fill out the nominal two-brigade structure of the force. UN Special Envoy Kofi Annan criticized the Security Council for authorizing little more than half the 9,300 troops that UN military advisors thought the operation needed to carry out its mandate. See David Stamp, "UN aide warns West on Croatian peacekeeping force," *Reuters* newswire, 28 December 1995, 2:10 P.M. EST.

SEVEN

THE POLITICS OF RECONCILIATION: THE UNITED NATIONS OPERATION IN MOZAMBIQUE

PAMELA L. REED

After concluding its struggle to gain independence from Portugal in 1975, the new government of Mozambique immediately faced another war against rebels supported by the minority-ruled governments in neighboring Rhodesia and South Africa. When Rhodesia transitioned to majority-rule in 1980, its support for the war in Mozambique ended. South African support continued throughout the decade, but had begun to taper off by the end of 1989, finally allowing Mozambique to resolve its conflict politically. Civil war formally came to a close in October 1992 when the government and the rebel movement signed the General Peace Agreement. The United Nations Operation in Mozambique (ONUMOZ) was established to oversee the impartial implementation of the agreement. After 16 long years of bloodshed, both Mozambique's populace and its soldiers were ready to embrace peace.

ORIGINS

Mozambique is located on the east coast of southern Africa (see figure 7.1). A country elongated north to south and encompassing around 800,000 square kilometers, it is roughly the combined size of Great Britain and France. It shares a border with six nations: Malawi, South Africa, Swaziland, Tanzania, Zambia, and Zimbabwe. Mozambique is one of the poorest countries in the world, but has the potential to overcome this lowly status. Its east-west rail lines and the major ports along its 2,470-kilometer coastline on the Indian Ocean offer trade access to its landlocked neighbors. In the past, Mozambique's beaches were a tourist mecca. If peace holds and the security situation improves, tourism may again contribute to Mozambique's revenue. Mineral deposits offer yet another source of foreign income earnings, and arable land could lead to self-sufficiency in production of staple food products with efficient management and the return of the people. Domestic, regional, and international circumstances have prevented Mozambique from capitalizing on these assets.[1]

Mozambique achieved its independence from Portugal in 1975. The Portuguese arrived in the region in the fifteenth century, but did not "govern [the territory] as a single administrative unit with a national economy" until 1941.[2] Portugal's colonial policy, moreover, left Mozambique ill equipped for self-management as an independent nation. Little infrastructure was built to connect the distant parts of the country. Major railways ran west to east, from inland African nations to the ports on the Indian ocean. Labor productivity was not directed toward internal development: Mozambicans were forced to grow export crops, such as cotton, neglecting staple foods; and they were hired out as laborers in neighboring countries. The Portuguese administration received a set percentage of South African goods through Mozambique's ports in return for supplying Mozambican workers for South African mines.

Assimilado status allowed Mozambicans to skirt these labor practices, but they had little access to the education required to become *assimilados* (by independence, *assimilados* comprised less than one percent of the African population). Moreover, Mozambicans had to compete with Portuguese citizens in the labor market. To ease economic and social problems at home, Portugal encouraged its lower class, peasant population to emigrate to Mozambique. They took the "semi-skilled and unskilled" positions usually filled by the indigenous populations in colonial systems and, thus, cut off another avenue for Mozambicans to advance.[3]

The War for Independence

Encouraged by Tanzania, exiled Mozambicans opposed to Portuguese rule formed the Frente de Libertaçao de Moçambique (FRELIMO) in Dar es Salaam in 1962. Eduardo Mondlane, educated in the West, was FRELIMO's first president. His program to eradicate the colonial structure and its practices led to the adoption of socialist policies: The support, and thus the empowerment, of the rural population was a necessary component of FRELIMO's success against the Portuguese as the peasants provided food, shelter, and intelligence to the liberation forces. Status within FRELIMO depended on active involvement in the liberation movement—the better to avoid creation of a political elite apart from the general populace and unappreciative of its needs. For example, Mozambicans who attended university had to work, in turn, to educate people in liberated zones.[4]

Fig. 7.1
MAP OF MOZAMBIQUE

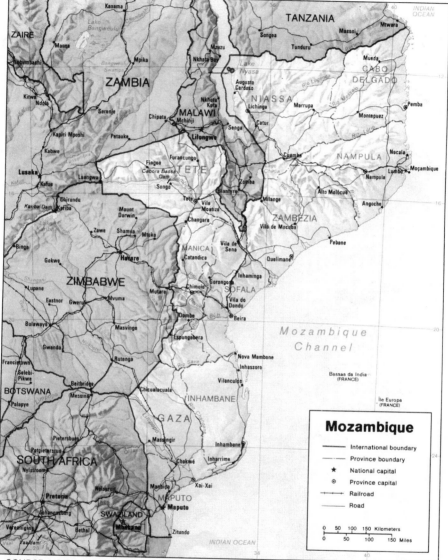

SOURCE: US Government

The struggle against the Portuguese began on 25 September 1964. FRELIMO operations were confined initially to the northern Cabo Delgado and Niassa regions. By 1968, it had opened fronts in Tete province, which gave it access to southern Mozambique. The larger Portuguese forces were unable to curtail FRELIMO activity, and in 1974 the struggle ended. The overthrow of the Portuguese right-wing government of Marcelo Caetano in April led to a cease-fire agreement between the new government and FRELIMO. Signed on 7 September 1974, the Lusaka Agreement established a transitional government pending full independence, which was granted on 25 June 1975.

FRELIMO's assumption of power resulted in the exodus of Portuguese nationals from the country. Its socialist economic ideals meant nationalization of property and loss of economic advantages. All sectors of the economy were subjected under centralized planning. Almost 90 percent of the colonials fled, stripping the country of all that they had "given" it. Cattle were slaughtered and machinery was destroyed. More important than the destruction of physical property, however, was the flight of Portuguese nationals, which deprived Mozambique of the educated and trained personnel necessary to build and manage the country. When FRELIMO came to power there were only "six economists and two agronomists, and fewer than a thousand black high school graduates."[5] According to another estimate, the country was left with only one black doctor and one "qualified" black agronomist.[6]

As the FRELIMO government set out to deal with these internal problems, a more troublesome problem was taking shape in Rhodesia (present-day Zimbabwe). The minority-ruled Rhodesian government of Ian Smith felt threatened by FRELIMO's rise to power. Its own nationalist independence movement, the Zimbabwe African National Union (ZANU), which had staged raids from Mozambican territory, now had the support of Mozambique's new majority-ruled government. In 1976, Mozambique began to enforce the UN-sanctioned embargo against Rhodesia, forfeiting the foreign revenue earned by Rhodesian use of the country's railways.

The War Against Independence

Ken Flower, head of the Rhodesian Central Intelligence Organization, established a paramilitary force purportedly to gather intelligence on ZANU's military wing, but also to disrupt the government of Mozambique. By 1976, radio broadcasts from Rhodesia hailed the successes of the "Mozambican rebel movement." Ex-Portuguese security personnel and disgruntled Mozambican nationals, who had expected to be amply rewarded for their role in the independence struggle, were recruited by the Rhodesian intelligence service to fight the new government. Thus came about the birth of the Resistência Nacional Moçambicano (RENAMO).

FRELIMO officially adopted Marxism-Leninism in 1977, the same year in which it signed a twenty-year treaty of cooperation and friendship with the Soviet Union. Although it planned to be nonaligned, Mozambique's close relations with the Soviet Union suggested a clear preference for the communist "camp." As the West distanced itself, Mozambique became more dependent on the Soviet Union and Eastern Europe for economic and military aid and more vitriolic in its rhetoric against the West.

Conditions approached crisis in the early 1980s.[7] The socialist agricultural policy was failing. The peasants, still producing for those in power instead of themselves, were disillusioned with the policy. The lack of skilled managers and workers to operate and maintain machinery squandered heavy investments in modern farming equipment. Economic benefits and support expected from the Soviet Union did not materialize as Mozambique's membership in the Council for Mutual Economic Assistance was refused in December 1981. Moreover, the extensive military aid required to quell rebel activity was not forthcoming.[8]

Although Zimbabwe gained independence in 1980, RENAMO's campaigns did not end as expected. South Africa, led by hardliner Pieter W. Botha, took over the reins. Afonso Dhlakama, a former FRELIMO soldier who escaped a reeducation camp where he had been jailed for theft, joined Flower's rebel movement and rose to become RENAMO's president. With South African aid, RENAMO, which had been disintegrating into small, disconnected armed bands, became a stronger, more highly trained, destructive rebel organization. By 1981, there were about 6,000 to 7,000 RENAMO fighters operating in Mozambique.[9]

South Africa set up training bases for RENAMO within its borders and airlifted soldiers and supplies into Mozambique. By mid-1981, nine of Mozambique's ten provinces were under attack. Mozambique's railway corridors were key RENAMO targets. RENAMO also attacked power supply systems, communication centers, hospitals, and schools. The Cabora Bassa Dam in Tete presented an easy target for RENAMO, and the loss of its electrical generation capacity was a costly blow to the government.

Civilians were treated no differently than physical property. RENAMO targeted doctors and teachers as symbols of FRELIMO's influence. Foreign aid workers and missionaries were captured and held for barter. Civilians were maimed, killed, kidnapped to serve as porters for RENAMO fighters, or forced to join the RENAMO army—where they were sometimes forced to commit brutal acts to make them accomplices.[10]

Although RENAMO professed as its goals multiparty democracy, a free-market economy, and freedom of religion, little political organization promoting these goals could be found within the country.[11] How much popular support RENAMO had was hard to gauge. Disenchantment with FRELIMO's policies did not necessarily convert into active support for RENAMO, but combined with a fear of RENAMO's brutality, it fostered passive opposition. The movement did, however, coopt the tribal chiefs, restoring their status, which FRELIMO had taken away in its efforts to centralize power. The Catholic Church, whose activities were prohibited by FRELIMO, supported aspects of RENAMO's policy, "especially where it allegedly [stood] for the growth of Church influence. . . . Some believe[d] that Catholic Church sympathy for RENAMO would put pressure on the government which . . . would lead it to moderate its anti-religious sentiments in an attempt to gain greater public support generally." Moreover, religious leaders were less often targeted by RENAMO than were teachers and health workers.[12]

Initiatives toward Conflict Resolution

At its Fourth Party Congress in 1983, FRELIMO took steps to restructure its economic policy. Family agricultural endeavors received more resources, and the private sector was strengthened. The government became a member of the International Monetary Fund and the World Bank in 1984. Foreign investors were attracted by more liberal economic policies, and more international aid was forthcoming. In 1984, Mozambique received more US emergency food aid than any other country.[13]

President Samora Machel, who succeeded the assassinated Eduardo Mondlane in 1969, also worked to find a political solution to South Africa's destabilization campaign. In the 1984 Nkomati Accord, South Africa and Mozambique agreed to discontinue all types of assistance to the other's rebel organization. Mozambique complied with the provisions, expelling members of the African National Congress from the country, but right-wing elements in the South African government who sympathized with RENAMO apparently continued to supply aid covertly.[14]

In 1986, Samora Machel was killed in a plane crash over South Africa. Joaquim Chissano, former prime minister for the 1974 transitional government and Mozambique's foreign minister thereafter, became president in November 1986. A pragmatic leader, he took bolder steps to stabilize conditions in Mozambique. Chissano believed that common economic interests could persuade South Africa to distance itself from RENAMO. In 1988, Chissano and President Botha signed an agreement in which South Africa pledged to assist in repairing the Cabora Bassa Dam, which could supply South Africa with 8 percent of its energy requirements. As hoped, South Africa warned its protégé RENAMO against further attacks on the installation.[15]

Improving relations with the West and South Africa gave the government the latitude to concentrate on marginalizing RENAMO. At its Fifth Party Congress in July 1989, FRELIMO renounced Marxism-Leninism and introduced plans for a multiparty political system. FRELIMO also announced its willingness to begin talks with RENAMO, which had also decided to work toward a negotiated settlement following its First Party Congress in June 1989.[16] Although disruptive, RENAMO did not have the capability to defeat the government. Moreover, South Africa's unprecedented political change further distanced it from RENAMO, which in turn distanced RENAMO from any aid.

Robert Mugabe, president of Zimbabwe, and Daniel arap Moi, president of Kenya, served as mediators for the government's initial dialogue with RENAMO. Mugabe owed much to the government of Mozambique for its unstinting support during his movement's independence struggle, and Zimbabwean troops had been stationed in Mozambique since 1985, providing security in the Beira and Limpopo rail corridors. Kenya, which had given refuge to Mozambican exiles since the 1960s, became a contact point with RENAMO for the government of Mozambique; Chissano believed that Moi could influence the rebel movement. The only country willing to issue RENAMO passports, Kenya also allegedly supplied logistical aid to RENAMO as South Africa's contributions decreased.[17]

The first talks were held in August 1989 in Nairobi, Kenya. Dhlakama attended as a member of RENAMO's delegation, but the government of Mozambique sent three church officials to present its proposals.[18] Both parties renounced violence and advocated the right to basic freedoms, but talks stalled over the refusal of the government and RENAMO to recognize each other's legitimacy. In July 1990, direct talks began in Rome to advance the peace efforts.[19]

The Sant' Egidio Community (a Catholic lay organization associated with the Vatican), the Italian government, and Bishop Jaime Gonçalves now mediated the talks, which resulted in a "limited," six-month cease-fire agreement in December. Zimbabwean troops were confined to a delimited area in the corridors, and RENAMO was to cease attack in these "corridors of peace."[20]

In February 1991, RENAMO fighters broke the cease-fire with attacks in the Limpopo corridor and the Tete transport corridor. Diplomatic intervention by Italy, the United States, and the Soviet Union convinced Dhlakama to return to the negotiation table in March 1991. Although fighting continued, a document on Fundamental Principles was signed on 18 October 1991. This document called for a tripartite commission, which would include the United Nations, to supervise the peace agreement.[21] By March 1992, the parties had signed two more protocols.

In June 1992, with the two parties to begin discussion of military issues, others nations were brought formally into the peace process. France, Portugal, the United Kingdom, the United States, and the UN were approved as official observers. Besides Italy, which played an instrumental role by hosting the peace talks, the United States was already playing a significant role at the negotiations as an unofficial observer. A US technical team advised on cease-fire provisions and elections; this team and the US observers consulted with the parties directly, and were consulted frequently by the mediators.[22]

In August 1992, following the encouragement of then US assistant secretary of state for African affairs Herman Cohen, Chissano and Dhlakama met for the first time at a Rome summit and promised to resolve all unanswered issues by 1 October. On 4 October 1992, they signed the General Peace Agreement (GPA). The accord went into effect on 15 October when it was ratified by the Mozambican National Assembly (see tables 7.1 and 7.2 for an outline of the GPA provisions).[23]

After 16 years of civil war, Mozambique was a ravaged country. An estimated 1 million people were dead as a result of the war. Between 1.5 and 1.8 million had fled the country, and the figure for internally displaced persons ranged from 4 to 5 million. The completion of the General Peace Agreement was a sign that the parties were ready to try peace. Their compliance with the accord would demonstrate the degree of their commitment to peace.

MANDATE

Security Council Resolution 797 of 16 December 1992 established the United Nations Operation in Mozambique. In the formulation of the operation's mandate, Secretary-General Boutros Boutros-Ghali divided the operational tasks into four interdependent components: political, military, humanitarian, and electoral. UN political responsibilities would be met by facilitating impartial implementation of the GPA's provisions, culminating in general elections. Timing of the elections was closely linked to implementation of the UN's military tasks. Boutros-Ghali stated that "in light of recent experience in Angola, it [was] of critical importance that the

Table 7.1

PROVISIONS OF THE GENERAL PEACE AGREEMENT (GPA)

Protocol I *Fundamental Principles*	• Government not to adopt any law contrary to negotiated agreements • RENAMO to refrain from armed combat
Protocol II *Political Parties*	• Parties to be "independent and national in scope"; to support democratic values • Parties representing exclusive interests not to be recognized
Protocol III *Principles for Electoral Law and Process*	• Government to draft electoral law in consultation with RENAMO and other parties • National Elections Commission (NEC) to organize and conduct electoral process • Freedom of the press, media access, organization, and movement • Government to assist RENAMO in obtaining offices, facilities, and transport needed to facilitate its transformation to political party
Protocol IV *Military Questions*	• Demobilization of current armed forces and reintegration into civil society • Withdrawal of foreign forces and disbandment of private and irregular forces • New, 38,000-strong army to be established before electoral campaign • Joint Commission for the Formation of the Mozambican Armed Forces (CCFADM), Cease-Fire Commission (CCF), and Reintegration Commission (CORE) to oversee these processes • Commission on Police Affairs (COMPOL) and Commission on Information (COMINFO) to monitor respect for civil rights, laws governing police force and intelligence services
Protocol V *Guarantees*	• Timetable for electoral process specified • Supervisory and Monitoring Commission (CSC) to oversee entire peace process; responsible for "the authentic interpretation of the agreement," with final authority over decisions of CCFADM, CCF, CORE[a]; final decisions in CSC to be made by government/RENAMO consensus • National Commission for State Administration to facilitate collaboration between state administration and RENAMO-controlled areas; public administration in both areas to obey laws already in force; institutions in RENAMO-controlled areas to employ residents in those areas • Government and RENAMO to allow political organization/campaigning throughout country
Protocol VI *Cease-Fire*	• Guidelines for cessation of armed conflict: cease-fire, separation of forces, concentration of forces, demobilization • Military commander from the corresponding party and representative from CCF monitoring group to be stationed in each assembly area • Some forces to be demobilized in situ at military facilities
Protocol VII *Donors' Conference*	• To raise funds for reintegration of ex-soldiers, displaced persons, and refugees, and for the electoral process • Italy to organize

NOTE: [a] The parties did not ask the UN to chair the CCFADM until June 1993. (Security Council, *Report of the Secretary General on the United Nations Operation in Mozambique*, S/26034, 30 June 1993, 7.)

SOURCE: Security Council, *The General Peace Agreement for Mozambique*, S/24635, annex, 8 October 1992.

elections should not take place until all military aspects of the agreement [had] been fully implemented."[24]

The military component was to monitor and verify the cease-fire; the separation and concentration of forces, their demobilization, and the collection, storage, and destruction of weapons; the complete withdrawal of foreign forces; and the disbanding of private

Table 7.2

MEMBERSHIP ON NON-UN COMMISSIONS

Commissions	Composition		
	Nominated by Government	Nominated by RENAMO	Nominated by government in consultation with Mozambique's political forces
National Elections Commission	two-thirds	one-third	N/A
Commission on Information	6	6	9
Commission on Police Affairs	6	6	9
National Commission for State Administration	4	4	N/A

SOURCE: Security Council, *The General Peace Agreement for Mozambique*, S/24635, annex, 8 October 1992.

and irregular armed groups. The military component would also provide security for United Nations and other international activities in support of the peace process.[25]

Humanitarian efforts were to be organized under the United Nations Office for Humanitarian Assistance and Coordination (UNOHAC). Its job was to coordinate the efforts of UN agencies and other nongovernmental organizations already present in Mozambique in order to implement a unified humanitarian strategy. UNOHAC's central task, however, was the reintegration of displaced persons, refugees, and soldiers into Mozambican society.

The Electoral Division was responsible for monitoring the entire electoral process. It was to verify the impartiality of the National Elections Commission (NEC) and to verify that all parties had freedom of organization and unrestricted access to media and that the electoral rolls were properly completed. It would observe registration, polling, and the counting of election results, report complaints and irregularities to the NEC, and press for action to resolve them, if necessary. To prepare Mozambican citizens for the electoral campaign, it would also conduct electoral education. In coordination with the electoral division, the United Nations Development Program would provide technical assistance, such as legal advice, advice on how to conduct the elections, and logistical planning.[26]

In February 1994, the Security Council passed Resolution 898, which authorized a civilian police contingent for the operation. In initial planning for ONUMOZ, the secretary-general had contemplated the possibility of deploying such a unit to monitor respect for human rights and civil liberties. RENAMO's later allegations that the government was transferring soldiers to the national police ranks resulted in both parties requesting UN civil police to monitor Mozambique's police activities. The police contingent would also provide technical support to the Commission on Police Affairs (COMPOL); verify the strength, location, and materiel of the Mozambican Police (PRM); and assist in the reorganization and training of the PRM's Quick Reaction Force.[27]

FUNDING

The Mozambique operation was a considerable undertaking with commensurate cost. The secretary-general estimated that the cost of ONUMOZ's first year of operation (October 1992 to October 1993) would exceed $264 million. The Advisory Committee on Administrative and Budgetary Questions gave the secretary-general authorization to expend up to $9.5 million so that he could act immediately after the Security Council approved the mission, but the actual budget was not approved by the General Assembly until mid-March 1993. The $140 million appropriated at that time covered expenses only until June. The General Assembly appropriated $54 million in September for the remainder of the first year. Total expenses for the first year were less than estimated, mainly due to the gradual deployment of military forces and civilian staff and to the deferment of other expenses because of this late deployment.[28]

The delay in implementation pushed the mission into a second year and ultimately incurred higher mission cost. The early estimated cost for the period 1 November 1993 to 15 November 1994 was $310 million. The Assembly appropriated $161 million on March 1994 for the period November 1993 - April 1994, and later $165 million for May 1994 to 15 November.[29]

Financial transactions in the field were constrained by actions in New York. The operation functioned without an approved budget for three months, and as noted, budgets for successive mandated periods were approved late. The peacekeeping account for Mozambique was also continually in deficit. By 31 December 1993, member states were in arrears for $81 million of $194 million appropriated for the operation's first year. By mid-November 1994, outstanding assessments were over $106 million.[30]

Assessed contributions for ONUMOZ were supplemented by voluntary contributions from the international community. A consolidated Humanitarian Assistance Program, devised by the government of Mozambique with the assistance of UNOHAC, envisaged programs for repatriation, emergency relief (food, clothing, tools), and restoration of essential services in rural areas to which the internally displaced persons and refugees returned. Funds for these programs were solicited at an International Donors' Conference. The first such conference was organized by Italy and held in December 1992; a second was held in June 1993.

Initially, $326 million was thought adequate to meet the assistance program's objectives. However, funding requirements increased as needs for health, education, and road repairs were reassessed, national agricultural output fluctuated, and the program for reintegrating soldiers was expanded. By December 1994, the international community had contributed 78 percent of the original $326 million, but by that time program requirements had risen to $650 million.[31]

Five trust funds managed by the UN and its agencies were established to collect funds donated for certain aspects of the peace process. The first one, managed by the UN Department of Humanitarian Affairs (DHA) dealt with humanitarian assistance and supported programs for mine-clearing activities and demobilization and reintegration of soldiers. The mine-clearance program cost $18.5 million; ONUMOZ contributed $11.6 million, which was applied to the national mine survey and the training of deminers. The remainder was donated by Italy, the Netherlands, and Sweden through the trust fund. Assessed UN funds for the demobilization of soldiers were allocated to such projects as setting up assembly areas and providing tarpaulins and blankets for soldiers, while the DHA voluntary fund supported such things as transportation of demobilized soldiers to their home regions.[32]

A second trust administered by the UN Development Program (UNDP) accepted contributions for a reintegration program that complemented the six-months' severance pay provided to demobilized soldiers by the government with another 18-months' pay to help former soldiers get a start in civilian life (and to discourage banditry). Originally budgeted at $18.1 million, its cost increased to $31.9 million because more soldiers were demobilized than planned. By late December 1994, only $8.9 million of the $27.6 million pledged had been received.[33]

In May 1993, the secretary-general established a third trust fund for the "implementation of the peace process in Mozambique" to help RENAMO secure accommodations, transport, and communications facilities to reorganize itself as a political party. The initial request for the trust fund was $10 million, but projected requirements increased to $19 million. By the end of August 1994, $13.6 million had actually been received. The United States, Denmark, Italy, and the European Union agreed to contribute the balance when RENAMO threatened not to participate in the elections unless the trust was fully funded. By 31 October 1994, over $17.7 million had been received and allotted.[34]

The fourth trust fund, for assistance to registered political parties, was established in April 1994. Parties that registered with the Ministry of Justice, including FRELIMO and RENAMO, received monetary assistance to "enable them to carry out various electoral activities. . . to ensure effective competition for elections." Contributions to this fund of more than $3 million were disbursed to the registered political parties by 31 October.[35]

A fifth and final trust fund supported the electoral process in general. With an original estimate of $71 million, the fund actually spent a bit less ($63.5 million). The international community paid $59.1 million, and the Mozambique state budget covered the remainder. The funds were used for registration and voting materials, air transport, civic education, and training of party personnel.[36]

PLANNING AND IMPLEMENTATION

President Chissano expected the UN force to assume its duties once the GPA and the cease-fire entered into force, but the Department of Peacekeeping Operations only began contracting for troop contributions after the Security Council authorized the mission on 16 December 1992. The secretary-general did, however, expedite the appointment of a special representative for Mozambique. Aldo Ajello from Italy arrived in Mozambique on 15 October with 21 military observers and worked to set up the apparatus for implementing the peace agreement. He arranged meetings between government and RENAMO officials, who had not met since the signing of the accords. His efforts enabled the Supervisory and Monitoring Commission and its three sub-commissions to be established in November 1992. The military observers began limited verification duties and performed reconnaissance tasks in the country's three regions.[37]

Size and Composition

ONUMOZ's authorized strength was almost 7,000 military personnel, the majority of whom were not deployed until May 1993. At its height, ONUMOZ had a combined strength of 6,843 military personnel and civilian police. Major General Lélio Gonçalves Rodrigues da Silva, the force commander, came from Brazil. After completion of his tour in March 1994, he was replaced by Major General Mohammad Abdus Salam of Bangladesh.

Five infantry battalions were deployed to provide security in the main transport corridors previously protected by Zimbabwe and Malawi. A Bangladeshi battalion deployed along the Nampula corridor in the north; Botswanan troops in the Tete province; Italian forces along the Beira corridor in central Mozambique; Zambian forces in the Limpopo corridor in the south; and a battalion provided by Uruguay along Highway One, which ran north from Maputo to Beira. By August 1994, an additional self-contained infantry company, provided by Brazil, was deployed in the Zambezia province, an area of increasing security problems. (For a complete list of troop contributors, see table 7.3).[38]

ONUMOZ was authorized 354 military observers from 19 countries. Their job was to verify compliance with the cease-fire, assist in preparation of assembly areas, and monitor troop assembly and demobilization.

The military component included a communications unit, a medical unit, three logistics companies, a movement control company, and a "substantial" aviation unit consisting of fixed-wing aircraft and helicopters. Portugal provided the communications unit. Argentina, Bangladesh, and Italy provided medical units for the three regional areas. Movement control personnel were provided by Japan. India sent an engineering company (to support the Zambian battalion), a logistics unit, and the ONUMOZ headquarters company. The Italian contingent also supplied its own air component at no cost to the UN.[39]

Linking UNOHAC's responsibilities to the military tasks, a civilian "technical unit" deployed people in each troop assembly area to work alongside military observers. Personnel were seconded from the World Health Organization, the United Nation's Children's Fund, the European Community, the International Organization for Immigration, and the Swiss Development Cooperation Agency. Technical unit personnel registered soldiers and issued personal documents; provided food, healthcare, and civilian clothing; and provided transportation to home districts and seeds and tools for resettlement.[40]

Table 7.3
ONUMOZ TROOP CONTRIBUTIONS

Country	May 1993 Infantry	May 1993 Observers	March 1994 Infantry	March 1994 Observers	Sept. 1994 Infantry	Sept. 1994 Observers
Argentina	40	8	40	8	40	8
Australia					4	
Bangladesh	1371	20	1458	30	1035	35
Botswana	747		757	13	750	2
Brazil	3	19	0	27	171	26
Canada		15		15		4
Cape Verde		15		18		16
China				10		10
Czech Republic		20		19		19
Egypt		20		20		20
Guinea Bissau		6		43		37
Hungary		18		23		22
India	670	19	918	18	88	18
Italy	1058		971		232	
Japan	53		53		53	
Malaysia		21		24		24
Netherlands			11		11	
New Zealand			2		9	
Portugal	282		277	1	153	1
Russian Federation		20		19		18
Spain		20		20		21
Sweden		19		20		13
United States			5		1	
Uruguay	844	10	842	34	832	27
Zambia	846		865	8	784	8
TOTALS	**6164**	**271**	**6569**	**370**	**4492**	**329**

SOURCE: UN Secretariat, Department of Peacekeeping Operations, monthly troop strength reports. (Mimeograph.)

In February 1994, the Security Council approved the secretary-general's request for 1,016 police observers, an addition to the 128 observers who were authorized initially (see table 7.4). To balance the added cost of the additional police, the Security Council asked the secretary-general to prepare proposals to reduce ONUMOZ by "an appropriate number of military personnel."[41] Reluctant to reduce the number of military observers—who were needed to verify compliance with the cease-fire and to dispose of weapons—the secretary-general decided to reduce military support elements. India and Bangladesh withdrew companies, and Portugal reduced its signals unit. Italy also withdrew its infantry units in April 1994.[42]

Table 7.4
POLICE OBSERVERS IN ONUMOZ

Country	March 1994	September 1994	Country	March 1994	September 1994
Australia	16	16	Jordan	45	80
Austria		20	Malaysia	35	70
Bangladesh	25	99	Nepal		50
Bolivia		10	Nigeria		40
Botswana		15	Norway	10	9
Brazil	35	67	Pakistan		65
Egypt	21	50	Portugal	7	30
Finland		5	Spain	14	40
Ghana		40	Sri Lanka		11
Guinea Bissau	25	65	Sweden	10	45
Hungary	10	20	Switzerland	1	3
India		75	Togo		5
Indonesia		15	Uruguay		15
Ireland	20	20	Zambia		50
TOTALS				274	1030

SOURCE: UN Secretariat, Department of Peacekeeping Operations, monthly troop strength reports.

In July 1994, the secretary-general submitted to the Security Council a plan for complete withdrawal of ONUMOZ, to start immediately after the elections. The international electoral observers were to be repatriated first. (The electoral component consisted of a director and 148 international electoral officers and support staff. To monitor the election itself, 1,200 short-term UN election observers were added to the roster, reflecting lessons learned from the 1992 debacle in Angola, where just 400 election observers were deployed, although the country is one-third larger than Mozambique.) The military drawdown began in mid-November and was completed by the end of January 1995.[43]

Command, Communications, and Logistics

Special Representative Ajello ran ONUMOZ: the force commander, the directors of the various UN components, and the chief police observer reported to him. In early 1994, Behrooz Sadry arrived in Mozambique to serve as deputy special representative and to deal with management and logistical problems. Sadry had served in the same capacity in the Cambodia operation, and his arrival freed Ajello to concentrate on the political problems then impeding implementation of the peace agreement.[44]

ONUMOZ headquarters were located in Maputo, Mozambique's capital. Regional offices were established in Matola, in the southern region; Beira, in the central region; and Nampula, in the north. The electoral, humanitarian, and police components also set up offices in each of the ten provinces; in addition, the police established posts in districts, and remote stations throughout the country.

The 16-year civil war had severely damaged Mozambique's infrastructure. The country did not have a nationwide communication system. Poor road conditions were exacerbated by mines, which had been strewn across the land. UN engineering companies cleared roads and bridges as required for ONUMOZ to fulfill its duties but 24 aircraft were included in the UN's aviation unit to compensate for road conditions. ONUMOZ used telephone links and secure and plain fax services but supplemented them with portable INMARSAT communication satellite systems; an internal high frequency radio network linking the major locations within the mission area; and shorter-range area networks operating in the VHF and UHF bands. Although the government was technically responsible for improving conditions in the assembly areas, UN units provided water and sanitation facilities.[45]

The UN used its aviation resources even more than had been anticipated. In addition to air patrols, aircraft were used for command liaison, investigations, and medical evacuations, to transport UN equipment and personnel, and to ferry government and RENAMO officers to training centers. ONUMOZ leased additional fixed-wing aircraft as they were more suited for these tasks than helicopters (and much cheaper).[46]

Original plans called for 355 international civilian administrative staff and 565 local hires. By November 1993, only 175 international staff and 291 local staff positions were filled. In January, the decision was made to reduce the authorized strength for international civilian staff to 255. UN volunteers were to offset this decrease, but civil staff, including UN volunteers, never reached planned levels; in April 1994, the vacancy rate for these administrative posts was 25 percent with no noticeable degradation in mission performance.[47]

Field Operations

The General Peace Agreement had outlined an ambitious timetable for implementation of the peace accords. General elections were planned for October 1993, a year after the GPA entered into force. The considerable tasks of humanitarian aid, repatriation of refugees, demobilization of existing armed forces, formation of the new national force, and conduct of elections were interconnected and tightly scheduled, leaving no room for error or delay. Without sufficient humanitarian aid, the security situation could deteriorate and demobilization might stall. Humanitarian aid could not be delivered without adequate military protection. The confidence required to demobilize, disarm, and carry out elections could be lost without sufficient political progress.[48]

Progress in implementing the military aspects of the peace agreement was crucial to moving the entire process forward. When the assembly and demobilization process stalled, the entire peace process was thrown off schedule. Even revisions made to compensate for delays were not strictly adhered to, as table 7.5 indicates.

Political Component

ONUMOZ's key responsibility was to create an environment in which the election process and its outcome would be judged "free and fair" by all parties. However, mistrust and noncooperation between the government and RENAMO made this a taxing undertaking for Special Representative Ajello. In addition to overseeing impartial implementation of the peace accords, Ajello constantly had to prod and cajole the parties to move the process forward.

Delay in deployment of the military component of ONUMOZ gave the parties a reason to delay implementing the accords. RENAMO initially conditioned demobilization on the deployment of 65 percent of the UN forces, the deployment of UN police monitors, and disbandment of irregular forces. However, both parties were more concerned with bettering their positions than cooperating to further the peace process. Chissano and FRELIMO held the advantage as the legitimate government of Mozambique and made certain they were dealt with as such. Dhlakama's efforts were geared toward amassing assets for RENAMO and maintaining what cards the party already held.

The funding promised by the peace agreement for accommodations, transport, and communications to help RENAMO transform itself into a political party was not immediately available, and the peace process was put on hold from March to May 1993 because RENAMO delegates could not set up shop in Maputo. At that point, trust fund number three was set up, and as contributions trickled in, Ajello constantly stressed to international donors the importance of this fund: their reneging on what was, realistically speaking, a slush fund for RENAMO's leaders would give RENAMO a reason not to participate in the peace process or to declare it unjust. As Ajello argued, RENAMO (and the other opposition parties) "[would] be less dangerous wielding position papers than AK-47 rifles."[49]

RENAMO strictly controlled access to the territory it occupied as a means to maintain political leverage, leaving the country divided into two de facto states. The GPA, through the National Commission for State Administration, tasked the two parties to work toward reintegration of the territories under a single, national administration, and the parties' pledge to allow freedom of movement should have aided in removing the boundaries. But RENAMO feared that freedom of movement would lead the people living in its areas to relocate, thereby weakening its power base. Moreover, restricted access to RENAMO-controlled zones required relief agencies and other organizations to deal directly with RENAMO officials, bypassing the government, and thereby sanctioning RENAMO's control of these "mini-states." A compromise September 1993 agreement stipulated that three RENAMO advisors would work with each provincial governor on decisions relating to RENAMO-controlled areas. Its implementation was delayed because RENAMO was late in nominating advisors and, once nominated, the government delayed appointing them formally.[50]

Table 7.5

GENERAL PEACE AGREEMENT IMPLEMENTATION TIMETABLE

	Peace Agreement	As of October 1993	Actual
Troop Assembly (beginning)	October 1992	November 1993	November 1993
Demobilization	November 1992–April 1993	January–May 1994	March–August 1994
Army Training (end)		August 1994	(incomplete as of early 1995)
Electoral Law	January 1993	November 1993	January 1994
Registration of Voters		April–June 1994	June–Sept 1994
Start of Electoral Campaign	September 1993	September 1994	mid-September
Elections	October 1993	October 1994	October 1994

SOURCES: Security Council, *Report of the Secretary General on the United Nations Operation in Mozambique*, S/1994/89, 28 January 1994, 2; Security Council, *Report of the Secretary General on the United Nations Operation in Mozambique*, S/1994/511, 28 April 1994, 2-3; Security Council, *Report of the Secretary General on the United Nations Operation in Mozambique*, S/1994/803, 7 July 1994, 2; and Security Council, *Report of the Security Council Mission Established Pursuant to the Statement Made By the President of the Security Council at the 3406th Meeting, Held on 19 July 1994 (S/PRST/1994/35)*, S/1994/1009, 29 August 1994, 5; Joseph Hanlon, Rachel Waterhouse, and Gil Lauriciano, "Demob Data," *Mozambique Peace Process Bulletin*, Issue 14 (February 1995): 11.

The Security Council, frustrated by these constant delays, passed a deliberately worded resolution attributing lack of progress mainly to RENAMO. Driving home the international community's impatience on a visit to Mozambique in October 1993, the secretary-general "threatened" UN withdrawal if GPA implementation did not pick up speed. The parties appeared to heed his warnings. They agreed to begin demobilization in November and resolved disagreements over membership on the non-UN commissions (state administration, NEC, COMPOL, and the Commission on Information). In December 1993, RENAMO submitted names for the provincial advisory positions.[51]

The secretary-general's visit did restore some momentum to the peace process but implementation remained slow. Provincial advisors did not report to posts until March 1994, and assembly and demobilization went forward unevenly, affecting the formation of the new armed forces. The schedule for general elections remained set, however. The Security Council strongly opposed postponing elections further and planned for the UN force to withdraw in November 1994.[52] Haunted by the spectre of Angola, Ajello wanted to prevent a similar outcome in Mozambique. However, he had to reconcile this objective with the international community's desire to terminate ONUMOZ in November. Ultimately, both goals were met.

Military Component

UN military personnel did three things in Mozambique. The infantry units helped maintain a secure environment in which ONUMOZ could carry out its duties and in so doing helped to strengthen Mozambicans' confidence in the peace process. UN military observers (UNMOs) monitored the cease-fire and oversaw the demobilization process. Training of a new integrated army, while not an ONUMOZ responsibility, is treated in this section for the sake of completeness.

Infantry Units. The infantry battalions patrolled along the main transportation corridors. They conducted air and motorized patrols; set up check points; monitored road movements; escorted convoys and trains carrying food supplies; and guarded food storage installations, weapons sites, and UN facilities.

Although Mozambique settled into general peace after the GPA was signed, banditry increased throughout the country as a consequence of the ready availability of weapons, the country's general state of disarray, and the presence of large numbers of now underemployed and underpaid soldiers and guerrilla fighters. Because they contributed to a sense of lawlessness and instability, incidents of banditry posed a greater threat to the peace process than cease-fire violations. ONUMOZ extended its military patrols outside the main corridors in response but its mandated tasks remained limited to patrolling, observing, and reporting. Force Commander da Silva, who interpreted the mandate narrowly, was reluctant to become involved in dealing with banditry, once reprimanding an Italian commander for intervening in a robbery and delivering the perpetrators to the Mozambican police.[53]

UN troops would probably have been more useful in more dispersed deployments rather than concentrated in the corridors. Although Mozambican police were responsible for internal security, a more extensive UN deployment might have served as a deterrent to some lawlessness even if the units could not formally uphold the peace. Because of the variance in the preparedness and capability of the different battalions, however, UN troops in several parts of the country might not have been able to respond effectively to serious challenges. (Zambia's unit arrived in Mozambique with no equipment, for example, and little capability for difficult missions, while Botswanan and Italian units, among others, arrived with full gear.) To avoid embarrassment to any troop contributing country, the UN took a lowest-common-denominator approach—if all units could not handle a responsibility, then it was not assigned to any unit.[54]

Military Observers and Demobilization. Principal duties of the military observers were to monitor compliance with the cease-fire, to prepare the camps in which the two sides' forces would assemble for demobilization, and to monitor the demobilization itself. A major cease-fire violation occurred in October 1993 when RENAMO forces occupied four towns in northern Mozambique. Government forces quickly retook them but violated the cease-fire as well, since the government bypassed the then functioning Cease-Fire Commission (CCF).[55] Formally confirmed violations were relatively few, however, and none were serious enough to threaten the peace process. Types of violations reported included illegal detention, alleged movements of troops, "unauthorized presence or misconduct of troops and militia, intimidating or aggressive behavior by soldiers," and irregularities in the assembly process, such as soldiers' registering twice.[56]

In the assembly areas (AAs), the military observers monitored the activities of the CCF joint monitoring groups stationed in each area. They were also responsible for the collection and storage of weapons and ammunition in the AAs.

A total of 49 assembly areas were located throughout the country, with 23 concentrated in the central region. Twenty-nine areas were allocated for government troops and twenty for RENAMO. When assembly began in November 1993, most government areas had been set up but only half of the ones in RENAMO's areas were ready. Many government AAs used old army bases but RENAMO's areas were out in the bush and harder to access. All assembly areas were set up and functioning by 21 February 1994.[57]

The UN initially estimated that over 61,000 government troops and close to 20,000 RENAMO troops would pass through the assembly areas, and that roughly 38,000 and 1,000, respectively, would be registered as "unassembled troops," that is, troops demobilized in situ at their normal bases. Initial numbers provided by the government for unassembled troops (14,000) were much lower than UN estimates. The government later reduced its estimate for assembled troops to 49,000, basing the discrepancy between its numbers and the UN's on the UN's inclusion of 12,000 men who had been demobilized in a unilateral program begun before the peace agreement. RENAMO accepted this new estimate with the stipulation that figures be "verified by the Cease-Fire Commission once demobilization is completed." RENAMO figures listed over 22,000 men to be demobilized, roughly 19,000 through AAs.[58]

Soldiers were expected to spend six to eight weeks in assembly areas. The demobilization process only began in March 1994, however, four months after troops had begun arriving at assembly points (see table 7.6). The lengthened stay contributed to overcrowding and food shortages in camps that were primitive to begin with, making them a hotbed for unrest that sometimes spilled outside the AAs. In July 1994, former RENAMO rebels blocked the main road between Maputo and Beira, looted the belongings of travelers, and took hostages, including UN police observers (all later released). ONUMOZ officers worked with the government and RENAMO officials to defuse the situation. In another incident, government soldiers "stormed a local police station" in Angoche in the Nampula district and shut off power to a rural town, demanding immediate demobilization.[59]

Troops arrived at the AAs in waves. Both parties were reluctant to assemble and demobilize forces from the central region where fighting had been heaviest. The soldiers processed first tended to be from marginal units that had been deployed in the south. Thus, the first groups of soldiers to arrive in the assembly areas came from units that had a higher percentage of troops demobilizing than did later demobilizing units, which contained soldiers the government and RENAMO wanted to keep for the new army. This tendency, in turn, delayed the formation and training of the new army.[60]

The final target date for completion of demobilization was 15 August 1994. The processing of troops at the assembly areas "was substantially concluded" on 22 August and all other unassembled troops had been registered in situ. A July decision by the government and RENAMO to permit all soldiers to demobilize who wanted to was

Table 7.6

CUMULATIVE TROOP ASSEMBLY AND DEMOBILIZATION

	Government	RENAMO
ASSEMBLY		
January 1994	9,895	6,714
April 1994	34,012	15,453
August 1994	43,297	17,466
Final	67,042	24,649
DEMOBILIZATION		
April 1994	12,195	561
July 1994	22,832	5,138
August 1994	52,242	17,847
Final	57,507	20,537

SOURCES: Security Council, *Report of the Secretary General on the United Nations Operation in Mozambique*, S/1994/89, 28 January 1994, 2; Security Council, *Report of the Secretary General on the United Nations Operation in Mozambique*, S/1994/511, 28 April 1994, 2-3; Security Council, *Report of the Secretary General on the United Nations Operation in Mozambique*, S/1994/803, 7 July 1994, 2; and Security Council, *Report of the Security Council Mission Established Pursuant to the Statement Made By the President of the Security Council at the 3406th Meeting, Held on 19 July 1994 (S/PRST/1994/35)*, S/1994/1009, 29 August 1994, 5; Joseph Hanlon, Rachel Waterhouse, and Gil Lauriciano, "Demob Data," *Mozambique Peace Process Bulletin*, Issue 14 (February 1995): 11.

partly responsible for the extra week needed to complete the process. A few soldiers remained in the assembly areas thereafter due to late registration, sickness, questions relating to their documentation, or pending transfer to the army.[61]

Private and irregular forces, totaling 155,600 and scattered throughout the country, were also demobilized. Responsibility for this process rested with the government. Teams from the Cease-Fire Commission verified the process and the collection of weapons.

Weapons collected from demobilized soldiers and paramilitary forces were placed under the control of UN military observers, then transferred to regional storage sites. Weapons were collected at an average of one per soldier, and most weapons were generally in poor condition. Post-demobilization verification teams visited 99 percent of government military locations but only 60 percent of RENAMO's before ONUMOZ's mandate expired. Although more than 180,000 weapons were collected, the UN did not expect that disarmament would be complete. Ajello admitted that the parties were probably keeping some weapon caches. His job, however, was to create an environment in which those guns would not be used for renewed conflict.[62]

Training of the Armed Forces. The joint commission that supervised the formation of the new armed forces was composed of government and RENAMO officials and representatives from France, Portugal, and the United Kingdom. Britain established a center in Nyanga, Zimbabwe, to train a corps of officers. France set up a training program for military engineers, and Portugal committed to training two marine and three special forces companies.[63]

The commission did not convene until July 1993. By early August, it had approved the timetable for the new military's formation, the rules and criteria for training of the instructors, and the structure of the military's high command. By October, documents were approved on the rules of discipline, the structure of the Joint General Staff, the staffing for the high command, and the working and instruction uniforms for the forces.[64]

Training at the Nyanga center commenced in August 1993 when 100 officers (50 from each party) arrived at the site. They were joined by another 440 recruits a month later. When training was completed in mid-December, ONUMOZ airlifted these new instructors to training centers within Mozambique: Dondo in Sofala province and Boane and Manhica in Maputo province. The slow demobilization process frustrated efforts to launch training programs for infantry, and in an attempt to accelerate the process, the parties decided to send 2,500 soldiers each to the centers without transiting through assembly areas. However, the government and RENAMO did not present their lists of soldiers to be trained until March. Disagreements on the salary for military personnel had to be resolved, and renovation of the training centers and late arrival of uniforms and course materials caused further delays. When the government failed to provide the funds for this purpose, Special Representative Ajello offered UN logistical assistance. Portugal restored the centers it was to use for its training, and Canada, Italy, and Sweden provided funds for other centers.[65]

Two principle features of the new national military—its size and its volunteer nature—were jeopardized by these delays. The new 30,000-strong force was to be fully operational by September 1994 but the training programs could graduate only 15,000 personnel before the elections, and the delays plaguing the program put even this goal in doubt. Former combatants showed a strong desire to return to civilian life, skeptical that life in the new army would be any different than life in the old ones. Struggling to reach full strength, both sides twisted arms. According to one report, "government soldiers arriving in Maputo on their way to start training for the new army said they were forced to go and really wanted to be demobilized. Meanwhile RENAMO soldiers said their leaders had sent them, but had not explained what for."[66] Ultimately, on 25 July, the government and RENAMO decided that all soldiers who wanted to demobilize could do so.[67]

By 16 August, although training for the new army was not completed, the old Mozambican armed forces were dismantled and "authority, equipment, and infrastructure" was transferred to the new military command. By late October, the new unified army had about 10,000 trained soldiers. Another 1,500 had enlisted by late December. Six infantry and three special forces battalions, one marine company, one company of sappers, and two logistics units had completed training.[68]

Police Component

Although the decision to include a civilian police (CIVPOL) component in ONUMOZ came late in the operation, the component was quick to establish itself within Mozambique. Full deployment was nearly achieved before the electoral campaign began.

The police unit established liaison with local COMPOL committees, all levels of the Mozambican police, and RENAMO advisers and officials. Unrestricted access to information, the public, prisons, and other police installations was required for the police observers to effectively discharge their duties but, initially, CIVPOL faced some obstacles. A CIVPOL seminar with COMPOL and police officials helped to improve, but not eliminate, access problems and lack of cooperation from the police. The government delayed access to the facilities of its Quick Reaction Force, for example, until two weeks before the elections. It was also difficult to obtain RENAMO's cooperation in reestablishing national police stations in RENAMO-controlled areas. The national police were reluctant to press the issue. UN officials purported that government police feared entering these areas and offered joint patrols with CIVPOL, but the Mozambican police still "did not become operational in the areas formerly held by RENAMO."[69]

The police observers investigated three categories of allegations: illegal detention of civilians, abuse of detainees' civil rights, and politically motivated criminal investigations. CIVPOL investigated 511 complaints. Those forwarded to COMPOL, the joint police commission, tended to sit unresolved.[70]

Because they were deployed in remote areas throughout the country and had to interact closely with the public to receive complaints of and to investigate alleged misconduct, the police observers often became ONUMOZ's most personal and accessible representatives. In addition to the tasks associated with the Mozambican police, the police observers monitored the elections and respect for the political rights of individuals and political groups.[71]

Humanitarian Component

Humanitarian efforts were an integral part of the peace operation. Improving the humanitarian situation in Mozambique became increasingly important to lasting peace as the country's immediate political and military problems were resolved. Key elements of ONUMOZ' humanitarian component dealt with resettlement of refugees and displaced persons, and with removal of land mines.

Resettlement. Cessation of armed conflict was a first step toward improvement of the humanitarian situation. Next, refugees made the journey home. UN estimates for the number of Mozambicans who fled to neighboring countries ranged from 1.5 to 1.8 million. (Table 7.7 provides a breakdown as of December 1992.) Spontaneous return accounted for a significant amount of repatriation, especially for refugees returning from Malawi to the Tete province. The United Nations High Commissioner for

Table 7.7

MOZAMBICAN REFUGEES, COUNTRIES OF ASYLUM

Country	Number of Refugees
Malawi	1,100,000
South Africa	250,000
Swaziland	25,000
Tanzania	72,000
Zambia	24,000
Zimbabwe	230,000
Other	1,000
TOTAL	**1,702,000**

SOURCE: Security Council, *Report of the Secretary-General on the United Nations Operation in Mozambique*, S/25044, 4 January 1993, 27.

Refugees (UNHCR) assisted these returnees in addition to launching organized repatriation programs. The Mozambican government and UNHCR had to negotiate with South Africa to obtain approval for repatriation efforts there because South Africa classified exiled Mozambicans as illegal aliens, not refugees. The International Organization for Migration worked with UNHCR, providing transportation assistance to resettle refugees in their districts. As table 7.8 shows, 73 percent had returned by the end of August 1994. By the end of March 1995, UNHCR had repatriated the last refugees from South Africa, and its operations in Swaziland, Tanzania, Zambia, and Zimbabwe had already closed. The Malawi government gave some 80,000 refugees there until September to return to Mozambique. As for internally displaced persons, about one million had not returned to their original area of residence by the end of 1994.[72]

Humanitarian operations based initially in refugee camps and settlements for displaced persons were soon transferred to rural areas. UNOHAC focused on involving the Mozambican people at the district and community levels, attempting to build an independent Mozambican capability to continue improving humanitarian conditions when ONUMOZ departed. It promoted projects for road repair, water supply and sanitation, health, education, and agricultural production. UNOHAC instituted humanitarian assistance communities in each province to expand contact between the government and RENAMO, promoting their joint cooperation with relief agencies to assess aid requirements at the district level. Similar groups were set up at higher levels for more comprehensive planning. By the end of August 1994, 40 nongovernmental organizations were present in RENAMO-controlled areas where before there had been only the International Committee of the Red Cross and the World Food Program.[73]

Table 7.8

CUMULATIVE RETURN/RESETTLEMENT OF MOZAMBICAN REFUGEES AND DISPLACED PERSONS

	Refugees Returned	Displaced Resettled
August 1993	326,000	
November 1993	400,000	1,200,000
January 1994	621,000	2,250,000
April 1994	800,000	3,000,000
August 1994	1,100,000	3,600,000

ª Where necessary, calculations of numbers and percentages for returned refugees and displaced persons are based on a total of 1.5 million refugees and 4.5 million displaced persons.

SOURCES: Security Council, *Report of the Secretary General on the United Nations Operation in Mozambique*, S/26385, 30 August 1993, 5; Security Council, *Report of the Secretary-General on the United Nations Operation in Mozambique*, S/26666, 1 November 1993, 8-9; Security Council, *Report of the Secretary General on the United Nations Operation in Mozambique*, S/1994/89, 28 January 1994, 8; Security Council, *Report of the Secretary General on the United Nations Operation in Mozambique*, S/1994/511, 28 April 1994, 11; Security Council, *Report of the Secretary General on the United Nations Operation in Mozambique*, S/1994/803, 7 July 1994, 8; and Security Council, *Report of the Security Council Mission Established Pursuant to the Statement Made By the President of the Security Council at the 3406th Meeting, Held on 19 July 1994 (S/PRST/1994/35)*, S/1994/1009, 29 August 1994, 10-11.

With assistance from UNOHAC, the Reintegration Commission (CORE) developed plans and procedures for reintegrating demobilized soldiers into civilian society. Programs approved by CORE focused on strategies for employing former soldiers in the agricultural sector and ways to finance job training for former soldiers who chose not to return to farming. Self-employment and the provision of subsidies to employers in the public and private sectors were other strategies considered to ease former soldiers back into the economic sector. CORE also approved a provincial fund to be used for community-based economic activities and "to provide small- and medium-sized grants for the employment of ex-soldiers."[74] Secondary to providing employment opportunities, these programs, if successful, would ease demobilization's disruptive effects on society. Because many of Mozambique's young soldiers had known no other job but war, this effort was crucially important to the future stability of the country.

Mine Clearance. The UN estimated that 2 million mines littered Mozambican territory. A report published by Africa Watch argued that the UN figure was inflated, but that hundreds of thousands of mines still presented a significant problem.[75] Roads and transit ways had to be cleared for delivery of humanitarian supplies and to reduce risks to returnees, and fields had to be cleared to encourage farmers to resume agricultural production. The UN humanitarian components worked with the Cease-Fire Commission, which had overall responsibility for mine clearance. The UN provided assistance in developing a national demining policy, and the CCF approved proposals for a national mine-clearance survey in December 1993. Halo Trust, a British nongovernmental organization (NGO), conducted the survey.

Startup of the UN mine-clearance program was delayed by turf battles between UNDP, which controlled the money for demining, and UNOHAC, which devised programs for demining. Funding was available at the end of 1992 but no significant progress was made until May 1994. At this time, a $4.8 million contract for clearing 2,000 kilometers of priority roads was awarded to Lonrho and Royal Ordnance of Great Britain, and Mechem (a South African company believed to have manufactured mines it was being paid to remove, and thus a controversial choice). Secretary-General Boutros-Ghali later transferred the remaining funds from UNDP's Office for Project Services to UNOHAC. Completed on 9 June 1994, the national mine survey noted "1,300 confirmed or suspected mine sites."[76]

Demining projects undertaken by NGOs were well underway before the UN mine-clearing program was launched. The European Community funded a demining project in Sofala. In Tete and Maputo provinces, demobilized soldiers trained as deminers worked on a project funded by Norway and supervised by Norwegian People's Aid. The US Agency for International Development (USAID) contracted Ronco Consulting Corporation to train mine-clearing personnel for a program in Sofala along the Zambezi River. The Halo Trust funded a mine-clearing project in Zambezia province.[77]

The United Nations also set up a Mine-Clearance Center to train demobilized soldiers. The first course commenced in April 1994. By the end of August, 119 Mozambicans had been trained at the center. By December 1994, 450 people, forming 10 demining teams, were working in Maputo province. The late start of the UN mine-clearance program left demining far from complete when ONUMOZ withdrew. To support a national capacity to continue the program, the UN donated its mine-clearing equipment to the demining program.[78]

Electoral Component

The NEC was responsible for organizing and conducting the elections. On 12 January 1994, the electoral law was finalized, a full year behind schedule. Various factors explain this holdup: the government's late presentation of the draft law, RENAMO demanding more time to review the law, the "unarmed opposition" demanding material and financial support from the government, and disagreement on NEC composition.[79] NEC members were appointed on 21 January 1994. Mr. Brazão Mazula, who was not affiliated with any party, was chosen as its chair on 2 February. President Chissano set the general election for 27-28 October 1994.[80]

The Technical Secretariat for Elections Administration was responsible for voter registration, which began on 1 June 1994. By that time, 1,500 of the planned 1,600 registration teams were available. About 32 percent of the voting population had registered by 4 July. Registration, scheduled to end on 15 August, was extended to 2 September to include as many eligible voters as possible. This scheduling change shaved ten days off the electoral campaigning period. When registration did end, 81 percent of the eligible population was registered to vote. In October, casting ballots at about 7,300 polling stations, they chose among 12 presidential candidates and 3,117 candidates representing the 14 political parties and coalitions standing for the election to the 250-seat national assembly.[81]

Technical errors such as "improper filling in of registration forms, registration books and voter cards"[82] were a problem initially, but guidance sheets provided to registration teams by the Technical Secretariat reduced their occurrence. There were also allegations of fraud, such as embezzlement of electoral funds and registration of minors and foreigners. Not all allegations were presented to the NEC as formal complaints, and most complaints that were investigated were not substantiated.[83]

Conditions "pose[d] a logistical nightmare for officials trying to run the first nationwide election[s]. . . . Poor roads, few telephones, and large areas without electricity [were] just a few obstacles. Transportation and minefields were others."[84] There was concern about the many uncollected weapons and unverified arms caches. Moreover, neither the government nor RENAMO had fully cooperated on inspections of some military bases and police installations. Access to some RENAMO-controlled areas was still restricted. In August, Secretary-General Boutros-Ghali had reported that "voter registration teams [had] gained access to all RENAMO-controlled districts," but other observers reported that "RENAMO-controlled zones in practice remain[ed] under separated administration." Opposition parties were not allowed to campaign in some areas. The electoral campaign itself was tense at times and spotted with violent incidents, but these "posed no serious threat to the democratic nature and fairness of the electoral process."[85]

However, the entire electoral process, and most importantly the two-year effort of the UN operation, was threatened on election eve when Dhlakama withdrew from the elections, challenging their "fairness." He called on RENAMO party supporters to boycott the elections, claiming that excess ballot papers and the participation of nonregistered voters would corrupt the election results. A flurry of diplomatic activity and promises to investigate his allegations and extend polling for an extra day convinced Dhlakama to reenter.[86]

Approximately 50 percent of the registered voters went to the polls on the first day of elections. Many in remote areas were not aware of the boycott and other RENAMO supporters who did know of the changed circumstances voted just in case Dhlakama reversed his decision. By the close of the second day, 80 percent of the eligible voters had cast their ballots. Because of the strong turnout on the first day, it is hard to tell whether Dhlakama's position had any impact on the voting, in either direction. Ultimately, however, with 90 percent voter participation, Mozambicans demonstrated a strong desire to participate in the consolidation of peace in their country.[87]

Special Representative Ajello declared the elections "fair and free" on 19 November 1994. Polling was carried out in a calm atmosphere without the disruptive violence threatened by some demobilized soldiers and national electoral workers demanding pay. About 2,300 international election observers had been dispersed throughout the country to verify the integrity of the process. Over 1,200 monitors were provided by ONUMOZ. Others were provided by UN member states, the diplomatic community in Maputo, nongovernmental organizations, the European Union, the Organization of African Unity, and other organizations. The NEC provided almost 50,000 national officials and 30,000 monitors from political parties. USAID provided funds for smaller parties to participate in verification of the process.[88] Thus, there was no lack of monitors to support, or contest if necessary, Ajello's pronouncement.

President Chissano and FRELIMO were declared the winners in Mozambique's first multiparty elections. Chissano obtained just over 53 percent of the presidential vote, and FRELIMO claimed 129 of the parliamentary seats. Dhlakama received about 34 percent of the vote, and RENAMO took 112 assembly seats. Choosing a different course than UNITA leader Jonas Savimbi in Angola (see chapter four in this volume), Dhlakama declared that, although the "elections were rife with irregularities," RENAMO "acknowledged that they were the only elections and we accept them with their deficiencies."[89]

ASSESSMENT AND CONCLUSIONS

Renewed civil war did not threaten the UN's effective discharge of its mandate in Mozambique. But for a year, implementation of the peace accords stagnated. After the second year, elections were successfully completed and a bevy of UN and international monitors acclaimed their fairness. This achievement was due in large part to the handiwork of Special Representative Aldo Ajello and his skillful maneuvering to steer the parties to act in their own best interest. Neither side had proven capable of winning the war, drought threatened both sides indiscriminately, the economy was in shambles depending mainly on foreign aid to stay afloat, and RENAMO's support was drying up. The only practical option for both sides lay in implementation of the peace plan.

Ajello openly criticized the government of Mozambique for not upholding its end of the bargain (which was supposed to include rehabilitation of the assembly areas and training centers and provision of funding for RENAMO), while responding to RENAMO's skirting of GPA stipulations with leniency. However, Ajello's leniency with RENAMO was understandable. RENAMO was in a much weaker position vis-à-vis the government than UNITA was vis-à-vis the government of Angola and had more hurdles to overcome to ensure its survival in postelection Mozambique. Chissano and FRELIMO were expected to win Mozambique's first elections; Dhlakama realized this also, but Ajello had to ensure that Dhlakama remained engaged in the process despite this fact. For this reason, he constantly stressed the importance of RENAMO's trust fund, from which Dhlakama was receiving over $300,000 a month for expenses. Ajello's comment supporting the legitimacy of the fund offers insight into his outlook: "The only way to make this mission a success was to forget conventional wisdom."[90]

Despite the successful conclusion of the elections, however, key aspects of the peace agreement remain incomplete. First, an unfinished weapons collection process has left an excess of arms circulating among the populace, contributing to the severity of crime throughout the country. (ONUMOZ is criticized for its slow progress in collecting weapons, but it did not have the mandate to disarm. As the CCF chairman noted, the Cease-Fire Commission, not ONUMOZ, was responsible for rounding up weapons.)[91] Second, as of mid-1995, the new joint army had only one-third of its planned personnel, and some units already trained were not fully operational. Lack of finance and logistics support explains some of this shortfall, and the principle of a volunteer army (supposedly) precludes coercive methods to increase enlistment.

Integration of the two territories into a single, national administration also remains a remote goal. RENAMO's obstruction of this goal was in clear violation of the peace accords. However, the consensus decision-making policy of the oversight commissions could not enforce full compliance with the peace accords, and in the absence of penalties for noncompliance, there was no formal redress for dealing with this problem. Moreover, the UN was not a member of the National Commission for State Administration. Thus, on the issue of territorial reintegration, the UN did not have the same leverage over the parties that it gained from chairing the four main commissions.

The problem of less-than-timely deployment of forces has long plagued the United Nations. In Mozambique, President Chissano expected the UN to deploy forces immediately after the General Peace Agreement was signed. The UN had more than sufficient notification of its pending role in implementation of the GPA, but ONUMOZ was not fully operational until six months after the peace agreement entered into force. This tardiness arrested the momentum of the two-year peace process as the parties retreated to their respective corners to await its arrival. More serious problems could have arisen if the local parties had not been basically committed to ending the conflict.

When UN troops did arrive they had no role in curbing what posed a greater threat to peace than the resumption of civil war, namely, the increase in crime and banditry. When indigenous police forces are not trusted by all local parties, and lack the skills and training to do their job well, then there may be a place for a UN operation that includes both a capacity and a mandate to help maintain a modicum of civil order. Cascading disorder in a fragile, post–civil war situation could otherwise disrupt the UN's mission and the peace process it supports. The use of infantry troops for this purpose would likely be opposed by UN member states as well as the host government, in most cases. Military police, without the "seize and hold ground" image of infantry forces, might be a more acceptable choice. UN civil police would, theoretically, be a logical choice as well, but the UN needs to do much more in the way of screening and training to improve both the competence and the image of the police components that it deploys in peacekeeping operations.

The UN made some progress in Mozambique with the management of humanitarian activities. It did a reasonably good job, for example, assisting in the resettlement of the majority of Mozambique's war refugees. ONUMOZ fell short, however, in managing the demining project and developing a coordinated humanitarian program. The UN mine-clearance program was not fully underway until just six months before the operation's mandate expired. It was neither the Mozambican parties nor funding but UN turf battles that delayed the startup of the program. Some critics have also contended that UNOHAC duplicated the efforts of other UN agencies and NGOs on the ground, and that at times it even delayed or blocked their work.[92]

Nonetheless, it clearly seems desirable to coordinate the humanitarian elements of a peacekeeping operation with the humanitarian efforts of other, independently funded agencies and organizations operating in the country, lest all of them work at cross-purposes. Some of the difficulty in doing so stems from the distinct "cultures" and objectives of postconflict peace building (direct political-military aid with a limited timeline), humanitarian relief (direct, apolitical aid), and humanitarian development (reconstruction and training efforts with a longer time horizon). These differences in focus produce different operational priorities.[93] Relief agencies, moreover, had been extensively involved in Mozambique before the peace accords were signed and would have viewed UNOHAC as the new kid on the block and something of an interloper. Although it may have failed to prevent duplication of effort, UNOHAC did help to bridge the immediate needs of the peace process and the longer-term needs of development, guiding, for example, food aid and healthcare toward demobilized soldiers (a political as much as a humanitarian necessity).

Finally, there is the question of the US role in peace operations like ONUMOZ. Some suggest that participation of US ground forces may be key to the success of some operations (especially the more difficult ones). In today's political environment, however, US troops for UN operations are harder to come by. Moreover, troops are not always the most useful contribution that the United States can make. In Mozambique, the United States seconded only five people to ONUMOZ, but it played an important role in resolving the conflict and implementing the GPA. The United States played a significant, albeit unofficial, part in advancing the peace talks before other western nations became involved. Once the implementation process was underway, the United States' seat on the UN-chaired commissions created by the GPA allowed it to influence the process without being in charge of it. Finally, the American ambassador used his office as a bully pulpit to help move the process past key sticking points.[94]

The United Nations presence in Mozambique helped build confidence in the peace process and helped the parties to work together despite mistrust. After the signing of the GPA, the efforts of the UN special representative, serving as an accepted intermediary, reopened dialogue between the two sides. What the UN accomplished in Mozambique, then, is what it probably does best: it provided an opportunity for erstwhile opponents to work toward, or to consolidate, resolution of differences through political channels.

However, peace and democracy are not consolidated solely with the holding of fair elections, especially in countries such as Mozambique where the political, economic, and social structures have been devastated by a war that involved the entire society and that left a whole generation knowing no other way of life but war and displacement. The UN and its member states need to pay continuing attention once a peace accord has been implemented, to help such countries build the institutions of civil society that are needed to consolidate stable democracy. Political stability is a prerequisite to the sort of investment, private and public, that can help rebuild a shattered economy. A stable economy is, in turn, the only sort in which democracy can put down strong roots and eventually thrive.

NOTES

1. Shaun Vincent, "The Mozambique Conflict (1980-1992)," in Michael Cranna, ed., *The True Cost of Conflict: Seven Recent Wars and Their Effect on Society* (New York: New Press, 1994), 106-107.

2. Alex Vines, *RENAMO: Terrorism in Mozambique* (Bloomington, IN: Indiana University Press, 1991), 7.

3. *Assimilados* were those Mozambicans who succeeded in assimilating into colonial Portuguese society. Hilary Andersson, *Mozambique: A War Against the People* (New York: St. Martin's Press, 1992), 7, 12; Gillian Gunn, "Learning from Adversity: The Mozambican Experience," in Richard J. Bloomfield, ed., *Regional Conflict and US Policy: Angola and Mozambique* (Algonac, MI: Reference Publications, Inc., 1988), 139.

4. Luis B. Serapio and Mohamed A. El-Khawas, *Mozambique in the Twentieth Century: From Colonialism to Independence* (Washington, D.C.: University Press of America, 1979), 128-132.

5. William Finnegan, *A Complicated War: The Harrowing of Mozambique* (Berkeley, CA: University of California Press, 1992), 30.

6. Vines, *RENAMO*, 8.

7. FRELIMO efforts were yielding positive results in the education and health sectors. At independence, adult illiteracy was around 93 percent and healthcare was available to few and virtually nonexistent for the rural community. FRELIMO began to remedy these problems with a massive infusion of funds. By 1980, the illiteracy rate had decreased by 23 percent and the number of students receiving primary and secondary education rose from about 650,000 in 1973 to 1.5 million in 1981. Mozambican healthcare improved, its emphasis shifting from curative to preventive care. Although the ratio of doctors to the population was still relatively low, Mozambique had over 300 doctors in 1985 compared to the 86 left after the Portuguese exodus. Healthcare workers had increased to 3800 from 2000 in 1975. Jens Erik Torps, *Mozambique: Economics, Politics and Society* (London: Printers Publishers, 1989), 88, 91-94; Andersson, *A War Against the People,* 40-41.

8. Kurt M. Campbell, "Soviet Policy in Southern Africa: Angola and Mozambique," in Richard J. Bloomfield, ed., *Regional Conflict and US Policy: Angola and Mozambique*

(Algonac, MI: Reference Publications, Inc., 1988), 104-106; Gunn, "Learning from Adversity," 156.

9. Vines, *RENAMO,* 19.

10. Finnegan, *A Complicated War,* 32; Vines, *RENAMO,* 87-90; see also Robert Gersony, *Summary of Mozambican Refugee Accounts of Principally Conflict-Related Experience in Mozambique* (Washington, D.C.: US Department of State, Bureau of Refugee Programs, April 1988); and Karl Maier, "Mozambican Foes Use Peasant as Pawn," *Washington Post,* 10 October 1993, A16.

11. Andersson, *A War Against the People,* 72.

12. Vines, *RENAMO,* 105, 109.

13. Gillian Gunn, "Post-Nkomati Mozambique," in Helen Kitchen, ed., *Angola, Mozambique, and the West* (New York: Praeger, 1987), 98-101.

14. Vines, *RENAMO,* 21-27.

15. Ibid., 28.

16. Witney W. Schneidman, "Conflict Resolution in Mozambique," in David R. Smock, ed., *Making War and Waging Peace: Foreign Intervention in Africa* (Washington, D.C.: United States Institute of Peace, 1993), 222-25.

17. Vines, *RENAMO,* 59-60; Schneidman, "Conflict Resolution in Mozambique," 226.

18. The church officials were Jaime Gonçalves, the Roman Catholic bishop of Beira; Alexandre dos Santos, the Roman Catholic bishop of Maputo; Anglican bishop Dinis Sengulane; and Pastor Osias Macache, chairman of the Mozambique Council of Churches. (Vines, *RENAMO,* 124.) FRELIMO's early relations with the Church had been strained by its belief that the Church had served as an agent of the former Portuguese administration. The relationship saw improvement in the 1980s, however, as the FRELIMO government adopted more liberal policies. The government also realized that its antichurch policy could hurt its image in the international community.

19. Vines, *RENAMO,* 125-26, 157-160.

20. Schneidman, "Conflict Resolution in Mozambique," 228; Vines, *RENAMO,* 128, 130. The government of Mozambique adopted a multiparty constitution in December 1990. David B. Ottaway, "Mozambique Enters Brave, New Uncertain World," *Washington Post,* 2 December 1990, A29.

21. Schneidman, "Conflict Resolution in Mozambique," 231-33.

22. For a detailed examination of the peace talks, see Cameron Hume, *Ending Mozambique's War: The Role of Mediation and Good* Offices (Washington, D.C.: United States Institute of Peace, 1994).

23. "Mozambique: Brag Poker in Rome," *Africa Confidential* 33, no. 16 (14 August 1992): 2; Alan Cowell, "Mozambique Leader and the Rebel Chief Talk Peace," *New York Times,* 6 August 1992, A5.

24. Joseph Hanlon, "Cease-fire Holds, But Election Delay Likely," *Mozambique Peace Process Bulletin,* Issue 1 (Amsterdam, Netherlands: AWEPA, January 1993): 1.

25. Security Council, *Report of the Secretary-General on the United Nations Operation in Mozambique,* S/24892, 3 December 1992, 5.

26. Ibid., 9-10, 12.

27. Security Council, *Report of the Secretary-General on the United Nations Operation in Mozambique,* S/26432, 13 September 1993, 4; Security Council, *Report of the Secretary-General on the United Nations Operation in Mozambique,* S/1994/89/Add.1, 28 January 1994, 4.

28. UN General Assembly, *Financing of the United Nations Operation in Mozambique,* A/47/881/Add.1, 8 February 1993, 4; UN General Assembly, *Financing of the United Nations Operation in Mozambique,* A/47/969, 28 June 1993, 4; UN General Assembly, *Financing of the United Nations Operation in Mozambique,* A/48/849, 17 January 1994, 4.

29. UN General Assembly, A/47/969, 51; UN General Assembly, *Financing of the United Nations Operation in Mozambique,* A/48/849/Add.1, 23 May 1994, 10; UN General Assembly, *Financing of the United Nations Operation in Mozambique,* A/49/649/Add.1, 23 November 1994, 22.

30. UN General Assembly, A/48/849, 8; UN General Assembly, A/49/649/Add.1, 22.

31. Security Council, *Report of the Secretary-General on the United Nations Operation in Mozambique,* S/25044, 4 January 1993, 13, 18-33; Security Council, *Final Report of the Secretary-General on the United Nations Operation in Mozambique,* S/1994/1449, 23 December 1994, 6.

32. Security Council, *Further Report of the Secretary-General on the United Nations Operation in Mozambique,* S/1994/1002, 26 August 1994, 8; Joseph Hanlon, Rachel Waterhouse, and Gil Lauriciano, "Demining Scandal," *Mozambique Peace Process Bulletin,* Issue 10 (July 1994): 10-11; UN General Assembly, *Financing of the United Nations Operation in Mozambique,* A/48/889, 2 March 1994, 3.

33. UN General Assembly, A/48/849/Add.1, 15; Security Council, S/1994/1449, 6.

34. Security Council, *Report of the Secretary-General on the United Nations Operation in Mozambique,* S/26666, 1 November 1993, 11; Security Council, S/1994/1002, 7; "Mozambique-Election," *Associated Press,* September 19, 1994, 6:52 A.M.; Joseph Hanlon and Rachel Waterhouse, "More Money," *Mozambique Peace Process Bulletin,* Issue 13 (11 October 1994): 6; UN General Assembly, *Financing of the United Nations Operation in Mozambique,* A/49/649, 8 November 1994, 6.

35. UN General Assembly, A/48/849/Add.1, 15; UN General Assembly, A/49/649, 7.

36. Security Council, *Report of the Secretary-General on the United Nations Operation in Mozambique,* S/1994/511, 28 April 1994, 8; Joseph Hanlon and Rachel Waterhouse, "Election Budget," *Mozambique Peace Process Bulletin,* Issue 14 (February 1995): 9.

37. Security Council, S/24892, 3 December 1992, 3; Security Council, *United Nations Operation in Mozambique: Report of the Secretary-General,* S/24642, 9 October 1992, 5.

38. Security Council, *Report of the Secretary-General on the United Nations Operation in Mozambique,* S/25518, 2 April 1993, 2; Security Council, S/1994/1002, 4.

39. Security Council, S/24892, 8; UN General Assembly, A/47/881/Add.1, 14; Rachel Waterhouse and Gil Lauriciano, "UN 'Blue Hats' Deployed," *Mozambique Peace Process Bulletin,* Issue 4 (June 1993): 3.

40. Security Council, S/24892, 7; Security Council, S/25518, 3; Security Council, S/25044, 31.

41. Security Council Resolution 882, 5 November 1993, 2; and Security Council Resolution 898, 23 February 1994, 2.
42. Security Council, S/1994/511, 6-7.
43. Security Council, S/24892, 15; Security Council, *Report of the Secretary-General on the United Nations Operation in Mozambique,* S/1994/803, 9-10; Security Council, S/1994/1449, 4.
44. Interview by William Durch, ONUMOZ headquarters, Maputo, Mozambique, November 1993.
45. UN General Assembly, A/47/969, 32-33; Security Council, S/24892, 8. INMARSAT is the International Maritime Satellite Organization.
46. Security Council, Documents S/26666, 7; UN General Assembly, A/49/649/Add.1, 15.
47. Interview by William Durch, ONUMOZ headquarters, Maputo, Mozambique, November 1993; UN General Assembly, A/48/849, 37, 59, 71; UN General Assembly, A/49/649/Add.1, 19.
48. Security Council, S/24892, 6.
49. Security Council, *Report of the Secretary-General on the United Nations Operation in Mozambique,* S/26034, 30 June 1993, 4; Bill Keller, "Rebels with a Quandary: What's the Cause Now?" *New York Times,* 26 February 1993, A4.
50. Security Council, S/26432, 2-3; Rachel Waterhouse and Gil Lauriciano, "Chissano-Dhlakama Summit," *Mozambique Peace Process Bulletin,* Issue 6 (October 1993): 2.
51. Security Council Resolution 863 (1993), 13 September 1993; Paul Taylor, "UN Finds Peace Has a Price in Mozambique," *Washington Post,* 24 October 1993, A35; "Problems Resolved: Boutros-Ghali Solutions," *Mozambique Peace Process Bulletin,* Issue 7 (December 1993): 2; "Advisers Take Up Posts," *Mozambique Peace Process Bulletin,* Issue 9 (April 1994): 3.
52. Paul Lewis, "UN Sets Deadline of November for Ending Role in Mozambique," *Washington Post,* 24 February 1994, A13.
53. Security Council, S/26666, 6; interview by William Durch, ONUMOZ headquarters, Maputo, Mozambique, November 1993.
54. Interview by William Durch, ONUMOZ headquarters, Maputo, Mozambique, November 1993.
55. The Cease-Fire Commission "receive[d], analyze[d], and rule[d] on complaints" of possible violations and "set itineraries for the movement of forces" to reduce risks of violations. It also monitored and verified the withdrawal of foreign troops and the disbandment of militia forces, and organized and supervised the demobilization process and the collection of weapons. Security Council, *General Peace Agreement for Mozambique,* S/24635, 8 October 1992, annex, 24, 28-29, 39-40.
56. "Four Towns Taken and Retaken," *Mozambique Peace Process Bulletin,* Issue 1 (January 1993): 3; Security Council, *Report of the Secretary-General on the United Nations Operation in Mozambique,* S/1994/89, 28 January 1994, 6; Security Council, S/1994/511, 5; Security Council, S/1994/803, 4.
57. Security Council, S/26666, 2; Security Council, S/1994/511, 2.

58. Ton Pardoel, Chief, Technical Unit, ONUMOZ, "Figures on Soldiers under the Peace Process Demobilization," Maputo, Mozambique, 5 November 1993 (mimeograph); "Former Mozambican Foes End Row over Army Figures," *Reuters* newswire, 18 June 1994, 12:36 P.M.

59. Iain Christie, "Mozambique Rebels Seize Hostages on the Main Road," *Reuters* newswire, 12 July 1994, 7:12 A.M.; Iain Christie, "Mozambican Rebels Begin Freeing Hostages," *Reuters* newswire, 13 July 1994, 3:01 P.M.; "Mozambican Mutineers Said to Paralyze Village," *Reuters* newswire, 21 July 1994, 4:04 P.M.

60. Security Council, S/1994/511, 3; Joseph Hanlon, Rachel Waterhouse and Gil Lauriciano, "Holding the Best for Last," *Mozambique Peace Process Bulletin,* Issue 10 (July 1994): 5.

61. Security Council, S/1994/1002, 2; Security Council, *Report of the Security Council Mission Established Pursuant to the Statement Made By the President of the Security Council at the 3406th Meeting, Held on 19 July 1994 (S/PRST/1994/35), S/1994/1009,* 29 August 1994, 5.

62. Joseph Hanlon, Gil Lauriciano, and Rachel Waterhouse, "Reluctance to Demobilize," *Mozambique Peace Process Bulletin,* Issue 8 (February 1994): 2; Security Council, S/1994/1449, 4; Joseph Hanlon and Rachel Waterhouse, "Demob Data," *Mozambique Peace Process Bulletin,* Issue 14 (February 1995): 11.

63. Security Council, S/25518, 6; Security Council, S/26666, 8. Later, Zimbabwe and Italy also provided support for the training program.

64. Security Council, *Report of the Secretary General on the United Nations Operation in Mozambique,* S/26385, 30 August 1993, 3-4; Security Council, S/26666, 8.

65. Security Council Document S/26385, 3; Security Council, S/1994/89, 6-7; Joseph Hanlon, Rachel Waterhouse, and Gil Lauriciano, "Training Yet to Start," *Mozambique Peace Process Bulletin,* Issue 8 (February 1994): 8; Gil Lauriciano and Rachel Waterhouse, "No Uniforms So No Training," *Mozambique Peace Process Bulletin,* Issue 9 (April 1994): 7.

66. Joseph Hanlon, Rachel Waterhouse, and Gil Lauriciano, "New Army," *Mozambique Peace Process Bulletin,* Issue 10 (July 1994): 4-5.

67. Security Council, S/1994/511, 28 April 1994, 4; Joseph Hanlon, Rachel Waterhouse, and Gil Lauriciano, "New Army," *Mozambique Peace Process Bulletin,* Issue 10 (July 1994): 4-5; Security Council, S/1994/1002, 2.

68. Security Council, S/1994/1002, 3; Security Council, S/1994/1196, 1; S/1994/1449, 4.

69. Security Council, S/1994/511, 10; Security Council, S/1994/803, 7; Joseph Hanlon, Rachel Waterhouse, and Gil Lauriciano, "No police," *Mozambique Peace Process Bulletin,* Issue 10 (July 1994): 7; Security Council, S/1994/1449, 5.

70. Security Council, S/1994/1002, 5.

71. Security Council, S/1994/1449, 5.

72. Rachel Waterhouse and Gil Lauriciano, "South Africa Break-Through," *Mozambique Peace Process Bulletin,* Issue 6 (October 1993): 7; Security Council, S/26666, 9; Security Council, S/1994/1449, 6; "Malawi Gives Mozambican Exiles September

Deadline," *Reuters* newswire, 27 March 1995, 2:25 P.M.; "Last Mozambican Refugees Head Home from South Africa," *Reuters* newswire, 29 March 1995, 6:20 A.M.

73. Security Council, S/25518, 7; Security Council, S/26666, 9; Security Council, S/1994/1009, 10.

74. Security Council, S/26666, 10; Security Council, S/1994/89, 7-8; Security Council, S/1994/1002, 8.

75. Gil Lauriciano and Rachel Waterhouse, "Slow Mine Clearance," *Mozambique Peace Process Bulletin,* Issue 9 (April 1994): 6; Human Rights Watch Arms Project, *Landmines in Mozambique* (New York: Human Rights Watch, March 1994), 14.

76. Security Council, S/1994/803, 8; Joseph Hanlon, Rachel Waterhouse, and Gil Lauriciano, "De-mining Scandal," *Mozambique Peace Process Bulletin,* Issue 10 (July 1994): 10-11.

77. Security Council, S/26666, 9-10; Security Council, S/1994/89, 9; Security Council, S/1994/511, 11; Gil Lauriciano and Rachel Waterhouse, "Slow Mine Clearance," *Mozambique Peace Process Bulletin,* Issue 9 (April 1994): 7.

78. Security Council, S/1994/511, 11; Security Council, S/1994/1002, 9; UN General Assembly, A/49/649/Add.2, 3, 5.

79. Rachel Waterhouse and Gil Lauriciano, "Transitional Government?" *The Mozambique Peace Process Bulletin,* Issue 4 (June 1993): 6. RENAMO and the unarmed opposition wanted the government, RENAMO, and the unarmed opposition each to nominate seven delegates, a proposal contrary to that outlined in the General Peace Agreement and a proposal that would have given its proponents veto power over the government. As a compromise, the government appointed ten members, RENAMO appointed seven, with three chosen by the other parties. An independent chairperson was to be selected by the appointees, or if no agreement was reached, by President Chissano from a list of five candidates chosen by the commission. (Security Council, S/26385, 6; Security Council, S/26666, 3.) For more information on the other political parties that constituted the "unarmed opposition," see Iain Christie, "Mozambique's Unarmed Opposition," *The Mozambique Peace Process Bulletin,* Special Supplemental, October 1993.

80. Security Council, S/1994/89, 1, 4; Security Council, S/1994/511, 8.

81. Security Council, S/1994/803, 6; Security Council, S/1994/1002, 6; Security Council, S/1994/1196, 1-2.

82. Security Council, S/1994/1002, 6.

83. Ibid.

84. "Mozambique-Ballot Blues," *Associated Press,* 25 October 1994, 11:56 P.M.

85. Security Council, S/1994/1002, 6-7; Jospeh Hanlon, Rachel Waterhouse, and Gil Lauriciano, "Two Countries," *Mozambique Peace Process Bulletin,* Issue 12 (September 1994): 5; Joseph Hanlon and Rachel Waterhouse, "Access Still Restricted," *Mozambique Peace Process Bulletin,* Issue 13 (11 October 1994): 3; Security Council, S/1994/1196, 2-3.

86. Judith Matloff, "RENAMO Pulls out of Mozambique's Multi-party Polls," *Reuters* newswire, 27 October 1994, 2:55 A.M.; "RENAMO Boycotts Mozambican Election,

United Press International, 27 October 1994, 11:22 A.M.; Keith Richburg, "Mozambique Ex-Rebel Joins Vote," *Washington Post* (wire service), 28 October 1994, 11:00 P.M.

87. Judith Matloff, "Mozambique Reports 90 Percent Voter Turnout," *Reuters* newswire, 29 October 1994, 1:31 P.M.

88. "Special Representative of Secretary General Declares Elections in Mozambique 'Free and Fair,'" UN Press Release, SG/SM/5488, 19 November 1994; Security Council, S/1994/1196, 3; "Dhlakama says 'no' to war after Mozambique polls," *Associated Press,* 25 October 1994, 3:41 P.M.

89. "Chissano Wins Mozambican Vote," *Washington Post,* 20 November 1994, A30.

90. Karen Gellen, "UN Broker's Peaceful Transitions in Angola, Mozambique," *Africa Recovery* 8, no. 3 (December 1994): 14.

91. "Mozambique War Is Over, But Shooting Continues," *Reuters* newswire, 21 December 1994, 12:24 A.M.

92. United States Department of State, "Lessons Unlearned—Or Why Mozambique's Peacekeeping Operation Won't Be Replicated Elsewhere." Mimeograph, US Embassy Maputo, 1994.

93. UN Undersecretary General Aldo Ajello, opening remarks at a seminar sponsored by the Council on Foreign Relations Study Group on "Lessons Learned in Peacekeeping: What Worked, What Didn't and Why?" (Session 6: The Case of Mozambique), Washington, D.C., 9 June 1995. Mimeograph.

94. Paul Taylor, "Rebel Vows Peace as Mozambique Moves toward First Election," *Washington Post,* 27 July 1994, A19.

EIGHT

INTRODUCTION TO ANARCHY: HUMANITARIAN INTERVENTION AND "STATE-BUILDING" IN SOMALIA

W I L L I A M   J .   D U R C H

Intervention in Somalia's civil war was a sobering experience for all concerned, even those parts of it that could be considered relatively successful. Somalia, ruled by one dictator and his extended family since 1969, had been a client of the Russians and then a client of the Americans and was well supplied with weapons. When its narrowly based government finally toppled in early 1991, no single group had legitimate claim to power and the country collapsed into Hobbesian anarchy. Broadcast images of mass starvation prompted international relief efforts that themselves became the targets of Somalia's quarrelsome clans. A small UN security force sent to escort relief was severely outgunned and, consequently, ineffectual. In late 1992, the United States led an armed international expedition to ensure that relief reached the neediest, which it did. But, fearful of becoming trapped in its own good deed, the United States pressed for rapid transfer of responsibility to the United Nations. The UN, fearful in turn of being outgunned once again, pressed the United States to disarm Somalia's militias and gangs. The United States declined, and the United Nations Operation in Somalia (UNOSOM) rapidly found itself in deep, shark-infested waters. Subsequent, US-led efforts to help produced more than

Fig. 8.1

MAP OF SOMALIA

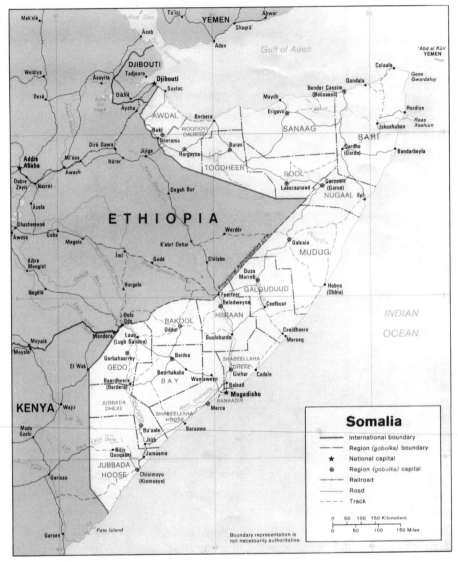

SOURCE: US Government

100 American battle casualties. In March 1995, the UN pulled out of Somalia with its assigned task of state-building unaccomplished and Somalis still at war with themselves.

ORIGINS

Until the mid-nineteenth century, Somalia was a land of indeterminate borders and largely nomadic pastoralists who grazed camels and cattle from the Indian Ocean coast well into what is now Ethiopia, and from northeastern Kenya to Djibouti at the mouth of the Red Sea. Somalis share a single ethnic background, a single language, and a single religion (Sunni Islam), but they are divided by clan, subclan, and family. Lacking central authority, Somali social and political relations were based on kinship—patrilineal blood-ties and marital ties—mediated by an unwritten social code, *heer,* and the precepts of Islam. This system kept Somali society in relative balance as long as outside influences were minimal.[1]

The British, having established a Crown Colony and coaling station in Aden across the water from northern Somalia, soon dominated the export trade there and, in 1866, looking toward the opening of the Suez Canal, established a protectorate. France soon did the same at Djibouti, creating French Somaliland. Italy joined the imperial land rush in the 1890s, establishing Italian Somaliland along the Indian Ocean coast in 1893, which abutted British holdings in Kenya that themselves included Somali-occupied territory.[2] Emperor Menelik of Ethiopia completed the nineteenth century division of traditional Somali lands by annexing the Ogaden region, which held the headwaters of Somalia's few rivers and seasonal pasturage that Somali herders were accustomed to using.[3]

With colonialism came centralized administration and commercialization. Over several decades, the old Somali sociopolitical system eroded, without replacement. When independence came in 1960, two of the European colonies—British and Italian Somaliland—were pasted together and declared to be a state. Somali areas of Kenya remained part of that state when it gained independence in 1963, and Djibouti remained separate as well, becoming independent in 1977. These "lost" lands were the natural targets of Somali irredentism, the closest thing to a nationalist sentiment to be found in newly independent Somalia.

For nine years, Somalia struggled to be a parliamentary democracy. The tendency of its politicians to line their pockets at the public's expense, combined with poor national economic performance, led to a bloodless military coup in October 1969 by Major General Mohamed Siad Barre.[4]

Siad Barre and company rapidly formed a Supreme Revolutionary Council that abrogated the constitution, banned political parties, and brooked no dissent. Having already received some military aid from the Soviet Union, the new regime turned in earnest to the Soviets for political and military support. The Soviets, looking for facilities to support their naval aspirations in the Indian Ocean, were happy to help. They abandoned their Somali hosts, however, when neighboring Ethiopia abolished its traditional monarchy and the new ruling military council severed longstanding ties with the United States and proclaimed a Marxist state.[5] The Soviet shift, in 1977, added urgency to Barre's goal of recovering the Ogaden for Somalia. By May 1977, Barre-supported guerrilla forces were attacking the territory and regular Somali forces soon followed. By hitting the Ethiopian military while it was in between arms suppliers, Barre hoped to finish the job quickly; he did not count on major intervention by the USSR and Cuba on Ethiopia's behalf. By October, they had indeed intervened with equipment and troops, respectively, to turn back the Somali assault.[6]

The Ogaden War, launched in part to shore up Siad Barre's increasingly unpopular regime, did so temporarily but its failure soon spawned opposition groups supported by Ethiopia. An abortive coup in April 1978 by army officers from the Mijerteen clan led to "communal reprisals" by the army that destroyed Mijerteen holdings in northeastern Somalia and drove clan members into exile. The exiles coalesced around the Somali Salvation Democratic Front (SSDF), led by Colonel Abullahi Yusuf, one of the April putschists. As the fissures in Somali society widened along clan lines, Siad Barre increasingly relied on the members of his own Marehan clan (which constituted less than 1 percent of the population at large) to staff the government and the army, such that by the late 1980s, government was looked upon by many Somalis as a Marehan support group, and the military as its enforcement arm.[7]

Siad Barre and Ethiopian head of state Mengistu Haile Mariam signed a "live and let live" accord in April 1988 in which each country pledged not to give haven to groups opposing the other's regime. Two Somali dissident groups based in Ethiopia, the SSDF and the Somali National Movement (SNM), found themselves without a patron. The SNM, based on the Isaaq clan, moved in force into the Isaaq-majority region of northern Somalia in May 1988 and seized three of its major cities (Hargeisa, Burao, and the port of Berbera). Siad Barre sent army forces led by his son-in-law, General Mohamed Siad Hersi (nicknamed "Morgan"), to quash the revolt, which they did with great brutality. An investigative report sponsored by the US State Department estimated that up to 5,000 Isaaq civilians were rounded up and killed by Morgan's forces, largely as a lesson to the rest. Hargeisa and Burao were bombed extensively. Some 300,000 Isaaq fled into Ethiopia. The army re-gained control of the cities but the SNM kept control of the countryside; the cities and Isaaq villages were systematically plundered. Thus the sort of devastation suffered in the southern part of the country in 1991-92 was visited upon the north two years prior.[8]

By mid-1989, the army itself was splintering. Colonel Omar Jess, an Ethiopian Ogadeni who commanded the government's northern forces, mutinied along with several thousand of his troops. In early 1990, Jess's troops, by then members of a loose coalition that included the SNM, SSDF, and a southern dissident group, the Ogadeni-based Somali Patriotic Movement (SPM), defeated Somali army units in several clashes along the border with Ethiopia.[9]

At the same time, other clans were forming their own political factions. One of the largest, the United Somali Congress (USC), was based on the Hawiye, who occupied a large swath of central Somalia that included Mogadishu, the capital.[10] In May 1990, a group of Mogadishu civic and business leaders (the "Manifesto Group") issued a call for a provisional government of reconciliation. Among them were Somalia's first president, Aden Abdullah Osman, and a Mogadishu hotelier, Mohamed Ali Mahdi, who became a principal political leader of the USC. Siad Barre had most of the signers arrested but might have done better to heed their call. In early October 1990, the three main opposition groups (USC, SNM, and SPM) agreed on the common objective of defeating Siad Barre.[11]

By late December, a largely lawless Mogadishu was under assault by the opposition militias. As the city collapsed into gunfire and looting, the expansive walled grounds of the American embassy became a last refuge for most of the foreigners remaining in the city, including Soviet diplomats. The United States mounted a brief rescue operation on 5-6 January 1991 that swept them all to safety.[12] On 27 January, Barre and his coterie fled south, and Somalia, which had no nationally accepted government for two years, now had no government at all, at least for a few days. On 1 February, USC leader Mohamed Ali Mahdi declared himself to be interim president. He did so, however, without consulting the USC's coalition partners or his military counterpart, General Mohamed Farah Aideed. Aideed rejected this move but was too busy fighting remnants of Barre's forces in southern Somalia to do much about it immediately.[13] In the north, in May, the SNM registered its rejection of the Ali Mahdi regime by declaring independence (its Somaliland Republic remained unrecognized by any outside power four years later).[14]

In early July, a USC congress offered a consolation prize to Aideed, electing him party chairman. A "reconciliation" conference shortly thereafter, co-sponsored by the presidents of Djibouti and Kenya, did not include Aideed, however. The conference endorsed a two-year transitional presidency by Ali Mahdi, which Aideed did not accept. In mid-August, Ali Mahdi had himself sworn in as president based on the Djibouti conference. Although he claimed national office, Ali Mahdi actually controlled little more than northern Mogadishu.[15]

Within weeks, Ali Mahdi's and Aideed's supporters came to blows in Mogadishu. Both sides brought in young fighters from the bush, giving them food and *qat* and equipping them with ad hoc urban fighting vehicles armed with antiaircraft cannon or recoilless rifles.[16] From roughly mid-November 1991 onward, these uninhibited predators turned Mogadishu into a free-fire zone, firing at anything that moved and most things that didn't. The city in which they fought had no public administration, no police, no courts, no power, and little of value that had not long since been looted.[17] Asked about his objective, Aideed replied that it was to "capture Mahdi."[18]

For most of 1991 and the first half of 1992, however, Aideed was primarily engaged fighting Barre's remnants, which included the forces of Barre's son-in-law Morgan, the "butcher of Hargeisa." Three times in this period, Barre's forces came relatively close to Mogadishu; in each case they were pushed back, adopting scorched earth tactics as they retreated across some of Somalia's most productive agricultural lands. This back and forth fighting displaced hundreds of thousands of Somali civilians and, compounding the effects of drought, was a direct cause of the Somali famine of 1992 and foreign military intervention. By July, the International Committee of the Red Cross (ICRC), engaged in energetic efforts to feed displaced Somalis despite the fighting, estimated that up to 2 million were at risk of starvation by the end of the year.[19]

Origins of UN Involvement

UN relief agencies pulled out of Somalia in January 1991; their staffs remained out of the picture, in Nairobi, in January 1992 when the UN sent its first political mediation mission to Somalia, headed by Undersecretary-General James Jonah. The Security Council also voted an arms embargo on Somalia—without practical effect, perhaps, but a vehicle by which to express Council disapproval of anarchy.[20]

Jonah's shuttle diplomacy efforts eventually produced a cease-fire agreement between Aideed and Ali Mahdi. Both men also agreed to the deployment of 50 unarmed UN observers in Mogadishu to monitor implementation of the cease-fire. It had effect, however, largely within Mogadishu; the rest of southern Somalia remained unaffected.[21]

The monitoring mission, part of the new UNOSOM, entailed the appointment of a resident special representative of the secretary-general (SRSG), Ambassador Mohammed Sahnoun of Algeria. Sahnoun, an energetic diplomat with an unruly, Einsteinian coif, settled into Somalia and began to work with clan elders to build the foundation for a country-wide peace.[22]

By Sahnoun's reckoning, the outside world had already missed three opportunities to stop Somalia's slide into the abyss (after the Hargeisa massacre in 1988, the Manifesto in 1990, and the Djibouti Conference in 1991). He was particularly critical of UN relief agency efforts in the first half of 1992, when the UN-backed World Food Program delivered just 19,000 of a planned 68,000 tons of foodstuffs, compared to 54,000 tons brought in by the ICRC in the same period. The UN, he complained, had done little to establish the necessary distribution networks and, as a result, those who cooperated with his reconciliation efforts could see no tangible improvement in their living conditions.

Over the summer, Sahnoun did manage to get Aideed and Ali Mahdi to agree to the deployment of 500 armed UN "security personnel" to protect aid coming through Mogadishu's port. Pakistan agreed to supply a battalion of lightly armed troops for this task, who began to arrive in Mogadishu on 14 September 1992.[23]

While the Pakistanis were enroute, however, the secretary-general asked the Security Council to increase UN forces in Somalia to 3,500 troops. Given the international reportage on conditions in Somalia and the secretary-general's earlier insistence that the Council pay more attention to the unfolding disaster there, this step undoubtedly seemed appropriate from New York's perspective, but Sahnoun was not notified in advance of this decision.[24] The Council approved Boutros-Ghali's request on 28 August. Sahnoun had spent most of the summer convincing his Somali interlocutors, particularly General Aideed, to accept the small security force; now, 3,000 more troops were to be dispatched without any advance consultation with the Somalis at all.

In a pattern that would be repeated many times over the next three years, Ali Mahdi and his relatively weak faction were basically delighted to see further foreign intervention, while Aideed was enraged. Seeing himself, not unreasonably, as the leader who had finally vanquished Siad Barre, Aideed believed that he had won the right to be president of Somalia. In August 1992, he formed his splinter of the USC into the Somali National Alliance (SNA) and recruited several smaller factions to join him; among them was Jess's faction. The SNA began to operate, particularly in

Mogadishu, as an organized political party as well as an armed faction. Although it included more than Habr Gedir members, that subclan remained dominant within the organization.[25]

With Boutros-Ghali, former foreign minister of Egypt and longtime Siad Barre ally, as secretary-general of the UN, Aideed suspected that the organization had a "hidden agenda" to establish a UN trusteeship and "eventually to restore Siad Barre" to power.[26] Aideed's suspicions were fueled by the actions of a Russian-built An-32 cargo aircraft bearing UN markings that made several deliveries in July 1992 to an Ali Mahdi-controlled airstrip north of Mogadishu. The former UN contractors flying the aircraft were freelancing, delivering cash and arms to Ali Mahdi. One of these flights crashed in October, suggesting that, formal protestations notwithstanding, the UN was not doing much to police its own contractors.[27]

Sahnoun had been consistently critical of the behavior of UN aid agencies in Somalia and now included UN headquarters in New York in his critiques. With private Swedish funding, he had organized a seminar of Somali intellectuals in the Seychelles, 1,000 kilometers offshore from Mogadishu, in an effort to generate ideas for reconciliation away from the din and guns. When he was upbraided by New York for (1) participating in the conference and (2) complaining publicly about the UN bureaucracy (which, like most organizations, likes to keep criticism "in the family"), Sahnoun asked for a redefined role that would allow him to report directly to the secretary-general, bypassing the UN bureaucracy. Receiving no reply to his request, he resigned his post.[28]

Sahnoun's replacement, longtime UN diplomat Ismat Kittani, dropped Sahnoun's policy of reaching out to Somali clan elders and faction leaders, inviting them instead to come to him—a "colonial" style adopted by his successor as well that some contend essentially doomed UN diplomacy in Somalia. Other observers suggest, however, that Sahnoun and UNOSOM had simply arrived six months too late to accomplish anything by diplomatic means; the social and political fabric of the country had so deteriorated by mid-1992 that negotiated agreements meant little.[29]

The Initial United States Role

In late April 1992, the Security Council approved deployment of 50 unarmed military observers to mind food shipments in Mogadishu after the United States objected to the cost of an armed force of 500. The State Department's argument—that Congress would not countenance yet another peacekeeping mission that year—was undercut by Senator Nancy Kassebaum's late July visit to central Somalia and subsequent public advocacy of an armed force to protect UN workers and food shipments. Within a month, the United States was pressing the Security Council to expand the armed element of UNOSOM.[30]

Also shortly after Senator Kassebaum's visit, Ambassador Sahnoun called for a UN relief airlift to complement the one run by the ICRC. The director of the State Department's Office of Foreign Disaster Assistance observed, after a brief visit to

Somalia, that since fighting in Mogadishu was mostly over control of relief supplies, airlifts to bring in more food would only increase the deadly competition for control of the country's new currency. There was a temptation, other State officials noted, to use airlifts "as a way of appearing to be doing something even though they may not achieve much."[31] Two weeks later, however, the United States announced a relief airlift that would run in parallel with the ICRC's airlift and a new airlift begun by the UN. The American effort, based in Mombasa, Kenya made its first deliveries on 28 August and was known as "Operation Provide Relief."[32]

As the international relief effort broadened and supplies reached the interior, two things became clear to relief agencies: (1) the scale of the suffering was much greater than expected, and (2) while more relief was getting into the country, widespread looting was keeping much of it from reaching the hungry and the sick. As the influx of aid increased, so did the looting—some of it to feed the looters, some of it to alter the balance of power between militias, and some of it at the behest of merchants who resold the supplies on Somalia's black market.[33]

The threat of looting in turn increased aid agencies' need for security guards, which even the military-averse ICRC hired to protect its shipments. Country-wide, ICRC estimated that it paid out $3,500 a week for protection in the fall of 1992, while the UN paid $150,000 a month for 900 security guards at Mogadishu port. Sometimes agencies sought out protection, while at other times Somalis made them offers they could not refuse. Negotiations with local gunmen to "protect" the arrival of the Pakistani battalion at Mogadishu airport, for example, resulted in demands on day one to hire 110 fighters. On day two, more than 200 claimed to have been hired and on day three, 489. The funds acquired by the gunmen were said to fuel new arms acquisitions by the factions. Thus, at least some of the aid intended to help the country get back on its feet was being used by the contestants for power to keep their contest going.[34]

As the situation in Somalia deteriorated through 1992, the United Nations was simultaneously engaged in implementing peace operations elsewhere of unprecedented size and scope. Nearly 20,000 military and civilian personnel were pouring into Cambodia to implement peace accords there; another 12,000 were deploying to separate Croats and Serbs in Croatia; and genocidal conflict in Croatia's neighbor, Bosnia, was drawing increased outside attention. In June 1992, the secretary-general issued his landmark report, *An Agenda for Peace,* which called for beefing up the UN's still-modest ability to conduct the sorts of missions that it was being given by the Security Council.

The Bush administration began crafting a reply to *Agenda for Peace* in early August, for presentation by the president at the opening of the UN General Assembly in late September. That speech laid out several areas in which peacekeeping required improvement, and areas in which the United States could render special assistance to the UN.[35] The Washington bureaucracy, seeing marching orders in the president's speech, fell to the task of turning his proposals into US policy. By November, more elements of the bureaucracy were attending to the problems and potential of peacekeeping than ever before. Thus the US government's preparedness to "do something" in Somalia grew while the plight of that country's people worsened and Americans became increasingly aware of it through media coverage.

The presidential election campaign complicated American decision-making. President Bush was being hectored by his principal opponent, Governor Bill Clinton, to do more in Bosnia; Clinton's platform called for aggressive use of American air power to stop the Bosnian Serbs. But presidents have always been wary of committing United States forces in election years: if things turn out well you may be a hero; if not, you will likely be accused of risking, and wasting, young American lives to further your own political career. As it was, relief organizations in Somalia were already criticizing Operation Provide Relief as a political stunt, noting that US cargo aircraft, in accordance with military regulations, usually flew with half loads of supplies.[36]

Several countries (among them Canada, Belgium, Egypt, and Nigeria) stood ready to send additional troops into Somalia but only if Somali faction leaders consented. Aideed did not consent, and the television images from Mogadishu came to include pictures of Pakistani troops trapped at the airport, surrounded by local "protection," unable to perform their tasks.

Several NATO countries (including Security Council permanent members France and Britain) had, by September 1992, volunteered troops to protect relief supplies going into Bosnia. They began to deploy in October and November.

One week after the 1992 presidential elections, won narrowly by Clinton, Assistant Secretary of State Robert Gallucci presented Acting Secretary of State Lawrence Eagleburger with a pair of choices: either the United States had to join the action in Bosnia, or it could take action in Somalia. Gallucci argued for intervention in Somalia under UN auspices; Eagleburger agreed.[37] Relief organizations also argued for greater protection, meeting with UN officials in New York and then sending a joint letter to the Bush administration. Representatives from Interaction, a coordinating group for aid providers, met weekly with staff of the State and Defense Departments to call for greater US action. On 20 November, the Deputies Committee (the number two officials from State, Defense, the Joint Staff, and other relevant agencies) held the first of four meetings on Somalia, discussing a Defense Department paper on the requirements for intervention. At the second meeting, on 21 November, Deputy Chairman of the Joint Chiefs Admiral David Jeremiah stated that, "if you think US forces are needed, [then] we can do the job." With the military willing to act, attention turned to the size, objectives, and end point of the operation. Brigadier General Frank Libutti, just done with a tour as head of Provide Relief, warned that US involvement could be lengthy, and thoughts turned to handing over the operation to the UN at the earliest feasible moment.[38] Had this exit option not been available, it seems unlikely that Operation Restore Hope would have been launched, and the Bush administration would have gone out not with a bang but a whimper.

UN officials did not like the idea of taking the bag from the United States, but what UN officials like and what the Security Council votes for are two different things. On 3 December 1992, the Council (after considerable lobbying of heads of state by President Bush), voted unanimously to authorize UN member states to "use all necessary means to establish as soon as possible a secure environment for humanitarian relief operations in Somalia."[39]

OPERATION RESTORE HOPE/UNIFIED TASK FORCE

This section presents a brief overview of Operation Restore Hope, known interchangeably in UN circles as the Unified Task Force (UNITAF). UNITAF entered Somalia on 9 December 1992 and handed over operational responsibility to the UN on 4 May 1993.

Political Support

Domestically, UNITAF was a big hit. In a *New York Times*/CBS poll taken a few days after President Bush's televised address announcing the operation, 81 percent of those interviewed agreed that "the US is doing the right thing in sending troops to Somalia to make sure food gets to the people there," while 70 percent agreed that the task was even worth possible loss of American lives. On the other hand, just 44 percent thought that the United States should stay in Somalia as long as it took to "make sure" that the country would "remain peaceful," suggesting that the Bush administration was well advised to stress an early exit.[40] The African Caucus at the United Nations also endorsed the secretary-general's initial call for military action in Somalia. And once the United States had made the commitment to send troops, nearly three dozen other states scrambled to join the operation. The anticipated presence of the Big Dog made it less risky for the rest.

Both Mohamed Ali Mahdi and Mohamed Farah Aideed welcomed UNITAF, though for different reasons. Ali Mahdi welcomed a counterweight to Aideed, and Aideed welcomed an alternative to his perceived nemesis, the UN.

Mandate

Although Security Council Resolution 794 legitimized Operation Restore Hope in the eyes of the world and to some extent constituted the mandate for the operation, its actual mandate was spelled out to the American people by President Bush the day after the Security Council acted:

> First, we will create a secure environment in the hardest-hit parts of Somalia so that food can move from ships overland to the people in the countryside now devastated by starvation. And second, once we have created that secure environment, we will withdraw our troops, handing the security mission back to a regular UN peacekeeping force. Our mission has a limited objective, to open the supply routes, to get the food moving, and to prepare the way for a UN peacekeeping force to keep it moving. . . . We will not stay one day longer than is absolutely necessary.[41]

Two things are clear from this presidential statement: the strictly limited, apolitical aims of the operation, and the alacrity with which the United States would attempt to hand the task over to the UN. The United States signaled clearly to Somali factions that any of them temporarily inconvenienced by the intervention could probably afford to wait it out, and that the United States was not proposing to fix what was broken in Somalia, but only to deal with the visible consequences of the breakdown that tore at Western consciences.

Boutros-Ghali wasted no time in objecting to UNITAF's limited mandate. He and his staffers knew only too well from ongoing experience in Cambodia and the former Yugoslavia that the UN could not forge the sort of operation that would be necessary to keep order in Somalia against determined resistance. The UN had neither the command and control structure nor the operating doctrine necessary to execute the Chapter VII peace enforcement operation that Resolution 794 authorized. More importantly, its member states were not in the habit of contributing forces to die for the UN Charter. Poor states contributed troops to make money from the UN's flat-rate reimbursements; richer states did it to feel good about themselves. Both groups contributed to the peace process in places like the Golan Heights, Cambodia, Mozambique, and Nicaragua, but neither wanted to lose troops in doing so.

To reduce the UN's risk in Somalia, Boutros-Ghali wanted UNITAF to disarm Somali militias.[42] Only with such a leg-up, he believed, would a follow-on UN operation have a prayer of maintaining order in the country. Disarmament carried a secondary requirement of quarantine: no point in taking guns away today that can be replaced tomorrow or next week from Kenya or Ethiopia. All states were already obliged by Security Council Resolution 733 not to sell arms to Somalia, but there was no enforcement mechanism and arms generally flowed as freely as *qat*. UNITAF eventually did a certain amount of disarmament in Mogadishu, but when operational responsibility was finally handed over to the United Nations in May 1993, southern Somalia probably contained about as many weapons as it had five months earlier.

Funding

UNITAF costs were borne by the participating states, defrayed in some cases by a trust fund for Somalia established by the United Nations. Total voluntary contributions to this fund for UNITAF totalled $105 million ($100 million from Japan and most of the rest from Austria, Denmark, Finland, and South Korea).[43] The United States received $27.5 million in UNITAF cost reimbursement from the trust fund. Unreimbursed incremental costs to the US Department of Defense for Operation Provide Relief and UNITAF amounted to $712 million.[44]

Planning and Implementation

Planning for Operation Restore Hope had both military and political dimensions. While military forces were maneuvered into position, diplomatic initiatives helped to assure that US-led forces would be welcomed and not actively opposed.

On the day of the first Deputies Committee meeting on Somalia, US Central Command (CENTCOM) notified the First Marine Expeditionary Force (I MEF) at Camp Pendleton, California, that it might be asked to undertake a humanitarian assistance mission on very short notice.[45] Two days of close collaboration between I MEF and CENTCOM produced a basic concept of operation briefed to President Bush on 25 November, the same day Secretary Eagleburger informed the UN of the United States' willingness to mount an operation in Somalia.

On 2 December, I MEF came under CENTCOM operational control, and the next day its commanding general was appointed commander of Joint Task Force Somalia. By 5 December, a Marine Amphibious Task Unit led by the helicopter assault ship USS *Tripoli,* and including two other amphibious transports and embarked Marines, was in position near Mogadishu, just over the horizon. Three days later, they were joined by a maritime prepositioning ship carrying heavy equipment. (These ships had been in the general vicinity of Somalia for several months, as part of the US Navy's fleet presence in the Indian Ocean.)

The Operational Plan

UNITAF's Operational Plan divided its tasks into four phases.[46] Phase One objectives included establishing a base of operations in Mogadishu; gaining control of relief supplies into and through the city; introducing other forces into the city; and securing the town of Baidoa. The plan allowed three weeks for completion of this phase; in fact it was finished in one week.

Phase Two of the plan called for expanding operations to additional ports and airfields (especially Baledogle, just northwest of Mogadishu); expanding security in the country's interior via relief convoy escort and creation of additional relief distribution sites; and establishing security and bases of operation at least in the towns of Gialalassi, Bardera, Belet Weyn, and Oddur. Phase Two was allowed 30 days in the plan, and took 12.

Phase Three called for further expansion of regional security and control of additional ports and airfields, especially Kismayo, in the south, which was hotly contested between forces loyal to Aideed and those loyal to Morgan, with the majority of its population caught in between. The plan specified no timetable for this phase, but it was considered complete roughly two months into the mission.

The final phase was the handoff to the UN, considered complete "when US forces had been relieved of their responsibilities in Somalia." The plan estimated 240 days from initial UNITAF deployment to complete the handover; officially, it occurred at the 146-day mark. US forces remained in Somalia in one or another combat capacity, however, for 470 days until their final withdrawal on 23 March 1994.

Initial Deployments

Uncertain of the welcome they would receive from Somali militias, the vanguard of US forces came ashore in the early morning hours of 9 December. Somali militias had been warned by their leaders to stay clear of the port and airport, thanks to the advance work of US ambassador Robert Oakley, a former ambassador to Somalia who knew most of the major players and arrived in Mogadishu a day ahead of time to clear a political path for the US-led intervention. It would be a pattern repeated frequently in weeks to come, as Oakley and a small staff traveled into the hinterland of Somalia, explaining to local leaders what was about to happen.[47]

The press did not get the word to stand back on 9 December, however, so US Navy commandos and Marine reconnaissance teams were met on the beaches of Mogadishu by throngs of cameramen with strobe and klieg lights, just in time for the evening news back home. The French, whose initial contingent for UNITAF arrived a bit later on the same day, caricatured the nighttime events as a "circus."[48] The timing was indeed curious, but given the clear discomfort of the first wave of reconnaissance troops, what the world saw on their screens was not so much a staged event as the carrying out of standard military operating procedures in support of a potentially opposed amphibious landing. Greater reliance on the political process (Oakley and company) to clear the beaches of the media as well as local fighters might have saved the US military this initial embarrassment, but had the first US troops marching into Somalia been ambushed while relying on such assurances, Task Force commanders would have been damned for their naivete.

Although relief agencies pressed US commanders to move swiftly into Somalia's interior, the first units of UNITAF only secured arrival areas for the main body of the force: first Mogadishu port and airport, then the Soviet-built Baledogle airstrip 160 kilometers northwest of Mogadishu. Into Baledogle flew the bulk of US and other UNITAF forces that subsequently fanned out to Baidoa, Bardera, Kismayo, and other locations in Somalia's southern "famine belt." Overall, the operation divided southern Somalia into nine Humanitarian Relief Sectors (HRS).[49]

Stretching the Mandate

It soon became clear that establishing a secure environment meant doing more than getting food to distribution centers, deterring gangs, and returning fire when fired upon. By late December, UNITAF began to require that heavy weapons in Mogadishu be cantoned or subject to seizure on sight. (Some weapons were cantoned; others were pulled out of the city.) When Somali factional leaders meeting for ten days in Addis Ababa (first under UN, then Ethiopian aegis) agreed to a cease-fire, UNITAF began to enforce it.[50] As Hirsch and Oakley relate,

> Once an internal Somali agreement was concluded, the US approach was to insist
> on its implementation, since experience soon showed that signing an agreement
> did not mean that either party necessarily intended to do anything about it, at
> least not of its own volition, or soon. It might mean a desire to appear cooperative,
> or that the elements in the agreement were not utterly unacceptable and might
> be implemented under certain circumstances. It rarely meant what the United
> States understood formal top-level agreements to mean.[51]

Even before the first Addis accord, however, UNITAF was responding forcefully to attacks, having warned factional leaders in advance that it would do so. On 7 January 1993, after shots were fired at US Marines from an SNA weapons compound, Marine loudspeakers announced in Somali impending retaliation. When machine gun fire answered the announcement, Marines returned fire with tanks, artillery, and Cobra helicopters launching antitank missiles. The firefight lasted less than an hour; the compound's defenders fled. UNITAF immediately reopened communications with Aideed, pointing out that the SNA had broken the rules regarding weapons use and had suffered the consequences, but offering to let bygones be bygones. The SNA agreed and communications channels to UNITAF remained open, allowing UNITAF, in days following this incident, to begin to shut down Mogadishu's arms bazaars.[52] At the same time, UNITAF and the US Liaison Office, headed by Oakley, facilitated almost daily meetings of a "joint security committee" of Aideed and Ali Mahdi military representatives that helped to keep the peace in Mogadishu. These meetings continued until UNITAF departed.[53]

The security situation in the rest of the country affected the visible levels of tension in Mogadishu. On 25 February, for example, General Aideed's supporters launched two days of destructive rioting in Mogadishu, not over anything that had happened in the city, but to protest UNITAF's handling of events elsewhere, particularly in Kismayo.[54]

The Kismayo region had seen protracted but inconclusive fighting between the forces of General Morgan, representing the old regime, and those of Colonel Jess, allied with the SNA and Aideed. Both sought control of a city that was home mostly to other clans, and neither wore a "white hat."[55] UNITAF dealt with Jess as the de facto power in Kismayo when US and Belgian forces deployed there at the end of December. When Morgan's forces attacked a Jess weapons compound on 24 January, UNITAF considered it a violation of the Addis cease-fire agreement and attacked Morgan's forces in turn. A month later, Morgan infiltrated fighters into Kismayo dressed as herders and attacked Jess, who fled town. British Broadcasting's (BBC) Somali language broadcast (which was perennially inflammatory, uncharacteristic of the BBC) claimed that Morgan had taken the town, implicitly with UNITAF consent. That claim, on top of a growing SNA realization that outsiders' encouragement of local political leaders undermined SNA influence, led to the Mogadishu riots by SNA supporters.[56]

UNITAF's Nigerian contingent, guarding a major downtown intersection, took fire from Somali snipers in this incident and returned it in recklessly high volume over a period of hours, with some stray bullets and shells landing in the UNITAF headquarters compound more than a mile away. Nigeria was held in particularly low regard by many Somalis, partly because it had given asylum to Siad Barre. The contingent's response to stress did not earn it any points either.[57]

There were relatively few other incidents during UNITAF's remaining weeks. Morgan and Jess fought briefly just as the March reconciliation conference began, but by and large UNITAF had established an environment in its areas of operation in which relief could reach the needy, hunger diminished, and fighting subsided. In several instances, to produce the secure environment called for in its mandate, UNITAF units did try to build up local leadership, and UNITAF reestablished elements of the Somali National Police, officially known as the UNITAF Auxiliary Security Force. By all accounts, the police had been one of the few respected national institutions in the country, neither clan-based nor coopted by Siad Barre's family values. The revised police force staffed checkpoints throughout Mogadishu and provided security and crowd control at feeding centers. They were generally considered an asset to the operation.[58]

Seeking Transition

The United States grew increasingly impatient to pull its forces out of Somalia. Operation Restore Hope had been billed as a short-term operation, and American commanders were anxious to set a date for transition to the UN. Otherwise, they faced the prospect of troop rotation at the six-month mark, an expensive and logistically complex proposition that would also entail transferring on the fly what had been learned in the field, through painful trial and error, to a new set of units.

UNITAF's ability to plan realistically for the handoff to UNOSOM was hampered to a degree by its staff's lack of familiarity with the United Nations, UN military operations, and UN rules. Some of UNITAF's early planning efforts suggested that it expected to hand off to an organization not unlike itself, that is, one with instant access to experienced people, adequate resources, and extant operational doctrine.[59] None of this was true. In early 1993, the UN's Department of Peacekeeping Operations remained a skeletal affair with a few dozen civilian and military officers on staff. The UN's logistics planners worked in a different UN Department. Seconded Western military officers helped them cope with the planning requirements, but the UN cannot purchase equipment or formally recruit people for a mission until that mission has a mandate, and UNOSOM II did not have a mandate until 26 March 1993.

The secretary-general did, however, have the authority to deploy up to 3,500 troops in Somalia under existing mandates. That he chose not to use his authority to facilitate the transition speaks to his misgivings about the mission and to his struggle with the United States over disarmament of Somali militias.

UN planners believed that only if Somalia were flatly pacified would it be susceptible to "regular peacekeeping." A conference of faction leaders in Addis Ababa in the last half of March 1993 appeared to produce a framework for peace, but it was just a framework, not a completed peace accord.

Assessment of UNITAF

In general, UNITAF performed its assigned tasks in an exemplary manner. Not only did US military professionalism show through but forces demonstrated adaptability to a difficult situation and an unfamiliar culture. Moreover, the United States provided effective, unified command and control for a variety of third-party forces deployed with widely varying equipment, training, and political constraints. Many contingents came with orders not to take any risks; UNITAF commanders posted them largely to guard the Mogadishu airport.

On the other hand, had UNITAF stayed longer, it might have felt the same cross-pressures brought to bear on UNOSOM II, and the United States would probably have been just as sensitive to casualties in its own operation as it proved to be in assisting the UN's operation. Early self-congratulations on fulfilling UNITAF's limited mandate took too narrow a view of Somalia's problems or were too willing to define success in terms of clearing self-defined sets of hurdles. The hunger there had been bested and some diseases checked only due to UNITAF's substantial deterrent (and occasionally punishing) presence. No political structure was left behind that could sustain UNITAF's results without the continuing crutch of strong outside military support. That was where the United Nations was supposed to come in. But US reliance on a UN-based exit strategy reflected US domestic political requirements and wishful thinking much more than a realistic appraisal of UN capabilities.

UNOSOM II

Rather than accept the inevitable transition, the UN Secretariat engaged in its own wishful thinking: that UNITAF would disarm a hypertrophied Somali gun culture, in the process neutralizing Somalia's rapacious faction leaders and making them suitably respectful of traditional peacekeepers. The Secretariat delayed active participation in transition planning until very late in the day and thus delayed presenting to the Security Council the framework for a mandate that, once passed, would authorize recruitment of peacekeeping units and mission staff. The upshot was a tardy, half-realized operation with a double dose of problems.

Political Support

Inasmuch as US needs impelled the creation of UNOSOM II, Washington's attitudes toward the operation receive the most attention here. But the near-universal lack of depth in the commitments of other troop contributors and the narrow, calculating attitudes of Somalia's warlords and their supporters also doomed the operation, almost from the start.

The United States

Although the United States wanted to pull its forces from Somalia as quickly as possible, the Clinton administration realized that the United States was the only power willing and able to provide the UN with the "force multipliers," particularly logistical and intelligence support, that it needed to carry the new burden that initial US action had thrust upon it. The United States insisted, in turn, on substantial American presence in the operation's command echelons. An American was appointed SRSG to succeed Ismat Kittani, and an American was appointed Deputy Force Commander (see further discussion under "Command and Control," below).

Resolution 814 established UNOSOM II at the high-water mark of the Clinton administration's support for "assertive multilateralism," a phrase coined by its UN representative, Ambassador Madeleine Albright. US actions in Somali exemplified this concept, which argued for continued, active US engagement in foreign affairs with maximum efforts to share that burden with others, especially through multilateral institutions. Albright called UNOSOM II "an historic undertaking. We are excited to join it and we will vigorously support it."[60]

Albright's enthusiasm may have been shared by her cabinet colleagues but no cabinet or subcabinet meetings weighed the implications of the UNOSOM II mandate either for the UN or for the United States before her supporting vote was cast in the Security Council. Moreover, few of the Clinton administration's mid- to upper-level political appointees in defense and foreign policy had been confirmed by the Senate by March 1993, so foreign policy decisions in the new administration lacked depth. Of course, the US military was acutely aware of Somalia's dangers, being hip-deep in them at the time, but UNOSOM II was the military's ticket out of the country and if it was delayed by political and security concerns, their exit was delayed. Lieutenant General Johnston and then Major General Zinni did brief their successors extensively on the pitfalls of peace enforcement in Somalia and especially on the risk of tangling with Aideed. But the impact of that message was dulled by the insistence of US diplomats who succeeded Robert Oakley in Mogadishu that Aideed was a dangerous character who had to be marginalized.[61]

Indeed, the Clinton administration did not articulate its reasons for being in Somalia until late summer. In a 27 August speech, Secretary of Defense Les Aspin laid out the 12-month history of US military involvement there, summarized the current situation in the country, and specified criteria for measuring mission success that would permit withdrawal of US forces.[62] But the president's full attention was not consistently engaged for another two weeks, reportedly stimulated by a long conversation at the White House with former president Jimmy Carter. Asked at a press conference, shortly thereafter, to present US goals in Somalia, President Clinton demurred, "because our position is not well enough formed yet."[63] At this point, US forces had been engaged in sporadic combat in Somalia for three months and US Army Rangers had been in the country for nearly one month on a semi-covert mission to capture General Aideed.

Somalia was not the only log on the administration's fire but it was the only place in the world where American combat troops were engaged in weekly firefights with dangerous, if underestimated, adversaries. It behooved the US administration to follow the course of the operation closely, at the highest levels. When the administration did decide, toward the end of September 1993, that UN and US policy in Somalia should de-emphasize military operations in favor of political initiatives, it neglected to pass the relevant orders to its troops in the field.[64]

When television images of gloating Somali gunmen replaced images of starving children, congressional leaders started to call for withdrawal of US troops, hoping to get out in front of demands from voters. But while congressional phone banks may have been temporarily swamped with such demands, opinion surveys showed a more evenly divided public, and one in which respondents were individually less inclined to withdraw in the face of casualties than they believed *the rest* of the public to be. Thus, while 68 percent agreed, in May 1993, that "the public" would quickly turn against any operation in which American troops were killed, only 41 percent, on average, called for immediate withdrawal from Somalia after 18 US soldiers died and 78 were wounded on 3 October 1993 in Mogadishu, and a majority supported President Clinton's temporary increase in troop strength.[65] Congress ultimately refused to allow spending on US forces in Somalia beyond 31 March 1994, the date that Clinton set for the final US withdrawal. Thereafter, active American support was limited to covering the final withdrawal of the UN force in March 1995.

Other Troop Contributing Countries

Several of the troop contributors to UNITAF agreed to stay on for UNOSOM II, but many of the best-equipped countries decided to withdraw even before the United States made its own decision, and the political commitment of most contributors was marginal at best. The political attention of the European contributors, particularly France, was increasingly drawn to the mess in Bosnia, where the UN operation was growing rapidly. The Belgians shifted their attention to their former colony, Rwanda, and sent a battalion to the new UN peacekeeping operation there. By mid-1994, all of the infantry units in Somalia came from developing countries.

Indian troops began to arrive in Somalia in September 1993 and Egyptian troops in late November. By spring 1994, India and Pakistan together were contributing two-thirds of the troops in the UN operation. Although India refused joint duty with Pakistan in Mogadishu, Pakistani helicopter units occasionally supported Indian troops, and the experience may have served as an operational confidence building measure between the two armies.[66]

From the earliest stages of the operation, the various troop contributing governments held differing views of Somali politics and how the UN should implement its mandate. While US civilian officials in Mogadishu and their counterparts in UNOSOM II backed a forceful, judgmental approach to the various factions, particularly Aideed's, Italian officials and their military representatives in Somalia balked at this approach.[67] Other contingents also phoned home to verify orders given to them by UNOSOM Force Command, a phenomenon common to other UN operations but a serious political limitation on the UN's ability to conduct dangerous peace enforcement missions.

In sum, one of the most difficult and dangerous missions ever assigned to United Nations-led forces was riven by political discord and undercut by shallow and distracted external political support. In previous UN operations, this had been a recipe for stalemate or failure; Somalia proved no exception.

The Local Parties

The complex politics of Somali anarchy were outlined earlier. When UNITAF handed over responsibility for keeping the peace in Somalia to the United Nations, nothing had become any simpler. All of the local militia-backed factions in southern Somalia attempted to manipulate both interventions to their own advantage. Because most factions were weaker than Aideed's SNA, they tended to see the outsiders as protectors and thus lined up behind outside efforts to keep the peace and cobble together a political settlement. Aideed and the SNA, at first welcoming of American military power as an alternative to the perceived anti-SNA machinations of the United Nations, came to realize that the outsiders' constraints on their use of force and their encouragement of local political initiative in the Somalia hinterland was eroding the SNA's power base.[68]

From Aideed's perspective, the successive outside interventions seemed calculated to throw obstacles in his path to the presidency of Somalia. From a Western perspective, neither he, nor Ali Mahdi, nor Jess, Morgan, or any other faction leader deserved to lead. None had much regard for anything other than their own power and that of their faction. All ignored the plight of those displaced from their farms and villages by the war.

Some observers suggested that by dealing with the factions and inviting their leaders to international peace conferences, outsiders gave them political legitimacy, whereas the UN should have done more to build up "traditional" Somali leaders.[69] But the long decline of Somali politics and culture into "clanism" had created a situation in which the factions had both the guns and the political organization. To fully supplant them required a complete social and political remake of Somalia for which outsiders had neither the stomach nor the patience. So they dealt with these de facto powers, as diplomats have done throughout history, while encouraging new structures that would cater to "the unarmed and vulnerable."[70] In the end, however, the United Nations proved too weak to protect either its clients or itself when the SNA finally mounted a serious armed challenge.

Here, then, is the dilemma of humanitarian intervention: either the outsiders feed, vaccinate, and stand aside, letting the local parties settle feuds in their own uniquely bloody way while providing some minimal protection to non-combatants; or the outsiders quash local power centers and look for more acceptable local alternatives. The "local alternatives," by definition, have not been strong enough to win on their own, which makes them wards of the intervention and prolongs anarchy until the new system grafted on by the outsiders can take hold. This approach obligates the international "surgeon" to complete the course of treatment, but he rarely has the time or attention span; in fact, he really has only the foggiest idea how to do the surgery and he fears the sight of blood, especially his own. Given these choices, the long-term prognosis for humanitarian intervention is not good.

Mandates

Like a number of other UN operations in dangerous locales, UNOSOM operated under a series of mandates that chart its rise and fall. UNOSOM II was the first attempt to enforce peace within a UN member state under Chapter VII of the UN Charter. Chapter VII, however, was designed to facilitate forceful international response to international aggression; it was not designed to catch a falling state.

This section discusses all relevant Security Council actions with regard to Somalia, from early 1992 through early 1994. It also discusses the March 1993 peace accords signed by Somali faction leaders.

Diplomacy and UNOSOM I

On 23 January 1992, one year after Siad Barre decamped from Mogadishu, the Security Council officially noticed that Somalia had a problem and, via Resolution 733, imposed a "general and complete embargo" on arms deliveries, and asked the UN secretary-general to appoint a coordinator for humanitarian relief efforts. On 17 March, in Resolution 746, the Council urged Somali factions to respect the cease-fire accord they had signed two weeks earlier, supported the dispatch of a UN technical survey team to Somalia, and asked the factions not to shoot at it. On 24 April, in Resolution 751, the Council decided to establish UNOSOM with 50 observers to monitor the cease-fire in Mogadishu, and agreed in principle to the deployment of a "security force" of unspecified size, under the direction of an SRSG, to secure relief shipments. Mohammed Sahnoun was appointed SRSG shortly thereafter; the security force materialized in September in the form of 500 Pakistani troops trapped at Mogadishu airport.[71]

On 27 July, in Resolution 767, the Council authorized a UN airlift of relief supplies into Somalia and dispatched another technical team. On 28 August, in Resolution 775, it raised the ceiling on UNOSOM to roughly 4,200 military and civilian personnel, at the urging of the United States, without consulting or notifying Ambassador Sahnoun, as noted earlier. No additional troops actually deployed under color of this latter resolution. Some of the units earmarked by their governments for UNOSOM deployed with UNITAF instead.

UNOSOM II

When the Security Council authorized deployment of UNITAF on 3 December 1992, it included in its Resolution 794 a determination "to restore peace, stability and law and order with a view to facilitating the process of political settlement under the auspices of the United Nations, aimed at national reconciliation in Somalia." The Council encouraged UN representatives "to promote these objectives," which went far beyond the accepted tasks of UNITAF and foreshadowed the more ambitious mandate of UNOSOM II. Resolution 794 also warned that those who violated international humanitarian law in Somalia would be "held individually responsible" for such acts, foreshadowing the UN's eventual, misguided manhunt for Mohammed Farah Aideed.

UNOSOM II was established initially on 26 March 1993 by Resolution 814, which passed unanimously (as did every Security Council resolution with respect to

Somalia). Its timing was interesting and most likely intended originally to dovetail with the outcome of a Somali Conference on National Reconciliation held in Addis Ababa, Ethiopia, that was scheduled to conclude on 19 March. When Resolution 814 passed, the conference was still underway, delayed by fighting in Kismayo. Rather than further delay the transition from UNITAF, the Council passed Resolution 814 while welcoming "any progress made" in Addis.

The conference did reach agreement; in fact, it reached two. The first accord, signed on 27 March, established a framework of broadly representative district and regional councils to jump-start local government. Each three-member regional council was to include at least one woman, "a marked departure from Somali tradition," as Hirsch and Oakley put it.[72] A "transitional national council" (TNC) was to act as the country's "supreme authority" for a period of two years, setting up a judiciary and overseeing the drafting of a "transitional charter" or constitution. The TNC was to include three representatives from each of the 18 administrative regions in Somalia (including the 5 that made up "Somaliland," which sent no representatives to the Addis meeting). Each political faction would also control 1 seat and Mogadishu would have 5, for a total of 74. There was nothing in the 27 March accord, however, about how members of the TNC, the regional councils, or the district councils were actually to be chosen. The accord also called for complete disarmament of the country within ninety days but did not provide a mechanism for implementing that either.[73]

On 30 March, a second document was signed by the 15 faction leaders in Addis. This document did specify a procedure for choosing members of the TNC: the three representatives from each administrative region would be appointed by the political factions in that region, and a mechanism was specified for resolving disagreements about nominees. The 30 March document did not mention representation for women and called for TNC nominations be made within 45 days (that is, by mid-May).[74]

The two Addis accords called for very different processes of political reconstruction. The 27 March document offered the possibility of an inclusive political process. The 30 March document divvied up political power among the 15 factions.

Resolution 814, passed before either of the Addis accords was signed, encouraged the SRSG in Somalia to press for broad participation by all sectors of Somali society in the search for a political settlement. Consistent with Resolution 814, UNOSOM II chose to actively implement the 27 March accord and to ignore the later one, making it appear to faction leaders that the UN mission, public pronouncements notwithstanding, was not implementing Somali political reconciliation plans but following its own agenda.

Resolution 814 had three parts. Part A dealt with political reconciliation and economic rehabilitation, in which UNOSOM II was to "assist the people of Somalia." Part B dealt with security issues and was explicitly linked to Chapter VII of the Charter. It authorized the expansion of UNOSOM II to a five-brigade force, emphasized "the crucial importance of disarmament," demanded full compliance with the 15 January 1993 cease-fire and disarmament accords, and asked the secretary-general to use the operation to implement the UN arms embargo and provide security for the repatriation of refugees and displaced persons. Part C continued the trust fund for Somalia and sought new, voluntary pledges from member states.

Resolution 814 was an ambitious document that applied to the whole country, including the northern part that did not think it needed outside help. UNOSOM II was also asked to do more than UNITAF with respect to disarmament and rebuilding legitimate government. The disarmament plan was developed in the field primarily by UNITAF with input from the few UNOSOM personnel then in Somalia. The plan called for the Somalis themselves to carry out voluntary cantonment of heavy weapons at designated sites; militia members would then congregate at "transition sites" some distance from the cantonments, where they would surrender personal weapons and register for "future . . . support . . . and training" of an unspecified nature. This process would be implemented region by region, with all militias within a given region disarming simultaneously. Weapons of those who refused to cooperate by a specified deadline, however, would be confiscated and/or destroyed by the UN.[75]

One month after it officially replaced UNITAF, UNOSOM II was already in hot water over weapons-related issues, the mission had suffered casualties at the hands of SNA gunmen and mobs, and its mandate was augmented. Resolution 837 of 6 June 1993 was drafted primarily by US government officials and passed the Security Council unanimously within 48 hours of the first casualties. Given the alacrity with which the Council acted, there was little opportunity to analyze the implications of its actions.

Resolution 837 singled out "forces apparently belonging to the United Somali Congress (USC/SNA)" and the SNA's "use of radio broadcasts . . . to incite attacks against United Nations personnel." It condemned "unprovoked armed attacks . . . which appear to have been part of a calculated and premeditated series of cease-fire violations," and stressed the need to neutralize "radio broadcasting systems that contribute to the violence and attacks directed against UNOSOM II." Finally, it "reaffirmed" that:

> the Secretary-General is authorized under Resolution 814 to take all necessary measures against those responsible for the armed attacks . . . [and] those responsible for publicly inciting such attacks . . . including . . . their arrest and detention for prosecution, trial, and punishment.[76]

This paragraph—made in the USA—set UNOSOM II on the path that led to the firefight of 3 October 1993, the US pullout from UNOSOM II, and an uproar in the United States over the role of American forces in UN peace operations.

In the latter part of September, US secretary of state Warren Christopher visited Secretary-General Boutros-Ghali to propose that UNOSOM's moribund political reconciliation efforts be resurrected. Back from its summer recess, the Congress was pressing the administration to explain itself on Somalia, and the administration, in turn, had finally become concerned that the fighting in Mogadishu was undercutting political and economic progress being made elsewhere in Somalia. One result was Security Council

Resolution 865, of 22 September 1993, which stressed that UNOSOM II's highest priority was assisting Somali national reconciliation while promoting the restoration of civil administration. Resolution 865 still stressed the need for disarmament, however, and reaffirmed that those who attacked UNOSOM would be held responsible. It remained silent on the issue of arresting and detaining those responsible for such attacks, thus letting previous instructions stand. The resolution also emphasized the urgency of reestablishing the Somali police, judicial, and penal systems.

On 16 November, the Security Council formally canceled UNOSOM II's mandate to arrest individuals implicated in attacks on UN forces (Resolution 885), and in early February 1994, UNOSOM II was given a modified mandate.[77] While still invoking Chapter VII of the Charter, Resolution 897 reduced the organization's military tasks to protecting lines of communication. Resolution 897 emphasized "encouraging and assisting" the process of national reconciliation and reconstruction, and directed UNOSOM to concentrate its efforts on those parts of the country that were most cooperative with international aid providers. Although the UN would thereafter continue diplomatic efforts to promote the rebirth of formal government in Somalia, its attempts to force the process had come to an end.

Funding

UNOSOM II was funded by assessed contributions from the UN's member states, like most peacekeeping operations. Total cost was $1.64 billion. Roughly half of that amount reimbursed governments for troops ($658 million) and for wear and tear on the military equipment that the troops brought with them ($184.5 million).[78]

After UNITAF departed, the trust fund for Somalia was reoriented to support the rebuilding of the Somali national police force and judiciary. UN member states contributed $21.5 million in cash, plus equipment and training support valued at $43.4 million (of which the United States contributed $37 million). As the security situation in Somalia deteriorated through 1994, however, that equipment was withdrawn.[79] UNOSOM II also incurred some nonstandard expenses. Like the nongovernmental organizations (NGOs), trying to work in Somalia, the UN had problems with local workers and building and vehicle leases, ending up, in effect, paying protection money to the local militias. It also had trouble with cash management.

Permanent Employees

In February 1993, a UN survey team established rates of pay for local UN hires (clerks, cooks, manual laborers, and drivers) that ranged from $215 to $1,461 per month. The monetized value of per capita monthly income in Somalia before the civil war, however, was only about $10. Thus the UN pay scale ranged from 20 to 150 times the average Somali's income. The impact of this pay rate was felt first by the NGOs, many of whom had been paying their guards less than half the UN scale; the guards of course demanded equal pay, or else.[80]

Second, because UNOSOM headquarters were deep in SNA territory at the site of the old US embassy in south Mogadishu, most of the local workers within the UN compound belonged to the SNA's major subclan, Habr Gedir—also Aideed's subclan. As one UN official put it, members of any other clans "would be killed on the road to work."[81] Thus the UNOSOM headquarters compound routinely swarmed with local eyes and ears for Aideed, with predictable consequences. In conducting some of its weapon sweeps in Mogadishu, for example, the US Quick Reaction Force reportedly found some of its own maps in buildings used by the SNA.

New Leases on Life

Building leases proved similarly unbreakable. The UN initially leased buildings (from whom is not clear, as legal ownership was difficult to sort out from de facto control) in several parts of Mogadishu, including the nonfunctioning university. After security deteriorated in June 1993, most of the UN civilians evacuated or moved in with the military at the embassy compound, but the leases on fifty to sixty buildings in south Mogadishu were maintained, some in the UN's south compound by the airport. A UNOSOM financial report justified their cost, an average of $3,000-$4,000 per month per lease, "to guarantee the safety and security of the mission headquarters in the Embassy compound. . . . The premises will be rented *until it is judged that the political situation has stabilized.*"[82]

For local transport until its fleet of UN-owned vehicles was delivered, and because it was deemed too dangerous to drive a white-painted automobile in Mogadishu, for a time UNOSOM rented a fleet of 100-200 cars and drivers at a daily rate of $75 (or $2,250 per month, per vehicle). Had the need been strictly vehicular, long-term leases might have been obtained offshore at some fraction of that cost. Here again, UNOSOM was maintaining a service that it could not safely refuse, "owing to the frequent threats if an attempt is made to replace a civilian hired car with a United Nations vehicle."[83]

Between workers' salaries and rental income from UNOSOM, the SNA doubt-lessly acquired plenty of cash with which to finance the flow of *qat* to its troops and the arms that it used to drive first the United States and then the UN out of the country.

Cash Flow

Cash, its acquisition and management, was a third problem that plagued UNOSOM II. Somalia had no functioning banking system, and UNOSOM never developed a secure alternative. To pay its local workers and the monthly "rent" and to make local purchases, it shipped in $1-3 million in cash from Djibouti every Tuesday and stored it, as one official put it, "under the mattress until the office opened" the next day;[84] 90 percent of it was disbursed within 24 hours. After a number of senior UNOSOM personnel left in March 1994, however, at about the same time that US forces withdrew, daily cash balances were allowed to accumulate. On 17 April, $3.9 million was discovered missing from the locked filing cabinet that functioned as a safe in the main compound cashier's office. The money was never recovered, nor were the perpetrators apprehended. UNOSOM's director of administration assumed responsibility and tendered his resignation, which was accepted and transformed into a summary dismissal. He and the operation's former chief financial officer, who had retired from UN service in March 1994, were both found grossly negligent. An appeals tribunal found, in November 1995, that the director of administration had been wrongfully singled out for punishment and asked that the secretary-general clear his record.[85]

Planning and Implementation

Most of the detailed planning for the transition from UNITAF to UNOSOM II was done in the field, as noted earlier, and most of the initiative came from UNITAF. Many aspects of the transition, from logistics, to infantry battalion handoffs, to intelligence, operations, and psychological warfare ("Psyops") posed problems for a UN uncomfortable with the operational tasks and aggressive nomenclature of a military mission. The logistics problem was solved temporarily by assigning 3,000 US support troops to UNOSOM II. To protect them, and to support other UN units as necessary, the United States left a battalion-sized, light infantry Quick Reaction Force (QRF) in Somalia, backed by a division-sized helicopter unit (transport and attack). The United States also contributed a sixty-person Intelligence Support Element (ISE). Both the QRF and the ISE remained under US command and control (see figure 8.2, below). Because the UN has no formal, institutional system for controlling classified information and because the UN command compound was frequented by many local people, management of intelligence information was a difficult problem.

When the UN did settle in to plan and staff the new mission, it was forced by circumstances, particularly the demands of the big, ongoing operations in Cambodia and former Yugoslavia and the new operation in Mozambique, to accept offers of troops from countries that perhaps should not have been part of UNOSOM II. Italy, for example, had old colonial ties there; Nigeria had given haven to Siad Barre; and Pakistan's earlier performance in UNOSOM I did nothing to enhance its image among the inhabitants of Mogadishu.

The pull of these other missions and concerns about the security situation in Somalia cut even more deeply into civilian recruitment for the mission. By the time it formally took over from UNITAF, UNOSOM II was at little more than half of its authorized strength on the military or the civilian side, which magnified every administrative and operational problem that it faced. The UN, an organization seriously in need of reform itself, was being made to do too much that was too hard and to do it all at once.

Command and Control

To make Washington more comfortable with UNOSOM II, an American was chosen to head the mission. In February, recently retired US admiral Jonathan Howe was asked by Anthony Lake, President Clinton's National Security Advisor, to be UN SRSG in Somalia. Howe was well-known to the US government, having dealt with Somalia on the Bush administration's National Security Council staff, and he reluctantly agreed to take the job. Given a one-year appointment by the UN, Howe arrived in Mogadishu on 11 March 1993 to replace Ismat Kittani. To his credit, he spent three of his first four weeks in Somalia personally familiarizing himself with the field situation outside Mogadishu in the company of UN relief officials with more than a year's experience in the country.

Howe, former commander of a nuclear ballistic missile submarine, was a student of international relations, a man with considerable experience in the ways of the Washington bureaucracy, and extensive ties to its defense community. He was also an inveterate organizer and perhaps the right person to set up such a difficult mission. He was not, however, a diplomat given to buttonholing local elders in dusty villages or dealing equitably with mercurial faction leaders who, by conventional Western standards, had much innocent blood on their hands. In other words, he might have been an ideal deputy SRSG, whose task it usually is to handle operational matters so that the special representative is free to deal with local politics and politicians.

In the case of UNOSOM II, the tasks of deputy and chief were reversed. A relatively young Guinean diplomat, Lansana Kouyate, was appointed deputy SRSG. Kouyate headed the UN's diplomatic efforts at the two Addis Ababa peace conferences in January and March 1993. While Howe organized the UN's field mission, Kouyate helped to create the fragile political framework on which UNOSOM was to build. Soon after UNOSOM II deployed, however, political outreach to Somalia's clans and factions essentially shut down and Kouyate took leave. He was still on leave (as was Force Commander Lieutenant General Cevic Bir) when UNOSOM II first exploded.

Civilian Components. The office of the SRSG included sections for operations, planning, analysis, and justice. Other offices included Political Affairs, Humanitarian Coordination, and Public Information. Political Affairs had responsibility for implementing the reconciliation provisions of the Addis accords and overseeing creation of district and regional councils. Although UNOSOM I's political officers reportedly interacted closely with UNITAF, the political division of UNOSOM II appears not to have been actively involved in policymaking during the crucial first six months of the operation's existence.

The Office for Coordination of Humanitarian Assistance ran a Humanitarian Operations Center that hosted daily meetings of thirty to fifty international NGOs and agencies in Mogadishu, giving them updated information on the food and medical needs in the outlying areas. A parallel Civil-Military Operations Cell (CMOC) coordinated convoy support for the NGOs and briefed them daily on the security situation in various parts of the country. CMOC played a vital coordinating role between the relief providers and UNOSOM's military contingents. The military preferred to plan its escort missions several days in advance, but most NGOs were not disposed to plan ahead and the fluid security and labor situations in Somalia,

Fig. 8.2
LINES OF RESPONSIBILITY, UNOSOM II

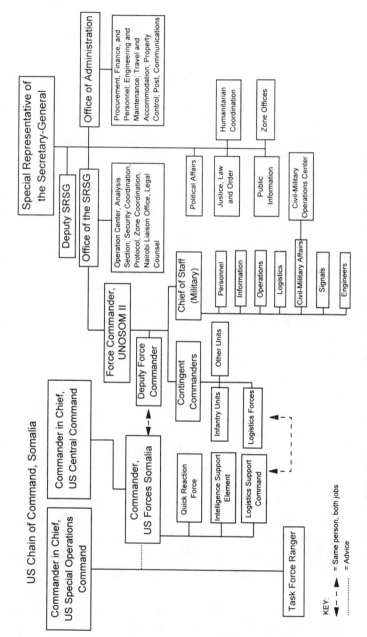

US Chain of Command, Somalia

Commander in Chief, US Special Operations Command

Commander in Chief, US Central Command

Commander, US Forces Somalia

Quick Reaction Force

Intelligence Support Element

Logistics Support Command

Task Force Ranger

Special Representative of the Secretary-General

Deputy SRSG

Office of Administration

Procurement, Finance, and Personnel; Engineering and Maintenance; Travel and Accommodation; Property Control; Post, Communications

Office of the SRSG

Operation Center, Analysis Section, Security Coordination, Protocol, Zone Coordination, Nairobi Liaison Office, Legal Counsel

Political Affairs

Justice, Law and Order

Public Information

Civil-Military Operations Center

Humanitarian Coordination

Zone Offices

Force Commander, UNOSOM II

Deputy Force Commander

Contingent Commanders

Infantry Units

Logistics Forces

Other Units

Chief of Staff (Military)

Personnel

Information

Operations

Logistics

Civil-Military Affairs

Signals

Engineers

KEY:
– – – ▲ = Same person, both jobs
▼ = Advice
·········· = Advice

SOURCES: Jarat Chopra, Åge Eknes, and Toralv Nordbo, *Fighting for Hope in Somalia* (Oslo, Norway: Norwegian Institute for International Affairs, 1995), 74-80; and UN General Assembly, *Financing of the United Nations Operation in Somalia II, Report of the Secretary-General*, A/47/916/Add.1, 29 June 1993, annex VII.

where workers and security guards were hired on a daily basis, reinforced this tendency.[86] CMOC bridged the gap.

The civilian Public Information Division held daily briefings for the press and published a daily newspaper, but most press attention was reserved for the separate military information office's daily press conference. Although Somalis were known to be avid radio listeners, often comparing news derived from several broadcasts, UNOSOM II planning did not include broadcast facilities.[87] Its initial budget allowed just $275,000 for all public information programs. It inherited a small radio station from UNITAF but its broadcasts did not reach beyond Mogadishu; additional equipment, still low-powered, arrived in late summer 1993. Despite field requests for higher-powered transmitters, UNOSOM II's budget (for the most part controlled in New York) continued to emphasize internal communications over outreach. While UNOSOM II continued to explain itself in writing to the relatively few Somalis who could read, it never did establish a presence on the airwaves that competed outside Mogadishu with Radio Mogadishu (Aideed) or the SNA-influenced broadcasts of the BBC. This inability to compete directly for the opinions of local listeners was a factor contributing to UNOSOM's decision to use military force to contest the operations of Radio Aideed.[88]

The Division of Administration handled the operation's procurement, finances, civilian personnel, engineering and maintenance tasks, ground transport and air operations, property management, postal services, and communications—representing, altogether, about half of UNOSOM II's civilian staff. Its cash flow problems were discussed earlier; its procurement difficulties were also considerable, but not much greater than in most of the newer UN operations in 1993. Some of the difficulty could be traced to UN procurement practice.

Most major purchases for UN field missions were handled through UN headquarters, which had a procurement staff of less than two dozen to support headquarters itself and field missions with 80,000 people and urgent requirements. Demand from the field to speed up the procurement process was constant (and largely justified), and bending the UN's procurement rules was, at the time, the only way to meet these demands. In mid-1993, eight procurement officers in New York were accused of improperly awarding air transport contracts on a sole-source (noncompetitive) basis to a Canadian firm, Skylink Aviation. Several procurement officers were put on suspension while an investigation (that turned up no evidence of fraud) went forward. In the meantime, other officers were afraid to sign new contracts. As a result, some of UNOSOM II's major fixed-wing aircraft (for example, a small fleet of Russian-built An-32 transports) were grounded in the fall of 1993.[89]

Military Component. The military side of UNOSOM II was unusual in that it contained two classes of forces: those that were American and all others. The non-American units were subject to the usual UN command procedures and rules of engagement. Although they came to the mission area with the usual nationally imposed limits on their freedom of action and use of force, their unit commanders all reported to the force commander of UNOSOM II. American units, on the other hand, operated differently.

Major General Thomas Montgomery, US Army, was appointed deputy force commander of UNOSOM II by the UN and, simultaneously, Commander, US Forces Somalia by US CENTCOM. The US officer in charge of the US Army logistics units that were left behind by UNITAF was at the same time commander of UNOSOM II Logistics Command and deputy commander, US Forces Somalia. The 3,000-strong US logistics unit was formally a part of the UNOSOM command structure.

The QRF was not. Rather, it was released by CENTCOM for specific operations in support of the UN, under the tactical control of Montgomery, not UN force commander Bir.[90]

In late August 1993, the United States dispatched a force of 400 US Army Rangers and Delta Force commandos to assist in the hunt for Mohamed Farah Aideed. The Rangers remained at all times under the operational and tactical control of US Central Command, exercised on-site by Major General William Garrison, commander, US Joint Special Operations Command, whose presence in Somalia was not publicly acknowledged at the time.

Thus, during the final months of the UN's war with the SNA, there were three distinct foreign military chains of command functioning in Somalia: UNOSOM II, the QRF, and Task Force Ranger. Bir had only informal say regarding the actions of the QRF, relying on Montgomery to coordinate US and UN actions. Montgomery, in turn, had a tacit veto over Ranger operations but no direct control over their actions. After the cease-fire with Aideed, the QRF merged into the much larger US Joint Task Force sent to oversee the truce, and the Rangers and Delta Force were withdrawn.

UNOSOM II consolidated UNITAF's nine Humanitarian Relief Sectors into five Areas of Responsibility (AORs). AOR Kismayo extended from Kismayo to Bardera near the Kenyan border. AOR Baidoa included Baidoa as well as Oddur and Baledogle. AOR Marka-Mogadishu included south Mogadishu and a stretch of territory southward to Kismayo. AOR Gialalassi extended from northern Mogadishu to a point 150 kilometers north of the city, where AOR Belet Weyn began and extended northward to the Ethiopian border. Altogether, these areas covered just 40 percent of Somali territory.

Initially, 27 countries contributed forces to UNOSOM II. (See table 8.1, which does not include the QRF or other US contributions not under UN command.) Most units were deployed in and around Mogadishu's port and airport or the main UN compound. All of the Western combat and support units were gone by the time the United States left in March 1994; by July of that year, just 12 countries were left in the force and two-thirds of the troops were from India and Pakistan.

Field Operations

UNOSOM II had a multiphased initial operational plan: transition from UNITAF, planned for May 1993; consolidating the nine relief sectors into five AORs, May–June; preparation for expansion into northeastern Somalia, June–August; expansion to the

Fig. 8.3

ATTACKS ON UNOSOM II, MOGADISHU, 5 JUNE THROUGH 22 OCTOBER 1993

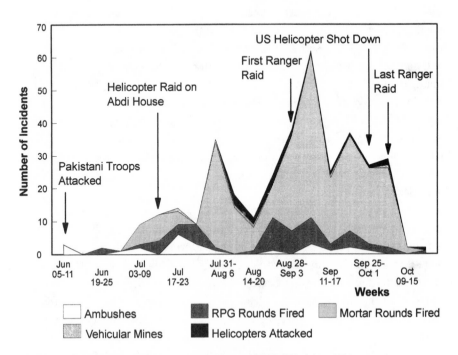

SOURCE: United Nations, *Note by the Secretary-General*, S/1994/653, 1 June 1994, annex 4.

northeast, August onward; expansion to the northwestern part of the country (schedule undeveloped); and withdrawal by March 1995. Because of its encounters with the SNA, UNOSOM II never got past the early stages of its planned third phase, and the sequence of events is better divided by time period: May–October 1993; November 1993–March 1994; and April 1994–March 1995.

May–October 1993. The 27 March 1993 Addis accords on national reconciliation that UNOSOM II chose to recognize had a number of loose ends (how to choose members of the TNC, regional councils, and district councils; the size of the regional and district councils; how to do disarmament; what kinds of training to offer to demobilizing militiamen; and how to set up the police). In most instances, the operation was to "assist" the Somalis, but in the security area it was to implement a Security Council "demand" that Somali factions disarm, to hold accountable Somalis who breached international humanitarian law, and to consolidate, expand, and maintain a "secure environment throughout Somalia."[91] So, was the task simply to be an honest broker extending a helping hand or was UNOSOM II to be an active political force and de facto trustee for the people of Somalia until the transitional political structures could reassert Somali sovereignty?[92]

Under UNITAF, the answer was "a firm helping hand," although that approach might not have been sustainable in a longer deployment. Under UNOSOM II, the public posture was a helping hand but the actions and attitudes of its top, mostly American, leadership veered toward actions consistent with trusteeship. Americans' distaste for making choices between relative evils probably contributed to a sense that the UN *ought to be* in charge because no prominent local "leader" was fit to lead. The same predisposition likely contributed to Admiral Howe's early decisions to "marginalize the warlords" and continue Kittani's arms-length style of dealing with them rather than Sahnoun's and Oakley's in-your-compound, in-your-face style.[93]

This arms-length style hobbled efforts to hold the meetings that were needed to flesh out the March 1993 Addis agreements, while the late start in transition planning meant that such political tasks took a back seat to the military transition and the effort to maintain order. When order in Mogadishu broke down one month into the operation, the political agenda was lost sight of entirely.

The run-up to the first major clash between the UN and the SNA can be interpreted in either of two ways. The first interpretation holds that General Aideed saw that the process of political reconciliation, now shepherded by the UN and his old nemesis Boutros-Ghali, was only bad news for him and the SNA and had to be stopped. Events in the spring of 1993 reinforced his intent: In the Morgan-Jess clash in Kismayo during the March Addis Ababa conference, UNITAF troops repulsed Jess's efforts to reenter the city; he failed again to dislodge Morgan from Kismayo in early May, repulsed by a Belgian contingent now operating under the UN flag. The UNOSOM Justice Division started to rebuild the Mogadishu judiciary, circumventing SNA-based judicial efforts and cutting SNA representatives out of the process. The SRSG declared the Somali Penal Code of 1962 to be the criminal law of Somalia, an extrapolation of UNOSOM's mandate to establish a secure environment, but this was a legal stretch that had UNOSOM acting like a government. UNOSOM also struggled with Aideed's people over the venue, participants, content, and management of a meeting called by Aideed to promote an alliance between his subclan and the Mijerteen of northeastern Somalia. Finally, UNOSOM instituted short-warning inspections of Aideed's declared weapons caches in Mogadishu. Because those caches had been substantially enlarged since the previous inspections by UNITAF in February, Aideed and the SNA would have expected UNOSOM's inspections to evolve rapidly into weapons seizure operations. The SNA moved to preempt them, possibly encouraged to act by the relative passivity exhibited by the UN in response to military challenges posed by the Bosnian Serbs and Cambodia's Khmer Rouge guerrillas.[94]

A second interpretation holds that Aideed "was ultimately prepared to accept the result of a democratic political process if for no other reason than because he saw himself as a natural leader [and] shrewd coalition builder."[95] Moreover, the 30 March Addis accord established a mechanism by which the SNA could wield a good deal of power on the Transitional National Council simply by moving forces into more of Somalia's regions and then claiming a say about who they nominated. UNOSOM II set this mechanism aside. In mid-May, Radio Aideed began broadcasting xenophobic diatribes accusing the UN of trying to recolonize Somalia. Soon thereafter, the Pakistani brigade of UNOSOM "was asked to draw up plans on how Radio Mogadishu could be shut down or otherwise silenced." The SNA became aware of these discussions within UNOSOM and "rumors spread within SNA circles that UNOSOM intended to seize" the station. UNOSOM's move to inspect weapons holdings that included the station seemed to confirm these rumors.[96]

UNOSOM was strongly supported in its suspicion of the SNA by the staff of the US Liaison Office (USLO), whose leadership changed hands in March 1993 as UNITAF was drawing to a close. Robert Oakley went home, replaced by Robert Gosende from the US Information Agency. With Washington's support, Gosende took a much harder line on Aideed and the SNA than had Oakley. His views coincided with Howe's, the views of Howe's mostly American "kitchen cabinet" (including senior political advisor April Glaspie), and the views of UN secretary-general Boutros-Ghali.[97]

Whether Aideed considered himself forced into a corner or planned all along to attack UN forces at an opportune time, events came to a head on 5 June 1993. On the previous day, two US Army officers serving as deputy chief of Intelligence and chief of the Cease-fire and Disarmament Division in UNOSOM II's Force Command, were authorized by Ambassador Glaspie (serving as deputy SRSG in Kouyate's absence) to give notice of impending UN weapons inspections to a representative of the SNA. At 5 P.M. on 4 June (Friday, the Islamic day of rest), they handed a letter to Mohamed Hassan Awale Qaibdid, chief of security for the SNA, that said UNOSOM would be inspecting five SNA Authorized Weapons Storage Sites the next morning. Qaibdid asked for more time to consult with his superiors, but was told the inspections would go forward, regardless. He replied that this would mean "war." The warning was passed to Major General Montgomery, then acting force commander in General Bir's absence.[98]

The inspections began early on the morning of 5 June, escorted by companies of troops from the Pakistani brigade. The Pakistanis did not expect trouble and were not told of the SNA's angry reaction to the notice of inspection the previous day; as a result, they traveled to the inspection sites in unarmored vehicles.[99]

After the troops at the radio station site completed their inspection at about 9:30 A.M., they encountered a crowd of 200 angry Somalis, but withdrew safely. About the same time, however, more than a kilometer away, another crowd of women and children with shooters behind them set upon a squad of Pakistani troops at a feeding station, killing four, severely maiming others, and taking half the squad hostage. Pakistani armored personnel carriers (APCs) sent from two directions to rescue these troops encountered roadblocks and heavy machine gun fire and withdrew. Other Pakistani-held strongpoints in the vicinity came under fire from gunmen who emerged from and then melted back into crowds of women and children. Around 11 A.M., the Pakistani brigade asked UNOSOM for armored backup from the Italian contingent.

After reportedly querying Rome for instructions, the Italians arrived at the feeding point at 4:30 P.M. to find only bodies.

A third weapons inspection team returning to base at 10:30 A.M. encountered roadblocks and heavy crossfire on 21 October Road, on the northwest edge of the city where much of the SNA militia was housed. Relief units, including members of the US Quick Reaction Force, were also subject to machine gun and rocket grenade attacks. Italian attack helicopters arrived two hours into this firefight but misperceived the ground situation and fired on Pakistani positions, wounding three troops, and were withdrawn. Altogether, on this first day of fighting, 24 Pakistani troops were killed and 57 wounded, as were 1 Italian and 3 American soldiers.

After Resolution 837 passed the Security Council, UNOSOM decided to strike back at the SNA, the assumed perpetrators of the incidents (which took place within SNA-held parts of Mogadishu). Civilian staff were evacuated or brought under the wing of the military component. Meanwhile, Aideed-controlled Radio Mogadishu alternated offers of mediation with condemnations of "wanton attacks by the UN-OSOM forces on peaceful Somali demonstrators."[100]

By 9 June, UNOSOM had been reinforced by four US AC-130H "Spectre" gunships equipped with several automatic cannon, a 105mm howitzer, and day/night vision equipment.[101] Starting at 4 A.M. on 12 June, AC-130s bombarded Radio Mogadishu and two of the weapon sites inspected on 5 June and destroyed them, while QRF troops attacked three SNA weapon sites and destroyed their contents. Over the next three days, UNOSOM's air force attacked clandestine SNA arms caches and chop shops holding about thirty "technicals," and destroyed a multi-tube barrage rocket launcher. One of two antitank missiles fired at the rocket launcher by a US Cobra helicopter gunship went astray and exploded in a civilian neighborhood, causing a dozen casualties.[102]

While these raids were underway, on 13 June, Pakistani soldiers confronted crowds of up to 3,000 Somalis, including many women and children, who converged on the Pakistanis' positions at the Kilometer 4 (K4) traffic circle on the main route from UNOSOM headquarters to the airport. Early reports had jittery troops without riot gear opening fire on an unarmed crowd, but subsequent investigation determined that militia gunmen were intermingled with the crowd and that Somali snipers positioned in cross streets near K4 also fired into the demonstrators to ensure a massacre that could be attributed to the UN. Given their experiences on 5 June, the Pakistanis were not about to let the crowd close to their positions. Human rights organizations reported at least twenty Somali dead, but how many deaths were due to UN action is not known: the UN made it a policy not to count Somali casualties. The front pages of Western newspapers the next day showed bodies scattered around K4 and blamed UNOSOM.[103]

This first phase of the war against the SNA concluded with a concerted air-ground operation on 17 June against Aideed's enclave in south Mogadishu, less than a kilometer from the main UN compound. Loudspeakers warned occupants to evacuate shortly before a 1:30 A.M. raid by the Spectre gunships. The several-square-block area was cordoned off by Moroccan and Italian UN troops while Pakistani troops conducted a weapons search. Meanwhile, armed crowds (women and children in front, militia behind) closed within 35 meters of exposed Moroccan lines and opened fire, as did militiamen positioned on nearby rooftops, including the roof of adjacent Digfer Hospital. General Aideed, escorted by a company of militiamen, was said to have slipped through the Moroccan lines while this deadly diversionary action was underway. Five Moroccan troops were killed and forty wounded in the hours-long firefight. Seven other UN troops were also wounded, including three Americans. It was to be the last large, multinational search operation conducted by UNOSOM II.[104]

Critics of UNOSOM's performance contend that, having destroyed much of Aideed's and the SNA's heavy weaponry at this point, it should either have pressed home the offensive to capture Aideed or explicitly halted operations and called for a truce, as UNITAF had done in its one major confrontation with Aideed. Instead, UNOSOM forces largely withdrew to barracks except for periodic weapons search operations, and Admiral Howe printed up and distributed a "wanted poster" that offered a $25,000 reward for information leading to the apprehension of General Aideed.

At the same time, Howe was also using back channels to the Pentagon to plead for US reinforcements. Perhaps coincidentally, on 5 June, the day of the first attacks, a team of US Army Rangers and Delta Force commandos began training for a mission in Somalia.[105]

As the struggle with the SNA continued, the process of state-building and economic rehabilitation elsewhere in Somalia stalled. Surveying the impact of the June fighting, one civilian UNOSOM advisor also noted that, "Communications within UNOSOM was nearly cut off and logistical support virtually terminated. . . . UNOSOM has inadvertently positioned itself to be held hostage by whichever faction controls" the adjacent sections of south Mogadishu.[106] With its headquarters in the heart of the inferno and most civilians shipped out of the country, UNOSOM had neither the attention span nor the staff to focus on its political reconciliation tasks.

In July, the character of the fighting in Mogadishu changed as the SNA began to take the offensive and UNOSOM's military component began to split along its national seams. Figure 8.3 illustrates the nature and tempo of SNA attacks, drawn from the report of the UN Commission of Inquiry. The increasing tempo through July, August, and September suggests rapid and substantial rearmament of SNA forces. (The count for rocket-propelled grenade attacks includes only those fired at UN installations, not those expended in general firefights.)

UNOSOM Force Command, meanwhile, was increasingly stymied by the reluctance of some contingents to implement operational orders, due to substantial differences on the parts of their governments with UNOSOM's decision to pursue Aideed. Pakistan and Italy, contributors of the two largest combat detachments in the UN force, shared major responsibility for security in Mogadishu, and both were reportedly satisfied with the level of "payback" visited upon the SNA by mid-June. In hindsight, a settlement with the SNA and the Habr Gedir at that point might have led to the appointment of a new leader, Aideed having lost face in the initial UN reprisals, which were far stronger than

Table 8.1

TROOP CONTRIBUTIONS TO UNOSOM II

Contributing Country	Unit(s) Contributed	Deployment Location(s)	Size November 1993	Size July 1994
Australia	Movement control	Mogadishu	48	55
Bangladesh	Infantry battalion	Afgoye	945	940
Belgium	Infantry battalion	Kismayo	948	---
Botswana	Infantry company	Bardera	326	420
Egypt	Infantry battalions	Mogadishu port, airport		1,665
France	Infantry battalion Logistics battalion	Oddur, Baidoa	1,107	---
Germany	Logistical units	Belet Weyn	1,726	---
Greece	Medical unit	Baidoa area	102	---
India	Infantry brigade	Baidoa, Kismayo	4,937	4,920
Ireland	Transport company	Baidoa	79	90
Italy	Infantry brigade	Belet Weyn, Gialilassi, Mogadishu	2,576	---
Korea (So.)	Engineer battalion	Mogadishu	252	---
Kuwait	Infantry company	Mogadishu	156	---
Malaysia	Infantry battalion	Mogadishu	871	955
Morocco	Infantry battalion	Brava	1,424	---
Nepal	Security company	Mogadishu	311	310
New Zealand	Supply unit	Mogadishu	43	---
Nigeria	Reconnaissance cpy.	Mogadishu, Merka	614	700
Norway	HQ company	Mogadishu	130	---
Pakistan	Infantry brigade	Mogadishu	5,005	7,055
Romania	Field hospital	Mogadishu	236	230
Saudi Arabia	Infantry battalion	Mogadishu	757	---
Sweden	Field hospital	Mogadishu	148	---
Tunisia	Infantry company	Mogadishu	142	---
Turkey	Infantry battalion	Mogadishu	320	---
UAE	Infantry battalion	Mogadishu	662	---
United States	Logistical unit	Mogadishu	3,017	---
Zimbabwe	Infantry battalion Signals company	Balad, Belet Weyn	958	900

SOURCES: Security Council, *Further Report of the Secretary-General Submitted in Pursuance of Paragraph 19 of Resolution 814 (1993) and Paragraph 5 of Resolution 865 (1993)*, S/26738, 12 November 1993, 12; Security Council, *Further Report of the Secretary General on the United Nations Operation in Somalia Submitted in Pursuance of Paragraph 2 of Security Council Resolution 923 (1994)*, S/1994/839, 18 July 1994, 8.

anything ventured by UN forces in Cambodia or the former Yugoslavia up to that time. But the United States was not satisfied with the level of payback and neither was the secretary-general, so the hunt continued and escalated.[107]

The Pakistani brigade, after taking more casualties in a late June weapons search, hunkered down to await delivery of armored vehicles. The Italian brigade commander, Brigadier General Bruno Loi, objected to UNOSOM's aggressive tactics and began to conduct (with support from Rome) his own, less-aggressive operation-within-an-operation, intended to show UNOSOM how experts dealt with Somalis.[108] The limits of the Italians' approach were demonstrated when they, too, were ambushed by the SNA during a weapons search on 2 July, suffering three dead and thirty wounded. A Force Command decision to "teach the SNA a lesson" on this occasion was frustrated, however, when the Italian contingent broke off the engagement and abandoned an adjacent UN strongpoint minutes before UN air support could be deployed. Loi further angered Force Command a week later by negotiating with the SNA for the contingent's unhampered return to the abandoned strongpoint in exchange for a promise not to conduct any more weapon searches in the area.[109]

Without the active cooperation of the Pakistani and Italian contingents, UNOSOM had to rely increasingly on the QRF for offensive operations in Mogadishu but the QRF, drawn from a light infantry division, had no armor. It did, however, have helicopters.

On 12 July 1993, helicopter gunships from the QRF staged a no-warning attack on an SNA headquarters where a meeting of top Aideed lieutenants was believed to be underway. Eleven TOW antitank missiles were launched at the so-called "Abdi House," first demolishing stairways, then the upstairs meeting area. The helicopter attack was followed up by QRF troops. The estimated number of Somali casualties in the raid varies from 20 (UNOSOM) to 215 (International Committee of the Red Cross[ICRC]). Crowds around Abdi House killed four international journalists who tried to cover the aftermath of the attack.[110]

The 12 July attack was a turning point for UNOSOM II. Italy threatened to withdraw completely from the force. The SNA escalated its attacks on the UN, targeting Americans in particular. Mortars, first used 6 July, were used extensively starting in early August. Use of command-detonated anti-vehicle mines also started in early August; on 8 August one of these killed four US soldiers.

That incident and a similar attack on 22 August led President Clinton to finally answer Howe's repeated requests and to dispatch the Rangers and the Delta Force, whose lead elements arrived in Mogadishu on 26 August. Over the next month, "Task Force Ranger" made six raids and captured a number of Aideed lieutenants, including financier Osman Atto.

While the Delta Force was conducting its independent mission, UNOSOM II continued to cope with the situation on the ground and inter-unit relations continued to be dysfunctional. Early on the morning of 5 September, a Nigerian company moved to replace Italian forces at UN Strongpoint 42 at the "Pasta Factory" in northeast Mogadishu (scene of the 2 July ambush of Italian troops). They were met by a crowd of Somalis and an elder who demanded that they negotiate permission to deploy, as the Italians had. This being the first that the Nigerians had heard about such a thing, the company commander demurred. The elder is said to have replied, "The Nigerian troops will see," and Somali gunmen opened fire. Nigerian reinforcements were discouraged from deploying by the Italian contingent, whose officers were said to be trying to calm the crowds at the Pasta Factory. The relief column pushed on nonetheless and was ambushed 500 meters short of its objective, with seven killed and eight wounded in a two-and-a-half hour engagement. The Nigerians charged that the Italian troops had failed to come to their assistance; the Italians claimed that they had failed to hear of the ambush, owing to differing radio networks.[111]

Four days later, Pakistani troops with tanks, APCs, and a bulldozer moved to clear roadblocks off 21 October Road, near one of the original 5 June ambush sites. Somali gunmen fired 106mm recoilless rifles to disable one tank, while men, women, and children hurled grenades. The tanks returned fire over several hours while two QRF helicopter gunships provided supporting fire, in the UN's heaviest single engagement in nearly three months. The SNA's tactic of mixing male fighters using firearms with women and children armed with grenades resulted in scores of dead and wounded Somalis who, having thrown their weapons at UN troops, appeared never to have been armed. The SNA's charge that the QRF fired on civilians thus could not easily be disproved, and given UNOSOM's policy of not counting Somali casualties, the UN was not able to challenge SNA casualty figures either.[112]

Task Force Ranger undertook its seventh assault on the afternoon of 3 October. The raid secured its objective—the capture of 24 SNA officials—and was about to bundle them back to Mogadishu airport by road when one of the supporting Special Operations transport helicopters was hit by a rocket-propelled grenade (RPG) and crashed.[113] Twenty minutes later, a second helicopter was hit and crashed.

At the first crash site, six of the eight crewmen and commandos survived. Two were scooped up by a Delta Force "Little Bird" helicopter, and a Blackhawk dropped a 15-man combat search and rescue team. Ranger ground forces also converged on the crash site, but took heavy casualties enroute. They remained there, supported and resupplied by air, until a relief column reached them early the next morning.

The third attempted relief effort was successful. The QRF tried twice to reach the crash sites in its relatively thin-skinned vehicles, but both efforts were ambushed and withdrew after heavy fighting. The final effort took five hours to organize and used APCs of the Malaysian contingent and some older tanks acquired from Turkey and operated by the Pakistanis. Both contingents immediately agreed to help with the rescue mission when asked to do so by Force Command, without consulting home governments. Neither contingent deployed night vision devices, however, and it was nearly midnight before the rescue mission was finally launched.[114] QRF troops disembarked from the Malaysian APCs about half a kilometer from the two crash sites and fought their way to the sites through heavy Somali fire, each soldier expending, on average, more than 1,000 rounds of ammunition over two hours.[115] The relief force reached the first crash site and its defenders around 2 A.M.; the body of the pilot pinned in the wreckage was freed some hours later and the entire force withdrew. At the second crash site, the rescuers found no survivors. Two Delta Force commandos who were landed at the crash site by helicopter received the Congressional Medal of Honor, posthumously, for giving their lives to defend the surviving pilot, Warrant Officer Michael Durant, who was captured and held hostage by the SNA for 11 days.

On 6 October, President Clinton announced that US troops would withdraw from Somalia, not immediately but in six months, and would be substantially reinforced with heavy armor in the meantime. Initially, the SNA worried that it had pressed the United States too hard and invited condign retaliation. Having taken over 1,000 casualties itself and expended large quantities of ammunition on the night of 3-4 October, the SNA was substantially weakened and potentially vulnerable and holding Durant as a hedge. Ambassador Robert Oakley and Major General Anthony Zinni returned to Somalia on 9 October to stress that the Clinton administration would not be cutting any deals for Durant's freedom. Habr Gedir clan elders convinced Aideed to release Durant to the ICRC on 14 October.[116]

When the newly arriving US forces did not take up the chase, it became clear that the SNA's battle with US forces was over. The main US objective in Somalia had become self-protection until departure.[117]

6 October 1993–March 1994. At UNOSOM II headquarters in early November there was no newfound liking for Aideed, and UN officials made an effort to behave as though the operation was back on track and moving forward. When US forces stood down, however, the other UN military contingents in Mogadishu stood down as well. Although UNOSOM's mandate under Resolution 837 had not yet been revoked, it could no longer be implemented. In Mogadishu, the operation closed in on itself, reinforcing the main walled compound, shell-proofing its prefabricated housing and administrative offices (recently acquired from the finished UN operation in Cambodia), and completing water and sewer lines. UNOSOM was digging in, completing the fort that it had needed the previous June. *Washington Post* reporter Rick Atkinson caught the Twilight Zone quality of the result:

> The World Inside the Walls is an 80-acre replica of America, a world of reserved parking, take-out pizza and manicured flower gardens. It is a world with street signs and shuttle buses and great rock-and-roll. . . . The World Outside the Walls . . . is very different. There is no electric power, no telephone network, no sewer system. There is no law, no order. . . . When it rains, the World Outside reeks with a charnel house stink because so many dead have been buried in shallow graves. [It] is chaos masquerading as a city, a Hieronymus Bosch painting of the Horn of Africa.[118]

In late November, when Atkinson wrote his piece, the situation outside of Mogadishu was still relatively stable, but when the UN gave up on "Mog" and the Western contingents packed up to leave, UN operations upcountry began to unravel as well. The departure of Western combat units and logistics caused both a real and a perceived degradation in the outsiders' power to affect events in Somalia, as had the transition from UNITAF to UNOSOM II. Along with these units went their governments' political engagement. The units that replaced them—the Indian brigade, Egyptian battalion, and additional Pakistani forces—tried to take a more conciliatory approach to Somalia and its factions. They found that the country's victims, like the farmers of the Rahanweyn clan in and around Baidoa, welcomed their efforts but that the bandit gangs and the more predatory subclans did not.

Indian troops were attacked with machine guns and mortars at an outpost 100 kilometers northwest of Kismayo one day after taking over the AOR from the Belgian contingent.[119]

As UNOSOM II drew in its horns, attacks on aid providers increased. In early January 1994, UN relief agencies evacuated offices in Mogadishu under threat of fire bombing; gunmen attacked the World Food Program (WFP) compound in Baidoa; and WFP offices in Bardera closed after staff were beaten. In February, grenade attacks drove aid workers out of Belet Weyn as German and Italian peacekeepers departed without replacement, and Morgan-Jess fighting resumed in Kismayo.[120]

UN efforts to encourage political reconciliation continued amidst the decaying security situation. UNOSOM sponsored a humanitarian aid conference in Addis Ababa in November 1993 at which Somali factions were warned by their host, Ethiopian president Meles Zenawi, and by international donors that the outside world had to see genuine political progress or it would cease its assistance. A political reconciliation conference promptly followed. Oakley caused a stir by flying Aideed to this conference in a US military VIP aircraft (since Aideed did not trust the UN); but the political meeting fizzled and the United States did not offer him a return flight. Other conferences were held in Nairobi and inside Somalia itself, and new agreements were signed and pledges made, but with little tangible effect.[121]

US forces quietly left Somalia in small detachments over a period of weeks in February–March 1994. By 25 March, just fifty Marines were left to guard a reduced US Liaison Office.[122]

April 1994–March 1995. To bolster UN forces after US troops departed, the United States leased to the UN thirty M-60A3 tanks, eighty M-113 APCs, and eight AH-1S Cobra antitank helicopter gunships. The tanks and helicopters came from National Guard stocks and National Guard teams went to Somalia to train Pakistani tankers and pilots. The UN paid $40 million for the lease. Pakistan's foreign minister complained that his country was being lent second-line equipment.[123]

After US forces withdrew, Somali looters began to work over Mogadishu's port and airport, brushing past guards from the Egyptian battalion. To stop the looters meant antagonizing their clans and the clans' militias and reigniting combat, which the new leadership of UNOSOM II did not wish to do, although some UN forces continued to respond to direct attacks.[124]

Such attacks escalated through 1994, mostly in SNA-controlled areas. Five Nepalese UN soldiers were killed in May when their convoy was attacked in south Mogadishu. Two Malaysian soldiers were killed and four others wounded in a similar ambush in mid-July. The Zimbabwean company deployed in Belet Weyn was overrun and stripped of its weapons, equipment, and uniforms in late July. An Indian army convoy was ambushed in southern Somalia on 22 August, suffering seven dead and nine wounded. A week later, a rifle grenade exploded inside the Indian-run hospital at Baidoa and three Indian doctors were killed.[125] At about the same time, the Indian brigade announced in Kismayo that it would no longer provide security for NGOs; General Morgan's militia promptly declared that the going rate for security guards would be $300 per day (the NGOs left Kismayo). On 9 September, the Zimbabwean contingent at Balad, north of Mogadishu, was surrounded by militia "technicals" and asked to surrender all of its equipment. This time, the Zimbabweans managed to drive off their attackers and withdraw with their equipment intact. Their camp was looted of anything else moveable immediately upon their departure.[126]

By May 1994, the UN had settled on March 1995 as the termination date for UNOSOM II. (That had been the planned withdrawal date all along but initial assumptions were that a new Somali government would be capable of maintaining at least minimal order by then.) The UN began to shrink its area of operations and its troop levels. By the end of September it had withdrawn from Bardera, Balad, and Belet Weyn and repatriated units from Botswana, Ireland, Romania, and one battalion from Pakistan. By the end of October, the Nepalese and Nigerians had left, and UNOSOM had an effective presence only in Baidoa, Kismayo, and north Mogadishu. Indian troops withdrew from Baidoa in late November and from Kismayo in early December, and departed Somalia entirely by the end of the month. On 6 December, Bangladeshi troops had to fight their way out of Afgoye, a town just west of Mogadishu, under cover of UN armored vehicles and helicopter gunships after militiamen blocked their withdrawal, demanding "back rent" for the two years of UN presence.[127]

By mid-January, all civilian UN staff in Mogadishu had been withdrawn from the main compound and relocated to the airport. A Pakistani battalion covered the removal of high-value equipment. When it fell back to the airport two weeks later, SNA militia quickly occupied the compound, which was shortly stripped once again of its windows, wiring, and anything else of value. When the Pakistanis pulled back from the airport at the end of February, enroute to leaving Somalia, airport facilities were gutted as well.[128]

By then, a US Marine evacuation force led by now Lieutenant General Anthony Zinni had arrived off Mogadishu and some 1,800 Marines had rolled ashore to cover, along with US Special Forces soldiers, UNOSOM's final withdrawal. After 73 hours ashore, and after waiting for the ship carrying the last Pakistani troops to clear Mogadishu harbor, US troops reboarded their vehicles and headed for home.[129]

Assessment of UNOSOM II

In Somalia, the UN was dealt a poor hand at a time when the organization knew that it was stretched as thin as paper. UNOSOM II was a quasi-enforcement operation assigned to an organization with no experience at doing law enforcement, let alone urban guerrilla warfare. All the normal problems of command and control experienced by a peacekeeping operation in calmer circumstances (lack of doctrine, nonstandard equipment and operating procedures, national checks on contingents' freedom to follow UN orders) were magnified by UNOSOM II's ambitious mandate and dangerous operating environment. Although Boutros-Ghali's deliberate delay of the UNITAF-UNOSOM transition contributed to UNOSOM's subsequent difficulties, his fears for the UN's ability to do the job were amply justified. The United States worried about getting bogged down in this place: Why should it have expected the United Nations to do any better?

Appointing an American to head the mission was not necessarily a bad idea but once it was done the operation became an American show; that is, it heavily reflected American culture and morality, which mix can-do pragmatism with a penchant for pigeonholing people as "white hats" or "black hats," allies or enemies. The Americans appointed to lead and support UNOSOM II were in that sense typical, but they were working in a country where alignments were complex and fluid and all the hats were dirty-gray, and they lacked the wheedling temperament needed to beat the local faction leaders at their own political-military game.

UNOSOM II's leadership misjudged the capacities of its adversaries and of its own forces, as well as the utility of US reinforcements. Events before, during, and after UNOSOM II suggested that General Aideed intended to be president of Somalia or, as one interviewee in Mogadishu put it, "die trying," yet UNOSOM II began to act against Aideed's interests seemingly without weighing the potential consequences, as though the moral authority of the United Nations carried weight enough. It acted like a strong organization before it was strong and asserted control that it could not maintain. In every previous UN-commanded field operation, success has depended on a high degree of local support for what the UN was trying to do, because no such operation has ever been strong enough to impose its will(s). What UNOSOM II had was not the support but the calculated compliance of most armed Somali factions, and not even that much from the strongest faction.

In these circumstances UNOSOM II had three potentially viable options: serve as honest broker among *the factions* (as opposed to Somali society at large); openly side with a faction or factions; or get out fast. Instead, it chose to function as arbiter of Somali politics and champion of the disempowered "Somali people," that is, as a kind of super-clan. UNOSOM II may have thought that it was merely impartially implementing the plan drawn up at the factions' March 1993 Addis meeting, but choosing to implement one version of that plan over the other put UNOSOM on a course to *supplant,* rather than accommodate, the factions (which is what many aid providers and human rights advocates wanted). In this effort, no faction was UNOSOM's ally as all stood to lose out to the political structures that UNOSOM was trying to build in the towns and villages of Somalia, unless those structures could be co-opted or hijacked. Thus clans and factions in contested areas battled for the privilege of nominating the members of district and regional councils, occasionally causing dozens of casualties; in fought-over towns like Kismayo, council-building was never really begun.[130]

The cost to the UN of occupying the moral high ground was substantial and would not have dropped appreciably had Aideed been apprehended, since it would have still had to deal with the Habr Gedir, and after them, the next most powerful Somali group, and then the next, all in the name of a "people," most of whom identified more strongly with one or another of these groups than with the concept of "Somalia."[131] There was, quite literally, not enough patience or money in the world for UNOSOM to have completed this task: a culture that developed over centuries and decayed over decades could not be reshaped in two years, especially to suit a political outcome that was "not invented here."

CONCLUSIONS

Perhaps vigorous, earlier intervention in Somalia by the UN or some other outside agency, seizing one of Sahnoun's lost opportunities, might have saved many lives. Perhaps earlier intervention in other preconflict situations could save lives as well, but recognizing appropriate opportunities ahead of time is not that easy. The current system is crisis-driven for a reason: situations in which lots of people *could* die, but are not dying yet, are not far above the norm for badly run countries, so situations in which lots of people *did* die usually look like candidates for early intervention only in retrospect. We can backtrack events to the point where action should have been taken in such instances, but without a convenient parallel universe in which to experiment with crisis prevention measures, it will always be difficult to know when early intervention might have made a difference. Moreover, because successful crisis prevention creates a self-denying prophecy (if it works, nothing happens), it is difficult to separate instances where prevention has worked from instances in which it was unnecessary. It is also difficult to convince people that they have a problem and need outside help to solve it when they do not see or will not acknowledge the problem, when they are not exercised about it, or when they think they can handle it.

Rather than draw lessons for preventive diplomacy from what was *not* done by the US/UN operations in Somalia, let us draw a few lessons for future interventions from what *was* done. The first lesson would be not to intervene in unstable countries without serious and sustained major power attention and backup. Second, pick a politically savvy mission head to handle local politics and diplomacy and to maintain contact with the major supporting powers. Give him or her a deputy to handle organizational and operational issues (a model followed in Cambodia and, belatedly, in Mozambique). Third, develop agreement on means and ends among troop contributing countries prior to deployment and consult with them regularly over the course of the operation. Fourth, do not push local parties beyond the mission's own capacity to defend itself or its capacity to sustain the push. Fifth, if the situation is so egregious that general conflict suppression is called for, do not run the operation through the UN: deputize a major power to serve as leader of a coalition. Sixth, if the coalition plans to hand responsibility for a diminished but not extinguished conflict to the UN, make sure UN planners and monitors are in on coalition operations from day one (a practice followed with good results in the US/UN operations in Haiti). And, seventh, make sure that coalition leaders are fully aware of both the capabilities and the shortcomings of UN-led missions. Had UNITAF fully appreciated the limitations of the UN operation to which it was handing over responsibility, it might have done much more to confiscate heavy weapons and to watch for replacements coming into the country.

Generally speaking, the United Nations has had the best luck with remedial operations, with efforts to restart polities after wars have burned themselves out and the former combatants need a hand up, outsiders need an escort to the border, and local politicians need an honest broker to count the ballots. Such operations do not stop famines or suppress civil wars, yet they are useful to the countries that need them and sometimes necessary to cement a peace. We should not discount their value, or the UN's ability to conduct them, because the organization failed in an impossible mission to make Somalia nice.

NOTES

1. Ahmed I. Samatar, "The Curse of Allah: Civic Disembowelment and the Collapse of the State in Somalia," in A. I. Samatar, ed., *The Somali Challenge: From Catastrophe to Renewal?* (Boulder, Colo.: Lynne Rienner Publishers, 1994), 109-111; and Terrence Lyons and Ahmed I. Samatar, *Somalia: State Collapse, Multilateral Intervention, and Strategies for Political Reconstruction,* Brookings Occasional Paper (Washington, D.C.: The Brookings Institution, 1995), 8-10.

2. Somali herders had not occupied that stretch of territory for long, however, having only crossed west of the Jubba River in the 1860s. Ken Menkhaus, "The Historical Roots of the Current Crisis: Patterns of Settlement and Displacement," UNOSOM "Lower Jubba Strategy" Briefing Paper No. 1 (Mogadishu, Somalia: July 1993), 2. (Mimeograph.)

3. Lyons and Samatar, *Somalia: State Collapse,* 11.

4. Samatar, "The Curse of Allah," 113-115; Lyons and Samatar, *Somalia: State Collapse,* 12-15. As Hirsch and Oakley note, the colonial heritage also played a role in democracy's early difficulties: "[N]either colonial power had prepared the country for self-government. Civil administrations in the north and south had inherited different European languages, cultures, and administrative structures from the colonial period. With no cohesive, trained civil service, and no accepted political norms, individual rivalries for power quickly took their toll." See John L. Hirsch and Robert B. Oakley, *Somalia and Operation Restore Hope: Reflections on Peacemaking and Peacekeeping* (Washington, D.C.: US Institute of Peace, 1995), 5.

5. Colin Legum, "Angola and the Horn of Africa," in Stephen S. Kaplan, ed., *Diplomacy of Power: Soviet Armed Forces as a Political Instrument,* (Washington, D.C.: The Brookings Institution, 1981), 610-611.

6. Ibid., 616-618.

7. Hirsch and Oakley, *Somalia and Operation Restore Hope,* 8; Lyons and Samatar, *Somalia: State Collapse,* 19; and Jarat Chopra, Åge Eknes, and Toralv Nordbo, *Fighting for Hope in Somalia,* Peacekeeping and Multinational Operations no. 6 (Oslo: Norwegian Institute of International Relations, UN Programme, 1995), 24-25.

8. Jane Perlez, "Report for US Says Somali Army Killed 5,000 Unarmed Civilians," *New York Times* (hereafter *NYT*), 9 September 1989, 1. In this article, an anonymous State Department official assessed Somalia to be in a state of "disintegration," but even so,

"still important to our interests" as a potential staging area for troops enroute to the Persian Gulf. However, the United States cut military aid to Somalia.

9. Neil Henry, "Rebels, Rights Groups Attack Somalia," *Washington Post* (hereafter *WP*), 18 February 1990, A23.

10. Lyons and Samatar, *Somalia: State Collapse,* viii; Samatar, "The Curse of Allah," 118.

11. Lyons and Samatar, *Somalia: State Collapse,* 20-21; Walter S. Clarke, *Somalia: Background Information for Operation Restore Hope,* SSI Special Report (Carlisle, Pa.: US Army War College, Strategic Studies Institute, December 1992), 30.

12. Helicopters carrying US Marines trained in special operations lifted off the amphibious assault ships USS *Guam* and USS *Trenton,* enroute to Somalia, sooner than planned because the embassy came under rocket attack. The rescue force was refueled twice in mid-air by US tanker aircraft flown down from Bahrain, more than 2,000 kilometers to the north. The tightly choreographed mission was completed without loss of life. Jane Perlez, "US and Italy Evacuating Foreigners in Somalia," *NYT,* 6 January 1991, A3; and R. Jeffrey Smith and Barton Gellman, "Daring Marine Helicopter Mission Rescued Foreigners from Somalia," *WP,* 9 January 1991, 8.

13. Although both men belonged to the Hawiye clan, Ali Mahdi belonged to the Abgal subclan and Aideed to the Habr Gedir subclan and thus represented different interests within the Hawiye and the United Somali Congress.

14. Clarke, *Background Information,* 33-34.

15. Ibid.; Hirsch and Oakley, *Somalia and Operation Restore Hope,* 15.

16. *Qat* is a popular stimulant of limited shelf life flown in daily from high-altitude growing areas in Kenya. The *qat* trade flourished throughout the conflict, and the urge for a daily dose of the stimulant drug also stimulated looting. See Jane Perlez, "Guns, Greed, and Khat [sic] Define Once-Graceful Somali City," *NYT,* 7 December 1992, A1.)

17. The copper in the city's electrical wiring and plumbing, for example, had been looted and sold for scrap.

18. Jane Perlez, "Factional Fighting in Somalia Terrorizes and Ruins Capital," *WP,* 8 December 1991, 1. The renewed fighting killed perhaps 30,000 people and drove at least 300,000 more into exile, this time to northern Kenya, itself seared by the drought then afflicting all of East Africa. "Fighting in Somali Capital Described as 'Murderous,'" *WP,* 22 November 1991, 36; and Keith B. Richburg, "Somalis Bring Refugee Crisis to Kenya," *WP,* 7 February 1992, A22. Although most analysts credit Aideed with far superior forces, he was never able to oust Ali Mahdi from north Mogadishu; perhaps too large a fraction of Aideed's militia was needed to keep Morgan at bay in the south, but wire services suggested that no more than one-fifth of the 20,000 fighters in Mogadishu were under an organization's control. Jane Perlez, "Somali Refugees Find Little Relief at Kenya Camp," *NYT,* 16 February 1992, 8. These gangs of *mooryaan* were strictly out for booty. Lyons and Samatar, *Somalia: State Collapse,* 22.

19. Lyons and Samatar, *Somalia: State Collapse,* 22. Populations outside the main towns were beset by the *mooryaan,* who looted property, including well pumps at oases, leaving livestock to die. Although the rains resumed in 1992, farmers had been

pushed off their lands either by such apolitical terror or by one or another militia. Jane Perlez, "Food Relief Grows but So Do Somalia's Dead," *NYT*, 19 July 1992, 8. Private relief providers hired some of these fighters at extortionate rates to safeguard their convoys. Lacking budget lines for "armed thugs to protect food shipments," agencies wrote off the cost to "technical assistance." Hence, Somalia's Road Warrior vehicles came to be known as "technicals."

20. Security Council Resolution 733, 23 January 1992; and Security Council, *The Situation in Somalia: Report of the Secretary-General*, S/23693, 11 March 1992, 1-9.

21. The initial cease-fire, signed by representatives of the two factions in New York on 14 February 1992, pledged "an immediate and effective cessation of hostilities and the maintenance of a cease-fire." But it did not specify where, when, or with respect to what opponent(s) the cease-fire would apply. Signatories represented the "Interim Government of Somalia" and the Central Committee of the United Somali Congress. That left a substantial number of political players and a substantial fraction of Somali territory unaffected. Security Council, S/23693, annex I.

22. Jonathan Stevenson, "Hope Restored in Somalia?" *Foreign Policy* 91 (summer 1993): 144-45.

23. *The United Nations and the Situation in Somalia*, Reference Paper DPI/1321/Rev.4 (New York: United Nations Department of Public Information, April 1995), 3. The vanguard of the Pakistani battalion was flown into Mogadishu by US Air Force Reserve and Air National Guard aircraft. "First US Troops Land in Somalia," *WP*, 15 September 1992, 12; and "2,400 US Marines Dispatched to Somalia," *NYT*, 17 September 1992, A16.

24. Mohamed Sahnoun, *Somalia, The Missed Opportunities* (Washington, D.C.: United States Institute of Peace, 1994), 38-39.

25. Clarke, *Background Information*, 13.

26. Chopra, Eknes, and Nordbo quote an interview with Aideed, conducted 20 February 1994, in which he contended that US-led intervention was preferable to a UN operation because the United States was not expected to "have colonial interests in Somalia." (*Fighting for Hope in Somalia*, 38.) Hirsch and Oakley confirm the bad blood between Aideed and Boutros-Ghali and the secretary-general's first envoy to Somalia, James Jonah. (*Somalia and Operation Restore Hope*, 19-20.)

27. Chopra, et al., *Fighting for Hope in Somalia*, 33. Sahnoun recounts that the same planes (or at least the same *types* of planes) making clandestine deliveries to Ali Mahdi also continued to bring UN VIPs into Mogadishu. (Sahnoun, *The Missed Opportunities*, 39.) The UN leases many An-32s, however, and unless Sahnoun was keeping track of tail numbers, there would be no way of knowing whether the VIP aircraft were also "freelancing" while still under UN contract.

28. Sahnoun, *The Missed Opportunities*, 40-41; Hirsch and Oakley, *Somalia and Operation Restore Hope*, 30-31; and Chopra, et al., *Fighting for Hope in Somalia*, 33. Although head of UNOSOM I, Sahnoun had no power over UN relief agencies in Somalia, much less private providers. His lack of authority to orchestrate diplomacy, relief, and security aspects of his mission contributed significantly to his frustration.

29. Hirsch and Oakley, *Somalia and Operation Restore Hope,* 32; and Lyons and Samatar, *Somalia: State Collapse,* 34-35.

30. Paul Lewis, "Reined in by US, UN Limits Mission to Somalia," *NYT,* 26 April 1992, 15; Jane Perlez, "Warring Factions' Agreement May Allow More Food Aid," *NYT,* 20 July 1992, A3; and Martin Sieff, "34 US Troops Fly to Kenya to Prepare for Somalia Airlift," *Washington Times,* 18 August 1992, 9.

31. Jane Perlez, "US Says Airlifts Fail Somali Needy," *NYT,* 31 July 1992, A9.

32. The airlift was announced, coincidentally, three days before the opening of the 1992 Republican National Convention. Ultimately, "Provide Relief" used a dozen cargo aircraft to fly in 28,000 metric tons of relief supplies to interior airfields of southern and central Somalia. See Kenneth Allard, *Somalia Operations: Lessons Learned* (Washington, D.C.: National Defense University, Institute for National Strategic Studies, January 1995), 14-15.

33. The food warehouse at the first destination of Operation Provide Relief, Belet Weyn, was looted on 21 September of all 870 tons of food that supplied 23 International Committee Red Cross (ICRC) feeding centers in the area by a subclan that felt cut out of the food distribution business. On the same day, gunfights broke out at the operation's second destination, Baidoa. Seasonal rains, breaking the long regional drought, also disrupted flights. In mid-October, Morgan's forces drove Aideed and the Somali National Alliance (SNA) out of Bardera, near the border with Kenya, and looted 800 of 1,000 tons of relief supplies as relief workers fled the area; local death rates soared. Aideed moved his headquarters to Mogadishu. Michael A. Hiltzik, "Gunfire, Thefts, Rains Crippling Somali Airlifts," *Los Angeles Times,* 23 September 1992, 1; and Jane Perlez, "UN Somalia Envoy Dismayed Over Aid," *NYT,* 13 November 1992, A5. To reduce the "currency" value of relief, the Red Cross preferred to distribute cooked food at feeding centers, rather than dry foodstuffs. As one report noted, "About half the dry food is lost to looters but cooked food . . . nearly always gets through." "The Map of Hunger," *The Economist,* 15 August 1992, 32. Another notion was to devalue food as a currency by making it abundant. This market-based approach proposed to sell relief at low prices to merchants who could resell it at "controlled and monitored prices inside the country." How proponents planned to control prices in a war zone while lacking any powers of enforcement is not clear. See Jane Perlez, "Theft of Food Aid Is a Business in Starving Somalia," *NYT,* 4 September 1992, A1.

34. Keith B. Richburg, "Somali Aid May Spur New Violence," *WP,* 26 September 1992, 1; and Jane Perlez, "Thievery and Extortion Halt Flow of UN Food to Somalis," *NYT,* 2 December 1992, A1. Fred Cuny, a consultant to the US Agency for International Development, claimed that a $1 million ICRC payment in mid-July 1991 to Aideed financier Osman Hasssan Ali ("Atto") for port security and cargo handling was mirrored by a request, a few days later for an "equivalent amount" of arms in Lisbon. Robert M. Press, "Somali Civil War is Fueled by Huge Stockpiles of Weapons," *Christian Science Monitor,* 14 October 1992, 1.

35. White House, "Address by President George Bush to the United Nations General Assembly," 21 September 1992, *Weekly Compilation of Presidential Documents* 28, no. 39 (1992): 1697.

36. Criticism to this effect tended to surface after the election. Press reports indicated that the United States was negotiating with private contractors to take over Provide Relief's routes. Liz Sly, "US Plans to Hand Off its Somalian Airlift," *Philadelphia Inquirer,* 12 November 1992, 11.

37. Don Oberdorfer, "The Path to Intervention," *WP,* 6 December 1992, A1, A36.

38. Ibid.; and Hirsch and Oakley, *Somalia and Operation Restore Hope,* 40-43.

39. Security Council Resolution 794, 3 December 1992, operative para. 10.

40. "Troops in Somalia: How Americans React," *NYT/*CBS News Poll of 1,333 adults, conducted 7-9 December 1992, *NYT,* 13 December 1992, 16.

41. "Bush's Talk on Somalia: US Must 'Do It Right'" (transcript of Bush's address), *NYT,* 5 December 1992, 4.

42. Elaine Sciolino, "UN Wants Somalia Disarmed before US Leaves," *NYT,* 11 December 1992, A23; and Security Council, *The Situation in Somalia: Report of the Secretary-General,* S/24992, 19 December 1992, 7-8. Boutros-Ghali set three conditions for transition: international control of the heavy weapons of each political faction; disarming of "lawless gangs"; and creation of a new, professional police force.

43. UN General Assembly, *Financing the Costs of the United Nations Operation in Somalia II, Report of the Secretary-General,* A/48/850, 19 January 1994, 9.

44. United States General Accounting Office (GAO), *Peace Operations: Cost of DOD Operations in Somalia,* GAO/NSIAD-94-88 (Washington, D.C.: GAO, March 1994), 4.

45. David J. Zvijac and Katherine A. W. McGrady, *Operation Restore Hope: Summary Report,* CRM 93-152 (Alexandria, Va.: Center for Naval Analyses, March 1994), 35-38. The US military's "unified commands," which operate US forces in the field, divide their responsibilities geographically; Central Command (CENTCOM) has responsibility for the Middle East, Persian Gulf, and the Horn of Africa.

46. This discussion is based on Jonathan T. Dworken, *Operation Restore Hope: Preparing and Planning the Transition to UN Operations,* CRM 93-148 (Alexandria, Va.: Center for Naval Analyses, March 1994), 7-10.

47. Keith B. Richburg and William Claiborne, "Navy, Marines Begin Landing in Somalia," *WP,* 9 December 1992, 1; and Hirsch and Oakley, *Somalia and Operation Restore Hope,* 55-60, 69-70. Given later events, it is interesting to note that, at this juncture, General Aideed was pointedly helpful to US forces, suggesting that, to make deployments into the hinterland go more smoothly, UNITAF forces always give clans advance warning of their approach and bring food along with them, so that they were not seen by locals as just another marauding band. Author's interview, command-level participant in Restore Hope, 5 April 1994.

48. Michael R. Gordon, "TV Army on the Beach Took US by Surprise," and Alan Riding, "French Fault 'Circus' Coverage of US Arrival," *NYT,* 10 December 1992, A18.

49. Hirsch and Oakley, *Somalia and Operation Restore Hope*, 65-67; Zvijac and McGrady, *Summary Report*, 42-43; and Lieutenant Colonel T. A. Richards, USMC, "Marines in Somalia," *US Naval Institute Proceedings*, May 1993, 133-6. The airlift of troops and supplies into Somalia relied heavily on regional refueling stops and access to air space. American cargo aircraft used airfields near Cairo, Egypt, and Jiddah, Saudi Arabia, as well as Ethiopia, Djibouti, Yemen, and Oman. Transports flying from the eastern United States required two or more refuelings and a change of crew to reach Mogadishu; those leaving from the west coast required three refuelings and a crew change. Michael R. Gordon, "African and Mideast Bases Aid Somalia Airlift," *NYT*, 18 December 1992, A9.

50. This meeting had been planned for some months, and diplomatic groundwork for it had been laid by Sahnoun. The cease-fire accord was reached on 15 January 1993. Some critics objected that this conference, and the follow-up March meeting that it scheduled, gave de facto international political recognition to Somalia's armed factions, rewarding the rule of the gun. On the other hand, no outside entity, including UNITAF, was willing to defang the factions so as to enable more traditional sources of authority in Somalia to come forward in safety.

51. Hirsch and Oakley, *Somalia and Operation Restore Hope*, 57.

52. Alison Mitchell, "US Troops Begin a Drive to Expand Hold on Mogadishu," *NYT*, 10 January 1993, A1; and Keith B. Noble, "Troops in Somalia Raid Big Arsenal," *NYT*, 12 January 1993, A3.

53. Paul Lewis, "For UN's 'Servant,' Undiplomatic Welcome," *NYT*, 7 January 1993, A9; Kenneth Noble, "400 US Marines Attack Compound of Somali Gunmen," *NYT*, 8 January 1993, A1; Author's interview, command-level participant, Restore Hope, 5 April 1994; and Hirsch and Oakley, *Somalia and Operation Restore Hope*, 57-58.

54. Diana Jean Schemo, "Rioting by Warlord's Supporters Creates Havoc in Somali Capital," *NYT*, 25 February 1993, A1; and Diana Jean Schemo, "Somali Warlord's Supporters On Rampage for Second Day," *NYT*, 26 February 1993, A1.

55. Morgan's responsibility for the northern Somalia massacres of the late 1980s was noted earlier; Jess was his chief of staff. When the first US Marines landed in Mogadishu, Jess's troops kidnapped and killed 100 elders of Kismayo's influential Harti subclan, attempting to eliminate legitimate competitors with whom the outsiders might wish to deal when they reached Kismayo. (The Harti, related to one of the major clans of northeastern Somalia, were primarily traders who had migrated to Kismayo in the late 1800s.) The number two man in Jess's organization served as night guard for the UNICEF food warehouse in Kismayo, which permitted "unofficial" distribution of food after hours. Jess also forced out all of the port workers at Kismayo, replacing them with his own men. In general, Somalis tended to compete for outsiders' business by killing their competitors, rather than trying to underbid them, and held onto the jobs they won by threatening their employers whenever layoffs or wage reductions loomed. Author's interview, Kismayo, Somalia, 9 November 1993.

56. Jane Perlez, "Somali Clan Killed Dozens of Rivals, US Officials Say," *NYT,* 29 December 1992, A1; "Somalia Factions Sign a Truce Pact," *NYT,* 16 January 1993, 2; and Hirsch and Oakley, *Somalia and Operation Restore Hope,* 76-77.

57. Diana Jean Schemo, "US and Nigerian Troops Halt Somali Shootings," *NYT,* 27 February 1993, 4. The Nigerians suffered two casualties in four hours of shooting. Hirsch and Oakley, *Somalia and Operation Restore Hope,* 77-78. The same contingent remained in Mogadishu under UNOSOM II. Pakistani forces suffered similarly in Somali eyes, their battalion for UNOSOM I having been easily corralled at the airport by Somali militias.

58. Dworken, *Preparing and Planning,* 24-31. Under Section 660 of the Foreign Assistance Act—passed by the Congress to curtail programs that had gained a reputation for training thugs—US forces were forbidden from funding or training the Auxillary Security Force (ASF). Although waivers have been granted, to assist Latin-American countries with narcotics control, none were granted for Somalia. (Ibid, 31.)

59. See, for example, Dworken, *Preparing and Planning,* 37ff.

60. "Statement by Ambassador Madeleine Albright to the UN Security Council, March 26, 1993," *Foreign Policy Bulletin* 3, no. 6 (January–April 1993): 48.

61. Keith B. Richburg, "Aideed Calls for Somalia Cease-fire," *WP,* 10 October 1993, A1, A44.

62. Aspin specified three criteria: settling "the security issue in South Mogadishu"; making "real progress toward taking heavy weapons out of the hands of the warlords"; and establishing "credible police forces in major population centers." "Speech by Secretary of Defense Les Aspin, August 27, 1993," *Foreign Policy Bulletin* 4, no. 3 (November–December 1993): 17-19.

63. Richburg, "Aideed Calls for Somalia Cease-fire," A44.

64. Michael R. Gordon, "US Officers Were Divided on Somali Raid," *NYT,* 13 May 1994, A8. Smith and Devroy argue that "Somalia never made the 'cut' that separated the big issues from ones considered less deserving of high-level attention in the administration." Russia and the Middle East were seen by the president as "far more significant than our operations in Somalia." R. Jeffrey Smith and Ann Devroy, "Inattention Led to US Deaths," *WP,* 17 October 1993, A29.

65. Steven Kull and Clay Ramsay, *US Public Attitudes on Involvement in Somalia* (College Park, Md.: School of Public and International Affairs, Program on International Policy Attitudes, 26 October 1993), 4-7.

66. Sidharth Bhatia, "Somalis Get a Taste of Compassion," *India Abroad,* 5 August 1994, 4-5.

67. Security Council, *Note by the Secretary-General,* S/1994/653, 78, 81-83. The note transmitted to the Council the report of the Commission of Inquiry appointed to investigate attacks on UNOSOM II personnel.

68. Alison Mitchell, "Marines in Somalia Try to Rebuild a Town Council," *NYT,* 18 January 1993, A3. Oakley referred to the process of gradual disempowerment of the warlords as "plucking the bird," one feather at a time. His remarks were picked up

and piped back to Somalia by the British Broadcasting Corporation's international service. Lyons and Samatar, *Somalia: State Collapse*, 48.

69. Lyons and Samatar, *Somalia: State Collapse*, 45-46.

70. Ibid., 46.

71. Security Council Resolution 733, 23 January 1992, operative para. 5; Security Council Resolution 746, 17 March 1992, operative para. 8; and Security Council Resolution 751, 24 April 1992, operative para. 4.

72. Hirsch and Oakley, *Somalia and Operation Restore Hope*, 98.

73. Security Council Resolution 814, 26 March 1993; Jennifer Parmalee, "Somalis Reach Peace Accord," *WP*, 28 March 1993, A22; Lyons and Samatar, *Somalia: State Collapse*, 50-52; and Hirsch and Oakley, *Somalia and Operation Restore Hope*, 191-97.

74. Security Council, S/1994/653, 17. No other accounts of events that I am aware of refer to the later Addis accord.

75. Dworken, *Preparing and Planning*, 20-24; and Security Council, *Further Report of the Secretary-General Submitted in Pursuance of Paragraphs 18 and 19 of Resolution 794*, S/25354, 3 March 1993, 13-15, paras. 59-69.

76. Security Council Resolution 837, 6 June 1993, operative para. 5.

77. Hirsch and Oakley, *Somalia and Operation Restore Hope*, 128; and Keith B. Richburg, "Aideed Calls for Somalia Cease-fire," *WP*, 10 October 1993, A1.

78. These numbers are drawn from a UN General Assembly report series entitled, *Financing of the United Nations Operation in Somalia II, Report of the Secretary General*, A/48/850, 19 January 1994; A/48/850/Add.1, 15 July 1994; A/49/563, 21 October 1994; and A/49/563/Add.2, 23 March 1995.

79. UN General Assembly, A/49/563, 8-9.

80. Somali employees routinely made death threats to foreign employees who tried to cut their pay or lay them off. Author's interview, UNOSOM II administrative offices, Mogadishu, 8 November 1993; and World Bank, *Social Indicators of Development, 1994* (Washington, D.C.: International Bank for Reconstruction and Development, 1994, electronic datafile).

81. Author's interview, UNICEF official, Mogadishu, 8 November 1993.

82. UN General Assembly, A/48/850/Add.1, 51. Bear in mind that Mogadishu had no running water and no functioning electric grid. When it did use rented housing, the UN had to provide all utilities separately.

83. Security Council, *Further Report of the Secretary-General Submitted in Pursuance of Paragraph 4 of Resolution 886 (1993)*, S/1994/12, 6 January 1994, 9.

84. Author's interview, UNOSOM administrative offices, Mogadishu, 8 November 1993.

85. UN General Assembly, *Financing of the United Nations Operation in Somalia II*, A/49/843, 2 February 1995. UNOSOM maintained a separate cashier's office for disbursing Somali shillings; paying in shillings, valued at 4,000 to the dollar, required enormous piles of banknotes because the largest denomination was a 1,000-shilling note. The half-million banknotes usually on-hand were stored in large bags in a strong room. That cash office was broken into as well, and robbed of 30 million shillings (worth about US $6,000-7,500), that is, robbed of at least 30,000 banknotes weighing

30 kilograms or about as much as one thief could carry away. See also Barbara Crossette, "Judges Find U.N. Unfair to Workers: Accusations False, Appeals Panel Says," *NYT*, 4 February 1996, 4.

86. Author's interview, UNOSOM headquarters, Mogadishu, 8 November 1993.

87. As the transition from UNITAF was being planned, the UN operation in Cambodia was having great success selling its mission with "Radio UNTAC"; although in that case, too, no advance provision had been made for high-powered transmitters in the mission's budget. (See chapter five in this volume for further discussion.)

88. Author's interviews, Mogadishu, 8 November 1993; and author's interview, Washington, D.C., May 1994.

89. Because Russian and other former East bloc equipment was the cheapest to lease, the UN used a lot of it in a number of operations. Usually their services were acquired through Western brokers like Skylink. By November 1993, contract aviation for UNOSOM II included 20 Mi-17 armored medium transport helicopters, 4 Mi-26 heavy lift helicopters, an I-76 heavy jet transport, and 3 L-100 cargo aircraft (civilianized C-130s), one configured as a tanker to fly fuel to outlying areas. In 1994, when Skylink's contracts were not renewed, this fleet was largely replaced by unarmored Bell-212 helicopters. General Assembly, A/48/850, 96; and General Assembly, A/48/850/Add.1, 100. See also *International Documents Review* 5, no. 4 (31 January - 4 February 1994), 3; and Crossette, "Judges Find UN Unfair to Workers."

90. Dworken, *Preparing and Planning*, 49-51.

91. Security Council Resolution 814, 26 March 1993, parts A and B.

92. American University Professor Tom Farer set up these alternatives very well in testimony before the US Congress. US Congress, House Committee on Armed Services, *Administration's Plan for Continued US Military Participation in UN Operations in Somalia*, 103rd cong., 1st sess., statement by Tom Farer, "United States Military Participation in United Nations Operations in Somalia," 14 October 1993, 32-61. Farer was the first to investigate the 5 June 1993 Mogadishu clash for the secretary-general.

93. Howe was also given to distributing written pronouncements with his full title addressed to "the Somali people." Intended or not, they had a viceregal flair.

94. Farer, "United States Military Participation," 43-47, 49, 52.

95. Ibid., 54.

96. Security Council, S/1994/653, 20-21. Only SNA cantonments were inspected, according to Farer, because other groups' official weapons holdings were already known to the UN. All groups maintained large stocks of undeclared weapons, however. Farer, "United States Military Participation," 25. Menkhaus concludes that whether UNOSOM's actions and attitudes prompted spontaneous SNA attacks or whether they were premeditated, "an armed confrontation was probably inevitable." Ken Menkhaus, "Getting Out vs Getting Through: US and UN Policies in Somalia," *Middle East Policy* 3, no.1 (1994): 156.

97. Glaspie had been US ambassador to Iraq in 1990 when Iraq invaded Kuwait.

98. Security Council, S/1994/653, 22-23; and Security Council, *Report Pursuant to Paragraph 5 of Security Council Resolution 837 (1993) on the investigation into the 5 June*

1993 attack on United Nations forces in Somalia conducted on behalf of the Secretary-General. Annex: Report of an investigation into the 5 June 1993 attack on United Nations forces in Somalia by Professor Tom Farer, S/26351, 24 August 1993, 5.

99. US Special Forces radio technicians accompanied the Pakistani teams inspecting Radio Mogadishu on 5 June. Security Council, S/1994/653, 20-21, 72. (Unless otherwise noted, the chronology of UNOSOM's war with General Aideed is taken from this document.) Neither UNITAF nor UNOSOM II anticipated urban guerrilla warfare as a worst case scenario. Both planned in terms of momentary civil disturbances of the sort experienced in late February in Mogadishu. See US Senate, Committee on Armed Services, *U.S. Military Operations in Somalia,* testimony of Major General Thomas Montgomery, 103d cong., 2d sess., S. Hrg. 103-846, 12 May 1994, 30; see also Security Council, S/1994/653, 41-42.

100. Security Council, S/1994/653, 27.

101. Douglas Jehl, "US Is Sending Planes to Bolster UN in Somalia," *WP,* 10 June 1993, A1.

102. Security Council, *Report of the Secretary-General on the Implementation of Security Council Resolution 837,* S/26022, 1 July 1993, 5-6; see also Keith B. Richburg, "Somali Warlord's Tactics Confound UN," *WP,* 16 June 1993, A1.

103. See, for example, Donatella Lorch, "20 Somalis Die When Peacekeepers Fire at Crowd," *NYT,* 14 June 1993, A1.

104. Keith B. Richburg, "In War on Aideed, UN Battled Itself," *WP,* 6 December 1993, A1.

105. US Senate, Committee on Armed Services (hereafter SASC), *US Military Operations in Somalia,* testimony of Major General William Garrison, Commander, US Joint Special Operations Command, 103rd Cong., 29th sess., S. Hrg. 103-846, 12 May 1994, 2.

106. Ken Menkhaus, "UNOSOM's Structure and the Issue of Decentralization," UNOSOM "Lower Jubba Strategy" Briefing Paper no. 4 (Mogadishu, Somalia, June 1993), 2-3. (Mimeograph.)

107. Author's interview, command-level participant, Restore Hope, 5 April 1994.

108. Donatella Lorch, "UN Troops Begin an Effort to Take Over Somali Streets," *NYT,* 11 July 1993, 14; Lorch, "Disunity Hampering UN Somalia Effort," *NYT,* 12 July 1993, A8; and Security Council, S/1994/653, 78.

109. Menkhaus asserts that Loi also agreed with the SNA "to hire security guards for their soldiers at strongpoints, [and] provide salaries for local 'elders' . . . in return for SNA agreement not to subject them to sniper fire." These and other deals cut by individual contingents with local political leaders facilitated the rearming of Somalia's factions, particularly the SNA. Menkhaus, "Getting Out vs. Getting Through," 152. The UN sought and eventually secured Loi's recall by the Italian government, and subsequently moved the Italian contingent out of Mogadishu.

110. Richburg, "UN Battled Itself," A1.

111. Security Council, S/1994/653, 31, 81-83; and Menkhaus, "Getting Out vs. Getting Through," 152. This incident terminated an apparent behind-the-scenes effort to negotiate an end to the war with moderate elements of the SNA and Habr Gedir. This

negotiation had gone forward without Howe's direct knowledge but with the support of Deputy SRSG Kouyate. On 3 September, Kouyate and political adviser John Drysdale presented to Howe an SNA proposal for a cessation of hostilities. The ambush of the Nigerians caused Howe to reject the initiative. John Lancaster and Keith B. Richburg, "UN Rejected Somali Overture," WP, 17 October 1993, A1.

112. Security Council, S/1994/653, 83-84. Keith B. Richburg, "US Helicopters Fire on Somalis," WP, 10 September 1993, A1; Richburg, "Somali Guerrillas Shell Peace Keepers," WP, 11 September 1993, A1; and Richburg, "US, UN Avoid Estimating Somali Deaths in Clashes With Peace Keepers," WP, 12 September 1993, A12. See also Eric Schmitt, "Somalis Faulted in Civilian Deaths," NYT, 11 September 1993, 3. This particular incident was reportedly deeply disturbing to CENTCOM's General Joseph Hoar, as well as to Clinton. Patrich J. Sloyan, "How the Warlord Outwitted Clinton's Spooks," WP, 3 April 1994, C 3.

113. The most detailed account of the events of 3-4 October is Rick Atkinson's two-part series, "The Raid That Went Wrong," WP, 30-31 January 1994, A1. The SNA had already downed a US Blackhawk helicopter with rocket-propelled grenades (RPGs) at night on 25 September even though the Blackhawk was flying at 130 knots and skimming the rooftops. Press reports indicate that Somali gunners fired large numbers of RPGs at once, creating a kind of shotgun effect. Three Americans were killed in the 25 September incident; the pilot and copilot survived the crash near Mogadishu port and were rescued after a four-hour firefight. SASC, US Military Operations in Somalia, 13; and Donatella Lorch, "Hunted Somali General Lashes Out," NYT, 26 September 1993, 22.

114. Defense Secretary Les Aspin was heavily criticized after the fact for his decision not to grant Major General Montgomery's September request for heavy armor reinforcements for the Quick Reaction Force, but Montgomery estimated that an all-US armored force would still have taken two to three hours to launch a rescue mission, versus the five hours required by the UN contingents. Most of the casualties saved would have been in the relief columns, had they had the option initially to go in under armor. SASC, US Military Operations in Somalia, 11, 54.

115. SFC Elroy Garcia, "We Did Right That Night," Soldiers (February 1994): 19-20.

116. Donatella Lorch, "Somali Chief Frees American Captive; Meets Reporters," NYT, 15 October 1993, A1.

117. Rick Atkinson, "Some Heavy Symbolism in Somalia," WP, 23 November 1993, A31. The United States shipped 30 M1-A1 tanks and 42 Bradley Fighting Vehicles to Somalia. Their presence seemed to calm intra-clan fighting in Mogadishu, but it increased again, along with carjackings and other varieties of armed robbery, once Somalis decided that the new force would not intervene to stop them.

118. Rick Atkinson, "UN Enclave, City Are Worlds Apart," WP, 26 November 1993, A1.

119. "Somali warlords test mettle of Indian UN Troops," Washington Times, 15 December 1993, 10; and "Somalis Striking at Rare UN Success Story," Reuters newswire, 1 September 1994, 12:16 P.M.

120. "2 UN Aid Agencies Shut Down Offices in Somalia's Capital," NYT, 4 January 1994, A5; "5,000 Are Driven From Port City By Fighting in Southern Somalia," NYT, 13

February 1994, 10; and Keith B. Richburg, "Aid Workers Under Fire in Somalia," *WP*, 13 February 1994, A27.

121. Aideed remained outside the country for the next six months, staying in Nairobi for the most part. "Aideed Cheered On His Return To Somali Capital," *WP*, 20 May 1994, A31. On political efforts, see Security Council, *Further Report of the Secretary-General on the United Nations Operation in Somalia Submitted in Pursuance of Paragraph 2 of Security Council Resolution 923 (1994)*, S/1994/839, 18 July 1994, 12-13; and Hirsch and Oakley, *Somalia and Operation Restore Hope*, 139-140, 144-145.

122. Donatella Lorch, "Americans Count Hours to End of Somali Mission," *NYT*, 28 February 1994, A3; and Rich Atkinson, "Today's Pullout Will Leave Only 50 US Marines in Somalia," *WP*, 23 March 1994, 24. The last American diplomats and their marine guards were pulled from Somalia six months later.

123. "US Cobra helicopters, tanks and APCs to be leased to UN," *Aerospace Daily*, 7 February 1994, 191; Katherine McIntire and Sean Naylor, "Guard return will meet Somalia pullout deadline," *Army Times*, 28 February 1994, 8; and "USA criticized as last troops leave," *Jane's Defence Weekly*, 26 March 1994, 12.

124. Keith B. Richburg, "Somalia Militia Tries New Role as Policing Force," *WP*, 5 April 1994, 14. Lieutenant General Bir left UNOSOM II in January 1994, replaced by Lieutenant General Aboo Samah bin Aboo Bakar of Malaysia. Major General Montgomery left in March, replaced by Major General Mike Nyambuya of Zimbabwe. Jonathan Howe officially completed his tour as SRSG on 8 March but was quietly replaced de facto in February by his deputy, Lansana Kouyate.

125. The field hospital at which the Indian doctors worked treated more than 100,000 Somalis over the course of a year. Indian troops' private contributions built recreation facilities for children and funded an orphanage in Baidoa. Indian vets tended Somali livestock and army "sappers" dug wells. Aidan Hartley, "Somalis striking at rare US success story," *Reuters* newswire, 1 September 1994, 12:16 P.M.

126. See the series Security Council, *Further Report by the Secretary-General on the United Nations Operation in Somalia*, S/1994/614, 24 May 1994, 5; and S/1994/839, 18 July 1994, 6. See also Security Council, *Report by the Secretary-General on the Situation in Somalia*, S/1994/1068, 17 September 1994, 5-6; and Ken Menkhaus, *Trip Report—Somalia*, September 1994, 1-3. (Mimeograph.)

127. Security Council, S/1994/1068, 4; Aden Ali, "UN tanks, helicopters clash with Somali parties," *Reuters* newswire, 6 December 1994, 09:48 A.M.; and Ali, "UN forces to quit southern Somali port next week," *Reuters* newswire, 24 November 1994, 09:40 A.M.

128. Tom Ashbrook, "Somalia nears a crossroads," *Boston Globe*, 7 February 1995, 1; Rick Atkinson, "Somalis Seize Airport Abandoned by UN," *WP*, 2 March 1995, A27; and Atkinson, "Marines Close Curtain on UN in Somalia," *WP*, 3 March 1995, A1.

129. Atkinson, "Marines Close Curtain," A1.

130. Keith B. Richburg, "Clashes in Somali Town Blamed on UN," *WP*, 21 November 1993, A29; and Rick Atkinson, "Mogadishu Calm As Attention Turns to Talks," *WP*, 28 November 1993, A33, citing AP.

131. Fresh evidence of these ties came after the death of Mohamed Farah Aideed on 1 August 1996. General Aideed was shot during street fighting in Mogadishu on 24 July. His son, Hussein Mohamed Aideed, a former US Marine who had served with UNITAF in December 1992, was appointed to succeed his father as head of the Somali National Alliance and quickly pledged to carry on his father's program. The elder Aideed had proclaimed himself president of Somalia in June 1995, but his claim went unrecognized by the international community and Somalia's other factions. At the time of his death, the SNA had been losing ground militarily to a coalition headed by Ali Mahdi Mohamed and former Aideed financier Osman Hassan Ali Atto. Nicholas Kotch, "Uncertain but with hope, Somalia enters new era," *Reuters* news-wire, 2 August 1996, 7:54 A.M.; and Stephen Buckley, "Son of Aideed Chosen to Head Somali Faction," *WP*, 5 August 1996, 13.

NINE

THE POLITICS OF GENOCIDE: PEACEKEEPING AND DISASTER RELIEF IN RWANDA

J. MATTHEW VACCARO

From October 1990 until August 1993, the government of Rwanda and a rebel group, the Rwandan Patriotic Front (RPF), engaged in a fitful civil war and sporadic peace negotiations. The eventual peace accord called for a neutral peacekeeping force to help implement a transitional period of power-sharing and subsequent free elections. The United Nations Assistance Mission for Rwanda (UNAMIR) was established for this purpose in October 1993. However, the reconciliation process broke down in April 1994 as extremists from within the government and its army reignited the civil war and instigated a three month period of genocide in which their militias killed an estimated 500,000 to 1,000,000 people and another 4.7 million people were forced to flee.

The UN peacekeeping force remained in the country throughout; however, as the situation changed, so did the mandate and composition of the force. When the war restarted and the genocide began, most of the peacekeepers were withdrawn and only a small mediation mission was left. Later, as the human toll became better known, the Security Council authorized an expanded force dubbed UNAMIR II to protect civilians. When UN Member States failed to contribute troops and equipment for that operation in a timely fashion, France initiated Operation Turquoise, a UN-authorized

Fig. 9.1

MAP OF RWANDA AND BURUNDI

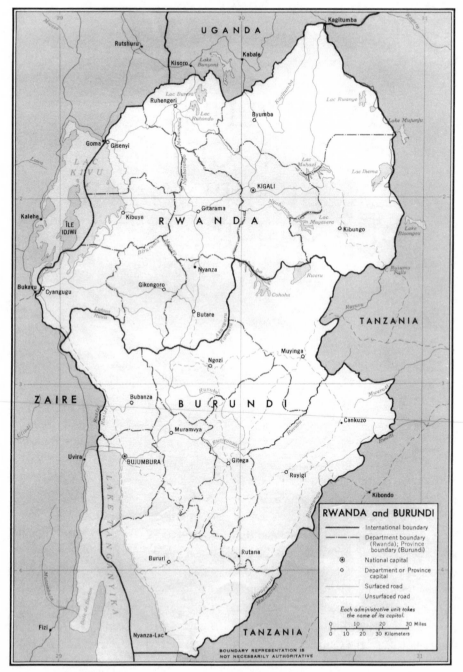

SOURCE: US Government

intervention in the southwestern part of Rwanda. In mid-July 1994 the RPF won the war, formed a new government, and pledged itself to reconciliation. Genocide and the flow of refugees ended, for the most part, with the end of the war, but humanitarian needs persisted. UN forces replaced the French. The new government was recognized by many states, as well as by the UN General Assembly. UNAMIR II attempted to work with the government to strengthen stability in the country. The government, however, grew wary of the UN's presence, and in June 1995, despite a precarious security situation, forced a gradual phase-out of the peacekeeping mission. UNAMIR withdrew from Rwanda in April 1996.

ORIGINS

The problems in Rwanda stemmed from many years of unresolved political confrontation combined with overpopulation and poverty. In 1992, the small, landlocked country of just under 25,000 square kilometers (see figure 9.1) was one of the poorest and most densely populated countries on the continent. With 329 persons per square kilometer and 90 percent of the workforce in agriculture, the competition for land was intense.[1]

A caste system based on ethnicity emerged 400 hundred years ago when wealthy Tutsi cattle herders moved into central Africa and established a monarchy that ruled over the poorer, but more numerous, Hutu farmers. The two ethnic groups, however, were not totally distinct from or antagonistic to each other. They shared language, culture, and religion; interethnic marriages were commonplace. Nonetheless, the society was class-based, with mostly Tutsi at the top, and only a slight degree of social mobility for the poor.

The first colonial power, Germany, retained the Tutsi monarchy and through it ruled Rwanda-Urundi, as the contemporary states of Rwanda and Burundi were then called. When Belgium took over the colony in 1916, indirect rule via Tutsi administrators was retained. Moreover, any social mobility of earlier times ended as Hutu were largely denied access to education, except training for the Catholic priesthood.[2] Under Belgian rule (1916-62), virtually the only indigenous people to gain wealth were Tutsi. These circumstances entrenched ethnicity into the political and social culture.[3]

In 1959, the Hutu revolted against the Tutsi and Belgian administrators of Rwanda-Urundi. Thousands of Tutsi fled to neighboring countries to escape the violence. In 1962, Rwanda and Burundi became separate states as they obtained independence from Belgium. In Rwanda, Belgium ceded power to a Hutu-dominated republic. However, democracy vanished quickly as President Grégoire Kayibanda, a Hutu, imposed single-party rule and concentrated power within a clique of supporters from his home region of central Rwanda. President Kayibanda dominated the country's politics for a little more than a decade. In 1973, Major General Juvénal Habyarimana, a Hutu from northern Rwanda, seized power in a coup and governed until he was killed in April 1994.

During the Hutu revolt and the period of Hutu rule, the Tutsi were blamed for almost all problems the country faced. Such scapegoating flared into ethnic massacres from time to time: notable incidents occurred in 1963, 1966, 1973, and 1990 through 1993. With each spate of violence more Tutsi fled Rwanda. Most became permanent exiles; few were ever allowed to reenter the country legally. In 1992 the Rwandan population of about 9.2 million was, overall, 83 percent Hutu and 17 percent Tutsi, but about half of the Tutsi population was in exile, or roughly 8 percent of the entire population.[4]

Origins of UN Involvement

In 1979, exiled Tutsi in Uganda and some Hutu who opposed the ruling party formed a revolutionary group called the Rwandan Alliance for National Unity. In 1986, its name was changed to the Rwandan Patriotic Front (RPF) but its activities remained limited and largely ineffective until 1990, when about 4,000 Tutsi who were serving in the army of Uganda formed the Rwandan Patriotic Army as a wing of the RPF.[5] Many of these Tutsi were descendants of the 1959 Rwandan exiles and had lived their entire life in Uganda, gaining military experience fighting in its civil war. Using their Ugandan military equipment and supplies, they invaded Rwanda together with 3,000 other exiles on 1 October 1990.

Rwandan Government Forces (FAR), with the support of French and Zairian troops, stopped and then turned back the invasion force just 30 kilometers north of Kigali.[6] At that point, the RPF attempted to seize and hold terrain, a strategic mistake since it did not have the force structure to win a conventional war. On 23 October 1990, government forces killed the rebels' two senior commanders and about 300 soldiers in an ambush. The RPF reverted to guerrilla tactics, taking cover in northern Rwanda and southern Uganda. Meanwhile, as sporadic skirmishes continued, under pressure from the International Monetary Fund and other aid donors, President Habyarimana formed a power-sharing arrangement with four opposition parties in April 1992; the RPF was not included. The five-party government was a nominal change because Habyarimana and his clique from northern Rwanda retained predominant authority.[7] A cease-fire agreement was reached in July 1992 with the assistance of international mediation sponsored by the Organization of African Unity (OAU) and led by the president of Tanzania, Ali Hassan Mwinyi.[8]

At the request of both the Rwandan five-party government and the RPF, the OAU established a peacekeeping observer mission in July 1992 to observe and verify compliance with the cease-fire agreement. The Neutral Military Observer Group (NMOG, later termed NMOG I) consisted of forty military officers, ten each from Mali, Nigeria, Senegal, and Zimbabwe plus five officers each from the FAR and RPF. The OAU observers were stationed in northern Rwanda along the cease-fire line between the rival armies.[9]

On 9 January 1993, official representatives of the five-party government and the RPF signed an agreement whereby the RPF would be worked into Rwanda's power-sharing arrangement, but President Habyarimana rejected it stating his dissatisfaction with the distribution of ministerial posts among the political parties.[10] Subsequent demonstrations by Habyarimana's supporters resulted in Rwanda's first well-documented case of "militias" being used to attack Tutsi and moderate Hutu civilians. The militias had been formed during 1992 from the youth wings of two political parties; Habyarimana's Movement for Reconciliation and Development (MRND) and the closely allied Coalition for the Defense of the Republic (CDR), a Hutu supremacist party. The term militia implies greater organization than these groups had. They did receive rudimentary training and light arms from the Rwandan Presidential Guard, but later proved themselves capable only of mob-type tactics against unarmed civilians. Together the militias are estimated to have numbered between 30,000 and 50,000.[11] Following Habyarimana's rejection of the five-party government's agreement with the RPF, the militias were unleashed against civilians near the cease-fire line. Over 300 people were killed and 4,000 displaced; they were mostly Tutsi.[12]

Equating the behavior of the militias with action by the FAR, the RPF launched an offensive on a broad front across the cease-fire line on 8 February 1993. This fighting was much heavier than the 1990 invasion because the FAR and the RPF had obtained heavier weapons during the cease-fire.[13] This round of fighting displaced over 650,000 persons and lasted until a new cease-fire agreement was signed on 9 March. Peace negotiations resumed, but the government of Rwanda and its patron, France, were concerned that the RPF might be using negotiations as a tactic to gain time to allow more weapons and supplies to be brought in via Uganda. The government of Uganda denied any complicity with the RPF and supported efforts to prove its statements. Following requests by Uganda and the five-party government of Rwanda, and with strong support from France, the UN Security Council, in June 1993, established a peacekeeping observer mission to verify that no military goods flowed from Uganda to Rwanda. The mission, the United Nations Observer Mission Uganda-Rwanda (UNOMUR), consisted of about 80 military observers based in southern Uganda.[14]

Meanwhile, peace negotiations had made progress in Arusha, Tanzania. On 4 August 1993, a comprehensive peace accord was signed by General Habyarimana and Colonel Alexis Kanyarengwe, chairman of the RPF (interestingly, a Hutu). The signing ceremony was witnessed by a broad group, including President Mwinyi of Tanzania, Salim Ahmed Salim, the secretary-general of the OAU, Vladimir Petrovsky, the director of the UN office in Geneva, the presidents of Uganda and Burundi, the prime minister of Zaire, and representatives from the remaining observer countries at the peace talks—Belgium, France, Germany, Nigeria, the United States, and Zimbabwe.[15]

The Arusha Accords were comprehensive. They entailed the creation of a transitional government in which 5 of 22 ministers would be allocated to the RPF; the establishment of a commission to oversee the return of refugees to Rwanda and to ensure their security; the formation of an integrated army with 50 percent of the high command and 40 percent of the troops coming from the RPF and the remainder from the FAR; and the organization of new parliamentary elections in 1995. Further, the accords included a request for a neutral international force to facilitate the implementation of the agreement. A timetable indicating when each of the prescribed reforms was to take place was written into the accords; unfortunately, it was unrealistic. For instance, the neutral peacekeeping force was to be operational by 10 September 1993, just 37 days after the accords were signed.[16]

The transitional government called for in the accords was never established, partly because of a dispute over the distribution of ministries. Habyarimana, in particular, disrupted the conciliation process, as he pitted the newer parties against each other. At one point, it looked as if a consensus had emerged, but Habyarimana refused to cooperate at the last moment. Reconciliation was the responsibility of the parties to the Arusha Accords, who were presumed to have signed in good faith. At least in Habyarimana's case, this was not so.

The UN secretary-general, in his report to the Security Council of 30 March 1994, linked the parties' failure to establish the transitional institutions with a deteriorating security situation.

> Owing in part to the continuing political stalemate, the period under review [January - March 1994] has seen a rapid and dramatic deterioration in the security situation in Kigali. January and February [1994] saw increasingly violent demonstrations, roadblocks, assassination of political leaders and assaults on and murders of civilians, developments that severely over stretched the resources and capabilities of the national gendarmerie.[17]

Implementation of the accords had faltered badly by late March. Tensions were increased by the use of hate radio by Hutu extremists. Just after the accords were signed the CDR party instituted a propaganda campaign through its newly established Radio/Television Libre des Mille Collines (RTLM). The station was owned and operated by members of Habyarimana's inner circle. The campaign opposed the accords from the start but became increasingly virulent and advocated violence against those supporting reconciliation. By the end of 1993, RTLM was regularly naming individuals who "deserved to die" and treated all Tutsi, and Hutu opposed to Habyarimana's party, as traitors and advocates of Tutsi monarchy.[18]

Six days after the secretary-general's field report, all hope of getting the Arusha Accords back on schedule vanished when Hutu extremists assassinated President Habyarimana and reignited the civil war using a strategy that included ethnic massacre.

Resumption of Civil War and Ethnic Massacre

The violence that erupted in Rwanda in April 1994 was part of a strategy by extremist Hutu officials to end the peace process and consolidate power in their own hands—in essence, a very bloody coup attempt. The assassination of President Habyarimana, who was viewed by the extremists as too willing to compromise with the RPF, was the first step of the strategy. On 6 April 1994, he was killed as his airplane, approaching Kigali, was hit by two missiles fired from the military camp at Kanombe, which was controlled by the Presidential Guard.[19] Within 45 minutes of this event the Presidential Guard, other FAR, and members of the militias of the MRND and CDR erected barricades on major thoroughfares in Kigali and began to kill Tutsi who attempted to pass. The Presidential Guard established road blocks that prevented UNAMIR forces from reaching the airport to investigate the crash site. Within a few hours, a self-proclaimed "interim government" had been formed by the extremists. Meanwhile, moderate members of the power-sharing government were sought out and killed by the Presidential Guard. The prime minister was killed along with ten Belgian members of UNAMIR who had been dispatched to protect her. On 8 April, the extremists' forces turned their attention from political opponents to Tutsi civilians in general. The systematic slaughter of Tutsi began in Kigali and spread to outlying areas. The militias, incited by hateful and inflammatory commands over RTLM, carried out most of the killing.[20]

Later, a UN commission determined that the extremists' strategy had constituted genocide. The commission's conclusion:

> Acts of genocide against the Tutsi group were perpetrated by Hutu elements in a concerted, planned, systematic and methodical way. These acts of mass extermination against the Tutsi group as such constitute genocide. . . . The Commission has not uncovered any evidence to indicate that Tutsi elements perpetrated acts committed with the intent to destroy the Hutu ethnic group as such.[21]

Concurrent with the attacks on civilians, the civil war between the two armies reignited. The RPF battalion, barracked in Kigali under the Arusha Accords, initiated battle against the government forces once it was evident that the FAR were killing Tutsi. The majority of RPF troops, who were in northern Rwanda, began a military advance south towards Kigali. Some arrived as soon as 12 April, causing the interim government to flee west to Gitarama.

POLITICAL SUPPORT

A review of the weak political support for reconciliation within Rwanda and the low interest within the Security Council for launching ambitious peace operations makes it clear why the country endured so much trauma in 1994.

Internal Actors

Only the RPF and its supporters seem to have had the political will to implement the original Arusha Accords, which were designed to bring the RPF into the government. The RPF hedged its bet, however, by maintaining preparedness for renewed fighting should the peace process collapse. In Rwanda, political affiliation more or less mirrored ethnicity. Hence the RPF and its mostly Tutsi supporters comprised less than 20 percent of the population, and about half of those supporters were exiles.

The second group key to events in Rwanda consisted of extremists within the ruling clique who wanted to stay in power despite the accords. General Habyarimana either endorsed or tolerated the acts of such extremists within his inner circle, as his government continued to commit politically motivated human rights violations against Tutsi and other political opponents in an effort to eliminate other contenders for political power.[22]

A UN Commission on Human Rights investigator concluded that government propaganda had created a situation in which "all Tutsi inside the country were collectively labeled accomplices with the RPF. . . . [T]here is a certain elite which, in order to cling to power, is continuing to fuel ethnic hatred." Concerning murders and small-scale massacres, the investigator concluded,

> such outbreaks were planned and prepared, with targets being identified in speeches by representatives of the authorities, broadcasts on Rwandan radio, and leaflets . . . [and] the persons perpetrating the massacres were under organized leadership. In this connection, local government officials have been found to play a leading role in most cases.[23]

Such actions by the governing party were antithetical to the spirit of reconciliation embodied in the Arusha Accords. Clearly, the extremist groups were working against the peace process.

External Actors

None of the external actors watching events in Rwanda had the necessary mix of capability and will to act in a timely enough fashion either to prevent the reemergence of violence in Rwanda or stop it once it flared. Of the two factors, political will was most often in short supply.

Rwanda had little intrinsic strategic value to outsiders, and few countries identified their national interests with the country or its people. The states with most at stake in Rwanda were its immediate neighbors: Burundi, Tanzania, Uganda, and Zaire. Stability and economic development in Rwanda would clearly serve their interests, but they had little capability themselves to influence either variable constructively. Burundi was preoccupied by its own, similar political-ethnic standoff between the Hutu masses and the Tutsi army. Uganda could not act as an honest broker because of President Museveni's historical ties with the RPF and the fact that the RPF had invaded Rwanda from Uganda. Zaire's state institutions had essentially ceased to function. Tanzania did at least act as a mediator during the peace talks.

The two other countries most interested in Rwanda were Belgium and France; Belgium as the former colonial metropole and France as the self-styled patron of all Francophone states in Africa. Belgium supported the Hutu government until 1990, when apparently weary of the government's corruption and human rights abuses, Brussels threw its political support to the newly resurgent RPF. Subsequently, the RPF set up its European headquarters there. During the initial RPF invasion in 1990, Belgium deployed 535 troops to Rwanda for one month ostensibly to protect its nationals living there. Although the FAR viewed the intervention as support for the RPF, the extent of Belgian material support to the RPF is unclear. France clearly cultivated a close relationship with Habyarimana and the FAR, providing substantial amounts of military training and equipment and political endorsement. The French are believed to have directly supported the FAR in the civil war against the RPF.[24]

Unfortunately for Rwanda, when its crisis occurred there was little outside enthusiasm for ambitious peace operations. The UN's experiences in Bosnia and Somalia had caused members of the Security Council to scrutinize new operations closely. UNAMIR operated under scrutiny from its inception. The mission was authorized just two days after the death of 18 Americans in Mogadishu, Somalia, the event that triggered a major US reassessment of the utility of peace operations. The Security Council authorized just two other UN peace operations in the two years following authorization of UNAMIR, in contrast with the nine new operations—among them three of the largest—in the two years preceding UNAMIR.[25] The international community seemed willing to help other countries resolve conflicts, but only at low cost and at the request of the local parties to those conflicts. To suppress genocide in Rwanda, coercive operations would have been required. Even Belgium and France, with their sentimental ties, did not have the political will to countenance such forceful and costly actions.

The US administration's growing doubts about coercive peace operations were made official on 5 May 1994 when the national security advisor, Anthony Lake, announced a new policy on reforming peace operations. Referring to conflicts that occur within states, he said:

> [T]hese kinds of conflicts are particularly hard to come to grips with and to have an effect on from outside, because basically, of course, their origins are in political turmoil within these nations. And that political turmoil may not be susceptible to the efforts of the international community. So, neither we nor the international community have either the mandate nor the resources nor the possibility of resolving every conflict of this kind.[26]

Later in the briefing Lake indicated that these conclusions governed US policy on peace operations during the period when UNAMIR was initiated.

Given this constellation of interests and attitudes, it should not be surprising that the Arusha Accords were disrupted. One of the internal actors, the Hutu extremists, did not support the process and retained the means (the FAR and militias) to revert to warfare. Once this happened, given the paucity of outside interests in Rwanda and the doubts prevalent about coercive peace operations, the Security Council reacted hesitantly whenever an expanded role for the UN in Rwanda was proposed. The failure of UN Member States to provide military units and equipment in a timely fashion once the mandate was expanded further demonstrates the reluctance of Member States to engage in coercive operations in Rwanda.

MANDATE

On 5 October 1993, the Security Council first authorized UNAMIR. The purpose of the operation was to assist in implementing the Arusha Accords. Its tasks were manifold: UNAMIR was to contribute to the security of the city of Kigali and monitor the overall security situation until national elections; monitor observance of the cease-fire and the formation of a new integrated army; and investigate alleged noncompliance with the accords and any incidents relating to the police or gendarmerie. UNAMIR also had a number of humanitarian tasks, including training local people to remove land mines, monitoring the repatriation of refugees, and assisting other UN agencies in coordinating humanitarian assistance. The operation was authorized up to 2,548 military personnel and 60 civilian police.[27] UNAMIR was to be conducted at the behest of the former belligerents and had their formal consent. Authorized as a consensual operation, the use of force was limited to self-defense. As events in Rwanda changed during the subsequent two years, the Security Council modified the mandate three times.

Initial Response to Violence

Following the outbreak of violence in April 1994, UNAMIR's mandate was no longer appropriate to the situation. The Security Council delayed modification of the mandate for 15 days, hoping that a cease-fire might be achieved. On 21 April 1994, as fighting continued, as Belgian troops were completing their withdrawal from the force, and as Bangladesh was indicating that it was about to withdraw, the Security Council unanimously voted to reduce the mandate and the force. UNAMIR was directed to mediate a cease-fire, and to evacuate all but 270 UN personnel.[28]

Mediation was the middle alternative of three proposed by the secretary-general. The other alternatives were to withdraw UN forces completely or to toughen up the mission under Chapter VII of the UN Charter to force a cease-fire. The first alternative was suggested by the US government but became viewed within the Council as capitulation and was consequently disregarded.[29] As the Nigerian representative stated, this alternative was "not acceptable to my delegation—first, because it is defeatist, and, secondly, because it would seriously undermine the credibility of the Security Council as the organ charged with the responsibility for maintaining international peace and security."[30]

The final alternative, escalation into peace enforcement, would have entailed "the immediate and massive reinforcement of UNAMIR and a change in its mandate so that it would be equipped and authorized to coerce the opposing forces into a cease-fire."[31] This alternative found little support within the Council; no member is on record as favoring it. The US government did not believe that the UN could mount an effective peace enforcement operation against the belligerents, and Ambassador Albright was determined not to set up false hopes in an impossible mission that would only lead to another failure.[32] The French representative to the Security Council expressed a similar sentiment following the vote to reduce UNAMIR's role. "We hope that the Rwandese [sic] parties will come to their senses and realize that the United Nations can neither take their place nor impose peace on them."[33] The US government was also reluctant to incur the expense of an operation that it believed could only fail.

At the same time UNAMIR's mandate and force structure were reduced by the Security Council, members of the Council focused on the resumption of the civil war between the two armies, not on the ethnic violence, apparently viewing the ethnic violence as a consequence of the breakdown in civil order rather than as an element of a military strategy. Yet ample information was available within the UN system and the international relief and human rights communities for officials to have predicted the violence that began in April 1994 and for them to have understood the genocidal nature of the violence. Additionally, some UN Member States probably had good intelligence of the situation in Rwanda during 1993 and 1994. France, with its close ties to the ruling party and the army, probably had an idea of what was going on within those circles.

The failure was twofold: not enough accurate analysis was available to the Council, and the information that was reported seems to have fallen on deaf ears. The recorded debate concerning the decision makes no mention of genocide. After the fact, the *Washington Post* reported that the Security Council was provided "blurred, sanitized summaries from Boutros-Ghali's staff depicting mutual and chaotic killing."[34] Indeed, the secretary-general's special report to the Security Council that outlined the alternatives described above did not stress the organized nature of the civil violence. The report simply termed the explosion of President Habyarimana's plane a "crash" and indicated that the crash set off ethnic killing in Kigali by "unruly" elements of the Presidential Guard.[35] These statements indicate that the UN, which had about 2,500 military personnel on the ground in Rwanda, did not yet realize (or was unwilling to state) that the events were part of a strategy of the Hutu extremists aimed fundamentally at the elimination of the Tutsi ethnic group and other political opponents. Initially, the events in Rwanda appeared similar to past ethnic massacres that had tended to erupt suddenly and just as suddenly peter out. Press reports leading up to the Council's vote to reduce UNAMIR suggested the scale of the killing. On 19 April, in the *New York Times,* a spokesman from the International Committee of the Red Cross reported "tens and tens of thousands of dead" and at least 400,000 persons displaced from their homes around Kigali. In the same article, a CARE representative reported that 26,000 people had sought refuge in neighboring countries.[36] However, the Council failed to recognize the systematic and one-sided nature of the ethnic massacres until a few weeks later when more numerous reports, relating death totals of much greater magnitude, became available.[37]

Expanded Mandate

As the violence continued, a number of smaller states, most prominently New Zealand, shamed the Council into action. On 17 May 1994, the Council voted unanimously to expand the mandate of what would be, effectively, the second UN attempt at peacekeeping in Rwanda. UNAMIR II was authorized up to 5,500 troops to establish secure humanitarian areas for civilians inside Rwanda; to provide security and support for the delivery of humanitarian supplies throughout the country; and to continue its efforts to negotiate a cease-fire. The Security Council resolution did not invoke Chapter VII of the UN Charter, but indicated that UNAMIR II might use lethal force to prevent the obstruction of its tasks in addition to the normal authorization to use force in self-defense.[38] New Zealand failed in an attempt to include a reference to genocide in the resolution. Evidently governments were concerned that the reference would impose a legal requirement on signatories of the Genocide Convention to take action to halt anything defined as genocide.

Some Council members felt that the United States was unnecessarily delaying action by demanding that the proposed new mandate satisfy the "factors of consideration" included in US Presidential Decision Directive 25, a new statement of US policy on peace operations. For its part, the United States was uncertain if adequate troops and equipment, complete consent of the belligerents, and coherent operational plans were available for the proposed mission.[39]

Four months after the war ended, the mandate was expanded again, on 30 November 1994, when the Council (under Resolution 965) directed that UNAMIR II provide protection to UN-affiliated personnel in Rwanda, including members of the International Tribunal set up to prosecute perpetrators of crimes against humanity during the war. The revised mandate also called for UNAMIR II's civilian police component to assist the Rwandan government in the establishment and training of a new, integrated national police force.

Phase-Out

Almost a year after the war had been won and the new government established, UNAMIR II was still authorized under its intrusive mandate of the war period. As it consolidated its rule, the government of Rwanda grew increasingly wary of the peacekeepers' activities within its borders and pressured the UN to limit the activities and size of the peacekeeping force. Since the operation was not a Chapter VII enforcement action and the situation did not justify one, the Security Council had little choice but to accept the reduced role proposed by the host government, even though the situation in Rwanda remained unstable.

On 9 June 1995, the Council realigned the mandate of UNAMIR II in accordance with Rwanda's wishes. The Rwandan government rejected any national security role for UNAMIR II, disallowing patrolling of the countryside, monitoring of its international borders, and protection of humanitarian convoys. The peacekeepers continued to protect UN-affiliated personnel in the country; to assist in the training of the national police force; to provide support to humanitarian activities; to provide monitors throughout the country to promote a climate of confidence that would facilitate the voluntary return of refugees; and to exercise its good offices to help achieve national reconciliation. The revised mandate directed that UNAMIR's troops be reduced to 2,330 by 9 September 1995, and further to 1,800 by 9 October 1995. The mandate for the force expired on 8 March 1996.[40]

FUNDING

The actual cost for the first six months of UNOMUR, the mission to monitor the Uganda-Rwanda border, was $2,354,100. Subsequent costs for UNOMUR, until it was disbanded in September 1994, were included in the budget for UNAMIR. The actual cost of the latter operation from 5 October 1993 to 4 April 1994 (from its establishment to just before the violence began) was $35,295,100. Expenditures for the period 5 April 1994 to 9 June 1995 were $261,302,200, and the mid-1995 cost estimate for the period 10 June 1995 to 31 December 1995 was $96,685,400. Altogether, from 22 June 1993 through 31 December 1995 UNOMUR and UNAMIR cost about $393,000,000.[41] These funds were provided by UN member states according to the standard UN peacekeeping scale of assessment.

The cost of the French-led coalition operation, Operation Turquoise, was born almost entirely by France, as no other major military or economic power participated. All told, $240 million—or approximately 1 percent of the French annual defense budget—was spent over the operation's sixty day duration.[42]

PLANNING AND IMPLEMENTATION

Within the constraints imposed by the Security Council, UNAMIR was a well-planned operation, reflecting newly developed competencies within the UN Secretariat and adequate discretionary funding authority. The secretary-general used that authority to deploy planning teams even before the Council had authorized the full operation. The prior experience of the OAU's peacekeeping force in northern Rwanda and of UNOMUR in Uganda, along Rwanda's border, fed into UN planning, as did the experience of numerous UN and private humanitarian agencies already active within the country. Officials from these ongoing efforts were able to offer advice and insight into the local situation and to contribute knowledgeable personnel to the new operation.

Fifteen days after the signing of the Arusha Accords, the reconnaissance team for the operation arrived in Rwanda. The chief military observer and head of mission from UNOMUR, Brigadier General Romeo A. Dallaire, a Canadian army officer, led the reconnaissance team with participants from the various Secretariat Departments that would take part in the potential operation: Peacekeeping Operations (DPKO), Political Affairs (DPA), Humanitarian Affairs (DHA), and the Office of the UN High

Commissioner for Refugees (UNHCR). The team remained in Rwanda for about two weeks, until 31 August 1993, gathering political information by meeting with the key officials within Rwanda and tactical information by surveying the military positions of the antagonists as well as the general condition of the population centers. Unlike reconnaissance missions for traditional military operations, the UN team operated with complete transparency.[43]

In addition to performing reconnaissance, the team met with representatives from all sides of Rwandan politics. The team made efforts to explain that it was not feasible for a UN force to be in place by 10 September 1993 as called for in the accords. Among the local parties, no viable alternatives were developed to deal with this anticipated delay.[44]

UNAMIR was to be a phased operation, both in the tasks assigned to the UN forces and, consequently, in the size of the UN force deployed. The phasing was supposed to ensure that the UN would commit resources to Rwanda only in proportion to local actors' ability to implement Arusha. As table 9.1 shows, shifting from Phase One to Phase Two depended on the local actors forming a transitional government. The UN planners determined that without such progress, the other elements of reconciliation could not proceed. So, during Phase One the objective of the UN force was to establish the conditions necessary to permit the "secure installation of the Transitional Government."[45] UNAMIR's initial military tasks derived from this objective and included: moving an RPF battalion into Kigali to counterbalance the FAR and deter aggression against RPF political leaders; monitoring the weapons of the RPF battalion and those of the FAR battalions in Kigali; providing security for the Kigali airport, the barracks of the RPF battalion, and government buildings; and deploying military observers around the country to begin monitoring. Only about half (56 percent) of the total authorized UN force was to be deployed to accomplish these tasks.[46]

Organization of UNAMIR I

UNAMIR was organized according to what has become a fairly standard model for contemporary peacekeeping operations designed to help implement peace accords. A special representative of the secretary-general, Jacques-Roger Booh-Booh from Cameroon, was given overall authority. Under him were three subordinate commands for the military units, the military observers, and the civilian police. General Dallaire, with his experience in the region from UNOMUR, was named force commander, and as such, he commanded the military units. UNAMIR was authorized up to 2,548 military personnel in three infantry battalions, one engineer company, a transportation section (with four utility helicopters), one logistics company, one medical platoon, and 331 military observers. The civilian police component was to be 60 personnel. UNAMIR assumed administrative responsibility for the ongoing UNOMUR and absorbed the OAU's military observer group. Since Rwanda had a constituted government and was at peace, more or less, humanitarian assistance was provided separately from the peacekeeping operation under the

Table 9.1

KEY ELEMENTS OF UNAMIR'S PHASED CONCEPT OF OPERATIONS

Phase One	
Objective	Establish the conditions necessary to institute transitional government.
Period	From Security Council authorization through D-Day[a] (Estimated: October 1993–December 1993).
Local Actors' Tasks	Continue cease-fire, install transitional government.
UNAMIR Tasks	Establish mission infrastructure. Absorb NMOG II; assume administrative control over UNOMUR; continue monitoring Uganda/Rwanda border and demilitarized zone. Escort an RPF infantry battalion into Kigali. Guard international airport, government buildings, and the RPF compound. Monitor a weapons secure area in Kigali (military armaments within 10km radius of city center to be cantoned and monitored).
UNAMIR Strength	1,217 troops and military observers.
Phase Two	
Objective	Prepare for disengagement, demobilization, and integration of former belligerents.
Period	D-Day to D-Day+90 (Estimated: January 1994–March 1994).
Local Actors' Tasks	Continue cease-fire; cooperate with preparations for disengagement, demobilization, and integration of forces.
UNAMIR Tasks	Continue to monitor DMZ, Uganda/Rwanda border; demarcate an expanded DMZ. Continue security tasks in Kigali. Demarcate assembly areas, cantonment sites, and integrated training centers.
UNAMIR Strength	2,217 troops and 331 military observers.
Phase Three	
Objective	Disengagement, demobilization, and integration of former belligerents.
Period	D-Day+90 to D-Day+360 (Estimated: April 1994–December 1994).
Local Actors' Tasks	Continue cease-fire; disengage, demobilize, and integrate forces.
UNAMIR Tasks	Continue to monitor DMZ and Uganda/Rwanda border; continue security tasks in Kigali; supervise troop movements to demobilization sites and monitor entire demobilization process.
UNAMIR Strength	By the end of Phase Three, approximately 1,240 military forces.
Phase Four	
Objective	Normalization and gradual withdrawal.
Period	D-Day+360 to D-Day+660 (Estimated: January 1995–October 1995).
Local Actors' Tasks	Integrate armed forces to assume security responsibilities. Respect human rights during electoral campaign.
UNAMIR Tasks	DMZ dissolved, Uganda/ Rwanda border monitoring ends. Assist in providing security during electoral campaign.
UNAMIR Strength	Approximately 850 troops and 80 military observers.

[a] D-Day was to be the day on which the Transitional Government was installed.

SOURCES: Security Council, *Report of the Secretary-General on Rwanda*, S/26488, 24 September 1993; and General Romeo Dallaire, presentation at Canadian embassy in Washington, D.C., 14 November 1994.

direction of the UN Development Program. However, UNAMIR was authorized to help in the coordination of humanitarian assistance.[47]

UNAMIR was slow to establish its operational capability. At the end of October 1993, only a nascent headquarters staff of 23 was in the country. In

November, the headquarters was strengthened and the first infantry battalion, a unit from Belgium with wheeled armored personnel carriers, began to arrive. In December, most of the second infantry battalion, a light unit from Bangladesh (with some trucks), deployed. Most of the military observers arrived gradually from November 1993 to February 1994.[48]

Despite the languid deployment schedule, UNAMIR was able to conduct all of its assigned tasks for Phase One, including escort of the RPF battalion into FAR-held Kigali and establishment of their barracks ahead of schedule and without incident. UNAMIR observers were co-located with the battalion. In addition to its forces in Kigali, UNAMIR also deployed military observers alongside the RPF and FAR in outlying areas.[49] The UN force demonstrated flexibility by establishing an unplanned sector of operations in the south of the country to mitigate instability caused by an inflow of 350,000 Hutu refugees who had fled ethnic violence in Burundi following a failed Tutsi-led coup there in October 1993.[50]

The local parties failed to form the transitional government in December 1993, as called for in the accords. Nonetheless, since it appeared that the transitional government would be formed in early 1994, the Security Council on 6 January 1994 authorized the peacekeepers to begin Phase Two tasks and deployment of the third infantry battalion.[51] Another light infantry battalion from Ghana (also with few vehicles) was deployed during February and March 1994.[52]

When violence broke out in Kigali in early April 1994, UNAMIR forces were at risk because they were stationed in the midst of the battlefield and exposed not only to small-arms fire but to poorly aimed artillery and mortar fire from both parties. Of even greater concern were threats and calls from the extremist Hutu to attack the Belgian contingent of the UN force. Officials of Habyarimana's party had considered Belgium partial to the RPF since 1990 when RPF military gains followed Belgium's withdrawal of troops from northern Rwanda.[53]

As soon as the fighting broke out UNAMIR could no longer conduct its mandated task. Because the force was expected to operate in a relatively benign environment, it had no war stocks, little ammunition, and except for the Belgian battalion, only poorly equipped forces.[54] The SRSG and the force commander focused the efforts of UNAMIR on self-protection and protection of other UN-associated personnel; on protecting, as far as possible without opposing the belligerents, Rwandan civilians who moved to UN facilities in Kigali for security; and on mediating between the belligerents to achieve a cease-fire. UNAMIR also assisted in the evacuation of non-Rwandan civilians by providing, when possible, armed escort to the Kigali airport and to land borders, and by negotiating with the belligerents to secure consent for French and Belgian forces that conducted independent operations to evacuate Europeans.[55]

Because of the threats against them and the fact that ten Belgian troops had already been killed on the first night of the violence, Brussels announced on 12 April that its contingent would be withdrawn from UNAMIR. Before the violence, Belgium provided about one-quarter of the total UN force but its contingent had been the

Table 9.2

CHANGE IN UNAMIR FORCE COMPOSITION, 30 MARCH–30 APRIL 1994

Country	Unit Type	30 March	30 April
Bangladesh	Infantry Battalion Engineer Company	883	4
Ghana	Infantry Battalion	817	324
Belgium	Infantry Battalion	418	0
Tunisia	Logistics Company	60	40
Romania	Staff Officers	5	0
Canada	Force Commander & Staff Officers	1	6
Numerous Countries	Military Observers	250	246[a]
Total		**2,434**	**620**

[a] Most military observers were moved to Kenya.

SOURCE: UN Department of Public Information, *United Nations Peace-keeping Information Notes, Update: May 1994* (UN Department of Public Information: New York, 1994).

backbone of the UN operation since it was the only fully equipped and competent *combat* unit. After Belgium's withdrawal, UNAMIR had little military capability or mobility.[56]

Following the Security Council decision to shrink UNAMIR's mandate, the organization of the field mission did not change. Though the SRSG, the force commander, and a few civilian and military staff officers remained in Kigali, they did not have many troops to command (see table 9.2). The only maneuverable forces under UNAMIR's control from late April to mid-August 1994 were two partially equipped companies of the Ghanaian infantry battalion, consolidated in Kigali. About half of the military observers were evacuated to Nairobi, Kenya.[57]

With barely enough soldiers for self-protection, the UN force was limited in its capabilities. Of course, its mandate was limited as well. General Dallaire attempted to mediate between the RPF and the interim government, but neither side would agree to a cease-fire. UNAMIR continued to help civilians in the capital whenever it was allowed to do so by the belligerents, such as during the initial days of the violence. Thousands of people, mostly Tutsi, sought safety from militias by gathering in large groups at various locations around the city: the sports stadium, the Milles Collines Hotel, the Tanzanian embassy, and the Sainte Famille church compound. Some huddled around the UN forces. Dallaire later recounted that he felt a moral responsibility to save as many of them as possible. UNAMIR was able to deter, more or less, attacks on the massed civilians whenever it could keep a small number of soldiers near such groups. UNAMIR forces also negotiated with the belligerents to move Hutu civilians to areas of Kigali under interim government control and Tutsi to RPF-held areas. Usually the warring factions consented to such actions as long as the exchanges were on a one-to-one basis. Dallaire estimated that about 25,000 lives in Kigali were saved by the presence and actions of the UN force.[58]

While the Rwandan crisis was bad in early April, by the end of the month it was worse. The human toll became more widely known to the outside world as media reporting surged. As the RPF swept from the north in an easterly arc toward the capital, the predominately Hutu population of areas coming under RPF control fled, presumably fearing atrocities from the mainly Tutsi RPF. On 29 April, UNHCR reported that 250,000 Rwandans had crossed into Tanzania over the previous 24 hours, marking the highest rate of refugee exodus ever recorded by the agency. In addition, UNHCR reported that 38,000 Rwandan refugees had crossed into Burundi, 5,500 into Uganda, and 3,300 into Zaire, for a total refugee exodus of almost 300,000. The UN estimated that 200,000 had been killed in civil violence up to that point and that at least 500,000 were displaced within Rwanda.[59]

The secretary-general appealed to the Security Council to reopen the debate on UN intervention in Rwanda. Unlike previous documents, which did not differentiate between the force-on-force civil war and the civil violence, this communication from the secretary-general indicated that most of the massacres were carried out by armed groups of civilians (the militias), implying a greater chance of success for a UN intervention to impose civil order and stop the massacres. The secretary-general noted that effective action to stop the massacres "would require a commitment of human and material resources on a scale which Member States [of the UN] have so far proved reluctant to contemplate," unusually pointed words from the chief executive to his board of directors.[60]

On 6 May, the Security Council, reacting to the growing crisis, asked for contingency plans to enable the delivery of humanitarian assistance within Rwanda and the provision of assistance to the growing population of displaced persons.[61] The secretary-general submitted a plan on 13 May.

Under Resolution 918 of 17 May, UNAMIR II received new authority to protect civilians but did not act on it because the mission lacked the forces to do so. After repeated efforts to obtain fully equipped troops, or to match equipment to offers of troops alone, the secretary-general admitted defeat on 19 June. Only 354 troops of the authorized 5,500 were volunteered by Member States and deployed to UNAMIR II. Secretariat officials, and in many cases the secretary-general himself, had approached over 50 countries with requests for troops. Only one country, Ethiopia, had offered to provide a ready unit (a motorized infantry battalion). Other offers of infantry units came from the Congo, Ghana, Malawi, Mali, Nigeria, Senegal, Zambia, and Zimbabwe; however, each of these countries required that the units be equipped by the UN. The Secretariat began to make arrangements to obtain the needed equipment but such an endeavor required still more time.[62]

Rwanda had no time to spare. By the time the secretary-general reported back to the Security Council on 20 June, 33 days after the Council had authorized the expanded mandate, the war and ethnic massacres had been ongoing for ten-and-a-half weeks. UNHCR was reporting over 514,000 refugees and more than 1.4 million internally displaced persons; unconfirmed reports of dead ranged from 200,000 to 500,000. In short, roughly one-quarter of the entire population was either dead or displaced. The internally displaced were left to fend for themselves since only two relief groups were operating inside Rwanda, and those only in Kigali.[63]

The secretary-general anticipated three more months would be required to give UNAMIR II the forces it needed to carry out its new mandate. Thus he supported the offer of the government of France to undertake a French-commanded, multinational intervention to implement the humanitarian provisions of the mandate assigned to UNAMIR II.[64]

The French Intervention: Operation Turquoise

On 17 June the government of France, in concert with its ally Senegal, offered to conduct a humanitarian intervention under Chapter VII of the UN Charter to accomplish the objectives laid out for UNAMIR II: specifically, "to protect civilians in the midst of the civil war, by creating safe areas, if needed, and to provide security so that humanitarian activities could be conducted."[65] The United States had set a precedent for coalition humanitarian intervention in support of UN objectives during Operation Restore Hope in Somalia from December 1992 to May 1993 (see chapter 8 in this volume). On 22 June, the Security Council authorized the French and Senegalese intervention, and placed few limits on the operation. The force was authorized to use "all means necessary" to achieve its humanitarian ends. Its size was not limited by the Council; France announced it intended to deploy about 2,500 troops. The operation was to be "coordinated" with the secretary-general and to be of no more than sixty days duration, at the conclusion of which UNAMIR II was supposed to be at full strength and capable of implementing its mandate.[66]

In contrast to the US-led coalition in Somalia, France was suspected by many of acting in bad faith in this endeavor. Many individuals and groups, especially humanitarian aid organizations, accused France of seeking to intervene in order to reinforce the armed forces of its client state, which was losing the war to the RPF. This seems to have been the perception of the two warring factions as well. The RPF announced that the French were not welcome and would be attacked. The extremists' radio hailed the intervention as a liberation from impending Tutsi monarchy. The Security Council was also divided on the issue of French motive.[67] It appeared that France would carry out the intervention with or without a UN authorization, since it had begun positioning forces in central Africa on 16 June. In the end, since there was little other recourse to stop the bloodshed, those with doubts—Brazil, China, New Zealand, Nigeria, and Pakistan—abstained from the vote to authorize the operation rather than oppose it.[68]

Operation Turquoise began the same day it was authorized (22 June) and ended on 21 August 1994. At its height on 13 July, the multinational coalition comprised 2,552 French troops and 508 African troops from 7 states (see table 9.3).[69]

Table 9.3

FORCES SUPPORTING OPERATION TURQUOISE

FRENCH GROUND FORCES	
Inter-Service Units	**No. of Personnel**
Theater Command Post	324
Quick Reaction Military Medical Unit	51
Specialist Detachment (5 helicopters)	218
Refueling Detachments (3)	34
Army Forces	
Tactical Headquarters (2)	104
Command and Services Co. (1)	150
Motorized Infantry Coys. (4)	580
Light Armored Car Sqdrn.	130
Heavy Mortar Sections (2)	118
Combat Engineering Section	25
Transport Helicopter Detachment (3 Puma transport helicopters)	60
Logistics Support Bn.	380
Subtotal, Army & Inter-Service:	**2,174**
AFRICAN GROUND FORCES	
Chad, Congo, Egypt, Guinea-Bissau, Mauritania, Niger, and Senegal	**508**
FRENCH AIR SUPPORT AVAILABLE	
Jaguar strike fighter (4)	C-130/C-160 Medium transport (5)
Mirage fighter (8)	SA-330 search and rescue helicopters (2)
C-135FR light transport (2)	Air force engineering unit
CASA-235 light transport (2)	Atlantique surveillance aircraft (1)
Subtotal air support personnel:	**340**

NOTE: This listing is short 38 persons compared to the maximum force level of 2,552; totals cannot be reconciled from the source documents.

SOURCES: Security Council, *Letter Dated 26 September 1994 from the Permanent Representative of France to the United Nations Addressed to the Secretary-General*, S/1994/1100, 26 September 1994; and Security Council, *Letter Dated 5 July 1994 from the Permanent Representative of France to the United Nations Addressed to the Secretary-General*, S/1994/795, 5 July 1994.

Operation Turquoise was commanded by French general Jean-Claude Lafourcade, who established an inter-service theater command post (similar to a US Joint Task Force) at Goma, Zaire. He reported directly to the Inter-Service Operational Center in Paris. Air support operated from a base near Kisangani, Zaire. Initially, French activities were not coordinated effectively with UNAMIR II because the UN forces were mostly confined to Kigali, in the center of Rwanda, the French were located on the western frontier of the country, and the RPF/FAR fighting front was between them. The two commanders (Lafourcade and Dallaire) finally met face-to-face in Goma eight days after Operation Turquoise began. Subsequently, UNAMIR II maintained a liaison officer in the French headquarters, while the French government and the UN stayed in contact via normal diplomatic channels at UN headquarters in New York.[70]

The first forces crossed into Rwanda from Zaire at Bukavu on 23 June and later at Goma. They conducted mounted patrols in the prefectures of Gisenyi, Kibuye, Cyangugu, and Gikongoro, all of which were still controlled by the interim government. (A Rwandan prefecture is similar to a US state; a commune is similar to a county.) The local population, mostly displaced Hutu who had fled the RPF advance on central Rwanda, greeted the French with open arms. Most of the genocide had ended by the time the French arrived because almost all the Tutsi in the west had already been massacred.[71] About 8,000 Tutsi were rescued on the first day of the operation in the city of Cyangugu, but after 13 days of the operation, only 1,325 more persons were identified as "at risk" and moved to safer areas.[72]

Just before Operation Turquoise was announced, the RPF advance had more or less stopped. General Dallaire believed that, up to that point, the RPF leadership had been content to control only half of the country; however, he contends the RPF was spurred to continue the advance by the French intervention, which the RPF believed was intended to support the FAR.[73] Following the announcement of the intervention, the RPF siege of Kigali intensified and its efforts to seize the rest of the country made substantial progress. Kigali came completely under RPF control on 4 July.[74] Kigali was important both as the national capital and because a large population of Tutsi civilians were massed there under nominal UN protection. Only 50,000 of a previous population of 300,000 remained in Kigali. Half of these 50,000 were displaced.[75]

The renewed RPF advance posed a military and humanitarian problem for the French, who had saved RPF supporters from Hutu militias. RPF officials, who had initially declared that the French would be attacked on sight, softened their rhetoric a bit, but as the RPF advanced toward the French area of operations, it was still unknown how the two forces would interact.

The RPF advance also caused thousands of Hutu civilians, encouraged by the extremists' radio, to flee southwest ahead of rebel forces. If the RPF took control of the entire country, this population would likely decamp to neighboring countries, worsening the humanitarian crisis.[76]

In early July, the RPF closed in on the southern city of Butare, thirty kilometers east of the French area of operations. The one recorded firefight of the entire French-led operation occurred on 3 July when the French ventured out of FAR-held territory and attempted to relocate a group of civilians just as the rebels moved in. The French patrol negotiated passage to and from the civilians with the local RPF leadership, but on the return trip RPF troops controlling a roadblock fired on the French. The French returned fire and broke contact by moving west to Gikongoro.

The next day, 4 July, the commander of the approximately 150 French troops at Gikongoro was ordered to prevent any indigenous armed groups from moving west of that town. French sector commander Colonel Rosier flew to Gikongoro to deliver the orders, telling reporters that the decision to prevent the RPF from entering the southwest portion of the country had been made by French president François Mitterrand. The unit in Gikongoro was reinforced by another 400 troops. Concurrently, in Paris, the French Ministry of Defense announced that the prefectures of Cyangugu and Gikongoro and the southern half of Kibuye prefecture was a "Humanitarian Protected Zone" (HPZ). No armed forces were to be allowed entry into the zone. (Resolution 929 had authorized the creation of safe areas in order to protect civilians.)

France informed RPF officials of these actions at their European headquarters in Brussels. The French armed forces chief of staff, Admiral Jacques Lanxade, indicated that he thought the RPF leadership had grudgingly accepted the French decision. The RPF did not attempt to enter the French-protected zone and no further confrontations occurred between RPF and Operation Turquoise forces. Although French officials stated the HPZ was created for humanitarian purposes only, many FAR troops were inside the zone when it was created. In effect, the French provided sanctuary for these forces as well.[77]

Bypassing the French zone, the rebels continued their push westward to gain control of the remainder of the country. As they did so, virtually the entire population of the northwestern part of Rwanda began to move west, away from the attacking forces. On 13 July, the RPF took control of Ruhengeri, the last stronghold of the interim government. Remnants of the interim government fled southwest to Gisenyi on the border with Zaire. On 14-15 July, as the RPF neared the international border, an estimated 1 million Rwandans fled to Goma, Zaire, creating a huge humanitarian crisis.[78] The rate at which the refugees poured across the border dwarfed the previous record set in April when Rwandans fled to Tanzania. On 20 July, the RPF, in control of the entire country except for the territory held by the French-led coalition, declared a unilateral cease-fire. The next day, in Kigali, the RPF announced a Broad-Based Government of National Unity (BBGNU). A number of political parties and both ethnic groups were represented in the new government. Two officials from the late president Habyarimana's party, MRND, were offered positions within the new government but did not accept.

With the de facto end of the civil war, the security situation improved dramatically in Rwanda. Not only was the war between the armies over but the ethnic violence largely ended as well, since the perpetrators—the militias—had fled into neighboring countries along with the interim government, the FAR, and a large proportion of the Hutu population. Indeed, the area controlled by the new government was relatively empty. On 24 July, UNHCR reported 2.1 million refugees, 1.4 million displaced persons in the

French zone, and 1.2 million displaced persons in the remaining three-quarters of the country. Estimates for the number of dead were coalescing at 500,000. Altogether, 60 percent of the population was either dead or displaced at the end of the war.[79]

As the war concluded, many countries endorsed the new RPF-backed government, ending a period of quandary for the international community since both of the belligerent parties had appeared unsavory at times and both were technically illegitimate. On 19 July, the permanent representative of Rwanda to the UN, who had been serving on the Security Council as a representative of the interim government, relinquished his position. On 24 July, the US ambassador returned to Kigali. The new government received formal recognition from the United States on the 29 July.

As the end of Operation Turquoise's sixty day authorization drew near, French officials, representatives of the relief community, and UNAMIR II leaders developed a plan to keep the population of the French zone stabilized as it passed to UN control and eventually to the new government. There was a well-established concern that, as the French pulled out, the remaining population would flee to Zaire and Burundi out of fear of the RPF. A less expected but substantial concern was the possibility of the civil war starting up again as the new regime confronted armed supporters of the defeated interim government. For these reasons, the transition plan entailed a strong UNAMIR II presence in the French-protected zone, delayed entry of the new government into the area, and increased relief supplies to entice the Hutu to remain.

On 11-13 August 1994, personnel from the UN Development Program and UNHCR entered the zone and began to coordinate the delivery of increased humanitarian assistance. The African units serving with France were organized into a combined unit and transferred to UNAMIR II, where they assumed responsibility for Kibuye prefecture. On 17 August, a Ghanaian infantry battalion took over French positions in Gikongoro, and an Ethiopian infantry battalion did the same in Cyangugu on 19 August. The French were out of Rwanda by 21 August. A small French logistics unit remained in Zaire, near Goma, and provided support to the inter-African unit by boat across Lake Kivu.[80] On 2 September 1994, UNAMIR II began voluntary weapons collection in an effort to reduce any threat to the new government from the Hutu militia. On 6 September, three newly appointed prefects, each accompanied by a UNAMIR II liaison officer and one platoon of RPF troops, reestablished government offices in Kibuye, Gikongoro, and Cyangugu. Five days later the troops were increased to one company per prefecture. The strategy to keep the population stabilized as the French zone gradually transitioned to government control was remarkably successful given the previous volatility of the Hutu population. During the transition only about 50,000 people, or less than 4 percent of the displaced population in the zone, fled to neighboring countries.[81]

Humanitarian Activities

The civil war and ethnic massacres caused massive human suffering. The extraordinary efforts to provide humanitarian assistance in Rwanda and neighboring countries by UN relief agencies, private relief agencies, and military forces have been well described elsewhere.[82] Rather than recount the details of these activities, this section will discuss the mechanisms established by the UN to coordinate the activities of the numerous aid providers.

Before the violence broke out in April 1994, several semi-autonomous UN agencies were providing different types of relief within Rwanda. These included the UNHCR, United Nations Children's Fund (UNICEF), the United Nations Development Programme (UNDP), the World Food Programme (WFP), the Food and Agriculture Organization (FAO), and the World Health Organization (WHO). Many private relief groups were also working there. In an unusual move toward unity of effort, the UN resident coordinator for Rwanda had been given the additional title of humanitarian coordinator. A small interagency staff was assembled to assist his efforts to coordinate the activities of the UN agencies, although "coordination" amounted at best to sharing of information among the UN agencies and the peacekeeping forces. Nonetheless, the precedent for coordination and cooperation and the necessary working relationships had been established among the agencies.[83]

When the violence broke out, almost all the foreign staff of the relief groups, both private and UN-related, evacuated the country. Most of the personnel went to neighboring countries from which they hoped to conduct relief activities into Rwanda. Most of the UN's coordinating team ended up in Nairobi, Kenya. Meanwhile, in Geneva on 14 April 1994, a new office called the UN Rwanda Emergency Office (UNREO) was created by the UN Department of Humanitarian Affairs and UNDP, with the cooperation of the other UN humanitarian agencies. The US government provided $349,000 through the US Agency for International Development (USAID) to help get UNREO established. The team working for the UN Humanitarian Coordinator in Rwanda became the "field office" of UNREO in Nairobi.[84]

During the period of open warfare (6 April - 18 July) humanitarian assistance activities within Rwanda gradually reemerged as the RPF took control of more terrain. The RPF allowed humanitarian agencies to provide relief but required that foreigners be escorted by RPF personnel at all times. Relief groups were pleased that access had been granted, but their actions were constrained by the unusual escorting requirement. Until 8 June, only two aid organizations had a presence in Rwanda, but by the end of the war 22 groups were active.[85] These limited relief efforts, however, did not meet all the needs of the populace. UNAMIR provided some aid in Kigali, but its supplies were largely cut off when the Kigali airport was closed by heavy fighting (5 June - 8 July).[86]

After the RPF captured Kigali on 4 July, UNREO field headquarters moved from Nairobi to Kigali. A satellite office remained in Nairobi. By this time, UNREO had established satellite offices near several major refugee centers—Kabale, Uganda; Bujumbura, Burundi; and Goma, Zaire. Many of the private relief organizations reestablished their local headquarters in Kigali. The USAID Disaster Assistance Response Team (DART) reported that UNREO was "fundamental in encouraging the coordination of NGOs and their activities, as well as in developing relationships with the RPF to formulate and implement relief efforts in RPF territories."[87]

In late July, the exodus into Goma, Zaire, created a humanitarian crisis that surpassed the capabilities of the Zairian government and the relief organizations alike. On 17 July, cholera, a disease caused by drinking contaminated water, broke out in the refugee camps and spread quickly in the squalid mass of people. Within a few days relief agencies were witness to the highest mortality rates (by far) ever recorded in a refugee population. Some 2,000 people were dying every day for lack of clean water and other basic needs. About 50,000 people died before the disease was brought under control by the efforts of the US military, a number of other countries' armed forces, and over 100 private relief groups.[88]

On 22 July 1994, President Clinton directed the commander in chief of US European Command to provide assistance to humanitarian organizations in order to stop the dying in Goma. A US humanitarian assistance operation, known as Operation Support Hope, was conducted from that day until 29 September 1994. A Joint Task Force was established in Entebbe, Uganda, under the command of Lieutenant General Daniel Schroeder. The forces under his control peaked near 2,500 in early August; mostly logistics troops, they also included, as a precaution, an infantry company that served as a small quick reaction force. The US forces purified water and dug mass graves and latrines in the Goma camps; increased the capacity of regional airports, including Kigali, which began around the clock operations on 30 July; and helped UNREO to coordinate the efforts of the numerous aid organizations.

In early August, UNREO opened a new office in Kigali and named it the On-Site Operations Coordinating Center (OSOCC). The OSOCC assumed and expanded the coordinating duties of UNREO's Kigali office. Arturo Hein became the senior UN representative and reported to Shaharyar Khan, who had been appointed SRSG on 1 July 1994. In an unprecedented move, the UN secretary-general had given the SRSG authority over all UN activities within Rwanda in order to strengthen the UN response to the Rwandan crisis.[89] In most situations an SRSG has authority only over the members of the peacekeeping operation, not the humanitarian agencies. However, the SRSG's direct control over humanitarian activities stopped at the OSOCC. The organizations that participated in the OSOCC were only required to coordinate with the UN (as depicted in figure 9.2).

The task of running the OSOCC was delegated to the deputy director of UNREO, who became a critical player in gaining the cooperation of the relief organizations. The infrastructure for the OSOCC (communications equipment, vehicles, office equipment) was provided by the government of Sweden. In addition to the US military cell, the US government provided a DART cell to operate within the OSOCC, an important move because a DART attracts the relief groups.[90] The US government spent over $400 million funding relief activities in Rwanda in fiscal years 1994 and 1995.

The OSOCC and its briefing room became the focal point for coordination of humanitarian assistance activities. Daily briefings were provided to the private relief groups on the security and humanitarian situation. Subgroups were established along functional lines—such as food provision, shelter provision, and children's needs—to facilitate coordination and synergy of efforts among the various relief groups.

Fig. 9.2
UNAMIR AND RELIEF EFFORTS IN RWANDA

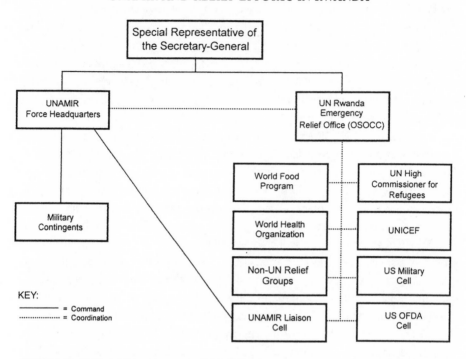

SOURCE: Colonel Karl Farris (US Army), Commander of US Civil Military Operations Center, Rwanda, interview by author, Carlisle Barracks, Pa., 1995.

Concurrent with the establishment of the OSOCC, the US military, as part of its separate humanitarian assistance operation, set up a Civil Military Operations Center (CMOC) in Kigali to liaise with the relief organizations. Not wanting to compete with the OSOCC or usurp any of its authority, the commander of the US CMOC, Colonel Karl Farris, opened a cell within the OSOCC with UNREO's approval. This arrangement worked quite well as it facilitated the US armed forces' provision of assistance to the UN coordination effort.[91] Within the OSOCC, US military personnel received air movement requests from private and UN-affiliated relief groups and UNAMIR II (the US military managed Rwandan air space while Support Hope was in progress); operated a special logistics cell that managed material requests for the population stabilization strategy in the French zone; and were seconded to the World Food Program to develop a warehouse inventory management system and to operate a movement control cell that coordinated the 800 trucks being used by the relief community in Rwanda.[92]

UNAMIR II: Since the End of the War

Since the establishment of the new government at the end of the war (July 1994), the international community has been working in conjunction with the government to enhance security and foster reconciliation throughout the country, according to a three part strategy: (1) resettle internally displaced persons and refugees; (2) develop governmental institutions and the country's infrastructure; and, (3) mete out justice for crimes against humanity. UNAMIR II, the UN relief agencies, more than 100 private relief organizations, and a field operation organized by the UN High Commissioner for Human Rights were the main tools used to implement parts one and two. The Security Council established an International Criminal Tribunal for Rwanda to address the third. Through mid-1995, however, little progress was made except on resettling the internally displaced.

UNAMIR II's primary task in the reconciliation process was to maintain a relatively secure environment within Rwanda, a necessary condition before any other progress could be made. The prompt withdrawal of the French component of Operation Turquoise in late August 1994 drove the UN to deploy its forces. After a mad scramble at the last minute, the UN managed to have an adequate number of replacements in theater before the French departed. By the end of August, UNAMIR II forces numbered 3,764.[93] Most of these troops were in the former French zone and in Kigali, but a small number were deployed in the northwest, near the border with Zaire.

A gradual build-up continued for the remainder of autumn. By the end of November 1994, UNAMIR II had 5,257 military troops, 333 military observers, and 55 civilian police. The military units were contributed by 15 different countries and included six infantry battalions (one each from Ethiopia, Ghana, India, Tunisia, and Zambia) and an Inter-African battalion composed of troops from Chad, the Congo, Guinea-Bissau, Niger, and Senegal. Three separate infantry companies were contributed by Mali, Malawi, and Nigeria. The forces were deployed throughout the country but were concentrated in the less stable areas (the southwest and northwest).[94] The command and control arrangements remained the same as for UNAMIR I, except that a new force commander, Major General Guy Toussignant from the Canadian army, replaced General Dallaire on 19 August 1994. Figure 9.3 shows the build-up and drawdown patterns of the various forces committed to Rwandan peacekeeping or relief through April 1995.

UNAMIR II provided support to the small human rights field mission operated under the auspices of the UN High Commissioner for Human Rights. This mission, run separately from the peacekeeping operation, was designed to support investigations into violations of human rights and to deter the commission of future violations. It was hoped that the presence of the monitors would encourage refugees and internally displaced persons to return to their homes. The government agreed to allow up to 147 monitors in the country—enough to give each commune at least one monitor.[95]

The Security Council voted to establish an International Tribunal on 8 November 1994 to investigate and prosecute the perpetrators of gross human rights violations during the war.[96] The tribunal operates independently of the peacekeeping force and is based in Arusha, Tanzania. The Rwandan government announced it would cooperate with the tribunal but was going to operate a parallel court so that the death penalty

Fig. 9.3

EVOLUTION OF PEACE OPERATIONS IN RWANDA
JULY 1993 THROUGH APRIL 1995

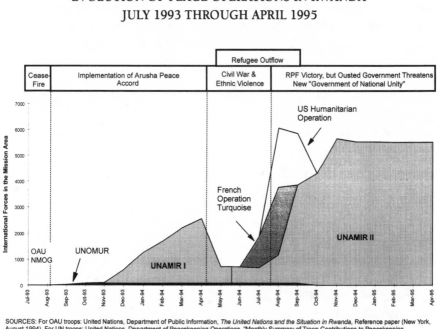

SOURCES: For OAU troops: United Nations, Department of Public Information, *The United Nations and the Situation in Rwanda*, Reference paper (New York, August 1994). For UN troops: United Nations, Department of Peacekeeping Operations, "Monthly Summary of Troop Contributions to Peacekeeping Operations," November 1993 through April 1995. Mimeograph. For American troops: US European Command, "JTF Support Hope: After Action Review," briefing to the Secretary of Defense, undated. Copy obtained by the author from Colonel Karl Farris, Director, US Army Peacekeeping Institute, US Army War College, Carlisle Barracks, Pa, 10 January 1995. For French troops: UN Security Council, *Letter Dated 5 July 1994 from the Permanent Representative of France to the United Nations Addressed to the Secretary-General*, S/1994/795, 5 July 1994; and Security Council, *Letter Dated 26 September from the Permanent Representative of France to the United Nations Addressed to the Secretary-General*, S/1994/1100, 26 September 1994.

could be imposed. (The tribunal is not authorized to invoke capital punishment.) As of this writing, the international efforts were still moving slowly. The Rwandan court had a huge backlog, and appeared to be delayed because the government lacked the personnel to prepare cases. Over 32,000 suspects had been detained by the government in terrible conditions in 11 known prisons. UN officials suspected the government was detaining and torturing others in secret detention centers.[97]

Since the government could not ensure the safety of the international personnel operating under UN auspices, the Security Council gave the task to UNAMIR II on 30 November 1994, expanding the mission's mandate.[98] The force incurred the responsibility to "contribute to the security of human rights officers and the International Tribunal." Given this additional task, the force commander of UNAMIR II redeployed some of his infantry forces to establish UN military presence in more localities. The force commander indicated that his forces were being stretch thin in the process.[99]

UNAMIR II also conducted training for 400 gendarmes and 20 police instructors from December 1994 to April 1995 and planned to provide training for 400 more gendarmes and, subsequently, 100 instructors. The secretary-general reported, however, that this part of the mandate—which was critical to fostering stability in

Rwanda—was severely limited by the failure of UN Member States to provide civilian police for the mission. As of 1 December 1995, only 85 of the authorized 120 civilian police had been provided.[100]

The UN troops also conducted infrastructure rebuilding. For instance, a 600-strong British contingent that served just after the war ended restored the water supply to the whole city of Ruhengeni, the third largest city in Rwanda; repaired several bridges on critical humanitarian supply routes; and provided medical assistance to some 80,000 persons.[101]

The situation in Rwanda gradually improved during the last six months of 1994. Commerce reemerged, some crops were being tended, and the government was remarkably moderate in behavior. By mid-January 1995, about 1 million of the internally displaced population had been returned, or had walked, to their home communes, and the displaced person camps within Rwanda had been reduced to 1.5 million people. The refugee population, however, remained close to its peak level at 2.1 million.[102] The militias and forces of the former government remained in control of the refugee camps and were preventing mass repatriation through intimidation and propaganda. Further, evidence emerged that these forces were preparing for renewed combat under the noses of Zairian authorities.[103]

In late January and early February 1995, tensions increased in Rwanda. With the RPF victory, over 600,000 "old case-load refugees," mostly Tutsi exiles who had been out of the country for many years, streamed back into Rwanda.[104] The return of the Tutsi complicated, and helped to deter, the return of the mostly Hutu population because the Tutsi returnees laid claim to much of the land on which the Hutu had previously lived and farmed. The Rwandan legal system was unable to deal with the competing property claims.

Further destabilizing the situation was an apparent threat of renewed fighting. In February, UNAMIR II strengthened its positions along the border with Zaire in order to detect and deter small groups of infiltrators that had been coming across the border and raiding civilian settlements. These cross-border raids were increasing and some believed that the extremists were beginning a new guerrilla war.[105] The attacks caused the new government to increase security measures throughout the country, that in turn increased tensions between the ethnic groups. For reasons that are not clear, government forces also became increasingly uncooperative with UNAMIR II and began to restrict its movements. On 15 February 1995, a UNAMIR II compound was attacked by unknown assailants, the first instance in which UN forces had been targeted since the end of the civil war. On 5 March another attack occurred. It was unknown whether the attacks were politically motivated or just the work of common outlaws.[106]

In late April 1995, the government apparently decided it could no longer tolerate the presence of the militias in the displaced person camps in the former French zone. The army closed the camps by force, abandoning a voluntary resettlement effort that had stalled. In the process of closing the Kibeho camp, an estimated 2,000 persons were killed in a clash between the government army and the militia that controlled the camp—essentially a long-delayed battle of the civil war. As of late May 1995, most of the internally displaced people had returned to their home communes but had not settled in; many remained on the move.[107]

In July 1995, UNAMIR II gave up the task of monitoring the international border with Zaire, in accordance with the wishes of the government. It also began a gradual withdrawal from Rwanda. Some 1.9 million refugees remained in camps (1,070,000 in Zaire; 602,000 in Tanzania; 230,000 in Burundi; and 4,000 in Uganda). Speculation that the former government's forces would launch a major attack on Rwanda was widespread, prompted by daily reconnaissance flights by a fixed-wing aircraft over Cyangugu Prefecture. The plane, believed to have been operating out of Zaire, reportedly flew out of the range of Rwandan antiaircraft capability. Its ownership was undetermined.[108]

ASSESSMENT

UNAMIR I accomplished its assigned tasks—indeed, initially it was ahead of schedule in making preparations for the demobilization and integration of the former belligerents. It would be difficult, however, to claim that the international community's strategy to bring reconciliation in Rwanda was successful. With its limited mandate and mission plan, UNAMIR I had little ability to gain the initiative from the extremists even before the April 1994 violence began. It was not endowed by the Security Council with the capacity to sway the situation in Rwanda. UNAMIR I was completely reactive. The mission could have been designed to seize the initiative by incorporating a large civilian component to develop grass-roots support for human rights and democracy, or by organizing an information campaign that could have been used to shape public opinion and compete with local hate radio. These types of activities are not often included, however, when a mission is planned to be as inexpensive as possible.

The experience of UNAMIR I puts into question the notion that peace operations should be phased in, with increases in the numbers and responsibilities of the peace force preceded by indicators that the parties to the conflict are, themselves, serious about reconciliation. If the parties can in fact achieve peace on their own, a peacekeeping force may be unnecessary, but most peace processes are not self-catalyzing. In these instances, the reconciliation process may be caught in a postconflict security dilemma in which the parties are sincere in their efforts at peace, but lack sufficient information to trust their former adversaries. Traditional peacekeeping was invented to help resolve this dilemma. A neutral, third-party force deployed between former belligerents or intermingled among them during a cease-fire or following a negotiated settlement can serve to assure each party of the other's compliance with the agreement and increase the confidence of each party in the sincerity of their antagonists. To rely on phased strategies or other strategies that wait for the local parties to take the first steps toward reconciliation is to risk the chance that the process will never get off the ground.

In Rwanda, the initial problem was not a security dilemma. The problem for the Arusha Accords was that extremists from President Habyarimana's party and the army did not support reconciliation with the RPF. UNAMIR I, as it was structured, could not overcome this fundamental obstacle to implementing Arusha. The extremists eventually created a pretext—the death of President Habyarimana—to scuttle the whole process and attempt to end Rwanda's ethnic division once and for all.

During the period in which UNAMIR was much reduced in size, its assigned task was to mediate a cease-fire, which proved impossible. The fact that UNAMIR was able to protect itself and some 20,000-25,000 civilians during the period of the worst massacres is highly commendable given the danger inherent in its situation and the minuscule capabilities of the force.

General Dallaire's successes in Kigali convinced him that civilians could have been protected in the same manner throughout Rwanda if an international force of sufficient numbers and mobility had been available. The validity of this judgment will never be known. It assumes the belligerents were indifferent to the plight of civilians. As events unfolded, it became clear that the interim government's forces, the FAR, and the militias were purposefully targeting civilians in large numbers. In Kigali, as long as UNAMIR's actions were inconsequential for the overall FAR campaign plan, they were tolerated by the extremists. If a larger UN force had been actively interfering with the extremists' genocidal activities, it would likely have been viewed by the FAR as a military opponent.

The UN force might have been able to protect more civilians during this phase of the operation had the Belgian contingent not been abruptly withdrawn. Although the best-equipped and most competent unit in the country—and as such, the backbone of the operation—the contingent withdrew after being targeted by extremist radio and suffering ten dead. Many Hutu believed Belgium to be partial to the RPF because it had been partial to the Tutsi during the colonial period, and because Hutu perceived Belgian military deployments during the Rwandan civil war as intended to support the RPF. A similarly competent UN contingent with less of a history in the local conflict would probably have provided a more sustainable core for UNAMIR. However, the extremists might have tried to force out any strong, third-party force, viewing it as a potential rival or the potential enforcement arm of the international community.

Belgium's abrupt withdrawal from UNAMIR I also illustrates how much UN security activities depend upon the willingness of Member States to provide the necessary muscle and, if necessary, take casualties to fulfill a UN mandate. As long as political will for robust peacekeeping operations is in short supply, such operations will continue to be hamstrung, which poses a dilemma for the UN. Peacekeeping theory calls for a neutral international force, yet the countries willing to commit forces to an operation must see their interests served by such participation, which may raise questions about their neutrality. If the interests served are unrelated to the conflict—a desire for international recognition, for example, or for financial gain—neutrality is enhanced but political will may not be.

Operation Turquoise

Even though the French and their allies behaved more or less as neutrals in the war zone, their presence and activities did, in fact, affect the outcome of the war. The zone under French control was not purged of militias or FAR troops. These combatants, with their weapons, were intermingled with the displaced civilians in the zone and later posed a significant problem for the new government when it closed the camps.

The French intervention could also have had serious consequences for UN-AMIR. The RPF opposed the French operation, and the RPF could have attacked UNAMIR in an attempt to exert leverage over the French. RPF forces did threaten UNAMIR troops from African countries that had endorsed the French operation. General Dallaire evacuated military observers from Senegal, Congo, and Togo in response to these threats. Further, RPF officials refused to meet with Dallaire from 23 to 29 June, disrupting his efforts to seek a cease-fire.[109]

Nonetheless, on balance, Operation Turquoise must be considered a success. If it had not occurred the remaining Tutsi in the southwest—who were among 11,500 persons directly protected or evacuated by the French—would likely have been killed. The establishment of the "humanitarian zone" stabilized the displaced population of 1.4 million that took refuge there. As long as the French were present, the Hutu believed they were safe from the RPF and did not flee further south into Burundi or west into Zaire. It was better (although not by much) for the displaced population to remain in their own country, spread throughout a wide area, than to have them huddled along the international border.[110] Within the French zone, the intervention forces provided humanitarian assistance that saved an undetermined number of lives. The French plan had been to provide a secure environment that would allow the relief organizations to offer the actual assistance. In the end, the French troops provided more assistance than they had planned because aid agencies were overwhelmed elsewhere and because many preferred not to operate under French auspices, remaining doubtful of French intentions until the very end.[111]

Humanitarian Activities

The coordination of humanitarian assistance activities for the Rwandan crisis was unprecedented. If the UN Department of Humanitarian Affairs had not established UNREO and then the OSOCC, Rwanda's agony would have been worse because some relief efforts would have been misdirected. The multidimensional strategy to keep the displaced population in the French area from fleeing as the French departed probably would not have been conceived or implemented without the OSOCC and the active participation of the humanitarian agencies and private groups.

The US government played a critical role in the coordination efforts by providing the seed money for UNREO and later deploying the DART and military cells to participate in the OSOCC. The government of Sweden provided a complete infrastructure package that included the specialists needed to operate communications equipment.

UNREO and the OSOCC were able to coordinate activities effectively only because most of the relief agencies and the private groups consented to their leadership. During the initial months of the crisis, the coordination team had valuable currency in its ability to gather, analyze, and provide information to the relief groups, which enabled it to develop strategy and set priorities rather than just being a venue through which relief groups could announce their intentions to each other. As the situation in Rwanda became less insane, the relief organizations' need for OSOCC's information decreased. Its effectiveness in developing strategy decreased in proportion as the relief agencies began to go their own way. If the coordination team had possessed a more durable currency, such as discretionary control of money, it would have remained effective for a longer duration.[112]

In the future, DHA should develop the capability to deploy a field coordination unit without relying on outside benefactors for people and equipment. Systems and procedures should be developed to routinize coordination rather than depend on the uncertain response of benefactors. Self-reliance would help to normalize the coordination efforts because DHA would be able to plan and train for such events and deploy common field equipment.

Assessing UNAMIR II

UNAMIR II was supposed to protect civilians from the ravages of civil war and from the direct attacks of militias. As already discussed, the UN was unable to deploy its force in a timely manner because the only Member States willing to provide troops for the mission did not offer troops who were properly equipped or trained. When UNAMIR II was finally deployed, the war was over and the killing had largely stopped. UNAMIR II did contribute to stability in Rwanda from the end of the war until June 1995, when the Rwandan government pressured the Security Council to reduce its mandate. Its wide deployment served to deter and mitigate tensions as the new government tried to rehabilitate the country and develop the infrastructure for a stable civil society (police, a justice code and courts, and economic opportunity). If UNAMIR II had not been present, it is likely that the forces of the old regime, some of which had escaped to the refugee camps in Zaire, would have counterattacked.

These remnants of the former government and its armed forces used the relative safety of the camps to reorganize, looking toward another round of warfare. Before Rwanda could hope for stability, these external groups had to be dealt with. The refugees needed to be brought home and provided the essentials to restart a basic life. Armed groups and their political leadership needed to be disbanded, and many deserved to stand trial for gross human rights violations. Within Rwanda, the new government needed to achieve a balance between redressing past wrongs against the Tutsi minority and respecting the rights of the Hutu majority. Further, the country's infrastructure needed to be rebuilt and much of the farmland needed to be cleared of mines. As of mid-1996, Rwanda was still a very long way from recovery.

CONCLUSIONS

Can (or should) the international community's response to future crises be made more effective? Three major shortcomings hindered that response in the case of Rwanda:

the strategy adopted for UNAMIR I was too passive; Security Council decision-making was ill informed; and the recent experience of dealing with civil war elsewhere made states with the capability to react speedily to the trauma in Rwanda reluctant to do so.

Inappropriate Mandate

The UN's experience in Rwanda suggests that its Member States should support strategies for field operations that help to motivate reconciliation, rather than strategies that leave the initiative for implementation with the local parties. Any such proactive strategy must be commensurate with the risk-adverse tendencies of most UN members, but risk aversion need not equal passivity. In particular, the capacity to conduct an information campaign should be part of the basic tool kit of every UN peace operation. In situations like Rwanda before April 1994, in which commitment to peace and reconciliation may be marginal, even feigned, on the part of one or more local parties, an effective information campaign could be used to guide public opinion, to shape the perceptions of the antagonists, and to undercut the appeal of extremists. An information campaign could also lend flexibility to the operation. The content of such a campaign can be shifted easily in response to the situation. It is much easier to reprogram the tone of a radio broadcast than to reposition troops.

The UN is currently reluctant to intrude on the airwaves of member states without their permission. The UN should overcome this reluctance. Chapter VII operations are legal interventions, overriding the UN Charter's strictures against intervention into "domestic jurisdiction" of states. The UN should interpret intervention to include intervention over the airwaves as well as over the ground. Chapter VI operations are more problematic because they are based on the consent of the host government(s) and other recognized parties. The UN should make it clear, however, that an information campaign consistent with the mandate of a peacekeeping operation is part and parcel of such an operation. The right to conduct such a campaign should be arranged before the Security Council authorizes a Chapter VI operation and should be a condition of such authorization. In Rwanda this did not occur, and the opening of a UN radio station was delayed for several months.

The UN is oversensitive to the accusation that an information campaign constitutes UN propaganda. In the aftermath of civil war, the UN is likely to be looked upon as a source of more objective information than any of the local antagonists about such things as election procedures and political rights.

An information campaign, however, is no panacea, especially once violence has erupted. In Rwanda, hate radio's propaganda so captured the militias and the general Hutu population that simply providing an alternative source of objective information would not have been enough to stop the slaughter. More aggressive actions were needed—destruction of the transmitters or jamming of their broadcasts. Such actions, however, may have precipitated a violent response against the intervenors, as was the case in Somalia. Thus, any force sent to take on hate radio would also have had to be strong enough to take on the interim government's army and militias, under a political mandate flexible enough to accommodate the RPF, lest it become an enemy in turn.

Ill-informed Decision-making

Ill-informed decision-making by the Security Council in the period immediately following the outbreak of violence also offers lessons for future crisis. Decisions are based in part on their expected potential consequences. Had Council members expected the Rwandan situation to become so deadly to civilians, encompassing genocide and precipitating costly follow-up humanitarian operations, they may have decided differently. Member States expect the Security Council and the Secretariat to make wise decisions concerning peace operations. In order to meet these expectations, the Council and its executive agent, the Secretariat, must be provided with good information.

A good deal of information concerning troubled states is already available within the UN. Hindsight concerning Rwanda has unearthed numerous indicators that what happened was going to happen. What is most needed is a mechanism to gather and assess the disparate bits of such information as it is reported from Member States, NGOs, the humanitarian and human rights agencies of the UN, and the media. Input from such a mechanism would supplement the intelligence that Member States prepare on their own to guide the votes of their Security Council representatives and would help guide the recommendations of the Secretariat to the Council.

Problems of Political Will

UNAMIR II was slow to deploy because states with the capability for rapid military response lacked the will to respond. UN missions already underway in Somalia and Bosnia had sensitized the Security Council to expect humanitarian interventions to be difficult, costly, and perhaps futile. The Somalia operation was clearly failing by the time Rwanda erupted (the United States had withdrawn its forces from that country not two weeks prior to the downing of President Habiyarimana's aircraft), and in Bosnia the UN was dealing with the Serbs' assault on the "safe area" of Gorazde. These two operations absorbed 75 percent of the 70,000 troops then committed to UN peacekeeping worldwide, an all-time high that had strained the organization's managerial capacity and tapped out its traditional sources of troops. Under these circumstances Security Council members, and the United States in particular, were reluctant to undertake yet another commitment in a conflict-ridden, failing state.

If, however, states in the region had forces trained and equipped for the sort of intervention needed in Rwanda, it is conceivable that the handful of UN members who pay the majority of peace-keeping costs would have supported a Security Council decision to send those forces into action. Advance training and access to prepositioned, UN-owned equipment would have lessened the region's dependence on outside powers—who currently have to take the risks associated with crisis intervention as well as shoulder the monetary burden. Shifting the risks to the region would make the monetary burden easier to bear. Whether regional states would in fact rise to the occasion is another matter, and before any investment in training and equipment is made, there must be evidence of regional powers' willingness to act constructively in future crises.

We do not know whether UNAMIR II could have substantially diminished the killing in Rwanda even if well-trained troops with appropriate equipment had been readily available. With hindsight, Brigadier General Dallaire's contention that timely deployments of UN troops might have quelled violence country-wide seems problematic, given the Hutu extremists' strategy and their determination to see it through. Although the French-led Operation Turquoise was successful, that success is somewhat misleading as an indicator of what might have happened to UN forces. Turquoise operated within territory held by France's erstwhile Rwandan allies, who expected French support and thus welcomed its intervention. UNAMIR II, if deployed in May 1994 as soon as it was authorized, would have faced much different circumstances.

NOTES

1. United Nations Development Programme, *Human Development Report, 1992* (Oxford: Oxford University Press, 1992), 20; and US Central Intelligence Agency, *The World Factbook, 1993-94* (New York: Brassey's, 1993), 289.

2. Guy Vassall-Adams, *Rwanda: An Agenda for International Action* (Oxford, UK: Oxfam Publications, 1994), 8.

3. Catherine Newbury, *The Cohesion of Oppression: Clientship and Ethnicity in Rwanda, 1860-1960* (New York: Columbia University Press, 1988).

4. US Central Intelligence Agency, *The World Factbook, 1993-94,* 289. US Department of State, *Annual Report on Human Rights, 1993* (Washington, D.C.: US Government Printing Office, 1993).

5. The thousands of Tutsi that allegedly defected en masse from Uganda's National Resistance Army (NRA) to join the RPF brought their uniforms, weapons, and ammunition with them. Although both RPF commanders and Ugandan president Yoweri Museveni denied that the NRA ever provided any direct support to the RPF, there is evidence to suggest a high degree of complicity between the two groups. Military rebels were allowed, after all, to carry out the invasion of a neighboring, sovereign state from Ugandan territory, using Ugandan weapons. The Ugandan government may also have allowed the RPF to transport arms and troops across its soil, as well as provided direct support in the form of ammunition and military equipment until May 1993, when peace talks were well under way. See Human Rights Watch Arms Project, *Arming Rwanda: The Arms Trade and Human Rights Abuses in the Rwandan War* (January 1994), 19-21; and

Catherine Watson, *Exile From Rwanda: Background to an Invasion* (Washington, D.C.: US Committee for Refugees, 1991), 2, 14.

6. Human Right Watch, *Arming Rwanda,* 23-24.

7. US Department of State, *Annual Report on Human Rights, 1993.*

8. Watson, *Exile from Rwanda,* 14-15.

9. Security Council, *Further Report of the Secretary-General on Rwanda,* S/26350, 24 August 1993, para. 8.

10. Human Rights Watch, *Arming Rwanda,* 10.

11. Human Rights Watch Africa, *Genocide in Rwanda: April–May 1994* (New York: Human Rights Watch, 1994), 2.

12. US Department of State, *Annual Report on Human Rights, 1993.*

13. Human Rights Watch, *Arming Rwanda,* 27.

14. Security Council Resolution 846, 22 June 1993.

15. Security Council, S/26350, para. 19. Since the signing of the peace accord, Uganda has scrupulously upheld its provisions.

16. Security Council, *Report of the Secretary-General on Rwanda,* S/26488, 24 September 1993, paras. 4-10, 24. The OAU's observer group was increased to 132 military observers and reauthorized as an interim measure until this neutral international force could be deployed. When the UN Security Council authorized this force, which became UNAMIR, most NMOG personnel were incorporated into it and the OAU operation was deactivated.

17. Security Council, *Second Progress Report of the Secretary-General on the United Nations Assistance Mission for Rwanda,* S/1994/360, 30 March 1994, para. 27.

18. Human Rights Watch Africa, *Arming Rwanda,* 2.

19. François Misser, "Who Killed the Presidents?" *New African* (June 1994): 14.

20. Security Council, *Letter Dated 1 October 1994 from the Secretary-General Addressed to the President of the Security Council,* S/1994/1125, 4 October 1994. annex.

21. Ibid., para. C.

22. Africa Watch, *Beyond the Rhetoric: Continuing Human Rights Abuses in Rwanda* (Washington D.C.: Africa Watch, 1993).

23. Bacre Waly Ndiaye, *Report to the UN Economic and Social Council, 11 August 1993,* quoted in Vassall-Adams, *Rwanda: An Agenda,* 26.

24. Francois Misser, "Belgium and France Beg to Differ," *New African* (June 1994): 15.

25. This counts the tandem UN operations in Cambodia as one and the operations in the former Yugoslavia as one, disregarding their March 1995 disaggregation into three distinct operations. See Pamela L. Reed, J. Matthew Vaccaro, and William J. Durch, *Handbook on United Nations Peace Operations* (Washington D.C.: The Henry L. Stimson Center, 1995), A-2-3.

26. White House, *Press Briefing, Policy on Multilateral Peacekeeping Operations,* Washington, D.C., 5 May 1994. Transcript by Federal News Service, Washington D.C., document number WL-05-01, 5 May 1994. Mimeograph.

27. Security Council Resolution 872, 5 October 1993.

28. Security Council Resolution 912, 21 April 1994. Although authorized a maximum of 270 troops after this decision, the force never dropped below 440 troops.

29. Paul Lewis, "Security Council Votes to Cut Rwanda Peacekeeping Force," *New York Times,* 22 April 1994, A1.

30. Security Council, *Minutes of the 3368th Meeting of the Security Council,* S/PV.3368, 21 April 1994.

31. Security Council, *Special Report of the Secretary-General on the United Nations Assistance Mission for Rwanda,* S/1994/470, 20 April 1994.

32. Colonel William Clontz, US Mission to the United Nations, interview by author, Buenos Aires, Argentina, 6 April 1995.

33. Security Council, S/PV.3368.

34. Julia Preston, "Rwandans Confound UN Security Council: Humanitarian Impulse as Mission Impossible," *Washington Post,* 8 May 1994, A25.

35. Security Council, S/1994/470, paras. 1, 3.

36. Associated Press Wire, "Massacres Spreading in Rwanda," *New York Times,* 19 April 1994, A3.

37. Clontz, author's interview, 6 April 1995.

38. Security Council Resolution 918, 17 May 1994.

39. Paul LaRose-Edwards, *The Rwandan Crisis of April 1994: The Lessons Learned* (Ottawa, Canada: International Human Rights, Democracy, and Conflict Resolution, 1994), 71.

40. Security Council Resolution 997 (1995), 9 June 1995; and Security Council Resolution 1029, 12 December 1995. The last peacekeepers departed Rwanda by 19 April 1996. "Last UN Peacekeepers Leave Rwanda," *New York Times,* 19 April 1996, A8.

41. UN General Assembly series, *Financing of the United Nations Observer Mission Uganda-Rwanda and Financing of the United Nations Assistance Mission for Rwanda,* A/49/375, 12 September 1994, 49-54; and A/49/375/Add.1, 11 October 1994, 3-4.

42. Colonel Daniel Bastien, French Air Force, Military Advisor at the French Mission to the United Nations, interview by author, New York, 31 July 1995.

43. Security Council, S/26488, paras. 2, 3, 18, and 19.

44. Ibid., paras. 12-17.

45. Ibid., para. 44.

46. Ibid., paras. 25-40.

47. Ibid.

48. General Romeo A. Dallaire, presentation at the Canadian embassy to the United States, Washington D.C., 14 November 1994; see also Barry M. Blechman and J. Matthew Vaccaro, *Training for Peacekeeping: The United Nations' Role* (Washington D.C.: The Henry L. Stimson Center, 1994), C-59-60.

49. Security Council, S/1994/360, paras. 23-32.

50. Alison Des Forges, "Burundi: Failed Coup or Creeping Coup?" *Current History* (May 1994): 206-207.

51. Security Council Resolution 893, 6 January 1994.

52. Security Council, S/1994/360, paras. 23-32.

53. Vassall-Adams, *Rwanda: An Agenda,* 29.

54. Dallaire, presentation at the Canadian embassy.

55. Security Council, S/1994/470, paras. 4-6.

56. Dallaire, presentation at the Canadian embassy.

57. UN General Assembly, A/49/375, 27.

58. Dallaire, presentation at the Canadian embassy.

59. UN Department of Public Information, *United Nations Peace-keeping Information Notes, Update: May 1994,* (New York: United Nations, 1994), 163.

60. Security Council, *Letter Dated 29 April 1994 from the Secretary-General Addressed to the President of the Security Council,* S/1994/518, 29 April 1994, para. 8.

61. Clontz, author's interview, 6 April 1995.

62. Security Council, *Letter Dated 19 June 1994 from the Secretary-General Addressed to the President of the Security Council,* S/1994/728, 20 June 1994, paras. 1-11. Undersecretary-General for Peacekeeping Kofi Annan indicated that some states tried to take advantage of the pressing need for troops and equipment by demanding exorbitant reimbursement for participation. See LaRose-Edwards, *The Rwandan Crisis of April 1994: The Lessons Learned,* 17.

63. US Agency for International Development, Bureau for Humanitarian Response, Office of U.S. Foreign Disaster Assistance, *Situation Report Number Two,* 8 June 1994. (This series is hereafter referenced as OFDA, *Situation Report #,* [date].)

64. Security Council, S/1994/728, para. 12.

65. Ibid.

66. Security Council, S/RES/929, 22 June 1994.

67. Clontz, author's interview, 6 April 1995.

68. Vassall-Adams, *Rwanda: An Agenda,* 46.

69. Security Council, *Letter Dated 26 September 1994 from the Permanent Representative of France to the United Nations Addressed to the Secretary-General,* S/1994/1100, 26 September 1994, annex, para. I.

70. Ibid.

71. "The French in Rwanda," *The Economist,* 2 July 1994, 39-40.

72. Security Council, *Letter Dated 5 July 1994 from the Permanent Representative of France to the United Nations Addressed to the Secretary-General,* S/1994/795, 5 July 1994, annex, para. 5.2.2.

73. Dallaire, presentation at the Canadian Embassy.

74. OFDA, *Situation Report #4,* 25 July 1994.

75. OFDA, *Situation Report #3,* 13 July 1994.

76. Raymond Bonner, "French Forces in Skirmish in Rwanda," *New York Times,* 4 July 1994, A2.

77. Julian Bedford, "Rebels Capture Rwanda's Capital and Key Town," *Reuters* newswire, 4 July 1994; Geoffrey Varley, "France Vows to Keep Rwanda Fighters out of Safety Zone," *Agence France Presse,* 4 July 1994; and Michela Wrong, "France Promises to Halt Rwandan Rebel Advances," *Reuters* newswire, 4 July 1994.

78. OFDA, *Situation Report #5,* 18 August 1994.

79. OFDA, *Situation Report #4*, 25 July 1994.

80. Colonel Karl Farris, interview by author, Carlisle Barracks, Pa., 10 January 1995.

81. Security Council, S/1994/1100.

82. Larry Minear and Philippe Guillot, *The Contributions of International Military Forces to Humanitarian Action in Rwanda* (Providence, R.I.: Brown University, Thomas Watson Institute, 1995).

83. Arturo Hein, interview by author, Buenos Aires, Argentina, 6 April 1995.

84. Hein, author's interview, 6 April 1995.

85. OFDA, *Situation Report #1*, 23 May 1994; *Situation Report #2*, 8 June 1994; *Situation Report #3*, 13 July 1994; and *Situation Report #4*, 25 July 1994.

86. OFDA, *Situation Report #3*, 13 July 1994.

87. OFDA, *Situation Report #4*, 25 July 1994.

88. Donatella Lorch, "A Year Later, Rwandans Stay and Chaos Looms," *New York Times*, 15 July 1995, A1.

89. The UN secretary-general announced through his deputy spokesman that "overall responsibility for the coordination of political, military, as well as humanitarian activities inside Rwanda rests with his Special Representative Mr. Shaharyar Khan." United Nations Secretariat, "Statement Attributable to the Deputy-Spokesman for the Secretary-General," 2 August 1994. Mimeograph.

90. Farris, author's interview, 10 January 1995. DARTs, among other duties, dispense US government funds directly to UN agencies, other international organizations, and private relief groups.

91. Farris, author's interview, 10 January 1995.

92. Colonel Karl Farris, "After Action Review: Civil Military Operations Center (CMOC)," memorandum, Carlisle Barracks, Pa., 1994. Mimeograph.

93. Reed, Vaccaro, and Durch, *Handbook on UN Peace Operations*, A-41-43.

94. Ibid.

95. Security Council, *Progress Report of the Secretary-General on the United Nations Assistance Mission for Rwanda*, S/1994/1133, 6 October 1994, paras. 11-14.

96. Security Council Resolution 955, 8 November 1994.

97. Donatella Lorch, "Rwanda Jails: No Space, No Food, No Justice," *New York Times*, 15 April 1995, A1.

98. Security Council Resolution 965, 30 November 1994.

99. Security Council, *Progress Report of the Secretary-General on the United Nations Assistance Mission for Rwanda*, S/1995/107, 6 February 1995, para. 29.

100. Security Council, *Progress Report of the Secretary-General on the United Nations Assistance Mission for Rwanda*, S/1995/297, 9 April 1995, para. 26-31; Security Council, *Report of the Secretary-General on the United Nations Assistance Mission for Rwanda*, S/1995/1002, 1 December 1995, para. 8.

101. "British Army brings much-needed help to Rwanda," *Army Quarterly and Defence Journal* 124, no. 4 (October 1994): 397-400.

102. OFDA, *Situation Report #3, Fiscal Year 1995*, 30 January 1995.

103. Security Council, S/1995/297, para. 8.

104. OFDA, *Situation Report #3, Fiscal Year 1995,* 30 January 1995.

105. Security Council, S/1995/107, para. 25.

106. Security Council, S/1995/297, paras. 20-22.

107. Donatella Lorch, "Rwandan Killings Set Back Effort to Provide Foreign Aid," *New York Times,* 26 April 1995, A3.

108. Department of Humanitarian Affairs (DHA) Integrated Operations Center, Kigali, *Humanitarian Situation in Rwanda,* no. 12, 19 July 1995, mimeograph; and Buchizya Mseteka, "Rwanda strongman appeals to Zaire over guerrillas," *Reuters* newswire, 9 November 1995, 10:55 A.M.

109. Dallaire, presentation at the Canadian embassy.

110. Security Council, S/1994/1100, section V.

111. Farris, author's interview, 10 January 1995.

112. Antonio Donini and Norah Niland, *Rwanda Lessons Learned: A Report on the Coordination of Humanitarian Activities, Prepared for the UN Department of Humanitarian Affairs,* November 1994, 6-10. Mimeograph.

TEN

KEEPING THE PEACE IN THE BORDERLANDS OF RUSSIA

KEVIN P. O'PREY

The region of the newly independent states (NIS) that emerged from the Soviet Union presents a major challenge to traditional notions of peacekeeping. Perhaps the paramount legacy of the Soviet Union has been the development of numerous deep-seated ethnic and political conflicts. In a region characterized by weak states, disputed political borders, a plethora of militias, and no shortage of weapons, the demand for international mediation and peacekeeping is enormous.

Yet the prospects for traditional approaches to peacekeeping in this region are not promising. These conflicts have developed at the same time that the United Nations' capacity to undertake new peacekeeping missions has been taxed to the limit. But more importantly, conflicts and their resolution in the newly independent states are dominated by the regional hegemon—the Russian Federation. While the Russian government welcomes endorsement and financial support from international organizations for its mediation and peacekeeping efforts, Moscow insists that it take the leading role diplomatically and militarily. Not surprisingly, its role is rarely impartial. Although the UN, the Organization for Security and Cooperation in Europe (OSCE),[1] and the United States have been involved in efforts to mediate NIS disputes, their limited means and Russia's occasional opposition have limited their effectiveness. Thus, the newly independent states represent a case in which there is a pronounced tension between the objective goal of peacekeeping and the interests of the great power that is most interested in, and most capable of, carrying out the mission.

Yet despite their sometimes suspect motivations and means, most of Russia's peacekeeping efforts need not be cause for great alarm. Each of the conflicts discussed here developed independently of Russian involvement. Moreover, having no interest in instability on its borders, the Russian government's peacekeeping efforts in most cases have aimed to limit conflicts in the NIS region. The problems have been a by-product of the baggage that Moscow brings to its role as peacekeeper: the pro-Russian concessions it demands from the conflicting parties for providing a public good, its refusal to allow outside parties to play a major role, and the often heavy-handed way that it enforces settlements. Although the United States, UN, and OSCE cannot—and should not—force their way into NIS peacekeeping, there are opportunities to influence Russia into pursuing a more balanced policy of peacekeeping that is consistent with international principles.

This chapter analyzes the particular features and challenges of international peacekeeping in the NIS. It excludes consideration of the use of military force *within* the borders of the Russian Federation—the conflict in Chechnya, in particular—because that is, in international legal terms, an internal Russian matter. The first section addresses the interests and capabilities of the external actors most interested in the region: Russia, the United States, the UN, and the OSCE. The next section considers the broad trends of conflict and peacekeeping in the NIS, as well as each of the current or likely peacekeeping operations in detail. The concluding section offers suggestions for external institutions and states seeking to encourage more positive behavior from Russia's peacekeeping efforts.

THE EXTERNAL ACTORS

Although they did not create the conflicts, the external actors discussed here have played a decisive role in the course and resolution of these conflicts. Ironically, each of these actors shares the common goal of peace, but the approaches with which they pursue this goal differ markedly. The most influential outside player is the Russian Federation, which, not coincidentally, is an interested party in each of the conflicts. The United States has peripheral interests in the region but has little inclination to pursue them actively in opposition to Russia, and has little leverage in any case. The United Nations has urged that Russia's mediation and peacekeeping efforts abide by UN standards, but its inability or unwillingness to provide UN troops or finances has hampered its effectiveness. The OSCE, meanwhile, has been more assertive in offering international peacekeeping forces and mediation. Although it, too, has thus far been unable to have much impact on Russian efforts in this region, it has the potential to make a substantial contribution.

The Russian Federation

Russia's approach to conflict mediation and peacekeeping in the NIS has been characterized primarily by insistence that Moscow remain the dominant player in regional politics and security. Although the Russian government seeks international recognition and financial support for its peacekeeping operations, it has jealously guarded its leading role.[2] Thus, instead of international peacekeeping forces dispatched by the UN, Moscow prefers that the UN support operations established by Russia or the Commonwealth of Independent States (CIS), the regional body that it tends to dominate. At times, Russia's diplomatic initiatives even appear to be oriented toward undermining alternative peace efforts, as in the Nagorno-Karabakh conflict. If the price for international recognition and support of its peacekeeping efforts is outside control, Russia seems to prefer to go it alone.

Russia's Foreign Policy in the NIS

An activist Russian foreign and security policy in the NIS appears to be inevitable for reasons ranging from national psychology to national interest. In the fractious realm of Russian domestic politics, one clear consensus among groups of all persuasions is that Russia should remain one of the world's "Great Powers." The perceived requirement for membership in the great power club is a sphere of influence in the so-called "near abroad."[3] Even if a Russian leader did not agree with this consensus, he would incur great political risk by pursuing policies that contradict it. Moreover, having lost Eastern Europe and the Soviet Union, Russian politicians and military officials are loathe to give up their historically leading role in what they consider to be their own backyard. In his September 1994 speech to the UN General Assembly, Russian president Boris Yeltsin explained that Russia considers its ties to the other members of the CIS to be a special "blood relationship." As a consequence, these states are Russia's foreign and economic policy priority.[4]

National pride, however, is not the only reason for Russian activism. Russia also has tangible national interests in developments in the other newly independent states. Most importantly, instability there potentially poses a threat to the unity of the Russian state itself. The armed conflict that broke out in December 1994 between Moscow and the separatist Russian republic of Chechnya underscores the sometimes shaky ethnic foundation of the Russian Federation. Beyond Chechnya, there are several Russian regions that to lesser degrees have rebelled against Moscow—for example, Tatarstan and the Komi Republic. In other regions—in North Ossetia and Ingushetia, for example—violence flares up periodically between competing ethnic groups. Given this multiethnic character and the potential for internal instability, permitting the redrawing of borders in the near-abroad states would set a dangerous precedent.[5] Refugee flight to Russia caused by NIS conflicts might also exacerbate internal Russian ethnic strains.

Furthermore, the Russian government seeks to protect the 25 million ethnic Russians who found themselves living in foreign lands after the sudden collapse of the USSR. A large number of Russian troops were similarly caught in the collapse, their bases relocated overnight, as it were, to foreign countries.[6] Also, Russia and the other newly independent states continue to have close—if not interdependent—economic ties. Although Russia has reduced its dependence on these economies, it nonetheless has a continued interest in their political and economic stability.

Finally, the Russian military is extremely sensitive to the involvement of non-CIS states in affairs of the countries on Russia's periphery. The security concerns that prompted Russian opposition to the expansion of NATO have been even more pronounced in their near abroad. Russian officials accurately perceive that Russia competes with a number of countries seeking a greater role in this region. Turkey and Iran seek to expand their influence in the Transcaucasus region, while Afghanistan and Iran are pursuing roles in the Central Asian states.

Thus, Russian military doctrine highlights a number of NIS scenarios as grounds for military action. These include any foreign territorial claims on the Russian Federation *or its allies*; current and potential "hot spots" of local wars and armed conflicts in the vicinity of Russian borders; the suppression of the rights, freedoms and interests of Russian speaking citizens in foreign states; and attacks on Russian armed forces and military facilities in foreign countries.[7] The common theme here, of course, is that Russia's military doctrine identifies Moscow's leading role in the NIS as necessitated by Russian *security* interests.

In order to defend regional interests, Russian Foreign and Defense Ministry officials in 1994 began pursuing a series of bilateral agreements with CIS states willing to permit Russian military bases on their territory. The aim was to create a Russian-guaranteed "zone of stability" in the NIS.[8] The Russian military believes that by maintaining bases in these regions, it will be able to deter foreign powers from becoming involved in the affairs of CIS states.[9] In a similar vein, Russian officials have increasingly referred to a perceived need to defend the CIS borders as if they were Russia's own.[10] Troops of the Russian Border Guards are already based on all of the CIS' outer borders except for those of Azerbaijan, Moldova, and Kazakhstan.[11]

Russia's Approach to Peacekeeping

An active, leading role in enforcing peace in NIS countries is a central component of Russia's regional strategy. By permitting conflicts on its periphery to persist, Moscow fears that it is inviting both interested foreign powers to gain a foothold in the region and instability to spill over Russian borders.[12] Foreign Minister Andrey Kozyrev highlighted these Russian concerns when he told the newspaper *Izvestiya* that plenty of Russia's Asian neighbors would be glad to infiltrate the former Soviet republics "under the guise of peacekeeping forces."[13] It is an unstated assumption in all these calculations that preventing or stopping conflict in the NIS region is a Russian obligation. In fact, Russian government officials often appear to be perplexed by Western criticism of their efforts to achieve peace in the region.[14]

Russia appears to prefer two coalition models—local or CIS—for its peacekeeping efforts in the NIS. In both cases, Russian officers possess operational control of the peacekeeping forces and Russian troops predominate. The local coalition model is based on Russian forces with supplementary troops contributed in roughly equal numbers by the parties to the conflict. These peacekeeping forces are usually mandated to maintain a demilitarized zone between the warring parties. This model is currently being employed in Moldova, Abkhazia, and South Ossetia.[15]

The CIS coalition model is based on Russian forces and command but includes troops from other members of the Commonwealth of Independent States who are not involved in the conflict. Moscow has been able to revitalize the initially stillborn CIS into a vehicle for providing a stamp of international legitimacy and outside material support for Russian peacekeeping activities in the NIS region. Russian forces predominate, however, as few of the other CIS members have military forces worthy of the name. The coalition model has been implemented in Tajikistan, where the Central Asian members of the CIS strongly support Russian action.[16]

Although these two models satisfy Moscow's desire for a leading role in NIS peacekeeping efforts, they share the common problem of imposing substantial financial and human costs on the Russian military. For the Abkhazia operation, Russia has had a difficult time getting anything more than an endorsement from its economically pressed allies. Although each of the CIS participants pays for its own forces in the Tajikistan operation, more than half of the troops and most of the actively engaged forces are Russian. Thus, the Russian military unhappily bears most of the cost of the Tajikistan mission and consistently complains that other CIS members do not help enough.[17]

Formally speaking, the Russian Ministry of Defense has dedicated two of its divisions—the 27th Motorized Rifle Division of Totskoye, Volga Military District and the 45th Motorized Rifle Division of Kamenka, Leningrad Military District—as well as an airborne battalion exclusively to peacekeeping tasks. Apparently, the motorized rifle elements of these two divisions are maintained at full strength, while the tank, artillery, and other units are maintained at a cadre level. Personnel in each are supposed to receive a five-month training program.[18]

Yet peacekeeping operations are nonetheless taking a substantial physical and material toll on all Russian forces. As the military failures in Chechnya during 1994-95 graphically indicated, the Russian armed forces are suffering from low levels of readiness, with many active units seriously undermanned.[19] Most of the operations discussed in this chapter have been carried out by Russian units already based in the so-called "hot spot." These units are usually at little more than cadre strength when they are initially called upon, so they must scrape together composite battalions from across the entire unit. For example, when the 145th Motorized Rifle Division in Batumi, Georgia, was called upon to provide forces for the peacekeeping mission in Abkhazia, it possessed only 3,000 personnel, instead of its standard allotment of 13,000. In order to put together two battalions for the peacekeeping mission, it had to use the bulk of the division's noncommissioned officers. Ironically, even the designated peacekeeping divisions appear to be suffering readiness problems. Regiments from the 27th Motorized Rifle Division performing six-month peacekeeping tours in Moldova are reportedly short of junior officers.[20]

The readiness problem is the product of the financial crisis afflicting the Russian Ministry of Defense. Even before the costly Chechnya debacle, the Ministry of Defense complained bitterly to the Chernomyrdin government that its budget could not support housing for Russian officers, much less a normal procurement and operations plan. The problem has been aggravated by the refusal of the two houses of the Russian legislature to create a separate peacekeeping budget. Thus, these operations are funded directly from the Ministry of Defense's already strapped budget.[21]

This financial crisis is one of the many reasons that Russia looks outside the NIS for peacekeeping support. Moscow has aggressively courted international organizations and the West for recognition and material support of CIS/Russian peacekeeping efforts because they ostensibly further international objectives. Another reason appears to be the psychological benefit to the Russian national image that would accompany international reaffirmation of their perceived great power status.

Yet Moscow has not been willing to sacrifice much control in return. Yeltsin, for example, has declared that the UN and other international organizations should grant Russia "special powers as a guarantor of peace and stability in the region of the former Soviet Union."[22] As explained by another Russian official, Moscow welcomes OSCE and UN support, but not supervision, of its peacekeeping missions: it wants these organizations to authorize peacekeeping operations by Russian or CIS forces; to provide logistical, financial, and other material assistance; and to support Russia's political mediation efforts. Although the international organizations are free to send observers, they should not interfere with Russian or CIS operations.[23]

Not surprisingly, Russia has had little success in gaining international support for its NIS activities. At best, it has succeeded in gaining UN "endorsement" of the Abkhazia peacekeeping mission. By fall 1994, Russian foreign ministry officials appeared to be giving up their attempts to gain international financing and were instead emphasizing their autonomy in NIS matters.

There are numerous reasons for the international reluctance to give a blanket endorsement to Russian leadership in NIS peacekeeping. First, Russia tends to have an exceptionally aggressive, heavy-handed, approach to peacekeeping that often ignores international norms. The Russian approach is distinct in its willingness to use military force to suppress hostilities. This approach is rarely "peacekeeping" strictly defined, but rather an open-ended, proactive form of peace enforcement that resembles Western concepts of counterinsurgency operations. Interestingly, there is as yet no word for "peacekeeping" in the Russian language: the commonly used term *mirotvorcheskiy* translates into English as "peacemaking."[24] Indeed, Foreign Minister Andrey Kozyrev argued that the UN's ideal model of peacekeeping is inappropriate for NIS conditions.[25] The more "appropriate," or Russian, approach was explained by the former commander of the 14th Army, Aleksandr Lebed, and echoed by the commander of the Volga Military District:

> The main experience in preparing peacekeeping forces consists in the following: If a decision is made to use troops, they must be employed decisively, firmly and without delay. And it must be clear to everyone that a force has arrived capable of putting every insolent, encroaching bandit in his place. *Anyone attempting to throw a wrench into the works will be arrested or destroyed.*[26]

Second, the same factors that generate Moscow's interest in these regions often make it something of a less than neutral party in the mediation, resolution, and implementation of agreements. Although Moscow's ultimate goal is virtually always to settle the conflict, the Russian government is not above taking advantage of its position to promote its own foreign policy interests. Russia refused to assist Eduard Shevardnadze's Georgian government in its war with Abkhazian separatists and the domestic opposition until Shevardnadze abided by Moscow's wish that Georgia join the CIS. Moscow also strong-armed Moldova's government with threats that it would weaken its peacekeeping commitment, in an effort to gain Moldovan flexibility on the issues of the Dniester breakaway region and the basing of Russian forces.

Perhaps more disturbing, Russian military forces at times have played a direct role in some of these conflicts. Most of these cases appear to have been the result of a breakdown in command and control between Moscow and forces in the field early in the conflicts. Russian forces still stationed in most of these regions were a steady source of weapons for the various hostile groups. Russian garrisons either sold their weapons to locals or gave them to friendly forces, a result of "freelancing" or corruption on the part of local commanders.[27] Proximity also made Russian units repeatedly susceptible to direct involvement in the conflicts. When Russian forces are fired upon—for whatever reason—Russian Ministry of Defense rules of engagement permit field commanders to defend themselves forcibly.[28] Early in the conflicts in Tajikistan and Abkhazia, for example, Russian commanders ordered punitive strikes against local forces.

But in at least one case—Moldova—Russian military forces on the ground have intervened decisively in a local conflict with, at least, the tacit acquiescence of the government in Moscow. In that case, when the local Russian military commander assumed a prominent role in local politics, the Ministry of Defense and the Yeltsin government were extremely reluctant to discipline him, and Moscow ignored Western efforts to mediate the conflict.

Evaluating Russia's Role and Interests

Although a number of observers argue that Russia is pursuing a renewed empire in the newly independent states, the truth is more complex.[29] Arguments that Moscow has a master plan for reclaiming the Soviet/Russian empire ignore the schizophrenia in Russia's actions. Although in some regions—like Moldova—Russian diplomatic and military efforts have interfered with sovereign governments and clearly violated international law, in other areas—such as South Ossetia—Russia has played a constructive role. Even within a single case—for example, Tajikistan—Russia has played both a negative and positive role depending upon the time and conditions. Perhaps more importantly, the Russian government has exercised restraint in a number of areas that offer opportunities for adventurism. In the dispute with Ukraine over the Crimea, in particular, Moscow has pursued a generally cautious and diplomatic policy. Arguably, if the Russian government wanted to encourage heightened confrontation on the ground in this dispute, it had plenty of opportunities.[30]

Russia's primary interests in all of the NIS disputes appear to be maintaining its role as the dominant player and containing conflict in the region. It has very little interest in fomenting strife on its borders. While Moscow is not above using economic and, occasionally, military bullying to press its interests in the region, its dominant preference is still the maintenance of the status quo, especially borders. Thus, Moscow has generally pressed for federal solutions to crises of secession—permitting the breakaway regions autonomy within the existing state.

The schizophrenic character of Russia's peacekeeping efforts has been most prominent in those regions where residual Russian military forces or ethnic Russians have found themselves, inadvertently, in the midst of local conflicts. In these cases, problems of command and control and Russian domestic politics have weighed heavily, resulting in constraints on the generally moderate Yeltsin government. In Moldova, in particular, the prominence of Russians in the breakaway Dniester region's leadership has generated enormous support from Russia's very vocal nationalist, imperialist, and even communist circles.

The United States

The US government has found itself with conflicting objectives in its approach to peacekeeping in the NIS. The Clinton administration believes there is a need for outside peacekeeping in the region and has serious misgivings about giving Russia a free hand. At the same time, the region is not high enough on the administration's list of priorities to warrant US—or even UN—peacekeepers or a direct challenge to Moscow. NIS peacekeeping ranks well below broader US objectives such as Russian political and economic reform or denuclearization. Short of threatening a rupture of the larger US-Russian relationship, the United States has very little leverage over Moscow's policies.

The pressing need for peacekeepers in the NIS developed at approximately the same time that the Clinton administration was reformulating its international peace-keeping policy to be much less activist.[31] The original draft of the administration's peacekeeping policy reportedly opposed extending peacekeeping authority to the CIS and making any UN payments to Moscow for its peacekeeping activities. Instead the United States proposed a voluntary international fund to underwrite such efforts.[32]

The Clinton administration ultimately adopted a policy of cautious support for some of Moscow's efforts. In September 1994, the US representative to the United Nations, Madeleine Albright, conceded that a significant Russian role is the only practical solution for policing conflicts in the region. While stressing that the "burden of proof" was on Russia to demonstrate that its peacekeeping activities were in fact benign, Albright announced US approval of Russia's peacekeeping role in the Transcaucasus region and Central Asia. Reportedly, the Clinton administration has expressed willingness in some cases to make financial contributions to a fund supporting the Russian operations.[33]

At the same time, the US government has been critical of Russian activities in other regions, seeking the withdrawal of Russian forces from Moldova.[34] Given that it has little leverage over Moscow in this area, a US policy of selective support is deemed the best way to encourage Russian peacekeeping to adhere to some international norms.

The United Nations

The United Nations has adopted a relatively "hands-off" approach to peacekeeping in the newly independent states. The UN has been willing to mediate negotiations between conflicting parties, as well as provide international observers, but refuses to become involved in armed peacekeeping missions. Although the Russian government and CIS officials have frequently and loudly requested a UN imprimatur and, perhaps more importantly, financial support, the UN has repeatedly demurred. Only after considerable Russian agitation did the UN Security Council finally "endorse" in July 1994 the Russian peacekeeping mission in Abkhazia, but without providing "blue helmet" status or financial assistance for the mission.[35]

There are three reasons for the UN's reluctance. First, the UN is short of money. Second, few of the conflicts in the NIS meet the standards for a United Nations peacekeeping mission. Russian/CIS missions in the region have a peace enforcement character, and where cease-fires exist they are either frequently violated or persist only because of a preponderance of Russian force. Third, and perhaps most important, the secretary-general and some members of the Security Council have been concerned about Russia's role in the conflicts themselves, their settlement, and their enforcement. The UN has been reluctant to bless Russia's self-proclaimed "special" or "leading" role in the NIS. Secretary-General Boutros-Ghali has stressed for some time that any UN peacekeeping operations there would have to be UN operations from the start, replete with UN commanders on the ground and restrictions on the number of troops from nonneutral states.[36]

Inevitably, the secretary-general and the UN have had to defer to Russia. Because the UN offers neither troops nor funds for CIS peacekeeping, it has very little leverage on Moscow or, for that matter, on the parties to the various conflicts. Evidently concluding that some Russian-led missions are better than nothing, the UN has sent observers to monitor Russian and CIS peacekeeping operations in Tajikistan and Abkhazia.

The UN has also worked to mediate lasting settlements to several of the NIS conflicts after Russia and/or the CIS have secured a cease-fire. In particular, UN mediators have played a prominent role in facilitating negotiations between the Georgian government and the Abkhaz leadership, as well as between the Tajik government and its political opposition.

The Organization for Security and Cooperation in Europe

The OSCE has been more energetic than the UN in attempting to mediate settlements and organize peacekeeping operations in the NIS but has often found its efforts hampered by Russian opposition, the intractability of some of the conflicts, and the organization's own somewhat lumbering nature. Like the UN, the OSCE has refused Russian requests that the organization endorse Russia's peacekeeping missions and has, on a number of occasions, sharply criticized Russian behavior.[37] In June 1994 the OSCE presented the Russian government with a list of preconditions for its endorsement of peacekeeping activities, all of which were rejected by Moscow, reportedly because of clauses that required all sides in a conflict to agree to the introduction of peacekeeping forces, forces that were not to remain indefinitely.[38]

In December 1994, the OSCE decided in principle to send a multinational peacekeeping force under its auspices to Nagorno-Karabakh. Russia's acceptance of the OSCE decision represented a significant precedent for outside forces to be used in NIS peacekeeping. As of mid-1996, however, the OSCE force existed only in spirit, as political differences between Russia and the OSCE, and the continued intransigence of the local parties delayed the signing of a peace agreement.

THE NIS CONFLICTS AND THE PEACEKEEPING EFFORTS

As of this writing there are four active operations in the NIS that the Russian government characterizes as "peacemaking": in the breakaway regions of South Ossetia and Abkhazia in Georgia, in Tajikistan, and in the Dniester region in Moldova. Russian peacekeepers are also likely to play a substantial role in the Nagorno-Karabakh operation. Four of the five conflicts derive from separatist movements seeking independence and/or unification with another state. The other conflict—Tajikistan—is a civil war with considerable foreign involvement. Only the Abkhazia and South Ossetia missions resemble true "peacekeeping" efforts, and the Abkhazia mission is the only one with United Nations endorsement.

The political instability in each of these regions predates the active involvement of Russia. The several-year collapse of the Soviet Union that concluded in December 1991 created a power vacuum in which ethnic and political groups could compete openly. But the weakness of the newly independent states, the divisions within them, and the abundance of weapons throughout these regions provided an extremely permissive environment for violent conflict.

Most of the new countries emerging from the Soviet order confront a difficult state-building problem. This is in part a legacy of Soviet ethnicity policies. In Central Asia and the Transcaucasus region, for example, republican boundaries were intentionally drawn to divide some large ethnic groups between two or more republics. Although this was a successful strategy for subjugating ethnic identities under a totalitarian regime, its legacy is weak political cohesion for each of these new states as well as a host of border disputes.[39]

The collapse of Soviet power also left these new states with weak or nonexistent political institutions at a time when local elites—traditionally supported by Moscow—confronted challenges from newly empowered political groups. The lack of an organized army or police force in many of these states contributed to the rise of many undisciplined, competing militias. Yet none of these groups has suffered for lack of

Table 10.1

OVERVIEW OF THE CONFLICTS AND PEACEKEEPING OPERATIONS

	SOUTH OSSETIA	ABKHAZIA	TAJIKISTAN	MOLDOVA	NAGORNO-KARABAKH
Type of Conflict	Separatist movement.	Separatist movement.	Civil war.	Separatist movement.	Separatist movement; undeclared interstate war.
Type/Size of Peacekeeping Contingent	Local Coalition: 700 Russian troops plus 700 Georgian and joint North/South Ossetian units.	CIS Coalition: 3,000 mostly Russian troops with minor Tajik contribution.	CIS Coalition: up to 25,000 troops, mostly Russian and Tajik; small Kazakh, Kyrgyz, and Uzbek contingents.	Local Coalition: 2-6 Russian battalions; 3 Moldovan battalions; 2 Dniester battalions.	OSCE Operation: 3,000-strong force to be deployed.
Date Initiated	July 1992	June 1994	August 1993 (second mission)	July 1992	(authorized, not deployed as of July 1996)
International Authorization	No: Trilateral agreement between Georgia, South Ossetia, and Russia in cease-fire and peacekeeping.	Yes: UN- and Russian-mediated cease-fire; UN and CIS endorsement of peacekeeping mission.	Yes: CIS-directed mission.	No: Bilateral agreement between Moldova and Russia.	OSCE authorization.
Other International Involvement	None.	UN Observer Mission; UN and OSCE Joint Commission to mediate.	UN-sponsored peace talks; OSCE mediation effort.	OSCE Observer Mission.	OSCE "Minsk Group" mediation effort; Turkey, Iran, and United States also involved.
Mandate	Police cease-fire and disengagement of forces along South Ossetia-Georgian border.	Separate factions and maintain demilitarized zone along Abkhaz-Georgian border.	Protect Afghan border and stop conflict within Tajikistan.	Separate factions along Dniester River.	OSCE mandate being negotiated.
Russian Interests Involved	Halt fighting; maintain border status quo.	Maintain existence of Georgia and keep it in CIS; seek federal solution to conflict.	Protect borders of CIS from Afghan incursions; maintain stability in Tajikistan.	Support Russian breakaway republic; prevent Moldovan union with Romania	Maintain Russian military presence and predominant military role in region; minimize influence of other foreign states.
Assessment of Russian Diplomacy and Peacekeeping	Positive: mission seems to have limited conflict but no signs of lasting political settlement.	Positive: mission appears to be engaged in honest peacekeeping effort.	Mixed: mission is primarily one of border defense; few signs of lasting settlement to conflict.	Negative: mission biased toward Dniester side and has obstructed OSCE monitoring.	

armaments. The ubiquitous presence of the Soviet military throughout the USSR resulted in large stocks of weapons being claimed—or seized—by political groups in each of the newly independent states.

The remainder of this section considers each of the active or prospective peacekeeping operations in detail. For each case, the origins of the conflict are discussed, with particular attention paid to the role played by Russia or other outside actors. The history and details of the peacekeeping operation are then analyzed. Each case concludes with an assessment of the success of, and lessons derived from, the particular peacekeeping mission. The order of the discussion is subjective, with those operations in which Russia is largely a positive force treated first and the cases in which Moscow's behavior is most suspect—Moldova and Nagorno-Karabakh—coming last. Table 10.1 provides an overview of the conflicts and peacekeeping operations. The table also serves as a frame of reference while reading through the details in the text.

South Ossetia

The peacekeeping mission in South Ossetia represents perhaps Russia's most positive involvement in conflicts in the NIS. The South Ossetia mission was Russia's first attempt to apply the local coalition model to peacekeeping. Moscow orchestrated the settlement and peacekeeping force directly with the conflicting parties—South Ossetia and Georgia. The CIS has played no role.

South Ossetia is the first of two conflicts that have threatened to tear the state of Georgia apart. One of the first union republics to declare itself independent of Soviet rule, Georgia has since been a tragedy of internal political divisions, external threats, and most of all, contradictions. Although Georgian nationalists argued in terms of self-determination and human rights in breaking from the USSR, they have been reluctant to adhere to the same standards in dealing with minorities in their own country. The first Georgian president, Zviad Gamsakhurdia, was a world famous dissident who became a paranoid autocrat once in office. The former Communist Party chief of the republic, Eduard Shevardnadze, returned as the savior of democracy and the Georgian nation. Among numerous other characters in the Georgian drama, there is Tengiz Kitovani, a sculptor-turned-minister-of-defense who later became a militia warlord opposed to the Tbilisi government. The conflicts played out among these and other characters have made Georgia highly vulnerable to secession movements and outside intervention by Russia.

Origins

The South Ossetian conflict is an excellent example of many of the state-and nation-building problems that are rife in the newly independent states. The contradictions between Soviet nationality policy and the forces of national self-determination are felt acutely here. The new Georgian state has sought to maintain its territorial integrity as defined in the Soviet period, but the excesses of Georgian nationalists drove minority

Fig. 10.1
MAP OF GEORGIA

SOURCE: US Government

ethnic groups like the Ossetians and Abkhazians, in their turn, to seek independence from Georgia.

Located in the north of Georgia along the border with Russia, during the Soviet period South Ossetia was an autonomous oblast within the Georgian Republic. It shared a border, however, with a separate autonomous republic—North Ossetia—that was part of the Russian Republic. Ethnic differences between North and South Ossetia were and are practically nonexistent while the differences between Ossetians and Georgians are substantial. For example, in 1989 only 14 percent of Ossetians claimed fluency in Georgian.[40]

Any misgivings that ethnic Ossetians had about the Soviet arrangement were reinforced by the nationalist character of the Gorbachev-era Georgian independence movement. Indeed, the movement appeared to have little tolerance for the rights or self-determination of ethnic minorities.[41] Open tension between Ossetians and Georgians developed in 1989 when South Ossetian intellectuals began agitating for independence from Georgia. Shortly thereafter Tbilisi initiated a republic-wide program for increased use of the Georgian language. This effort provoked bitter recriminations, charges of discrimination, and a request to Moscow from South Ossetian patriotic groups to permit their unification with North Ossetia. Increased agitation against Georgian rule provoked Tbilisi to deploy its Interior Ministry troops to South Ossetia in November 1989. Thereafter, the Georgian parliament and the South Ossetian Supreme Soviet engaged in a war of laws and charges that spurred conflict at the grass-roots level in Ossetia. In August 1990, the South Ossetian Supreme Soviet declared its sovereignty, and the next month it proclaimed the region to be a "Soviet Democratic Republic."[42]

The Georgian Supreme Soviet, having elected Zviad Gamsakhurdia as its chairman in October 1990, abolished the "autonomous" status of the South Ossetia oblast in December. When South Ossetian radicals killed several ethnic Georgians in response, Gamsakhurdia declared a state of emergency in the South Ossetian capital. Moscow urged flexibility, but by mid-1991 there was interethnic war replete with blockades, hostage-taking, and artillery attacks by the Ossetian guerrillas.[43]

Because of open rebellion brought on by his erratic rule, Gamsakhurdia was forced to flee Georgia in January 1991. Ironically, Gamsakhurdia's ouster and replacement by Eduard Shevardnadze as Georgian head of state in March 1992 did little to improve South Ossetian-Georgian relations. Although he had been the most radical of Gorbachev's reformers and a champion of human rights, Shevardnadze was also a Georgian patriot who would not tolerate the disintegration of his state.[44]

The conflict ultimately came to a head at Moscow's instigation. Chafing at the influx of refugees into Russia and worried about the risk of the conflict spreading north, Speaker of the Russian Supreme Soviet Ruslan Khasbulatov in June 1992 demanded that Georgia cease its provocations and allow refugees to return home. Otherwise, he warned, Russia would be forced to consider incorporating South Ossetia into the Russian Federation. Although Shevardnadze denounced Russia's political intervention into the conflict, he agreed to meet with Russian president Boris Yeltsin as well as representatives from the two Ossetias in late June 1992 at Dagomys, outside the Russian city of Sochi. At this meeting the parties agreed to a cease-fire and the deployment of a joint peacekeeping force.[45]

The Peacekeeping Mission

The South Ossetian mission was the first application of Russia's local coalition model of peacekeeping. The peacekeeping force is comprised of troops from both sides of the conflict as well as from North Ossetia and Russia. Although a joint command supervises the operation, because Russia provides the largest share of troops, it dominates. The Russian component of the peacekeeping force is 700 troops; Georgia and South Ossetia together contribute another 700 or so.[46]

The initial mission of the peacekeeping force was to separate the warring sides by creating a 14-kilometer-wide buffer zone separating South Ossetia and Georgia. The peacekeepers maintained 12 observation posts and 20 control posts in the conflict zone, and on a number of occasions, reportedly had to use force to separate the warring factions.[47]

By June 1993 the operation appears to have expanded to a more general policing function throughout South Ossetia. A document from the Joint Military Command described the primary mission of the peacekeepers as stopping "criminal activity of destructive forces striving to exacerbate the situation [in the region] and striving to renew armed clashes."[48] The Russian commanders complain that because the South Ossetian government has not been able to assert any control over its territory and its local militia/police force is ineffective, all parties look to the peacekeepers to protect them from widespread crime in the region. By the fall of 1994, the lack of a settlement and demands for troops elsewhere drove the Russian command to reduce its contribution of peacekeepers to about 500.[49]

The Dagomys agreement stipulated that compliance would be overseen by a specially created Mixed Oversight Commission comprised of representatives from Russia, Georgia, and North Ossetia. Although this commission was fairly successful in handling critical problems such as prisoner exchanges, confiscating weapons, and providing food for the local population, since the spring of 1993 its function has diminished except for occasional short inspection trips.[50]

Assessment

The Russian-led operation has suppressed the wide-scale conflict in South Ossetia but, reflecting a pattern in Russian peacekeeping efforts, it has done little more than enforce peace. There has been slight progress toward resolving the underlying conflict between Georgia and the South Ossetians. As a consequence, South Ossetia continues to be characterized by sporadic violence and is, generally speaking, an unpleasant place to live. In June 1994 the then Russian deputy minister of defense for peacekeeping, Colonel General Georgiy Kondrat'yev, complained that the delivery of food to the region had been meager, the crime situation had been deteriorating rapidly, and paper currency had been virtually withdrawn from circulation.[51]

Abkhazia

Organized and implemented almost entirely by Russia alone, the peacekeeping effort in Abkhazia is to date the only NIS mission that has received the endorsement of the United Nations. The conflict is a clear case of Moscow using mediation and a Russian-led peacekeeping mission to achieve a foreign policy objective: in this case, coaxing a resistant Georgian government to join the CIS and permit Russian bases on its territory. Nonetheless, since Georgian head of state Eduard Shevardnadze requested Russian military support in the fall of 1993, the Russian role has become very constructive.

Origins

The conflict in Abkhazia pitted a minority separatist movement in the Abkhaz Autonomous Republic against the Georgian government in Tbilisi. Although there are relatively few Abkhazians, outside support for their cause and the weakness of the Georgian government contributed to a near-death experience for Georgia in the fall of 1993. Over the next nine months, the conflict caused 3,000 deaths and created 200,000 refugees.[52]

During the 1920s, Abkhazia was formally a union republic (SSR) with the same status as Georgia. In 1931, however, Joseph Stalin downgraded Abkhazia's status to that of an autonomous republic within Georgia. Due to Georgian migration in the 1940s and 1950s, Abkhazians accounted for only 17 percent of the population of their titular republic before hostilities broke out. Nonetheless, Abkhazians were permitted to run the republic's government, and for the last thirty years of the Soviet period, agitated for a return to their status as a union republic independent of Georgia. The agitation intensified during the Gorbachev period, generating counterdemonstrations in Tbilisi in March 1988 by patriotic Georgians opposed to Abkhazia's secession. In April 1988, a hunger strike by Georgian protesters in Tbilisi was broken up by Soviet troops, leading to the deaths of twenty civilians and the acceleration of Georgian efforts to break from the Union.[53]

Just as in South Ossetia, tensions between the Abkhazians and Georgians escalated in response to repressive, pro-Georgian measures adopted by Zviad Gamsakhurdia and the Georgian Supreme Soviet. In August 1990, the Abkhazian Supreme Soviet declared the region to be a full republic independent of Georgia at the same time as South Ossetia. The Georgian Supreme Soviet responded by annulling the decision. The battle was waged largely with legal measures until July 1992, when the Abkhazian parliament revived its 1920s-era union republic constitution and again declared itself independent of Tbilisi.

Under circumstances that are still unclear, the following month Georgian defense minister Tengiz Kitovani ordered Georgian forces to deploy into Abkhazia. The initial pretext of the operation was to attack forces of deposed Georgian president Gamsakhurdia, who were allegedly allied with Abkhazian separatists. But it quickly became an effort to crush Abkhazian resistance to Georgian rule. Kitovani's forces seized the Abkhazian capital, Sukhumi, and shelled the parliament building.[54]

What followed was an armed confrontation between the separatists and forces allied with the Tbilisi government, punctuated by a series of failed attempts at cease-fire. Moscow was instrumental in getting the two sides to agree to a short-lived cease-fire in September 1992. Yeltsin's subsequent order for Russian forces to seize control of strategic railroads along the Abkhazian coast, ostensibly to protect Russian interests, outraged Georgian nationalists. Subsequently, Shevardnadze complained that Russian forces were supporting the separatists, preventing Georgia from using its air force and navy to quash the rebellion.[55]

In March 1993 the Abkhazians sought to retake Sukhumi in an offensive reportedly supported by fighter aircraft with Russian markings.[56] Yeltsin, Shevardnadze, and the Abkhazians agreed on cease-fires in May and July 1993, both of which were violated almost immediately by the Abkhazians. On the second occasion, the Abkhazian forces pushed Georgian forces out of Sukhumi.

This defeat nearly caused the dismemberment of Georgia. Having been routed in Abkhazia, Shevardnadze's forces suddenly found themselves under attack from the militias loyal to deposed president Zviad Gamsakhurdia ("Zviadists"). Shevardnadze had never been able to consolidate the disparate militias and their warlords into a coherent Georgian army and Ministry of Defense. The Georgian leader on a number of occasions appealed for NATO and/or UN peacekeepers to be dispatched to the conflict zone, without success.[57] As his army collapsed, Shevardnadze requested Russian intervention and accepted membership in the CIS as the price of that support. Russia then embraced Shevardnadze and intervened to turn back the Zviadists. In early December 1993, with the Gamsakhurdia forces defeated, the Georgians and Abkhazians reached a new cease-fire. The negotiations dragged on through the following April when, under Russian mediation in Moscow, the two sides agreed to repatriate refugees and deploy a peacekeeping force.

Although the agreement called for a force under UN auspices, Secretary-General Boutros-Ghali, who was present at the signing, refused to endorse either UN military units or UN funding of CIS/Russian peacekeeping operations. The UN, however, did send additional observers to the region and endorsed the Russian peacekeeping mission. The CIS conferred its official endorsement in October 1994 and later extended the mandate of the mission twice.[58]

The Russian Role

Russia's role in the Abkhaz-Georgian conflict has shifted considerably over time from manipulator to relatively honest peacekeeper. Moscow has primarily reacted to developments in the region, although always in a manner that promotes Russian interests. If Moscow had consistent strategic goals, they were (1) to freeze the conflict and perhaps return to the *status quo ante,* albeit with increased autonomy for Abkhazia within a federal Georgia, and (2) to secure Georgia's joining the CIS as the price of Russian assistance. Although a number of Western analysts have argued that 93,000 Abkhazians could not possibly have defeated a nation of 3.8 million without substantial support from Russia, it does not appear that Russia ever allied with the Abkhazians.[59] Moscow refused to support Abkhaz claims of independence or even requests to join the Russian Federation. The virtue of the federal solution was there were neither outright winners nor losers in the conflict. Russia apparently opposed an Abkhaz victory because of the dangerous precedent that it would set for separatist movements in Russia, yet Moscow also would not tolerate a Georgian victory that resulted in Tbilisi's complete subjugation of Abkhazia.[60]

The participation of Russian forces in the conflict appears to have been primarily a locally directed phenomenon with occasional encouragement from central authorities in Moscow. Russian forces stationed throughout the region inevitably became part of the hostilities, caught in crossfires, defending strategic sites of Russian interest, or fending off raids by local fighters seeking weapons.[61] In other cases, weapons ended up in the hands of Abkhazian fighters, transferred from sympathetic Russian units or sold by corrupt ones.

As long as neither side seemed poised to win, the Russian Ministry of Defense appears to have tolerated or, at times, even encouraged the anti-Georgian actions of local commanders. The Russian military has carried a particular grudge against Shevardnadze, whom the high command blames for negotiating their humiliating withdrawals from Eastern Europe. Local Russian forces, furthermore, appear to have soured long ago on Georgia's militias. Thus, when Kitovani's forces attacked Sukhumi in August 1992, local Russian commanders, eager to punish him and other anti-Russian segments of the Georgian hierarchy, supported the Abkhazian defense. Russian defense minister Grachev justified Russian air force bombing runs against Georgian forces in Sukhumi as retaliation for attacks against a Russian defense research center in Eshera.[62]

Ultimately, Moscow was able to turn the Abkhaz-Georgian conflict to its benefit in a number of ways. Although Russia would probably have prevented the capitulation of the Georgian side in any event, it nevertheless withheld its support to extract concessions. As the Georgian state was collapsing under the two-pronged assaults of Zviadists and Abkhazians, Russian defense minister Grachev responded to Shevardnadze's pleas for help by insisting that Georgia first join the CIS. Since accepting the deal, the Tbilisi government has had to reconcile itself to a long-term Russian presence on its territory. In February 1994, Shevardnadze signed a treaty with Yeltsin that permitted Russia to maintain three military bases on Georgian soil past 1995.[63]

Since it took on its formal peacekeeping role in the region, Russia's behavior has been far more evenhanded. Then Russian deputy minister of defense, Colonel General Georgiy Kondrat'yev, strongly pressed the Abkhazian side in the fall of 1994 to permit the full and immediate repatriation of Georgian refugees to Abkhazia. When negotiations between Georgia and Abkhazia appeared to be breaking down, Minister of Defense Grachev and later Yeltsin himself intervened diplomatically to push for continued negotiations.[64] By September 1994, Shevardnadze was reportedly praising Yeltsin and Grachev for their help in resolving the dispute.[65]

The UN Role

The UN was not active diplomatically in the Abkhazian conflict until the summer of 1993. In May of that year the secretary-general dispatched a special envoy and in July and August the Security Council unanimously approved sending military observers to Georgia to monitor the imminent cease-fire.[66] After the short-lived 27 July cease-fire agreement, the UN provided a venue for further peace talks, but the Security Council became extremely critical of Abkhazian cease-fire violations and it consistently expressed support for the territorial integrity of Georgia. In UN-sponsored talks after the December 1993 cease-fire, the two sides agreed to repatriate refugees, create a demilitarized zone along their border, and invite UN peacekeeping forces to monitor the truce.[67]

Yet the UN has consistently refused to provide peacekeepers for the Abkhazian mission. Initially Secretary-General Boutros-Ghali argued that no UN force would be sent until substantial progress was made toward a political settlement. Later, in March 1994, Boutros-Ghali went so far as to suggest that Russian troops go into the region first without UN approval.[68]

The Security Council had been very reluctant to "approve" or even "authorize" the Russian operation.[69] However, bowing to the reality that the Russian mission was the only realistic solution, on 21 July 1994 the Security Council endorsed the Russian deployment, but without giving Russia a blank check: it simultaneously authorized 136 UN military observers to monitor the Russian peacekeepers.[70]

Since that time the United Nations has been active in mediating talks between the two sides aimed at a permanent settlement. The UN High Commissioner for Refugees also dispatched a representative to oversee and facilitate the repatriation of Georgian refugees to Abkhazia.[71]

The US Role

The case of Abkhazia is a good example of the limits of US power in the region. Throughout the Abkhaz conflict, the United States has expressed support for the Georgian government and been suspicious of Russia's intentions, but Washington has been unwilling to intervene either diplomatically or with peacekeepers. In March 1994, during Shevardnadze's visit to Washington, President Clinton told the Georgian leader that he endorsed the proposal to dispatch a UN peacekeeping force to Abkhazia on the condition that substantial progress is made toward a political settlement; the proposed peacekeeping force would include only a limited Russian contingent and no US troops.[72]

Later, Washington reportedly opposed UN endorsement of a Russian-led force but had to relent when Russia threatened to veto Security Council support for a US invasion of Haiti.[73] Although the Clinton administration recognized that it had no alternatives to the Russian-led force, it nonetheless insisted that there were limits to its support for Russia in this area. In fact, during her September 1994 visit to Georgia, the US ambassador to the UN, Madeleine Albright, stressed that Russian peacekeeping in Georgia must be temporary and kept under international scrutiny.[74]

The Peacekeeping Mission

In contrast to other peacekeeping efforts in the NIS, the Abkhazia mission is based entirely on Russian troops, albeit with UN and CIS mandates. Georgian and Abkhaz representatives agreed in late June 1994 to deployment of a CIS peacekeeping force.

Although the force was supposed to operate under CIS command, Tajikistan was the only state other than Russia willing to provide troops. Thus, the Russian forces already deployed in Georgia became the de facto CIS force.[75] The Russian peacekeepers began deploying on 24 June 1994, to police a "security zone" 56 kilometers in width and 78 kilometers in length along the Inguri River, which divides Abkhazia and Georgia. The area is divided into two zones.[76]

According to Russian colonel general Georgiy Kondrat'yev, the security zone would be stripped of all "heavy" combat hardware, which would be withdrawn into collection areas monitored by UN observers.[77] In addition, the peacekeeping agreement stipulated that all armed formations would withdraw to a distance of 12 kilometers from the Inguri River, beyond artillery and tank range of one another. To facilitate this disengagement, Russian peacekeepers were ordered to protect facilities and main transportation routes and safeguard the return of refugees. The conflict had produced approximately 250,000 Georgian refugees from Abkhaz territory.[78]

Following Russia's broad definition of peacekeeping, Russian troops are permitted to open fire if fighting flares again, even if they are not directly under attack. As one general explained, "We are under orders to suppress any seats of fire, after a warning."[79] In addition to forces based at a number of observation posts, the Russian peacekeepers have organized four helicopter-mobile groups for rapid reaction to outbreaks of violence.[80]

A total of 3,000 Russian troops deployed, most of whom were allocated from units already in the region: two motorized rifle battalions from the 145th Motorized Rifle Division based in Batumi, Georgia, and a composite battalion from the 345th Airborne Regiment. Russia's designated peacekeeping divisions, the 27th Motorized Rifle Division in Totskoye and the 45th Motorized Rifle Division in Kamenka, also deployed one battalion each.[81]

Responsibility for funding the operation appears to fall on the already strapped regular budget of the Russian Ministry of Defense, as the Russian Council of Federation refused the Ministry's request for a special line-item for the Abkhaz mission in the federation budget. The Ministry of Defense estimates that the cost of peacekeeper salaries alone will be 1 billion rubles per month (approximately $526,000).[82] It is not surprising, therefore, that some of the loudest calls for international funding of Russian peacekeeping missions have come from the Ministry of Defense.

Assessment

Georgian and some Western officials express concern that one of the aims—or at least one of the results—of the Russian peacekeeping mission has been the reinforcement of Abkhazia's de facto independence. Shevardnadze has increasingly called for the size of and the mandate for the peacekeeping mission to be expanded to include police functions in the border zone and to guarantee the repatriation of Georgian refugees to their homes in Abkhazia.[83] The repatriation issue, of course, is controversial for both sides because of the effect that it will have on popular support for independence or federation within Abkhazia.

Although the agreement and the decision to join the CIS was a bitter pill for Georgians, peace has held within Georgia for the first time in years. Indeed, the Russian intervention and peacekeeping operation almost certainly saved the Shevardnadze regime. The prospects for a lasting political settlement, however, have been mixed. On the positive side, in UN-mediated talks, the Abkhazians apparently dropped their insistence on independence and accepted the prospect of a federation within Georgian borders. But the Abkhazians have blocked the return of Georgian refugees, demonstrating that achieving a permanent settlement between the two sides may be extremely difficult.[84]

Tajikistan

The current peacekeeping effort in Tajikistan is the result of Russian and Central Asian fears that the civil war in that country will spill over into neighboring states. The conflict—and CIS fears—have been exacerbated by the ties between Tajikistan's Islamic opposition and radical groups in Afghanistan. Of all the governments in the NIS, Tajikistan's has had the greatest difficulty in consolidating control of its territory. As a consequence, until the fall of 1993, the Islamic resistance and their Afghan supporters were able to ship weapons and operate back and forth across the Tajik-Afghan border practically at will.[85]

The large-scale Russian and CIS intervention is less a peacekeeping operation than a coalition defense of CIS borders. The peacekeepers have succeeded, to varying degrees, in sealing off the border and enforcing a cease-fire within Tajikistan. In the process, however, the country has become something of a Russian protectorate. Today the government of Imomali Rakhmonov—a former Communist who became head of state in late 1992—depends heavily upon Moscow for financial and military support.

Origins

Tajikistan has experienced precious little political stability since it became independent in September 1991. In contrast to the majority of union republics, Tajikistan had not sought independence from the USSR, and the Communist regime there was one of the few groups to support the attempted putsch against Gorbachev in August 1991. Located in extremely mountainous terrain that makes travel and communication very difficult, the country was the poorest and most underdeveloped republic in the USSR.[86] Thus, although the government has changed hands several times, no administration has succeeded in extending its control much beyond the capital of Dushanbe. From 1991 through 1994, a bitter civil war raged between competing political factions. Apparently, all sides of the conflict have been guilty of atrocities such as ethnic cleansing and murder of civilians. One estimate holds that by January 1993 the conflict had caused 50,000 deaths and produced at least 500,000 refugees.[87]

Fig. 10.2

MAP OF TAJIKISTAN

SOURCE: US Government

On the surface, the conflict has been political, pitting a series of governments run by Communists against an opposition coalition of democrats and Islamic groups. In fact, the conflict is based on historical, regional, and clan rivalries that have intensified in the quasi-anarchical post-Soviet environment. Throughout the Soviet period, the Leninabad (now renamed Khojand) province—the most economically developed part of Tajikistan—provided the elite that controlled the government in Dushanbe. This elite enjoyed the support of Tajikistan's large ethnic Uzbek minority and the pro-Communist clans of the southern Kulyab region. Largely excluded from any political or economic benefits were the Garmis, who were based in the Garm Valley in the east and the southwest province of Kurgan-Tyube, and the Pamiris, who lived in the mountainous eastern region. Kurgan-Tyube and the Pamir region were perhaps the poorest areas in Soviet Tajikistan, and belief in Islam was strong in both.[88] Although it ultimately held little affinity for Communism, after independence the traditional elite nevertheless showed no interest in relinquishing its exclusive hold on the government. The Garmis and Pamiris united in opposition with intellectuals and democrats in Dushanbe, as well as pro-Islamic groups.[89]

In the fall of 1991, what began as competing pro- and anti-government mass demonstrations in the central squares of Dushanbe quickly deteriorated into a bloody civil war. The opposition demonstrations forced the Communist president, Kakhar Makhmamov, to resign. When his successor banned the Communist Party, the holdover Tajik Supreme Soviet replaced him with the former leader of the Tajik Communist Party, Rakhmon Nabiyev. Although Nabiyev won the popular election for president in November 1991, his efforts to restore Communist rule produced bloody clashes in Dushanbe between his supporters and the opposition. Nabiyev tried to create a government of national reconciliation that included 33 representatives from opposition groups, but by this time pro-Communist, anti-Communist, and regional militias were ignoring Dushanbe and fighting it out on the ground. In September 1992 opposition forces captured Nabiyev and forced him to resign at gunpoint. The pro-Communist Supreme Soviet—having fled the capital—responded by abolishing the presidency in November 1992 and installing Supreme Soviet chairman Rakhmonov as head of state. In December 1992, Communist forces recaptured Dushanbe and retired the government of "national reconciliation."[90]

Having consolidated his hold over the Dushanbe government, Rakhmonov and his supporters set about to crush those regions that were supporting the opposition. Rakhmonov's forces and allies reportedly razed entire villages in opposition strongholds such as Kurgan-Tyube and pushed at least 100,000 Tajiks into Afghanistan.[91] As the civil war persisted, the Tajik opposition gained greater direct support from Afghan Mujaheddin forces across the border who were interested in promoting an Islamic republic in Tajikistan or were at least fiercely anti-Russian. According to one Russian estimate, in August 1994 there were roughly 4,000-5,000 opposition fighters operating within Tajikistan and another 13,000 joint Tajik-Afghan guerrillas based just over the border in Afghanistan.[92]

By 1993-94, the Dushanbe government appeared to control the western half of the country but was having difficulty rooting out guerrillas in the mountainous eastern regions. The ferocity of the civil war abated somewhat as the focus of the battle shifted to preventing the infiltration of guerrillas through the Afghan border. A significant diplomatic breakthrough occurred when UN, Russian, and Iranian mediation helped the Tajik government and the Islamic opposition agree to a cease-fire in talks in Tehran on 17 September 1994.[93]

Continued international mediation efforts kept the two sides talking and the formal cease-fire in place. Yet actions by both the Tajik government and opposition forces continued to aggravate the situation on the ground. The government went forward with presidential (in November 1994) and parliamentary (in February 1995) elections despite boycotts by the main opposition parties and substantial international criticism of their being neither free nor fair.[94] Furthermore, in January 1995, the government violated the truce by moving its forces into the Gorno-Badakhshan region in order to suppress a strong guerrilla presence.[95] The opposition, for its part, violated the cease-fire in the spring of 1995 by escalating its armed infiltration from Afghanistan and its attacks on border guards.

The Russian Role in the Tajik Conflict

Russia initially had an indirect role in the Tajik civil war because it controlled a number of former Soviet military units based in the country, and it had an interest in the 40,000 ethnic Russians still living there. Although a number of Western critics have charged that the Russian forces intervened to support the Communist side in the civil war, it appears that commanders of the main Russian unit in Tajikistan—the 201st Motorized Rifle Division (MRD)—sought to remain neutral in the conflict throughout the most intense fighting in 1992.[96] Because they possessed a large quantity of weapons that local forces coveted or because they occupied strategic positions, Russian units frequently came under attack by all sides. Finding their troops in the middle of the fighting and feeling compelled to defend themselves, these units intervened against forces of all sides in the conflict.[97] At one point, the 201st weighed an armored attack on both sides as a warning not to engage in violence against Russian forces. Russian border guard units—organizationally separate from the Russian Ministry of Defense— appeared to side more often with the former Communists, if only because they frequently engaged opposition forces infiltrating from Afghanistan.[98]

The watershed event for Russian involvement in Tajikistan occurred on 13 July 1993, when Tajik opposition forces and their Afghan supporters captured a border outpost manned by Russian border guards. The attack and subsequent fighting resulted in the deaths of 28 Russian troops and 6 Tajik soldiers, as well as the destruction of a nearby village of 700 residents.[99] The Russian deaths and the brazenness of the attack infuriated the Russian government, which concluded that its interests were under direct threat and that radical measures were necessary. Russian minister of defense Pavel Grachev depicted the attack as "an undeclared war *against Russia*" and ordered an immediate expansion of the Russian military presence. Russian border guards were authorized to fire across the border because, according to Russian security minister Viktor Barannikov, they had "the moral right to raid Afghan territory" if border violations continued.[100] Foreign Minister Andrey Kozyrev described Russia's goals in Tajikistan as (1) guaranteeing the security and legal rights of the 200,000 Russians living there; and (2) stopping the spread of regional, clan, and Islamic extremism in Central Asia. He later added to this list a historic Russian "duty" to guard the Tajik border.[101]

By instituting a wide-scale peace enforcement effort, Russia's actions thereafter inevitably supported the Rakhmonov government: any efforts to stabilize the military situation involved quashing the opposition militias. Russian officers joined the staff of the new Tajik Ministry of Defense, and since the summer of 1993, Russian forces appear to have carried out some operations against rebel forces within Tajikistan.[102] During the border fights of the spring and summer of 1995, Russian Border Guards carried out major combat operations, including air strikes on rebel bases in Afghanistan.[103]

To Russia's credit, at the same time that it was defending the border and maintaining stability within Tajikistan, it was also pressing for a dialogue between the Rakhmonov government and the opposition.[104] Russia pressed the Rakhmonov government throughout 1994 to accept opposition participation in the fall 1994 presidential election. When the opposition initially balked at participation, Moscow successfully urged the Rakhmonov government to postpone the election. Furthermore, as the situation deteriorated in early 1995, the head of the Collective Peacekeeping Forces, Colonel General Valeriy Patrikeyev, strongly criticized the Dushanbe government for violating the truce.[105]

The United Nations' Role

Despite pleas from the participants, the United Nations has generally resisted active involvement in the Tajik conflict and peacekeeping operations. Although the UN has helped mediate a cease-fire and dispatched observers to monitor and verify compliance, it has not been willing to send armed peacekeepers or to endorse the CIS peacekeeping force. After the July 1993 border attack, Rakhmonov appealed to the UN to force Afghanistan to stop the rebels and their Afghan backers, while Afghanistan sent a letter to the UN demanding that the expansion of Russian deployments on its borders be stopped. Russia then notified the Security Council that it would help Tajikistan defend itself against attacks launched from Afghan territory.[106] In August 1993, CIS foreign ministers expressed hope that the UN would support the CIS peacekeeping coalition in Tajikistan. Tajikistan and the Kazakh foreign minister subsequently requested that peacekeeping forces on Tajik territory be recognized as UN forces.[107]

The UN response to these various requests and initiatives has been lukewarm. Secretary-General Boutros-Ghali reported that he was willing to seek a peaceful solution to the conflict through the good offices of a special envoy. In August 1993, the president of the Security Council expressed concern over the continuing violence in Tajikistan, terming it a threat to peace in Central Asia. But the statement limited UN involvement to calling for negotiations aimed at an early cease-fire and eventual national reconciliation.[108]

After the delay, beginning in June 1994 the UN organized talks between the government and the opposition aimed first at a cease-fire, then at an exchange of prisoners, and ultimately at a political settlement. Held in Tehran and Islamabad, the talks include mediators or observers from Russia, Iran, and Pakistan.[109] In October 1994, a team of 15 UN military observers was dispatched to monitor the September 1994 truce reached as a result of these talks. The Security Council formally established the Tajikistan observer mission in a 16 December 1994 resolution. By June 1995 the size of the mission numbered 72 personnel, including 39 military observers.[110] The joint commission of government and opposition representatives that was created by the Tehran agreement is chaired by the head of the UN mission in Tajikistan. The commission is mandated to work closely with the cease-fire monitors and to handle technical issues such as exchange of prisoners.[111]

The Peacekeeping Missions

There have been two distinct CIS military operations in Tajikistan. The first began in December 1992, was small in scale, and appears to have been a relatively honest attempt by the CIS countries to stabilize the military and political environment in Tajikistan. It originated in a meeting of the CIS defense ministers on 30 November 1992, when the ministers of Kazakhstan, Kyrgyzstan, Uzbekistan, and Russia joined the commander in chief of the CIS Joint Armed Forces, Yevgeniy Shaposhnikov, and Tajik president Rakhmonov in calling for a CIS peacekeeping force for Tajikistan.[112]

The first peacekeeping mission did not formally include the 201st MRD and Russian border guards units. Instead, the operation consisted of one reinforced Russian battalion and two Uzbek battalions. Kazakhstan and Kyrgyzstan promised to contribute one battalion each, but ultimately failed to do so.[113] The mission was mandated to settle the conflict first and foremost through a systematic disarming of "illegal" groupings.[114] The force was not to be deployed until a cease-fire between the warring factions was reached. In the end, a cease-fire never occurred but the mission went forward anyway. It is not clear what effect, if any, this small force had on preventing continued conflict and atrocities.

The second effort was a much larger response to the collapse of order on the Tajik-Afghan border in July 1993. It represented a full-scale intervention by Russia and the Central Asian states into the Tajik conflict, ultimately making Tajikistan a de facto Russian/CIS protectorate. Following the bloody 13-14 July fight, Russia and the Central Asian states agreed to create a new, larger peacekeeping force through the CIS mechanism. In an early August CIS meeting, the participants in the CIS Collective Security Treaty expressed great concern regarding the inviolability of borders and pledged to send more troops to defend the Afghan border. By 25 August, five of the six signatories of the CIS Collective Security Treaty agreed to set up a "coalition" peacekeeping force for Tajikistan. The CIS subsequently extended the mandate for the operation through June 1995.[115]

This second CIS peacekeeping operation dwarfed the first in terms of size and mandate. The entire coalition force numbered approximately 25,000 troops. Russia contributed the combat-strength 201st MRD reinforced by an additional 6,000 personnel.[116] Tajikistan allocated its interior troops to the task. Kazakhstan, Kyrgyzstan, and Uzbekistan contributed one battalion (approximately 350-400 men) each. However, at least one of the Kyrgyz units is still based on Kyrgyz territory and is operationally useless.[117]

The national peacekeeping contingents sent to Tajikistan retain their uniforms and are fully financed by the state sending them. Only the command of the Collective Peacekeeping Forces (KMS) and combat support units are financed from a joint budget, to which each participating state contributes on the basis of agreed quotas.[118] Initially, the CIS states considered a proposal for quotas governing each state's contribution of troops, funds, fuel, technical details, and so on. However, they ultimately opted for an arrangement in which each republic and its defense ministry would itself decide on the forces and facilities that it would contribute and the sectors of the country or roles for which it would be responsible.[119]

Command and control of the coalition forces, at least initially, appears to have had serious limitations. The KMS command is supposed to have operational control over the 201st MRD and the Uzbek, Kazakh, and Kyrgyz battalions. But in practice, each of these units answers formally to their respective national command structures. Therefore, according to the first commander of the KMS, Russian colonel general Boris P'yankov, planned operations would be coordinated with member states' defense ministers and would be carried out only with their approval. Only in special "emergency" cases was the KMS commander given the right to use the force's entire arsenal to repel an attack.[120]

As a general rule, it appears that the KMS command has had some difficulty imposing its will on the Russian contingents, which constitute the bulk of the force. While he was commander of the KMS, Colonel General P'yankov communicated with the commander of the 201st MRD, Colonel General Viktor Timofeyev, only through the chain of command in Moscow, with persons "of the highest military ranks" serving as intermediaries. This arrangement leaves the Russian contingent commander with considerable freedom of action. Upon their arrival in Tajikistan, for example, the Uzbek unit demanded fuel and ammunition from the KMS, which turned to Timofeyev for help only to receive a cold shoulder. P'yankov was replaced as commander of the KMS by Colonel General Valeriy Patrikeyev, but it is not clear that the problem of operational control of the national contingents has been resolved.[121]

The mandate of the second peacekeeping mission was quite broad: to "stabilize the situation in Tajikistan and maintain peace." By early 1994, however, as the domestic situation appeared to stabilize, the mandate may have actually shrunk to border protection.[122] According to P'yankov, the main objective of the coalition force was to protect and defend Tajikistan's—and CIS—borders, participate in the negotiating process, and protect humanitarian aid columns. But, he stressed, they would provide no military assistance to local groupings.[123] Indeed, in September 1994 fighting, in which Tajik government forces suffered setbacks at the hands of the rebels, the CIS forces stayed out of the fighting, arguing that their mission was only to defend the border. It appears that the non-Russian units are devoted largely to this mission, albeit as reinforcements for front-line Russian border guards.[124]

Assessment

Since the first authorized peacekeeping effort in December 1992, the role and goals of CIS and Russian peacekeepers have shifted considerably. Initially an effort to separate the warring factions and introduce an element of stability to Tajik politics, since mid-1993 the peacekeeping mission has increasingly become a CIS collective security operation aimed primarily at defending the Tajik-Afghan border.[125]

The success of the CIS intervention has been limited. Despite the establishment of a truce and a process of internationally mediated talks, the situation on the Afghan border shows no sign of improvement and low-intensity conflict persists in the east.[126] The Rakhmonov government has demonstrated virtually no interest in accepting the opposition's main demand: a power-sharing arrangement while a new constitution is written. And although the opposition has adopted a relatively constructive approach in the negotiating process, it continues to prosecute the guerrilla war on the border with vigor. Furthermore, as long as Afghanistan continues to be unstable, it is hard to imagine that there will not be radical elements in that country willing to support and fight with the Tajik government's most hardline opponents.

By mid-1995, the apparent intractability of the conflict appeared to be wearing on all of the outside participants. The UN special envoy threatened to withdraw the UN mission because neither side appeared willing to compromise.[127] Despite their fears of spreading political instability and radicalism in the region, the Central Asian participants in the CIS peacekeeping force were also showing signs of wanting to withdraw.[128] Even Russian defense minister Pavel Grachev, whose attention had clearly turned to crises closer to home, showed signs of having had enough when he refused to reinforce the Border Guards or permit an increase in their number in April 1995.[129]

Russia's role in the internal conflict in Tajikistan has varied over time. Yet throughout Moscow appears to have sought, above all else, stability and an end to the conflict. Recalling the intervention into the civil war in Afghanistan and, more recently, the conflict in Chechnya, Russian officials apparently do not want another military and political quagmire within the borders of the CIS. Although it has backed the Rakhmonov government, Moscow would probably support any government save an Afghan-backed Muslim one.

Moldova

The situation in Moldova and the breakaway Dniester region represents the most egregious example of Russian meddling in the internal affairs of a former Soviet republic. On one hand, Moscow has played a productive role in helping to police a cease-fire between Moldova and Dniester forces. Yet any positive contribution has been overshadowed by the actions of the Russian Federation's 14th Army, which has actively intervened in the conflict in support of the Dniester region. The schizophrenia in Russia's policy toward this area is largely the product of the political popularity of the Dniester cause among many Russians and some key members of the Russian military. As a consequence, despite international condemnation of Russia's activities in Moldova, the prospects for an internationally acceptable resolution of the conflict appear dim at least in the near future.

Origins

The Dniester conflict is based on the efforts of residents of the east bank of the Dniester River to secede from Moldova and create their own republic.[130] The dispute is unique among conflicts in the NIS because it is as much based on politics as on ethnic

Fig. 10.3
MAP OF MOLDOVA

SOURCE: US Government

differences. Although ethnic Russians and Ukrainians are overrepresented in the Dniester leadership, 70 percent of the Russians in Moldova live—apparently quite contently—on the west bank of the Dniester. At the same time, the largest group living on the east bank are ethnic Moldovans who evidently back the Dniester leadership. Both sides of the dispute are Orthodox Christians.[131]

The two regions have a tradition of being separate political entities, however. The east bank of the Dniester was always a part of the USSR. Although the west bank,

Bessarabia, had been part of the Russian Empire, at the time of the Russian civil war it became part of Romania. The USSR regained Bessarabia in 1940 through the Molotov-Ribbentrop Pact, and linked it to the east bank region to create the new Union Republic of Moldova.[132]

As Moldova moved toward independence in the late 1980s, these historical ties became significant. Popular movements and the Moldovan Republic leadership, based in Chisinau, agitated for reunification with Romania and passed laws replacing Cyrillic with Latin script and reintroducing Romanian/Moldovan as the state language. The east bank, which had used the Cyrillic alphabet since the fourteenth century and had never been part of Romania, generally reacted to these developments with great alarm.[133]

In September 1990, the east bank proclaimed itself to be the Dniester Moldavian SSR, a constituent part of the USSR—not Moldova—with Tiraspol as its capital.[134] Dniester independence became a cause célèbre of unionists and nationalist Russians throughout the collapsing USSR, and a great number of Cossacks and other volunteers filtered into the Dniester region to join the separatist militias. In the fall of 1991, separatist paramilitary groups lay siege to east bank police stations, demanding that the police either join them or cross the river. Tensions increased between the two sides until March 1992, when Moldovan president Mircea Snegur issued an ultimatum to east bank leaders, demanding full compliance with Moldovan laws. When the Dniester leaders ignored the ultimatum, Snegur declared martial law throughout Moldova.[135]

In the wide-scale fighting that ensued, the commander of the Russian 14th Army, a holdover from the Soviet period based in the Dniester capital of Tiraspol, permitted separatist groups to take large quantities of weapons, ammunition, and equipment from his arsenal.[136] Although President Yeltsin put the 14th Army directly under his control and replaced its commander with the fiery Lieutenant General Aleksandr Lebed, by summer 1992 elements of the 14th Army were directly supporting the Dniester forces in combat.[137] Entire units of the 14th Army were reportedly transferred to the control of Dniester forces.[138]

The Moldovan government's war effort was neither successful on the battlefield nor popular with the public. As a result, the Moldovan leadership agreed to direct negotiations with Russia that began on 3 July 1992 in Moscow. Having participated as observers, not negotiating partners, Dniester representatives joined Russian and Moldovan envoys in signing an immediate cease-fire on 7 July. In another example of Moscow's local coalition model for mediation and peacekeeping, Yeltsin and Moldovan president Snegur agreed to act as joint guarantors of peace. The lengthy communique from the Russian-Moldovan agreement stressed the sovereignty and territorial integrity of Moldova as well as noting that the Russian 14th Army should be gradually withdrawn. However, the communique also stipulated that if Moldova were to change its status as a state—that is, reunify with Romania—the east bank of the Dniester would have the right to secede.[139]

Only Russia was willing to contribute peacekeepers to the Moldovan mission. The CIS and several Eastern European states planned to send in peacekeepers, but the initiative collapsed when participating states Belarus, Romania, and Bulgaria all backed out of the process and called for the use of OSCE mechanisms. The 9-10 July 1992 OSCE summit in Helsinki refused the Moldovan government's request for a OSCE peacekeeping force. Thus, on 21 July, Chisinau had to accept a Russian proposal of a tripartite—Russian, Dniester, and Moldovan—force that was called a CIS peacekeeping force.[140]

Although the cease-fire has held, movement toward a lasting political resolution to the conflict has been slow. Since the war's end, Moldova has pursued a conciliatory policy toward the separatists, offering them a substantial degree of autonomy. Although Russian and Dniester fears of Moldovan reunification with Romania may have been warranted initially, since 1992 at least, most Moldovan political groups—including, most prominently, President Snegur—have opposed reunification.[141] Nonetheless, the Dniester leadership demands the functional equivalent of its own state with its own currency and armed forces, and will accept nothing more than nominal confederal status with Moldova. They oppose any agreement that would result in the withdrawal of the 14th Army.[142] More generally, they seek unification with Russia, an aspiration complicated by the lack of common borders or access to the sea.

The Russian Role

Moscow's Moldova/Dniester policy has veered between an evenhanded diplomatic course and outright military intervention in support of the Dniester separatists. If the Yeltsin government's policymaking were free of Russian domestic politics, it would likely pursue a federal solution for Moldova and Transdniester, which would be acceptable to the Moldovan government. In addition to the long-lasting cease-fire agreed to in 1992, Yeltsin and the Moldovans agreed, in August 1994, to a three-year timetable for complete withdrawal of the 14th Army. Furthermore, the Yeltsin government has little reason to sympathize with the Dniester cause. It has not recognized the breakaway region as independent in part because of the implications for independence-minded regions within Russia. Moreover, the east bank leadership supported the putschists during the August 1991 Moscow coup and the October Events of 1993, while Chisinau backed the Yeltsin government on both occasions.[143]

Unfortunately, Russia's Moldovan/Dniester policy is not made in a vacuum. The Yeltsin government's moderate line has consistently been overcome by the strong pro-Dniester feelings of many Russians and, especially, by the activities of the 14th Army's leadership. As a consequence, the Russian government has frequently reversed policy or, perhaps worse, tolerated seemingly blatant insubordination from its troops in the region.

The Dniester conflict has become a lightning rod for Russian nationalists angered by the collapse of the Soviet Union. Indeed, the dispute between the two sides in part has reflected a conflict over the fate of the Soviet Union. The Dniester leaders have largely clung to the concept of a unified Soviet state, while ethnic Moldovans are generally anti-Communist and anti-Union. Thus, Russian nationalists have embraced the east bank as brethren seeking to restore the Russian empire. When they discuss the conflict, it is as though all of the east bank population is ethnic Russian, seeking reunification with the motherland and a break with pro-Romanian infidels.[144] More broadly, the Russian press also appears to view the conflict as a struggle of ethnic Russians against the Moldovan government. Despite its inaccuracy, this view led even the most liberal Russian commentators toward a positive assessment of the 14th Army's and Lebed's behavior in the Dniester region.

The Russian Ministry of Defense has grown less enamored of the Dniester cause than have the Russian nationalists, but it has consistently intervened in ways that support it. The key player here has been Lieutenant General Lebed, an officer who was extremely popular among the ranks of the Russian army and permitted the 14th Army to become de facto the Dniester military. According to Lebed, by July 1994, 51 percent of the officers and 79 percent of noncommissioned officers were locals.[145] Lebed himself briefly held a seat in the Dniester parliament before he broke with the leadership over their support for the anti-Yeltsin forces during the October 1993 rebellion. Although he became extremely critical of the Dniester leadership, Lebed was clearly contemptuous of the Moldovan government and is adamantly opposed to the withdrawal of the 14th Army from the region.

Until June 1995, Boris Yeltsin and his government appeared unwilling to challenge Lebed and his nationalist bedfellows.[146] One of the reasons for Yeltsin's reluctance appears to have been respect for Lebed's popularity in the Russian military. Senior Russian officers appear to support Lebed's demands that the 14th Army be based in Moldova permanently.[147] Thus, under pressure from Lebed and the nationalist opposition, Yeltsin began backing away from the August 1994 agreement to withdraw the 14th Army before the ink was dry.[148]

After much temporizing and substantial international pressure, Yeltsin finally challenged Lebed in April 1995. Despite the general's threats of resignation, Yeltsin and Grachev ordered the downgrading of the 14th Army to a single division, thereby requiring the transfer of Lebed to a more senior post. Lebed issued his resignation, and to the surprise of many, Yeltsin accepted it. Yeltsin and Grachev dispatched a strong Yeltsin ally, Major General Valery Yevnevich, to take over the remains of the 14th Army.[149]

The United States, UN, and OSCE

Virtually all of the major external actors are critical of Russia's behavior in the Dniester region and are generally supportive of the Moldovan government's position in the conflict. For example, no foreign country recognizes the Dniester region as a sovereign state. While visiting Moldova in November 1994, Secretary-General Boutros-Ghali appeared to support the Moldovan government's position by condemning "separatist trends" and applauding Moldova's proposals on the Dniester issue.[150] During a September 1994 visit to Moldova, US representative to the UN, Madeleine Albright, joined President Snegur in condemning "separatism." She also handed over a message from President Clinton stressing support for Moldova's independence, territorial integrity, and democratic development. The message affirmed that the United States regarded withdrawal of the 14th Army from Moldova as a "matter of primary importance." The Parliamentary Assembly of the OSCE also criticized Russia's reluctance to withdraw the 14th Army.[151]

In early 1993, the OSCE established a mission to promote dialogue among the main political actors, encourage the withdrawal of foreign troops, and monitor human rights conditions and the implementation of any settlement. The mission has had modest success in helping to resolve a dispute over a new language law. It has also helped facilitate a preliminary agreement on negotiations concerning the eventual status of the Dniester region within Moldova.[152] But, as described below, the mission's observer functions have been consistently obstructed by the Russian and Dniester "peacekeepers."

The Peacekeeping Mission

The July 1992 cease-fire agreement provided for a tripartite peacekeeping force comprised of six Russian battalions (approximately 2,000 troops), three battalions from the Moldovan army, and two battalions from the Dniester forces. The Russian share of the force is distinct from the 14th Army and is comprised instead of units from the 27th Motorized Rifle Division at Totskoye that are rotated into the area for six-month tours.[153] The agreement also created a Joint Control Commission to monitor the armistice.

The peacekeepers were deployed in late July and August 1992 in a zone separating Moldovan and Dniester forces. The zone is 225 kilometers long and from 4 to 15 kilometers deep. The peacekeepers established a checkpoint control regime, observation posts, and mobile groups to patrol the zone.[154]

Although there has been no outbreak of large-scale hostilities since the peacekeeping operation began, the mission has been anything but impartial. In contrast to other examples of the Russian local coalition model of peacekeeping, Russia's activities in this operation have been largely unilateral and generally biased: consistently ignoring Dniester violations of the truce agreement and interfering with the OSCE Observer Mission's effort to investigate Dniester behavior.[155]

Furthermore, citing costs, the Russian side unilaterally began to reduce its commitment to the trilateral peacekeeping force. Over the protests of the Moldovan government, beginning in September 1994 Moscow withdrew two of its six battalions and did not replace them. In November, Moscow replaced the remaining four with only two new battalions, arguing that their peacekeeping functions could be taken on effectively by the 14th Army. The Moldovan government protested the cuts because their unilateral character contravened the trilateral convention. More importantly, the Moldovan government feared that it was losing an important buffer between its military and the superior Dniester forces, which appeared poised to occupy the positions vacated by the departing Russian units.[156]

Assessment

Overall, Moldova is the worst example of Russian meddling under the guise of peacekeeping. The peacekeeping mission there has helped to preserve the cease-fire, but has done little else that is positive. The pro-Dniester bias of the majority-Russian forces illustrates the limitations of Russia's local coalition model for peacekeeping. Furthermore, the effectiveness of the operation has been thoroughly undermined by the activities of Russia's 14th Army. In this light, Russian proposals to transfer peacekeeping responsibility to the 14th Army appear to be completely disingenuous.

The resolution of the conflict between the Dniester region and Moldova appears to be tied to the future disposition of the 14th Army. During Lebed's tenure, the Dniester forces clearly benefited from training in and armaments from that unit. Less explicitly, the Dniester leadership was almost certainly emboldened with the knowledge that Lebed would not permit Moldova to resolve the dispute by force.

The departure of the army poses potentially serious problems. In particular, the fate of the army's many arms depots and stockyards could well determine whether the Dniester-Moldovan dispute becomes a violent conflict again. While the Moldovan government lays claim to 35 percent of the 14th Army's property, the Dniester leadership claims all of it. In fact, by May 1995 the Dniester armed forces had surrounded many of the army's depots, refusing to permit the transfer of the arms back to Russia.[157]

Nagorno-Karabakh

The conflict over the Nagorno-Karabakh region in Azerbaijan was the only one of the five disputes discussed here that, by mid-1996, had yet to see a foreign peacekeeping force deployed. The interstate war between Armenia/Nagorno-Karabakh and Azerbaijan has proven to be one of the more intractable conflicts in the NIS. Although a variety of international organizations (such as the OSCE and UN) and foreign governments (such as Russia, the United States, Turkey, and Iran) have tried their hands in resolving the conflict, none has found a formula for peace that is acceptable to all the parties. By August 1994, the conflict had taken more than 15,000 lives and caused more than 1 million refugees.[158]

Nagorno-Karabakh has been the subject of some of the most blatant attempts by Moscow to monopolize a mediation and peacekeeping process. Although Russian military forces and diplomatic efforts played little role in spurring the initial dispute over Nagorno-Karabakh, by 1994 Russian diplomatic initiatives increasingly undercut the efforts of other regional states and the OSCE to resolve the conflict. A potentially substantial and precedent-setting breakthrough occurred when Russia supported in principle an OSCE-organized peacekeeping force in December 1994.

Origins

At the root of the conflict is the presence of a large enclave of ethnic Armenians, formerly the Autonomous Oblast of Nagorno-Karabakh, within the territory of Azerbaijan. Open animosity between Armenians (a non-Slavic group that is predominantly Christian) and Azeris (a Muslim people of mixed Turkish, Iranian, and Caucasian ancestry) has a long history, aggravated by Soviet nationality policy. Partly

Fig. 10.4
MAP OF NAGORNO-KARABAKH

SOURCE: US Government

to divide and rule the Armenian population and partly to reward the Azeris for their
support of the Reds in the Civil War, the Bolshevik government in 1921 placed
Nagorno-Karabakh—the permanent population of which was 94 percent ethnic
Armenian—under the administrative control of Azerbaijan. Armenians never accepted

this decision, and by the 1960s, Nagorno-Karabakh was one of the few issues in the Soviet Union that generated public political demonstrations, some of which turned into violent clashes between Armenian and Azeri protestors.

As glasnost and perestroika lifted political restraints in the late 1980s, control over Nagorno-Karabakh became a central issue for nationalist forces in both Armenia and Azerbaijan. A war of laws between the Nagorno-Karabakh government and Azerbaijan helped contribute to a cycle of anti-Armenian pogroms in Azerbaijan and anti-Azeri demonstrations in Armenia. Azerbaijan put Armenia in an economic stranglehold by blockading its rail and ocean links. A Moscow-imposed state-of-emergency in Azerbaijan later stopped the pogroms, but did nothing to resolve the hostilities.

When Azerbaijan declared its independence from the USSR in August 1991, the Nagorno-Karabakh government declared itself to be an independent Soviet republic. Although the Armenian government, fearful of Moscow's response, distanced itself from this declaration, the dispute between rival militias intensified. The Nagorno-Karabakh Armenian forces quickly gained the upper hand and by May 1992 had achieved a nearly total military victory over Azeris in the oblast. Ultimately, Armenian military forces joined in and were able to seize all of the Azeri territory separating Nagorno-Karabakh from Armenia. Nagorno-Karabakh forces also pushed eastward, expanding their territory at the expense of Azerbaijan. Foreign diplomatic efforts produced a number of cease-fire agreements, that either were not implemented or quickly collapsed.

Russian mediation of the conflict finally produced a cease-fire agreement in Moscow in May 1994. Although the agreement also called for deployment of observers from the three sides, from Russia, and from the CIS, all to be safeguarded by CIS/Russian troops, by mid-1995 only the cessation of hostilities had been implemented.[159]

This plan provoked mass demonstrations in Azerbaijan by groups opposed to the potential deployment of Russian or CIS peacekeepers.[160] Although General Grachev changed the proposal to reduce Russian participation in the CIS force, Azerbaijan president Aliyev subsequently opposed the deployment of any Russian peacekeeping forces in Azerbaijan without a mandate from the OSCE.[161] By the summer of 1994, Azeri representatives were proposing a formula in which no single country would provide more than 30 percent of the peacekeeping troops. The leadership of Nagorno-Karabakh has been strongly opposed to any Turkish presence in the peacekeeping force, and Armenian president Levon Ter-Petrossyan has stressed that Russian peacekeepers are the only forces that could guarantee stability in Karabakh. So far, only Russia and Turkey have offered to participate in the force.[162]

Russian Involvement

Since before the collapse of the Soviet Union, Russia has sought a diplomatic resolution of the conflict in Nagorno-Karabakh.[163] As the conflict has persisted and foreign states and organizations have attempted to assume a larger role in its resolution, Russia has increasingly asserted its perceived right to a leading role. For example, Moscow has rejected Turkish proposals that the two countries field a joint peacekeeping force in the region. A cease-fire proposal advanced by Grachev in April 1994 included OSCE peacekeepers but evidently only as an addition to a CIS force.[164]

At times Moscow appears to have purposely undermined foreign initiatives by pressing its own competing diplomatic proposals. The May 1994 Moscow meeting that produced the cease-fire was apparently convened with the goal of excluding the OSCE Minsk Group (see below). Responding to foreign criticism on this score, the Russian ambassador-at-large for Nagorno-Karabakh argued that some representatives of the group are more interested in the "distribution of roles"—or who gets credit for achieving a settlement—between OSCE, the CIS, and Russia than in the essence of the conflict.[165] Moscow adopted a more cooperative diplomatic stance by the end of 1994 and through much of 1995. At the December 1994 Budapest Summit of the OSCE, the Russian government relented on its insistence that it lead any peacekeeping force in Nagorno-Karabakh. Instead, Russia accepted in principle the deployment of an OSCE organized peacekeeping force in which the plurality of forces would almost certainly be Russian. Moscow also appeared to abandon its effort to compete with the OSCE mediation efforts as it assumed cochairmanship of the Minsk Group (see below).[166]

Other Regional Powers

Having ethnic and historical ties to Azerbaijan, Turkey has supported Baku politically in the conflict. In May 1992, for example, the Turkish government threatened to cut off land routes to Armenia in order to scare Yerevan into abandoning its fight for Nagorno-Karabakh. When Armenian forces succeeded in creating a landbridge between Armenia and Nagorno-Karabakh, Ankara called for the UN Security Council to intervene while threatening its own political and military intervention.[167] Turkey has also pursued a diplomatic resolution, joining the United States and Russia in a tripartite mediation effort under the auspices of the OSCE in May 1993, while consistently offering troops to serve as peacekeepers in any settlement. Turkey also joined the OSCE and the United States in their criticism of Russia's efforts to resolve the crisis on its own.

By 1994 Iran had become active in the diplomatic process as well.[168] Despite its concerns about Islamic fundamentalism, Moscow has been somewhat accommodating to Iran's interests in the region in order to counterbalance Turkey.

The OSCE, the UN, and the United States

The OSCE has sought a central mediation and peacekeeping role in Nagorno-Karabakh. The OSCE established the Minsk Conference—or the "Minsk Group"—in March 1992, composed of Belarus, France, Germany, Hungary, Italy, Russia, Sweden, and Turkey. The mediation effort focused on the establishment of a cease-fire and the deployment of OSCE peacekeepers, rather than a fundamental political settlement. An advance delegation of OSCE observers arrived in the region in April 1993 to prepare for the eventual arrival of more permanent international observers.[169]

By the fall of 1994, many OSCE members appeared to have become irritated at Russia's efforts to exclude it from the mediation and peacekeeping process. At a September meeting of the OSCE's Committee of Senior Officials, committee members from NATO and neutral countries complained that Russia had held a summit meeting in Moscow that month between the warring parties without informing the OSCE; that it had snubbed a meeting organized by the Minsk Group; and that it had pressed for a Russian/CIS peacekeeping force to be deployed in Karabakh, rather than an OSCE-sponsored multinational force.[170]

At the Budapest Summit in December 1994, the OSCE members may have achieved a substantial breakthrough by approving an OSCE-organized peacekeeping force for Nagorno-Karabakh. If carried out, the Nagorno-Karabakh mission would be the OSCE's first attempt at peacekeeping. Although the summit's statement did not specify details on the makeup of the force or when it would deploy, the participants called for the establishment of a high-level planning group to organize the force.[171] Other reports stated that the peacekeeping force would be composed of 3,000 troops and would cost approximately $40 million for the first six months. Furthermore, in order to placate Azeri and Western fears of excessive Russian influence, the parties reportedly agreed that no single country would contribute more than 30 percent of the force. Azeri, Armenian, and Nagorno-Karabakh officials warmly welcomed the plan.[172]

However, by mid-1996, the deployment of the peacekeeping mission still appeared to be far from a done deal. The Vienna planning group responsible for organizing the mission had released its report of the mission's operational requirements, but fundamental decisions such as which countries would participate had not been hammered out. Furthermore, the situation on the ground showed no signs of resolution. The Azeris, the Karabakh Armenians, and the Armenians continued to disagree on key issues such as whether the Karabakh Armenians were, in fact, an independent party to the conflict.[173] Furthermore, by the end of 1995 Russia appeared to cool again toward the idea of an OSCE-brokered peace agreement in the region. The politics of oilfields and pipelines and who controls them had renewed Moscow's interest in a leading role in any peace operation.[174] The web of intertwined local and international issues provided little room for optimism that the OSCE mission could be deployed in the near future.

The United Nations, meanwhile, has sought on a number of occasions to assist in the Nagorno-Karabakh mediation. In March 1992, the United Nations dispatched former US secretary of state Cyrus Vance on a fact-finding mission and, in October of that year, named a special envoy to the region. An April 1993 offensive by Armenian forces provoked a Security Council resolution calling for the cessation of hostilities and specifically condemning Armenian incursions into Azeri territory outside of Nagorno-Karabakh. In November 1994, Secretary-General Boutros-Ghali reaffirmed support for the OSCE's peace plan.[175]

The United States has taken a special interest in the Nagorno-Karabakh conflict. The US government has favored the OSCE and, in particular, the Minsk Group, as the appropriate forum for a Nagorno-Karabakh settlement. As a result, the Clinton administration has taken a cautious stance regarding Russia's desire to lead the process. After the May 1994 Moscow agreement, the United States joined Turkey in supporting the rival OSCE proposal.[176] At the September 1994 Clinton-Yeltsin summit in Washington, the issue of a peacekeeping force was discussed behind closed doors and the Clinton administration did not openly criticize the Russian position. Later, Yeltsin told Russian television that Clinton had clarified that no US troops would take part in peacekeeping in Nagorno-Karabakh, but that the United States might be willing to contribute financing to a mission.[177] Pressure by President Clinton at this summit and after may have played a decisive role in convincing Moscow to accept the OSCE-sponsored peacekeeping force in December 1994.[178]

Assessment

If implemented, the OSCE mission in Nagorno-Karabakh could become one of the most promising developments in peacekeeping in the NIS. It would represent an important precedent of Russia permitting outside forces to oversee peacekeeping and political mediation in the region. As of the beginning of 1995, the multinational peacekeeping mission was hardly a done deal. Although 18 countries had offered personnel or equipment to the force, it remains to be seen whether these commitments will be adequate or whether the usual problem of insufficient non-Russian commitment to peacekeeping in the NIS will develop again in Nagorno-Karabakh.[179] If outside parties do not commit sufficient troops, the Nagorno-Karabakh mission, like other operations in the NIS, will likely come to be dominated by Moscow. Furthermore, the parties to the dispute seem far from any agreement on a political settlement. In particular, in early 1995 Azerbaijan continued to refuse to consider Nagorno-Karabakh forces to be independent parties to the conflict. The Azerbaijan government also feared that the introduction of a peacekeeping force *before* the withdrawal of Armenian and Nagorno-Karabakh forces from Azeri territory would legitimize ethnic cleansing.[180]

CONCLUSIONS

Conflicts within the newly independent states seem sure to persist for the foreseeable future. The collapse of the Soviet Union has created an environment rife with territorial and ethnic disputes, and the means to wage war. Because of the political instability that these conflicts cause along its borders, the Russian Federation will continue to view an activist diplomatic and military role in its "near abroad" as imperative. In particular, for reasons of national interest, national pride, and domestic politics, Russia will continue to insist that formerly Soviet territory is its international sphere of influence and that foreign powers defer to its leading role as both mediator and peacekeeper. Although Russian actions were not the cause of these conflicts, Moscow generally imposed its interests when settling them. And in two cases—Moldova and

Nagorno-Karabakh—Russia's diplomatic and peacekeeping efforts appear to have delayed the settlement of the dispute.

The Russian approach to peacekeeping in the NIS has rightly been the cause for some international concern. The same factors that make Russia the practical choice for leading peacekeeping missions in the NIS—proximity, a large military, and a willingness to provide forces—also make it at times a far less than altruistic peace-keeper. Furthermore, the Russian approach to "peacekeeping" is more force-prone than that of the United Nations or most of its members.

But arguably Russian activism in the NIS may at times be a good thing. In fact, in a number of cases Russian activities may be in the interests of the international community and may facilitate political resolutions if only because they will not permit a military dispute. One of the virtues of Russia's activist-peace enforcement approach is that it achieves cease-fire agreements quickly. Russia's current missions in Abkhazia and South Ossetia have reduced the violence in those regions. Although Russian behavior in Tajikistan may be suspect from an international legal perspective, it perhaps serves US interests by containing ethnic and religious conflict in the Central Asian tinderbox. More generally speaking, Russia's interest in preventing the redrawing of borders may also serve international interests in the general stability of the NIS region.

In coping with Russian activism in the NIS, the United States and the international community have limited influence. Because neither the United Nations nor the United States has been able or willing to provide troops for NIS peacekeeping efforts, Russia inevitably dominates these missions.

Although Russia is not likely to surrender its leading role in this region, through inducements the international community can perhaps encourage more consistent and constructive behavior. The Russian government has repeatedly appealed for foreign financial assistance and endorsement of its peacekeeping activities in the NIS. A trade of UN endorsement for Russia's full cooperation with international mediators and observers might be a useful approach. Considering the financial crisis in the Russian military after the war in Chechnya, perhaps an even more effective arrangement would be international financing—either through the UN or OSCE—of peacekeeping efforts in the NIS. In exchange for international financial assistance, the Russian government or CIS might be expected to permit greater transparency and accountability in these operations. For example, international observers could be attached to peacekeeping units in order to monitor their adherence to agreed rules of engagement.

Although none of these arrangements is an ideal solution to the problem of objective peacekeeping in the NIS, they represent perhaps the best that can be expected under the circumstances. Russia shares with the United States, United Nations, and OSCE the goals of peace and stability for the newly independent states. With greater international transparency and accountability, Russian peacekeeping missions could provide an international service that would otherwise be absent. Russia's agreement in principle to an OSCE-led peacekeeping force in Nagorno-Karabakh represents one promising development. It suggests that under the right conditions, Russia might be willing to allow outside parties some role in settling conflicts in the NIS. In the wake of the military debacle in Chechnya and considering the escalating costs of Russia's existing peacekeeping operations, it appears quite likely that Moscow will be compelled to become more flexible in the future.

NOTES

1. Until 1 January 1995, the Organization for Security and Cooperation in Europe (OSCE) went by the name of the Conference on Security and Cooperation in Europe (CSCE). In order to avoid confusion, I will use the current title throughout the text of this chapter regardless of the period.

2. In his September 1994 speech to the UN General Assembly, Russian president Boris Yeltsin explained, "We are interested in active participation of the world community in settling this difficult problem. But the main peacekeeping burden in the territory of the former Soviet Union lies upon the Russian Federation." See Boris N. Yeltsin, President of the Russian Federation, "Peace Keeping Burden in the Former Soviet Union Lies Upon the Russian Federation," reprinted in *Vital Speeches of the Day,* vol. LXI, no. 1, 15 October 1994.

3. Aleksey Arbatov notes that support for the Russian "Monrovskiy Doctrine" ranges from pro-Western liberals, to centrists, to moderate conservatives. See Aleksey Arbatov, "Russian National Interests," in Robert D. Blackwill and Sergei A. Karaganov, eds., *Damage Limitation or Crisis? Russia and the Outside World,* CSIA Studies in International Security no. 5 (Washington, D.C.: Brassey's, Inc., 1994), 55, 60.

4. See Boris N. Yeltsin, "Peace Keeping Burden." In a more crass formulation, Foreign Minister Andrey Kozyrev stressed that Russia should not permit anyone to undermine "geopolitical positions that took centuries to conquer." See Maksim Yusin, Andrey Kozyrev: "Polgoda Nazad Rutskoy Skazal Mne: 'Ya Ikh Nenavizhu Etikh Krasno-Korichnevykh'" (Six months ago Rutskoy told me: 'I hate them, these red-browns'), *Nezavisimaya Gazeta,* 8 October 1993, 3.

5. See Foreign Minister Kozyrev's worries on this subject with respect to the danger of a dismemberment of Georgia, in Maksim Yusin, "Andrey Kozyrev"; and Maxim Shashenkov, "Russian Peacekeeping in the 'Near Abroad,'" *Survival* 36, no. 3 (autumn 1994): 48-49.

6. In early 1994 there were roughly 175,000 troops still stationed in the non-Russian members of the Commonwealth of Independent States (CIS). See Bruce D. Porter and Carol R. Saivetz, "The Once and Future Empire: Russia and the 'Near Abroad,'" *The Washington Quarterly* (summer 1994): 77, 82.

7. See "Voyennaya doktrina Rossii," (The military doctrine of Russia), excerpts printed in *Rossiyskiye Vesti,* 18 November 1993, 1-2.

8. Georgia agreed in February 1994 to permit Russia to keep three military bases on its territory past the original 1995 deadline for their withdrawal. Russia intends to maintain one base each in Armenia and Azerbaijan, although the latter state has expressed great reluctance. See Celestine Bohlen, "Russia and Georgia Sign Military Cooperation Treaty," *New York Times,* 4 February 1994, 3; and Steven Erlanger, "Yeltsin's On-and-Off Decrees on Bases Cloud the Policy Outlook," *New York Times,* 8 April 1994, 5.

9. See the editorial in the Russian army's newspaper, "Perspektivy razvitiya SNG i positsiya Zapada" (Prospects for development of the CIS and the position of the West), *Krasnaya Zvezda,* 28 September 1994, 3; and John W. R. Lepingwell, "The Russian Military and Security Policy in the 'Near Abroad,'" *Survival* 36, no. 3 (autumn 1994): 77.

10. See Minister of Defense Pavel Grachev's characterization of Russian Security Council discussions on Russian borders in Pavel Fel'gengauer, "Staryye granitsy i <novyye> bazy: Strategicheskoye otstupleniye armii zakanchivaetsya" (Old borders and 'new' bases. The army's strategic retreat is ending), *Segodnya,* 16 September 1993, 3.

11. Azerbaijan, Kazakhstan, and Moldova are the only CIS states not participating in a CIS joint-border defense regime. Furthermore, according to the deputy chief of staff of Russia's Border Troops, Russian border guards are only "observing," not "guarding," Ukraine's outer borders. See Vladimir Socor, "One Border for All," *Radio Free Europe/Radio Liberty (RFE/RL) Daily Report* (online), 29 November 1994; and Lieutenant Colonel N. Lobodyuk, "The Situation is Stably Complex," *Pogranichnik* no. 6 (June 1994) [signed to press 24 April 1994]: 14-22, translated in *Joint Publications Research Service—Central Eurasia Military Affairs* (hereafter, *JPRS-UMA*) 94-042 (19 October 1994): 29-35.

12. *Krasnaya Zvezda,* "Perspektivy razvitiya."

13. *Krasnaya Zvezda,* "Perspektivy razvitiya"; and Maksim Yusin, "Andrey Kozyrev."

14. Shashenkov, "Russian Peacekeeping," 46.

15. Ibid., 52.

16. Partly through Russian cajoling of the former Soviet republics to join, the CIS now includes 12 of the 15 former Soviet republics. Russia blocked the establishment of a CIS military force, however. See Porter and Saivetz, "The Once and Future Empire," 76; and Stephen Foye, "End of CIS Command Heralds New Russian Defense Policy?" *RFE/RL Research Report* (2 July 1993): 45-49.

17. See Steven Erlanger, "In Ex-Soviet Lands, Russian Army Can be a Protector or an Occupier," *New York Times,* 30 November 1993, 1; Yuriy Kushko, "Blue Helmets Also Go with Kyrgyz Boots," interviewing Colonel General Boris P'yankov, *Rossiya,* no. 4 (26 January - 1 February 1994): 5, in *JPRS-UMA* 94-009 (4 March 1994): 19-20; Oleg Falichev, "General-polkovnik Boris P'yankov: V Oktyrbre kollektivnye sily pribudut v Tadzhikistan" (Colonel-General Boris P'yankov: Collective forces will go to Tajikistan in October), *Krasnaya Zvezda,* 29 September 1993, 1; and Colonel General Gennadiy Miranovich, "Bezopasnost' SNG: Rossiya gotova podelit'sya

noshey. Ne vse gotovy eyo prinyat" (CIS security: Russia is ready to share the burden. Not everyone is ready to accept it), *Krasnaya Zvezda,* 20 July 1994, 1.

18. The first six weeks are devoted to all-arms training and the remainder to peacekeeping training specifically. See Michael Orr, "Peacekeeping—A New Task for Russian Military Doctrine," *Jane's Intelligence Review* (July 1994): 307.

19. See, for example, the comments of the commander of the Russian ground forces, Colonel General Vladimir Semyenov, in Pavel Fel'gengauer, "Nikto ne khochet byt' mirotvortsem v Karabakhye" (Nobody wants to be a peacekeeper in Karabakh), *Segodnya,* 20 May 1994, 2.

20. Michael Orr, "Peacekeeping and Overstretch in the Russian Army," *Jane's Intelligence Review* (August 1994): 363-65. Another source reports that overall the 27th Motorized Rifle Division has only 8,500 troops, a deficit of at least 2,000 from normal combat strength. See Dr. Roy Allison, "Russian Peacekeeping—Capabilities and Doctrine," *Jane's Intelligence Review* (December 1994): 545.

21. As a result, the head of Russia's peacekeeping forces complained that during 1993 alone the military was forced to allocate more than 26 billion rubles of its funds on peacekeeping activities. See Colonel General Georgiy Kondrat'yev, Russian Deputy Minister of Defense, "Mirotvorcheskaya Rol' Rossii" (The peacemaking role of Russia), *Krasnaya Zvezda,* 21 June 1994, 1-2.

22. Strengthening Democratic Institutions Project (hereafter, SDIP), *Report on Ethnic Conflict in the Russian Federation and Transcaucasia* (Cambridge, Mass.: John F. Kennedy School of Government, Harvard University, July 1993), 105; and Boris N. Yeltsin, "Peace Keeping Burden."

23. See the interview of Yuriy Ushakov, Russia's chief delegate to the CSCE Review Meeting in Budapest, in Vladimir Socor, "Russia Does Not Want 'Supervision' of Its Peacekeeping," *RFE/RL Daily Report,* 13 October 1994.

24. Russian doctrine also refers to "operations to maintain peace" (*operatsii po podderzhaniyu mira*). See Michael Orr, "Peacekeeping—A New Task," 307; and United Nations Institute for Disarmament Research (hereafter, UNIDIR), *Russian Approaches to Peacekeeping Operations,* Research Papers no. 28 (New York: United Nations, 1994), 5-8.

25. Kozyrev argues that, "'Classical' yardsticks which the United Nations applied to peacekeeping operations dozens of years ago are now unsuitable. . . . We should . . . proceed from real life, not from a scheme, all the more so because new approaches have already proved their efficiency, as in the Dniester Region and South Ossetia." See Foreign Minister Andrey Kozyrev, "Rossiya fakticheski v odinochku neset bremya real'nogo mirotvorchestva v konfliktakh po perimetru svoikh granits: i nikto za neyo eto ne sdelaet" (Russia actually bears the burden of peacemaking in conflicts on the perimeter of its borders alone: And no one will do this for her), *Nezavisimaya Gazeta,* 22 September 1993, 1.

26. Author's italics. The statement was cited approvingly by Lieutenant Colonel G. Zhilin in "The Problem Demands a Solution: Troops of Peacekeeping Forces Must Operate Decisively, Firmly, and Without Delay," *Voyennyy Vestnik,* no. 9 (September 1993)

[signed to press 20 August 1993]: 17-19, translated in *JPRS-UMA* 94-005 (9 February 1994): 32-34; see also Volga Military District 1st Deputy Commander Lieutenant General Anatoliy Aleksandrovich Shapovalvov, interview by Colonel A. Bondarenko, "The Volga Soldiers Try on the 'Blue Helmets,'" *Voyennyy Vestnik,* 22 March 1993, 2-5, translated in *JPRS-UMA* 93-026 (28 July 1993): 21-24.

27.   Ironically, Russian units may have even sold weapons to the Chechen militia, which, of course, turned around and used them on Russian forces. See, for example, Robert Orttung, "More Revelations About the Beginning of Chechen War," *Open Media Research Institute Daily Digest* (online), 8 February 1995; and Doug Clarke, "Military Main Source of Criminals' Weapons," *Open Media Research Institute Daily Digest* (online), 5 April 1995.

28.   This policy dates to the Gorbachev period when Soviet Minister of Defense Dmitriy Yazov announced that Soviet troops would be permitted to fire upon civilians if it were in self-defense. The policy at the time was partly a response to forces harassing Soviet troops in Georgia. See Statement by Defense Minister Army General Dmitriy Timofeyevich Yazov, from the "Vremya" newscast, Moscow Television, 18:00 GMT, 27 November 1990, translated in *Foreign Broadcast Information Service Daily Report: Soviet Union* (hereafter, *FBIS-SOV*) 90-229 (28 November 1990): 68.

29.   For analyses that are critical of Russia's policy in the NIS, see, for example, Fiona Hill and Pamela Jewett, *"Back in the USSR": Russia's Intervention in the Internal Affairs of the Former Soviet Republics and the Implications for United States Policy toward Russia* (Cambridge, Mass.: Strengthening Democratic Institutions Project, John F. Kennedy School of Government, January 1994), 2; Zbigniew Brzezinski, "The Premature Partnership," *Foreign Affairs* (March - April 1994): 71-75; Yuri N. Afanasyev, "Russia's Vicious Circle," *New York Times,* 28 February 1994, 17; and William S. Cohen, "The Empire Strikes Back," *Problems of Post-Communism* (January - February 1995): 13-18.

30.   The election of a Russian nationalist as president of Crimea in January 1994 presented an opportunity for Moscow to encourage separatism by the ethnic Russian majority. There have also been a number of cases of political terrorism as well as confrontations between Ukrainian and Russian units, in particular, in the disputed Black Sea Fleet. In all of these cases, Moscow has not only passed on the opportunity to stir up trouble, it has encouraged a diplomatic solution to the dispute. See, for example, Lee Hockstader, "Brush with Black Sea Naval Battle Heightens Russo-Ukrainian Tensions; Warships, Fighter Jets Dispatched in Weekend Confrontation," *Washington Post,* 11 April 1994, 10; and Lee Hockstader, "Separatist Storm Brewing in Crimea; Return to Russia Beckons as Promises of Ukraine Independence Falter," *Washington Post,* 14 May 1994, 16.

31.   See, for example, the account of the politics of Presidential Decision Directive 25 (PDD-25) in Elaine Sciolino, "New US Peacekeeping Policy Deemphasizes Role of the UN," *New York Times,* 6 May 1994, 1.

32.   See R. Jeffrey Smith and Barton Gellman, "U.S. Will Seek to Mediate Ex-Soviet States' Disputes; Aim Is to Avert Russian Military Intervention," *Washington Post,* 5 August 1993, 1. The public white paper summarizing PDD-25 is perhaps purposefully

unclear on this point. See US Department of State, Bureau of International Organization Affairs, *The Clinton Administration's Policy on Reforming Multilateral Peace Operations,* Publication 10161 (Washington, D.C.: May 1994). For further discussion of the development of PDD-25, see chapter two in this volume.

33. John Thornhill, George Graham, and Chrystia Freeland, "US Approves Role of Russian Troops within CIS States," *London Financial Times,* 7 September 1994, 16; and Smith and Gellman, "US Will Seek to Mediate."

34. Thornhill, Graham, and Freeland, "US Approves Role of Russian Troops."

35. *Reuters,* "U.N. Endorses Russian Troops for Peacekeeping in Caucasus," *New York Times,* 22 July 1994, 2.

36. Suzanne Crow, "Results of Boutros-Ghali Visit," *RFE/RL Daily Report,* 6 April 1994.

37. For example, in December 1993 the OSCE Foreign Ministers' meeting in Rome rejected a Russian request for blanket authorization of Russian-led peacekeeping efforts in the former Soviet Union (FSU). The meeting insisted that the OSCE assess each case according to whether it meets OSCE objectives. See Konrad J. Huber, "The CSCE's New Role in the East: Conflict Prevention," *RFE/RL Research Report,* 12 August 1994, 29. In June 1994 senior diplomats criticized Russia for not withdrawing its troops from Moldova and for obstructing the work of the OSCE observer mission there. See Vladimir Socor, "Kozyrev Qualifies His Remarks On Troops In Moldova," *RFE/RL Daily Report,* 16 June 1994.

38. See John W. R. Lepingwell, "CSCE on Russian Peacekeeping," *RFE/RL Daily Report,* 15 June 1994.

39. For example, the border between North Ossetia, an autonomous republic in Russia, and South Ossetia, an autonomous oblast in Georgia, is completely artificial. See Karen Dawisha and Bruce Parrott, *Russia and the New States of Eurasia: The Politics of Upheaval* (Cambridge, Mass.: Cambridge University Press, 1994), 53.

40. SDIP, *Report on Ethnic Conflict,* 95.

41. See SDIP, *Report on Ethnic Conflict,* 90; and Dawisha and Parrott, *Russia and the New States,* 87.

42. SDIP, *Report on Ethnic Conflict,* 95-96; and UNIDIR, *Russian Approaches to Peacekeeping Operations,* 25.

43. The conflict forced 23,000 Georgians in South Ossetia to flee to Georgia and at least 50,000 Ossetians to flee to North Ossetia from the south and Georgia. See Daniel C. Diller, *Russia and the Independent States* (Washington, D.C.: Congressional Quarterly, Inc., 1993), 154; and SDIP, *Report on Ethnic Conflict,* 96-97.

44. Gamsakhurdia's tenure as president was characterized by practically daily mass demonstrations led by Georgian liberals and intellectuals who opposed him. In late December 1991, armed opposition forces lay siege to the Government House in Tbilisi, where Gamsakhurdia was holding out. In early January 1992, Gamsakhurdia fled to Armenia, and then to Russia's Chechen Republic. Thereafter, he led a rebellion against the Shevardnadze regime. See Diller, *Russia and the Independent States,* 273; Dawisha and Parrot, *Russia and the New States of Eurasia,* 153-154; and SDIP, *Report on Ethnic Conflict,* 97.

45. See SDIP, *Report on Ethnic Conflict,* 97-98.

46. The first estimate is from Dmitriy Trenin, "Blessed Are the Peacemakers . . . ," *Novoye Vremya,* no. 24 (June 1993): 8-12, translated in *JPRS-UMA* 93-024 (14 July 1993): 26. Another estimate suggests 600 Russian troops, one Georgian battalion of approximately 300, and a joint North-South Ossetian battalion of 400-500. See Michael Orr, "Peacekeeping—A New Task." A third report estimates one Russian paratroop battalion and some Interior Ministry troops (altogether approximately 700 troops); a regiment of Georgian National Guard (320 troops), North Ossetian Interior Ministry troops, and some South Ossetian volunteers (totaling roughly 470 troops). See James M. Greene, "Russia's Peacekeeping Doctrine: The CIS, Russia, and the General Staff," Central and East European Defence Studies, Supreme Headquarters Allied Powers Europe (SHAPE), 11 January 1993 (mimeograph), cited in Shashenkov, "Russian Peacekeeping," fn 24.

47. Shashenkov, "Russian Peacekeeping," 52; and SDIP, *Report on Ethnic Conflict,* 98.

48. Order of Joint Military Command of Composite Peace and Law and Order Forces, 16 June 1993, city of Tskhinvali, *Prikaz Obyedininennogo Voyennogo Komandovaniya SSMP,* 16 June 1994, 1-7, translated in *JPRS-UMA* 94-040 (28 September 1994): 14-17.

49. Yuriy Gladkevich, "Gody Bez Voyny: Oni tak i ne prinecli zhitelym Yuzhnoy Osetii ni spokoystviya, ni dostatka" (The years without war: They brought neither peace nor prosperity to the inhabitants of South Ossetia), *Krasnaya Zvezda,* 10 November 1994, 2; and *Iberia,* 14:30 GMT, 20 June 1994, translated in *Foreign Broadcast Information Service Daily Report—Central Eurasia (FBIS-SOV)* 94-119 (21 June 1994): 69.

50. Aleksandr Iskandaryan, "Hot Spot: Three Questions from Tskhinvali or the Trigger Has Not Been Pulled Yet . . . ," *Novoye Vremya,* no. 20 (May 1994), translated in *Foreign Broadcast Information Service Report—Central Eurasia* (hereafter, *FBIS-USR*) 94-063 (14 June 1994): 9-10.

51. Colonel General Georgiy Kondrat'yev, "Mirotvorcheskaya Rol' Rossii"; Dmitriy Trenin, "Blessed are the Peacemakers"; Michael Orr, "Peacekeeping—A New Task," 309; and Yuriy Gladkevich, "Gody Bez Voyny."

52. Lee Hockstader, "Russian Peacekeepers Approved for Georgia; Moscow to Send 3,000 Troops to Rebel Province," *Washington Post,* 22 June 1994, 16.

53. Diller, *Russia and the Independent States,* 274; and SDIP, *Report on Ethnic Conflict,* 101-102.

54. Several authoritative reports have stated that the assault on Sukhumi was a personal initiative of Kitovani. See, for example, Elizabeth Fuller, "Paramilitary Forces Dominate Fighting in Transcaucasus," *RFE/RL Research Report* (18 June 1993): 81.

55. SDIP, *Report on Ethnic Conflict,* 101-104.

56. Georgian forces downed an aircraft piloted by a member of the Russian air force, prompting Shevardnadze to declare in Georgian parliament: "I can boldly state that we are in fact dealing with a Russian-Georgian conflict. Thousands of Russian citizens, mercenaries, and regular army men are directly involved in military hostilities against

Georgia." See SDIP, *Report on Ethnic Conflict,* 105-106. UN observers reportedly confirmed that the downed flier was a Russian air force officer. See Helsinki Watch, *War or Peace? Human Rights and Russian Military Involvement in the "Near Abroad"* 5, no. 22 (December 1993): 7.

57. SDIP, *Report on Ethnic Conflict,* 106.

58. The first extension was through 15 May 1995. The second extension endorsed the mission through the end of 1995. See Suzanne Crow, "Results of Boutros-Ghali Visit," *RFE/RL Daily Report,* 6 April 1994; Elizabeth Fuller, "Transcaucasia Peacekeeping," *RFE/RL Daily Report,* 9 June 1994; Vladimir Socor, "'Peacekeeping' Update," *RFE/RL Daily Report,* 26 October 1994; Elizabeth Fuller, "Abkhaz-UN Talks Deadlocked," *RFE/RL Daily Report,* 18 November 1994; and Elizabeth Fuller, "Shevardnadze on Abkhazia, South Ossetia," *OMRI Daily Digest,* 30 May 1995.

59. See Hill and Jewett, *"Back in the USSR,"* 48; Helsinki Watch, *War or Peace?* 6; Thomas Goltz, "Letter from Eurasia: The Hidden Russian Hand," *Foreign Policy* (fall 1993): 92-116; and Lepingwell, "The Russian Military."

60. See Maksim Yusin, "Andrey Kozyrev;" and Helsinki Watch, *War or Peace?* 7.

61. Even some of the sharpest critics of local Russian military forces concede that Georgian militias at various times attacked Russian bases and engaged in considerable human rights abuses. See, for example, Hill and Jewett, *"Back in the USSR,"* 50.

62. Dawisha and Parrott, *Russia and the New States of Eurasia,* 239; and Helsinki Watch, *War or Peace?* 7. The Russian general in charge of the Eshera facility argued similarly that he ordered artillery strikes against Georgian forces that had been shelling him first. See Colonel Vladimir Zhitarenko, "General'skoye delo" (General's Business), *Krasnaya Zvezda,* 20 March 1993, 3.

63. Stephen Foye, "Grachev on Georgia, Doctrine, 4 October," *RFE/RL Daily Report,* 20 October 1993; and Celestine Bohlen, "Russia and Georgia Sign Military Cooperation Treaty," *New York Times,* 4 February 1994, 3.

64. Aleksandr Pel'ts and Pyotr Karapetyan, "Rossiya, pokhozhe, uvodit Gruziyu i Abkhaziyu ot novogo voyennogo protivostoyaniya" (Russia, it seems, is leading Georgia and Abkhazia away from a new military confrontation), *Krasnaya Zvezda,* 20 September 1994, 1; and Aleksandr Koretskiy, "Three-Way Talks Could Not Be Held," *Kommersant-Daily,* 20 September 1994, 3, translated in *FBIS-SOV* 94-183 (21 September 1994): 41-43.

65. Teymuraz Mamaladze, "V Abkhazii sozrel khoroshiy urozhay 'Izabelly'" (A fine crop of 'Isabells' were harvested in Abkhazia), *Izvestiya,* 20 September 1994, 1-2.

66. Security Council Resolution 849, 9 July 1993; Security Council Resolution 854, 6 August 1993; and Security Council Resolution 858, 24 August 1993. Resolution 858 formally established the United Nations Observer Mission in Georgia (UNOMIG).

67. Security Council Resolution 876, 19 October 1993; Security Council Resolution 896, 31 January 1994; and Elizabeth Fuller, "Abkhazia, Georgia Request UN Peacekeepers," *RFE/RL Daily Report,* 14 January 1994.

68. Elizabeth Fuller, "No UN Peacekeepers for Georgia," *RFE/RL Daily Report,* 1 February 1994; Elizabeth Fuller, "Abkhazia Sets Conditions for Resuming Talks," *RFE/RL*

Daily Report, 24 March 1994; and Elizabeth Fuller, "No UN Peacekeeping Troops for Abkhazia," *RFE/RL Daily Report,* 6 May 1994. Initially consisting of less than 10 observers, the mission expanded to 55 by mid-1994 and to 126 by November 1994. See Security Council Resolution 858; and *United Nations Peace-keeping Information Notes* (New York: United Nations Department of Public Information, Update, December 1994), 171.

69. Initially, diplomats predicted that the Security Council would do nothing more than "take note of Russia's intentions to send peacekeepers." See Paul Lewis, "Russia Seeking U.N. Backing for Caucasus Force," *New York Times,* 27 May 1994, 3; and Elizabeth Fuller, "UN Endorses Russian Peacekeeping Mission in Abkhazia," *RFE/RL Daily Report,* 22 July 1994.

70. Security Council Resolution 937, 21 July 1994, stated that the Security Council "[w]elcomes the contribution made by the Russian Federation, and indications of further contributions from other members of the CIS, of a peace-keeping force."

71. See the report series, Security Council, *Report of the Secretary-General Concerning the Situation in Abkhazia, Georgia,* S/1995/10, 6 January 1995; S/1995/181, 6 March 1995; and S/1995/342, 1 May 1995; and Elizabeth Fuller, "Repatriation of Georgian Refugees Gets Under Way," *RFE/RL Daily Report,* 13 October 1994.

72. Thomas W. Lippman, "U.N. Force for Ex-Soviet Georgia Wins Clinton Support; Funds Sought," *Washington Post,* 8 March 1994, 9.

73. See Williams, "Moscow's Troubling Intervention; U.S. Fears Troops in Former Republics May Lead to Expansion," *Washington Post,* 21 June 1994; and Lally Weymouth, "Yalta II," *Washington Post,* 24 July 1994, C7.

74. Williams, "Moscow's Troubling Intervention"; and Elizabeth Fuller, "Georgian-Abkhaz Talks Focus on Refugees," *RFE/RL Daily Report,* 2 September 1994.

75. Elizabeth Fuller, "Shevardnadze, Opposition, Clash Over Abkhazia," *RFE/RL Daily Report,* 24 May 1994; and Elizabeth Fuller, "CIS Defense Ministers Fail to Agree on Abkhaz Peacekeepers," *RFE/RL Daily Report,* 20 July 1994.

76. Within the peacekeeping area, the Russian forces set up five checkpoints to regulate the flow of returning refugees and bar the passage of weapons into the security and arms limitation zones. In addition, 22 observation posts were created throughout the entire territory. Viktor Litovkin, "Glavnymi mirotvortsami v Zakavkaz'ye naznacheny desantniki" (Paratroopers named as chief peacekeepers in Transcaucasus), *Izvestiya,* 23 June 1994, 2.

77. Heavy hardware is defined as artillery weapons and mortars in excess of 80 mm, as well as tanks, armored personnel carriers, and armored fighting vehicles. See Gennadiy Sobolev, "Russian Peacekeeping Forces Move into Zone of Georgian-Abkhaz Conflict," *Rossiskiye Vesti,* 25 June 1994, 1, translated in *FBIS-SOV* 94-123 (27 June 1994): 15.

78. Viktor Litovkin, "Glavnymi mirotvortsami"; and Chris Bird, "Peacekeeping Role New One for Russia," *Los Angeles Times,* 28 June 1994, 3.

79. Vladimir Sarishvili, "They Came for the Sake of Peace," *Trud,* 28 June 1994, 5, translated in *FBIS-SOV* 94-125 (29 June 1994): 9-10.

80. Litovkin, "Glavnymi mirotvortsami."

81. Orr, "Peacekeeping and Overstretch," 365.

82. Litovkin, "Glavnymi mirotvortsami." Although a half million dollars per month would not appear to be much to the average observer, it is nonetheless a substantial sum for the cash-strapped Russian military. An American report cites a cost of approximately $1 million per month. See Lee Hockstader, "Russian Peacekeepers Approved for Georgia; Moscow to Send 3,000 Troops to Rebel Province," *Washington Post,* 22 June 1994, 16.

83. Bird, "Peacekeeping Role New One for Russia"; Liana Minasyan, "Tbilisi is Still in Need of Moscow's Help: Russian Peacekeepers on the Inguri River Have Had Little Success as Yet," *Nezavisimaya Gazeta,* 18 May 1995, 1, translated in *East View Press Digest* (online), 18 May 1995.

84. Elizabeth Fuller, "Progress Toward Abkhaz Settlement?" *Open Media Research Institute Daily Digest,* 14 February 1995. The UN Security Council deplored the Abkhaz leadership's continued obstruction of the return of refugees. See Security Council Resolution 993, 12 May 1995.

85. Dawisha and Parrott, *Russia and the New States of Eurasia,* 222-23.

86. Diller, *Russia and the Independent States,* 257.

87. Raymond Bonner, "Tajik Civil War Fades, but the Brutality Goes On," *New York Times,* 26 November 1993, 3; and Bess Brown, "Central Asia: The First Year of Unexpected Statehood," *RFE/RL Research Report* (1 January 1993): 35.

88. Justin Burke, "Regional, Religious Rivalries Rend Tajikistan," *Christian Science Monitor,* 14 September 1992, 1; Serge Schmemann, "War Bleeds Ex-Soviet Land at Central Asia's Heart," *New York Times,* 21 February 1993, 1; and Bonner, "Tajik Civil War Fades."

89. The Pamiris and Garmis joined with the nationalist Rastokhez Popular Front (which had been formed by a number of writers and intellectuals), the Islamic Renaissance Movement, and new pro-democracy parties.

90. See Bess Brown, "Tajikistan to Restore Presidency," *RFE/RL Research Report* (12 August 1994): 12; and Ann Sheehy, "Nabiyev Resignation Accepted," *RFE/RL Daily Report,* 23 November 1992, 3.

91. See Leon Aron, "Yeltsin's Vietnam: A Central Asian Quagmire May Wreck Russian Reform," *Washington Post,* 22 August 1993, C1; and Bonner, "Tajik Civil War Fades."

92. Captain Igor Chernyshov, "Tajikistan: Concerns and Hopes," *Oriyentir* no. 2 (August 1994) [signed to press 12 August 1994]: 12-17, translated in *JPRS-UMA* 94-043 (26 October 1994): 30; and Steve LeVine, "Afghan, Arab Muslim Militants Back Rebels in Ex-Soviet State," *Washington Post,* 27 April 1993, 10.

93. Elizabeth Fuller, "Tajik Cease-fire Agreement Reached," *RFE/RL Daily Report,* 19 September 1994. The cease-fire apparently did not enter into force until the arrival of 11 UN military observers on 19 October 1994. It was subsequently extended on repeated occasions. See Bess Brown, "Tajik Talks Resume," *RFE/RL Daily Report,* 20 October 1994; Elizabeth Fuller, "Tajik Cease-fire Extended," *RFE/RL Daily Report,* 11

November 1994; and Bruce Pannier, "Tajik Talks Yield Results," *Open Media Research Institute Daily Digest,* 31 May 1995.

94. See Bess Brown, "Tajik Elections Criticized," *RFE/RL Daily Report,* 10 November 1994; and Elizabeth Fuller, "Elections in Tajikistan," *Open Media Research Institute Daily Digest,* 27 February 1995.

95. See Security Council, *Report of the Secretary-General on the Situation in Tajikistan,* S/1995/390, 12 May 1995; and *Interfax,* 11:29 GMT, 19 April 1995, reprinted in *FBIS-SOV* 95-076 (20 April 1995): 1.

96. See Helsinki Watch, *War or Peace?* 12; and Hill and Jewett, *"Back in the USSR,"* 40-42. Hill and Jewett argue that Russia intervened directly in the civil war in order to restore the pro-Communist, pro-Moscow Rakhmonov regime; and Bess Brown, "Central Asian States Seek Russian Help," *RFE/RL Research Report* (18 June 1993): 83-88.

97. Russian troops and citizens were occasionally kidnapped and murdered by the warring parties during this period. While there are reports that Russian units intervened against the opposition militia (especially during the fight for the southern city of Kurgan-Tyube), in December 1992 units of the 201st division allegedly drove off an attack on Dushanbe by pro-Communist forces. See *Itar-TASS World Service,* in Russian, 11:40 GMT, 4 December 1992, translated in *FBIS-SOV* 92-235 (2 December 1992): 23; Bess Brown, "Russian Troops in Dushanbe Stop Pro-Communist Attack," *RFE/RL Daily Report,* 7 December 1992; Bess Brown, "Russian Border Guards Clash with Tajik Government Supporters," *RFE/RL Daily Report,* 16 December 1992; Bess Brown, "Russian-Speakers Taken Hostage in Dushanbe," *RFE/RL Daily Report,* 17 December 1992; Bess Brown, "Moscow Condemns Murder of Russian Servicemen in Tajikistan," *RFE/RL Daily Report,* 29 December 1992; and Helsinki Watch, *War or Peace?* 12-13.

98. Brown, "Russian-Speakers Taken Hostage in Dushanbe"; and Brown, "Central Asian States Seek Russian Help."

99. See Keith Martin, "Russian Troops Retake Tajik Post," *RFE/RL Daily Report,* 15 July 1993; and Keith Martin, "Tajikistan: Russians Come" *RFE/RL Daily Report,* 19 July 1993.

100. Author's italics. Martin, "Tajikistan: Russians Come"; and Keith Martin, "Tajik Developments," *RFE/RL Daily Report,* 21 July 1993.

101. See Minister of Foreign Affairs Andrey Kozyrev, "Chego khochet Rossiya v Tadzhikistanye" (What Russia wants in Tajikistan), *Izvestiya,* 4 August 1993, 4; and Suzanne Crow, "Joint Session of CIS Foreign and Defense Ministers," *RFE/RL Research Report,* 17 March 1994. The commander of the Collective Peacekeeping Forces, Colonel General Valeriy Patrikeyev, later provided a similar assessment of Russia's interests in Tajikistan, emphasizing a fear of an instability "domino-effect," in particular. See Mumin Shakirov and Otakhon Latifi, "The Tajik Knows: Two Views on the Situation," *Literaturnaya Gazeta,* no. 31 (3 August 1994): 11, translated in *FBIS-USR* 94-091 (21 August 1994): 103-106.

102. For example, on 19 July 1993 Russian aircraft reportedly participated in the bombing of a strategic rebel stronghold east of Dushanbe. Despite repeated denials, Russian

forces may also have joined Tajik units in fighting the rebels in July 1994. See Keith Martin, "Tajik Update," *RFE/RL Daily Report,* 20 July 1993; the comments of Russian deputy minister of defense Georgiy Kondrat'yev in Keith Martin, "Russian Official on Tajik Situation," *RFE/RL Daily Report,* 8 June 1994; Keith Martin, "Tajik Forces Attack 'Rebels,'" *RFE/RL Daily Report,* 22 June 1994; Keith Martin, "More on Tajik Fighting," *RFE/RL Daily Report,* 27 July 1994; and Oleg Panfilov, "<Soldatskiye Materi> Sankt-Peterburga Protiv Generala Gracheva: Storoniki Abdulladzhanova obvinyayut Rakhmonova v narushenii zakona o vyborakh" ('Soldier's mothers' of St. Petersburg against General Grachev: Abdulladzhanov's supporters accuse Rakhmonov of violating the law on elections), *Nezavisimaya Gazeta,* 28 September 1994, 3.

103. Reportedly, Russian peacekeeping units were not involved in these operations. See Lowell Bezanis, "Tajik Roundup," *Open Media Research Institute Daily Digest,* 11 April 1995; and Bruce Pannier, "Many Casualties in Bombing in Northern Afghanistan," *Open Media Research Institute Daily Digest,* 18 April 1995.

104. In late July 1993, Foreign Minister Kozyrev was named as Russia's special representative to the conflict, with a top priority of opening up a dialogue between the conflicting parties. See Bess Brown, "Kozyrev Appointed Special Russian Representative on Tajikistan," *RFE/RL Daily Report,* 29 July 1993; and Kozyrev, "Rossiya fakticheski."

105. Bess Brown, "Tajik Election Date Postponed," *RFE/RL Daily Report,* 8 September 1994; and *Interfax,* 11:29 GMT, 19 April 1995, reprinted in *FBIS-SOV* 95-076 (20 April 1995): 1.

106. See Martin, "Tajikistan: Russians Come"; and Keith Martin, "Update on Tajik situation," *RFE/RL Daily Report,* 22 July 1993.

107. See Boris Sitnikov, *Itar-TASS,* in English, 20:27 GMT, 31 August 1993, reprinted in *FBIS-SOV* 93-169 (2 September 1993): 1; Bess Brown, "Tajikistan Update," *RFE/RL Daily Report,* 6 October 1993; and Bess Brown, "Central Asian, Russian Foreign Ministers Confer on Tajikistan," *RFE/RL Daily Report,* 15 March 1994.

108. Elizabeth Fuller, "UN Security Council Discusses Tajik Situation," *RFE/RL Daily Report,* 24 August 1994.

109. Keith Martin, "Tajik Peace Talks Begin," *RFE/RL Daily Report,* 21 June 1994.

110. Security Council, *Report of the Secretary-General on the Situation in Tajikistan,* S/1994/1363, 30 November 1994, 1. Personnel of the United Nations Mission of Observers in Tajikistan (UNMOT) are based in the cities of Dushanbe, Garm, Kurgan-Tyube, and Pyanj. See also Security Council Resolution 968, 16 December 1994; and Security Council, *Report of the Secretary-General on the Situation in Tajikistan,* S/1995/472, 10 June 1995.

111. Bess Brown, "Tajik Government-Opposition Commission Meets," *RFE/RL Daily Report,* 15 November 1994.

112. Bess Brown, "CIS Peacekeeping Force for Tajikistan," *RFE/RL Daily Report,* 1 December 1992.

113. Kyrgyzstan sent its battalion in March 1993, but withdrew it the next month. See Shashenkov, "Russian Peacekeeping," 54; and Mikhail Shevtsov, *Itar-TASS,* in En-

glish, 19:24 GMT, 4 December 1992, reprinted in *FBIS-SOV* 93-235 (2 December 1993): 1.

114. Aleksandr Karpov, "Soglasheniye o vvodye mirotvorcheskikh sil SNG v Tadzhikistan dostignuto" (Agreement is reached on sending CIS peacekeeping forces to Tajikistan), *Izvestiya,* 1 December 1992, 1.

115. The five signatories that contributed forces were Russia, Kazakhstan, Kyrgyzstan, Uzbekistan, and Tajikistan. Only Armenia did not join the CIS coalition agreement. See Stephen Foye, "Collective Security Signatories Widen Cooperation," *RFE/RL Daily Report,* 25 August 1993; and Vladimir Socor, "Military Decisions," *RFE/RL Daily Report,* 24 October 1994.

116. Formally speaking, only one battalion of the 201st Division has been designated a peacekeeping unit. Nonetheless, for the purposes of this paper the entire division will be considered to be assigned to peacekeeping. See Allison, "Russian Peacekeeping," 544.

117. Larisa Kudryavtseva, "Peacemaking is a National Concern," interviewing Colonel General Georgiy Kondrat'yev, *Chestu Imeyu,* no. 5-6 (May - June 1994) [signed to press 10 July 1994]: 2-6, translated in *JPRS-UMA* 94-041 (12 October 1994): 4-7; and Kushko, "Blue Helmets."

118. The quotas are: Russian Federation, 50 percent; Uzbekistan, 15 percent; Kazakhstan, 15 percent; Kyrgyzstan, 10 percent; Tajikistan, 10 percent. See Falichev, "General-polkovnik Boris P'yankov." The operation's command staff consists of about 200 people. "Stars Descend on Dushanbe," *Komsomolskaya Pravda,* 21 December 1993, 2, translated in *JPRS-UMA* 94-003 (26 October 1994): 40.

119. Igor Chernyak, "'Afghan War:' Act Two? CIS Troops Are to Be Transferred to Tajikistan before First Snowfall," *Komsomolskaya Pravda,* 25 August 1993, 1, translated in *FBIS-SOV* 93-164 (26 August 1993): 2-3.

120. The only limitation, in this case, was a need to make a subsequent report to the heads of state and defense ministers. See Falichev, "General-polkovnik Boris P'yankov."

121. *Komsomolskaya Pravda,* "Stars Descend on Dushanbe"; and Panfilov, "<Soldatskiye Materi>." Patrikeyev himself was replaced by Lieutenant General Valentin Bobryshev in May 1995. See Rodion Morozov, "General Will Be Promoted," *Obshchaya Gazeta* no. 22/98 (1 June 1995): 2, translated in *East View Press Digest,* 1 June 1995.

122. See, for example, Valeriy Nikishin, "In Hours of Calm, X-Hour Comes to Mind; The Campaign in Preparation for the Impending Tajik Presidential Elections Has Evoked a Sharp Reaction of the Opposition Forces," *Kazakhstanskaya Pravda,* 8 September 1994, 1, 4; and Vadim Makhin, "On the Firing Line: Reportage from the Tajik-Afghan Border," *Sovety Kazakhstana,* 7 September 1994, 2, both translated in *JPRS-UMA* 94-040 (28 September 1994): 22-27.

123. Kushko, "Blue Helmets."

124. Bess Brown, "Tajikistan Update," *RFE/RL Daily Report,* 12 September 1994; Nikishin, "In Hours of Calm;" and Makhin, "On the Firing Line."

125. Shashenkov, "Russian Peacekeeping," 54-55.

126. Between August 1993 and August 1994, border units reportedly engaged hostile forces 400 times. See Captain Igor Chernyshov, "Tajikistan: Concerns and Hopes," *Oriyentir* no. 2 (August 1994): 12-17, translated in *JPRS-UMA* 94-043 (26 October 1994): 28-32.

127. See Bruce Pannier, "UN Threatens to Withdraw Mission from Tajikistan," *Open Media Research Institute Daily Digest,* 29 May 1995.

128. On 20 April 1995, the presidents of Uzbekistan and Kazakhstan announced that they were considering pulling their peacekeeping units out of Tajikistan. The Uzbek president is said to have personally admonished Rakhmonov at a May 1995 CIS meeting for not being more flexible with the opposition. See "Moscow Criticizes Uzbek, Kazakh Positions on Tajikistan," *Jamestown Monitor* (online), 23 May 1995; and Lowell Bezanis, "Rakhmonov, Karimov Tangle?" *Open Media Research Institute Daily Digest,* 6 June 1995.

129. Grachev's resistance to helping the Border Guards was, no doubt, also influenced by a running political feud between him and the head of the Russian Border Guards. See Igor Korotchenko, "Is the Defense Ministry Ignoring Border Guards' Requests for Help?" *Nezavisimaya Gazeta,* 14 April 1995, 1.

130. Most press accounts refer to the western, Moldovan side of the river as the "right bank" and the side on which the Trans-Dniester Republic is based as the "left bank." These descriptions, based on the direction in which the Dniester River flows, cause confusion when looking at a north-south-oriented map of the conflict.

131. Ethnic Russians make up some 25 percent of the population of the Dniester Republic, while ethnic Ukrainians constitute 28 percent. See Pal Kolsto and Andrei Edemsky with Natalya Kalashnikova, "The Dniester Conflict: Between Irredentism and Separatism," *Europe-Asia Studies* 45, no. 6 (1993): 975-76, 979.

132. Until this time, the east bank had been part of the Union Republic of Ukraine. See Kolsto, et. al., "The Dniester Conflict," 977-81.

133. The east bank was occupied briefly by Romania during World War II. Ibid., 979-81.

134. Still later the republic was renamed the Dniester Moldovan Republic. Ibid., 983.

135. Ibid., 987.

136. Diller, *Russia and the Independent States,* 155.

137. For example, the 14th Army joined Dniester forces in seizing the city of Bendery, on Moldovan territory on the west bank of the Dniester. See Vladimir Socor, "More Postmortems on Dniester War," *RFE/RL Daily Report,* 30 August 1994.

138. This claim was made by the Dniester Republic's Defense Minister, Lieutenant General Stanislav Khazheev, as cited in Socor, "More Postmortems on Dniester War."

139. Kolsto, et al., "The Dniester Conflict," 994.

140. Vladimir Socor, "Cease-fire Agreement in Moldova," *RFE/RL Daily Report,* 9 July 1992; Vladimir Sokor "CIS 'Peacemaking' Plan for Moldova Stillborn," *RFE/RL Daily Report,* 14 July 1992; Shashenkov, "Russian Peacekeeping," 53; and Kolsto, et. al., "The Dniester Conflict," 994.

141. See, for example, Dawisha and Parrott, *Russia and the New States of Eurasia,* 79; and Kolsto, et. al., "The Dniester Conflict," 986.

142. William D. Jackson, "Imperial Temptations: Ethnics Abroad," *Orbis* (winter 1994): 6-7; Vladimir Socor, "Russia Content With Stalemate in Moldova?" *RFE/RL Daily Report,* 24 August 1994; and Vladimir Socor, "Dniester Autonomy Talks Launched," *RFE/RL Daily Report,* 30 September 1994.

143. Kolsto et. al., "The Dniester Conflict," 993.

144. While Moldovan authorities refused to permit the March 1991 Soviet referendum on the future of the Union to take place on their territory, the referendum was administered on the east bank. The Dniester side reported that support for the Union on its territory was greater than 93 percent. (See Kolsto et. al., "The Dniester Conflict," 984, 992.) The east bank also continues to use the hammer and sickle as its symbols and has not removed its Soviet monuments, as other republics have. Dniester leader Igor Smirnov describes the defense of his region as a cause for both Communists and Russian monarchists. See Henry Kamm, "Russian Troops Quitting a Hot Spot in Moldova," *New York Times,* 28 October 1994, 12; and Vladimir Socor, "'Dniester' Leader Hails Russian Pan-Orthodoxism," *RFE/RL Daily Report,* 13 October 1994.

145. Furthermore, in a clear violation of international law, the Russian 14th Army drafted local Moldovan-Dniester citizens into its ranks. See Svetlana Gamova, "Aleksandr Lebed': Sama Zhizn' Zastavlyaet Generalov Zanimat'cya Politikoy" (Aleksandr Lebed: Life itself compels generals to engage in politics), *Izvestiya,* 20 July 1994, 1, 4.

146. In an example of Yeltsin's deference to Lebed, in October 1993 the Russian president awarded medals to approximately 200 servicemen of the 14th Army, most of whom had taken part in the 1992 Dniester operations. See Vladimir Socor, "Lebed Licensed to Run Own Show?" *RFE/RL Daily Report,* 6 October 1993. Also, in a startling rebuke to his minister of defense, Yeltsin overruled Grachev's reassignment of Lebed in August 1994.

147. For example, the commander of the Russian ground forces, Colonel General Vladimir Semyenov, told the press that the Transdniester area was "native Russian territory" and urged the creation of a Russian military base on the basis of the 14th Army. See Pavel Fel'gengauer, "Voyennyye gotvyatsya k bor'be za den'gi" (The military is preparing itself for a battle for money), *Segodnya,* 29 October 1994, 4. The former chief of Russian peacekeeping forces, Colonel General Kondrat'yev, also proposed reducing the tripartite peacekeeping force and transferring its functions to the 14th Army. See Vladimir Socor, "More on Russian Military Demands on Moldova," *RFE/RL Daily Report,* 22 February 1994. There are even reports that Grachev himself in mid-1992 signed a bilateral agreement with Dniester leaders that transferred weapons to the separatists. See Helsinki Watch, *War or Peace?* 10.

148. For details on the agreement to withdraw the 14th Army, see Sergey Knyaz'kov, "Tri goda na sbory: Rossiya i Moldaviya okonchatel'no soglasovali tekst soglasheniya o vyvodye 14-i armii" (Three years in the making: Russian and Moldova finally agree on the text of an agreement on the withdrawal of the 14th Army), *Krasnaya Zvezda,* 19 October 1994, 3. Lebed's considered reaction was that his troops "would like to spit on this agreement." See Kamm, "Russian Troops Quitting a Hot Spot in Moldova," 12. Civilian analyst Sergey Rogov argues that President Yeltsin finds it safer politically

to let the military do what it wants in situations such as this. See Erlanger, "In Ex-Soviet Lands."

149. Robert Orttung, "Yeltsin Accepts Lebed's Resignation," *Open Media Research Institute Daily Digest,* 15 June 1995. Lebed subsequently turned to politics. He ran for president of the Russian Federation in spring 1996, winning a surprisingly high 15 percent of the vote in first-round balloting. In return for Lebed's backing in the run-off election, Yeltsin appointed him chairman of the president's Security Council.

150. Porter and Saivetz, "The Once and Future Empire"; and Vladimir Socor, "Boutros-Ghali Condemns 'Separatism' in Moldova," *RFE/RL Daily Report,* 9 November 1994.

151. Throughout the Moldovan conflict, the United States has maintained that the 14th Army must be withdrawn. In July 1994, the CSCE Parliamentary Assembly called for a rapid, unconditional, full withdrawal of the Russian 14th Army from Moldova. See Vladimir Socor, "Albright Stresses US Support to Moldova on Russian Troops," *RFE/RL Daily Report,* 1 September 1994; and Vladimir Socor, "CSCE Forum Calls for Russian Withdrawal From Moldova," *RFE/RL Daily Report,* 7 July 1994.

152. See Huber, "The CSCE's New Role," 28.

153. Orr, "Peacekeeping and Overstretch," 363-65.

154. See Kondrat'yev, "Mirotvorcheskaya Rol' Rossii."

155. See, for example, Vladimir Socor, "Russia Criticized for not Withdrawing from Moldova," *RFE/RL Daily Report,* 16 June 1994; Vladimir Socor, "CSCE's Moldova Mission Shows Meager Results," *RFE/RL Daily Report,* 10 November 1993; and Porter and Saivetz, "The Once and Future Empire," 84-85.

156. Vladimir Socor, "Russia Sharply Cutting Peacekeeping Force in Moldova," *RFE/RL Daily Report,* 17 November 1994; and Vladimir Socor, "Renewed Hostilities Feared in Moldova," *RFE/RL Daily Report,* 1 December 1994.

157. Brian D. Taylor, "The Transdniester Conflict and Russia's Fourteenth Army," in Alexei Arbatov, Abram Chayes, Antonia Handler Chayes, and Lara Olsen, eds., *Ethnic Conflict in the Former Soviet Union* (Cambridge: MIT Press, forthcoming 1996); and Rodion Morozov, "Dniester Region: A Crime in the Making," *Obshchaya Gazeta,* no. 20/96 (18-24 May 1995): 1, translated in *East View Press Digest,* 18 May 1995.

158. Steven Greenhouse, "Armenia Says It Would Welcome Russian Peacekeeping Offer," *New York Times,* 12 August 1994, 3. Azerbaijan president Aliyev told the OSCE 1994 Budapest summit that over 20,000 Azeris had been killed in the conflict, while UN sources report that 6,000 people were killed in the conflict between December 1994 and December 1995. See Jonathan Rugman, "Oil Fuels Enclave Peace Initiative," *The Guardian,* 28 December 1994, 11.

159. See Elizabeth Fuller, ". . . And for Nagorno-Karabakh," *RFE/RL Daily Report,* 8 June 1994; and Elizabeth Fuller, "Karabakh Cease-fire Agreement Signed," *RFE/RL Daily Report,* 17 May 1994.

160. Elizabeth Fuller, "Aliev Holds Out against Russian Peacekeepers," *RFE/RL Daily Report,* 24 May 1994; and A. D. Horne, "Armenian Leader Argues for Russian Truce Force," *Washington Post,* 11 August 1994, 24.

161. The revised Grachev proposal limited Russian participation in the force to one-third of all troops. See Fuller, "And for Nagorno-Karabakh"; and Elizabeth Fuller, "Grachev in Security Talks with Azerbaijan," *RFE/RL Daily Report,* 13 June 1994.

162. Elizabeth Fuller, "Progress towards a Karabakh Settlement?" *RFE/RL Daily Report,* 12 July 1994; Elizabeth Fuller, "Karabakh Political Settlement Imminent?" *RFE/RL Daily Report,* 29 June 1994; Elizabeth Fuller, "Russia Opposes Turkish Peacekeepers for Karabakh," *RFE/RL Daily Report,* 11 July 1994; and Horne, "Armenian Leader Argues."

163. Beginning with a peace mission organized by Kazakhstan president Nursultan Nazarbayev and Russian president Boris Yeltsin in the fall of 1991 and another mission in September of the following year, the Russian president or his representatives negotiated several cease-fire agreements between Armenian and Azeri leaders, none of which succeeded. Russian defense minister Pavel Grachev also tried his hand at forging a settlement, but without any success. See SDIP, *Report on Ethnic Conflict,* 79-80.

164. Elizabeth Fuller, "Russia/Turkey/US/Karabakh," *RFE/RL Daily Report,* 10 September 1993; Elizabeth Fuller, "Azerbaijan Conditionally Agrees to Karabakh Cease-fire," *RFE/RL Daily Report,* 27 April 1994; and Roland Eggleston and Elizabeth Fuller, "Russia Demands Responsibility for Karabakh Peacekeeping," *RFE/RL Daily Report,* 25 October 1994.

165. Aleksandr Kuzmin, *Itar-TASS,* in English, 17:41 GMT, 19 August 1994, reprinted in *FBIS-USR* 94-162 (22 August 1994): 1.

166. Interviews by author with US government officials, Washington, D.C., December 1994 and July 1995.

167. See SDIP, *Report on Ethnic Conflict,* 77-78.

168. Elizabeth Fuller, "Russian-Iranian Talks on Karabakh," *RFE/RL Daily Report,* 27 June 1994.

169. The team held negotiations with leaders of Nagorno-Karabakh to hammer out logistical concerns and secure a permanent cease-fire. See SDIP, *Report on Ethnic Conflict,* 77, 79, 82; and Huber, "The CSCE's New Role," 27.

170. See Huber, "The CSCE's New Role," 27; and Vladimir Socor, "CSCE Reacts to Russian Stance on Karabakh," *RFE/RL Daily Report,* 20 September 1994.

171. The summit decision statement linked the beginning of the mission to a political agreement on the cessation of hostilities beyond the existing cease-fire. See *CSCE Budapest Decisions,* December 1994.

172. Richard Balmforth, "CSCE Approves Peacekeeping Force for Karabakh," *Reuters* newswire, 6 December 1994, 11:49 A.M. See also Azerbaijan president Aliyev's comments in *Turan,* in English 14:45 GMT, 8 December 1994; the comments of the acting press secretary for Armenian president Ter-Petrossyan in *Interfax,* 18:57 GMT, 8 December 1994, both reprinted in *FBIS-SOV* 94-237 (9 December 1994): 51-52; and the comments of the "foreign minister" of the Mountainous Karabakh Republic (MKR) in *Noyan Tapan,* 16:46 GMT, 12 December 1994, reprinted in *FBIS-SOV* 94-239 (13 December 1994): 48.

173. Interviews by author with US government officials, Washington, D.C., July 1995; and Ara Tatevosyan and Vladimir Yemelyanenko, "Karabakh's Bosnian Intransigence," *Moskovskiye Novosti* no. 8 (25 February-3 March 1996): 9, translated in *East View Press Digest,* 27 February 1996.

174. See, for example, Armen Khanbabyan, "Moscow Uniterested in Success of OSCE Mission. Peace in Karabakh Now as Remote as It Was 18 Months Ago," *Nezavisimaya Gazeta,* 1 December 1995, 3, translated in *East View Press Digest,* 1 December 1995, part 1; and Armen Khanbabyan, "The Pendulum of Russian Sympathies. In the Caucasus, This Time It Has Swung Toward Azerbaijan," *Nezavisimaya Gazeta,* 26 January 1996, 3, translated in *East View Press Digest,* 26 January 1996.

175. SDIP, *Report on Ethnic Conflict,* 77-80; Elizabeth Fuller, "Boutros-Ghali in Baku," *RFE/RL Daily Report,* 2 November 1994; and Security Council Resolution 822, 30 April 1993.

176. Elizabeth Fuller, "Karabakh Mediation Update," *RFE/RL Daily Report,* 20 May 1994.

177. The White House Press Office, however, clarified that any US contribution would be directed toward an OSCE mission, not a Russian peacekeeping effort. Yeltsin as cited in Vladimir Socor, "Russian Assessments of the Washington Summit," *RFE/RL Daily Report,* 5 October 1994; and author interview, White House Press Office, December 1994.

178. Author interview with US government official, Washington, D.C., 6 January 1995.

179. Boris Vinogradov, "3000 mirotvortsev dolzhny sozdat' usloviya dlya uregulirovaniya v Karabakhye" (3,000 peacekeepers should create the conditions for a settlement in Karabakh), *Izvestiya,* 9 December 1994, 3; Bruce Clark and Virginia Marsh, "CSCE agrees to Karabakh peace operation," *Financial Times,* 7 December 1994, 2; and Rugman, "Oil Fuels Enclave Peace Initiative."

180. See the comments of the Azerbaijan Foreign Ministry's senior negotiator on Nagorno-Karabakh in Rugman, "Oil Fuels Enclave Peace Initiative."

BIBLIOGRAPHY

REPORTS, BOOKS, AND ARTICLES

Africa Watch. *Beyond the Rhetoric: Continuing Human Rights Abuses in Rwanda.* Washington D.C.: Africa Watch, 1993.

Akashi, Yasushi. "UNTAC in Cambodia: Lessons For U.N. Peacekeeping." The Charles Rostov Annual Lecture on Asian Affairs. Johns Hopkins University, Paul H. Nitze School of Advanced International Studies, Washington, D.C., 14 October 1993.

Allard, Kenneth. *Somalia Operations: Lessons Learned.* Washington, D.C.: National Defense University, Institute for National Strategic Studies, 1995.

Allison, Roy. "Russian Peacekeeping—Capabilities and Doctrine." *Jane's Intelligence Review* (December 1994).

Amnesty International. *Angola: An Appeal for Prompt Action to Protect Human Rights.* New York: Amnesty International Publications, May 1992.

———. *Angola: Assault on the Right to Life.* New York: Amnesty International Publications, August 1993.

Andersson, Hilary. *Mozambique: A War Against the People.* New York: St. Martin's Press, 1992.

Arbatov, Aleksey. "Russian National Interests." In Robert D. Blackwill and Sergei A. Karaganov, eds., *Damage Limitation or Crisis? Russia and the Outside World.* CSIA Studies in International Security no. 5. Washington, D.C.: Brassey's, 1994.

Arbuckle, Tammy. "Yugoslavia: Strategy and Tactics of Ethnic Warfare." *International Defense Review* (January 1992).

Arend, Anthony Clark and Robert J. Beck. *International Law and the Use of Force.* London: Routledge, 1993.

Azimi, Nassrine, ed. *The United Nations Transitional Authority in Cambodia: Debriefing and Lessons.* London: Kluwer Law International, 1995.

Bebler, Anton. "Yugoslavia's Agnony." *International Defense Review* (September, 1992).

Bender, Gerald. "Washington's Quest for Enemies in Angola." In Richard J. Bloomfield, ed. *Regional Conflict and US Policy.* Algonac, MI: Reference Publications, 1988.

Berkowitz, Bruce D. "Rules of Engagement for UN Peacekeeping Forces in Bosnia." *Orbis* (fall 1994).

Bhatia, Sidharth. "Somalis Get a Taste of Compassion." *India Abroad,* 5 August 1994.

Birmingham, David. *Frontline Nationalism in Angola & Mozambique.* Trenton: Africa World Press, 1992.

Blechman, Barry M. and J. Matthew Vaccaro. *Training for Peacekeeping: The United Nations' Role.* Washington D.C.: The Henry L. Stimson Center, 1994.

Bloomfield, Richard J., ed. *Regional Conflict and US Policy: Angola and Mozambique.* Algonac, MI.: Reference Publications, 1988.

Brenner, Michael. "The United States Perspective." In Mario Zucconi, ed., *Western Responses to the Conflict in Yugoslavia.* New York: St. Martin's Press, forthcoming 1997.

Bridgland, Fred. *Jonas Savimbi: A Key to Africa*. Edinburgh, UK: Mainstream Publishing Co., 1986.

"Brioni Declaration." *Yugoslav Survey* 32, no. 2 (1991).

"British Army Brings Much-Needed Help to Rwanda." *Army Quarterly and Defence Journal* 124, no. 4 (October 1994).

Brown, Frederick Z. *Cambodia and the Dilemmas of U.S. Policy*. Critical Issues series 1991 2/3. New York: Council on Foreign Relations Press, 1991.

Browning, David. "El Salvador—History." In *South America, Central America and the Caribbean*. London: Europa Publications, 1995.

Brzezinski, Zbigniew. "The Premature Partnership." *Foreign Affairs* (March - April 1994).

Campbell, Kurt M. "Soviet Policy in Southern Africa: Angola and Mozambique." In Richard J. Bloomfield, ed. *Regional Conflict and US Policy: Angola and Mozambique*. Algonac, MI: Reference Publications, 1988.

Carnegie Endowment for International Peace. *The Other Balkan Wars: A 1913 Carnegie Endowment Inquiry in Retrospect*. Washington, D.C.: The Carnegie Endowment, 1993.

Carney, Timothy. "UNTAC's Information/Education Programme." In Nazrine Azimi, ed. *The United Nations Transitional Authority in Cambodia: Debriefing and Lessons*. London: Kluwer Law International, 1995.

Chopra, Jarat. *United Nations Authority in Cambodia*, Occasional Paper no. 15. Providence, RI: Thomas J. Watson Institute, Brown University, 1994.

Chopra, Jarat, Åge Eknes, and Toralv Nordbo. *Fighting for Hope in Somalia*. Peacekeeping and Multinational Operations no. 6. Oslo: Norwegian Institute of International Relations, UN Programme, 1995.

Cohen, William S. "The Empire Strikes Back." *Problems of Post-Communism* (January - February 1995).

Cohen, Lenard J. *Broken Bonds: The Disintegration of Yugoslavia*. Boulder, CO: Westview Press, 1993.

Coker, Christopher. "Experiencing Southern Africa in the Twenty-first Century." *International Affairs* (1991).

Collelo, Thomas, ed. *Angola: A Country Study*. Washington, D.C.: Library of Congress, 1989.

Council for a Livable World Education Fund. "The United Nations Financial Crunch: The US Role in Creating the Crisis." Washington, D.C., October 1995. Mimeograph.

Crocker, Chester A. *High Noon In Southern Africa: Making Peace in a Rough Neighborhood*. New York: W. W. Norton, 1993.

———. "Peacemaking in Southern Africa: The Namibia-Angola Settlement of 1988." In David D. Newsom, ed. *The Diplomatic Record 1989-1990*. Boulder, CO: Westview Press, 1991.

Cuny, Frederick C. "An Analysis of Serb Violations of the Sarajevo Exclusion Zone." *Intertect*, 28 May 1994. Mimeograph.

Damrosch, Lori Fisler, ed. *Enforcing Restraint: Collective Intervention in Internal Conflicts*. New York: Council on Foreign Relations Press, 1993.

Damrosch, Lori Fisler and David J. Scheffer, eds. *Law and Force in the New International Order*. Boulder, CO: Westview Press, 1991.

Daniel, Donald C. F. and Bradd C. Hayes, eds. *Beyond Traditional Peacekeeping*. New York: St. Martin's Press; London: Macmillan, 1995.

Dawisha, Karen and Bruce Parrott. *Russia and the New States of Eurasia: The Politics of Upheaval*. Cambridge, MA: Cambridge Univ. Press, 1994.

De Soto, Alvaro and Graciana del Castillo. "Obstacles to Peacebuilding." *Foreign Policy* 94 (spring 1994).

———. "El Salvador: Still Not A Success Story." June 1994. Unpublished manuscript.

Des Forges, Alison. "Burundi: Failed Coup or Creeping Coup?" *Current History* (May 1994).

Diehl, Paul F. *International Peacekeeping*. Baltimore: Johns Hopkins Univ. Press, 1993.

Diller, Daniel C. *Russia and the Independent States*. Washington, D.C.: Congressional Quarterly, Inc., 1993.

Dobbie, Colonel Charles. "A Concept for Post - Cold War Peacekeeping." *Survival* 36, no. 3 (fall 1994).

Donia, Robert J. and John V. A. Fine, Jr. *Bosnia and Hercegovina: A Tradition Betrayed.* New York: Columbia Univ. Press, 1994.

Doyle, Michael W. *UN Peacekeeping in Cambodia: UNTAC's Civil Mandate.* London: Lynne Rienner, 1995.

Doyle, Michael W. and Nishkala Suntharalingam. "The UN in Cambodia: Lessons for Complex Peacekeeping." *International Peacekeeping* 1, no. 2 (summer 1994).

Durch, William J. "United Nations Forces and Regional Conflicts." In Patrick M. Cronin, ed. *From Globalism to Regionalism: New Perspectives on US Foreign and Defense Policies.* Washington, D.C.: National Defense University Press, 1993.

———. "The Components of Peace Operations and Their Impact on Economic Development and Welfare." Background paper for the Organization for Economic Cooperation and Development Workshop on Peacekeeping Operations and Development, Paris, November 1993. Mimeograph.

———. "Structural Issues and the Future of UN Peace Operations." In Donald C. Daniel and Bradd Hayes, eds. *Beyond Traditional Peacekeeping.* New York: St. Martin's; London: Macmillan, 1995.

———, ed. *The Evolution of UN Peacekeeping: Case Studies and Comparative Analysis.* New York: St. Martin's Press, 1993.

Durch, William J. and Barry M. Blechman. *Keeping the Peace: The United Nations in the Emerging World Order.* Washington, D.C: The Henry L. Stimson Center, March 1992.

Dworken, Jonathan T. *Operation Restore Hope: Preparing and Planning the Transition to UN Operations.* CRM 93-148. Alexandria, VA: Center for Naval Analyses, March 1994.

Findlay, Trevor. *Cambodia: The Legacy and Lessons of UNTAC.* SIPRI Research Report no. 9. Oxford: Oxford Univ. Press, 1995.

Finnegan, William. *A Complicated War: The Harrowing of Mozambique.* Berkeley: Univ. of California Press, 1992.

Fortna, Virginia Page. "United Nations Angola Verification Mission I." In William J. Durch, ed. *The Evolution of UN Peacekeeping: Case Studies and Comparative Analysis.* New York: St. Martin's Press, 1993.

———. "United Nations Transition Assistance Group in Namibia." In William J. Durch, ed. *The Evolution of UN Peacekeeping: Case Studies and Comparative Analysis.* New York: St. Martin's Press, 1993.

Franck, Thomas M. "The Emerging Right to Democratic Governance." *American Journal of International Law* 46 (1992).

Garcia, SFC Elroy. "We Did Right That Night." *Soldiers* (February 1994).

Ghali, Mona. "United Nations Interim Force in Lebanon: 1978-Present." In William J. Durch, ed. *The Evolution of UN Peacekeeping: Case Studies and Comparative Analysis.* New York: St. Martin's Press, 1993.

Glenny, Misha. *The Fall of Yugoslavia: The Third Balkan War.* Revised and updated ed. New York: Penguin Books, 1993.

Gow, James. "Deconstructing Yugoslavia." *Survival* 33 no. 4 (July - August 1991).

Gunn, Gillian. "Learning from Adversity: The Mozambican Experience." In Richard J. Bloomfield, ed. *Regional Conflict and US Policy: Angola and Mozambique.* Algonac, MI: Reference Publications, 1988.

Gunn, Gillian. "Post-Nkomati Mozambique." In Helen Kitchen, ed. *Angola, Mozambique, and the West.* New York: Praeger, 1987.

Gutman, Roy. *A Witness to Genocide.* New York: Macmillan, 1993.

Hall, Brian. *The Impossible Country: A Journey through the Last Days of Yugoslavia.* Boston: David R. Godine, Publisher, 1994.

Heininger, Janet E. *Peacekeeping in Transition: The United Nations in Cambodia.* New York: The Twentieth Century Fund, 1994.

Helsinki Watch. *War or Peace? Human Rights and Russian Military Involvement in the "Near Abroad."* Vol. 5, no. 22 (December 1993).

Hill, Fiona and Pamela Jewett. *"Back in the USSR": Russia's Intervention in the Internal Affairs of the Former Soviet Republics and the Implications for United States Policy Toward Russia.* Cambridge, MA: Strengthening Democratic Institutions Project, John F. Kennedy School of Government, January 1994.

Hirsch, John L. and Robert B. Oakley. *Somalia and Operation Restore Hope: Reflections on Peacemaking and Peacekeeping.* Washington, D.C.: US Institute of Peace, 1995.

Holiday, David and William Stanley. "Building the Peace: Preliminary Lessons from El Salvador." *Journal of International Affairs* 46, no. 2 (winter 1993): 43

Human Rights Watch Africa. *Genocide in Rwanda: April - May 1994.* New York: Human Rights Watch, 1994.

Human Rights Watch Arms Project. *Arming Rwanda: The Arms Trade and Human Rights Abuses in the Rwandan War.* New York, January 1994.

———. *Landmines in Mozambique.* New York, March 1994.

Hume, Cameron. *Ending Mozambique's War: The Role of Mediation and Good Offices.* Washington, D.C.: United States Institute of Peace, 1994.

Jackson, William D. "Imperial Temptations: Ethnics Abroad." *Orbis* (winter 1994).

Jeldres, Julio A. "The UN and the Cambodian Transition." *Journal of Democracy* 4, no. 4 (October 1993).

Johnsen, William T. *Deciphering the Balkan Enigma: Using History to Inform Policy.* Carlisle, PA: US Army War College, Strategic Studies Institute, 25 March 1993.

Kaplan, Robert D. *Balkan Ghosts: A Journey through History.* New York: Vintage Books, 1993.

Karl, Terry Lynn. "El Salvador's Negotiated Revolution." *Foreign Affairs* (spring 1992).

Kawakami, Takahisa. "Exercising the Transitional Authority." In Nassrine Azimi, ed. *The United Nations Transitional Authority in Cambodia: Debriefing and Lessons.* London: Kluwer Law International, 1995.

Kiernan, Ben. "The Failures of the Paris Agreement on Cambodia, 1991-93." In Dick Clark and William Nell, eds. *The Challenge of Indochina: An Examination of the U.S. Role.* Queenstown, MD: The Aspen Institute, 1993.

Kohut, Andrew and Robert Toth. "Arms and the People." *Foreign Affairs* 73, no. 6 (November - December 1994).

Kolsto, Pal and Andrei Edemsky with Natalya Kalashnikova. "The Dniester Conflict: Between Irredentism and Separatism." *Europe-Asia Studies* 45 no. 6 (1993).

Kull, Steven and Clay Ramsey. *U.S. Public Attitudes on UN Peacekeeping. Part I: Funding.* College Park, MD: Program on International Policy Attitudes, Univ. of Maryland, March 1994.

———. *U.S. Public Attitudes on Involvement in Somalia.* College Park, Md.: Program on International Policy Attitudes, Univ. of Maryland, October 1993.

LaRose-Edwards, Paul. *The Rwandan Crisis of April 1994: The Lessons Learned.* Report prepared for the Canadian Department of Foreign Affairs and International Trade, Ottawa: International Human Rights, Democracy, and Conflict Resolution, 30 November 1994.

Lawrence, Roger C. "Economics/Rehabilitation." In Nassrine Azimi, ed. *The United Nations Transitional Authority in Cambodia: Debriefing and Lessons.* London: Kluwer Law International, 1995.

Legum, Colin. "Angola and the Horn of Africa." In Stephen S. Kaplan, ed. *Diplomacy of Power: Soviet Armed Forces as a Political Instrument.* Washington, D.C.: The Brookings Institution, 1981.

Lepingwell, John W. R. "The Russian Military and Security Policy in the 'Near Abroad.'" *Survival* 36 no. 3 (fall 1994).

Los Angeles World Affairs Council. "Remarks by Governor Bill Clinton." Los Angeles, CA, 13 August 1992. Mimeograph.

Lyons, Terrence and Ahmed I. Samatar. *Somalia: State Collapse, Multilateral Intervention, and Strategies for Political Reconstruction.* Brookings Occasional Paper. Washington, D.C.: The Brookings Institution, 1995.

Vincent, Shaun. "The Mozambique Conflict (1980-1992)." In Michael Cranna, ed. *The True Cost of Conflict: Seven Recent Wars and Their Effect on Society.* New York: New Press, 1994.

MacInnis, Major General John A. "The Rules of Engagement for UN Peacekeeping Forces in Former Yugoslavia: A Response." *Orbis* (winter 1995).

Mackinlay, John and Jarat Chopra, *A Draft Concept of Second Generation Multinational Operations 1993.* Providence, RI: The Thomas J. Watson Institute, Brown University, 1993.

Magas, Branka. *The Destruction of Yugoslavia: Tracking the Breakup, 1980-92.* London: Verso, 1993.

Maley, Michael. "Reflections on the Electoral Process in Cambodia." In Hugh Smith, ed., *Peacekeeping: Challenges for the Future.* Canberra: Australian Defence Force Academy, 1993.

Maxwell, Kenneth. "The Legacy of Decolonization." In Richard J. Bloomfield, ed., *Regional Conflict and US Policy: Angola and Mozambique.* Algonac, MI: Reference Publications, 1988.

McNamara, Dennis. "UN Human Rights Activities in Cambodia: An Evaluation." In Alice H. Henkin, ed. *Honoring Human Rights and Keeping the Peace: Lessons from El Salvador, Cambodia and Haiti.* Queenstown, MD: The Aspen Institute, 1995.

Menkhaus, Ken. *Trip Report—Somalia.* September 1994. Mimeograph.

Minear, Larry and Philippe Guillot. *The Contributions of International Military Forces to Humanitarian Action in Rwanda.* Providence, RI: The Thomas Watson Institute, Brown University, 1995.

Misser, François. "Who Killed the Presidents?" *New African* (June 1994).

———. "Belgium and France Beg to Differ." *New African* (June 1994).

"Mozambique: Brag Poker in Rome." *Africa Confidential* 33, no. 16 (14 August 1992).

Munro, David and Alan J. Day. "El Salvador." In *A World Record of Major Conflict Areas.* Chicago, IL: St. James Press, 1990.

Newbury, Catherine. *The Cohesion of Oppression: Clientship and Ethnicity in Rwanda, 1860-1960.* New York: Columbia Univ. Press, 1988.

Orr, Michael. "Peacekeeping and Overstretch in the Russian Army." *Jane's Intelligence Review* (August 1994).

———. "Peacekeeping—A New Task for Russian Military Doctrine." *Jane's Intelligence Review* (July 1994).

Pazzanita, Anthony J. "The Conflict Resolution Process in Angola." *Journal of Modern African Studies* 14 (1991).

Pillar, Paul. *Negotiating Peace: War Termination as a Bargaining Process.* Princeton, NJ: Princeton Univ. Press, 1983.

Pinson, Mark, ed. *The Muslims of Bosnia-Herzegovina: Their Historic Development from the Middle Ages to the Dissolution of Yugoslavia.* Cambridge, MA: Harvard Univ. Press, 1994.

Porter, Bruce D. and Carol R. Saivetz. "The Once and Future Empire: Russia and the 'Near Abroad.'" *The Washington Quarterly* (summer 1994).

Power, Samantha. "Guns and Pigs." *The New Republic,* 22 May 1995.

———, comp. *Breakdown in the Balkans: A Chronicle of Events, January 1989 to May 1993.* Washington, D.C.: The Carnegie Endowment for International Peace, 1993.

Prasso, Sheri. "Cambodia: A $3 Billion Boondoggle." *The Bulletin of the Atomic Scientists* (March–April 1995): 36-40.

Ratner, Steven R. *The New UN Peacekeeping: Building Peace in Lands of Conflict After the Cold War.* New York: St. Martin's Press, 1995.

Reed, Pamela L., J. Matthew Vaccaro, and William J. Durch, *Handbook on UN Peace Operations.* Washington, D.C.: The Henry L. Stimson Center, April 1995.

Reed, Laura W. and Carl Kaysen, eds. *Emerging Norms of Justified Intervention.* Cambridge, MA: Committee on International Security Studies, American Academy of Arts and Sciences, 1993.

"Remarks by Governor Bill Clinton." Los Angeles: World Affairs Council, 13 August 1992.

"Remarks Prepared for Delivery by Governor Bill Clinton." New York: Foreign Policy Association, 1 April 1992.

"Resolving Civil Conflicts: The Lessons of El Salvador." Proceedings of an academic workshop hosted by The Center for Latin American Studies and The Center for International Security and Arms Control, Stanford University, 5-7 May 1993.

Richards, Lieutenant Colonel T. A., USMC. "Marines in Somalia." *US Naval Institute Proceedings* (May 1993).

Rieff, David. *Slaughterhouse: Bosnia and the Failure of the West.* New York: Simon and Schuster, 1995.

Samatar, Ahmed I. "The Curse of Allah: Civic Disembowelment and the Collapse of the State in Somalia." In A. I. Samatar, ed. *The Somali Challenge: From Catastrophe to Renewal?* Boulder, CO: Lynne Rienner Publishers, 1994.

Sanderson, Lieutenant General John M. "Preparation for Deployment and Conduct of Peacekeeping Operations: A Cambodia Snapshot." In Kevin Clements and Christine Wilson, eds. *UN Peacekeeping at the Crossroads.* Canberra: Australian National University, 1994.

———. "UNTAC: Successes and Failures." In Nassrine Azimi, ed., *The United Nations Transitional Authority in Cambodia: Debriefing and Lessons.* London: Kluwer Law International, 1995.

Schear, James A. "Beyond Traditional Peacekeeping: The Case of Cambodia." In Donald C. F. Daniel and Bradd C. Hayes, eds. *Beyond Traditional Peacekeeping.* New York: St. Martin's Press; London: Macmillan, 1995.

Schneidman, Witney W. "Conflict Resolution in Mozambique." In David R. Smock, ed. *Making War and Waging Peace: Foreign Intervention in Africa.* Washington, D.C.: United States Institute of Peace, 1993.

Schraeder, Peter J. *United States Foreign Policy Toward Africa: Incrementalism: Crisis and Change.* Cambridge, UK: Cambridge Univ. Press, 1994.

Serapio, Luis B. and Mohamed A. El-Khawas. *Mozambique in the Twentieth Century: From Colonialism to Independence.* Washington, D.C.: University Press of America, 1979.

Shashenkov, Maxim. "Russian Peacekeeping in the 'Near Abroad.'" *Survival* 36, no.3 (fall 1994).

Shawcross, William. *Cambodia's New Deal.* Washington, D.C.: Carnegie Endowment for International Peace, 1994.

Sivard, Ruth, *World Military and Social Expenditures, 1993.* Washington, D.C.: World Priorities, 1993.

Smith, Anthony D. "The Ethnic Sources of Nationalism." *Survival* 35, no. 1 (spring 1993).

Snyder, Jack. "Nationalism and the Crisis of the Post-Soviet State." *Survival* 35, no.1 (spring 1993).

Spence, Jack and George Vickers. *Toward a Level Playing Field? A Report on the Post-War Salvadoran Electoral Process.* Washington D.C.: Hemisphere Initiatives, January 1994.

Spikes, Daniel. *Angola and the Politics of Intervention.* Jefferson, NC: McFarland & Co., 1993.

Stanley, William. *Risking Failure: The Problems and Promise of the New Civilian Police Force in El Salvador.* Washington, D.C.: Hemisphere Initiatives and Washington Office on Latin America, September 1993.

Stedman, Stephen John. "The New Interventionists." *Foreign Affairs* 72, no. 1 (winter 1992-93): 1-16.

———. *Peacemaking in Civil War: International Mediation in Zimbabwe, 1974-1980.* Boulder, CO: Lynne Rienner Publishers, 1990.

Steinberg, James B. "International Involvement in the Yugoslavia Conflict." In Lori Fisler Damrosch, ed. *Enforcing Restraint: Collective Intervention in Internal Conflicts.* New York: Council on Foreign Relations, 1993.

Stevenson, Jonathan. "Hope Restored in Somalia?" *Foreign Policy* 91 (summer 1993).

Stockholm International Peace Research Institute. *SIPRI Yearbook 1993: Armaments, Disarmament, and International Security.* Oxford and New York: Oxford Univ. Press, 1993.

Stockwell, John. *In Search of Enemies.* New York: W.W. Norton, 1978.

Strengthening Democratic Institutions Project. *Report on Ethnic Conflict in the Russian Federation and Transcaucasia.* Cambridge, MA: John F. Kennedy School of Government, Harvard University, July 1993.

Times Mirror Center for the People and the Press. *America's Place in the World: An Investigation of the Attitudes of American Opinion Leaders and the American Public about International Affairs.* Washington, D.C., November 1993.

Torps, Jens Erik. *Mozambique: Economics, Politics and Society.* London: Printers Publishers, 1989.

Tvedten, Inge. "US Policy Towards Angola Since 1975." *Journal of Modern African Studies* 31 (1992).

———. "The Angolan Debacle," *Journal of Democracy* 4, no. 2 (April 1993).

"UN Broker's Peaceful Transitions in Angola, Mozambique." *Africa Recovery* 8, no. 3 (December 1994).

Van Der Waals, Ws. *Portugal's War in Angola: 1961-1974.* Johannesburg, South Africa: Ashanti Publishing. 1993.

Vassall-Adams, Guy. *Rwanda: An Agenda for International Action.* Oxford: Oxfam Publications, 1994.

Vickers, George and Jack Spence. *Endgame: A Progress Report on Implementation of the Salvadoran Peace Accords.* Cambridge, MA: Hemisphere Initiatives, 3 December 1992.

Vines, Alex. *Renamo: Terrorism in Mozambique.* Bloomington, IN: Indiana Univ. Press, 1991.

Wainhouse, David W. *United Nations Peacekeeping at the Crossroads.* Baltimore, MD: Johns Hopkins Univ. Press, 1973.

Washington Office on Latin America (WOLA). *El Salvador Peace Plan Update #3: Recent Setbacks in the Police Transition.* Washington, D.C., 4 February 1994.

Watson, Catherine. *Exile From Rwanda: Background to an Invasion.* Washington, D.C.: US Committee for Refugees, 1991.

Weiner, Lauren. "El Salvador Confronts the Truth Commission Report." *Freedom Review* 24, no. 6. (November - December 1993).

Wilson, Brigadier General John. "Lessons from UN Operations in Yugoslavia." In Hugh Smith, ed. *Peacekeeping: Challenges for the Future.* Canberra: Australian Defence Studies Centre, 1993.

Wolfers, Michael and Jane Bergerol. *Angola in the Frontline.* London: Zed Press, 1983.

Woodward, Susan. *Balkan Tragedy: Chaos and Dissolution After the Cold War.* Washington, D.C.: The Brookings Institution, 1995.

World Bank. *Social Indicators of Development, 1994.* Electronic datafile. Washington, D.C.: International Bank for Reconstruction and Development, 1994.

Zametica, John. *The Yugoslav Conflict,* Adelphi Paper 270. London: IISS, 1992.

Zartman, I. William, ed. *Illusive Peace: Negotiating an End to Civil Wars.* Washington, D.C.: The Brookings Institution, 1995.

Zvijac, David J. and Katherine A. W. McGrady. *Operation Restore Hope: Summary Report.* CRM 93-152. Alexandria, VA: Center for Naval Analyses, March 1994.

NEWSPAPERS, NEWSWIRES, NEWSLETTERS, AND NEWS MAGAZINES

ABC News
Aerospace Daily
Agence France Presse (newswire)*
Army Times
Associated Press (newswire)*
Boston Globe
Christian Science Monitor
Defense News

East View Press Digest (Minneapolis, Minn.)

The Economist

Federal News Service (Washington, D.C.)

Financial Times (London)

Foreign Broadcast Information Service Daily Report

Free Choice: Electoral Component Newsletter (United Nations, Phnom Penh)

The Guardian

The Independent

International Documents Review (New York)

Izvestiya (Moscow)

Jamestown Monitor (Washington, D.C.)

Jane's Defence Weekly

Joint Publications Research Service

Kazakhstanskaya Pravda (Moscow)

Krasnaya Zvezda (Moscow)

National Public Radio

The New York Times

Newsweek

Nezavisimaya Gazeta (Moscow)

Open Media Research Institute Daily Digest (Prague)

The Philadelphia Inquirer

Radio Free Europe/Radio Liberty Daily Report

Reuters (newswire)*

Segodnya (Moscow)

United Press International (newswire)*

UNPAs Monitor (UN, Zagreb)

UNPROFOR News (UN, Zagreb)

UNPROFOR Magazine (UN, Zagreb)

Voyennyy Vestnik (Moscow)

The Washington Post

(* The time zones of the date-time stamps indicated in the newswire reports vary by news organization, and by the zone in which the report was filed. For a copy of any newswire report cited, contact the editor of this volume.)

GOVERNMENT DOCUMENTS

Albright, Madeleine K. "Remarks to the National War College." Fort McNair: National Defense University, 23 September 1993.

———. "A Strong United Nations Serves U.S. Security Interests." Address before the Council on Foreign Relations, New York, 11 June 1993. Reprinted in *Dispatch* (formerly the Department of State *Bulletin*) 4, no. 26 (28 June 1993).

Aspin, Les. *Annual Report of the Secretary of Defense to the President and the Congress*. Washington, D.C.: GPO, 1994.

Australia. Department of Foreign Affairs and Trade. *Informal Meeting on Cambodia: Issues for Negotiation in a Comprehensive Settlement*, Jakarta, Indonesia, 26-28 February 1990. Working Papers. Canberra, 1990.

———. Senate. "Prospects for a Cambodian Peace Settlement." Statement by Foreign Minister Gareth Evans. Canberra, 6 December 1990.

Bennet, Douglas J. "Statement at Confirmation Hearing before the Senate Foreign Relations Committee." 7 May 1993. Reprinted in *Dispatch* 4, no. 20 (17 May 1993).

Bush, George H. W. *National Security Strategy of the United States.* Washington, D.C.: The White House, January 1993.

———. *The President's Report on "An Agenda for Peace,"* a report to Congress by the president pursuant to section 1341 of the National Defense Authorization Act for FY1993. Washington, D.C.: White House, Executive Office of the President, 19 January 1993.

Canada. Department of Foreign Affairs and International Trade and Department of Defence. *Towards A Rapid Reaction Capability for the United Nations.* Ottawa, September 1995.

Christopher, Warren. "Building Peace in the Middle East." Address at Columbia University, 20 September 1993. Reprinted in *Dispatch* 4, no. 39 (27 September 1993).

Clarke, Walter S. *Somalia: Background Information for Operation Restore Hope.* SSI Special Report. Carlisle, Pa.: US Army War College, Strategic Studies Institute, December 1992.

Clinton, William J. *A National Security Strategy of Engagement and Enlargement.* Washington. D.C.: The White House, February 1995.

Dallaire, General Romeo A. Presentation at the Canadian Embassy to the United States, Washington, D.C., 14 November 1994.

Gersony, Robert. *Summary of Mozambican Refugee Accounts of Principally Conflict-Related Experience in Mozambique.* Washington, D.C.: Bureau of Refugee Programs, US Department of State, April 1988.

House Republican Caucus. "National Security Restoration Act." *Legislative Digest* (27 September 1994).

Lake, Anthony. "From Containment to Enlargement." Remarks at the Johns Hopkins University School of International Studies. Washington, D.C.: The White House, 21 September 1993.

NATO/Western European Union. *Fact Sheet: Operation Sharp Guard.* Naples, Italy: NATO AFSOUTH Public Information Office, 5 January 1995.

NATO. Press Release 93, no. 52. Brussels: NATO Press Service, 9 August 1993.

———. Press Release 94, no. 15. Brussels: NATO Press Service, 9 February 1994.

———. Press Release 94, no. 31. Brussels: NATO Press Service, 22 April 1994.

———. Press Release 94, no. 32. Brussels: NATO Press Service, 22 April 1994.

"Speech by Secretary of Defense Les Aspin, August 27, 1993." *Foreign Policy Bulletin* 4, no. 3 (November–December 1993).

"Statement by Ambassador Madeleine Albright to the UN Security Council, March 26, 1993." *Foreign Policy Bulletin* 3, no. 6 (January–April 1993).

Supreme Headquarters Allied Powers Europe. *ACE Doctrine for Peace Support Operations.* ACE Directive No. 80-62. Draft Revision. Mons, Belgium, 22 September 1995.

US Agency for International Development. Bureau for Humanitarian Response. Office of US Foreign Disaster Assistance. *Situation Report [Rwanda].*

    No. 1, 23 May 1994.

    No. 2, 8 June 1994.

    No. 3, 13 July 1994.

    No. 4, 25 July 1994.

    No. 5, 18 August 1994.

US Army. *Peace Operations.* Field Manual 100-23. Washington, D.C.: Headquarters, Department of the Army, December 1994.

US Central Intelligence Agency. *The World Factbook, 1993-94.* New York: Brassey's, 1993.

US Congress. General Accounting Office. *UN Peacekeeping: Lessons Learned in Managing Recent Missions.* GAO/NSIAD-94-9. Washington, D.C.: GAO, December 1993.

————. *Peace Operations: Cost of DOD Operations in Somalia.* GAO/NSIAD-94-88. Washington, D.C.: GAO, March 1994.

————. *United Nations: How Assessed Contributions for Peacekeeping Operations Are Calculated.* GAO/NSIAD-94-206. Washington, D.C.: GAO, August 1994.

US Congress. House. *H.R. 7—To Revitalize the National Security of the United States.* 104th Cong., 1st sess., February 1995.

————. Committee on Armed Services. *United States Military participation in United Nations Operations in Somalia: Roots of the Conflict with General Mohamed Farah Aideed and a Basis for Accommodation and Renewed Progress.* 103 Cong., 1st sess., 14 October 1993.

————. Committee on Foreign Affairs. "Conferees Agree on State Department, Peacekeeping Bill." News Release. 20 April 1994.

————. Committee on Foreign Affairs. *The Foreign Relations Authorization Act for Fiscal Years 1994 and 1995,* 103rd Cong., 2nd sess., 1994. H.Doc. 103-482.

————. Committee on Foreign Affairs. *US Participation in United Nations Peacekeeping Activities.* Hearings before the Subcommittee on International Security, International Organizations and Human Rights. 103rd Cong., 1st sess., 21 September 1993.

————. Committee on Foreign Affairs. *US Participation in United Nations Peacekeeping Activities.* Hearings before the Subcommittee on International Security, International Organizations, and Human Rights, 103rd Cong., 2nd sess. Statement by Amb. Madeleine K. Albright, 24 June 1994, 3-21.

US Congress. Senate. Committee on Armed Services. *International Peacekeeping and Peace Enforcement.* Hearing before the Subcommittee on Coalition Defense and Reinforcing Forces. 103d Cong., 1st sess., 14 July 1993.

————. Committee on Armed Services. *U.S. Military Operations in Somalia.* 103d Cong., 2d sess., May 1994. S. Hrg. 103-846.

————. Committee on Foreign Relations. *Foreign Policy Overview, Budget Requests for FY94, Hearing to Review . . . the Administration's FY94 Authorization Request For Foreign Aid Programs.* 103rd Cong., 1st sess. Statement by Secretary of State Warren H. Christopher, 20 April 1993, 2-39.

————. Committee on Foreign Relations. *US Participation in Somalia Peacekeeping.* 103rd Cong., 1st sess. Statement made by Amb. Madeleine K. Albright, 20 October 1993.

US Department of State. *Annual Report on Human Rights, 1993.* Washington, D.C.: GPO, 1993.

US Department of State. Bureau of International Organization Affairs. *The Clinton Administration's Policy on Reforming Multilateral Peace Operations.* Publication 10161, Washington, D.C., May 1994.

US Embassy, Maputo. "Lessons Unlearned—Or Why Mozambique's Peacekeeping Operation Won't Be Replicated Elsewhere." Maputo, Mozambique, 1994. Mimeograph.

White House. "Address by President George Bush to the United Nations General Assembly," 21 September 1992. In *Weekly Compilation of Presidential Documents* 28, no. 39 (1992): 1697.

————. "The President's News Conference with Prime Minister Morihiro Hosokawa of Japan in New York City," 27 September 1993. In *Weekly Compilation of Presidential Documents* 29, no. 39 (1993): 1908.

————. "Remarks of President Clinton to the 48th Session of the United Nations General Assembly in New York City," 27 September 1993. In *Weekly Compilation of Presidential Documents* 29, no. 39 (1993): 1901.

————. "Address to the Nation on Somalia," 7 October 1993. In *Weekly Compilation of Presidential Documents* 29, no. 40 (1993): 2022.

————. "The President's News Conference," 14 October 1993. In *Weekly Compilation of Presidential Documents* 29, no. 41 (1993): 2068.

————. "President Clinton Signs New Peacekeeping Policy." Statement by the Press Secretary. 5 May 1994.

———. "Press Briefing. Policy on Multilateral Peacekeeping Operations." Washington, D.C., 5 May 1994. Transcript by *Federal News Service,* Washington D.C., no. WL-05-01, 5 May 1994. Mimeograph.

UNITED NATIONS DOCUMENTS

General

Boutros-Ghali, Boutros. *An Agenda for Peace, 1995.* 2nd ed. New York: United Nations, 1995.

United Nations. Department of Public Information. *The Blue Helmets: A Review of United Nations Peace-Keeping.* 2nd Edition. New York, 1990.

United Nations General Assembly. *An Agenda for Peace: Preventive Diplomacy, Peacemaking, and Peacekeeping: Report by the Secretary-General of the United Nations.* A/47/277, June 1992.

ONUSAL (El Salvador)

United Nations. Department of Public Information. *The Agreement on Human Rights.* ONUSAL Fact Sheet No. 5. DPI/1149E. New York, July 1991.

———. *El Salvador.* ONUSAL Fact Sheet No. 7. DPI/11449G-40697. New York, July 1991.

———. *ONUSAL: Mexico Agreements.* DPI/1149D-40697. New York, July 1991.

United Nations General Assembly. *Report of the Economic and Social Council: Situation of Human Rights in El Salvador: Note by the Secretary-General.* A/45/630, 22 October 1990.

———. *Financing of the United Nations Observer Mission in El Salvador: Report of the Advisory Committee on Administrative and Budgetary Questions.* A/45/1021, 12 June 1991.

———. *Financing of the United Nations Observer Mission in El Salvador: Report of the Secretary-General.* A/48/842/Add.1, 27 July 1994.

A/49/518 annex I, 14 October 1994.

———. *Letter dated 26 September 1991 from the Permanent Representative of El Salvador to the United Nations Addressed to the Secretary-General.* A/46/502, 26 September 1991.

———. *Letter dated 4 October 1991 from the Permanent Representative of El Salvador to the United Nations Addressed to the Secretary-General.* A/46/502/Add.1, 7 October 1991.

———. *Second Report of the United Nations Observer Mission in El Salvador. Annex: Report of the Director of the Human Rights Division.* A/46/658, 15 November 1991.

———. *The Situation in Central America: Threats to International Peace and Security and Peace Initiatives: Annex: Report of the Director of the Human Rights Division.* A/46/935, 5 June 1992.

———. *The Situation in Central America: Threats to International Peace and Security and Peace Initiatives: Note by the Secretary-General.* A/45/1055, 16 September 1991.

United Nations Security Council. *Central America—Efforts Toward Peace: Report of the Secretary-General.*

S/22031, 21 December 1990.

S/22494, 16 April 1991.

S/23402, 10 January 1992.

———. *Further Report of the Secretary-General on the United Nations Observer Mission in El Salvador.* S/26581 annex 1, 14 October 1993.

S/26790, 23 November 1993.

———. *Note by the President of the Security Council.* S/26695, 5 November 1993.

———. *Report of the Secretary-General on the United Nations Observer Mission in El Salvador.*

S/24833, 23 November 1992.

S/23642, 25 February 1992.

S/23999, 26 May 1992.

S/25006, 23 December 1992.

S/25812, 21 May 1993.

S/26606, 20 October 1993.

S/1994/179, 16 February 1994.

S/1994/304, 16 March 1994.

S/1994/375, 31 March 1994.

S/1994/536, 4 May 1994.

S/1994/561/Add. 1, 18 May 1994.

United Nations. Secretary-General. "Presentation of the report of the Commission on the Truth." New York, 15 March 1993.

UNAVEM II (Angola)

United Nations General Assembly. Resolution 1603. UN General Assembly Official Record A/Res/1603, 20 April 1961.

United Nations General Assembly. *Financing of the United Nations Angola Verification Mission: Report of the Secretary-General.*
A/47/744, 2 December 1992.

A/48/836, 4 January 1994.

A/49/433, 27 September 1994.

———. *Verification in All its Aspects: Study on the Role of the United Nations in the Field of Verification.* A/45/372, 28 August 1990.

United Nations. Press Release.
SC/5387, 24 March 1992.

SC/5435, 7 July 1992.

SC/1966, 19 October 1992.

SC/5567, 12 March 1993.

United Nations Security Council. *Peace Accords for Angola.* S/22609, 17 May 1991.

———. *Further Report of the Secretary-General on the United Nations Angola Verification Mission II (UNAVEM II).*
S/23671, 24 March 1992.

S/24145, 24 June 1992.

S/24556, 9 September 1992.

S/24858, 25 November 1992.

S/25840, 25 May 1993.

S/26434, 13 September 1993.

S/1995/97/Add.1, 6 February 1995.

———. *Lusaka Protocol.* S/1994/1441, 22 December 1994.

———. *Report of the Secretary-General on the United Nations Angola Verification Mission II (UNAVEM II).*
S/23191, 31 October 1991.

S/24245, 7 July 1992.

S/1995/97, 1 February 1995.

———. Resolution 163 (S/Res/163), 9 June 1961.

S/Res/387, 31 March 1976.

S/Res/428, 6 May 1978.

S/Res/626, 20 December 1988.

S/Res/696, 30 May 1991.

S/Res/747, 24 March 1992.

S/Res/832, 27 May 1993.

S/Res/864, 15 September 1993.

S/Res/952, 27 October 1994.

S/Res/976, 8 February 1995.

UNTAC (Cambodia)

Sanderson, Lieutenant General John M. Press conference by the Force Commander, UNTAC Headquarters. Phnom Penh, Cambodia, 13 November 1992. Mimeograph.

———. Remarks to UN volunteers. Phnom Penh, Cambodia, 20 April 1993. Mimeograph.

United Nations. *Agreements on a Comprehensive Political Settlement of the Cambodia Conflict.* New York, 1991.

United Nations. Department of Public Information. *The United Nations and Cambodia, 1991-1995.* New York, 1995.

———. *United Nations Transitional Authority in Cambodia.* DPI/1352. New York, March 1993.

United Nations General Assembly. *Letter Dated 11 September 1990 from France and Indonesia, as Co-chairmen of the Paris Conference on Cambodia, Transmitting a Joint Statement on Cambodia Issued at the End of Talks Held in Jakarta, 9-10 September 1990.* A/45/490, 17 September 1990.

———. *Financing of the United Nations Transitional Authority in Cambodia: Report of the Secretary General.* A/47/733/Add. 1, 27 July 1993.

———. *Report of the Secretary General on the Financing of the UN.* A/48/701, 8 December 1993, Annex II.

United Nations Security Council. *First Progress Report of the Secretary-General on the United Nations Transitional Authority in Cambodia.* S/23870, 1 May 1992.

———. *Second Progress Report of the Secretary-General on UNTAC.* S/24578, 21 September 1992.

———. *Third Progress Report of the Secretary-General on UNTAC.* S/25154, 25 January 1993.

———. *Fourth Progress Report of the Secretary-General on UNTAC.* S/25719, 3 May 1993.

———. *Further Report of the Secretary-General on the Implementation of Security Council Resolution 745 (1992).* S/26529, 5 October 1993.

———. *Report of the Secretary-General on Cambodia.* S/23613, 19 February 1992.

———. *Report of the Secretary-General in Pursuance of Paragraph 6 of Security Council Resolution 810 (1993) on Preparations for the Election for the Constituent Assembly in Cambodia.* S/25784, 15 May 1993.

———. *Report of the Secretary-General on the Conduct and Results of the Election in Cambodia.* S/25913, 10 June 1993.

———. *Report of the Secretary-General on the Implementation of Security Council Resolution 783.* S/24800, 15 November 1992.

———. *Report of the Secretary General on Cambodia.* S/23613/Add. 1, 11 October 1994.

———. *Second Special Report of the Secretary-General on UNTAC.* S/24286, 14 July 1992.

———. *Special Report of the Secretary-General on UNTAC and Phase II of the Cease-fire.* S/24090, 12 June 1992.

————. *Statement by the President of the Security Council Concerning the Successful Completion of the Mandate of UNTAC.* S/26531, 5 October 1993.

United Nations Security Council. Resolution 717 (S/Res/717), 16 October 1991.

    S/Res/718, 31 October 1991.

    S/Res/745, 28 February 1992.

    S/Res/766, 21 July 1992.

    S/Res/792, 30 November 1992.

    S/Res/810, 8 March 1993.

    S/Res/826, 20 May 1993.

United Nations Transitional Authority in Cambodia. *Report of the Special Representative to the Supreme National Council.* Phnom Penh, 10 June 1992. Mimeograph.

————. "Statement of Special Representative Yasushi Akashi to the Supreme National Council." Phnom Penh, 10 June 1992. Mimeograph.

————. "Statement of H.E. Mr. Khieu Samphan to the Supreme National Council." Phnom Penh, 10 June and 24 August 1992. Mimeograph.

————. *Report on UNTAC's Activities: The First Six Months, 15 March-15 September 1992.* Phnom Penh, September 1992. Mimeograph.

————. *Impact of UNTAC on Cambodia's Economy.* Report by the Economic Advisor. Phnom Penh, December 1992. Mimeograph.

————. *United Nations Electoral Legislation for Cambodia: Amendment Law no. 2.* Phnom Penh, January 1993. Mimeograph.

UNPROFOR (The Former Yugoslavia)

United Nations. Department of Information. *The United Nations and the Situation in the Former Yugoslavia.* New York, May 1993. Revised 15 March 1994.

United Nations. High Commissioner for Refugees. *Information Notes on Former Yugoslavia.* Zagreb: Office of the Special Envoy for former Yugoslavia.

    Issue 5/93, 25 April 1993.

    Issue 6/93, 25 May 1993.

    Issue 7/93, 30 June 1993.

    Issue 8/93, 1 August 1993.

    Issue 1/94, January 1994.

    Issue 1/95, January 1995.

    Issue 7/95, July 1995.

United Nations Security Council. *Further Report of the Secretary-General Pursuant to Security Council Resolution 721 (1991).* S/23592, 15 February 1992.

————. *Report of the Secretary-General Pursuant to Security Council Resolution 721 (1991).* S/23280/Annex III, 11 December 1991.

————. *Further Report of the Secretary-General Pursuant to Security Council Resolution 749 (1992).* S/23844, 24 April 1992.

————. *Further Report of the Secretary-General Pursuant to Security Council Resolution 752 (1992).* S/24188, 26 June 1992.

————. *Further Report of the Secretary-General Pursuant to Security Council Resolution 757 (1992), 758 (1992), and 761 (1992).* S/24263, 10 July 1992.

————. *Further Report of the Secretary-General Pursuant to Security Council Resolution 743 (1992) and 762 (1992).* S/24600, 28 September 1992.

————. *Further Report of the Secretary-General Pursuant to Security Council Resolution 743 (1992).* S/24848, 24 November 1992.

S/26470, 20 September 1993.

————. *Letter Dated 6 August 1993 from the Secretary-General Addressed to the President of the Security Council.* S/26260, 6 August 1993.

————. *Letter Dated 3 March 1994 from the Permanent Representatives of Bosnia and Herzegovina and Croatia to the United Nations Addressed to the Secretary-General.* S/1994/255, 4 March 1994.

————. *Letter Dated 30 March 1994 from the Secretary-General Addressed to the President of the Security Council.* S/1994/367, 30 March 1994.

————. *Letter Dated 21 September 1994 from the Permanent Representatives of France, Germany, Russian Federation, United States of America, and the United Kingdom of Great Britain and Northern Ireland to the United Nations Addressed to the Secretary-General.* S/1994/1081, 21 September 1994.

————. *Letter Dated 15 November 1995 from the Permanent Representative of Croatia to the United Nations Addressed to the Secretary-General.* S/1995/951, 15 November 1995.

————. *Report of the Secretary-General on the Situation in Bosnia-Herzegovina.* S/24333, 21 July 1992.

S/24540, 10 September 1992.

————. *Report of the Secretary-General Pursuant to Security Council Resolution 762 (1992).* S/24353, 27 July 1992.

————. *Report of the Secretary-General Pursuant to Security Council Resolution 781 (1992).* S/24767, 5 November 1992.

————. *Report of the Secretary-General on the Activities of the International Conference on the Former Yugoslavia: Peace Talks on Bosnia and Herzegovina.* S/25479, 26 March 1993.

————. *Report of the Secretary-General Pursuant to Security Council Resolution 815 (1993).* S/25777, 15 May 1993.

————. *Report of the Secretary-General Pursuant to Security Council Resolution 836 (1993).* S/25939, 14 June 1993.

————. *Report of the Secretary-General Pursuant to Security Council Resolution 795.* S/26009, 13 July 1993.

————. *Report of the Secretary-General to the Security Council Pursuant to Security Council Resolution 871 (1993).* S/26828, 1 December 1993.

————. *Report of the Secretary-General to the Security Council Pursuant to Security Council Resolution 900 (1994).* S/1994/291, 11 March 1994.

————. *Report of the Secretary-General Pursuant to Security Council Resolution 947.* S/1995/222, 22 March 1995.

————. *Report of the Secretary-General Submitted Pursuant To Paragraph 4 of Security Council Resolution 981 (1995).* S/1995/320, 18 April 1995.

————. *Report of the Secretary-General Pursuant to Security Council Resolutions 981 (1995), 982 (1995), and 983 (1995).* S/1995/987, 23 November 1995.

————. *Report of the Secretary-General Pursuant to Security Council Resolution 1019 (1995) on Violations of International Humanitarian Law in the Areas of Srebrenica, Zepa, Banja Luka, and Sanski Most.* S/1995/988, 27 November 1995.

————. Resolution 713 (S/Res/713), 25 September 1991.

S/Res/721, 27 November 1991.

S/Res/743, 21 February 1992.

S/Res/749, 7 April 1992.

S/Res/752, 15 May 1992.

S/Res/753, 18 May 1992.

S/Res/754, 18 May 1992.

S/Res/755, 20 May 1992.

S/Res/757, 30 May 1992.

S/Res/758, 8 June 1992.

S/Res/760, 29 June 1992.

S/Res/761, 29 June 1992

S/Res/762, 30 June 1992.

S/Res/764, 13 July 1992.

S/Res/769, 7 August 1992.

S/Res/770, 13 August 1992.

S/Res/771, 13 August 1992.

S/Res/776, 14 September 1992.

S/Res/779, 6 October 1992.

S/Res/780, 6 October 1992.

S/Res/781, 9 October 1992.

S/Res/786, 10 November 1992.

S/Res/787, 16 November 1992.

S/Res/795, 11 December 1992.

S/Res/802, 25 January 1993.

S/Res/807, 19 February 1993.

S/Res/808, 22 February 1993.

S/Res/815, 30 March 1993.

S/Res/816, 31 March 1993.

S/Res/819, 16 April 1993.

S/Res/820, 17 April 1993.

S/Res/824, 6 May 1993.

S/Res/827, 25 May 1993.

S/Res/836, 4 June 1993.

S/Res/838, 10 June 1993.

S/Res/844, 18 June 1993.

S/Res/847, 30 June 1993.

S/Res/900, 4 March 1994.

S/Res/908, 31 March 1994.

S/Res/914, 27 April 1994.

S/Res/941, 23 September 1994.

S/Res/942, 23 September 1994.

S/Res/943, 23 September 1994.

S/Res/947, 30 September 1994.

S/Res/958, 19 November 1994.

S/Res/959, 19 November 1994.

S/Res/981, 31 March 1995.

S/Res/982, 31 March 1995.

S/Res/983, 31 March 1995.

S/Res/1021, 22 November 1995.

S/Res/1022, 22 November 1995.

S/Res/1023, 22 November 1995.

S/Res/1026, 30 November 1995.

S/Res/1031, 15 December 1995.

S/Res/1035, 21 December 1995.

S/Res/1037, 15 January 1996.

ONUMOZ (Mozambique)

United Nations Operation in Mozambique. "Figures on Soldiers Under the Peace Process Demobilization." Ton Pardoel, Chief, Technical Unit, ONUMOZ. 5 November 1993. Mimeograph.

United Nations General Assembly. *Financing of the United Nations Operation in Mozambique.*

A/47/881/Add.1, 8 February 1993.

A/47/969, 28 June 1993.

A/48/849, 17 January 1994.

A/48/889, 2 March 1994.

A/48/849/Add.1, 23 May 1994.

A/49/649, 8 November 1994.

A/49/649/Add.1, 23 November 1994.

United Nations Security Council. *Final Report of the Secretary-General on the United Nations Operation in Mozambique.* S/1994/1449, 23 December 1994.

———. *Further Report of the Secretary-General on the United Nations Operation in Mozambique.* S/1994/1002, 26 August 1994.

———. *General Peace Agreement for Mozambique.* S/24635, 8 October 1992.

———. *Progress Report on the United Nations Operation in Mozambique.* S/1994/1196, 21 October 1994.

———. *Report of the Secretary-General on the United Nations Operation in Mozambique.*

S/24892, 3 December 1992.

S/25044, 4 January 1993.

S/25518, 2 April 1993.

S/26034, 30 June 1993.

S/26432, 13 September 1993.

S/26666, 1 November 1993.

S/1994/89/Add.1, 28 January 1994.

S/1994/511, 28 April 1994.

S/1994/803, 7 July 1994.

———. Resolution 863 (S/Res/863), 13 September 1993.

S/Res/882, 5 November 1993.

S/Res/898, 23 February 1994.

———. *United Nations Operation in Mozambique: Report of the Secretary-General.* S/24642, 9 October 1992.

UNOSOM (Somalia)

Menkhaus, Ken. "The Historical Roots of the Current Crisis: Patterns of Settlement and Displacement." UNOSOM "Lower Jubba Strategy" Briefing Paper no. 1 (July 1993). Mimeograph.

———. "UNOSOM's Structure and the Issue of Decentralization." UNOSOM "Lower Jubba Strategy" Briefing Paper no. 4 (June 1993). Mimeograph.

United Nations. Department of Public Information. *The United Nations and the Situation in Somalia*. DPI/1321/Rev.4. New York, April 1995.

United Nations General Assembly. *Financing of the United Nations Operation in Somalia II: Report of the Secretary-General*.

A/48/850, 19 January 1994.

A/48/850/Add.1, 15 July 1994.

A/49/563, 21 October 1994.

A/49/563/Add.2, 23 March 1995.

———. *Financing of the United Nations Operation in Somalia: Progress of the Investigation and Action Thereon to Determine Responsibility for the Theft of US$ 3.9 million in the United Nations Operation in Somalia II*. A/49/843, 2 February 1995.

———. *Further Report of the Secretary-General Submitted in Pursuance of Paragraphs 18 and 19 of Resolution 794*. S/25354, 3 March 1993.

———. *Further report of the Secretary-General Submitted in Pursuance of Paragraph 4 of Resolution 886 (1993)*. S/1994/12, 6 January 1994.

———. *Further Report of the Secretary-General on the United Nations Operation in Somalia Submitted in Pursuance of Paragraph 14 of Security Council Resolution 897 (1994)*. S/1994/614, 24 May 1994.

———. *Further Report of the Secretary-General on the United Nations Operation in Somalia Submitted in Pursuance of Paragraph 2 of Security Council Resolution 923 (1994)*. S/1994/839, 18 July 1994.

———. *Report of the Secretary-General on the Implementation of Security Council Resolution 837*. S/26022, 1 July 1993.

———. *Report Pursuant to Paragraph 5 of Security Council Resolution 837 (1993) on the Investigation into the 5 June 1993 Attack on United Nations Forces in Somalia Conducted on Behalf of the Secretary-General*. S/26351, 24 August 1993.

———. *Report of the Commission of Inquiry Established Pursuant to Security Council Resolution 885 (1993) to Investigate Armed Attacks on UNOSOM II Personnel*. S/1994/653, 1 June 1994.

———. *Report by the Secretary-General Concerning the Situation in Somalia*. S/1994/1068, 17 September 1994.

———. *The Situation in Somalia: Report of the Secretary-General*.

S/23693, 11 March 1992.

S/24992, 19 December 1992.

———. Resolution 733 (S/Res/733), 23 January 1992.

S/Res/746, 17 March 1992.

S/Res/751, 24 March 1992.

S/Res/767, 27 July 1992.

S/Res/775, 28 August 1992.

S/Res/794, 3 December 1992.

S/Res/814, 25 March 1993.

S/Res/837, 6 June 1993.

S/Res/865, 22 September 1993.

S/Res/885, 16 November 1993.

S/Res/897, 4 February 1994.

UNAMIR (Rwanda)

Donini, Antonio and Norah Niland. *Rwanda Lessons Learned: A Report on the Coordination of Humanitarian Activities*. Prepared for the UN Department of Humanitarian Affairs, New York, November 1994. Mimeograph.

United Nations. Department of Humanitarian Affairs. *Humanitarian Situation in Rwanda*. no. 12. Integrated Operations Center, Kigali, Rwanda, 19 July 1995.

United Nations. Department of Public Information. *United Nations Peace-keeping Information Notes, Update: May 1994*. New York, 1994.

United Nations General Assembly. *Financing of the United Nations Observer Mission Uganda-Rwanda and Financing of the United Nations Assistance Mission for Rwanda*.

    A/49/375, 12 September 1994.

    A/49/375/Add.1, 11 October 1994.

    A/49/501/Add.1, 30 March, 1995.

————. *Financing of the United Nations Assistance Mission for Rwanda*. A/50/712, 1 November, 1995.

United Nations Security Council. *Further Report of the Secretary-General on Rwanda*. S/26350, 24 August 1993.

————. *Letter Dated 29 April 1994 from the Secretary-General Addressed to the President of the Security Council*. S/1994/518, 29 April 1994.

————. *Letter Dated 19 June 1994 from the Secretary-General Addressed to the President of the Security Council*. S/1994/728, 20 June 1994.

————. *Letter Dated 5 July 1994 from the Permanent Representative of France to the United Nations Addressed to the Secretary-General*. S/1994/795, 5 July 1994.

————. *Letter Dated 26 September 1994 from the Permanent Representative of France to the United Nations Addressed to the Secretary-General*. S/1994/1100, 26 September 1994.

————. *Letter Dated 1 October 1994 from the Secretary-General Addressed to the President of the Security Council*. S/1994/1125, 4 October 1994.

————. *Minutes of the 3368th Meeting of the Security Council*. S/PV.3368, 21 April 1994.

————. *Report of the Secretary-General on Rwanda*. S/26488, 24 September 1993.

————. *Progress Report of the Secretary-General on the United Nations Assistance Mission for Rwanda*.

    S/1994/360, 30 March 1994.

    S/1994/1133, 6 October 1994.

    S/1995/107, 6 February 1995.

    S/1995/297, 9 April 1995.

————. *Special Report of the Secretary-General on the United Nations Assistance Mission for Rwanda*. S/1994/470, 20 April 1994.

————. Resolution 846 (S/Res/846), 22 June 1993.

    S/Res/872, 5 October 1993.

    S/Res/893, 6 January 1994.

    S/Res/912, 21 April 1994.

    S/Res/918, 17 May 1994.

    S/Res/929, 22 June 1994.

    S/Res/955, 8 November 1994.

    S/Res/965, 30 November 1994.

    S/Res/997, 9 June 1995.

United Nations Development Programme. *Human Development Report, 1992*. Oxford: Oxford Univ. Press, 1992.

Peacekeeping in the Newly Independent States

United Nations Security Council. *Report of the Secretary-General Concerning the Situation in Abkhazia, Georgia.*
    S/1995/10, 6 January 1995.
    S/1995/181, 6 March 1995.
    S/1995/342, 1 May 1995.
————. *Report of the Secretary-General on the Situation in Tajikistan.*
    S/1994/1363, 30 November 1994.
    S/1995/390, 12 May 1995.
    S/1995/472. 10 June 1995.
————. Resolution 849 (S/Res/849). 9 July 1993.
    S/Res/854, 6 August 1993.
    S/Res/858, 24 August 1993.
    S/Res/876, 19 October 1993.
    S/Res/896, 31 January 1994.
    S/Res/968, 16 December 1994.
    S/Res/993, 12 May 1995.
United Nations Institute for Disarmament Research. *Russian Approaches to Peacekeeping Operations.* Research Paper no. 28. New York: United Nations, 1994.
United Nations. Department of Public Information. *United Nations Peace-keeping Information Notes.* New York: Update, December 1994.

INDEX

Abdus Salam, Major General Mohammad, 286

Abkhazia, 413-15, 418, 448: conflict origins, 424; Russian role in, 425, 427; UN role in, 417, 426; United States and, 427

Afghanistan, 12, 412, 436: Tajikistan conflict and, 431

African National Congress, 280

Aideed, General Mohamed Farah, 26, 48, 56, 315-17, 319, 320, 322, 324, 327-30, 334, 339, 341, 343-44, 348-49, 351

air power, 8, 20

Ajello, Aldo 285, 288, 290-91, 294-95, 300: crucial role of, 301; RENAMO and, 301

Akashi, Yasushi: and Cambodia, 151, 163, 167, 170-72, 174; and former Yugoslavia 226, 238, 241-42, 244

Albright, Madeleine, 12, 40, 41, 46, 47, 55-57, 59, 246, 327, 377, 416, 427, 440

Algeria, and Angola, 105

Ali Mahdi, Mohamed, 314-17, 320

An Agenda for Peace, 24, 37, 318

Angola, 12, 18, 22-25, 291, 301: anti-colonial struggle, 104-6; civil war (battle of Cuito Cuanavale, 107; decimated infrastructure, 106, 112, 119; origins of, 106; resumption of, 120-21); integrated armed forces (FAA), 109, 120; election results, 120; European Community aid, 117

Angola, peace process: Alvor Accord (1975), 106; December 1988 accord, 107; Bicesse Peace Accords, (1991), 108-109, 121-22, 124 (Joint Political Military Commission [CCPM], 109, 122; Joint Verification and Monitoring Commission [CMVF], 109, 118; National Elec-toral Commission [NEC] 115, 117, 119; Protocol of Estoril, 109; UNITA/MPLA mistrust, 112); 1992-93 peace talks, 121; Lusaka Protocol (1994), 122

Angola, political factions: Front for the Liberation of the Enclave of Cabinda (FLEC), 104; National Front for the Liberation of Angola (FNLA), 104, 106; National Union for the Total Independence of Angola (UNITA), 104, 106, 108 (demobilization delays and, 118; arms embargo on, 122); Popular Movement for the Liberation of Angola (MPLA), 104, 106, 108, 120-21

Annan, Kofi, 11, 48, n. 198, 274

Anstee, Margaret Joan, 114, 121

Argentina, 88: and Mozambique, 286

Armenia, 442

Aspin, Les, 41, 57: and Somalia, 327

Association of Southeast Asian Nations (ASEAN), 137, 141, 176

Australia, and Cambodia, 141
Austria: and former Yugoslavia, 203; and Somalia, 321

Austro-Hungarian Empire, 196

Azerbaijan, 412, 442, 444

Badinter, Robert, 204

Baker, James, 200

Balkans: as crossroads, 196; geography, 196

Bangladesh: and former Yugoslavia, 239; and Mozambique, 286-87; and Somalia, 350; and UNAMIR I, 376, 382

Barannikov, Viktor, 432

NOTES ON CONTRIBUTORS

WILLIAM J. DURCH is a senior associate at the Henry L. Stimson Center. He is former assistant director of the Defense and Arms Control Studies Program, Massachusetts Institute of Technology, and has taught at Georgetown University. He has held research appointments at MIT, Harvard University, and the Center for Naval Analyses, and has served in government at the US Arms Control and Disarmament Agency. He has lectured on peace operations at the US Air, Army, and Naval War Colleges, NATO, the National Defense University, and Columbia University. He is editor and coauthor of *The Evolution of UN Peacekeeping: Case Studies and Comparative Analysis* (St. Martin's Press), coauthor of studies on arms control in Europe and US military roles and missions, and author of several studies of strategic and theater ballistic missile defense. He is a graduate of the Georgetown University School of Foreign Service and holds a PhD in political science from MIT.

IVO H. DAALDER is associate professor at the School of Public Affairs and director of research at the Center for International and Security Studies, both at the University of Maryland. As a Council on Foreign Relations fellow, he served as director for Global Affairs on the National Security Council staff and as executive secretary to the Executive Committee on Implementation of the Bosnian Peace Settlement. He has written widely on questions of international security, including arms control, peacekeeping, and military intervention. His most recent publications include *Rethinking the Unthinkable: Future Directions for Nuclear Arms Control* (Frank Cass & Co.), *The Development of the Clinton Administration's Policy Toward Multilateral Peace Operations* (Pew Studies in International Affairs), and chapters on the former Yugoslavia and US policy toward military intervention in Michael Brown, ed., *International Implications of Internal Conflict* (MIT Press). He is a graduate of the University of Kent (Canterbury) and holds a PhD in political science from MIT.

FEN OSLER HAMPSON is associate professor of international affairs at Norman Paterson School of International Affairs, Carleton University, Ottawa, where he teaches courses on conflict analysis and strategy and security and his research focuses on international negotiation and conflict resolution. He has also taught at Georgetown University and been a research fellow at the US Institute of Peace (USIP) and the Center for Science and International Affairs, Harvard University. He is author of *Multinational Negotiations* (USIP), *Unguided Missiles* (W.W. Norton), *Forming Economic Policy* (St. Martin's), and articles in *International Journal* and *International Security*. He is a graduate of the University of Toronto, and holds a PhD in government from Harvard.

YVONNE C. LODICO is a lawyer and founding director of the Galileo Institute for Global Cooperation, New York. She has extensive field experience in UN peacekeeping operations, having served as legal advisor and special assistant to the Director of the Office of Humanitarian

Affairs in the third Angola Verification Mission; member of the US delegation to the UN Observer Mission in South Africa; legal advisor to the electoral division of the UN Operation in Mozambique; and liaison officer with the second Angola Verification Mission. Before joining these operations, she worked in the UN Secretariat's Office of Outer Space Affairs and was a telecommunications and satellite communications consultant in developing countries, especially Brazil and China. She holds a JD from American University, an LLM from New York University, and an MA in international affairs from Columbia University.

KEVIN P. O'PREY is an associate at DFI International and a member of the Project on Post-Soviet Security at MIT, where he is completing a doctoral dissertation. He researched and drafted this report while a guest of the Foreign Policy Studies Program at the Brookings Institution. He is also author of *A Farewell to Arms? Russia's Struggle with Defense Economic Conversion* (The Twentieth Century Fund) and *The Arms Export Challenge: Cooperative Approaches to Export Management and Defense Conversion* (The Brookings Institution). He is a graduate of Grinnell College.

PAMELA L. REED, a research associate at The Henry L. Stimson Center, worked on the Center's project on peacekeeping and US foreign policy. She also assessed UN peace operations in 1993 and 1994 for the Verification Technology Information Center (VERTIC), a London-based, independent, nonprofit organization. She is a graduate of Rice University and holds an MPIA from the University of Pittsburgh.

JAMES A. SCHEAR is a resident associate and Abe Fellow at the Carnegie Endowment for International Peace and formerly a senior associate at The Henry L. Stimson Center. From 1989 to 1995, he served as a policy consultant to United Nations Undersecretary-General Yasushi Akashi. In this capacity, he worked for the UN Transitional Authority in Cambodia and UN Peace Forces in former Yugoslavia, conducting assessments of field operations in the areas of peacekeeping, public security, humanitarian relief/human rights monitoring and civil affairs. He has held research appointments at the International Institute for Strategic Studies, Harvard University, and the Brookings Institution, and served as a program coordinator for the Aspen Institute's Strategy Group. He is a graduate of The American University and holds a PhD in international relations from the London School of Economics.

J. MATTHEW VACCARO works as a political-military planner in the Office of the Deputy Assistant Secretary of Defense for Peacekeeping and Humanitarian Assistance. When his contribution to this volume was prepared, he was an employee of DFI International, where he conducted studies on conflict resolution, and was also an adjunct fellow at the Henry L. Stimson Center. Formerly, as a US Army officer, he served in Somalia during Operation Restore Hope and was called back to active duty to serve on the Defense Department's Haiti Task Force, which developed policy to restore democracy in that country. He is a graduate of Stanford University.